Baltimore County, Maryland

DEED ABSTRACTS

1659–1750

Robert Barnes

HERITAGE BOOKS
2016

HERITAGE BOOKS
AN IMPRINT OF HERITAGE BOOKS, INC.

Books, CDs, and more—Worldwide

For our listing of thousands of titles see our website
at
www.HeritageBooks.com

Published 2016 by
HERITAGE BOOKS, INC.
Publishing Division
5810 Ruatan Street
Berwyn Heights, Md. 20740

Heritage Books by Robert W. Barnes
and Bettie Stirling Carothers

1783 Tax List of Baltimore County

Index of Baltimore County Wills, 1659–1850

Heritage Books by Robert W. Barnes:

Baltimore and Fell's Point Directory of 1796

Baltimore County, Marriage References, 1659–1746

Baltimore County, Maryland Deed Abstracts, 1659–1750

Gleanings from Maryland Newspapers, 1776–85

Gleanings from Maryland Newspapers, 1786–90

Gleanings from Maryland Newspapers, 1791–95

Index to Marriages and Deaths in the
Baltimore County Advocate, *1850–1864*

Cover illustration is a map by George Horvath.
It shows a portion of western Baltimore County, Maryland.

International Standard Book Numbers
Paperbound: 978-1-58549-340-1
Clothbound: 978-0-7884-6343-3

INTRODUCTION

Tracing the descent of specific tracts of land has often revealed family relationships, or clues to possible relationships, that may not be apparent from other sources. Ruth Dryden has followed this approach in her volumes of Somerset, Worcester, and Wicomico County land records.[1]

A great deal of work on Baltimore County Land Records has been done by earlier scholar Louis Dow Scisco abstracted early deeds and published them in *The Maryland Historical Magazine.* These have been reprinted by The Genealogical Publishing Company.[2] William B. Marye, author of many articles in *The Maryland Historical Magazine,* used land records copiously to help locate long vanished streams, paths, and early roads.

Several people, including Mr. Marye, have plotted the location of early land grants. Thomas D. Penniman and Malcolm W. Waring created a number of plats showing the location of early tracts. The names of these plats are given below. Unfortunately these plats do not show modern roads, towns, or other landmarks. In recent times, George Horvath has created a series of maps showing the location of early tracts in Baltimore and Carroll Counties. The names of these maps and a brief description are also given below. The latest contribution to this aspect of research has been made by R. Carlton Seitz, whose volume *Maps of Land Patents in Northern Baltimore and Carroll Counties,*[3] with two maps of land grants in northern Baltimore and Carroll Counties, has pinpointed the location of several hundred tracts. Fortunately both Mr. Horvath and Seitz have located their plats on maps showing roads, churches, streams and other landmarks.

The present work was based on the abstracts of land records done by the late Dr. Richard Miller. He abstracted deeds from 1659 to about 1745, working through Liber TB#E. The compiler has expanded that to include deeds through 1750/1. One of the early volumes, Liber IS#K, was practically illegible and so the entries from the Index to Baltimore County Land Records, located at the Maryland State Archives, were used to augment missing data.

Entries in this volume are arranged by name of tract and then a chronological listing of transactions from Baltimore County Deed Books at the Maryland State Archives. Many times the date of survey, name of person for whom surveyed and names of early owners, as found in *The Rent Rolls of Maryland: Baltimore and Anne Arundel Counties,*[4] have been included. At other times Peter Wilson Coldham's three volumes, *The Early Settlers of Maryland, 1679-1700, 1701-1730,* and *1731-1750,*[5] have been used to provide the date of the patent, and name of the patentee.

If a tract has been plotted on one of George Horvath's maps, or other tract maps, the nam of the map is given.

There are occasional references to the Provincial Court Land Records, the 1750 Debt Book, and F. Edward Wright's *Inhabitants of Baltimore County, 1659-1762.*[6]

When the words Addition or Resurvey are used in the tract name, in this volume they follow the name of the tract. Thus "Addition to Good Will" or "Resurvey on Friendship" will be found under "Good Will, Addition to," or "Friendship, Resurvey on."

NOTES

1. *Land Records of Somerset County.* By Ruth Dryden. Repr.: Westminster: Family Line Publications, 1992. *Land Records of Wicomico County, 1666-1810.* By Ruth Dryden. Repr.: Westminster: Family Line Publications, 1992.

Land Records of Worcester County, 1666-1810. By Ruth Dryden. Repr.: Westminster: Family Line Publications, 1992.

2. *Baltimore County Land Records, 1665-1687, From the Maryland Historical Magazine.* By Louis Dow Scisco. Baltimore: Genealogical Publishing Co., Inc., 1995.

3. Westminster: Family Line Publications, 1995.

4. Baltimore: Genealogical Publishing Co., Inc. Repr.: Baltimore: Clearfield Co., 1996.

5. Baltimore: Genealogical Publishing Co., Inc., 1995-1996.

6. Westminster: Family Line Publications, 1987.

BIBLIOGRAPHY

A: "Baltimore County, Maryland, Land Grants," by Raymond B. Clark, Jr., *The Maryland and Delaware Genealogist,* 12:37+.

B: *Woodlawn, Franklintown and Hebbville: Three Communities--Two Centuries.* Woodlawn Recreation and Parks Council, 1977.

C: "The Great Maryland Barrens," by William B. Marye, *The Maryland Historical Magazine*, 50: 11-23+.

ABBREVIATIONS (Sources)

DB: Debt Book; at MSA.

HO: Horvath.

IBC: *Inhabitants of Baltimore County, 1692-1762.* By F. Edward Wright. Westminster: Family Line Publications.

KN: Sue Knight and Ellen Niball.

MPL: Maryland Patent Liber.

MRR: Maryland Rent Rolls, esp.: *The Rent Rolls of Maryland: Baltimore and Anne Arundel Counties.* Baltimore: Genealogical Publishing Co.

PCLR: Provincial Court Land Records; originals at MSA.

PW: Penniman and Waring.

PLATS

HO Plat: *Early Cox's Town (Now Hampstead).* 1978. The map takes in tracts on both sides of the Hanover Road from Manchester in the north to Dover Road on the south. Most of the tracts are in Carroll County. Hampstead and Snydersburg are shown.

HO Plat: Early Land Owners, 1798. This plat takes in tracts between Liberty Road on the south and Gamber Road on the north, and extending west from Ivy Mill Road, to Gamber.

HO Plat: *Early Owners Near Wards Chapel Church.* 1978. The map extends from west of Randallstown on the east, along Liberty Road to Wards Chapel Road on the west.

HO Plat: *Early Patents and Roads.* 1976. The plat is centered around Reisterstown, and extends from St. Thomas' Church on the south to Glen Falls and Hanover Pike on the north. Tracts on both sides of Reisterstown and Hanover Roads are shown.

Ho Plat: *Eldersburg.* 1979. The map shows tracts on both sides of Liberty Road, from the Old Potomac Baptist Church on the east to beyond the Johnsville and Freedom Roads on the west. It matches the Gamber Map on the north, and Gamber and Wards Chapel Maps on the east, the Sykeville Map on the south, and the Winfield Map on the west.

HO Plat: *Elkridge to Ellicott's Upper Mills.* 1985. The plat takes in tracts bounded by I-70, the Baltimore City Line, US Rte 1, and the Patapsco River.

HO Plat: *Finksburg to Westminster.* 1980. The plat shows tracts west from the Patapsco River, along Md. Rte 140 to that road's intersection with Md. Rte 97. It also shows tracts along The Indian Road, Gamber Road, George Ogg's Road (later Joppa Road and then Deer Park Road).

HO Plat: *Granite.* 1985. The plat extends from Rolling Road on the east to a point west of Granite on the west, and from Liberty and Marriottsville Roads on the north to the Patapsco River on the south. It matches the Ellicotts Upper Mill Map on the east, the Elk Ridge Map on the south, the Baltimore/Carroll County Map on the west, and the Wards Chapel Area Map on the north.

HO Plat: *Greenspring Valley.* 1980. The map shows tracts in the area bounded roughly by Falls Road, Caves Road, the Baltimore Beltway, and Reisterstown Road. It matches the Reisterstown Map on the north and the Towson Map on the east.

HO Plat: *Owings Mills.* 1982. The plat extends west from the intersection of Reisterstown and McDonogh Roads, west to Deer Park Road, and north from Winands Road to a point north of the Old Tollgate Road. It matches the Reisterstown Map on the north, Green Spring Valley Map on the east, and the Randallstown Map on the south.

HO Plat: *Pikesville Map.* 1981. The plat extends from the intersections of Old Court Road and Seven Mile Line on the north to the intersections of Reisterstown Road and Rogers Avenue on the south, and from Greenspring Avenue on the east to the Baltimore Beltway on the west. It matches the Mt. Washington and Towson Maps on the east, Green Spring Valley Map on the north, and the Randallstown Map on the West.

HO Plat: *Randallstown Map.* 1981. The plat extends west from the Baltimore Beltway west to a line beyond Chapman Road, and from Mt. Wilson and Winands Roads on the north to Windsor Mill Road on the south. It matches the Green Spring Map on the north, the Pikesville Map on the East, Wards Chapel and Granite Maps on the west, and the Plat in the Woodlawn Book (KN Plat WO) on the south.

HO Plat: *From Rayville to Maryland Line (Along the Middle York Road (Middletown Road), Old York Road, and the Great York Road.* 1986. The plat extends from Middletown, BA Co., on the west, to the Great York Road on the east, and from the PA Line on the north to Rayville on the south.

HO Plat: *Ruxton-Riderwood.* 1979. The map shows plats in the area bounded roughly by the Baltimore Beltway, the Jones Falls Expressway, and York Road, south towards the Baltimore City Line.

HO Plat: *Sykesville Area Map.* 1984. The plat shows those tracts located between Liberty Road, The Patapsco River, The Carroll-Howard County Line, and a line drawn about a mile west of Md Rte 32. On the north it matches the Eldersburg Plat.

HO Plat: *Union Bridge, south towards Johnsville.* 1983. The plat extends from Md. Rte 75 on the north to the Clemson cemetery on the south, and from Winter's Lutheran Church on the east to the Carroll-Frederick Line of 1837.

HO Plat: *Winfield, South to the John Gillis Land.* n.d. The plat shows tracts from Washington Road and Berrett on the east, west to Md. Rte 27, south to Hood's Mill Road, and north to New Liberty Road, Md. Rte 26. It matches the Sykesville and Eldersburg area maps on the east, and the Taylorsville and Winfield Map on the north.

HO Plat: *Winfield to Eldersburg.* 1979. The map shows plats located on both sides of Liberty Road and Md. Rte 97. It matches the Gamber Map on the east, the Eldersburg Map on the south, and the Westminster Map on the north.

KN Plat WO: "Land Grant Map of Woodlawn and Vicinity, 1694 to 1846," in *Woodlawn, Franklintown and Hebbville: Three Communities--Two Centuries.* Woodlawn Recreation and Parks Council, 1977.

PW Plat AR: "Mount Joy."

PW Plat AS: "My Lady'a Manor."

PW Plat AT: "Land of Charles, Lord Baltimore."

PW Plat AU: "Cullin's Lot."

PW Plat B: "Frederick Stadt."

PW Plat B2: "Brunswick."

PW Plat C: "Clark's Park."

PW Plat D: "Darnall's Camp."

PW Plat E: "Long Valley."

PW Plat G: "Gassaway's Ridge."

PW Plat H: "Hampton, Northampton."

PW Plat HB: "Labyrinth."

PW Plat J: "John's Chance."

PW Plat L: "Elledge's Farm."

PW Plat M: "Mesopotamia."

PW Plat N: "White Oak Bottom."

PW Plat P: "Price's Delight."

PW Plat R: "Mansell's Purchase."

PW Plat W: "Welsh's Cradle."

PW Plat WH1: "Wester Ogle."

PW Plat WH1A: "Howard's Square."

PW Plat WH2: "Brooklandwood."

PW Plat WT: "Cockey's Meadow."

OTHER ABBREVIATIONS

AA Co. = Anne Arundel County

a. = acres

acc. = according

ackn. = acknowledged

adj. = adjacent or adjoining

afsd. = aforesaid

als. = alias

atty. = attorney

BA Co. = Baltimore County

betw. = betw.

bro(s). = brother(s)

CE Co. = Cecil County

cert. = certificate

ch. = children

CH Co. = Charles County

CV Co. = Calvert County

co. = county

cons. = consent or consented

cont. = containing

conv. = conveyed

dau. = daughter

dec. = deceased

d. = died

d. s.p. = died without issue

DE = Delaware

desc. = descended

e. = east

exch. = exchange or exchanged

exec. = executor

extx. = executrix

FR Co. = Frederick County

HA Co. = Harford County

inher. = inherited

KE Co. = Kent County

LWT = last will and testament

n. = north

orig. = originally

p/a = power of attorney

pt. = part

pat. = patented

pet. = petitioned

poss. = possibly, possible

Prov. = Provincial

purch. = purchased

R. = River

s. = son or south

SM Co. = St. Mary's County

s.p. = without issue

surv. = surveyed

TA Co. = Talbot County

VA = Virginia

w. = wife or west or with*

* = name of subject tract

AARON'S SPRING

15 June 1747: James Phillips, s. and heir of Col. James Phillips, conv. pt. (*) to Josias Middlemore. JP's w. Sarah cons. (TB#E: 453).

ABBOTT'S FOREST

16 June 1684: 1000 a. surv. for George Abbott on w. branch of Bush R.; later possessed by the heirs of Abbott; still later by Alexander Parran (MRR: 16).

1738: Isaac Webster conv. 200 a. to Thomas Jackson, weaver. Edmond Morris assigned his half to John Webster (Archer Notes).

22 May 1739: Hudson Davidge (who bought the tract from Isaac Webster) conv. 300 a. to John Brice (HWS#1-A: 234).

ABELL'S LOT

15 July 1684: 300 a. surv. for Abell Brown on e. side of Bush R.; later possessed by the orphans of Brown; still later by Robert Brown (MRR: 48).

24 Nov 1715: Robert Brown, Gent., of AA Co., conv. (*) to William Bond and John Bond.

1720: William Bond, conv. to Mary Bond on behalf of her s. Benjamin, who was the s. of Mary and her dec. husband John Bond (TR#DS: 270).

4 Aug 1746: Benjamin Bond and w. Clemency conv. 150 a. (*), orig. surv. for Abell Brown, to Thomas Bond (TB#E: 206).

1750: 150 a. held by Sarah Bond (1750 DB).

ABERLA

Poss. taken up by Charles Gorsuch.

4 Nov 1701: John Francis Holland and w. Jane Frances conv. (*) to Sarah Stairs (HW#2: 96).

4 Nov 1701: John Francis Holland and his w. Jane Francis Holland, conv. 240 a. Steir's Progress (formerly taken up by Charles Gorsuch and called Aberle), also pt. William, to Sarah Steirs, spinster (HW#2: 96).

ABERLY LODGE

3 June 1697: 242 a. surv. for Thomas Preston (HW#2: 133).

2 March 1701 Thomas Preston, Sr., conv. 242 a. to Charles Baker; Preston's w. Mary cons. (HW#2: 133).

3 Nov 1703: Preston and w. Mary conv. the tract to Julian de Lappe, widow, adj. land once in possession of Abraham de Lappe (HW#2: 291).

7 March 1716: James Isham and w. Julian conv. 200 a. of the land to Lewis Nowell [sic] (TR#A: 455). (Julian was the 2nd w. of Abraham de Lappe, Jr.) (BCF: 168).

4 March 1723: Lewis Nowell [sic] and w. Jane conv. (*), 100 a. Crow Perches and two parcels of John's Interest to Henry Wetherall (IS#G: 277).

ABINGDON'S ENLARGEMENT

1750: Abraham Eaglestone owned 210 a. (*) (1750 DB: 30).

ABINGTON

12 June 1682: 100 a. surv. for Charles Gorsuch; later held by Francis Holland; later by John Rouse (MRR: 88).

31 July 1697: Roger Newman, merchant, conv. pt. (*) and pt. Willin to John Francis Holland, 238 a. in all (IS#IK: 145).

ABNER'S CAMP

10 July 1743: 50 a. pat. to Abner Baker (MPL: EI#6: 641, LG#E: 160; TB#E: 242).

11 May 1746: Abner Baker conv. 50 a. (*) to Thomas Leaven (TB#C: 537).

18 Aug 1746: Thomas Levens conv. 50 a. (*) to William Hammond; Levens' w. Ann cons. (TB#E: 242).

ABRAHAM'S DELIGHT

1747: 230 a. granted to George Ashman (Plat WH1A).

ABSOLOM'S CHANCE

18 Oct 1756: Benjamin Barney conv. 100 a. (*) to Nicholas Merryman (BB#I: 596).

ABSOLOM'S MEADOW

20 March 1757: 16 a. surv. for Absolom Price (B).

ABSOLOM'S PLACE

18 March 1746: Absolom Baker and w. Mary conv. 40 a. (*) to Peter Gosnell (TB#E: 330).

1763/4: Peter Gosnell listed as owning (AHAL: 36, MHS).

ABSOLUTE (TOWN OF)

7 March 1693: William Wilkinson conv. to John Smith of Biteford, Co. Devon, Lot # 3 of the Town of Absolute on Patapsco R. Wilkinson had built on the land. (The deed mentioned an Act of the Assembly) (RM#HS: 414).

ADAM THE FIRST

8 April 1687: 500 a. surv. for Adam Shipley on Elk Ridge, on northeast side of the head of a branch of Patapsco; later held by Richard Shipley (MRR: 101).

29 Sep 1712: Richard Shipley and w. Susannah conv. 103 a., pt. (*) now called Eve's Dower, to James Barnes (TR#A: 210).

29 Sep 1712: Richard Shipley and w. Susannah conv. 91 a., now called Robert's Delight, pt. of a larger tract called (*), to Robert Shipley (TR#A: 212).

18 April 1713: James Barnes and w. Keturah mortgaged 114 a. (*), now called Eve's Dower, to John Brice of AA Co., merchant; tract was first pat. by Adam Shipley, and sold to James Barnes by Richard Shipley (TR#A: 242).

ADAM'S ADDITION
(See also GOD'S PROVIDENCE)

16 Nov 1703: Charles Adams conv. 10 a. (*) to Thomas Chamberlain; may have also been called Prospect (HW#2: 348).

2 Oct 1713: Thomas Chamberlain, Gent., conv. 20 a. (*) to Charles Carroll of Annapolis (TR#A: 399).

9 Aug 1716: Thomas Chamberlain and w. Mary conv. 20 a. (*), and 140 a. God's Providence, to Richard King (TR#A: 402).

ADAM'S GARDEN

1754: 1212 a. granted to Adam Shipley (Plat J).

On Horvath Plats: Eldersburg and Sykesville.

1 Sep 1755: Adam Shipley conv. 397½ a. to John Elder. Adam's w. Ruth cons. (BB#I: 456).

ADDITION (1660)

24 Oct 1668: 400 a. surv. for Walter Tucker; later held by Peregrine Brown of London (MRR: 10).

14 Oct 1717: Maurice Burchfield, Surveyor General of His Majesty's Customs in the Southern District of America, and Joseph Brown, late of London, merchant, s. and heir of Peregrine Brown, late of London, dec., conv. 400 a. (*) to James Phillips; the deed stated that Peregrine Brown made a will naming w. Margaret as extx.; the following tracts in MD were owned by Peregrine Brown at the time of his death: (*) 400 a.; Bachelor's Addition 50 a.; Bachelor's Hope 400 a.; Chilbury 250 a.; Waters' Neck 100 a. the MD Court of Chancery decreed that these tracts should be held to satisfy the debts of Browne (TR#A: 485).

ADDITION (1668)

19 July 1668: 101 a. surv. for Richard Sampson; later held by Isaac Sampson (MRR: 97).

ADDITION (1679)

10 Oct 1679: 50 a. surv. for John Boring (Card Index to Patents, MSA).

ADDITION (1695)

6 Oct 1695: 200 a. surv. for John Miles on n. side of eastern branch of Back (Bush?) R. (MRR: 5).

ADDITION (1695)

11 Nov 1732: William Cook and w. Hannah conv. 200 a. to Roger Matthews (adj. tract is Mile End) (IS#L: 328).

8 Aug 1733: Roger Matthews and w. Elizabeth conv. 200 a. of (*), pat. 1 Oct 1695, to Edward Wakeman (IS#L: 411).

5 June 1751: Edward Wakeman, Gent., conv. to Robert Patterson 5 a. (*), (TR#D: 243).

ADDITION (1702)

Oct 1702: 166 a. surv. for Benjamin Williams (MRR: ?).

ADDITION (1702)

1702: 140 a. surv. for Thomas Bale.

10 Oct 1704: Pat. to Thomas Bale (MPL WD:396, DD#5, 144).

See PW Plats WH1 and WH1A; Horvath Plat: Green Spring Valley.

ADDITION (1704)

15 Dec 1704: 52 a. surv. for Patrick Murphy (Card Index to Patents).

ADDITION (THE)

10 Jan 1705: Surv. for 52 a. (IS#L: 318).

5 March 1732; Samuel Maccubbin of BA Co. and w. Mary conv. 100 a. Cuckoldmaker's Palace, 98 a. Murphy's Pleasure, surv. 10 Jan 1705, and 52 a. (*), to John Parrish (IS#L: 318).

ADDITION

29 March 1723: 100 a. surv. for Isaac Butterworth (MRR#II: 530).

ADDITION

30 March 1749: 60 a. pat. to William Gist (MPL TI#4: 170, BY#1: 237).

See PW Plat W; Horvath Plat: Owings Mills.

(Unplaced Tracts named Addition)

18 April 1704: James Carroll conv. 125 a. (*), also called the Cow Land, to Christopher Gardner (TR#RA: 428).

19 Feb 1711: Thomas Randall and w. Hannah conv., 140 a. (*) and 100 a. Rich Land to George Ogg (TR#A: 176).

19 Nov 1724: William Dawkins of CV Co., and w. Ann (dau. and devisee of Richard Smith of CV Co., dec.), and James Dawkins, s. and heir of said William and Ann conv. 500 a. (*) plus 1250 a. (being ½ of the Valley of Jehosophat), to Daniel Dulany of Annapolis (IS#H: 22).

8 March 1738: Richard Gist conv. 216 a. (*), which he had surv., to his s. Thomas Gist (HWS#1-A: 189).

18 Aug 1743: Abraham Boyd and w. Hester, and John Giles and w. Sarah conv. 100 a. (*) to Isaac Butterworth (TB#C: 406).

2 Nov 1743: Isaac Webster and w. Margaret conv. 50 a. (*) to Henry Thomas (TB#C: 420).

9 June 1744: William and Ruth Lewis conv. 50 a. (*) and 100 a. The Mistake to Andrew Scriber of PA (TB#C: 634).

1750: Richard King Stevenson owned 94 a. (1750 DB).

12 Aug 1756: Richard Hooker of Samuel, bro. and heir at law of Samuel Hooker, Jr., dec., conv. 100 a. (*), laid out for afsd. Samuel Hooker on 30 March 1748, to John Ensor, Jr. (BB#I: 580).

ADDS BUDS PROSPECT

1 Feb 1742: Henry Sater conv. 50 a. (*) to Henry Loveall, preacher of the Gospel. Henry's w. Dorcas cons. (TB#C: 240).

18 April 1749: Henry Loveall of BC, preacher, conv. 50 a. (*) to Thomas Sligh. HL's w. Martha cons. (TR#C: 215).

ADVENTURE (1681)

16 June 1681: 1000 a. surv. for George Lingan on the s. side of the Great Falls of Gunpowder; by c1707 the tract was possessed: 500 a. by Henry Butler and 500 a. by Josiah Wilson (MRR: 39). (See PW Plat D).

23 Oct 1705: George Lingan by his LWT left land to his son-in-law Henry Boteler and w. Katherine (MWB 12:248).

27 Aug 1713: Henry Boteler made a will leaving the land to his s. Edward (MWB 13:595).

21 July 1738: Edward Boteler of PG Co., conv. 500 a. to Thomas Sheredine; no w. cons. (HWS#1-A: 160).

2 May 1740: Charles Boteler of PG Co., and w. Sophia granted quitclaim to Sheredine (HWS#1-A: 402).

10 Jan 1740: Thomas Sheredine and w. Tabitha conv. 500 a. (*) to John Galloway (HWS#1-A: 465).

1750: Heirs of John Galloway owned 1000 a. (*) (1750 DB).

ADVENTURE

5 March 1718: Francis Street conv. 100 a. (*) to Richard Gist (TR#RA: 482).

18 Feb 1742: Christopher Gist and w. Sar(--) conv. pt. (*) to William Kelley (TB#C: 185).

4 July 1743: Christopher Gist conv. 2 a. (*) to William Hamilton, Samuel Owings, Christopher Randall and Nicholas Haile, to build a chapel of ease. CG's w. Sarah cons. (TB#C: 274).

ADVENTURE (Pt. of YATES' FORBEARANCE)

1 July 1710: John Yate and w. Elizabeth conv. 100 a. (*) being pt. of Yates' Forbearance, to Joshua Sewell of AA Co. (TR#A: 84).

12 Nov 1716: Joshua Sewell of AA Co. and w. Mary conv. 100 a. (*) to Richard Colegate (TR#A: 511).

ADVENTURE (1727)

1727: 725 a. granted to Richard Gist.

23 March 1728: 725 a. pat. by Richard Gist (MPL PL#7: 157, IL#B: 400).

See PW Plat W; Horvath Plats Green Spring Valley and Owings Mills.

ADVENTURE (1729)

6 Oct 1729: Pat. to Charles Yate (TR#C: 295).

30 Sep 1740(?): John Ensor and w. Elizabeth conv. 50 a. (*) to Charles Yates (HWS#1-A: 463).

6 Feb 1742: Charles Yates of BC, planter, and w. Jane, conv. 50 a. (*) to John Ensor (IS#L: 387).

12 March 1742: Charles Yates conv. 50 a. (*) to his son-in-law John Stone; no w. cons. (TB#C: 269).

16 July 1743: John Stone and w. Mary conv. (*) to Moses Rutter (TB#C: 295).

9 Feb 1746: Moses Rutter conv. 20 a. pt. (*) to Charles Ridgely; no w. cons. (TB#E: 296).

ADVENTURE

(unplaced tracts named Adventure)

1 April 1725: Richard Lenox conv. 418 a., (*), and Martin's Choice to Thomas Hatchman, innholder (IS#H: 77).

15 Dec 1739: Michael Gilbert and w. Mary, dau. of Martin Taylor, Sr., and heir of Martin Taylor, Jr., both dec., conv. ⅓ of (*) and 60 a. (⅓ of) Wittby, in all 178 a., to Benjamin Bond (HWS#1-A: 324).

4 Nov 1742: Jonathan Hughes, taylor, and w. Jane, dau. of Martin Taylor, Jr., dec. conv. ⅓ of (*) and ⅓ of Wittly(?) to Benjamin Bond (HWS#1-A: 164).

ADVENTURE

1798: 98 a. held by Joseph Killey; 30 a. held by Joseph Evans, 191 a. held by Thomas Gist; (B).

ADVENTURE, ADDITION TO

1683: 300 a. surv. for George Lingan (MRR: 47; on PW Plat D).

12 May 1747: Thomas Lingan of AA Co. conv. 300 a. (*) to William Andrew (TB#E: 566).

AFFINITY

4 Sep 1683: 1500 a. surv. for John Darnall and later held by Col. Henry Lowe (MRR: 43).

1 June 1727: Henry Darnall of PG Co., conv. ½ of (*) to John Digges of PG Co. (IS#I: 69).

1729: Henry Darnall and Charles Diggs et al. conv. (*) to John Diggs (IS#K: 91).

11 June 1734: John Digges of PG Co., conv. 1500 a. (*) to Samuel Hyde, exec. of John Hyde of London, merchant (HWS#M: 198).

AGREEMENT

1687: 525 a. surv. for Thomas Thurston.

1 March 1691: Thomas Thurston, Gent., conv. to dau. Elizabeth, relict of John Walley and now w. of Charles Ramsey of BA Co., planter, 400 a. (*); deed mentions grantor's w. Mary, but no w. signed (RM#HS: 340).

9 Nov 1691: Charles Ramsey and w. Elizabeth leased the land to Michael Judd for 1 year, Judd to have liberty to build a house there and keep the property in repair (Archer Notes).

3 March 1713: Thomas Ramsey, s. and heir of Charles Ramsey of BA Co., dec., conv. 200 a., being ½ (*) to Jarvis Gilbert, and ½ the tract was given by Thurston to his dau. Elizabeth and Charles Ramsey on 1 March 1691; the other half was sold by Charles and Elizabeth on 20 June 1706 (TR#A: 270).

9 Aug 1723: Simon Pearson and w. Elizabeth conv. 100 a. pt. (*) to Patrick Ruark (IS#G: 183).

1731: John Gallion devised 100 a. (*) to s. James, and lower pt. (*) to s. Joseph (MWB 20:263).

13 Dec 1732: John Gallion, eld. s. of John, dec., divides property among his bros. (IS#L: 324).

13 May 1752: James Gallion, s. of John, conv. 50 a. (*) to William Barton; mentioned 50 a. formerly sold by James to his uncle Solomon Gallion; James' w. Ruth cons. (TR#D: 330).

A HA AT A VENTURE

7 May 1687: 200 a. surv. for John Hathaway; later held by Humphrey Jones (MRR: 21).

16 June 1748: John Hughes conv. 200 a. (*) and 100 a. Jones' Addition to Thomas White (TB#E: 725).

AHA THE COW PASTURE

3 May 1687: 194 a. surv. for John Hathaway; later held by John Webster and William Howard; still later held by Christopher Cox (MRR: 53).

8 April 1695: George Smith and w. Hannah conv. 194 a. (*) to William Howard and John Webster (RM#HS: 453).

22 Nov 1704: William Howard and w. Martha and John Webster and w. Hannah conv. 1984 a. (*) to Christopher Cox (IR#AM: 3).

22 May 1744: Robert Bishop and w. Elizabeth, dau. and heir of Christopher Cox, conv. (*) to John Day (TB#E: 63).

1746: Robert and Elizabeth Bishop conv. (*) to Thomas White (TB#E: 63).

AIRY HILLS

23 July 1733: 100 a. surv. for Charles Wells (B).

AITROPP (See also EIGHTROPP)

1758: Walter Ashmore of BA Co., assigned a lease to Samuel Hughes for 62 a. Beautiful Island (B#G: 109).

25 Aug 1763: Frederick Ashmore was a surety for Joseph Renshaw for Abraham Ayres, Jr., admin. of James Maxwell (MDTP 39:22).

ALBROUGH

13 Aug 1670: 350 a. surv. (as Old Burrough) for Peter Sterling at the head of a creek on the n. side of Sterling's Branch; later possessed by Luke Raven (MRR: 72).

26 Dec 1671: Peter Sterling, chirurgeon of Gloucester Co., VA, conv. (*) to Luke Raven, blacksmith of same co.; also 100 a. Tryangle (G#J: 232, 235).

26 Dec 1671: Peter Sterling appoints Thos. Long his atty. to acknowledge sale of land.

11 June 1722: Luke Raven, Sr., conv. 350 a. (*) to his s. Isaac, but reserves the right to revoke the gift (IS#H: 270).

ALDERWOOD

1672: A. surv. for John Woodvine who d. s.p.; no heirs, the land uncultivated (MRR: 92).

ALIEN'S REST

1727: An Act of the Legislature stated that the tract had been sold by Bartholomew and Sebra Atkinson to John Hurd who has since left the Province (ARMD 38:405).

ALLEN'S REST

25 Nov 1697: Maurice Baker conv. 100 a. (*), pt. of Baker's Addition, to Robert Allen; Maurice's w. Elizabeth cons. (TR#RA: 406).

ALTOGETHER

15 March 1720: Henry Ridgely of AA Co., Gent., conv. 300 a. (*), pt. of 1200 a. surv. in partnership with Thomas Worthington, to Lancelot Todd of BA Co. (TR#DS: 264).

AMBROSE LOT

23 Jan 1730: 100 a. surv. for Ambrose [Geoghegan?] (B).

AMBROSE'S LOT AUGMENTED
(Resurvey of AMBROSE'S LOT)

20 Feb 1752: Surv. for Ambrose (Geoghegan?); Located e. of Rolling Road, betw. Liberty and Dogwood Roads.

See KN Plat WO; and Horvath Plat: Randallstown.

AMON'S INHERITANCE

19 Aug 1784: Joseph Murray of FR Co. and w. Nancy conv. 14 a. (*) to Richard Owings (WG#V: 512).

AMOS' DELIGHT

9 June 1744: Thomas Amos mortgaged 92 a. (*) in Lord Baltimore's Reserve to Robert Bishop and Josias Slade (TB#E: 91).

8 March 1772: William Lux, exec. of Nicholas Ruxton Gay, conv. 92 a. (*) to George Chocke (AL#G: 176).

AMOS' DESIRE

9 June 1744: Thomas Amos mortgaged 79 a. (*) to Robert Bishop and Josiah Slade (TB#E: 91).

AMOS' OUTLET

1763: Thomas Amos assigned 80 a. to James Amos (B#L: 219).

1763: Thomas Amos conv. (*) to Nicholas D. Amos (B#L: 217).

ANDERSON'S ADDITION

----: Pat. to Andrew Anderson (See TB#E: 149).

19 June 1705: Andrew Anderson conv. 66 a. (*) to James Crooke; and in another deed, all his goods and chattels real and personal to said Crooke (IR#AM: 15, 17).

4 June 1746: Charles Crook conv. 66 a. (*) to Charles Carroll of Annapolis, chirurgeon (TB#E: 149).

ANDERSON'S ADDITION

1704: Surv. for John Anderson (See TR#DS: 151).

4 Nov 1719: William Anderson, s. and heir of John Anderson, conv. 50 a., surv. in 1704 for John Anderson, to William Bond (TR#DS: 151).

ANDERSON'S BARRENS

1755: Leonard Anderson conv. 100 a. to Oliver Matthews (BB#I: 460).

1756: Leonard Anderson conv. same to Oliver Matthews (BB#I: 586).

ANDERSON'S CAMP

19 June 1705: Andrew Anderson conv. 34 a. (*) to James Crooke (IR#AM: 15).

ANDERSON'S LOT

15 Oct 1685: 400 a. surv. for John Anderson of SO Co.; later held by Howard's orphans (MRR: 51).

ANDOVER

12 Sep 1677: 1640 a. surv. for Nicholas Painter; later held by Francis Leafe; still later held by James Greeneff's orphans (MRR: 74).

11 Aug 1707: John Greeneff and w. Ruth conv. pt. (*), now called Knowles' Purchase, to Henry Knowles (RM#HS: 567).

6 July 1724: Adam Shipley conv. 100 a. pt. (*) to Lancelot Todd (IS#G: 299).

ANDREWS' ADDITION

10 March 1747: Andrew Thompson conv. 50 a. (*) to Thomas Thompson; AT's w. Elizabeth cons. (TR#C: 13).

26 Jan 1749: Thomas Thompson of BA Co. deeds 25 a., pt. (*), to James Preston. TT's w. Sarah cons. (TR#C: 207).

ANDREW'S CONQUEST (See also Hall's Park).

10 Sep 1683: 780 a. surv. for Andrew Matson, adj. Cook's Chance; Matson dead; no heirs; greater pt. of land taken away by an elder surv.; no heirs appear; query if there are any heirs (MRR: 17).

17 May 1689: Andrew Matson and w. Jane conv. tract (name illegible to Samuel Underwood (RM#HS: 267).

10 June 1689: Samuel Underwood conv. 300 a. pt (*) to Nicholas Rogers; [Underwood appears to have purch. the tract but the folios have holes in them] (RM#HS: 267).

24 July 1719: Samuel Underwood of Newcastle Co., PA, conv. 300 a. (*) to Edward Hall (TR#DS: 73).

24 July 1719: John Matson, als. Defoss, of Newcastle Co., PA, eld. s. of Matthias Matthiason, als. Matson, late of CE Co., blacksmith, dec., conv. 480 a. (*) to Edward Hall (TR#DS: 76).

9 July 1744: Abarilla Hall, widow and extx. of Col Edward Hall conv. (*) to Col. John Hall; deed stated that Edward Hall had purch. 480 a. (*) in 1719 and claimed the other 300 a. as escheat for want of heirs of Nicholas Rogeir, als. Rogers, and had the two tracts surv. in 1734, which now included 1152 a. in all (TB#C: 531).

ANGEL'S FORTUNE

1752; 112 a. surv. for James Welsh.

See Horvath Plat: Ruxton and Riderwood.

ANN CATHERINE'S NECK

23 July 1658: 400 a. surv. for George Hack; pat. in May 1659 (Archer Notes).

ANN'S DELIGHT

July 1700: 200 a. surv. for Henry Wriothesley (Card Index to Patents).

29 Sep 1713: Ann Wriothesley, widow, conv. 200 a. (*) to William Brown of CE Co., merchant (TR#A: 259).

5 Aug 1732: Esther Brown, widow of Chester Co., PA, widow of William Brown, conv. 200 a. (*) to

Hannah Johns; deed stated that the cert. of surv. was dated 26 July 1703 (IS#L: 268).

8 Aug 1746: Sutton Sickelmore conv. 200 a. (*), orig. granted 24 April 1701 to Henry Wriothesley, to Stephen Onion (TB#E: 159).

27 Sep 1749: William Brown, late of Nottingham Twp., Chester Co., PA, s. and heir of William Brown of Nottingham Twp., dec., in order to quiet the title, conv. his right to (*) to Col. John Hall and w. Hannah (who was widow and devisee of Abraham Johns) (TR#C: 288).

ANN'S DOWRY

22 Sep 1683: 200 a. surv,. for Ann Grove or Gross (MRR: 46).

ANN'S LOT

8 June 1683: 500 a. surv. for Miles Gibson on w. side of Susquehanna; later held by Thomas Thurston; still later by Francis Smith who sold it to Thomas Edmonds who d. without heirs (MRR: 26).

5 July 1684: Miles Gibson conv. 500 a. (*) to Thomas Thurston (RM#HS: 91).

2 Nov 1702: Thomas Thurston conv. 500 a. (*) to Francis Smith (HW#2: 189).

20 Oct 1704: Francis Smith sells 500 a. (*) to Thomas Edmonds (HW#2: 362).

ANTHONY AND ANN

28 Feb 1704: Surv. (TR#DS: 299).

8 March 1720: Anthony Asher conv. (*) to James Crooks (TR#DS: 299).

ANTHONY'S DELIGHT (1722)

20 July 1722: 100 a. pat. to Anthony Coffery (MPL FF#7: 376, CE#I: 402).

See Horvath Plat: Green Spring Valley.

ANTHONY'S DELIGHT (1728)

15 Nov 1728: 75 a. pat. by Anthony Brayfoot (MPL PL#7: 20, IL#B:23).

1729: Anthony Brayfoot conv. 75 a. (*) to John Cockey (IS#K: 65).

11 Dec 1813: James Davis of Fred. Co., VA and w. Sarah Jekyll Davis, deeded land in BA Co., including (*) to Dennis A. Smith (WG#126: 557).

ANTIOCH

9 Dec 1718: Thomas Bond conv. 214 a. (*) to Thomas Preston; Bond's w. Ann cons. (TR#DS: 125).

5 June 1725: Thomas Preston conv. 100 a. (*) to William Grafton, with cons. of w. Elizabeth (IS#H: 167).

6 April 1733: Thomas Preston and w. Elizabeth conv. 50 a. (*) to William Davis (IS#L: 396).

6 Nov 1735: William Grafton and w. Margaret conv. pt. (*) to Maurice Baker (HWS#M: 333).

9 May 1737: Thomas Preston conv. 64 a., remainder of (*) to William Davis (HWS#M: 5; cons. of w. Elizabeth is on folio 301).

ANYTHING AT ALL

1794: 13 a. pat. by John Boring.

23 Aug 1794: John Boring and w. Sarah conv. 13 a. (*) to George Keller of Mannheim Twp., York Co., PA (WG#PP: 238).

AQUILA'S ADVENTURE

26 March 1773: Aquila Carr conv. 300 a. to James Franklin (AL#H: 92).

AQUILA'S INHERITANCE

(also AQUILA'S INHERITANCE RESURVEYED)

1699: 732 a. surv. for John Hall (MRR: 8).

1735: Resurv. as Aquila's Inheritance Resurveyed, and included Hall's United Addition, Hall's Addition, and Poor Man's Beginning (Archer Notes).

19 Oct 1761: Nicholas Kroesen conv. 50 a. (*), pt. of the land conv. to Kroesen by John and Mary Keene, to his s. Richard Kroesen (B#I: 345).

ARABIA FELIX

1750; surv. for Joshua Sewell.

See Horvath Plat: Eldersburg.

ARABIA PETREA

History and location discussed by W. B. Marye (C:122-123).

10 Oct 1723: 4735 a. surv. for Dr. Charles Carroll.

6 Sep 1733: Dr. Chas. Carroll of Annapolis, chirurgeon, conv. (*), pat. 10 Oct 1723, plus Neighborhood and Stone Hill, to Jacob Giles and Isaac Webster (HWS#M: 12).

20 Feb 1734: 6340 a. resurv. for Isaac Webster and Jacob Giles; they divided it into 31 tracts of 40 to 400 a. It was located 5 miles betw. Deer Creek and Broad Creek (Archer Notes).

10 March 1735: Isaac Webster and w. Margaret and Isaac [sic] Giles and w. Hannah conv. 323 a., being ½ of (*) and Neighborhood, to Michael Webster (HWS#M: 394).

10 March 1735: Michael Webster conv. 372 a. (*) and Neighborhood to Henry Jones of Chester Co., PA, sadler. MW's w. Elizabeth cons. (HWS#M: 397).

25 March 1737: IW and JG conv. 236 a., pt. (*) to Alexander Hill (IS#IK: 373).

25 March 1737: same grantors conv. 165 a. to William Jenkins (IS#IK: 385).

25 March 1737: same grantors conv. 417½ a. to Samuel Wallis (IS#IK: 388).

13 Aug 1737: Webster and Giles conv. (*) as follows:
237 a. to John Briarly (IS#IK: 520).
400 a. to Walter Ashmore (IS#IK: 524).
400 a. to William Coale (IS#IK: 528).
300 a. to Richard Wells (HWS#1-A: ?).
64 a. to Richard Dallam (HWS#1-A: 2).
100 a. to Charity Spencer (HWS#1-A: 7).
100 a. to Gregory Farmer (HWS#1-A: 8).
100 a. to Rebecca Hawkins (HWS#1-A: 10).

20 Oct 1737: IW and JG conv. 166 a. to Joseph Jones (HWS#1-A: 18).

29 Sep 1738: Grantors and wives conv. as follows:
183 a. to Seaborn Tucker (HWS#1-A: 126).
100 a. to John Willson (HWS#1-A: 133).
199 a. to John Dunn, blacksmith (HWS#1-A: 175).
170 a. to John Dunn (HWS#1-A: 178).
51 a. to John Dunn (HWS#1-A: 180).
96 a. to Thomas Bradley (HWS#1-A: 182).

5 Jan 1739: Henry Jones conv. 60 a. pt. (*) to John Wooley. HJ's w. Eleanor cons. (HWS#1-A: 345).

1 May 1739: IW and JG conv. as follows:
100 a. to Thomas Litten (HWS#1-A: 222).
74 a. to Abraham Ayres (HWS#1-A: 226).
67 a. to Francis Jenkins (HWS#1-A: 228).

28 June 1740: Michael Webster conv. 30 a. pt. (*) and 167 a. pt. Neighborhood to Richard Dallam. MW's w. Elizabeth cons. (HWS#1-A: 423).

20 Aug 1740: IW and JG conv. 284 a. pt. (*) to Edward Ward. Wives Margaret and Joh. cons. (HWS#1-A: 427).

30 March 1742: IW and JG conv. 200 a. (*) to Thomas Veazey (TR#A: 121).

7 June 1742: Gregory Farmer, Jr., and w. Rachel conv. 102 a. to Rebecca Hawkins (TB#A: 177).

2 Nov 1743: Francis Jenkins and w. Mary conv. 67 a. (*) to Alex. Hill (TB#C: 343).

24 Jan 1744: Henry Jones conv, 110 a. to George Jones. HJ's w. unnamed, cons. (TB#E: 4).

3 Sep 1744: Rebecca Hawkins, widow, conv. two 100 a. parcels of (*) to Michael Montgomery of PA (TB#C: 570).

12 May 1746: Joseph Jones and w. Patience conv., 58 a. pt. of 165 a. (*) to Joseph Rogers (TB#E: 56).

12 May 1746: Joseph Rogers with cons. of w. Charity, mortgages 58 a. (*) to Thomas White (TB#E: 59).

2 May 1747: IW and JG conv. 50 a. to Thomas Phillips (TB#E: 392).

2 May 1747: Giles and w. Johanna, and Webster and w. Margaret, conv. 100 a. (*) to Martha Paca, dau. and devisee of Aquila Paca; assignee of Timothy Keen (TB#E: 412).

10 May 1747: Michael Montgomery of Chester Co., PA conv. 100 a. to William Beavour. MM's w. Ann cons. (TB#E: 607).

10 May 1747: MM and w. Ann conv. 102 a. to Joseph Lee (TB#E: 626).

16 Aug 1749: George Jones, with cons. of w. Elizabeth, conv. 110 a. pt. (*) to Skipwith Coale (TR#C: 306).

19 Sep 1749: Joseph Crockett and Samuel Crockett conv. 66 a. (*) to Edward Neale, Ralph Falkner, and William Bennett, ironmasters. Jean and Esther Crockett cons. (TR#C: 309).

1750: Walter Ashmore mortgages 400 a. to Thomas White (TR#D: 391).

1750: John Ayres conv. 174 a. to John Allender (TR#D: 424).

1762: John Allender conv. 174 a. to Thomas Foster (B#K: 128).

ARDEN'S (ARDINGTON'S) ADVENTURE

15 March 1676: 100 a. surv. for John Arden on the s. side of Back R.; later held by Richard Sampson (MRR: 90).

2 Nov 1682: John Arden and w. Sarah conv. 100 a. (*) to Richard Sampson (RM#HS: 14).

11 March 1708: Isaac Sampson conv. (*) plus Addition to Arden's Adventure, to Richard Sampson,. but if Richard dies s.p., land is to revert to Isaac (RM#HS: 650).

14 Feb 1725/6: Thomas Stone conv. (*) to his son-in-law Richard Sampson (IS#H: 385).

26 Dec 1741/2: Philip Cordeman, bricklayer, leases (*) top William Holmes for 7 years, but Johanna Impy is to be allowed to graze her cattle on the plantation (TB#A: 57). [N.B.: Philip Cordeman m. Ann Sampson on 5 Feb 1735: St. Pauls', 155).

ARDEN'S ADVENTURE, ADDITION TO

11 March 1708: Isaac Sampson conv. (*) plus Arden's Adventure, to Richard Sampson,. but if Richard dies s.p., land is to revert to Isaac (RM#HS: 650).

ARDEN'S MARSH

1686: 28 a. surv. for John Arden; later held by Nicholas Haile for Arden's orphans (MRR: 97).

6 March 1739: Richard Gist purch. (*), resurv. on Martinson, Walton, and Addition to Walton's Nest from John Arden, resurv. them into Triple Union. On this day he sold 137 a. Triple Union to Luke Trotten and 88 a. of Triple Union to Philip Jones (HWS#1-A: 355, 358).

ARDINGTON

1679: 50 a. surv. for John Arden; later held by Nicholas Haile for Arden's orphans (MRR: 96).

5 Aug 1712: Samuel Arden conv. 50 a. (*) to Stephen Bentley (TR#A: 195).

ARDINGTON

20 May 1714: Cert. of surv. (IS#H: 85).

9 Nov 1724: Amy Fenton of BA Co., widow, conv. 100 a. to Thomas Stanborough (IS#H: 85).

ARNOLD'S ARBOUR ENLARGED

See Horvath Plat: Finksburg to Westminster.

ARNOLDS CHANCE

1740/41; 50 a. surv. for Anthony Arnold.

See Horvath Plat: Granite.

ARNOLD'S CHOICE

19 June 1742: Anthony Arnold conv. 50 a. to William Odell., Arnold's w. Margaret cons. (TB#C: 50).

1750: William Odell's heirs owned 50 a. (*) (1750 DB: 66).

ARNOLD'S HARBOR

1750: Anthony Arnold owns 50 a. (*) (1750 DB: 87).

17 Aug 1752: Anthony Arnold and w. Margaret, now of FR Co., conv. 50 a. (*) to Joseph Arnold of BA Co. (TR#D: 428).

ARRESSES ADDITION

5 Aug 1703: Enoch Spinks and John Cutchin conv. 64 a. made up of (*) and Addition to Privilege to James Crook (HW#2: 265).

ARTHUR'S CHOICE

20 Aug 1683: 300 a. surv. for Arthur Taylor on the w. branch of Gunpowder; later possessed as follows: 75 a. by Lawrence Richardson, 75 a. by Lawrence Richardson for the orphans of James Greer, 150 a. by Walter Bosley; still later pt. by Oliver Harreot (MRR: 64).

3 March 1683/4: Arthur Taylor agrees with his w. Frances to conv. 150 a. (*) to James Smithers, s. of Frances Taylor, from the warrant taken up 20 April 1683, out of a warrant orig. assigned to Nicholas Painter, assigned to Maj. Thomas Trueman, who assigned it to Thomas Lightfoot, who assigned it to the grantor (RM#HS: 68).

6 June 1687: Arthur Taylor conv. 75 a. (*) to James Greer and w. Ann (RM#HS: 261).

6 June 1687: Arthur Taylor conv. 75 a. (*) to Richard Smithers (RM#HS: 262).

29 Oct 1696: James Smithers conv. 150 a., pt. of 300 a. (*) orig. taken up by Arthur Taylor, to Lawrence Richardson (IS#IK: betw. pp. 88-100).

3 Nov 1696: Lawrence Richardson and w. Ann conv. 150 a. (*) to Walter Bosley (IS#IK: 108).

9 June 1699: Richard Smithers conv. 75 a. (*) to Lawrence Richardson (TR#RA: 362).

2 Nov (or 2 Aug.) 1699: Walter Bosley and w. Mary conv. 45 a. Hopewell, pt. of (*), to Charles Whitehead of AA Co. (TR#RA: 378).

4 March 1714: John Greer and w. Sarah conv. 75 a. (*) to Walter Bosley (TR#A: 332).

7 Aug 1723: Thomas Richardson and w. Sarah conv. 75 a. (*) to John Hatch (IS#G: 313).

5 Aug 1729: Joseph and John Bosley released 100 a. pt. (*) to William Wood (IS#K: 47).

9 March 1738: Charles Bosley conv. 50 a. (*) to William Andrews (HWS#1-A: 193).

4 Aug 1741: William Andrews conv. 50 a. (*) to William Wood (HWS#1-A: 532).

1741: William Andrews conv. 50 a. (*) and 100 a., being $\frac{1}{2}$ of Bosley's Expectation to Francis Watkins (HWS#1-A: 534).

1750: John Arnold owned 75 a. (*) (1750 DB: 76).

31 Aug 1751: John Hatch, als. Arnold of KE Co., conv. to Francis Watkins 75 a. (*), the same 75 a., which Thomas Richardson and w. Sarah conv. to JH on 7 Aug 1743 (TR#D: 177).

ARTHUR'S DELAY

1688: Thomas Richardson assigned 10 a. (*) to Samuel Sickelmore (Archer Notes).

5 Nov 1707: Samuel Sickelmore and w. Sarah conv. 14 a. (*) to John Ewings (RM#HS: 616).

20 Nov 1708: John Ewing and w. Elizabeth conv. 14 a. (*) and 200 a. Foster's Neck to John Roberts (RM#HS: 565).

22 Nov 1742: Stephen Roberts, s. and devisee of John Roberts, dec., conv. his interest in 14 a. (*) plus 200 a. Goldsmith's Neck, pt. Wolf Harbor Necks, and Lots 6 and 17 of Joppa, to John Roberts, another s. and devisee of John Roberts, dec. (TB#C: 219).

21 May 1744: John Roberts mortgages 14 a. (*) to Alexander Lawson (TB#C: 476).

1750: John Roberts owns 14 a. (*) (1750 DB: 49).

ARTHUR'S LOT

14 March 1746: Avarilla Day, widow of Edward Day, conv. 72 a. Z(*) to her dau. Avarilla Day and the heirs lawfully begotten; if she d. s.p., then land to go to grantor's dau. Anna (TB#E. 335).

1750: Patrick Lynch holds 72 a. (*) plus other tracts (1750 DB: 25). [Patrick Lynch m. Avarilla Day on 20 April 1747: St. John's Parish].

ASHER'S PURCHASE

7 Sep 1745: Anthony Asher of BA Co. mortgaged 220 a. (*) to John Philpott and Edward Lee of London, merchants (TB#E: 349).

1750: Anthony Asher owned 220 a. (*) (1750 DB: 7).

1755: John Asher conv. 220 a. (*) to John Philpott and Edward Lee (BB#I: 353).
26 Oct 1765: Anthony Asher, s. of Anthony Asher, dec., (who had land resurv.), conv. 110 a. (*) to Charles Carroll of Annapolis (PCLR DD#4: 1).

ASHMAN'S DELIGHT

1747: 230 a. granted to George Ashman.
See PW Plat WH1; Horvath Plat: Green Spring Valley.
4 Aug 1750: George Ashman of BA Co. conv. 18 a. (*) to Cornelius Howard. GA's w. Jemima cons. (TR#C: 519).
1750: George Ashman conv. 8 a. (*) to John Shermadine (Shelmerdine?) (TR#D: 292).
1765: George Ashman conv. 8.25 a. (*) to John Shelmedine (B#O: 315).

ASHMAN'S HOPE

30 Nov 1694: 512 a. surv. for George Ashman on the n. side of Patapsco at Hunting Ridge; later held by the Widow Ashman for the orphans of George Ashman; later held by Thomas Cromwell (MRR: 99). Tract is on s. side of Dogwood Road, n. of Ingleside Ave.
See KN Plat WO, Horvath Plat: Elkridge.
28 April 1744: John Ashman granted quitclaim of 157 a. (*) to George Ashman; on the same day George grants quitclaim of 257 a. (*) to John Ashman; both men were sons and devisees of John Ashman of AA Co., dec., who left the tract to his two sons (TB#C: 632, 633).
12 Feb 1744 [/5?]: John Ashman conv. 250 a. pt. (*) to Zachariah Maccubbin (TB#E: 25).
17 Jan 1746: George Ashman conv. 257 a. (*) to Thomas Harrison; GA's w. Jemima cons. (TB#E. 307).
1798: Pt. held by Zachariah Maccubbin; pt. held by William Clem (B).

ASHMAN'S RETIREMENT
(See ASHMORE'S RETIREMENT)

ASHMORE'S PRIVILEGE

31 Aug 1747: William Rail (Rayle) conv. (*) to Walter Ashmore, a resurv. of the lease granted 15 Aug 1746 by Benjamin Tasker, for 102 a. (TB#E. 644).

ASHMORE'S RETIREMENT

7 Sep 1745: 100 a. pat. by John Porter (MPL PT#2: 144).
12 June 1766: John Porter conv. 100 a. (*) to William Crooks (B#P: 212).
1765: William Crooks conv. 100 A. Ashman's Retirement to John Porter (B#P: 212).

ASKIN'S HOPE

1 Aug 1749: William Askins of SM Co. conv. 100 a. (*) to John Paca. WA's w. Elizabeth cons. (TR#C: 326).

ASTON AND DEALE'S CHANCE

29 Nov 1728: Surv. for William Deale (HWS#M: 203).
5 March 1734: William Deale conv. 100 a. (*) to Samuel Bull, with cons. of Deale's w. Eleanor (HWS#M: 210).
5 March 1734: William and Eleanor Deale conv. 100 a. Rachel's Delight, being pt. of (*) to Henry Donahue (HWS#M: 203).
27 March 1742: Henry Donahue and w. Rachel conv. 100 a. (*) to Benjamin Wheeler (TB#A: 134).

ATHALIAH'S LOT (See ETHELIAH'S LOT)

ATHOL

12 Nov 1694: 617 a. surv. for James Murray on the n. side of Patapsco R.; later possessed: 100 a., Hector Maclane, 303 a. Thomas Beale, and 214 a. by Thomas Odin (or Odell) (MRR: 98).
See KN Plat WO. and Horvath Plat: Elkridge. The tract is on the s. of Ingleside Ave., southwest of Dogwood Road.
8 April 1698: James Murray conv. 100 a. (*) to Hector Maclane, in exch. for MacLane's Hope (IS#L: 254).
7 May 1718: Thomas Odell, Gent., of PG Co., conv. 210 a., pt. (*) to George Bailey; TO's w. Sarah cons. (TR#RA: 453).
23 May 1741: Michael Taylor of PG Co., conv. to George Bailey 37 a. (*) adj. to the land that Bailey bought from Thomas Odell (HWS#1-A: 525).
27 Aug 1763: Sarah Bailey, widow of George Bailey, and dau. of Hector MacLane conv. 80 a. (*) (which MacLane left by will to his dau. Sarah) to Elijah and Samuel Bailey (B#L: 468).

ATHOLBOROUGH

1684: 600 a. surv. for George Thompson; later held by the orphans of Giles Blissard (MRR: 75).

AUSTEN AND DEAL'S CHANCE

28 Nov 1728: Surv. for William Deale (TR#D: 286).
18 Dec 1751: Samuel Bull, with cons. of w. Elizabeth, conv. 100 a. (*) to John Bull (TR#D: 286).

AUSTIN

1685: 300 a. surv. for Thomas Thurston (Archer Notes).

AVARILLA'S GARDEN

6 March 1727/8: Edward Day and w. Avarilla conv. 150 a., being ½ of (*), to Nathan Pumphrey (IS#I: 60).

10 Nov 1732: Edward Day conv. 100 a. (*) to Richard Hendon; Hendon's portion now to be called Hendon's Hope (IS#I: 305).

8 June 1747: John Starkey and w. Ann conv. 150 a. (*) to Mark Guishard of AA Co. (TR#C: 22-23).

17 Oct 1747(?): James Crouch of PG Co., conv. 150 a. pt. (*) to John Starkey (TB#E: 561).

AXELL'S NECK (See OXELL'S NECK)

AYRES' ADDITION

28 April 1688: 100 a. surv. for Edward Ayres; later held by Abraham Taylor (MRR: 33).

7 Nov 1694: John Devagh and w. Elizabeth (dau. of Edward Ayres who left the land to his dau. Elizabeth), conv. 100 a. (*) to Abraham Taylor of KE Co., blacksmith (RM#HS: 439).

7 Nov 1719: Abraham Taylor conv., 100 a. (*) (spelled Heirs' Addition), where John Taylor now lives, to the said John Taylor (IS#H: 140).

7 Nov 1719: Abraham Taylor granted quitclaim to John Taylor for the same tract (TR#DS,. 127).

15 March 1726/7: John Taylor conv. 100 a. (*) to Thomas Bond of London, merchant (IS#H: 415).

7 March 1732: John Taylor, devisee of Abraham Taylor, dec., conv. 100 a. (*) to Mary Tolley, extx. of Thomas Tolley (IS#L: 351).

AYRES' DESIRE

Tract is on n. side of Great Falls of Patapsco, w. of Ben's Run, and Dogwood Road (KN Plat WO).

25 Oct 1746: Nathaniel Ayres and w. Rhoda sell 28 a. (*) and 15 a. Nathaniel's Hope, to Charles Ridgely of BA Co., merchant (TB#E: 286).

AYRES' LOT

8 March 1731: Nathaniel Ayres and w. Rhoda, conv. 100 a. (*) to Jacob Bull, bricklayer (IS#L: 206).

5 June 1740: Jacob Bull and w. Rachel conv. 100 a. (*) to s. John Bull (HWS#1-A: 385).

BACHELOR'S ADDITION

28 April 1673: 50 a. surv. for William Tomson; later held by Peregrine Brown of London, merchant (MRR: 10).

14 Oct 1717: Maurice Burchfield, Surveyor General of His Majesty's Customs in the Southern District of America, and Joseph Brown, late of London, merchant, s. and heir of Peregrine Brown, late of London, dec., conv. 50 a. (*) to James Phillips; the deed states that Peregrine Brown made a will naming w. Margaret as extx.; the following tracts in MD were owned by Peregrine Brown at the time of his death: Addition, 400 a.; (*) 50 a.; Bachelor's Hope 400 a.; Chilbury 250 a.; Waters' Neck 100 a. the MD Court of Chancery decreed that these tracts should be held to satisfy the debts of Browne (TR#A: 485).

BACHELOR'S BEGINNING

6 June 1734: John White, carpenter, conv. 100 a. (*) to Seaborn Tucker; JW's w. Priscilla cons. (HWS#M: 69).

BACHELOR'S CHANCE

Sep 1709: 200 a. surv. for Enoch Spinks (Card Index to Patents).

BACHELOR'S CHOICE (1730)

27 Oct 1730: 400 a. pat. to John Stinchcomb (MPL PL#7: 614, IL#B: 289).

7 Feb 1744: John Stinchcomb conv. 150 a. (*) to Michael Miller (TB#E: 57).

7 Feb 1744: John Stinchcomb conv. 150 a. (*) to Samuel Bucknall (TB#E: 59).

7 Feb 1744: John Stinchcomb conv. 100 a. (*) to Nicholas Corver, farmer (TB#E: 61).

BACHELOR'S CHOICE (1743)

8 Sep 1743: 100 a. pat. by Thomas Levens (MPL LG#B: 769, LG#E: 140).

11 Oct 1746: Thomas Levens and w. Ann sell 100 a. (*), to James Richard (TB#E: 219).

6 March 1749: Jacob Cox and w. Elizabeth conv. 50 a. (*) to Charles Bosley (TR#C: 391).

BACHELOR'S DELIGHT

22 June 1671: 260 a. surv. for Edward Smith on the s. side of Bush R.; later possessed by Nicholas Haile for the orphans of John Arden (MRR: 96).

1693: John Arden of BA Co., conv. 50 a. (*) and tract Haberston to Richard Thompson, planter (RM#HS: 437-439).

6 June 1710: Samuel Arden conv., 41 a. Norton's Addition, being pt. of (*) to John Norton (TR#A: 67).

6 June 1710: Samuel Arden, s. and heir of John, conv., 56 a. Smith's Addition, pt. of Bachelor's Delight, to Thomas Smith of BA Co., planter (TR#A: 69).

4 Nov 1710: Samuel Arden conv. 260 a. (*) (except for what has already been sold) to Samuel Hinton (TR#A: 122).

1728: Thomas Harryman conv. 50 a. (*) to Ralph Brodach [Broadricks] (IS#K: 56).

1729: Ralph Broaduck conv. 50 a. (*) to Thomas Harryman (IS#K: 56).

5 Nov 1729: Ralph Broadducks [Broadricks] of BA Co., with cons. of w. Elizabeth, conv. 50 a. (*) to Dorcas Sutton (IS#K: 125).

11 Feb 1734: Sarah Hinton Olive conv. 325 a., being ½ of (*) to Elizabeth Stone, being the same land which she inher. from Samuel Hinton, by his will dated 4 April 1730 (HWS#M: 163).

10 Sep 1741: James Backford/Bagford and w. Comfort conv. 133 a. (*) to Patrick Lynch (TB#A: 38).

8 July 1744: James Bagford conv. 100 a. to William Lynch (TB#C: 642).

1750: Patrick Lynch owned 133 a. (1750 DB: 25).

BACHELOR'S FANCY

14 June 1737: Thomas Taylor of BA Co., and w. Sarah, conv. 400 a. (*), being pt. of Friend's Discovery, to Henry Morgan (HWS#1-A: 20).

BACHELOR'S FEAR

26 July 1744: 256 a. surv. for Zachariah Maccubbin and Edward Norwood (B; Shown on PW Plat B).

13 Nov 1749: Edward Norwood, planter, mortgaged 256 a. (*) and 44 a. Partnership, to Edward Dorsey (TR#C: 336).

1 April 1751: Zachariah Maccubbin of BA Co. conv. to Daniel Dulany, Esq., and Co., ½ of (*), cont. 250 a. in all; the half of which became the right of Zachariah Maccubbin by a grant from His Lordship to ZM and Edward Norwood. ZM's w. Sarah cons. (TR#D: 163).

BACHELOR'S GOOD LUCK

Nov 1703: 1000 a. surv. for Enoch Spinks.

4 Feb 1709: Enoch Spinks of BA Co., conv. 1000 a. (*) to Col. William Holland of AA Co., except for 100 a. already sold to Martin Depost and Anthony Demasters (TR#A: 50).

22 July 1710: Martin Depost of BA Co. conv. 50 a. (*) (being ½ the 100 a. sold to Depost and Anthony Demasters by Enoch Spink) to James Crawford also of BA Co. (TR#A: 90).

26 June 1741: William Holland of CV Co., conv. 1000 a. (*) and 50 a. pt. Jones' Adventure to Henry Chew; WH's w. Anne cons. (TB#A: 17).

4 Nov 1741: Henry Chew of BA Co., Gent., conv. 300 as. pt. (*) to Thomas Hawkins (TB#A: 33).

13 Feb 1741/2: Henry Chew of BA Co., Gent., conv. pt. (*) and pt. Jones' Adventure, in all about 100 a., to Joseph Chew (T#A, 100).

21 Oct 1742: Henry Chew of CV Co., Gent., conv. 309 a. pt. (*) to James Rigbie; tract was taken up by Enoch Spinks who sold it to William Holland who left it to his s. William, who sold it to the said Chew (TB#C: 43).

20 April 1747: James Rigbie of BA Co. mortgaged 217 a., pt. (*) (bought from Henry Chew) to Josias Middlemore (TB#E: 387).

BACHELOR'S HOPE (1664)

7 Feb 1664: 550 a. surv. for Edward Gilfe and Richard Meriday; lands was taken away by an elder surv. (MRR: 92).

BACHELOR'S HOPE (1668)

28 April 1668: 400 a. surv. for William Tomson on the e. side of Bush R. and the w. side of Bush Hunting Creek Branch; later possessed by Peregrine Brown (MRR: 10).

7 Sep 1669: Lodowick Williams, planter, conv. to Walter Tucker and Co., merchants, of England, tract (*), 400 a.; also an unnamed tract of 50 a. (IR#PP: 76).

14 Oct 1717: Maurice Burchfield, Surveyor General of His Majesty's Customs in the Southern District of America, and Joseph Brown, late of London, merchant, s. and heir of Peregrine Brown, late of London, dec., conv. 400 a. (*) to James Phillips; the deed states that Peregrine Brown made a will naming w. Margaret as extx.; the following tracts in MD were owned by Peregrine Brown at the time of his death: Addition, 400 a.; Bachelor's Addition: (*) 400 a.; Chilbury 250 a.; Waters' Neck 100 a. the MD Court of Chancery decreed that these tracts should be held to satisfy the debts of Browne (TR#A: 485).

3 Aug 1725: John Vines of AA Co., conv. 25 a. (*) in BA Co., to John Brown of AA Co.; JV's w. Elizabeth cons. (PCLR PL#6: 87).

20 Dec 1737: John Stinchcomb of BA Co. deeds to Nathaniel Stinchcomb tracts (*) and Addition to Bachelor's Hope (HWS#1-A: 41).

BACHELOR'S HOPE (1679)
(See DENTON'S HOPE)

27 May 1679: 200 a. surv. for James Denton as 2 parcels of land called Salt Peter Neck and Bachelor's Hope; later called Denton's Hope and possessed by William Denton (MRR: 65).

BACHELOR'S HOPE (B)

2 May 1750: Thomas Jarman of BA Co. conv., to John Denton his moiety or half of Bachelor's Hope, Bachelor's Meadow, and Salt Peter Neck, lately owned by William Denton, dec. TJ's w. Mary cons. (TR#C: 482).

2 May 1750: John Denton and w. Rachel, in exch. for 100 a. called Violin, conv. his moiety of Bachelor's Hope, Bachelor's Meadow, and Salt Peter Neck (TR#C: 510).

BACHELOR'S HOPE, ADDITION TO

14 April 1721: 50 a. surv. for John Stinchcomb.

20 May 1725: 50 a. pat. by John Stinchcomb (MPL PL#6: 310, IL#A: 201).

20 Dec 1737: John Stinchcomb of BA Co. deeds to Nathaniel Stinchcomb tracts (*) and Bachelor's Hope (HWS#1-A: 41).

BACHELOR'S MEADOW

2 May 1750: Thomas Jarman of BA Co. conv., to John Denton his moiety or half of Bachelor's Hope, (*), and Salt Peter Neck, lately owned by William Denton, dec. TJ's w. Mary cons. (TR#C: 482).

2 May 1750: John Denton of BA Co., and w. Rachel, in exch. for 100 a. called Violin, conv. his moiety of Bachelor's Hope, Bachelor's Meadow, and Salt Peter Neck (TR#C: 510).

24 May 1751: William Denton of BA conv. to John Davis of William a ½ moiety of Denton's Hope (311 a. in all) and ½ of Bachelor's Meadows. WD's w. Elizabeth cons. (TR#D: 176).

3 March 1757: John Davis s. of Walter conv. (*) to William Andrew (B#G: 16).

BACHELOR'S NECK

Jan 1716: 50 a. surv. for Abr. Vaughan (Card Index to Patents).

5 Sep 1738: Abraham Vaughan conv. 50 a. (*) (surv. 21 Oct 1718 [sic]) to William Wheeler; AV's w. Edith cons. (HWS#1-A: 101).

BACHELOR'S NECK, ADDITION TO

8 Aug 1744: Abraham Vaughan, with cons. of w. Edith, conv. 24 a. pt. (*) to William Wheeler (TB#C: 549).

6 March 1747: Abraham Vaughan conv. 140 a. (*) (except for 24 a. already sold to William Wheeler) to William Rogers; AV's w. Edith cons. (TB#E: 430).

9 May 1747: Abraham Vaughan leases (*), pt. of His Lordship's Reserve, to William Rogers of BA Co., innholder (TB#E: 442).

17 Feb 1752: William Rogers gave to his s. Nicholas Tempest Rogers 166 a. (*) (TR#D: 279).

BACHELOR'S RANGE

25 July 1725: Thomas Broad of BA Co., planter, conv. 50 a. (*) to William Rogers of BA Co., cordwainer (IS#H: 135).

4 Sep 1730: William Rogers and w. Sarah of BA Co., conv. 50 a. (*) to William Cox (IS#L: 184).

3 Aug 1736: William Cox, for love he bears his dau. Elizabeth, w. of Charles Bosley, conv. her 50 a. (*); WC's w. Mary cons. (HWS#M: 418).

BACHELOR'S RIDGE

4 Dec 1742: Robert Harryman of BA Co., planter, conv. 100 a. (*) on White Maple Run, to Thomas Hines; TH's w. Elizabeth cons. (TB#C: 196).

6 March 1744: Thomas Hines of St. Paul's Parish, conv. 100 a. (*) and 16 a. Hines Desire to Edward Fell, the sale to take effect after the death of said Hines and his w. Elizabeth (TB#C: 20 (or 70).

31 May 1763: Edward Fell, s. of William Fell, dec., conv. 100 a. (*) and 16 a. Hines Desire to Richard Fowler (B#L: 235).

BACHELOR'S VINEYARD

29 Sep 1712: Richard Shipley, with cons. of w. Susannah, conv. (*) to Peter Shipley (TR#A: 213).

BACK LINGAN (See also BACK LINGHAM)

6 Nov 1682: 525 a. surv. for George Lingan; later including 450 a. held by Edward Butler (MRR: 41).

22 Jan 1735: Bigger Head of CV Co. and w. Martha, dau. of Edward Butler, late of sd. co., conv. (*) to William Andrew and his s. Andrew (TB#E: 1).

17 Nov 1745: Thomas Swan and w. Elizabeth, (dau. of Edward Butler) of SM Co., conv. 450 a. (*) to Alexander Lawson and Co. (TB#E: 412).

1760: William Andrew conv. 450 a. (*) to Alexander Lawson and Co. (B#H: 412).

BAGFORD

7 March 1733/4: Samuel Chew gives receipt for 100 a. (*) and numerous other tracts to Thomas Todd (HWS#M: 20).

BAGFORD'S (BAYFORD'S) FORTUNE

17 Dec 1726: Thomas Stone and w. Elizabeth conv. 80 a. (*) to Luke Stansbury (IS#H: 328).

1750: William Lynch owned (*) (1750 DB: 43).

BAIRE'S GRIME (See BEAR'S GRIME)

BAKER'S ADDITION

25 Nov 1697: Maurice Baker conv. 100 a. Allen's Rest, being pt. (*), to Robert Allen. MB's w. Elizabeth cons. (TR#RA: 406).

BAKER'S CHANCE

16 July 1685: Tract was pat. (TR#A: 154).

1 June 1703: Charles Baker and w. Hannah conv. pt. (*) (or Baker's Choice) to John Rattenbury (BCF: 20).

8 Aug 1711: William Baker of BA Co., tailor with cons. of w. Ann, conv. 50 a. pt. (*) to James Drane of BA Co. (TR#A: 154).

1750: Indimeon Baker owned 50 a. (*) (1750 DB).

22 Sep 1753: Indimeon Baker of BA Co. deeds 50 a. (*) (orig. granted to said Baker), to Richard Wilmot. IB's w. Katherine cons. (BB#I: 135).

BAKER'S DELIGHT

21 Feb 1722/3: John Baker and w. Margaret conv. 40 a. (*) to John Buckingham (IS#G: 165).

29 July 1758: Benjamin Buckingham and w. Aberilla conv. 40 a. (*) to James Hood (B#G: 209).

BAKER'S DISCOVERY

28 Oct, 1762: Robert Gilchrist of BA Co. conv. 15 a. pt. (*) to John Evans of BA Co.; Robert's w. Helen cons. (B#K: 385).

BAKER'S INDUSTRY

10 April 1762: John Baker of BA Co. deeds 178 a. (*) to Vachel Dorsey; John's w. Elizabeth cons. (PCLR DD#2, 35).

BAKER'S PLEASURE

1742: Charles Baker leased 115 a. (*) on Gunpowder Manor for the lives of Charles and his s. and dau. Charles and Providence; in 1767 Charles was age 63, and Charles, Jr., was age 26; in 1785 it was resurv. for James Baker and contained 125 a. (Slattery: 2).

BALD HILL

15 Sep 1741: Benjamin Wheeler conv. 80 a. St. Omers, with a plantation called Bald Hill, to his dau. Ann Wheeler (HWS#1-A: 558).

BALD HILLS

1750: William Hamilton owned 50 a. (*) and East Lothian (1750 DB).

BALE'S DISCOVERY

10 Nov 1703: 300 a. pat. to Thomas Crossing (MPL CD#4: 60, DD#5: 125).

See Horvath Plats: Ruxton and Riderwood, and Green Spring Valley.

13 Jan 1731: John Crossing of Exon, tailor, bro. and heir, and admin. of Thomas Crossing of Exon, ironmonger, conv. 300 a. (*) to John Smith of MD (IS#L: 271, 273).

14 Jan 1731: John Crossing of the city of Exon, tailor, bro. and heir and admin. of Thomas Crossing, dec., gave to Robert Babb of London, p/a to conv. (*) in MD to Col. John Smith (IS#L: 270).

18 Jan 1731: Susannah Richards, now w. of Edmond Richards, and relict of Francis Crossing late of Exon, cordwainer, dec., made an affidavit that John Crossing, tailor, her son, was next heir to her s. Thomas Crossing, formerly of Exon, ironmonger, who d. at sea (IS#L: 275).

14 Nov 1743: Capt. John Smith of CV Co., merchant, conv. 300 a. (*) plus 700 a. The Groves and 424 a. pt. Addition to Poor Jamaica Man's Plague, to Walter Smith of the Freshes, Patuxent R., s. and heir of Walter Smith, dec., in exch. for 636 a. of Hall's Craft in CV Co. (TB#C: 416).

BALL'S ADDITION

11 Feb 1683/4: Thomas Everest, planter, and w. Hannah, conv. 60 a. (*) to John Bennett, merchant, of AA Co.; the tract was orig. pat. to Richard Ball, cordwainer, of BA Co., dec. (RM#HS: 74).

13 May 1699: William Herbert and w., conv. (*) to Nicholas Fitzsimmons; also Bennett's Range, formerly taken up by John Bennett, and Thomas' Range, formerly taken up by John Thomas (HW#2: 21).

BALL'S ENLARGEMENT

9 Oct 1676: William Ball of AA Co. conv. 100,a. (*) to William Cockey; tract had been pat. by Ball on 20 July 1674 (IR#PP: 6).

23 Feb 1723: William Farrall and w. Mary conv. 1/5 of 100 a. (*) and 93 a. Cockey's Enlargement to Charles Hall; a note excepts the dowry of Mary Pumphrey, late widow of William Cockey (IS#H: 32).

BALLESTONE

7 Aug 1677: William Ball appointed Nicholas Ruxton of MD his atty. to acknowledge sale of land to Thomas Long; on 4 June 1678 Ruxton, of Patapsco, atty., for William Ball of Lancaster Co., VA, conv. 420 a. (*) to Major Thomas Long at Middle R. in Gunpowder R., said tract having been pat. 24 Sep 1663 to Ball (IR#PP: 24).

6 March 1733: John Long of BA Co. conv. 420 a. (*) to Stephen Body (HWS#M: 29).

6 June 1733: John Long conv. pt. (*) to Joseph Ward (IS#L: 378).

25 June 1737: Thomas Sheredine conv. 150 a. pt. (*) to Buckler Partridge (HWS#M: 27).

25 Sep 1740: John Long of BA Co. conv. pt. (*) to Buckler Partridge; Long's w. Eleanor cons. (HWS#1-A: 449).

BANKS

4 Nov 1668: Thomas Bastock and w. Jane conv. (*) to James Magregor, on the w. side of Bohemia R. (IR#PP: 70).

BANKS' DELIGHT

1732: 77 a. granted to William Banks (PW Plat W).

10 May 1747: William Banks of BA Co. conv. 77 a. (*) to Darby Lux; Banks' w. Elizabeth cons. (TB#E: 394).

BARE HILLS

28 Jan 1741: Thomas Litton and w. Ann conv. 100 a. (*) to James Rowland (TB#A: 97).

BARE HILLS (1752)

1752; 175 a. granted to Daniel Dulany

See PW Plats H and HB, Horvath Plats: Ruxton and Riderwood and Green Spring Valley.

BARKER'S CHOICE

12 June 1705: John Barker dated his will leaving (*) to Dr. John Rattenbury (BAWB 1:).

BARKER'S INHERITANCE

10 July 1701: John Gadsby of AA Co., planter, and w. Jane, conv. 130 a. (*) (being pt. of 1000 a. Browne's Adventure which Lord Baltimore granted to Thomas Browne on 10 June 1699, and Browne conv. the tract to Gadsby) to John Barker of AA Co., carpenter (HW#2: 99).

BARNES' LEVEL

1743: Surv. for Benj. Barnes.

See Horvath Plat: Finksburg to Westminster.

18 March 1746: Benjamin Barnes and w. Martha conv. 50 a. (*) to William Gosnell (TB#E: 328).

31 Oct 1752: William Gosnell and w. Elizabeth conv. 50 a. (*) to Thomas Walton (TR#D: 448).

BARNEY'S PURCHASE

11 June 1743: John Jamison conv. 130 a. (*), 100 a. London, and 100 a. Pitchcraft and Polecat Ridge, to Samuel Howell. JJ's w., unnamed, cons. (TB#C: 258).

18 Aug 1748: Samuel Howell conv. 130 a. (*) and 100 a. London to William Savory. SH's w. Sarah cons. (TR#C: 54).

BARNEY'S TIMBER RIDGE

25 March 1757: date of cert. of surv. (B#I: 94).

6 April 1761: Benjamin Barney of BA Co., planter, conv. 100 a. (*) to Benjamin Wheeler. Barney's w. Delilah cons. (B#I: 94).

27 June 1761: Benjamin Barney of BA Co., with w. Delilah's cons., conv. 200 a. (*) to Jacob Cox (B#I: 359).

19 July 1793: Benjamin Wheeler conv. 100 a. (*) to Mordecai Wheeler (WG#MM: 378).

BARRAND POINT

4 June 1677: James Ives, planter, conv. 50 a. (*) to Henry Haslewood, at the head of Muskeeto Creek. W. Martha Ives signed with grantor (IR#PP: 13).

BARRETT'S ADDITION

14 April 1718: Alice Barrett, extx. of last will of John Barrett, conv. 190 a. (*) to John Talbott of AA Co., merchant (TR#RA: 426-427).

BARRETT'S DELIGHT

14 April 1718: Alice Barrett, extx. of last will of John Barrett, conv. 200 A. (*) to John Talbott of AA Co., merchant (TR#RA: 426-427).

BARRETT'S REST. (pt. of DEAR BIT)

26 Feb 1712: William Farfarr of Back R., conv. 256 a. (*) to John Barrett. Farfarr's w. Eleanor cons. (TR#A: 219).

3 Sep 1733: Nicholas Corbin and w. Eleanor conv. 125 a. (*), (which John Barrett devised by his will of 21 June 1717 to said Corbin), to Philip Sindall (IS#L: 421).

5 Nov 1734: John Royston and w. Mary conv., 125 a. (*) to Thomas Creen (HWS#M: 126).

BARTON'S CHANCE

17 March 1727: Thomas Barton conv., ⅓ of (*) to Peter Carroll; Barton's w. Elizabeth cons. (IS#I: 324) [both pages of the deed are illegible].

1750: Peter Carroll owned 15 a. pt. Barton's Chance; William Robinson "of Gunpowder" owned 100 a. pt. of the same tract (1750 DB).

BARTON'S HARBOR

5 April 1748: John Barton of BA Co. assigned to Ashael Hitchcock the residue of the lease made 1 Sep 1742 from Benjamin Tasker for 50 a. (*), pt. of His Lordship's Reserve, for 99 a. (TB#E: 698).

BARTON'S MOUNT

19 Sep 1750: Selah Barton conv. 15½ a. (*) to James Brown. Selah's w. Comfort cons. (TR#D: 22).

BATCHELOR'S ... (See BACHELOR'S ...)

BATSON'S FELLOWSHIP

6 Jan 1698: 150 a. surv., for Edward Batson (MRR: 27).

BATSON'S FOREST

26 March 1707: (*) surv. for Edward Battson (HWS#1-A: 68).

20 Aug 1709: Edward Battson conv. (*) or Newfoundland, to Richard Dallam (HWS#M: 139).

23 Nov 1734: Amey Battson of PG Co., dau. of Edward Battson, dec., conv. (*) to Richard Dallam, s. of the above Richard Dallam (HWS#M: 139).

26 Nov 1734: Richard Dallam conv. 500 a. (*) to William Dallam (HWS#1-A: 68).

9 June 1738: William Dallam conv. 250 a., being $\frac{1}{2}$ of (*) to John Gill. (HWS#1-A: 78).
9 June 1738: William Dallam conv. 250 a., $\frac{1}{2}$ of (*), to William Rogers (HWS#1-A: 79).
12 Jan 1744: William Rogers conv. 125 a. pt. (*) to John B[axter?]. Rogers' w. Sarah cons. (TB#E: 42).
12 Jan 1744: John Baxter and w. Mary conv. 62$\frac{1}{2}$ a. (*) to Thomas Hudson (TB#E: 27).
12 Jan 1744: William Rogers conv. 125 a. (*) to Stephen Gill. William's w. Sarah cons. (TB#E: 38).

BAYLEY

22 June 1661: Godfrey Bayley conv. 300 a. (*) to Nathaniel Stiles, merchant (RM#HS: 1).
7 March 1670/1: Nathaniel Stiles conv. 300 a. (*) to Richard Whitton (Scisco, "BA Co. Land Records of 1671," MHM 27:125).
5 March 1683: Elias Robertson of CE Co., conv. 200 a. pt. (*) to Andrew Mattson of BA Co., carpenter. (RM#HS: 87).

BAYS TOWN

c1763/4: Mordecai Gosnell owned 10 a. (ALAH at MHS).

BEAL'S CAMP

22 Sep 1683: 1000 a. surv. for Ninian Beale at the head of Bush R.; later held by Archibald Edmondson (MRR: 18).
29 Oct 1713: Archibald Edmondson and w. Jane of PG Co., conv. 200 a. pt. (*) to Daniel Scott (TR#A: 245).
30 Aug 1714: same grantors conv. 100 a. to Daniel Scott, Jr. (TR#A: 307).
1718: same grantors conv. 199.5 a. (*) to Jacob Bull of BA Co., turner (TR#RA: 450).
13 Jan 1719: same grantors conv. 100 a. (*) to Thomas Smithson (TR#DS: 135).
19 Feb 1721: same grantors conv. 100 a. (*) to John Steel (IS#G: 14).
30 Aug 1722: same grantors conv. 100 a. (*) to John Corbin (IS#G: 188).
29 April 1726: same grantors conv. 400 a. (*) to Daniel Scott (IS#H: 232).
13 Sep 1726: same grantors conv. 100 a. (*) to Jacob Bull of BA Co. (IS#H: 347).

BEAL'S PURCHASE

5 Dec 1735: Christopher Randall conv. (*) to John Moale. CR's w. Katherine cons. (HWS#M: 356).

BEAR NECK (1671)

7 July 1671: 100 a. surv. for William Ball on the s. side of Patapsco R. at Curtis Creek; later possessed by William Cromwell (MRR: 99).
13 Aug 1706: William Cromwell and w. Mary conv. 140 a. (*) as Bare Neck) to Thomas Foster, schoolmaster (RM#HS: 613).

BEAR NECK (1682)

8 Feb 1682: 146 a. surv. for Robert Proctor on s. side of Bodkin Creek; later 100 a. possessed by William Foreman and 46 a. by the orphans of Nicholas Lamb (MRR: 104).

BEAR NECK (1685)

1695: Cert. for 200 a. laid out for Edward Felkes (RM#HS: 42).

BEAR NECK (1697)

10 Oct 1697: 500 a. surv. for Walter Smith on n. side of Back R., near the place called Newport (MRR: 54).
31 Sep 1727: Elinor Addison of PG Co., widow,. conv. 250 a., being $\frac{1}{2}$ of (*) to her bro. Richard Smith of CV Co. The parcel was her half of 500 a. granted on 10 Nov 1695 to her father Walter Smith, dec.; he bequeathed the land to his daus. Elinor and Anne (IS#I: 6).

BEAR RANGE

19 Nov 1728 pat. to Thomas Johnson for 100 a. (HWS#M: 30).
6 March 1733: Thomas Johnson of The Land of Nod, conv. (*) to John Poteet. TJ's w. Alice cons. (HWS#M: 30).
1750: John Poteet owned 100 a. Bear Range (Debt Book)
1755 (no day or month given): James Poteet conv. 100 a. Bear Racing (Bear Range?) to John McGouern. James' w. Elizabeth cons. (BB#I: 414).

BEAR'S GRIME

28 Feb 1669/70: John James, Gent., conv. 100 a. (*), near the head of Steelpone Creek, to Charles James (IR#PP: 77).

BEAR'S THICKET

29 Oct 1737: Thomas Preston of AA Co. conv. (*) to Benjamin Larkin (HWS#M: 29).

BEAUTIFUL ISLAND

1758: Walter Ashmore conv. 62 a. (*) to Samuel Hughes (B#G: 109).

BEAVANS' ADVENTURE

5 Nov 1734: Joseph Beavens, with cons. of w. Rebecca, conv. 100 a. (*) to William Andrews (HWS#M: 188).

BEAVER NECK

28 March 1663: 200 a. surv. for John Collett on the w. side of Musketa Creek; 125 a. later held by James Ives; still later 75 a. held by John Hall and 125 a. held by John Stokes (MRR: 25).

4 March 1667/8: John Collett, Gent., conv. 100 a. (*), being the northern half, to John Taylard (IR#PP: 62).

3 May 1670: Sarah Tilliard gave p/a to James Ives to acknowledge sale of 100 a. (*) to John Mascord (IR#PP: 99).

11 Nov 1670: John Tilliard, planter, conv. 100 a. (*), the northern half, to John Mascard (IR#PP: 99).

28 Jan 1670/1: John Collett conv. 100 a. (*) to Matthew Knivington (IR#PP: 94).

2 Aug 1673: John Mascord and Jane Mascord (w.?) and Matthew Knivington conv. 200 a. (*) to Bernard Utie (G#J: 176; TR#RA: 127).

5 June 1676: Thomas Overton and w. Jane conv. to Peter Ellis 75 a. pt. of (*), lately in poss. of Bernard Utie and now occupied by Edward Jackson [Is Jane the widow or dau. of John Mascord?] (G#J: 300; TR#RA: 235).

4 June 1679: Henry Haslewood made a will leaving 125 a. (*) to his w. Elizabeth and then to his s. Henry, Jr. (MCW#I, 96).

2 Aug 1679: Peter Ellis, planter, and w. Elizabeth, conv. 75 a. (*) to Simon Dawkins; tract was lately possessed by Bernard Utie, Thomas Overton and w. Jane, and now by Edward Jackson (IR#PP: 41).

13 April 1703: William Loney and w. Jane conv. (*) to Thomas Capell; being ½ of the tract formerly belonging to Bernard Utie, later sold to Peter Ellis, who sold to Simon Dawkins, and now in poss. of Thomas Capell (HW#2: 351).

4 March 1703/4: James Ives of BA Co. made his will leaving (*) to Susanna Wells and her heirs (MCW#III, 30).

29 Dec 1708: John Stokes, the elder, conv. 125 a. (*) to John Stokes the younger, which desc. to JS the elder's w. Susanna by the will of James Ives (RM#HS: 632).

17 March 1718: John Stokes and w. Susanna conv. 125 a. (*) and 102 a. Mosquito Proof to John Clarke (TR#RA: 422).

2 Nov 1723: John Clarke conv. 125 a. (*) and 102 a. Mosquito Proof to John Hall (deed traces descent of property from Bernard Utie who devised to Henry Haslewood, Sr., who devised to Henry Jr., who devised it to James Ives, who devised to Susanna Wells now w. of John Stokes and sold by them to John Clark (IS#G: 212).

4 Jan 1728: John Hall made his will leaving pt. of (*) to his s. John (MCW#VII: 221).

BEDFORD

22 Sep 1730: William Logsdon and w. Honour (Oner) conv. 100 a. to Matthew Coulter, tailor (IS#L: 46).

29 May 1742: Matthew Coulter of BA Co., tailor, conv. 240 a. (*) to Thomas Bond (TB#A: 169).

BEDFORD RESURVEYED

15 July 1747: Thomas Bond and w. Phebe conv. 100 a. made up of pt. (*) and pt. Logsdon's Adddition to Patrick and Elizabeth Gray (TB#E: 494).

25 July 1747: Thomas Bond and w. Phebe conv., 62.5 a. (*) and 37.5 a. [Logsdon's Addition?] to Benjamin Bond (TB#E: 494).

11 April 1748: Benjamin Bond and w. Sophia conv. 37.5 a. (*) to Richard Croxall (TB#E: 706).

21 April 1750: Benjamin Bond of BA Co. conv. 62½ a. (*) to Richard Croxall, being the same land which Thomas Bond conv. to the grantor on 25 July 1747. BB's w. Sophia cons. (TR#C: 427).

1750: Benjamin Bond owned 62½ a. (*) (1750 DB: 83).

7 April 1757: William Shrider and w., Susanna conv. 100 a. pt. (*) and pt. Logsdon's Addition to Thomas Johnson (B#G:162).

BEDLAM (Pt. of EXPECTATION)

21 March 1702/3: John Elliss conv. 50 a. (*), pt. of Expectation, to Miles Hannes (HW#2: 287).

3 Feb 1706: Miles Hannis of BA Co. conv. 50 a. (*) to Tobias Eminson (RM#HS: 541).

2 March 1708: Tobias Eminson conv. 50 a. (*) back to Miles Hannis (RM#HS: 648).

BEDNALL GREEN

9 Aug 1733: William Hitchcock, Sr., conv. 100 a. (*) to WH, Jr. (IS#L: 412).

3 March 1752: William Hitchcock conv. (*) to Isaac Hitchcock (TR#D: 305).

BEEDLE'S RESERVE

22 Sep 1680: 100 a. surv. for Edward Beedle; later held by the orphans of George Utie, and still later by John Hall (MRR: 4).

30 Dec 1696: John Hall and w. Martha, one of the daus. and coheirs of Edward Beedle, dec., conv. to Mary Utie, relict of George Utie, and sister of Martha Hall, 130 a. pt. Carter's Rest and 100 a. (*) (IS#IK, 241, 245).

17 July 1722: Francis Holland and w. Susanna, conv. 60 a. (*) to Benjamin Osborn (IS#G: 92).

18 July 1722: Francis Holland and w. Susanna conv. 60 a. (*) to Thomas Gash (IS#G: 84).

28 Nov 1737: Thomas Gash and w. Hannah conv. 60 a. (*) to Benj. Osborne of William (HWS#1-A: 43).

BEGRUDGED

1764: Thomas Cockey conv. 45 a. (*) to Charles Gorsuch (B#N: 288).

BELINDA

26 Oct 1765: John Ford of BA Co. conv. 9 a. pt. (*) to Nicholas Orrick and Alexander Wells (B#O: 557).

BELT'S HILLS

22 May 1719/20: 800 a. surv. for John Belt of AA Co. (RM#HS: 685).

1720: John Belt of AA Co., with cons. of w. Lucy, conv. 400 a. (*) to Benjamin Stevens of BA Co. (RM#HS: 685).

BELT'S POINT

12 Jan 1719/20: Cert. of surv.

25 June 1726: John Belt, Sr. conv. 112 a. (*) to his natural dau. Mary who is about to marry Greenbury Dorsey of John (IS#H: 236).

1 May 1727: John Belt of BA Co. conv. 112. a. (*) to his son-in-law Greenbury Dorsey (son of Col. John Dorsey and w. Comfort) (IS#H: 441).

BELT'S PROSPERITY

29 April 1685: Thomas Lightfoot, surveyor, conv. 300 a. (*) to John Belt of AA Co., being pt. of 1000 and 500 a. tracts, both called Expectation. Rebecca Lightfoot signs with grantor (RM#HS: 123).

21 Sep 1745: Joseph and Benjamin Belt, of PG Co., conv. 300 a. (*) to Stephen Onion. JB's w. Martha cons.; JB is conv. only his right to 100 a. (TB#E: 334).

BENGER'S ADDITION

31 May 1681: Robert Benger of Gunpowder R. gave bond to Thomas Harris of Herring Creek, AA Co., that he will conv. 30 a. (*) and 150 a. Oliver's Reserve to said Harris (IR#AM: 134).

BENGER'S ADDITION TO PRIVILEGE

15 Aug 1688: 58 a. surv. for Robert Benger (TR#A, 278).

4 Feb 1713: Alexander Graves, late of KE Co., conv. (*) to John Harris of KE Co. (TR#A: 278-279).

5 Feb 1713: Alexander Graves gave p/a to Charles Hynson to acknowledge above sale (TR#A: 178-179).

BENGER'S PRIVILEGE

15 Jan 1700: John Shaw conv. 180 a. (*) and other lands to Alexander Graves of BA Co. (HW#2: 53).

4 Feb 1713: Alexander Graves, late of KE Co., conv. (*) to John Harris of KE Co. (TR#A: 278-279).

5 Feb 1713: Alexander Graves gave p/a to Charles Hynson to acknowledge above sale (TR#A: 178-179).

BENITON

3 Aug 1688: Charles James, merchant, conv. to John James, Gent., 200 a. (*) at Steelpone Creek (IR#PP: betw. 65-69).

BENJAMIN'S ADDITION

1 June 1764: James Chambers and w. Mary, dau. of John Tipton, conv. 50 a. (*) to John Ridgely (B#O: 247).

BENJAMIN'S BEGINNING

See Horvath Plat: Ruxton and Riderwood.

1720: Benjamin Martin conv. 100 a. (*) to Richard Wheeler (RM#HS: 667).

24 Aug 1730: Richard Wheeler conv. 100 a. (*) to John Tipton (IS#L: 18).

BENJAMIN'S CAMP

15 Sep 1741: Benjamin Wheeler conv. 100 a. pt. (*) to dau. Ann Wheeler (HWS#1-A: fol. 558).

15 Sep 1741: Benj. Wheeler conv. 67.5 a. (*) to s. Ignatius Wheeler, mentions daus. Eliz., Mary, and Ann (HWS#1-A: 549).

15 Sep 1741: same grantor conv. 67.5 a. (*) to s. Leonard Wheeler (HWS#1-A: 551).

BENJAMIN'S CHOICE (1678)

11 May 1678: 400 a. surv. for Col. George Wells at a bounded white oak; sold to George Utie; later held by John Hall and Mark Richardson for the orphans of Utie; later held by John Hall (MRR: 4).

7 Aug 1694: George Wells of BA Co., Gent., and w. Blanch conv. 400 a. (*) to George Utie (RM#HS: 409).

28 Feb 1716: Francis Holland of BA Co., Gent., and w. Susanna conv. 400 a. (*) to James Phillips; tract was surv. for Col. George Wells, who sold it to George Utie, father of Susanna Holland (TR#A: 472).

29 Sep 1738: James Phillips of BA Co., Gent., conv. 100 a. pt. (*) to Joshua Wood (HWS#1-A: 107).

7 Dec 1739: James Phillips, s. and heir of Col. James Phillips, dec., conv. 500 a. pt. (*) and pt. James Park to his sister Johanna, w. of Jacob Giles (HWS#1-A: 310).

BENJAMIN'S CHOICE (1683)

25 Sep 1683: 254 a. surv. for Thomas Hedge; later held by his heirs (MRR: 17).

1690/1: Thomas Hedge of BA Co., clerk, conv. 254 a. (*) to his s. Henry Hedge of BA Co. (IR#AM: 70).

31 May 1726: Samuel Hedge, merchant of Salem Co., NJ, conv. 254 a. (*) to Roger Matthews (IS#I: 169).

1729: Roger Matthews conv. 254 a. (*) to William Smith (IS#K: 141).

20 March 1736: William Smith conv. (*), orig. granted to Thomas Hedge,. to Helen Newsom, in exch. got 200 a. Contrivance and 50 a. Newsam (HWS#1-A: 299).

1 Sep 1738: Mary Smith, widow of William Smith, conv. 254 a. (*) to John and Helen Bailey (HWS#1-A: 271).

18 Sep 1739: John Bailey and w. Helen conv. 250 a. (*) to Joshua Wood (HWS#1-A: 280).

23 Feb 1748: Joshua Wood of BA Co. conv. to Abraham Taylor 254 a. (*), and other lands, which his father, Joshua Wood, d. possessed of (TR#C: 157).

BENJAMIN'S DELIGHT

21 Sep 1754: Benjamin Hooker conv. 75 a. (*) to William Bell (B#I: 1).

9 Oct 1762: Mordecai Price and Samuel Price of BA Co. lease 65 a., (*), to Mordecai Ford (B#L: 114).

BENJAMIN'S PROSPECT

10 June 1734: 50 a. pat. to Benjamin Davis (MPL EI#2: 14, EI#3: 317).

16 April 1750: Benjamin Davis of Augustus [sic] Co., VA, conv. 50 a. (*) to John Risteau. BD's w. Margaret cons. (TR#C: 424).

BENNETT'S HOPE

14 March 1681/2: Thomas Everest and w. Hannah conv. 100 a. (*) to John Bennett adj. to East Humphreys (IR#AM: 173).

BENNETT'S RANGE

11 Feb 1683/4: Thomas Everest of the Cliffs, CV Co., and w. Hannah conv. 50 a. (*) to John Bennett, of AA Co. (RM#HS: 75).

13 May 1699: William Herbert and w. Mary conv. (*), formerly taken up by John Bennett of AA Co., to Nicholas Fitzsimmons (HW#2: 21).

BENSON'S PARK

5 Aug 1723: Daniel Benson of CE Co., Daniel Gears and w. Elizabeth, and James Huggins and w. Jane (said Daniel Benson, Jane and Elizabeth being ch. of Daniel Benson of AA Co., dec.), conv. 250 a. (*) in Elk Ridge to Lancelot Todd of BA Co. (Daniel Benson the elder d. leaving 150 a. to s. Daniel and 50 a. to each of his daus.). (IS#G: 172).

BEST ENDEAVOR

16 Oct 1705: Thomas Hammond and w. Rebecca give p/a to Francis Dallahide to acknowledge the following indenture: they conv. 100 a. Friend's Enlargement, being pt. of Best Endeavor, to John Webster (IR#PP: 195).

4 March 1718: John Hammond, Gent., conv. 100 a. (*), pt. of a 400 a. tract, to John Webster (TR#RA: 534).

4 June 1744: Comfort Dorsey, John Hammond Dorsey and Vincent Dorsey, execs. and heirs of John Hammond, conv. to John Webster the residue of (*) not already purch. by Webster (TB#C: 542).

BEST SUCCESS

10 March 1705: Thomas Hammond and w. Rebecca conv. 250 a. Success, pt. of Best Success, orig. taken up by Thomas Lightfoot, to Matthew Hawkins (IR#AM: 8).

18 May 1710: Joshua Merriken, s. of Hugh, dec., and Joshua's w. Elizabeth, conv. to John Brice of AA Co., merchant, Merriken's Purchase, being pt. of (*), purch. from Thomas Lightfoot on 6 Nov 1686 (TR#A: 79).

23 Sep 1723: Thomas Noland and w. Mary, John Cole and w. Dinah, Thomas Broad and w. Anna, and Rebecca Hawkins, conv. 250 a. (*), bought by Matthew Hawkins, late of BA Co., from Col. Thomas Hammond (and adj. Brother's Kindness), to Lancelot Todd, except for 90 a. deeded by Matthew Hawkins to Joseph Hawkins (IS#G: 208).

BETHEL

1 Aug 1731: John Cole of BA Co., and w. Dinah, conv. 100 a. (*) to Charles Gorsuch (IS#K: 328).

10 Dec 1737: Charles Gorsuch conv. 100 a. (*) to his s. John Gorsuch (HWS#M: 45).

BETTER HOPE

28 May 1707: Francis Watkins of BA Co., planter, conv. (*), Hopewell and Surplus, to James Crooke, yeoman (RM#HS: 559).

4 Jan 1730: Joseph Elledge and w. Elizabeth conv. 100 a. (*) (or Better Hopes) to John Taylor (IS#L: 59).

BETTOR HOPES (1731)

17 Oct 1731: 100 a. pat. to Joseph Elledge who later sold it to John Taylor. In his will Taylor empowered his w. and extx. Keziah to sell the land to settle his debts (TR#C: 250).

2 Aug 1749: Joshua Hardesty and w. Keziah, widow of John Taylor mentioned above, conv. to Greenbury Dorsey 100 a. (*) (TR#C: 250).

26 March 1752: Greenbury Dorsey, with cons. of w. Sarah, conv. 100 a. (*) (TR#D: 318).

BETTY'S ADVENTURE

7 Aug 1722: Edward Reaston and w. Johanna conv. 100 a. pt. (*) to John Gardner of Clapham, on Patapsco R. (IS#G: 30).

10 Sep 1743: Luke Trotten and William Hamilton, execs. of John Gardener, conv. 100 a. (*), and 25 a. Miller's Choice, to John Bosley (TB#C: 404).

BETTY'S CHOICE

20 July 1678: 480 a. surv., for George Yates; later held by Benjamin Burgess, and later by John Watkins' orphans (MRR: 34).

24 Jan 1680/1: George Yate, Gent., of AA Co., conv. 480 a. (*) to Robert Hooper, cooper, as pat. 18 July 1679 to Yate; Yate's w. Mary cons. On the same day Yate gave bond to Hooper he would perform the covenants (RM#HS: 80).

10 June 1683: Robert Hooper, cooper, of AA Co., conv. (*) to Col. William Burgess, and on the same day gave bond to Burgess, and appoints Thomas Hedge his atty. (RM#HS: 86).

28 May 1725: Charles Burgess of PG Co., and w. Elizabeth conv. 480 a. (*) to Edward Hall of BA Co. (IS#H: 165).

BETTYS DELIGHT

1729: Cadwallader Jones released (*) to Bloyce Wright (IS#K: 128).

BETTY'S INHERITANCE
(May be one of several)

4 Aug 1714: James Richardson conv. 200 a. (*) to Thomas Hutchins of BA Co., innholder (TR#A: 336).

16 Jan 1717: Mary Stevenson of BA Co., widow, conv. (*) (as pt. of Morgan's Delight) to dau. Elizabeth Barney. Appended is an Act of Assembly authorizing William Barney, s. of Elizabeth Barney, to have the deed recorded (TB#E: 512).

11 April 1720: Robert Chapman of BA Co. conv. 100 a. (*) to John Hall. Chapman's w. Elizabeth cons. (TR#DS: 191).

20 April 1741: James Lenox of BA Co., planter, conv. 200 a. (*) to Heathcote Pickett. JL's w. Mary cons. (HWS#1-A: 509).

BETTY'S LOT

21 Feb 1722: granted to John Durbin, Sr. (TB#E: 141).

22 Sep 1743: mentioned in will of John Durbin.

31 July 1746: John Durbin of BA Co., Sr., s. of John Durbin, dec., mortgaged (*) to Thomas White (TB#E: 141).

7 Aug 1750: John Durbin and w. Mary conv. (*) and Treble (Triple?) Union to William Husband of CE Co. (TR#D: 19).

7 Aug 1750: John Durbin of BA Co. conv. to John Stump of CE Co., 50 a. pt. Betty's Lot, and 150 a. pt. of Durbin's Chance. JD's w. Mary cons. (TR#D: 16).

BILBERRY HALL (See CHILBERRY HALL)

8 July 1741: Pat. to John Brice, Jr. (TB#E: 23).

28 Nov 1744: John Brice of Annapolis, Gent., conv. (*) to Samuel Durham; Brice's w. Sarah cons. (TB#E: 23).

c1754: Samuel Durham owned pt. Edmund's Camp; Bilbury Hall; Durham's First Addition to D'o; D'o Second Addition to D'o; D'o Third Addition to D'o; pt. Edwin's Contrivance, and Friend's Advice (IBC: 63).

BILLINGATE

14 Oct 1694: 79 a. surv. for Francis Whitehead (MRR: 28).

6 May 1735: William Ingram and w. Phoebe conv. 33 a. pt. (*) to Samuel Howell (HWS#M: 193).

BIRD CAGE

See Horvath Plat: Randallstown.

5 Oct 1749: Matthew Coulter of BA Co., tailor, conv. 50 a. (*) to Thomas Ricketts (TR#C: 312).

17 July 1750: Thomas Ricketts of BA Co. conv. to Samuel Owings 50 a. (*), orig. taken up by Matthew Coulter and conv. by him to Ricketts. TR's w. Mary cons. (TR#C: 516).

BIRR (or BINN)

10 Sep 1712: James Carroll of AA Co., conv. 200 a. Pt. (*) to Frances, Anna, and Catherine Rhodes, daus. of Henry Rhodes, dec.; Henry had paid 10/0/0 for the land, but no deed was made, and now the mother of the girls, their cousin Thomas Stockett, and others, alleged it was Henry's intention to let the girls have the land (Ref.?).

13 March 1730/1: Michael Taylor conv. 200 a. pt. (*) to Lewis Potee, Jr.; tract was granted to James Carroll, who devised it to the said Taylor (IS#L: 68).

Same day; Michael Taylor conv. 120 a. (*) to Benjamin Norris (IS#L: 76).

Same day: Michael Taylor conv. 100 a. (*) to Daniel Scott (IS#L: 78).

9 Aug 1734: Henry Rhodes, eld. s. of Henry and Catherine Rhodes, conv. 2/3 of 200 a. (*) to John Nelson (HWS#M: 94).

7 Nov 1734: Henry Rhodes, s. and heir at law of Henry Rhodes, dec., conv. 200 a. (*) to his sister Catherine, w. of William Osborne, and to his sisters Frances and Ann, at the instance of their mother Catherine, widow of HR, Sr. (HWS#M: 131).

5 Nov 1745: Daniel Scott, s. of Daniel Scott who purch. pt. (*) from Michael Taylor, now conv. 100 a. (*) and other lands (Scott's Close, and Scott's Improvement) to James Scott (TB#E: 345).

1750: Lewis Potee owned 200 a. pt. Binn (1750 DB).

BITE THE BITER

6 May 1743: Pat. to Talbot Risteau (TB#E: 235).

2 Nov 1746: Talbot Risteau of BA Co. conv. (*) to Nicholas Ruxton Gay (TB#E: 235).

BITERS BITT

11 Jan 1734: John Talbott of AA Co., and w. Prudence, conv. 320 a. (*) to William Dallam (HWS#M: 168).

BLACK ISLAND

12 May 1662: 100 a. surv. for John Collett; later held by the orphans of Col. Wells, and later in poss. of Thomas Frisby (MRR: 6).

1 June 1669: John Collett, Gent., conv. 100 a. on (*) to Richard Collins, smith (IR#PP: 73).

4 Jan 1669/70: Richard Collins, smith, conv. 100 a. (*) to Capt. George Wells (IR#PP: 79).

BLACK SNAKE POINT

25 April 1737: Richard Horner of AA Co., conv. 100 a. (*) to Luke Stansbury, Gent. (IS#IK, 429).

BLACK WALNUT

Vulgar name of 300 a. Richardson (q.v.).

12 June 1702: James Todd of BA Co. conv. 300 a. (*) to Mark Swift (HW#2: 153).

6 March 1704: James Todd gave p/a to John Harryman to dispose of livestock and land, including Todd's right to a plantation to Mr. Oulton, and Todd's plantation (*) to the care of John Shaw, planter (HW#2: 337).

BLACK WALNUT (NECK)

10 Feb 1659: 300 a. were surv. for Capt. Thomas Todd on the n. side of Patapsco R., on the e. side of Welchman's Creek; later possessed by James Todd, and still later by Mark Swift (MRR).

12 June 1702: James Todd conv. 300 a. to Mark Swift (HW#2: 153).

6 March 1704: James Todd gave p/a to John Harryman to dispose of Todd's plantation to John Shaw (HW#2: 337).

BLACK WOLF NECK

8 June 1667: 150 a. surv. for Richard Furendall in Gunpowder R., later possessed by Edward Felkes, and then by Ann Felkes (MRR: 64).

11 Oct 1667: 150 a. granted to Richard Farrendoll (HWS#1-A: 104).

4 Aug 1668: Richard Farendall conv. land at Black Wolf Neck to Robert Chapman (IR#PP: 69).

19 June 1738: Edward Pigg of Spottsylvania Co., VA, conv. (*) and 200 a. Felks Range and 200 a. Good Hope to Samuel Maxwell (HWS#1-A: 104).

15 Oct 1738: Samuel Maxwell conv. 150 a. (*) and other tracts, to Buckler Partridge of BA Co., surgeon (HWS#1-A: 184).

14 June 1740: Samuel Maxwell conv. 150 a. (*) to Walter James; Maxwell's w. Jane cons. (HWS#1-A: 396).

BLACKWELL'S SEARCH

1 March 1718: Capt. John Dorsey conv. 439 a. (*) to Andrew Norwood of BA Co.; tract was granted to Thomas Blackwell by patent dated 10 Nov 1695, and left by Blackwell to said Dorsey (TR#RA: 504).

BLADEN'S MANOR

1783: Benjamin Rogers owns 193 a. pt. (*) in Gunpowder Upper Hundred (1783 TL).

BLATHNIA CAMBRIA

Thomas Bladen of London, per atty. Benjamin Tasker, leased pts. of (*) as follows:

10 Dec 1736: 100 a. to William Gadd for lives of William, his w. Mary and s. Abraham (IS#IK, 435).

10 Dec 1736: 50 a. to James Boring for lives of James, his w. Rebecca and their dau. Ann (IS#IK, 438).

10 Dec 1737: 100 a. to Daniel Shaw of BA, blacksmith, for lives of Shaw, Elizabeth Shaw, and William Hall, s. of Thomas and Ann Hall (HWS#M: 72).

10 June 1738: 60 a. to Ralph Bradake for lives of said Ralph, w. Elizabeth, and their dau. Ann (HWS#1-A: 118).

10 Dec 1738: 200 a. to James Standiford for lives of said James, w. Martha, and dau. Chloe (HWS#1-A: 166).

21 June 1739: 100 a. to William Ditto for lives of William, w. Jane, and dau. Elizabeth (HWS#1-A: 321).

24 July 1739: 100 a. to Thomas Burk for lives of Thomas, w. Sarah, and Richard, s. of Ulick Burke who was the father of Thomas (HWS#1-A: 327).

24 Sep 174-(?): Benjamin Tasker leases 250 a. to Thomas Franklin (TB#E: 230).

BLOCKSEDGE

June 1680: 50 a. surv. for Thomas Heath and later held by Henry Matthews (MRR: 39).

3 Aug 1697: Thomas Heath and w. Sarah conv. 50 a. (*) to Henry Matthews (IS#IK: 154).

BLUNDER

10 June 1734: 100 a. pat. to Alexander Macmillan (MPL EI#2: 81, EI#3: 319).

See Horvath Plat: Pikesville.

15 Dec 1737: Alexander Macmillan conv. 100 a. (*) to Thomas Gibbins (HWS#M: 62).

BLUNTVILLE

29 Nov 1666: Nathaniel Stiles, Gent., conv. 175 a. (*) to William Stanley, planter, on the eastern side of the Bay, opposite Pool's Island (IR#PP: 57).

29 Nov 1667: Stanley, of TA Co., conv. 175 a. (*) to Richard Foxum, planter (IR#PP: 57).

BODY'S ADVENTURE

3 Jan 1718; Thomas Welsh of BA Co., planter, conv. 75 a., pt. (*) to John Cromwell (TR#RA: 495).

3 Jan 1718: Thomas Welsh conv. 67 a., pt. (*) to John Gardiner, Gent. (TR#RA: 502).

16 March 1731/2: John Gardiner of AA Co., conv. (*) and Gardiner's Addition to his dau. Susanna Walker (PCLR PL#8: 89).

4 June 1747: Samuel Hart of AA Co., conv. to Dr. James Walker of AA Co. and Dr. William Lyon of BA Co. 1560 a., ½ of (*) and ½ of Neighbour's Affinity, with p/a to pay his debts with the property (TB#E: 402).

BOHEMIA MANOR

4 Aug 1668: Augustine Herrman conv. to Robert Chapman, cooper, a tract in Bohemia Manor, on the s. side of Bohemia Back Creek als. Back R. (IR#PP: 93).

3 Jan 1670/1: Robert Morgan, cooper, and w. Bennett, conv. to Richard Chapman the tract purch. from Augustine Herman, lying within the mouth and on the s. side of Back Creek or Back R. (IR#PP: 94).

BOLD ADVENTURE

1719: John Boring pat. 50 a.

29 --- 1752: John Ensor, with cons. of w. Elizabeth, conv. to William Wheeler 100 a. (*) (TR#D: 302).

BOLD VENTURE

1767: James Dougherty conv. 25 a. (*) to John Conaway (B#Q: 231).

BOLEALMANACK NECK

12 Aug 1684: John Hawkins, planter of AA Co., eld. s. and heir of John Hawkins, dec., conv. to Henry Constable, merchant, 100 a. (*) on the s. side of Patapsco R., formerly taken up by grantor's father (RM#HS: 103).

BOND'S ADDITION (1733)

19 Jan 1733: 158 a. pat. by William Bond (MPL AM#1: 152, EI#1: 353).

7 Jan 1744: Barnett Bond of BA Co., mariner, conv. (*), orig. surv. for his father, William Bond, and Bond's Lot, in all 460 a., to Thomas Johnson and Walter Billingsley (TB#C: 666).

5 Nov 1747: Walter Billingsley conv. (*) to Thomas Johnson (TB#E: 590).

BOND'S ADDITION (unplaced)

18 March 1733: Charles Wells of BA Co. leased the messuages and tenements of (*) and of Wells' Chance to Pater Sailor or Sartor, cordwainer, for 18 years (HWS#M: 37).

BOND'S ADVENTURE

25 Aug 1720: 150 a. surv. (TB#E: 263).

6 March 1721: William Bond and w. Mary conv. 50 a. (*) to Joseph Johnson (RM#HS: 676).

6 March 1721: William and Mary Bond conv. 100 a., pt. of 150 a. (*), to Thomas Yates (RM#HS: 675).

1729: Thomas Yates conv. 100 a. (*) to Richard Ruff (IS#K: 228).

6 Dec 1746: Joseph Johnson of BA Co., conv. 50 a. pt. (*) to Richard Ruff (TB#E: 263).

BOND'S BEGINNING

26 Nov 1751: Thomas Bond conv. to Edward Mattingly 100 a. Francis Delight, 210 a. Bond's Choice, 109 a. (*), 122 a. Good Neighbor, and 56 a. pt. Bond's Fortune. TB's w. (unnamed) cons. (TR#D: 257).

BOND'S CHOICE

24 July 1746: Thomas Bond of BA Co. conv. (*) and two other tracts to s. Thomas Bond, Jr. (TB#E: 112).

26 Nov 1751: Thomas Bond conv. to Edward Mattingly 100 a. Francis Delight, 210 a. (*), 109 a. Bond's Beginnings, 122 a. Good Neighbor, and 56 a. pt. Bond's Fortune. TB's w. (unnamed) cons. (TR#D: 257).

BOND'S DESIRE

30 Jan 1729: Mary Wooton of Exmouth, Co. Devon, England, through Christopher Randall, her atty., conv. 222 a. (*) to John Swynyard; she had inher. the tract from her bro. Thomas Bale (IS#L: 429).

BOND'S FOREST

20 Oct 1708: Peter Bond and w. Eleanor conv. 300 a. (*) to Stephen Bentley (TR#A: 60).

3 June 1741: Thomas Bond conv. 82 a., pt. (*) to Henry Hicks, with cons. of TB's w. Ann (HWS#1-A: 527).

7 June 1743: Thomas Bond conv. 141 a. to John Holland; no w. cons. (TB#C: 253).

10 July 1746: Thomas Bond conv. 500 a., pt. (*) to his s. John. On the same day he conv. 400 a. (*) to his s. William; no w. joins him (TB#E: 103, 105).

12 Oct 1751: William Robinson, with cons. of w. Temperance, conv. to Laban Ogg 100 a. Hicks Adventure, and 82 a. Bond's Forest (TR#D: 250).

6 Nov 1751: Thomas Bond. conv. (*) near land of Henry Hicks to s. John; no w. (TR#D: 231).

16 March 1759: Joshua Bond of Thomas conv. 167 a. (*) to Samuel Higginson, brass founder (B#G: 340).

c1765: David Malsby conv. 100 a. pt. (*) and 100 a. Hicks' Adventure to Charles Baker (B#C, 225).

BOND'S FORTUNE

151 a. surv. for Thomas Bond. Jr.

7 March 1743: Thomas Bond, Jr., conv. 95 a., pt. (*) to Walter Billingsley (TB#C: 455).

26 Nov 1751: Thomas Bond conv. to Edward Mattingly 100 a. Francis Delight, 210 a. Bond's Choice, 109a. Bond's Beginnings, 122 a. Good Neighbor, and 56 a. pt. (*). TB's w. (unnamed) cons. (TR#D: 257).

1753: Walter Billingsley conv. 95 a. (*) to John Love (BB#I: 103).

BOND'S GARRISON

1754: Surv. for Thomas Bond.
See Horvath Plat: Pikesville.

BOND'S GIFT

9 March 1732/3: John Taylor and w. Mary conv. to William Talbot 200 a. (*) and Ogg King of Bashan for the life of Mary Taylor, relict of Edward Talbot (IS#L: 392).

5 Feb 1735: Edmund Talbot conv. 100 a. pt. (*), orig. taken up by his father Edmund Talbott, dec., to his bro. William. ET's w. Mary cons. (HWS#M: 363).

5 Feb 1735: Edmund Talbott and w. Mary conv. 100 a. Vardre, being pt. of 800 a. tract (*) to John Higginson (HWS#M: 373).

5 Feb 1735: William Talbott conv. 100 a. Vardre's Addition, being pt. of (*) to John Higginson. WT's w. Mary cons. (HWS#M: 376).

12 Feb 1738/9: John Talbott gave bond he will conv. 100 a. (*) to (?) (HWS#1-A: 169).

21 March 1738/9: John Talbot of BA Co. gave bond to Robert Mackilvain he will conv. 100 a. (*) with all his plantation his father left him (TR#C: 279).

5 March 1739: John Rockhold and w. Elizabeth conv. 200 a. pt. (*) to Edmund Talbott (HWS#1-A: 353).

6 Aug 1740: John Parker of BA Co. and w. Mary conv. 100 a. (*) to Walter Billingsley. In all 800 a. (*) was surv. for Edward Talbott who devised it to his s. John, who sold it on 6 Aug 1740 (HWS#1-A: 415).

3 March 1741/2: John Rockhold and w. Elizabeth Eleanor conv. 139 a. pt. (*) to Edmond Talbot (TB#A: 111).

14 May 1745: Robert Mackilwaine mortgaged 100 a. (*) to Joshua Bond (TB#E: 102).

BOND'S HOPE

2 Nov 1743: Jacob Giles and Isaac Webster conv. 31 a., pt. (*), to James Balch. Giles' w. Johanna and Webster's w. Mary cons. (TB#C: 387).

29 April 1752: James Balch, with cons. of w. Anne, conv. to William Jenkins 31 a., pt. (*) (TR#D: 325).

10 Oct 1753: Samuel Webb conv. 69 a. pt. (*) to John Allen (BB#I: 140).

BOND'S INCREASE

20 Oct 1709: Peter Bond of BA Co., conv. 10 a., pt. (*) to John Wells. Peter's w. Eleanor cons. (TR#A: 494).

27 April 1739: Charles Wells conv. 24 a. (*) to Benjamin Tasker, except for ½ a. reserved for a burying ground, 1/5 for use of Benj. Tasker; 1/5 to Chas. Carroll of Annapolis; 1/5 to Daniel Dulany; 1/5 to Charles Carroll, chirurgeon, and 1/5 to Charles Carroll, s. of Daniel (HWS#1-A: 244).

BOND'S INDUSTRY

28 Oct 1760: John Bond of BA Co. conv. 40 a. pt. (*) to William Tipton. Bond's w. Keturah cons. (B#H: 424).

BOND'S LAST SHIFT

16 Dec 1723: Tract was surv. (IS#H: 297).

2 Nov 1726: Thomas Coale conv. 125 a., pt. (*) to Lewis Puttee (IS#H: 297).

7 June 1727: Thomas Bond and w. Anne conv. 225 a. pt. (*) to Thomas Cole (IS#H: 418).

1750: Lewis Potee owned 125 a. pt. Bond's Last Shift (1750 DB).

BOND'S LOT

8 June 1723: Thomas Bond and w. Ann conv. 510 a. (*) to William Bond; tract was surv. for Thomas Bond on 20 Jan 1720; if 30 a. are taken

away by elder surv., William Bond is to be compensated (IS#G: 148).
3 Nov 1730: William Bond of BA Co. conv. 200 a. pt. (*) to his dau. Else, w. of Thomas Johnson (IS#L: 56).
7 Jan 1744: Barnett Bond of BA Co., mariner, conv. 460 a. including pt. of (*) to Thomas Johnson and Walter Billingsley; tract had orig. been surv. for Thomas Bond who conv. it to William Bond, father of the grantor (TB#C: 666).
7 Nov 1744: Thomas Johnson and w. Alice conv. 510 a. (*) to Thomas Bond; deed stated that on 8 June 1723 T. Bond sold (*) to William Bond, who on 3 Nov 1730, conv. (*) to his dau. Alice Johnson; she found that the tract Turkey Range took away pt. of her land and lodged a complaint; Thomas Bond paid her £37 common money in compensation (TB#C: 662).
5 Nov 1747: Thomas Johnson conv. 230 a. pt. (*) to Walter Billingsley (TB#E: 587).
5 Nov 1747: Walter Billinglsey conv. 230 a. (*) and Bond's Addition to Thomas Johnson (TB#E: 590).
20 Oct 1750: Thomas Johnson and w. Alice conv. 200 a. (*) to their s. William Johnson (TR#D: 32).

BOND'S MANOR
8 Aug 1739: Capt. Thomas Cresap conv. 200 a. pt. (*) and 150 a. Pleasant Garden to Jacob Mires. TC's w. Hannah cons. (HWS#1-A: 243).
8 Aug 1739: Thomas Bond, merchant, conv. 200 a. (*) to Edward Evans. No w. joined (HWS#1-A: 260).
8 Aug 1739: Thomas Bond, merchant, conv. 165 a. pt. (*) to Thomas Cresap (HWS#1-A: 159).
8 Aug 1739: Thomas Bond conv. 100 a. pt. (*) to William Cameron (HWS#1-A: 262).
28 Feb 1745: William Cannon of BA Co. and w. Frances conv. 100a. (*) to John Meyer of Lancaster Co., PA (TB#E: 76).

BOND'S PLEASANT HILLS
8 July 1730: Peter Bond conv. 100 a. (*) to Peter Johnson. No w. joined (IS#L: 24).
21 Feb 1735: John Bond conv. 100 a. pt. (*) to William Wells, bricklayer (HWS#M: 196).
1783: 198 a. in Middlesex Hundred owned by Philip Rogers (1783 TL).

BOND'S PROSPECT
2 Aug 1749: Thomas Bond conv. 1. a. pt. Bond's Prospect to Thomas Bond, Jr., and John Bond for themselves and for the Society called Quakers to build a meeting house; no w. cons. (TR#C: 276).

BOND'S WHARF
2 Nov 1743: Samuel Webb, tanner, purch. 69 a. pt. (*) from Jacob Giles and Isaac Webster (TB#C: 347).

BONNER'S PURCHASE
23 Dec 1697: Henry Bonner of AA Co., and w. Elizabeth conv. 200 a. (*) to Nicholas Waterman of AA Co. (TR#RA: 305).
19 Jan 1729: Mary Wootten of Exmouth, Co. Devon, England, widow, conv. (*) to Roger Matthews; tract had been devised to Mary by her bro. Thomas Bale; on 26 Nov 1731: MW appointed Christopher Randall her atty.; 8 March 1732: deed ackn. in court (IS#L: 379, 382).

BOODEN'S LIBERTY
(See BOWDEN'S LIBERTY)

BORING'S CHOICE
1769: Absolom Boring patents 23 a. (*) (Caron, Boring Notes).
6 Aug 1795: Surv. again for Absolom Boring , who assigns it to Michael Armacost (MPL IC#K: 199).

BORING'S CONVENIENCE
1742: 175 a. pat. by John Boring.

BORING'S DELIGHT
22 Sep 1716: John and Francis Thornborough, sons and heirs of Rowland Thornbury, dec., conv. 200 a. Selsed, now called (*) to John Boring (TR#RA: 499).

BORING'S FOREST
1721: 300 a. pat. by John Boring (Card Index to Patents).
1747: 355 a. resurv. for John Boring (Card Index). On PW Plat H.
1750: Held by John Boring, Jr. (1750 DB).
12 March 1763: Avarilla Boring, widow, conv. to Nicholas Britton her right of dower, ⅓ interest in (*), Boring's Gift and Cuckoldmaker's Hazard (B#L: 116).
27 July 1765: Absolom Boring and w. Ann conv. (*) to Charles Ridgely, John Ridgely, and Charles Ridgely, Jr. (B#O: 331).

BORING'S GIFT
1730: 50 a. for Johm Boring; on PW Plat H.
28 Aug 1742: John Boring, Jr., conv. pt. (*) to Charles Merryman and Richard Miller Cole (TB#C: 29).
28 Aug 1742: Charles Merryman and w. Millicent and Richard Miller Cole and w. Sabina, in exch. for 100 a. (*), conv. to John Boring, Jr., 00 a. Haile's Folly, for the lifetimes of John Boring, Jr.,

John Boring, Sr., and the latter's w. Sarah (TB#C: 18).
16 March 1746: John Boring, Jr., of BA Co, conv. to Richard Miller Cole pt. of (*). JB's w. Abarilla cons. (TB#E: 478).
16 March 1746: John Boring, Jr., and w. Abarilla, and Charles Merryman and w. Millicent conv. to Charles Ridgely pt. (*) (TB#E: 481).
12 March 1763: Avarilla Boring, widow, conv. to Nicholas Britton her right of dower, ⅓ interest in (*), Boring's Gift and Cuckoldmaker's Hazard (B#L: 116).

BORING'S MEADOW

31 Oct 1749: John Boring for love he bore his grandson John, s. of his s. John, conv. him 100 a. (*) (TR#C: 371).

BORING'S MEADOWS, ADDITION TO

1744: Capt. John Boring pat. 100 a. (Boring notes comp. by Caron).
1748: John Boring, in consideration toward my loving s. John, and my grandsons: William and Reuben Boring sons of my s. Thomas, and John Boring, s. of my s. John, grant to s. John: Lot 18 in Baltimore Town, and to grandsons, lot 17 in Baltimore Town, and to godson John, 100 a. (*) (TR#C: 371).
1750: John Boring, Jr., owned 100 a. (1750 DB).
1755: John Boring pat. 25 a. Addition to (*).

BORING'S PASSAGE

1684: John Boring pat. 50 a. (Card Index to Patents, MSA).
27 Nov 1686: John Boring pat. 109 a. (*) (Card Index to Patents, MSA).
30 July 1713: James Boring and w. Jane, and John Boring and w. Mary, conv. 109 a. (*) to Joseph Hoare (TR#A: 233).
18 Feb 1725: John Boring and w. Presiota, and James Boring and w. Jane conv. 50 a. (*) and other lands to William Buckner (IS#H: 218).
18 Feb 1726: John Boring and w. Pretiosa and James Boring and w. Jane conv. 50 a. (*) to Thomas Buckner (IS#H: 218).
30 Aug 1735: Thomas Buckner of VA conv. 50 a. (*) and four other tracts back to John Boring (HWS#M: 294).
1735: Thomas Buckner conv. 50 a. back to John Boring (HWS#M: 294).
13 Jan 1737: John Boring of BA, and w. Sarah conv. 50 a. (*) to Alexander Lawson (HWS#1-A: 48).

BORING'S PASTURE

10 Oct 1682: John Boring surv. 50 a. (*) (Card Index to Patents).
18 Feb 1725: John Boring and w. Pretiosa, and James Boring and w. Jane conv. 50 a. (*), 50 a. Boring's Range, and 80 a. Swan Harbor, and 189 a. pt. Ferry Range to William Buckner (IS#H: 218).

BORING'S RANGE

10 Oct 1679: 50 a. surv. for John Boring; 1680: 50 a. pat. by John Boring; later poss. by John Boring; and later by the orphans of John Boring.
18 Feb 1725: John Boring and w. Pretiosa, and James Boring and w. Jane conv. 50 a. Boring's Pasture, 50 a. (*), and 80 a. Swan Harbor, and 189 a. pt. Ferry Range to William Buckner (IS#H: 218).
30 Aug 1735: Thomas Buckner conv. 50 a. to John Boreing (HWS#M: 294).
13 Jan 1737: John Boring and w. Sarah sell 50 a. to Alexander Lawson (HWS#1-A: 48).
1750: 50 a. poss. by Wm. Alexander Lawson (1750 DB).

BORING'S STRUGGLE

1740: Thomas Boring, Jr., pat. 50 a. (MPL BC&GS#10: 449).

BOSLEY'S EXPECTATION

On 10 Oct 1696/7 Bosley surv. 200 a. Bosley's Expectation on the s. side of Gunpowder (MRR: 64).
c1715: Walter Bosley willed the property to his s. James Bosley (MCW#IV: 79).
5 Nov 1738: James Bosley and w. Elizabeth conv. 100 a. (*) to William Andrews (HWS#1-A:164).
1741: William Andrews conv. 100, being ½ of (*) to Francis Watkins (HWS#1-A: 534).
31 Aug 1751: William Bosley of BA Co., planter, conv. to Thomas Sligh (*), left to said WB by will of his father Walter Bosley (TR#D:183).

BOSLEY'S GOOD LUCK

14 Jan 1748: Joseph Bosley leased 51 a. (*) to John Merryman. The tract had been leased to Bosley by Benjamin Tasker (TR#C: 151).

BOSLEY'S PALACE
(See TAYLOR'S PALACE)

1 April 1712: Thomas Taylor conv. 100 a. Taylor's Palace, now called (*), to Walter Bosley (TR#A:183).
c1715: Walter Bosley devised this tract to his s. Joseph Bosley (MCW#IV: 79).
13 Dec 1746: Joseph Bosley conv. 100 a. (*) to Charles Robinson (IS#H: 305).
1750: Charles Robinson owned 100 a. (*) (1750 DB).

BOUGHT DEAR

26 Feb 1732: Teague Tracey pat. 50 a. (*) out of 50 a. assigned to Tracey by Nicholas Haile (MPL AM#1: 152; EI#1: 19).

4 Nov 1745: Teague Tracey conv. to William Fell 50 a. (*); also 50 a. Round About; also 84 a. pt. of 100 a. sold to Teague Tracey in 1741 called Cole's Contrivance, and 16 a. pt. Cole's Chance (TB#D: 353).

1752: Joseph Taylor and others conv. (*), Roundabout Neighbors, Cole's Chance, and Cole's Contrivance to John Gorsuch (TR#D: 373).

BOUGHTON'S FOREST

29 Aug 1677: 575 a. surv. for Richard Boughton. Later 400 a. were held by Edward Smith and 175 a. held by Joseph Peake's orphans (MRR: 40).

1 Aug 1699: Joseph Peake and w. Jane conv. 575 a. to Edward Smith (TR#RA: 384).

7 March 1716: Edward Smith and w. Bridget conv. 400 a. of 575 to Richard Burrough (TR#A: 428).

13 Oct 1739: John Kemp, Mary w. of John Caggill, and Jemima, w. of John Broad, grandchildren of Joseph Peake, conv. 575 a. (*) to Daniel Dulany (HWS#1-A: 336).

10 March 1720: Richard Burrough of BA Co., merchant, conv. 575 a. (not named: possibly Boughton's Forest) to Daniel Dulany of Annapolis (TR#DS: 244).

4 Feb 1739: Catherine Stone of CH Co., widow, dau. and sole surviving heiress of Richard Boughton of CH Co., dec., gave quitclaim on 575 a. (*) to ... (not named) (HWS#1-A: 341).

22 April 1747: 575 a. orig. granted to Richard Boughton, at head of Back R. John Wamsley of AA Co. and w. Abigail, conv. 575 a. (*) to James Russell, James Wardrope, James Johnson, and Alexander Lawson (TB#E, f: 525).

BOURNE

13 Nov 1703: Thomas Stockett of AA Co., Gent., and w. Damaris conv. (*) to Richard Smithers (IR#AM: 34).

16 Sep 1716: Richard Smithers, Gent., leased (*) to Matthew Moulton (TR#A: 442).

18 Feb 1718: Richard Smithers, Gent., conv. 200 a., ½ (*), to John Stokes, being tract formerly sold by Thomas Stockett to the said Smithers (TR#RA: 506).

23 May 1721: Richard Smithers, Gent., and w. Mary conv. 400 a. (*) to John Stokes (TR#DS: 307).

2 July 1726: Thomas Stockett, Sr., of AA Co., confirmed and made good the title to 400 a. (*) owned by John Stokes; on 13 Nov 1703 Thomas Stockett and w. Damaris sold tract to Richard Smithers who later sold it to Stokes (IS#H: 255).

15 Oct 1731: John Stokes, Gent., conv. 400 a. (*) to Philip Smith of London; w. Susanna cons. (IS#L: 172). (Deed also conv. 200 a. Ebenezer's Lot, and 220 a. Shrewsbury.)

25 May 1737: Philip Smith of London, now living in AA Co., s. and heir of Philip Smith, late of London, and holding his father's p/a to sell 400 a. (*), and 220 a. Shrewsbury, and 200 a. Ebenezer's Lot, to Jacob Giles; later tract was sold to Philip Smith on 15 Oct 1731 by John (Stokes?) of BA Co. (IS#IK: 432).

7 Aug 1741: John Stokes, s. and heir of John Stokes, dec., conv. (*) and Johnson's Delay, als. Shrewsbury, to Jacob Giles (HWS#1-A: 538).

BOWDEN'S (BOODEN'S) LIBERTY

11 Oct 1707: 50 a. surv. for John Bowden (B).

5 Nov 1718: John Booden of BA Co., and w. Bridgett conv. 50 a. (*) to John Teall (TR#RA: 521).

BOWEN'S PROSPECT

7 April 1744: Benjamin Bowen of BA Co. conv. 100 a. (*) to Samuel Bowen (TB#C: 582).

19 June 1758 or 1759: Samuel Bowen conv. 50 a. (*) to Joel Higginbotham (B#G: 183).

BRANDON

1663: Cert. for 250 a. to Paul Kinsey (RM#hs, 240).

17 Aug 1663: 250 a. surv. for Paul Kinsey on the s. side of Patapsco on the northwest side of Deep Creek; later possessed by John Lockett for Richard Gwinn's orphans (MRR: 107).

Feb 1663/4: Paul Kinsey and w. Katherine assigned their interest in a patent to William Guyn (RM#HS: 11).

2 May 1711: Thomas Gwinn conv. 60 a. (*) and 153 a. Cromwell's Island to Thomas Crocus (TR#A. 142).

2 May 1711: Thomas Crocus, planter, conv. 60 a. pt. of 250 a. (*) to Thomas Gwinn. TC's w. Frances cons. (TR#A: 144).

BRANTER'S RIDGE

1760: James Amos conv. 4½ a. (*) to John Bowen (B#H: 406).

1761: Thomas Amos conv. 72 a. (*) to William, Benjamin, and Joshua Amos (B#I: 407).

1763: Thomas Amos mortgaged 85 a. (*) to Robert Adair (B#L: 317).

BRASHER'S DESIRE

1 May 1739: Isaac Webster conv. 100 a. (*) to William Grafton. IW's w. Margaret cons. (HWS#1-A: 224).

BRICE'S ENDEAVOR

5 Aug 1741: Samuel Brice conv. 200 a. (*) to Thomas Montgomery (HWS#1-A: 523).

BRIDEWELL DOCK

5 April 1667: 100 a. surv. for Francis Trippas; later held by Mary Frizzell for the orphans of William York (MRR: 63).

26 March 1670: Francis Trippas and w. Ann conv. 150 a. (*) to William York; the said 150 a. covered by two patents (Scisco, 96:230).

23 Nov 1690: William York of BA Co. d. leaving a will in which he left his lands to his ch.: William, Oliver, John, George and James (IS#G: 204).

2 Feb 1702: George York of BA Co. conv. 100 a. (*) to John Ewings (HW#2: 295).

2 March 1709: John Ewings of BA Co. conv. 50 a. (*) (formerly taken up by Francis Trippas) to George York (RM#HS: 644).

June 1723: Elizabeth York, dau. of William York,s. of the testator of 1690, conv. her share of (*) to her uncle George York (IS#G: 204).

20 April 1750: George York conv. 20 a. (*) and 62 a. York's Chance to Edward York (TR#D: 12). Same day he conv. 25 a. (*) and 62 a. York's Chance to John York (TR#D: 124).

5 Aug 1762: James Meades and w. Ann conv. pt. (*) to Samuel Ricketts (B#K: 285).

BRING ME HOME

19 Sep 1752: Michael McDowell late of Halifax Co., VA, conv. his share of 100 a. (*) to Josephus Murray (TR#D: 507).

BRISTOL FOLLY

24 April 1717: Col. John Thomas and w. Sarah conv. 150 a. (*) to Buckler Partridge of Bristol, England, surgeon (TR#A: 445).

BROAD NECK (1664)

20 Sep 1664: 100 a. surv. for William Hollis; later held by William Pritchett (MRR: 23).

1690: William Hollis and w. Mary conv. 100 a. (*) to William Pritchard (RM#HS: 324).

15 March 1735: Abraham Cord and w. Mary (sister of Joseph Pritchard, lately dec.), conv. 100 a. (*) to John Atkinson, in exch. for money and JA's agreeing to maintain MC for the rest of her natural life (HWS#M: 401).

17 Feb 1736: Abraham Cord and w. Mary, sis. of Joseph Pritchard, dec., conv. (*) and other lands to John Atkinson (IS#IK: 358).

BROAD NECK

c1672: Thomas Bradford of London asked Lord Baltimore to aid in his recovery of the estate of his uncle John Bradford who d. about 3 years ago at Bush R. without any heirs except the petitioner (IS#IK: 49).

21 Nov 1672: Lord Baltimore stated he is satisfied by testimony that Thomas Bradford is legal heir to the dec. (IS#IK: 49).

19 Oct 1674: Thomas Bradford and w. Mary of London, for £19 conv. to Thomas Thurston 250 a. (*) formerly owned by John Bradford. 20 Oct 1674: Thomas Bradford appoints Miles Gibson his atty. (IS#IK:49).

BROAD'S CHOICE

7 June 1723: Edward Cox and w. Jean conv. 86½ a. (*) to Thomas Broad; land was taken up by John Broad and willed by him to his dau. Jean (IS#G: 194).

BROAD'S DESIRE

1758: Thomas Broad assigns 40 a. (*) to Abraham Ensor. No w. cons. (B#G: 244).

BROAD'S IMPROVEMENT

1694: 173 a. was surv. for John Broad (data from Daniel P. Redmond, cites MPL C#3: 276).

1721: Tract was resurv. (MPL AM#1: 146).

21 July 1724: Thomas Broad of BA Co., planter, conv. 102 a. (*), now called Merryman's Purchase, to John Merryman. TB's w. Ann cons. (IS#H: 159).

2 Sep 1729: Thomas Broad, and w. Ann conv. 105 a., pt. (*) to John Miller (IS#K: 176).

1734: Tract was resurv. again and increased to 474 a. (Redmond data, cites MPL EI#5: 365).

22 March 1738: John Merryman conv. 102 a. (*), also called Merryman's Purchase, back to Thomas Broad (HWS# 1-A: 197).

23 March 1738: Thomas and Ann Broad conv. 102 a. back to John Merryman (HWS# 1-A: 199).

2 Oct 1742: Thomas Broad and w. Anne, conv. 105 a., pt. (*) to Richard Miller, s. of John. This deed is to correct errors in the deed of 2 Sep 1729 of the 105 a. from Broad to John Miller (TB#C: 162).

10 Nov 1742: Thomas and Ann Broad conv. 170,a., pt. (*), to John Hunt (TB#C: 66).

20 June 1749: John Hunt of BA Co. conv. 170 a. pt. (*) to Daniel Barnett and Peter Mirer. JH's w. Dorcas cons. (TR#C: 236).

1750: Daniel Barnett owning 170 a. (*); John Merryman, Jr., owned 102 a. (*); Richard Miller of John owned 105 a. (*) (1750 DB).

13 April 1752: Daniel Barnett, with cons. of w. Catherine, conv. to Peter Mirer 170 a. (*) (TR#D: 332).

BROAD STREET

6 Nov 1694: Thomas Hedge conv. 46 a. (*) and other lands (Common Garden and Mate's Neck) to s. Henry Hedge (RM#HS: 435).

29 June 1724: Samuel Hedge of Salem Co., West Jersey conv. pt. (*) and other lands totalling 180 a. to Roger Matthews (by virtue of a p/a from Hedge to Thomas Sheredine) (IS#G: 358).

BROADWELL (BRODWELL) HILL

288 a. surv. 16 October 1695 for Thomas Preston on the s. side of Bush R. by Sam's Cove (MRR: 62).

15 Feb 1709: Thomas Preston, Sr., of BA Co., planter, conv. 288 a. to John Stokes of BA Co., clerk; Preston's w. Mary cons. (TR#A: 56).

7 Oct 1713: John Stokes conv. the entire 288 a. to Jacob Loton, planter (TR#A: 281).

6 April 1714: Jacob Loton gave p/a to Jonathan Massey to "sell the tract and all other things I shall leave in the country;" Loton mortgaged the tract to Massey, who gave Loton a release on the mortgage in May 1722 (TR#A: 292).

6 July 1719: Jacob Looten of BA Co., mariner, conv. the tract to John Crockett (TR#DS: 63).

8 July 1719: James Maxwell gave bond to John Crockett to protect him from any mortgage; Loton conv. the 288 a. to Crockett on this day, but Looten had mortgaged it to Jonathan Massey on 6 April 1714 (TR#DS: 36).

May 1722: Massey gave Looten a release on the mortgage (TR#A: 292).

16 Nov 1733: John Crockett pet. for a land commission to determine the boundaries of Brodwell's Hills, Samuel's Hills, and Smith Range. On 30 March 1734, James Isham, aged c62, deposed that about 30 years earlier Thomas Preston and Cornelius Herrington showed him the bounds (Land Commissions, HWS#3: 202-204).

BROKEN ISLANDS

30 March 1713: John Deaver, planter, conv. 93 a. pt. Deaver's Endeavor, being pt. The Broken Islands, to Richard Deaver. The tract was surv. 5 April 1705. JD's w. Hannah cons. (IS#I: 182).

15 Oct 1746: Richard Deaver and w. Mary conv. 133 a. (*) where James Lee lived, to Jacob Giles and Co. (TB#E: 224).

BROOKS CROSS

23 Sep 1684: 1500 a. surv. for Roger Brook; located at the Head of Gunpowder R.; later 1000 a. possessed by John Brooke, and 50 a. by Basil Brooke (MRR: 49).

BROOM'S BLOOM

5 Aug 1684: 1000 a. surv. for John Broom; located on the e. side of Bush R. betw. Bynam's Branch and James' Branch; later possessed by the orphans of said Broom (MRR: 48).

14 Sep 1753: William Smith, Gent., conv. 100 a. pt. (*), adj. Sedgely, to John Beaver. WS' w. Elizabeth cons. (BB#I: 76).

21 March 1763: John Majors and w. Rebecca conv. (*) to Moses Ruth; tract was devised to Rebecca by her father John Pollard by his LWT, dated 29 Feb 1761 (B#L: 103).

BROTHERLY LOVE (1697)

28 Aug 1697: 100 a. surv. for Richard Perkins and William Lofton, and later held by Lofton's [Logsdon's?] orphans (MRR: 27).

10 Sep 1697: 100 a. pat. by Richard Perkins (MPL 38:20).

15 June 1737: Thomas Lofton, s. and heir at law of William Lofton, and Richard Perkins, s. and heir at law of Richard Perkins, conv. 100 a. (*) to John Poloke (IS#IK: 461).

15 Jan 1742: William Logsdon (and w. Ann), John Logsdon (and w. Sarah), and Edward Logsdon (and w. Sarah) of PG Co. [now FR Co.?] conv. 300 a. (*) to John George Counts of Little Conewago, farmer. Hannah Logsdon, mother of the grantors, also cons. (TB#C: 183).

15 July 1745: John George Counts of Little Conewago conv. 150 a. (*) to Philip Morningstar and his heirs by his present w. (TB#E: 190).

7 July 1746: John George Counts of Little Conewago, conv. 150 a. pt. (*), to Adam Hoopard and his heirs lawfully begotten in marriage (TB#E: 193).

BROTHERLY LOVE (1717)

10 Sep 1717: 189 a. pat. by John Parrish of AA Co. (MPL EE#6: 320, PL#4: 315).

5 April 1738: John Parrish conv. 189 a. (*) and 138 a. Rich Neck to Charles Ridgely. JP's w. Catherine cons. (IS#L: 80).

BROTHERLY LOVE (1730)

9 July 1730: 83 a. pat. by William Rogers of BA Co. (MPL PL#8: 35, IL#B: 286).

See Horvath Plat: Reisterstown.

1 Jan 1763: Thomas Stocksdale conv. to John Reister 80 a. called (*), orig. granted to William Rogers in 1743(?) (B#L: 5).

BROTHERLY LOVE (Unplaced)

31 May 1750: John Pogue and w. Sarah conv. (*) and Johnson's Rest to Jacob Giles (TR#D: 3).

BROTHER'S CHOICE

1735: Surv. for Mathew Colter.

See Horvath Plat: Pikesville.

24 Oct 1748: Matthew Coulter conv. 200 a. (*) to John Anter (TR#C: 130).

1754: John Anter conv. 200 a. (*) to Christopher Carnan (BB#I: 295).

BROTHER'S DISCOVERY

15 Dec 1730: (*) surv. for Jacob Giles and Isaac Webster and later pat. (IS#IK, 417).

8 Aug 1734: Jacob Giles and Samuel Webster conv. 50 a. pt. (*) to Job Barnes (HWS#M: 87).

25 March 1737: Isaac Webster (and w. Mary), and Jacob Giles and (w. Hannah) conv. 134 a. pt. (*) to Thomas Renshaw (IS#IK, 417).

2 Nov 1743: Jacob Giles and Isaac Webster (w. cons. of their wives Johanna and Margaret), conv. 100 a. pt. (*) to Hugh Morgan, assignee of James Cannon (TB#C: 413).

3 Sep 1744: Thomas Renshaw and w. Jane conv. 134 a. (*) to James Rigbie (TB#C: 567).

3 Sep 1744: Thomas Renshaw and w. Jane conv. 100 a. (*) to Nathaniel Porter (TB#C: 572).

25 Jan 1744[/45]: Nathaniel Porter and w. Sarah conv. 100 a. (*) to William Montgomery of PA (TB#E: 16).

19 June 1747: John and William Montgomery of New London Twp., PA, conv. 100 a. (*) to David Maxfield. WM's w. Fortune cons. (TB#E: 457).

29 April 1751: John Renshaw of BA Co., conv. 79 a., pt. (*) to Samuel Webb, tanner and currier (TR#D: 204).

BROTHER'S EXPECTATION

6 Nov 1702: George Hollingsworth, planter, conv. 100 a. (*) to Thomas Knighton; GH's w. Margaret cons. (HW#2: 337).

2 Aug 1704: Thomas Knighton of CE Co. conv. (*) to Humphrey Lewis; (*) was granted to Geo. Hollingsworth by Lord Baltimore ((HW#2: 339).

3 March 1713: James Hollingworth of BA Co., planter, conv. 50 a. (*) to William Hamilton (TR#A: 274).

5 Oct 1738: William Hamilton conv., 50 a. pt. (*) and Christian's Lot to Thomas Floyd. WH's w. Sarah cons. (HWS#1-A: 137).

14 Jan 1747: George Hollingsworth, s. and heir of James H., and surviving heir of George Hollingsworth, the Elder, who was father of Geo., Otho, Charles and James Hollingsworth of BA Co., dec., conv. 250 a. (*) to Charles Carroll of Annapolis in trust for him and the company in the Ironworks. Hollingsworth's w. Hannah cons. (TB#E: 633).

11 June 1756: John Floyd, Thomas Floyd, and TF's w. Rachel conv. 50 a. pt. (*) to William Jessop. Henry Maynard and w. Zepporah ackn. receiving full satisfaction for Zepporah's right of dower (BB#I: 570).

BROTHER'S GOODWILL
(Pt. of COUNTERSCARPE)

6 July 1711: Josephus Murray of BA Co. conv. 100 a. (*) to his sister Zipporah Gist (TR#A: 140).

14 March 1743: Christopher Gist mortgaged above tract as well as others.

28 March 1746: James Richard, atty. for Stephen Theodore Jannsen, conv. the above tracts to William Cromwell and Tobias Stansbury who have paid the mortgaged (TB#E: 438).

BROTHER'S GOOD WILL, ADDITION TO
(Pt. of COUNTERSCARPE)

31 Oct 1724: Josephus Murray conv. to Richard Gist all that land called (*), being pt. of Counterscarpe, adj. to Brother's Good Will, which JM had already conv. to his sister Zipporah Gist. JM's w. Ruth cons. (IS#H: 69).

28 July 1746: Tobias Stansbury of BA Co., merchant, conv. 100 a. (*) to George Ashman. TB's w. Mary cons. (TB#E: 113-117).

21 Nov 1748: George Ashman of BA Co. conv. 100 a. (*) to Richard Croxall. GA's w. Jemima cons. (TR#C: 124).

BROTHER'S INHERITANCE

4 June 1747: William Hammond conv. 377 a. (*) (except 148½ a. now called Hammond's Purchase), 109¼ a. Hammond's Purchase Resurveyed (except for 19½ a. sold to Benjamin Tasker) and 100 a. Hammond's Struggle (except for 11 a. taken away) to Charles Carroll. WH's w. Sarah cons. (TB#E: 448).

BROTHER'S KINDNESS (A)

14 April 1705: Matthew Hawkins conv. 90 a. (*) to his bro. Joseph Hawkins (IR#AM: 12).

7 Dec 1725: Joseph Hawkins leaves 90 a. (*) to his w., and residue of his personal estate to her for life; if she remarries then to his ch.: John, Augustine, Jemima and Elizabeth (MCW#V: 210).

BROTHER'S KINDNESS (B)

27 May 1735: Lawrence Hammond, s. and devisee of Col. Thomas Hammond, conv. his share of Dearing's Increase, 200 a. Health, and 100 a. Spring Point, which LH had resurv. into Brother's Kindness, in all 371 a., to his bro.

William Hammond. LH's w. Abarilla cons. (HWS#M: 313).

BROWNING'S PLANTATION

21 July 1664: Pat. to Abraham Morgan, who conv. it to Thomas Browning, father of John Browning, below (G#J: 117; TR#RA: 82).

6 April 1672: John Browning and w. Elizabeth conv. to Richard Nash 300 a. near Bohemia R. (G#J: 117; TR#RA: 82).

BROWNE'S ADVENTURE

10 Oct 1694: 1000 a. pat. by Thomas Browne (MPL 27:300).

See Horvath Plat: Elkridge.

10 June 1699: Thomas Browne conv. 1000 a. to John Gadsby (HW#2: 99).

10 July 1701: John Gadsby of AA Co., planter and w. Jane, conv. 130 a. (*) to John Barker; land is now called Barker's Inheritance (HW#2: 99).

BROWN'S CHANCE

23 Jan 1719: James Brown of BA Co., conv. 190 a. (*) and other lands to James Phillips (TR#DS: 109).

18 Feb 1719: Samuel Brown conv. his interest in (*) and other lands to James Phillips, except for a lease to David Thomas (TR#DS: 111).

4 June 1744: George Brown of BA Co., planter conv. 150 a. (*) and pt. Chevy Chase, to Robert North. Brown's w. Mary cons. (TB#C: 479).

BROWN'S DELIGHT

1 Sep 1746: Benjamin Tasker leased 100 a. (*) to William Brown of BA Co. (TB#E: 236).

BROWN'S ENTRANCE

24 May 1735: Gabriel Brown leased 60 a. (*) to Richard Scott, including the improvements made by Mary Keen (HWS#M: 268).

31 Oct 1741: Thomas Browne, s. and heir of John Browne, late of BC, dec., conv. 400 a. (*) to Gabriel Browne; tract had been devised to TB by his father (TB#A: 45).

25 Nov 1742: Gabriel Brown and w. Mary conv. 400 a. (*) to John Paca (TB#C: 221).

2 Jan 1746: John Paca of BA Co., and w. Elizabeth, conv. 400 a. (*) to Benjamin Culver (TB#E: 271).

BROWN'S FOREST

7 April 1725: Amos Garrett of AA Co., merchant, conv. 200 a. pt. (*), formerly belonging to Thomas Brown, father of the grantee, to Valentine Brown of BA Co. (IS#H: 111).

BROWN'S LOT

4 Aug 1730: Benj. Jones conv. 100 a. to John Browne (IS#L: 1).

10 Nov 1732: Benjamin Jones and John Brown conv. 100 a. (*) to Nathaniel Ayres (IS#L: 344).

29 March 1735: Nathaniel Ayres and w. Rhoda conv. 100 a. (*) to Rowland Vine (HWS#M: 271).

BROWN'S PROSPECT

10 May 1731: Cert. of surv. for 50 a. (See TR#C: 388).

24 May 1746: William Brown of BA Co. conv. 50 a. (*) to William Lyon and Samuel Hart of AA Co.; Brown's w. Esther cons. (TB#E: 83)

10 Feb 1749: William Brown conv. 50 a. (*)to John Bond. WB's w. Esther cons. (TR#C: 388).

1750: John Bond owned 50 a. (*) (1750 DB).

BROWNE'S SURVEY

25 May 1704: Richard Kimble (or Kirkland) conv. 200 a. (*) to Alexander Delmeyrosa of AA Co., innholder (HW#2: 342).

BRUSH'S NECK BOTTOM

26 Oct. 1690: William Luffman of Severn R., AA Co., conv. 100 a. (*) and also Sefton, being ½ the old pat. land on the s. side of Magothy R. (HW#2: 240).

BRYAN'S CHANCE

27 Sep 1746: Henry Morgan, merchant, mortgaged (*) and other tracts to Christopher Grindall (TB#E: 182).

BRYANT'S CHOICE

2 Feb 1750: Capt. Henry Morgan of BA Co., mariner, conv. to James Bryant 50 a. (*). HM's w. Sarah cons. (TR#D: 105).

BUCK'S ADVENTURE

10 Dec 1714: granted to John Buck (RM#HS: 673).

13 Nov 1721: John Buck conv. 148 a. (*), adj. to Bachelor's Hope, to Daniel Scott (RM#HS: 673).

BUCK('S) FOREST

16 Aug 1742: 200 a. granted to George Ogg (See TR#C: 396).

19 Feb 1749: George Ogg conv. 200 a. (*) to Robert Chapman, wheelwright. GO's w. Mary cons. (TR#C: 396).

5 May 1759: Robert Chapman of BA Co. and w. Margaret conv. 50 a. (*) to Nathan Chapman (B#G: 380).

1764: Francis Brothers conv. pt. (*) to Nathan Chapman (B#N: 318).

18 Aug 1764: Nathan Chapman and w. Rebecca conv. 50 a. (*) and 25 a. Nathan's Desire to Francis Brothers (B#N, 318).

BUCK NECK

3 March 1666(?): William Pearce, planter, conv. 150 a. (*) to Daniel Sillvain, on the e. side of the Bay; pt. of 550 a. formerly taken up by Joseph Hopkins (IR#PP: 62).

5 Sep 1671: Daniel Silvaine, planter, gave quitclaim on his purchase (*) to William Pierce (G#J: 54; TR#RA: 39).

BUCK RIDGE

23 March 1750: William Hammond of BA Co., Gent., conv. $20+\frac{1}{2}$ a. pt. (*) to Charles Croxall. WH's w. Sarah cons. (TR#D: 125).

BUCK'S PARK

13 Dec 1750: Peter Bond and w. Susanna conv. 50 a. (*) to John Sadden (TR#D: 141: FSH).

[post 1750]; John Sadden, with cons. of w. Margaret, conv. 50 a. (*) to William Anderson (TR#D: 338).

BUCK'S PURCHASE (Pt. of SELSED)

1716: John Thornbury, late of BA Co., MD, now of Lancaster Co., VA, conv. 100 a. (*), pt. of Selsed, to Nicholas Rogers, who agreed to pay land rents owing for past 16 years (TR#DS: 260).

14 Dec 1733: Nicholas Haile and Roland Thornborough conv. (*) pt of Selsed, to Henry Sater (HWS#M: 20).

7 Nov 1734: Henry Sater conv. 100 a. (*) to John Beassey [Basey] (HWS#M: 129).

BUCK['S] RANGE (1687)

6 Feb 1687: 750 a. surv. for 19 Oct 1611 [sic] for John Fanning who d. with no heirs (MRR: 39).

BUCK['S] RANGE (1687)

6 Feb 1687: Surv. for John Fuller at the head of Back R. (MRR: 39, 70).

3 March 1702: John Fuller and w. Sarah conv. 148 a. (*) to John Anderson; tract formerly bel. to John Fuller, Sr. (HW#2: 265).

4 Nov 1719: William Anderson, of BA Co., carpenter, s. and heir of John Anderson, late of BA Co., dec., conv. 148 a. (*) to William Bond; tract had been conv. by John Fuller and w. Sarah to John Anderson on 3 March 1702 (TR#DS: 151).

1 Nov 1750: John Hanson and w. Jane of CH Co., conv. 291 a., pt. (*) to Nicholas Carew et al., all of Great Britain (TR#D: 114).

BUCK RANGE['S] (1701)

3 Nov 1701: Surv. for Matthew Hawkins on the drafts of the Patapsco (MRR: 39).

See Horvath Plat: Elkridge.

14 April 1705: Matthew Hawkins conv. (*) to John Israel of BA Co., factor (IR#PP: 156).

6 Nov 1706: John Israel of BA Co., planter, conv., to William Foreman 100 a. (*), pt. of which Matthew Hawkins conv. to JI in 1705 (RM#HS: 573).

5 Oct. 1748: Matthew Hawkins of BA Co., s. and heir at law of Matthew Hawkins, Sr., conv. 160 a. (*) to Charles Carroll, Esq. MH's w. Elizabeth cons. (TR#C: 101).

BUCK'S RANGE (1745)

18 Oct 1745: 45 a. surv. for Nathaniel Ayres (B).

BUCK RANGE RESURVEYED

28 Aug 1773: Henry Pemberton of BA Co. conv. to Henry Stevenson of Edward 172 a. pt. (*) (AL#H: 193).

BUCK RIDGE

4 May 1727: Christopher Gardiner and w. Sibrah conv. 400 a. (*) to John Giles (IS#H: 409).

BUCKINGHAM'S GOOD WILL

1756: 520 a. surv. for Benj. Buckingham.

See Horvath Plat: Finksburg to Westminster.

29 July 1758: Benjamin Buckingham, and w. Aberilla conv. pt. (*) to John Buckingham (B#G: 192).

29 July 1758: Benjamin Buckingham, and w. Aberilla conv. 96 a. pt. (*), to George Bramwell, schoolmaster (B#G: 193).

BUCKINGHAM'S PREVENTION

2 Nov 1740: Benjamin Buckingham of BA Co. conv. 50 a. (*) to Edward Stocksdale. His w. Avarilla cons. (TR#C: 303).

28 Aug 1762: Edward Stocksdale conv. 50 a. pt. (*) to Solomon Stocksdale (B#K: 278).

BUCKNER'S IMPROVEMENT

30 Aug 1735: Thomas Buckner of VA conv. (*) and other lands to John Boring of BA Co. (HWS#M: 294).

BUFFALO

11 Sep 1756: Leonard Anderson conv. 49 a. (*) to Thomas Broad (BB#I: 585).

BULFORD

4 Dec 1687: Thomas Richardson, Deputy Surveyor, granted cert., for 76 a. (*) to Robert Benger (RM#HS: 34).

BUNHILL'S MAKESHIFT

6 Dec 1749: George Bunhill leased 95 a. (*) to Joshua Bond (TR#C: 149).

BUNKER'S HILL

26 April 1776: 50½ a. surv. for Zachariah Maccubbin (B).

BURCHFIELD'S VENTURE

1730: Adam Burchfield conv. 50 a. (*) to Thomas Price (IS#K: 231).

1729 [sic]: Thomas Price conv. 50 a. (*) to Samuel Howell (IS#K: 241).

10 Sep 1746: Samuel Howell and Sarah Durbin entered a prenuptial contract; in consideration of their marriage he gave her (*) and other lands, and a child's portion of his personal estate, to her and her heirs by him. If she d. without heirs by him the above tracts were to be divided among his male heirs. She relinquished her dower right to ⅓ of his estate (TB#E: 177).

BURGES' CAMP

21 Sep 1683: 1000 a. surv. for George Burgess; located on the head of Bush R.; later possessed by Charles Carroll (MRR: 48).

BURMAN'S FOREST

12 Feb 1685: 350 a. surv. for Robert Burman of London, merchant; later 100 a. by Joseph Perregwa and 100, a. by Richard Watkins for Ebenezer Blakiston (MRR: 93).

7 May 1687: Robert Burman of KE Co., merchant, and w. Ann, conv. 350 a. (*) to Matthew Hudson (RM#HS: 271).

27 Dec 1688: Matthew Hudson made a will leaving (*) to his w. Jane (RM#HS: 345).

17 Oct 1716: Ebenezer Blackstone of KE Co. and w. Sarah conv. 100 a. Goodwill, being pt. of (*) to Edward Peregoy (TR#A: 412).

17 Oct. 1716: Ebenezer Blackstone of KE Co. and w. Sarah conv. 97 a. Interest, being pt. (*) to Joseph Peregoy (TR#A: 413).

17 Oct 1716: Ebenezer Blackstone of KE Co. and w. Sarah conv. 100 a. Success, being pt. (*) to Henry Peregoy (TR#A: 414).

17 Oct 1716: Ebenezer Blackstone of KE Co. and w. Sarah conv. 48 a. Green's Lot, being pt. (*) to Robert Green (TR#A: 414-416).

9 Aug 1737: George With conv. to John Bowen 50 a. (*), bought from John Miller (HWS#1-A: 7).

BURMAN'S INDUSTRY

20 Dec 1690: Robert Burman conv. 120 a. (*), 100 a. The Cross, and 150 a. Guttering's Addition to James Dryden (IR#AM: 113).

BURNEY'S PURCHASE

11 June 1743: John Jamison conv. 130 a. Burney's Purchase, 100 a. London, and 100 a. Pitchcraft and Polecat Ridge, to Samuel Howell. JJ's w., unnamed, cons. (TB#C: 258).

BUSH FORK

20 Nov 1695: Tract pat. (HW#2: 8).

15 May 1700: John Richardson conv. 200 a. (*) to James Crooke of BA Co. (HW#2: 8).

BUSH GROVE

10 Oct 1745: Pat. as Timber Grove (TB#E: 383).

5 March 1746: John Bond and w. Aliceanna conv. (*) to William Wilson, Jr., of AA Co., and to Henry Wilson of CV Co. (TB#E: 383).

BUSHWOOD

15 Aug 1659: 150 a. surv. for Abraham Holman on the w. side of Bush R.; later poss. by John Hall (MRR: 30).

1 April 1693: John Hall and w. conv. 150 a. (*) to Richard Adams (RM#HS: 366).

8 April 1693: Richard Adams and w. Mary, conv. 150 a. (*) to John Hall (RM#HS: 368).

8 June 1710(?): John Hall and w. Martha conv. 150 a. (*) and 1200 a. Galler's Bay to James Maxwell (TR#DS: 86).

BUSHY NECK

20 March 1696: 200 a. pat. to John Richardson (MPL 37: 421).

BUSHY NECK BOTTOM

14 Sep 1693: Edward Batson, surveyor of CV and AA Co. has surv. 238 a. (*) for John Hurst; land is in AA Co., and the warrant of surv. was dated 24 April (HW#2: 244).

27 Aug 1701: John Hurst of Patapsco R., BC, assigned (*) to John Busvargus of London, upholsterer, in case Hurst did not repay certain bills of exch. (HW#2: 241).

BUSSELLS (THE)

21 June 1757: Thomas Broad and w. Ann deed to John Ensor, Sr., and to Abraham Ensor 49 a. (*), and other lands (B#G: 9).

BUTTS FORTUNE

3 Dec 1750: Mary Butts, for love and affection, conv. to Peter Black a tract of land in His Lordship's Reserve, called (*) on the n. side of Broad Creek, and other prop. (BACT 1:21?).

CABIN BRANCH HILLS AND VALES

25 Sep 1747: Samuel Hughes leased (*) and Hughes' Cabin to Roger Perryman for 99 years. Hughes had leased the land from Benjamin Tasker on 18 July 1746 for 222 a. (TB#E: 629).

CABIN'S NECK

2 June 1671: John Collett conv. 100 a. (*) on w. side of Bush R. to William Yorke (IR#PP: 102).

7 March 1750: George York of BA Co., conv. 100 a. (*) to William Savory, merchant (TR#D: 143).

CADWALLADER (Pt. EXPECTATION)

8 Sep 1683: 100 a. surv. for Thomas Jones; later held by Charles Jones, and still later held by Edward Smith for the orphans of Charles Jones (MRR: 39).

24 March 1702: John Ellis conv. 100 a. (*), pt. of Expectation, to Cadwalader Jones (IR#PP: 132).

30 June 1705: Cadwallader Jones, with cons. of w. Mary, conv. 100 a. (*) to William Norris.

28 Dec 1705: William Norris and w. Sarah conv. 100 a. (*) to Samuel Jackson (IR#AM: 18).

9 March 1722: Theophilus Jones conv. 126 a. pt. (*), included in the resurv. called Jones Inheritance (IS#G: 184).

CAIN'S ADDITION

10 May 1758: Edward Lloyd, Agent for Lord Baltimore, leased to James Cain 80 a. called (*) for 99 years (Proprietary Leases 1:230).

CAIN'S CHANCE

26 April 1758: Edward Lloyd, Agent for Lord Baltimore, leased 30 a. (*) to William Cain for 99 years (Prop. leased, 1:238).

CALEB'S NECESSITY

6 Nov 1751: Robert Collins of BA Co., conv. his estate, right, title, and interest in (*) to Edward Flanagan. The tract had orig. been granted to Joseph Ellidge on 1 Aug 1745. RC's w. Jemima cons. (TR#D: 229).

CAMP (THE)

27 Feb 1703: 100 a. surv. for Edward Hooke (1723 RR).

3 May 1709: Edward Hooke and w. Jane conv. 100 a. (*) to James Crooke (TR#A: 66).

CAMPBELL'S ADVENTURE

14 Dec 1708: John Campbell of BA Co. makes 300 a. (*) over to Ruth Robinson, Phillis Campbell and James Campbell (TR#A: 70).

CAMPBELL'S ISLAND

4 Nov 1708: John Campbell and w. Eleanor conv. 48 a. (*) to John Ewings (RM#HS: 625).

CANAAN (1729)

8 Nov 1729: 100 a. pat. by Edward Stevenson (MPL PL#7: 207, IL#B: 74).

7 March 1743: Edward Stevenson conv. 100 a. (*) to Charles Gorsuch. Stevenson's w. Susanna cons. (TB#C: 536).

CANAAN (1743)

4 Oct 1743: 150 a. pat. by Edward Stevenson (MPL EI#6: 616, LG#E: 163).

1750: Edward Stevenson owned 150 a. (1750 DB).

CANNON'S DELIGHT

10 June 1706: granted by Lord Baltimore to John Cannon.

See Horvath Plat: Elkridge.

20 July 1710: John Israel and w. Barbara conv. 150 a. (*) to Amos Garrett of BA Co. (TR#A: 97).

CAROLINA FELIX

19 Oct 1747: 645 a. pat. by James Richard (MPL LG#C: 668, BT: 192).

See Horvath Plats: Wards Chapel and Baltimore/ Carroll Co.

13 Oct 1748: James Richard of BA Co., merchant, mortgaged to Charles Ridgely and Joseph Taylor, execs. of William Fell 646 a. (*) and other lands (TR#C: 82).

CARPENTER'S PLAIN

29 May 1717: Cert. of surv. (IS#H: 115).

12 May 1725: Joshua Wood of BA Co., carpenter, conv. 100 a. (*) to Charles Anderson. Joshua's s. cons. (IS#H: 115).

CARRICKFERGUS (also called CURGAFURGUS)

1734: Surv. for 400 a.

See Horvath Plat: Finksburg to Westminster.

12 April 1740: William Hammond conv. 200 a. (*), being ½ the tract to Joseph Cornelius. WH's w. Sarah cons. (HWS#1-A: 417).

28 Oct 1741: William Hammond conv. 200 a., being ½ of (?)...urg... to George Ogg (TB#A: 14).

12 May 1744: Joseph Cornelius and w. Elizabeth, conv. ½ of (*) to Thomas Stocksdale (TB#C: 539).

12 May 1744: Joseph Cornelius conv. to Robert Cross 100 a. (*). (TB#C: 673).

27 Oct 1749: Robert Cross of BA Co., planter, and w. Jemima, deed 57 (51?) a. pt. of (*) to William Mattox (TR#C: 317).

20 Feb 1749: George Ogg, Sr., makes a deed of gift to his s. George, Jr., 200 a. pt. (*). GO's w. Mary cons. (TR#C: 498).

1750: George Ogg, Jr., owned 200 a. Carrickfergus (1750 DB).

CARR'S LOT

14 Oct 1743: Thomas Carr conv. 90 a. (*) to John Stansbury (TB#C: 336).

CARR'S PLEASURE

See Horvath Plat: Ruxton and Riderwood.

6 Nov 1716: Thomas Hooker of BA Co. conv. 100 a. (*) to Benjamin Carr. The tract is pt. of a larger tract called Samuel's Hope (TR#A: 452).

CARROLLTON

10 Feb 1702: Cert. of surv. for (*), laid out for (or by) James Carroll, Deputy Surveyor (TR#RA: 490).

CARTER'S CHOICE

1747: 50 a. surv. for John Carter.

See Horvath Plat: Randallstown.

26 Aug 1751: John Carter of BA Co., cooper, conv. 50 a. pt. (*) to William Wright. JC's w. Frances cons. (TR#D, 227).

CARTER'S REST (See JAMES FOREST)

25 July 1661: 400 a. surv. for Edward Carter on the s. side of Musketo Creek; 130 a. sold to Edward Beedle, and now held by John Hall and Mark Richardson for the orphans of George Utie; still later 130 a. held by John Hall, 180 a. by Anthony Drew, and 90 a. held by Samuel Jackson (MRR: 4, 11, 12).

29 May 1675: Nathaniel Utie and w. conv. 90 a. (*) to Robert Jones (G#J: 361, and IR#PP: 1).

29 May 1675: Hon. Col. Nathaniel Utie and w. Elizabeth conv. 130 a. (*) to Edward Beedle, adj. 90 a. sold to Robert Jones (G#J: 315).

29 May 1675: Nathaniel Utie and w. Elizabeth conv. 180 a. (*), pt. of 400 a. granted to Edward Carter, to Ruthen Garrett; deed mentions 130 a. sold to Edward Beedle (IR#PP: 2).

29 April 1685: Thomas Lightfoot, surveyor, conv. to Edward Carter of AA Co., 500 a. on the s. side of the n. branch of the head of Gunpowder R., 500 a. called (*), being pt. of two tracts, 500 a. and 1000 a., both called Expectation. Rebecca Lightfoot signed with the grantor (RM#HS: 125).

15 Nov 1696: Lodwick Martin and w. Mary conv. 90 a. pt. of 400 a. (*) to Samuel Jackson (IS#IK: 62).

30 Dec 1696: John Hall and w. Martha, one of the daus. and coheirs of Edward Beedle of BA Co., dec., 130 a. (*) and 100 a. Beedle's Reserve, to Mary Utie, relict of George Utie, sister of said Martha Hall, and coheir of said Beedle (IS#IK: 241, 245).

29 Aug 1698: Garrett Garrettson of St. George's Parish conv. 180 a. (*) to Anthony Drew, being the same land formerly purch. by Ruthen Garrett from Col. Nathaniel Utie (HW#2: 245).

21 May 1699: Anthony Drew, of St. George's Parish, and w. Mary Ann, conv. 180 a. (*) to Capt. Nicholas Lydstone or Leadstone of London, merchant (TR#RA: 344).

31 May 1703: Roger Matthews and Thomas Cord of Spesutia Hundred, trustee of the will of Mary Utie, have viewed the property belonging to Susanna Utie, orphan of George and Mary Utie; property included pt. of (*), Utie's Addition and Utie Rumley (HW#2: 235).

14 June 1703: Garrett Garrettson of BA Co. again conv. 180 a. of (*) to Anthony Drew, since the deed of 29 Aug 1698 does not seem to have been recorded. GG's w. Elizabeth is mentioned in the deed, but did not sign the deed (HW#2: 245).

20 March 1716: Anthony Drew of BA Co. conv. 180 a. (*) to Francis Holland. AD's w. Margaret cons. (TR#A: 433).

28 May 1725: Francis Holland and w. Susanna conv. 180 a. (*), orig. bought by Ruthen Garrett from Col. Nathaniel Utie, and 120 a. which Utie sold to Edward Bedell, to a [John Stokes]. (IS#H: 130).

20 July 1725: John Stokes conv. two parcels of (*), 130 a. and 180 a., conv. to him on 28 May 1725, to John Clarke; deed excludes 1 a. set aside for a family burial ground (IS#H: 173).

8 June 1726: John Stokes of BA Co again conv. the two parcels to John Clark (IS#H: 247).

19 Nov 1731: Mary Foster conv. 90 a. of (*) (pt. of the 400 a. tract which Robert Jones purch. from Col. Nathaniel Utie) to James Taylor; she also conv. 100 a. Jackson's Outlet (IS#L: 165).

28 Feb 1740: William Carter and w. Ann of St. Paul's Parish, conv. 100 a. (*) to William Fell (HWS#1-A: 469).

25 May 1743: William Carter of AA Co., shipwright, heir at law of Edward Carter, dec., conv. 500 a. (*) to Talbot Risteau; the deed mentions the 1685 deed of gift from Thomas [Lightfoot] to Edward Carter, recorded in RM#HS: 125. (TB#C: 226).

1750: William Wright of Patapsco owned 50 a. (*) (1750 DB: 84).

31 Oct 1767: Samuel Bonham of Hanover Co., NC, and w. Tomlinson, granddaughter and sole heir of Edward Carter of BA Co. The deed states that on 7 Oct 1750 Bonham and w. sold 200 a. (*) to Henry Garrett of Johnston Co., NC, and later on 12 July last, sold by Isaac Garrett, heir of said Henry, and w. Mary sold the land to Samuel Bond. Now Bonham and w., conv. the land to Bond again to quiet the title (B#Q: 290).

CARVELL'S ISLAND

20 June 1733: Bloyce Wright made his will leaving 150 a. (*) and other lands to his eld. s. Thomas (MCW#VII: 232).

1 Sep 1741: William Wright (and w. Sarah) conv. (*) and other lands (which he inher. from his father Bloyce Wright) to Abraham Jarrett (HWS#1-A: 560).

CASWELL'S VENTURE

16 Jan 1745: Richard Caswell conv. 98 a. (*) and 230 a. Sterling's Purchase to William Dallam. RC's w. Christiana cons. (TB#D: 422).

8 Aug 1750: William Dallam, merchant, conv. to John Hatton, planter, 98 a. (*) and 200 a. Mate's Affinity (TR#D: 71).

CAVAN

6 Aug 1718: granted to Owen Sullivan (TB#C: 299).

9 March 1726/7: Owen Sullivan and w. Anne conv. 100 a. (*) to Thomas Price (IS#H: 315).

1730: Thomas Price conv. 100 a. (*) to Adam Burchfield (IS#K: 256).

7 May 1743: Adam Burchfield and Mary conv. 100 a. (*) to Guy Little (TB#C: 299).

9 Nov 1749: Guy Little of BA Co. conv. 100 a. (*) to Edward Garrettson; land had orig. been granted 6 Aug 1718 to Owen Sullivant (TR#C: 324).

CHADWELL'S OUTLET

4 July 1676: Cert. of surv.

Nov 1729: John Jones and w. Margaret, dau. of John Chadwell, s. and heir of John Chadwell of BA Co., dec., conv. 45 a. (*) to Bloyce Wright (IS#K: 157).

1750: The land (called Chadwick's Outlet) was owned by the heirs of Thomas Wright (1750 DB: 16).

CHADWELL'S RANGE

1 Oct 1675: Pat. by John Chadwell (TB#C: 469).

1 Nov 1698: John Chadwell of BA Co., planter, s. and heir of John Chadwell, dec., conv. 80 a. (*) to Robert Benger, cordwainer (TR#RA: 300).

4 Feb 1713: Alexander Graves, late of KE Co., conv. 80 a. (*), laid out for John Chadwell, dec., to John Harris of KE Co. On 5 Feb 1713 Graves gave p/a to Charles Hynson to acknowledge this deed (TR#A: 178, 179).

1729: John Jones and w. conv. (*) and Bettys Delight to Bloyce Wright (IS#K: 128).

6 April 1744: Thomas Norris and w. Abarilla conv. (*) to Anthony Asher (TB#C: 469).

CHALKLEY'S WELL (or WILL)

16 May 1705: 200 a. surv. for Thomas Chalkley; 20 Jan 1706: 200 a. pat. to Chalkley (MPL CD#4: 261).

CHAMBERLAIN'S IMPROVEMENT

17 Jan 1743: Benjamin Tasker leased to John Chamberlaine 106 a., pt. of HL Manor of Baltimore, called Chamberlaine's Improvement. The lease to run for the lifetimes of Thomas, Elizabeth, and Mary, ch. of said John Chamberlain (TR#C: 486).

CHAMBERLAIN'S MEADOW
(Pt. of HIS LORDSHIP'S RESERVE)

23 Oct 1745: Benjamin Tasker, Agent for Lord Baltimore, leased 75 a. (*) to John Chamberlain for 99 years (TB#E: 88).

CHANCE (1663)

Oct 1663: 100 a. in AA Co. surv. by William Frizzell (MRR).

CHANCE (1669)

(There is almost certainly more than one tract of this name).

150 a. surv. 10 Aug 1669 for Joseph Herves (Hughes) on the w. side of Bush R., on the n. side of a marsh near Hog Neck, and now in the possession of Preston who married the heiress of the said Hughes (MRR: 62).

June 1727: Thomas Cross pet. the court that he possessed (Hughes') Chance, laid out for Joseph Hughes on 1 Aug 1669, in right of his TC's w. Sarah (BALC, HWS#3: 15).

2 April 1728: Thomas Cross of BA Co., cordwainer, and w. Sarah, conv. 50 a. of the tract to James Standiford (IS#I: 77).

Nov 1728: James Standiford, with cons. of w. Mary conv. 50 a. to William ...(?). (IS#I: 222).

9 March 1731: Catherine Whayland, dau. of Henry Matthews, conv. 50 a. to Thomas Lego; Henry Matthews by his LWT devised 100 a. to his dau. Sarah Matthews, and 50 a. to his dau. Catherine (IS#L: 208).

5 June 1734: Thomas Cross, with cons. of his w. Sarah, conv. 10 a. out of the 50 a. (pt. of 150 a.) to which he is entitled, to William Rhodes (HWS#M: 67).

8 Aug 1734: William Rhodes conv. 60 a. to Theophilus Jones and w. Elizabeth. Rhodes had bought 50 a. from Thomas League (who bought it from Patrick Whayland and w. Catherine, who had inher. it from her father Henry [Matthews]; and 10 a. from Thomas Cross who m. Sarah, dau. of said Henry [Matthews]. WR's w. Mary cons. (HWS#M: 90).

Theophilus Jones d. by 3 March 1735 and his widow and extx. Elizabeth married Thomas Lloyd [Barnes; BCF, 1659-1759, p. 373]

14 May 1748: Sarah Price, widow of Thomas Price, conv. 40 a. pt. (?), in all a 150 a. tract, to Edward Brucebanks (TR#C: 16).

19 Nov 1748: Elizabeth Lloyd, widow, of BA Co. made her will leaving to Thomas Durbin 60 a. on Bush R., adj. the plantation belonging to Matthew Beck and Joseph Smith (A: cites MWB 25: 475).

1750: Edward Brucebanks owned 40 a. pt. (*) (1750 DB).

1750: Thomas Durbin owned 60 a. (*) (1750 DB: 53).

1754 Debt Book: Thomas Durbin is listed as owning pt. Preston's Deceit and (*) (IBC: 60).

CHANCE (THE) (1676)

43 a. surv. 12 July 1676 for Edward Reeves on the n. side of Gunpowder R., and later held by Thomas Preston (MRR: 61).

7 Nov 1677: Edward Reeves, planter, conv. 43 a. to Thomas Preston. ER's w. Anne cons. (IR#PP: 19).

13 Jan 1717: Richard Gist of BA Co. conv. 120 a. (*), pt. of Turkey Cock Hall, to Thomas Taylor. RG's w. Zipporah cons. (TR#RA: 444).

14 Jan 1717: Thomas Taylor and w. Elizabeth, conv. 120 a. (*), pt. of TCH, to Samuel Merryman (TR#RA: 430).

1 July 1717: Thomas Preston conv. the 43 a. to John Bond, describing the tract as "land where Capt. Thomas Preston formerly resided." No w. cons. (TR#A: 425).

24 June 1738: Samuel Merryman of BA Co. conv. 120 a. (*), pt. of TCH, to Edward Riston (HWS#1-A: 91).

2 Feb 1740: Absolom Browne leased to Owen Maccan and w. Elizabeth for 21 years, 66 a. pt. of (*), taken up by Samuel Browne (HWS#1-A: 467).

CHANCE (1701)

Dec 1701: 969 a. surv. for Robert Kirkland (Card Index to Patents).

CHANCE (1704)

1704: Tract was surv. for Charles Smith (HWS#M: 166).

3 Feb 1734: Henry Fitch conv. $\frac{1}{2}$ of (*) to dau. Mary Parlett. After dau. Mary's death, land was to pass to Fitch's grandson William Parlett. HF's w. Mary cons. (HWS#M: 166).

CHAPMAN'S FELLOWSHIP

5 June 1700: 150 a. pat. to James Chapman of PG Co. (MPL 34:252, 38:157).

6 Nov 1730: James Chapman of DO Co. carpenter, conv. 150 a. (*) to Edward Wright (IS#L: 33).

CHARITY'S DELIGHT
(Pt. REBECCA'S DELIGHT)

10 Sep 1687: Rebecca Lightfoot conv. 106 a. (*) to George Ashman (RM#HS: 283).

CHARLES' FOREST

19 Aug 1720: Morris Baker of BA Co. conv. 295 a. (*), formerly in AA Co., now in BA Co., to Lancelot Todd of BA Co.; Maurice's w. Sarah cons. (TR#DS. 272).

CHARLES' NEIGHBORS

8 Nov 1743: Edward Thorpe purch. 329 a. (*) from Aquila and John Paca (TB#C: 389).

CHARLES' PURCHASE

15 Feb 1676/6: Nicholas Gassaway has a warrant for 450 a. of land (IR#PP: 34).

27 Feb 1677/8: Gassaway patents 300 a. (*) (IR#PP: 34).

9 April 1679: Nicholas Gassaway of South R., AA Co., appointed Miles Gibson his atty., to assign title and deliver 300 a. to Robert Love. 3 June 1679: Nicholas Gassaway, Gent., of AA Co. conv. 300 a. (*) to Robert Love (IR#PP: 34).

CHARLOTTE TOWN

12 April 1744: 2 lots to William Wright; for WW c27, w. Sarah c14, and dau. Mary c18 mos. (TB#C: 496).

20 April 1744: 1 lot to John Bull for ... JB c28, John Bacon s. of Martin age 1, c3 (Ibid: 499).

26 May 1744: Thomas Brerewood, Sr., leased 1 lot in (*) to Charles Cole for lives of Cole, age c22, his bro. Joseph, c18, and bro. Matthew, c12 (TB#E: 360).

28 May 1744: 2 lots plus 1⅓ a. to Thomas Hamilton, for ... TH c50, s. TH, Jr. c14, and dau. Margaret c17 (Ibid: 559).

12 Sep 1744: To Paul Garron for ... PG c25, s. John 12, and s. James 9 (folio 598).

20 Sep 1744: 4 lots to William Carson, for WC 24, w. Elizabeth 16, and her bro. Andrew Johnson c8 (Ibid: 601).

20 Sep 1744: 2 lots to Thomas Oakley for ... TO c30, w. Prudence c28, and TO, Jr. c2 (Ibid: 603).

20 Sep 1744: To Nicholas Seavers for ... NS c38, Eliz. S. c33, and Nicholas, Jr., c1 (TB#C: 606).

20 Sep 1744: 4 lots to John Wood for ... JW c50, w. Ann c44, and Charles Seaver of Nicholas c9 (Ibid: 610).

20 Sep 1744: 4 lots to Thomas Hamilton for ... same lives as on 28 May 1744 (TBEC: 613).

1 Oct 1744: To Robert Whitehead for ... RW c45, w. Elizabeth in 40s, and s. Thomas c4 (TB#D: 180).

-- Dec 1744: Thomas Brerewood leased 4½ lots to William Wright for lives of said WW, w. Sarah, and dau. (unnamed), age c2 (TB#D: 194).

26 March 1745: 3 lots to Nicholas Seavers, for ... (much of deed is missing) (TB#C: 170).

10 June 1745: Thomas Brerewood leased 3 lots in (*) to Cornelius Stewart for lifetimes of Stewart, age 41, Arthur Brownlee, Jr., c10, and Joseph Brownlee, age c7 (TB#E: 362).

10 Oct 1746: Brerewood leased 11 lots in (*) to Jonathan Ady of BA Co. for lives of Ady, age c27, w. Rebecca, c22, and s. William (4 years? 14 mos.?), The 11 lots had orig. been leased to Nicholas Seaver (TB#E: 352).

CHASE (THE)

1745: Surv. for Henry Morgan.

See Horvath Plat: Reisterstown.

27 Sep 1746: Henry Morgan, merchant, mortgaged 300 a. (*) and other land to Christopher Grindall (TB#E: 182).

CHEAPSIDE

4 March 1718: Thomas Preston and James Preston of BA Co., planters, conv. 500 a. (*) to Thomas Bond. JP's w. Elizabeth cons. (TR#DS: 21).

CHELSEA

10 March 1676: 125 a. surv. for James Phillips; located on the n. side of Bush R. adj. a tract called Crab Hill; later 100 a. sold and possessed by George Smith, and residue by James Phillips; still later as Chelsea Resurveyed, 100 a. held by David Thomas for George Smith's orphans and 25 a. possessed by James Phillips (MRR: 14).

4 June 1681: James Phillips and w. Susanna conv. 100 a., pt. of 125 a. (*) to George Smith and w. Elizabeth (IR#AM: 129).

2 Feb 1716: William Smith, s. and heir of George Smith conv. 100 a. (*) and 100 a. Mates Angles to James Phillips. Hannah, now w. of David Thomas, cons. (TR#A: 477).

CHENOWETH'S ADVENTURE

8 Oct 1761: Richard Chenoweth of BA Co. conv. to John Daughaday, blacksmith, 201 a. (*). RC's w. Keziah cons. (B#I: 337).

CHENYCHE

25 Sep 1666: Land was pat. by William Peirce, who sold it to John Willis (G#J: 248).

2 June 1674: John Willis, planter, conv. 200 a. (*) to Joseph Hopkins; land is on the s. side of Chirne Creek (G#J: 248).

CHERRY GARDEN

1710/1: Robert Gardner left the tract to his s. Alexander (MCW#III: 206).

1750: John Gardner owns 50 a. (*) (1750 DB: 89).

1763/4: John Gardner owned 50 a. (*) (AHAL: 77).

CHESTNUT LEVEL

6 March 1754: Richard Richards conv. 50 a. (*) to Zebulon Loveall (BB#I: 174).

CHESTNUT NECK (1662)

29 July 1662: 150 a. surv. for Oliver Sprye; possessed by James Maxwell (MRR: 37).

CHESTNUT NECK (1673)

3 May 1673: 100 a. surv. for John Chadwell; later owned by Daniel Scott, Sr., who had it resurv. as pt. of Scott's Improvement (q.v.) (MRR: 67; TB#E: 534).

17 Sep 1701: John Chadwell and w. Mary conv. to Daniel Scott 100 a. (*) and 190 a. Stanharket (HW#2: 95).

21 July 1724: John Jones of BA Co., and w. Margaret, dau. and sole heir of a certain John Chadwell the Younger conv. (*) and Stanharket (orig. surv. for John Chadwell, Sr.), Harmer's Hope and Hunting Creek, surv. for Godfrey Harmer and Oliver Spry and sold to John Chadwell, Sr., grandfather of Margaret Jones (IS#C: 352).

CHESTNUT NECK (1678)

4 May 1678: 100 a. surv. for William Westbury on the s. side of Gunpowder R.; later possessed by his orphans, and still later by Simon Pearson (MRR: 36).

8 March 1710: John Butteram and w. Elizabeth and William Bond and w. Mary conv. to Simon Pearson, weaver, their interest in lands formerly belonging to Thomas, Daniel, and William Westbury, dec., said Elizabeth and Mary being the heirs thereof (TR#A: 63).

24 Nov 1713: Simon Pearson and w. Emma conv. 150 a. (*) on s. side Gunpowder R. to Francis Dallahide (TR#A: 254-255).

3 Aug 1720: Francis Dallahide conv. 150 a. (*) to Jacob Groce (TR#DS: 227).

10 Aug 1734: Isaac Groce conv. 150 a. (*) to John Maccubbin, Jr. (HWS#M: 100).

4 June 1734: Isaac Grice and Rosanna Stanton give quitclaim to Anthony Asher for all accounts (HWS#M: 216).

10 July 1744: William Maccubbin and Zachariah Maccubbin of BA Co. conv. to George Presbury 150 a. (*) which Isaac Groce sold to John Maccubbin, bro. of William and Zachariah on 10 Aug 1734 (TB#C: 546).

CHESTNUT RIDGE

9 Oct 1724: Joseph Howard of AA Co. conv. 242 a. (*) and 200 a. Howard's Ridge to John Swinyard; w. Margery cons. (IS#G: 391).

26 March 1725: Joshua Wood, carpenter, and w. Martha conv. 90 a. (*) to Isaac Wood, carpenter (IS#H: 113).

CHEVY CHASE (1695)

26 July 1695: 400 a. tract surv. for John Thomas in the woods adj. to Edward Felkes' land; later poss.; 100 a. Elisha Sedgwick, 100 a. Joshua Sedgwick and 200 a. Seaborn Tucker (MRR: 55).

15 April 1703: John Thomas of BA Co. and w. Jane conv. ½ of 200 a. (*) to Elisha Sedgwick of CV Co. (HW#2: 225).

15 April 1703: John Thomas and w. Jane conv. 200 a. to Seaborn Tucker; Jane Thomas gave p/a to William Reid to acknowledge above sale as her "infirmity, impotence, and old age" make it impossible for her to travel to the co. court (HW#2: 227, 229).

16 April 1703: Elisha Sedgwick of CV Co. conv. 100 a. (*) to Joshua Sedgwick of same co. (HW#2: 229).

1 July 1712: Seaborn Tucker of AA Co., planter, conv. 200 a., being ½ of (*), to Samuel Groom of London, merchant (TR#A: 217).

10 Aug 1713: Elisha Sedgwick and w. Grace of CV Co. conv. 100 a. (being ½ the land conv. to said Elisha on 15 April 1703 by John and Jane Thomas) to John Thomas of BA Co., Gent. (TR#A: 247).

26 April 1742: Benjamin Sedgwick of CV Co. conv. 100 a. pt. (*) to John Ensor; tract had been sold by Elisha Sedgwick to Joshua Sedgwick, father of Benjamin (TB#A: 142).

20 Jan 1743: Daniel Johnson Lowe of Prince William Co., VA, conv. 200 a. (*) to Edward Evans (TB#C: 385).

4 July 1743: Thomas Bond and w. Phebe conv. 100 a. pt. (*) to John Ensor (TB#C: 270).

1 Jan 1762: Abraham Ensor leased pt. (*) to Edward Wigley (B#K: 445).

CHEVY CHASE (1734)

10 June 1734: 277 a. pat. by Henry Sater (MPL EI#3: 303; EI#4: 199).

30 Aug 1740: Henry Sater conv. 200 a. pt. (*) to George Brown (HWS#1-A: 479).

4 June 1744: George Brown of BA Co. planter, and w. Mary conv. 200 a. (*), formerly surv. for Henry Sater, to Robert North (TB#C: 479).

1 June 1745: Henry Sater and w. Dorcas conv. 200 a. pt. (*) to Robert North (TB#D: 261).

CHEW'S BOUNTY

7 Oct 1712: Samuel Chew of AA Co. conv. 200 a. (*) (pt. of Chew's Vineyard) to niece Sidney Pierpoint and the heirs of her body lawfully begotten, i.e., John and Francis Pierpoint (TR#A: 207).

CHILBURY

2 Feb ---: 250 a. surv. for William Orchard on the e. side of Bush R., and later held by Peregrine Brown of London, merchant (MRR: 10).

5 March 1667/8: William Orchard conv. to Walter Tucker 250 a. (*) [called ---ilberry] (IR#PP. 64).

17 Jan 1690/1: John Burridge of Lyme Regis, Dorset, merchant and exec. of Walter Tucker, conv. to John Cary of London, 1200 a. of land including 600 a. (*) 600 a. of other land. Deed states that James Gundrey, factor or agent for Walter Tucker, purch. (*) from William Orchard in 1666 (IR#AM: 101).

22 April 1717: John Cary of London, merchant, John Burridge of Lyme Regis, Dorset, and George Cole of London, merchant, conv. 600 a. (*) to Peregrine Brown of London, merchant (TR#RA: 436).

14 Oct 1717: Maurice Burchfield, Surveyor General of His Majesty's Customs in the Southern District of America, and Joseph Brown, late of London, merchant, s. and heir of Peregrine Brown, late of London, dec., conv. 250 a. (*) to James Phillips; the deed states that Peregrine Brown made a will naming w. Margaret as extx.; the following tracts in MD were owned by Peregrine Brown at the time of his death: Addition, 400 a.; Bachelor's Addition 50 a.; Bachelor's Hope 400 a.; (*) 250 a.; Waters' Neck 100 a. the MD Court of Chancery decreed that these tracts should be held to satisfy the debts of Browne (TR#A: 485).

CHILBURY, ADDITION TO

5 April 1743: James Phillips leased 100 a. (*) to George Hollandsworth for 15 years (TB#C:198).

CHILBURY HALL

15 June 1668: 250 a. tract surv. for John Lee on the n. side of Bush R., 125 a. later possessed by Anthony Drew, and 125 a. unclaimed by anyone; still later in possession of Anthony Drew (MRR: 15).

3 March 1670/1: John Lee, planter, conv. ½ of (*) to Richard Collins, who is to choose the pt. he likes the best (IR#PP: 99).
16 Jan 1673/4: Richards Collins, blacksmith, for natural love and affection conv. to friend Anthony Brispo 125 a. (*), giving possession by affixing a six pence to the seal (G#J: 227; also TR#RA).
5 June 1693/4: James Durham of BA Co., planter, and w. Elizabeth (dau. of John Lee) conv. ½ of 550 a. tract laid out for John Lee called (C...)bery (Hall), to John Durham (RM#HS: 350).
25 March 1699: John Durham of St. John's Parish, and w. Sarah conv. to Anthony Drew 125 a., being ½ of 250 a. (*) (TR#RA: 335).
1 March 1703: John Ewings of BA Co. conv. 210 a. Chilberry Hall, and 400 a. Ewings' Contrivance to John Brice of AA Co.; John Swynyard who is now in possession of (*) to be allowed to dwell and remain there for three years (HW#2: 312).
14 March 1704: John Brice paid 29 shillings for alienation of 361 a. pt. Ewings' Contrivance, and 194 a. (Chilberry) Hall. 19 May 1704: John Ewings gave a receipt (HW#2: 373).
4 April 1715: Anthony Drew of BA Co., Gent., conv. 21 a. pt. (*) to Aquila Paca; tract was formerly taken up by John Lee (TR#A: 348).

CHOATE'S ADVENTURE

28 May 1742: Christopher Choate, Sr., and CC, Jr., conv. pt. (*) and pt. Green Spring Traverse, in all 108 a., to Nathaniel Gist. CC's w. Flora cons. (TB#A: 155).

CHOATE'S CONTRIVANCE

3 July 1734: Lloyd Harris was given a warrant for 100 a. On 12 Feb 1734/5 it was renewed for 6 mos. On 13 July 1735 the warrant was assigned to William Rogers who assigned the 100 a. to Augustin Choate.
25 July 1737: 100 a. pat. by Augustine Choate (MPL EI#2: 635, EI#5: 219).
See Horvath Plat: Green Spring Valley.
29 May 1742: Christopher Choate, Jr., heir at law of Augustine Choate, late of BA Co., dec., conv. 100 a. (*) to William Lewis, in exch. for land conv. by Nath. Gist to James Kelley (TB#A: 202).
30 Oct 1742: William Lewis and w. conv. (*) to Thomas Norris.
7 May 1753: Thomas Norris and w. Avarilla conv. pt. (*), and pt. of Norris' Chance, to Dr. John Stevenson (TR#D: 550).

CHOATE'S FANCY

18 Aug 1722: Richard Gist of BA Co. and w. Zepporah conv. to Christopher Choate (*), being pt. of Green Spring Traverse, and pt. of Street's Adventure (IS#G: 111).

CHOICE TRIPPAS

2 Nov 1726: Lewis Puttee and w. Katherine, dau. and coheir of Matthew Green, and granddaughter of Jane Boone, conv. to Thomas Coale, pt. of (*), Green's Chance, and Levy's Tribe (IS#H: 290).
1729: Ann Cowdry conv. (*), Greens Range and Levy's Tribe to Thomas Coale (IS#K: 193).
8 March 1732: William Hill of BA Co., and w. Martha, dau. and coheir of Matthew Green, and also one of the granddaughters of Jane Boone, sell to Thomas Coale pt. of (*), Green's Chance, and Levy's Tribe (IS#L: 326).

CHRISTIAN'S LOT (1696)

1 May 1696: 100 a. pat. to John Christian (MPL 37:354).
See Horvath Plat: Elkridge.
2 Aug 1709: John Christian conv. 100 a. (*), adj. to Expectation, to Thomas Randall (TR#A: 7).
13 Nov 1715: Thomas Randall and w. Hannah conv. 100 a. pt. of tract, to William Hamilton; land on n. side of Patapsco, adj. to Brother's Expectation (TR#A: 363).
5 Oct 1738: William Hamilton conv. to Thomas Floyd tracts Christian's Lot and pt. Brother's Expectation. WH's w. Sarah cons. (HWS#1-A: 137).
18 Oct 1738: Thomas Floyd conv. to William Hamilton 100 a. (*) and 50 a. Tucker's Fountain. TF's w. Zipporah cons. (HWS#1-A: 137).
11 June 1756: John Floyd, Thomas Floyd, and TF's w. Rachel conv. 100 a. (*) to William Jessop. Henry Maynard and w. Zepporah ackn. receiving full satisfaction for Zepporah's right of dower (BB#I: 570).

CHRISTOPHER'S CAMP

10 June 1685: 1000 a. (*) was granted to Christopher Beanes who by his LWT left the land to his ch. William, Anne (m. Alphonso Cosden and left one s. and heir at law Alphonso), and Mary, m. John Parker of CV Co., dec. (IS#H: 101).
12 March 1724: William Beans of PG Co., Alphonso Cosden and Mary Parker of CV Co., conv. 1000 a. (*) to Isaac Johns of CV Co.
20 March 1750: Abraham Johns of CV Co., shipwright, conv. to Isaac Webster of BA Co., 250 a., pt. of (*). AJ's w. Elizabeth cons. (TR#D: 148).

CHRISTOPHER'S LOT

6 Aug 1746: Thomas Cole of BA Co. conv. to his s. Thomas, pt. of (*) and Thomas's Lot (TB#E: 120).

CLAPHAM'S POINT

4 Nov 1700: Jane Thomas gave p/a to Nathaniel Ruxton to conv. 100 a. (*) to John Gardner (HW#2: 44).

6 Nov 1700: John Thomas of Patapsco R., Gent., conv. 102 a. of (*), pt. of 500 a. granted to William Clapham, to John Gardner. JT' w. Jane gave cons. (HW#2: 45).

CLARK'S DEMURRER
(Also DONMURENINTRUM,
DUMMARY ANTIAM,
CLARK'S DONMURENTON)

25 Aug 1732: James Bond of KE Co., cooper, conv. (*) to Thomas Renshaw of CE Co. (IS#L: 313).

6 March 1744: Thomas Renshaw, Sr., conv. (*) and Giles and Webster's Discovery, in all 250 a. to his s. Thomas Renshaw, Jr. (TB#D: 47).

10 Feb 1749: Joseph Renshaw of BA Co. conv. to Isaac Webster, iron master, 6 a. (*) or some such a name, formerly surv. for John Clark (TR#C: 415).

CLARKE'S FOREST

2 May 1732: Owen Smithson of SM Co., and w. Ann (dau. of Thomas Jackson late of SM Co., dec., and sis. of Geo. Jackson also of SM Co., dec.), conv. 500 a. (*) to James Bisco of SM Co., s. of Ann Smithson by a former marriage; the tract had been conv. by Gilbert Clark of SM Co., to Thomas Jackson of Plymouth, merchant, who conv. it to his s. George, who d. leaving it to his sis. Ann afsd. (IS#L: 256).

21 May 1740: James Bisco of SM Co., conv. 200 a. (*), orig. granted to Thomas Jackson of Plymouth, England, to Thomas Gittings of BA Co. (HWS#1-A: 392).

CLARK'S PARK

31 July 1746: Robert Clark conv. 100 a. (*) to Thomas Wheeler. Clark's w. Selinah cons. This seems to have been an exch. for 100 a. Wheeler's Union which Thomas and Sarah Wheeler conv. to Clark (TB#E: 106, 109).

CLARK'S TOBACCO

17 March 1718: John Clark and w. Elizabeth conv. 100 a. (*) and 145 a. Hall's Pipe to Lawrence Draper (TR#RA: 515).

7 Oct 1727: Lawrence Draper and w. Mary conv. 70 a. (*) and 145 a. Hall's Pipe to Gervase Gilbert (IS#H betw. 20 and 26).

17 Sep 1735: Gervase Gilbert conv. 60 a. (*), 40 a. pt. Gilbert's Chance, and 145 a. pt. Hall's Pipe to his s. Michael Gilbert. Gervase Gilbert's w. Mary cons. (HWS#M: 302).

4 April 1743: Michael Gilbert of BA Co., s. of Garvase Gilbert, conv. to his bro. Charles 60 a., pt. (*), devised to MG by his father in such a way that he only has a life interest in it, and also 60 a. Union, lately surv. for Michael Gilbert; latter's w. Mary cons. (TB#C: 201-206).

CLARKSON'S FOREST

20 March 1746: Clarkson Bowen and w. Rosanna conv. 100 a. pt. (*) to James Sinclair (TB#E: 378).

1750: James Sinclair owned (acreage not given) (1750 DB).

CLARKSON'S HOPE

28 Sep 1683: 600 a. surv. for Robert Clarkson; later held by his heirs, and still later by Edward Reynolds (MRR: 44). See PW Plat G.

10 May 1706: John Bowen of BA Co., conv. 600 a. (*) to Edward Reynolds; tract had been granted to Robert Clarkson of AA Co., who left it to his dau. Milcah, now w. of Bowen. "Mildor" Bowen gave her cons. (RM#HS: 549).

10 Nov 1707: John Bowen and w. Milcah grant quitclaim for 600 a. (*) to Edward Reynolds (RM#HS: 566).

21 Feb 1718: Edward Reynolds conv. (*) to William Hickman of CV Co., in exch. for 300 a. of land in CV Co. (300 a. The Old Plantation, and 300 a. Gassaway Ridge). ER's w. Ann cons. (TR#DS: 67).

3 Feb 1736/7: William Hickman made a will leaving 300 a. (*) to his dau. Mary, w. of William Ireland (MCW#VII: 206).

24 Sep 1748: Joseph Lane of AA Co. conv. $\frac{1}{2}$ of 600 a. (*), which William Ireland and w. Mary sold to said JL, to Stephen Onion. JL's w. Rachel cons. (TR#C: 96).

1750: Thomas Reynolds of CV Co. owning 300 a. (*) (1750 DB: 104).

CLARKSON'S PURCHASE

24 Sep 1683: 600 a. tract surv. for Robert Clarkson on the s. side of the w. branch of Bush R.; belonging to the heirs of Robert Clarkson; still later 400 a. held by Henry Wright, and 200 a. held by John Bowen (MRR: 45).

8 June 1711: John Bowen of BA Co., and w. Milcah conv. 200 a. (*) to Henry Wright, being pt. of a

600 a. tract laid out for Robert Clarkson on 24 Oct 1683 (TR#A: 136).

3 June 1713: John Bowen and w. Milcah conv. 200 a. pt. (*) to William Bond; tract was laid out as before, but date was given as 4 Oct (TR#A: 225).

2 March 1715: William Bond and w. Mary conv. 200 a. (*) to Charles Simmons (TR#A: 326).

2 March 1715: John Bowen and w. Milcah conv. 100 a. pt. (*) to Charles Simmons (TR#A: 327).

8 March 1715: Henry Wright of BA Co. conv. 200 a. (*) to William Amos; tract was granted by cert. of surv. dated 14 Oct 1683 to Robert Clarkson who d. leaving an only dau. Milcah, now w. of John Bowen; Bowen and his w. conv. the land to Wright (TR#A: 391).

4 March 1741: George (and w. Elizabeth), John, and Thomas Symonds, sons and devisees of Charles Symonds, and Charles Symonds' widow Hannah, conv. 180 a. pt. (*) to John Taylor, son-in-law of afsd. Hannah Symonds (TB#A: 105).

9 Oct 1742: Charles Symonds, s. and devisee of Charles Symonds, conv. 60 a. pt. (*) to John Taylor (TB#C: 178).

20 June 1752: Charles Taylor conv. pt. (*), left Charles Simmons [sic] by his father, to Joshua Hardesty; also 32 a. Timber Swamp granted to John Taylor; CT's w. Elizabeth cons. (TR#D: 366).

15 July 1754: Josias Simmons conv. 64 a. (*), left him by his father, Charles, to Margaret James (BB#I: 272).

24 Oct 1754: Josias Simmons conv. 64 a. (*) to Margaret Hunn, w. of Francis Hunn, and late widow of Nicholas James (BB#I: 333).

CLAY

See Horvath Plat: Reisterstown.

7 June 1732: John Rutledge conv. (*) to John Teye. JR's w. Jane cons. (IS#L: 250).

30 March 1741: John Tye of BA Co., conv. 50 a. (*) and 50 a. The Park to Richard Clark. JT's w. Preciosa cons. (HWS#1-A: 492).

29 July 1746: John Bell and w. Susanna conv. to Richard Clark all that tract called Clay, near Soldier's Delight, which was conv. to Susanna Bell by her father John Tye (TB#E: 119).

CLAYBANK

1 Dec 1696: John Kemp of BA Co. made his will leaving (*) to his dau. Mary (MCW#II: 11).

15 Sep 1711: John Boring and w. Mary and Richard Kemp, all of BA Co., sell (*) to John Gardner (TR#A: 171).

CLEMENT

15 Sep 1666: 50 a. surv. for William Orchard; in Rumley Creek; later in poss. of John Savory; later held by William Prichard (MRR: 12).

31 Dec 1666: William Orchard, cooper, conv. 50 a. (*) to John Bradford (IR#PP: 58).

11 May 1681: George Skipwith, planter, and w., Elizabeth, conv. 50 a. (*) to Edward Reeves; Skipwith and w. Elizabeth both appt. James Phillips as their atty. (IR#AM: 125).

14 Dec 1702: John Savory and w. Ann conv. 50 a. (*) and 100 a. Clement's Dean to William Prichard (HW#2: 211).

15 March 1735: Abraham Cord and w. Mary (sister of Joseph Prichard, lately dec.), conv. 50 a. (*), 100 a. Broad Neck, and 100 a. Clement's Dean, to John Atkinson, in return for his agreeing to maintain Mary Cord for the rest of her natural life (HWS#M: 401).

17 Feb 1736: Abraham Cord and w. Mary, sis. of Joseph Prichard, dec., conv. (*) to John Atkinson [again?] (IS#IK: 358).

CLEMMENS DENN

(More properly ST. CLEMENT DANE'S: q.v.)

CLERK'S WOODYARD (THE)
(Pt. HOLLAND'S ADVENTURE)

15 April 1727: Robert Cutchin conv. 40 a. (*) to John Stokes. RC's w. Dorothy cons. (IS#H: 379).

24 Jan 1744: Mary Stokes of BA Co., widow and admnx. of Humphrey Wells Stokes conv. 40 a. (*) plus house and lots in Joppa to Stephen Onion, ironmaster. The tract (*) was bought by John Stokes, father of Humphrey Wells Stokes (TB#D: 75).

CLYNMALIRA

2 Nov 1739: Charles Carroll of Annapolis leased 150 a. pt. (*) to William Lowe for the lives of William, John, and Thomas Lowe (HWS#1-A: 367).

2 Nov 1739: Charles Carroll of Annapolis leased 100 a. pt. (*) to Thomas Johnson, for the life times of Israel, Melchisedek, and Nathan, sons of Thomas Johnson (HWS#1-A: 371).

16 Jan 1743: Charles Carroll of Annapolis leased 100 a. pt. (*) to John Low for the lifetimes of John, Thomas and William Lowe (TB#C: 392).

16 Jan 1743: Charles Carroll of Annapolis leased 100 a. pt. (*) to Nehemiah Hicks for lives of sons Isaac, Nehemiah, and Jacob Hicks (TB#C: 371).

16 Nov 1743: Charles Carroll of Annapolis leased 100 a. (*) to Aquila Greer for the lives of Aquila, and Elizabeth, and Sarah Greer (TB#C: 460).

16 Nov 1743: Charles Carroll of Annapolis leased 100 a. (*) to Jacob Johnson s. of Thomas, for the life times of Jacob, Aaron and Jacob Johnson (TB#C: 418).
16 Nov 1743: Charles Carroll of Annapolis leased 100 a. (*) to Jno. Standiford for lives of Jno. Standiford, Skelton, and William Standiford (TB#C: 457).
17 Sep 1745: Charles Carroll of Annapolis leased 150 a. pt. (*) to Henry Hicks for the lives of his sons James, Laban, and Henry Hicks (TB#D: 425).

COAKINGTON (See OAKINGTON)

COBB'S CHANCE (or CHOICE)
13 April 1741: James Cobb of BA Co., planter, conv. 150 a. (*) (cert. of surv. dated 1 Sep 1734) to George Buchanan (HWS#1-A: 476).
1750: Samuel Durbin owned (*) (1750 DB: 81).
c1754: Samuel Durbin owned Cobb's Choice (IBC: 65).

COBB'S DELIGHT
7 June 1738: James Cobb of BA Co., planter, conv. 100 a. (*) to Samuel Wallis. Cobb's w. Ruth cons. (HWS#1-A: 85).
1750: Samuel Wallis owned 100 a. (*) (1750 DB: 35).

COBB'S NECESSITY
29 June 1747: Joseph Elledge and w. Mary conv., 100 a. (*) to James Amos and Richard Rhodes (TB#E: 650).

COCK CROW THRICE
6 Sep 1668: John Cocks, planter, conv. to Bartlett Hendrickson, 200 a. (*) (IR#PP: 69).

COCKEY'S ENLARGEMENT
23 Feb 1724: Charles Hall purch. 1/5 of 93 a. (*) from William Farrell and w. Mary. A note stated that the dowry of Mary Pumphrey, late widow of William Cockey, was excepted (IS#H: 32).

COCKEY'S TRUST
8 April 1696: 300 a. surv. for William Cockey (GSV, 1:9).
See Horvath Plats: Ruxton and Riderwood, and Green Spring Valley.
29 March 1745: Sarah Hall, widow, Joseph Pumphrey, of AA Co. and w. Anne, Mark Johnson of AA Co., and w. Elizabeth, O'Neal Johnson and w. Mary, coheirs of William Cockey, conv. 300 a. (*) to John Cockey (TB#D: 250).

COCKFELL (or COCKSELL)
Nov 1707: 200 a. surv. for John Jones; 2 Nov 1710: 200 a. pat. to John Jones (MPL DD#5: 649, PL#3: 324).

COCK PITT
17 June 1773: Joseph Ellis conv. (*) to Stephen West of PG Co., merchant (AL#G: 344).

COCKIN'S LOT
7 March 1720: John Cockin of BA Co. planter, conv. 104 a. (*) to William Noble, and w. Elizabeth (RM#HS: 681).

COHEIR'S LOT
(Resurv. on 800 a. Goldsmith's Hall, 24 a. Mathew's Neglect, 200 a. Timber Proof, and 81 a. Watson's Addition).
13 Feb 1726/7: John Smithers of KE Co., Gent., eld. s. of Blanche Smithers, a dau. of Col. George Wells, dec., and one of the coheirs of George Wells, Jr.), conv. his interest in (*) plus 200 a. Timber Proof, to John Stokes (IS#H: 385).
11 Nov 1736: George Stokes, s. of John Stokes, conv. 2/3 of (*) to Humphrey Wells Stokes in exch. for Harman's Town and Montserada (IS#IK: 334).

COHEIRS LOT REVISED
(Surv. of several tracts including pt. of Goldsmith's Hall and other tracts owned jointly by Humphrey Wells Stokes, his mother Susanna Stokes, and Peregrine Frisby).
7 June 1735: Humphrey Wells Stokes owned ⅓ of several tracts now called (*), and conv. the southern half to Aquila Paca (HWS#M: 227).

COLD COMFORT
24 Feb 1661/2: 50 a. pat. to Lovelace Gorsuch on the middle branch of Patapsco; since conv. to Charles Gorsuch (IR#PP: 104).
8 Nov 1670: Lovelace Gorsuch appointed his bro. Charles Gorsuch his atty. to sell land at Patapsco R. (IS#IK: 38).
1 Feb 1669/70: Charles Gorsuch, planter, conv. 50 a. Cold Comfort and 100 a. Rich Level to Thomas Roper. Lovelace Gorsuch also signed the deed (IR#PP: 104; see also IS#IK: 39).
8 Nov 1670: Lovelace Gorsuch of TA Co. appointed his bro. Charles Gorsuch his atty. to sell land at Patapsco R. (IS#IK: 38).
1 Nov 1675: Thomas Roper of AA Co. conv. to Anthony Demondidier also of AA Co. 295 a. in three parcels: 50 a. (*), 100 a. Rich Neck Level (both conv. to Roper on 1 Feb 1669/70), and 145 a. Ropers Range. TR's w. Mary released seisin on 2 Nov 1675 (G#J: 316).

7 Sep 1698: Anthony Demondidier of BA Co. and w. Mary conv. 50 a. Cold Comfort, 100 a. Rich Level, and 145 a. Roper's Range to Margaret Kiersted of CV Co., widow, and her s. Hance Kiersted (HW#2: 33).

6 March 1699: Anthony Demondidier conv. above three tracts to Samuel Sickelmore and Henry Wriothesley in trust for above named Margaret and Hance Kiersted (HW#2: 29).

14 Oct 1715: Margaret Gray, widow of George Gray of CV Co., conv. 50 a. (*) to Thomas Taylor of BA Co. (TR#A: 257).

19 May 1724: Thomas Taylor and w. Elizabeth conv. 50 a. Cold Comfort, 100 a. Fox Hall, and 100 a. Rich Level to Philip Smith (IS#G: 318).

COLE'S ADDITION

10 Nov 1698: 67 a. granted to John Cole (See TR#C: 500).

15 March 1711: John Cole conv. (*) to Robert Green (Se TR#C: 500).

2 July 1750: William Green of BA Co., eld. s. and heir at law of Robert Green, dec., conv. 67 a. (*) to William Hammond. WG's w. Hannah cons. (TR#C: 500).

COLE'S ADVENTURE

1 Nov 1710: 300 a. pat. to John Cole (MPL DD#5: 675, PL#3: 219).

3 Aug 1719: John Cole conv. (*) to Susanna Noden, w. of John Noden; JC's w. Dinah cons. (TR#DS: 18).

25 May 1732: Susanna Moorcock conv. 100 a. pt. (*) to Thomas Demmett and 100 a. pt. (*) to John Demmett (IS#L: 264, 266).

23 July 1734: Susanna Moorcock for love she bears her s. Thomas Demmett conv. all her property to him except for 100 a. (*) already conv. to her s. Richard Demmitt (HWS#M: 85).

COLES BANKS

19 May 1676: Thomas Thurston, in consideration of marriage made by his dau. Ann to Miles Gibson conv. to MG 600 a. in TA Co. embracing tracts (*) and Moorefields (G#J: 330).

COLE'S CHANCE

20 Oct 1702: John Cole and w. Johanna conv. 809 a. (*) to Richard Owen of Herring Creek, AA Co. (HW#2: 183).

28 June 1731: John Cole of BC, planter, conv. 220 a. pt. (*) and Contrivance to Cole's Chance? to George Buchanan. JC's w. Dinah cons. (IS#L: 121).

29 July 1738: Dr. George Buchanan and w. Eleanor and John Cole deed 220 a. pt. (*) and Cole's Contrivance to Charles Gorsuch (HWS#1-A: 94).

6 June 1744: John Cole, Sr., conv. 80 a. pt. (*), 12 a. pt. Contrivance to Cole's Chance, and 276 a. Cole's Search, to Robert North (TB#C: 485).

15 Dec 1744: John Cole, Sr., conv. 100 a. pt. (*) and pt. Contrivance to Cole's Chance to John Gorsuch. JC's Dinah cons. (TB#C: 486).

25 March 1745: John Cole, Sr., and w. Dinah, conv. 100 a. pt. (*) taken up by John Cole on 3 Sep 1724, to Darby Lux (TB#D: 107).

20 May 1745: John Gorsuch conv. 16 a. pt. (*) to Teague Tracey (TB#D: 110).

4 Nov 1745: Teague Tracey conv. 16 a. pt. (*) to William Fell, as well as pts. of Bought Dear, Cole's Contrivance, and Round About (TB#D: 353).

1752: Joseph Taylor and others conv. pt. Cole's Chance, Cole's Contrivance, Bought Dear, and Roundabout Neighbors, to John Gorsuch (TR#D: 373).

1766: Robert Lux conv. 100 a. (*) to Charles Gorsuch (B#P: 271).

1766: Charles Cole conv. 100 a. to Charles Gorsuch (B#P: 273).

COLE'S CONTRIVANCE

(See CONTRIVANCE TO COLE'S CHANCE)

29 July 1738: Dr. George Buchanan and w. Eleanor conv. 220 a. pt. (*) and Cole's Chance to Charles Gorsuch. John Cole also joins the grantors (HWS#1-A: 94).

12 Sep 1741: Charles Gorsuch of BC conv. (*) to Teague Tracey. CG's w. Sarah cons. (TB#A: 19).

28 Nov 1741: Charles Gorsuch and w. Sarah conv. 120 a. pt. (*) to s. John Gorsuch (TB#A: betw. 74 and 80).

4 Nov 1745: Teague Tracey conv. to William Fell 100 a. pt. (*), as well as pts. of Bought Dear, Cole's Chance, and Roundabout (TB#D: 353).

1752: Joseph Taylor and others conv. pt. (*) and pts. of Bought Dear, Cole's Chance, and Round About to John Gorsuch (TR#D: 373).

COLE'S CONTRIVANCE TO COLE'S CHANCE

6 June 1744: John Cole, Sr., conv. 80 a. pt. Cole's Chance, 12 a. pt. Contrivance to Cole's Chance, and 276 a. Cole's Search, to Robert North (TB#C: 485).

COLE'S HARBOR

28 April 1667: 550 a. surv. for George Yates; assigned to David Poole on the n. side Patapsco R.; later possessed by James Todd; still later Richard Colegate possessed 185 a.; possessed by James Carroll; and John Hurst is the possessor at present (MRR: 95).

8 Dec 1679: Charles Gorsuch of TA Co. conv. to David Jones three parcels of land totalling 1200 a., as inher. by his w. Sarah under the will of Thomas Cole; 1st 550 a. (*); 2nd 450 a. Maiden's Choice, 3rd 200 a. Maryebon, formerly laid out for George Hixon; 4 Feb 1679/80: Miles Gibson appeared in court as atty. for Charles and Sarah Gorsuch, and to take acknowledgement of 380 a. sold by Jones to Gorsuch; Gibson also appears as atty. for David Jones' w. Ann (IR#PP: 46).

1 Aug 1682: Sarah Gorsuch, w. of Charles Gorsuch, and sole heir of Thomas Cole, late of Patapsco R., gave quitclaim to David Jones for all of above tracts; her cons. was not inserted in former deed (IR#AM: 185).

3 March 1701: James Todd of BA Co. conv. pt. Cole's (Harbor), 135½ a., and 160 a. (pt. Mounteney's Neck) to John Hirst (HW#2: 123).

13 Oct 1702: John Hurst of BA Co. and w. Hannah conv. 135½ a. (*) and 164½ a. land formerly belonging to Alexander Mounteney, (Mountenay's Neck) to Richard Colegate (HW#2: 196).

9 June 1711: Charles Carroll conv. 31 a. pt. (*), now called Hanson's Improvement, to Jonathan Hanson (TR#A: 138).

19 Feb 1741: Jonathan Hanson of BC, planter, conv. 30 a. (*) to Richard Fottrell; JH's w. Sarah cons. (TB#A: 101).

19 Feb 1741/2: George Walker conv. to Edward Fottrell: a) 20 a. (?) leased from Lord Baltimore on 4 Sep 1735, and b) his int. in 30 a. Cole's Harbor, bought by Jonathan Hanson, dec., from Charles Carroll, in right of dower of his (GW's) w. to said land (TB#A: 103).

19 March 1749: John Hurst of BA Co. conv. to Thomas Sheredine and Thomas Sligh: a) 135 a., (*), and b) 164 a. [Mountney's Neck?] formerly belonging to Alexander Mounteny and purch. by James Todd (TR#C: 419).

15 Nov 1750: John Colegate and Thomas Colegate conv. 300 a. including pts. of (*) and Mounteny (which Richard Colegate left to his sons) to Thomas Sheredine and Thomas Sligh. TC's w. Cassandra cons. (TR#D: 61).

8 June 1759: Thomas Sligh conv. to Abraham Ensor pt. of (*) which was earlier resurv. and called Todd's Range (B#G: 447).

COLE'S MOUNTAIN

1742: 33 a. leased to Thomas Cole (WG#63).

2 May 1781: Thomas Cole conv. to s. Christopher all his goods and chattels, including his lease of tract (Cole's) Mountain (WG#G: 332).

COLE'S OPPOSITION

29 Nov 1760: John Ensor assigned to Thomas Cole a lease for 100 a. (*) (B#I: 96).

COLE'S SEARCH

6 June 1744: John Cole, Sr., conv. 80 a. pt. Cole's Chance , 12 a. pt. Contrivance to Cole's Chance, and 276 a. (*), to Robert North (TB#C: 485).

1745: John Coale, Sr., conv. 68 a. pt. (*) to John Gorsuch (TB#D: 162).

3 March 1747: Joseph Taylor, exec. of William Fell, exec. of John Cole, Sr., assigned lease of 276 a. (*) to William Nowland (TB#E: 667).

COLEGATE'S INDUSTRY

5 May 1733: Richard Colegate of BA Co., Gent., conv. 88 a. (*) to Peasley Ingram (HWS#M: 1).

COLEGATE'S LAST SHIFT

23 April 1707: 163 a. surv. (IS#L: 82).

25 April 1717 [sic]: Pat. to Richard Colegate (HWS#1-A: 453).

6 April 1731: John Talbot and w. Prudence of AA Co. conv. (*) to William Buckner (IS#L: 82).

30 Aug 1735: Thomas Buckner of VA, Gent., conv. 163 a. (*) to Thomas Bond of BA Co., Gent. (HWS#M: 288).

5 Nov 1737: Thomas Bond and w. Ann conv. 163 a. (*) to George Elliott (HWS#1-A: 54).

5 Nov 1737: George Elliott and w. Patience conv. 163 a. (*) and 500 a. Friend's Discovery, to Benjamin Wheeler (HWS#1-A: 35).

25 Nov 1740: Benjamin Wheeler and w. Elizabeth conv. 163 a. (*) pat. on 25 April 1717 to Richard Colegate, to Benjamin Colegate (HWS#1-A: 453).

pt. of 130 a. held by Thos. Colegate, 8 wh. inhabs., (1783 TL).

COLINGHAM

4 Nov 1658: 100 a. surv. for John Collett on the w. side of Spesutia Creek; sold to John Ireland being gone away; now in possession of Ralph Gillian; land liable to an escheat; still later called Greenfields, in possession of Thomas Greenfields (MRR: 5). Archer's Notes calls this tract Collington.

18 Jan 1676: Henry Haslewood and w. Elizabeth conv. 100 a. (*) on w. side Spesutia Creek; formerly taken up by John Collett, Sr., now occupied by Ireland, and adj. land laid out for George Goldsmith; other being the 8 a. tract Haslewood's Retirement. HH's w. Elizabeth gave cons. when sale was aknowledged on 5 June 1677 (IR#PP: 10).

COLLESTON

26 July 1670: John Collett, Gent., conv. to Joseph Hopkins 200 a. (*) on the s. side of Church Creek (IR#PP: 83).

COLLETON

15 Feb 1659/60: Pat. to Richard Collett (See G#J: 189; TR#RA: 138).

... Richard Collett assigned tract to John Hawkins (See G#J: 189; TR#RA: 138).

30 May 1673: Robert Hawkins, heir and admin. of John Hawkins, dec., conv. 700 a. (*) to William Dunkerton and Thomas Overton (See G#J: 189; TR#RA: 138).

COLLETT'S NECK

2 Feb 1704: John Armstrong of BA Co. conv. 60½ a., pt. (*), and 41 a. Hopewell (formerly in poss. of Michael Judd); to Abraham Taylor, blacksmith. JA's w. Mary cons. (IR#PP: 143).

6 Feb 1717: Mary Wells, widow, conv. 200 a., being ½ of (*) to Aquila Paca (TR#RA: 433).

COLLETT'S NEGLECT
(See COLLIER'S NEGLECT)

19 Aug 1677: 300 a. tract surv. for George Holland, on the n. side of Gunpowder R.; adj. land formerly laid out for Edward Reeves and Lodwick Williams; later 150 a. held by John Rawlins, and 150 a. held by John Armstrong; still later 191 a. held by Jno. Rawlins and 78 a. held by Abra. Taylor who resurv. it and found no more (MRR: 31). (The original transcription says Collier's Neglect, but later deeds seem to refer to it consistently as Collett's Neglect).

19 April 1680: George Holland, Gent., of AA Co. conv. to Michael Judd and w. Jane the 300 a. tract, on n. side of Gunpowder, adj. United Friendship; same date George Holland appointed Jacob Jenifer his atty. to acknowledge and record a deed (IR#PP: 52).

22 June 1681: Michael Judd, carpenter, and w. Jane conv. 150 a. of the 300 a. tract to Thomas Cannon, planter (IR#AM: 122).

14 Jan 1680/1: James Thompson Smith, states he has received from Michael Judd 164 lbs. tobacco in payment of two years' rent of the 300 a. tract (*), and 180 a. Norberry, and also 120 lbs. tobacco for alienation of (*) (RM#HS: 61).

9 April 1685: Michael Judd and w. Jane conv. 150 a. (*) to Miles Gibson (adj. to United Friendship); the conv. land being the grantors' dwelling plantation, pat. to George ... (page torn), and conv. 19 April 1680 to Judd. 10 April 1685: Michael and Jane appoint Samuel Browne their atty. to acknowledge their conv. to Gibson (RM#HS: 130).

2 Nov 1686: Miles Gibson conv. 150 a., being ½ of the tract, to John Rawlings (RM#HS: 210).

2 Aug 1698: Thomas Cannon, s. of Thomas Cannon, late of BA Co., planter, conv. 150 a. (*), 300 a. in all, to William Ebden (TR#RA: 282).

30 Sep 1698: William Ebden and w. Elizabeth conv. 150 a. of above tract to John Armstrong of AA Co. (TR#RA: 289).

4 Aug 1703: John Armstrong conv. 41 a. (pt. of 150 a. parcel) to John Rawlings (HW#2: 263).

10 April 1707: Abraham Taylor of BA Co., blacksmith, conv. to Gaen Stevenson of Chester Co., PA, malster, 76½ a. (*), and 41 a. pt. Hopewell, being the two parcels together of 117½ a., lately in possession of John Armstrong (RM#HS: 536).

1 March 1708: Abraham Taylor of BA Co., blacksmith, and w. Jane, conv. 76½ a. (*), and 41 a. Hopewell to William Howard, planter (RM#HS: 637).

COLLETT'S POINT
(See STONY POINT)

30 April 1668: 400 a. surv. for John Collett on the e. side of Bush R. betw. the Northwest Branch and the Middle Branch; Collett and all his heirs being dead, the land is liable to an escheat (MRR: 10).

20 Nov 1668: 300 a. surv. for John Collett near an island called the Black Island, formerly surv. for John Collett; now possessed by the orphans of Col. Wells; still later possessed by George Wells (may have been called Wells Neck, conv. 1100 a.); in possession of Thomas Frisby (MRR: 7).

4 June 1672: John Collett conv. 320 a. (*) to George Wells, near Black Island; land was pat. by Collett on 1 Nov 1671; notation by sheriff Thomas Charleton that on 27 March 1674 he had received from Capt. George Wells 39 lbs. tobacco for alienation (TR#RA: 3).

----: Martha, w. of James Presbury, and Mary, widow of (James?) Marshall, were coheirs of 400 a. (*) (ARMD 38: 417).

1 Nov 1709: James Presbury posted notice that no one was to hunt over his land, (*), with dogs or gun, without his permission (TR#RA: 15).

4 Feb 1718: William Marshall, Gent., and w. Mary conv. the res. of (*) to Aquila Paca (TR#RA: 488).

4 April 1725: Richard Smithers of BA Co., Gent., conv. 450 a. Stony Point, being pt. Planter's Delight, and pt. (*), formerly occupied by Col. George Wells, dec., to John Stokes; adj. the land bequeathed by Col. George Wells to dau. Frances and s. George (IS#H: 124).

27 Dec 1728: James Presbury and w. Martha conv. 400 a. (*) to Mary Marshall (IS#I: 41).

COLLIER(BY ?)

11 June 1663: John Collier and w. Ann conv. to John Bruer the tract (*) (RM#HS: 6).

COLLIERS' MEADOW

27 Sep 1709: Jonathan Massey and w. Ann sell 150 a. (*) to Francis Barney (TR#A: 28).

9 Oct 1726: Joseph Barney of KE Co. conv. 150 a. (*) to St. Leger Codd of KE Co. (IS#H: 349).

9 April 1750: Col. St. Leger Codd d. leaving heirs: Mary, w. of Esau Watkins, of Chester Co., PA, and Beatrice Johnson, widow of KE Co., all of whom now conv. 150 a. (*) to James Phillips (TR#C: 405).

COLLIER'S NEGLECT
(Sometimes called COLLETT'S NEGLECT)

19 Aug 1677: 300 a. surv. for George Holland on the n. side of Gunpowder R., adj. land formerly laid out for Edward Reeves and Lodwick Williams; later 150 a. held by John Rawlins and 150 a. held by John Armstrong (a later Rent Roll called this Colett's Neglect), and 191 a. was held by Jno. Rawlins and 78 a. by Abraham Taylor who resurv. the same and found no more (MRR: 31).

30 Sep 1698: William Ebden and w. Elizabeth conv. 150 a. of (*) to John Armstrong (TR#RA: 289).

4 Aug 1703: John Armstrong conv. 41 a. of the tract to John Rawlings (HW#2: 263).

10 April 1707: Abraham Taylor of BA Co., blacksmith conv. to Gaen Stevenson of Chester Co., PA, 76½ a. (*) and 41 a. pt. Hopewell, being two parcels totalling 117½ a., lately held by John Armstrong (RM#HS: 536).

COLLINBOURNE

Orig. granted to Henry Howard (See HWS#M: 56).

21 Jan 1726/7: John Dorsey mortgaged 200 a. (*) and (?) a. Joshua's Lot (mortgage to run until 1 July 1727) to Richard Snowden of AA Co., merchant (IS#H: 353).

18 May 1734: Richard Snowden of AA Co., merchant, conv. (*) to Joshua Starkey (HWS#M: 56).

COLLINS CHOICE

1750: Henry Adams owned 100 a. (*) (BCF).

COLLINS' FIRST SHIFT
(Pt. HIS LORDSHIP'S RESERVE)

16 Aug 1742: Benj. Tasker, Agent for Lord Baltimore, leased (*) to Robert Collins for 99 years (TB#E: 209).

6 Sep 1745: Collins assigned the lease to William Few (TB#E: 212).

19 May 1746: William Few assigned the lease of (*) to William McComas of John (TB#E: 200).

COMBINES CHOICE

5 March 1760: Michael Taylor, eld. s. of Abraham Taylor who d. testate. And left 150 a. (*) to s. Thomas, 150 a. s. Aquila, and 66 a. to s. Michael. Aquila d. under age, and his share passed to Michael, who now conv. 216 a. (*) to Garrett Garrettson. Michael's w. Mary cons. (B#H: 87).

COME BY CHANCE (1671)

9 June 1671: 200 a. surv. for James Bynum on James' Branch of Bush R.; in 1684 granted to Thomas Thurston by virtue of a madamus; later 167 a. held by Thomas Thurston and 33 a. by Robert Love (MRR: 60).

10 Nov 1686: Pat. to Thomas Thurston (IS#I: 189).

6 March 1703: Thomas Thurston, s. of Thomas Thurston, dec., conv. 200 a. (*) to William Love (HW#2: 332).

9 June 1726: John McComas and w. Anne conv. 20 a. pt. (*) to William Bradford, in exch. for 20 a. pt. Enlargement (IS#H: 239, 244).

6 June 1728: John McComas and w. Anne conv. 80 a. (*), pat. to Thomas Thurston on 10 Nov 1686, and now known as Ruff's Enlargement to Richard Ruff (IS#L: 189).

5 Sep 1731: John McComas and w. Anne conv. 1 a. pt. (*) to Isaac Webster for use as a mill (IS#L: 292).

7 Nov 1739: Ann McComas, widow, conv. 1 a. pt. (*) to William Bradford (HWS#1-A: 305).

10 Dec 1741: Ann McComas, widow of John, conv. pt. (*) to her ch. William and Alexander; also mentions her ch. Daniel, Mary, and Anne (TB#A: 57).

27 Feb 1746: William McComas, s. of John, conv. 49 a. (*) (which his mother had owned at the time of her death) and 32 a. pt. Whitacre's Enlargement to Col. John Hall, Jacob Giles, and Isaac Webster, assignees of Col. Thomas White. William's w. Hannah cons. (TB#E: 310).

12 Nov 1746: Alexander McComas of BA Co. conv. 49 a. (*) to Thomas White; being the same land which he and his bro. William inher. from their mother Ann, widow of John McComas. Alexander's w. Deborah cons. (TB#E: 244).

15 April 1749: Alexander McComas, s. of John conv. pt. (*) to John Hall, Isaac Webster, and Jacob Giles (TR#C: 183).
7 June 1749: Thomas White granted release to John Hall, Isaac Webster, and Jacob Giles for pt. (*) (TR#C: 224).

COME BY CHANCE (1694: 257 a.)

24 Feb 1694: 257 a. surv. for John Ferry on the n. side of Back R.; later belonging to the orphans of John Boring (MRR: 109).
16 Feb 1710/11: Thomas Boring gave p/a to John Norton to conv. (*) and Long Point to John Boring (TR#A: 135).
6 Feb 1711: Thomas Boring of VA, by John Norton, his atty., conv. (*) to John Boring of Back R. all 257 a. that John Ferry left to Thomas Boring (TR#A: 151).
5 Aug 1719: John Boring of BA Co. conv. 109 a.pt. (*) to Thomas Boring (TR#DS: 89).
2 May 1732: John Boring of BA Co. conv. (*), laid out for 257 a., to Thomas Hines, except for 109 a. John previously sold to his bro. Thomas. JB's w. Pretiosa cons. (IS#L: 236).
2 July 1737: James Boring of BA Co. conv. 100 a. of (*) to Dutton Lane (IS#IK: 477).
29 Sep 1739: Dutton Lane of St. Paul's Parish conv. 109 a. pt. (*) to Abraham Eaglestone. DL's w. Dinah cons. (HWS#1-A: 287).
1750: Abraham Eagleston owned 109 a. (1750 DB).

COME BY CHANCE (1694: 282 a.)

24 Nov 1694: 282 a. surv. for John Richardson on the w. side of Jones Falls; later poss. by the afsd. JR, and still later by John Cole (MRR: 79).
5 Aug 1701: John Richardson conv. 282 a. (*) to Moses Edwards (HW#2: 74).
2 June 1702: M(oses?) Edwards conv. 282 a. (*) to John Cole (HW#2: 256).

COME BY CHANCE (1706)

3 Aug 1715: 100 a. surv. for John Leakins (HWS#1-A: 507).
3 Aug 1715: John Larkin [sic] conv. 50 a. (*), being ½ of the tract, to Robert German or Jarman (TR#A: 352).
2 June 1741: William Jarman conv. 50 a., being ½ of (*) to Robert Parks. By several transfers it came from John Leakins to Robert Jarman, father of William Jarman. After the dec. of WJ the land was to be divided betw. his two sons Thomas and William; Thomas, the eld. s. has settled on the western half and has agreed to sell. WJ's w. Sarah cons. (HWS#1-A: 507).

COME BY CHANCE (1719)

See Horvath Plat: Green Spring Valley.
31 July 1727: John Dorsey conv. 50 a. (*) to James Catcham. (*) had been surv. 16 Jan 1719 for William Bennett (IS#I: 44).

COME BY CHANCE (200 a.)

1723: 200 a. granted to Thomas Cole (P&W).

COME BY CHANCE (Unconnected)

14 March 1743: Thomas Shea of BA Co conv. 105½ a. (*) to Henry Beach. TS's w. Ann cons. (TB#C: 563).
6 Dec 1744: John Derumple and w. Sarah of BA Co., conv. 50 a. (*) to Samuel Owings (TB#C: 683).
24 Dec 1745: Samuel Richardson, exec. of Samuel Coale, late of BA Co., dec., conv. 200 a. (*) to John Holt (TB#E: 6).
10 March 1747: Henry Beach conv. 16 a. (*) to John Paca. Beach's w. Jane cons. (TB#E: 693).
25 Aug 1748: Henry Beach of BA Co. conv. 89½ a. (*) to John Paca. HB's w. Jane cons. (TR#C: 57).
24 April 1756: Samuel Hooker, with cons. of w. Sarah, conv. 307 a. (*) to Jonathan Hanson (BB#I: 536).

COMES' ADVENTURE

20 Oct 1715: Robert Parker of BA Co., planter, conv. 100 a. (*), and 26 a. Margaret's Delight, to Mary Scutt, devisee of Henry Knowles (TR#A: 370).
7 July 1720: William Douglas and w. Mary conv. 100 a. (*) and 26 a. Margaret's Delight to Tobias Emminson (TR#DS: 338).
1729: George Goodwin and w. conv. 100 a. (*) and 26 a. Margarets Delight to Edward Fell (IS#K: 103).

COMMON GARDEN (See COVENT GARDEN)

COMPANY'S ADVENTURE

1734: 400 a. surv. for Levin Gale et al. (P&W).

CONCLUSION

1750: John Day of Edward owned 360 a. pt. (*) (1750 DB: 80).

CONQUEST (See CONTEST)

CONSTANT FRIENDSHIP

6 July 1722: John Hutchinson of PG Co., conv. 1000 a. being ⅓ of (*) to John Shepherd. Deed recites the descent of property from Robert Doyne of CH Co., who was granted the property. Doyne d. intestate leaving the property to his ch.; Wharton Doyne, William Doyne, Sarah, Verlinda,

Elinor, and Mary Doyne; land desc. to Wharton Doyne who d. overseas intestate; land then desc. to his bro. William who d. intestate and without heirs; land then desc. to his sisters, but Elinor d. intestate and s.p., and her share went to her three sisters; Sarah m. William Hutchinson and had six ch.: John, Ann, Mary, William, Elizabeth, and George; she survived her husband and land desc. to her youngest s. George, he d. s.p., and the land then desc. to his eld. bro. John who hereby conv. 1000 a. being one-third of the tract (IS#G: 88).

20 March 1734: Verlinda Brown and Mary Dawson of PG Co., and William Penson of PG Co., agree they all have equal rights to 641 a. of (*). This deed sets off William Penson's share (HWS#M: 42).

15 March 1736: William Penson/Pawson of PG Co., and w. Elizabeth conv. 238 a. of (*) to Zachariah Wade, eld. s. of grantor's w. (IS#IK: 427).

25 March 1747: Thomas Dawson of PG Co. conv. 150 a. pt. (*) to Thomas Harrison of BA Co.; Doyne d. possessed of 1000 a. which desc. to his three daus.: Mary Dawson, Verlinda Taylor, and Sarah Hutchinson. Later Mary Dawson, Verlinda Brown, and William Penson partitioned the land; Mary Dawson d. and her share desc. to her s. Thomas Dawson, the present grantor. His w. gave her cons. to the sale (TB#E: 340).

27 March 1747: Samuel Taylor of PG Co. and w. Mary conv. Verlinda Brown's pt. (150 a.) of (*) to Thomas Harrison (TB#E: 344).

CONTEST (Also called CONQUEST)

22 Aug 1683: 100 a. surv. for Samuel Brand at the head of Swan Creek; belonging to the orphans of Capt. Henry Johnson (MRR: 18).

9 Feb 1684/5: Samuel Brand, blacksmith, conv. 100 a. (*) to Capt. Henry Johnson. Mary Brand signed with SB (RM#HS: 131).

2 May 1712: Joseph Johnson conv. 100 a. to Thomas Bucknall (TR#A: 186).

18 July 1734: Henry Bucknall leased his 50 a., half of (*) to his sister Mary; tract was bequeathed to Henry by his father Thomas; the lease was to run for 13 years (HWS#M: 86).

23 Oct., 1744: Francis Bucknall conv. 50 a., being $\frac{1}{2}$ of (*) to John Hall. FB's w. Blanch cons. (TB#C: 653).

1 Nov 1744: Francis Bucknall, with cons. of w. Blanche, conv. 50 a. (*) and 50 a. Hall's Park to John Hampton and Daniel Pologe (TB#C: 660).

CONTRIVANCE (See Notebook)
(See also CONTRIVANCE TO COLE'S CHANCE and CONTINUANCE ...)

18 Dec 1701: James Phillips conv. 200 a. (*) to Thomas Newsom (HW#2: 149).

20 March 1736: Helen Newsom agrees to conv. 200 a. (*) and 50 a. Newsom's Meadow to William Smith, in exch. for 254 a. Benjamin's Choice (HWS#1-A: 299).

CONTRIVANCE TO COLE'S CHANCE

28 June 1731: John Cole and w. Diana conv. 200 a. pt. (*) and Cole's to George Buchanan (IS#L: 121).

15 Dec 1744: John Cole, Sr., and w. Diana conv. pt. (*) to John Gorsuch (TB#C: 486).

20 May 1745: Teague Tracey conv. 16 a., pt. Contrivance to John Gorsuch (TB#D: 132).

14 June 1796: John Gorsuch of John conv. $6\frac{1}{4}$ a. (*) to Elijah Merryman. The tract was bequeathed to the grantor by John Gorsuch. JG's w. Belinda cons. (WG#XX:).

CONVENIENCY

20 Oct 1740: Michael Taylor of PG Co., Gent., prisoner in PG Co. jail, conv. 200 a. (*) and other lands to John Hepburn, High Sheriff of PG Co. (TB#E: 374).

8 Dec 1746: John Hepburn of PG Co., formerly High Sheriff, conv. 200 a. (*) and other lands to Thomas White (TB#E: f. 375).

COOK'S CHANCE

13 May 1678: 158 a. surv. for John Cooke on the s. side of Swan Creek; later poss. by William Jeffs, and still later by Thomas Brown (MRR: 25).

2 Aug 1680: John Cooke conv. 150 a. (*) at Cooke's Cove to Patrick Dew of CV Co. JC's w. Sarah cons. (IR#AM: 153).

27 Dec 1698: David Morgan of CV Co. planter conv. 150 a. (*) to William Jeffs of BA Co., boatwright (TR#RA: 317).

19 Nov 1703: William Geffe of BA Co., carpenter, conv. 150 a. (*) to Thomas Browne (HW#2: 323).

10 April 1711: John Olivell of AA Co., and w. Elizabeth (late w. of William Jeffs of BA Co., carpenter, dec.), conv. 150 a. (*) to John Brown (TR#A: 162).

9 Aug 1734: Augustus Brown conv. 150 a. (*) to Edward Hall, being the same land the grantor inher. from his father, John Brown (HWS#M: 143).

25 June 1743: Thomas Brown of BA Co. granted quitclaim on (*) to Avarilla Hall, widow and extx. of Edward Hall, to correct any errors in deed from John Browne, now dec., to Edward Hall (TB#C: 262).

COOK'S DOUBLE PURCHASE

8 May 1748: Jeremiah Cook of BA Co., s. and heir of William Cooke, and bro. of John Cooke, dec., conv. 159 a. (*) to Amos Garrett who owned the land which took away the tract by an elder surv. formerly belonging to John Copson (TB#E: 708).

COOKS NECK

10 Sep 1683: 100 a. surv. for John Cooke; later possessed by John Cooks orphans, and still later by Thomas Cord (MRR: 18).

COOK'S REST

5 Dec 1704: John Cook conv. 100 A. (*) to Thomas Cord (IR#PP: 141).

9 March 1743: Abraham Cord granted quitclaim to 100 a. (*) to bro., Jacob Cord; parties are sons of Thomas Cord who brought the land from John Cook (TB#C: 386).

COOM'S ADVENTURE

26 Nov 1750: George Goodwin, cordwainer, of BA Co., conv. 100 a. (*) to Isaac Webster (TR#D: 128).

COOPER'S PARADICE

20 Aug 1748: William Shepard, s. and heir of Nathaniel Shepard, conv. 100 a. (*), orig. granted to NS, to Stephen Onion (TR#C: 63).

COOPER'S RANGE

1729: John Cooper conv. 50 a. (*) to Abraham Each (IS#K: 184).

COPE (See HOPE)

COPUS' HARBOR

6 Sep 1683: 100 a. surv. for John Copus and later held by Thomas Copus (MRR: 84).

1 May 1703: Thomas Copus (s. and heir of John Copus late of BA Co., dec.), and w. Jane, conv. 100 a. (*) to Thomas Hedge (IR#PP: 135).

29 May 1728: Samuel Hedge of Salem Co., NJ, conv. 100 a. (*) to Lloyd Harris of BA Co. (IS#I: 146).

8 Nov 1730: Lloyd Harris of BA Co. conv. 100 a. (*) to William Fell; LH's w. Eleanor cons. (IS#L: 47).

CORBIN'S FOREST

1766: Nicholas Corbin conv. 18 a. pt. (*) to William Winchester (B#P: 253).

CORBIN'S REST

26 July 1680: 200 a. pat. to Nicholas Corbin (HWS#M: 13).

29 Oct 1723: Thomas Gostwick, and w. Elizabeth, conv. 50 a. (*) to Edmond Baxter (IS#G: 208).

10 Sep 1737: Edward Corbin and w. Jane conv. 150 a., pt. (*), bequeathed to said Edward in will of Nicholas Corbin, and 50 a. pt. Jonas' Range, to Thomas Sligh of BA Co. (HWS#1-A: 13).

20 July 1746: Thomas Sligh and w. Sophia conv. 150 a., pt. (*), 48 a. Rider's Industry, and 50 a. pt. Jonas' Range to Peter Dowell (TB#E: 196).

31 Oat. 1754: Peter Dowell sold 227 3/4 a. (*) and Jonas' Range, 45¼ a. Rider's Industry to Joseph Sollers (WG#154: 361).

CORCELL HILL

19 Sep 1716: Edward Corbin of BA Co. and w. Jane conv. pt. (*) to John Bowen (TR#A: 431).

CORD'S PURCHASE

1 April 1727: Thomas Cord gave bond to Abraham Cord he will let Abraham occupy the designated pt. of (*), French Plantation, and Peter's Addition, which they inher. from their father Thomas Cord, and which they have divided (IS#H: 402).

1 April 1727: Abraham Cord gave bond to Thomas Cord he will guarantee the right of TC to occupy the specified half of land bequeathed them by their father Thomas Cord (IS#I: 58).

2 Nov 1743: Abraham Cord leased pt. (*), pt. French Plantation, 19 a. Ten Pound Purchase, and pt. French Plantation to Abraham Taylor (TB#C: 365).

CORDWAINER'S HALL

10 March 1695: 300 a. surv. for Nicholas Fitzsimmons (B).

See: PW Plat B; Horvath Plat: Elkridge.

10 March 1701: Nicholas Fitzsimmons, cordwainer, conv. 300 a. (*) to Richard Cromwell (HW#2: 157).

CORNCHASTON

(no date) Godfrey Bayley, with his w.'s cons., has assigned to William Fisher 100 a. (*) on Sassafras R. (RM#HS: [16?]).

CORNELIUS AND MARY'S LOT

3 March 1728/9: Edmund Howard conv. 100 a., being ½ of (*), to Cornelius Howard. EH's w. Ruth cons. (IS#I: 261).

21 June 1758: Charles Howard conv. 100 a. (*) to William Igo (B#G: 202).

COSTERS HARBOR (Now in CE Co.)

1664: 300 a. pat. to Abraham Morgan (MPL 7:157).

3 Nov 1663: Abraham Morgan, with cons. of w. Ann, conv. 300 a. on s. side of Bohemia R. to Thomas Browning (IR#PP: 59).

COTTERELL'S PURCHASE

1 Sep 1701: Henry Bourne or Bourke of BA Co. conv. to John Cotterall 100 a., pt. (*), being pt. of M...acoess [?] (HW#2: 140).

COUNTERSCARPE

1743: Surv. for Josephus Murray.

See Horvath Plat: Green Spring Valley.

14 March 1743: Christopher Gist mortgaged 100 a. (*), 83 a. Milford, Gist's Inspection, 500 a. Joshua's Lot, 50 a. Gist's Meadows, and 2 lots in Baltimore Town. (TB#D: 438).

28 Oct 1743: Josephus Murray conv. 100 a., pt. (*) and Hurd's Camp, to his dau. Jemima Ashman (TB#C: 340).

28 March 1746: James Richard, atty. for Stephen Theodore Jannsen, conv. 100 a. (*), 83 a. Milford, Gist's Inspection, 500 a. Joshua's Lot, 50 a. Gist's Meadows, and 2 lots in Baltimore Town to William Cromwell and Tobias Stansbury, who have paid the mortgaged (TB#D: 438).

25 July 1747: Josephus Murray conv. 439 a. (*) and 340 a. Oulton's Garrison to Richard Croxall. JM's w. Ruth cons. the same day. Zipporah Gist granted a quitclaim on the two tracts to Josephus Murray (TB#E: 464, 468).

21 Nov 1748 Richard Croxall of BA Co. conv. 20 a. (*) to George Ashman (TR#C: 122).

1 Sep 1750: Josephus Murray granted a release of (*) and Oldton's Garrison to Richard Croxall, which Murray had earlier sold to Gist; the terms being that Zeporah Gist shall live at Brother's Good Will (TR#D: 13).

COURANT

30 June 1677: Thomas Hooker had surv. 31 a. called (*) in the woods on the back of Brownton. The land was later possessed by Thomas Hooker of BA Co. (MRR: 151).

COVE TRACT

7 Jan 1664/5: 100 a. pat. to Nathaniel Stiles (IR#PP: 124).

7 Nov 1671: Nathaniel Stiles, Gent., conv. 100 a. (*) on the e. side of Steelpone Creek to Thomas Howell, Gent. (IR#PP: 124).

COVENT (or COMMON) GARDEN

3 June 1667: 450 a. tract surv. for William Osborn and John Lee on Bush R.; granted to said Osborn by patent in 1678; 100 a. held by James Phillips; 100 a. sold to William Osborn, Jr., and mortgaged to said Phillips; 40 a. in possession of Henry Hedge; 170 a. still in possession of William Osborn, Sr.; 40 a. held by Henry Jackson; still later Covent Garden held as follows: 150 a. Thomas Hanson; 50 a. James Phillips; 40 a. Henry Hedge; 40 a. John Roberts; 170 a. held by the orphans of said Osborn (MRR: 24).

2 Aug 1681: Miles Gibson, Gent., conv. to Thomas Hedge; 1st 100 a. bought from Lee and Osborne (unnamed); 2nd 140 a. Common Garden bought from Lee and Osborn; 3rd 100 a. Mile End; grantor ackn. in court on 6 Dec 1681; Ann Gibson cons. before Edward Bedell (IR#AM: 162).

3 Nov 1686: Thomas Hedge, Gent., conv. 100 a. Common Garden to William Osborne, adj. the land of William Osborne, Sr., and purch. by the grantor from Miles Gibson; N. B.: 4 Oct 1688: Sheriff Thomas Long receives from William Osborne, Jr., a year's rent in alienation (RM#HS: 195).

18 Feb 1685/6: William Osborn of Rumley Creek, planter, assigned his right and title to 100 a. Common Garden, to Mark Richardson (RM#HS: 296).

6 Nov 1694: Thomas Hedge conv. to s. Henry Hedge, 46 a. Broad Street, 40 a. Common Garden, 100 a. Mates Neck, and two tracts on Rumley Creek taken up by Thomas Hedge (RM#HS: 435).

11 Sep 1696: William Osborne, planter, conv. (mortgaged?) Covent Garden to James Phillips (HW#2: 60).

15 Sep 1698: William Osborn of BA Co., planter, and w. Margaret, conv. 40 a. Common Garden to Henry Jackson, tanner (TR#RA: 370).

1 March 1703/4: James Phillips, Gent., and w. Bathia conv. 100 a. Covent Garden (mortgaged to Phillips by William Osborn, who has not paid his debts) to Thomas Hanson; also 100 a. pt. of a tract in possession of Phillips on Rumley Creek, adj. to Covent Garden (probably Lambert's Marsh) (IR#PP: 118).

18 March 1703/4: Thomas Hanson granted to ... (unnamed) release of interest in "afsd. land" ... grantee and name of tract not specified (HW#2: 322).

23 Feb 1706: Edward Jackson of BA Co., conv. 40 a. Common Garden to John Roberts, but Edward Jackson may live in the kitchen house until 1 Oct 1707 (RM#HS: 535).

10 April 1708: John Roberts of BA Co., conv. 40 a. (*) to James Phillips of BA Co., Gent.. JR's w. Mary cons. (RM#HS: 602).

3 March 1719: Benjamin Hanson conv. 40 a. (*), pt. of a 100 a. tract, to Roger Matthews; BH held land by right of dower due to Sarah Cockey, relict of Thomas Hanson, dec. BH's w. Sarah cons. (TR#DS: 95).

COW LANE (THE) (Also called THE ADDITION)
18 April 1704: James Carroll conv. 125 a. (*) to Christopher Gardner (TR#RA: 428).

COWAN'S ADDITION
15 April 1743: John Cowen, Sr., conv. 100 a. (*) to his s. Thomas (TB#C: 216).
14 April 1750: Thomas Cowan of BA Co. conv. 100 a. (*) to Edward Mitchell (TR#C: 422).
8 Feb 1752: Edward Mitchell conv. 100 a. (*) to William Mitchell (TR#D: 300).

COWAN'S SETTLEMENT
15 April 1743: John Cowen, Sr., conv. 76 a., pt. (*), to his s. John Cowen, Jr. (TB#C: 215).

COX'S ENLARGEMENT
3 Aug 1703, Christopher Cox and w. Mary conv. 200 a. Cox's Enlargement and 200 a. Cox's Range to Luke Reed (HW#2: 271).

COX'S FANCY
28 Jan 1717/8: Cert. of surv. (mentioned IS#G: 367).
6 Aug 1719: Pat. to Edward Cox (mentioned TB#E: 126).
3 June 1724: Edward Cox and w. Jane conv. 100 a. (*) to Robert North of London, mariner (IS#G: 263).
7 Aug 1724: Robert North of London, mariner, conv. 100 a. (*) to Luke Stansbury (IS#G: 367).
31 July 1746: John Hall and w. Bethia conv. 100 a. (*) and other lands to Abraham Raven (TB#E: 126).

COX'S FOREST
4 Nov 1724: Edward Cox and w. Jane conv. 100 a. (*) to Ulick Burke (IS#G: 2980.

COX'S HOPE
23 July 1745: Edward Cox and w. Necis of BA Co. conv. 30 a. (*) to John Holloway (TB#D: 343).
2 Dec 1745: John Holloway (or Hollowan) of BA Co. conv. 30 a. (*) and other land to John Macoll of CV Co.; JH's w. Elizabeth cons. (TB#D: 392).

COX'S PROSPECT
30 March 1725: Edward Cox of BA Co. and w. Jean conv. 100 a. (*) to James Nicholson of AA Col (IS#H: 74).

COX'S RANGE
3 Aug 1703, Christopher Cox and w. Mary conv. 200 a. Cox's Enlargement and 200 a. Cox's Range to Luke Reed (HW#2: 271).
2 April 1757: Jacob Cox and w. Elizabeth conv. 50 a. (*) to Charles Bosley (BB#I: 655).

CRAB HILL (1665)
23 March 1665: 100 a. surv. for John Lee on the e. side of Bush R., at the southernmost bounds of Upper Eling; later held by James Phillips (MRR: 14).
4 March 1667/8: John Lee and William Osborne, conv. 100 a. (*), pat. to Lee and Osborne, to Oliver Spry (IR#PP: 67).
27 Oct 1676: Godfrey and Mary Harmer conv. 100 a. (*) to Richard Morgan and John Hall (IR#PP: 87).
1 Aug 1671: John Hall, planter, conv. 50 a. (*) to Richard Morgan, being ½ the land Hall and Morgan purch. from Godfrey Harmer (IR#PP:108).
6 Feb 1673/4: Richard Morgan conv. 100 a. (*) to Anthony Brispo (G#J: 225; also TR#A).

CRAB HILL (1678)
16 May 1678: Pat. to George Smith; adj. to Upper Eling (IR#PP: 26).
6 Aug 1678: George Smith and w. Elizabeth conv. 100 a. (*) to James Phillips, innholder (IR#PP: 26).

CRAB HILL (1678)
16 May 1678: Pat. to George Smith (IR#PP: 26)
6 Aug 1678: George Smith and w. Elizabeth conv. 100 a. (*) to James Phillips. The tract is adj. to Upper Eling. GS's w. Elizabeth gave her cons. before Edward Bedell (IR#PP:26).

CRABTREE'S LOT
4 June 1728: William Crabtree of BA, for love he bore her, conv. to his dau. Grace Hays 100 a. (*) on the s. side of Deer Creek (IS#K: 20).
1729: William Crabtree conv. (poss. same land) to Thomas Crabtree (IS#K: 22).

CRANBERRY HALL
14 Oct 1694: 1547 a. surv. for John Hall (MRR: 8).
17 Dec 1741: Edward Hall conv. pt. (*), pt. Jericho and pt. Sophia's Dairy to his bro., Parker Hall; both are sons of John Hall, dec. (TR#A: 63).

CREDENTIA
1701: 311 a. pat. by William Talbott (MPL DD#5: 37).
See Horvath Plat: Green Spring Valley.
18 March 1736: Benjamin Hammond conv. all his interest in (*), in right of his w. Margaret, dau. of said William Talbott, to John Risteau, who m. Catherine, relict of Talbott (IS#IK: 377).

CREED (or CREED'S BEGINNING)

10 Oct 1709: Bennett Creed of CV Co., mortgaged 223 a. (*) and other land to William Holand of AA Co. for 2000 years (TR#A: 92).

13 Feb 1745: William Holland of CV Co., Gent., surv. exec. of William Holland assigned mortgage on (*) and other land to Isaac Webster (TB#E: 20).

22 Feb 1745: Francis Holland, s. of Francis, granted title to (*) and other lands to Isaac Webster. FH's w. Cordelia cons. (TB#E: 25).

CREEK PLANTATION

26 Nov 1729: Nathaniel Daugherty conv. 24/94? a. Dougherty's Chance and 50 a. (*) to Gregory Farmer (IS#K: 152).

2 March 1733: Gregory Farmer, Sr., conv. 50 a. (*) and 10 a. pt. Dougherty's Chance, to s. John Farmer (HWS#M: 27).

1750: James Death owned 54 a. (*) (1750 DB).

CROCK AND PILL

3 June 1669: Peter Jones, shopman, conv. 250 (*) to John Glover; tract is on the n. side of the Sassafras R. (IR#PP: 720).

CROMWELL'S ADVENTURE

12 Dec 1670: Cert. of surv. was issued (IS#H: 179).

6 Dec 1714: Joshua Cromwell and William Cromwell agree to divide the land (TR#A: 329).

13 Aug 1725: Joshua Cromwell conv. 150 a. pt. (*) to Benjamin Tasker (IS#H: 179).

CROMWELL'S CHANCE

15 Dec 1727: Thomas Cromwell conv. 305 a., being $\frac{1}{2}$ of (*) to William Hammond. TC's w. Eleanor cons. (IS#I: 38).

12 Jan 1745: Oliver Cromwell conv. quitclaim to $\frac{1}{2}$ of (*), which Thomas Cromwell left to his sons Thomas, (who has already conv. his $\frac{1}{2}$ to William Hammond), and to Oliver Cromwell (TB#D: 420).

CROMWELL'S ISLAND

2 May 1711: Thomas Gwin conv. 153 a. (*) and 60 a. Brandon to Thomas Crocus (TR#A: 142).

2 May 1712: Thomas Crocus and w. Frances conv. lands back to TG (TR#A: 144).

5 June 1712: Thomas Gwin of BA Co. conv. 153 a. (*) to Peter Bond (TR#A: 190).

18 April 1747: Thomas Bond and Richard Bond conv. 130 a. (*) to Capt. Darby Lux (TB#E: 350).

CROMWELL'S PARK

3 Sep 1757: John Cromwell of AA Co. and w. Elizabeth conv. (*) to Samuel Tipton (B#G: 44).

CROSS (THE)

Orig. surv. for Warner Shudall (ment. RM#HS: 113).

24 Dec 1684: John Shudall of TA Co. appointed Thomas Scudamore his atty. to conv. land to Robert Burman (RM#HS: 113).

26 Feb 1684/5: Thomas Scudamore, atty. for John Shudall, conv. 100 a. (*) to Robert Burman, merchant of London (RM#HS: 113).

20 Dec 1690: Robert Burman of merchant of MD, conv. 100 a. (*) and other land to James Dryden of London, merchant (IR#AM: 113).

CROSS' CHANCE

19 Aug 1752: John Wheeler and John Cross deeded to Abraham Raven 50 a. Wheeler's Beginnings, surv. 7 Oct 1716; also 50 a. (*), surv. 6 Feb 1743; JW's w. Elizabeth and JC's w. Dinah cons. (TR#D: 408).

1 June 1753: Robert Cross of BA Co. and w. Hannah conv. 19 a. (*) to Richard Griffee (WG#H: 416).

CROSS'S FOREST

9 Aug 1704: John Cross and w. Elinor conv. 357 a., pt. (*) to David Mackelfresh (HW#2: 346).

CROSS'S LOT

1750: William Cross owned 23 a. (1750 DB).

10 Jan 1756: William Cross and w. Anne conv. 23 a. (*) and 50 a. Level Bottom to Samuel Lane (BB#I: 493; See also MHM 15:346).

CROSS'S OUTLET

3 June 1734: John League of BA Co. conv. (*) to Anthony Asher (HWS#M: 66).

CROSS'S PARK

19 Aug 1752: John Cross, Sr., for love he bears his s. John Cross, Jr., conv. him 50 a. (*), lying in the Barrens of Baltimore (TR#D: 407).

CROW PERCHES

4 March 1723: Lewis Nowell [sic] and w. Jane conv. Aberly Lodge, 100 a. Crow Perches and two parcels of John's Interest to Henry Wetherall (IS#G: 277).

CROWLEY CONTRIVANCE

11 March 1699: 200 a. surv. for Daniel Crowley (WHC, App. 1, p. 1).

14 June 1704: Daniel Crowley of BA Co. gave bond to Patrick Murphy he would conv. all land over 200 a. (*) that might be found within the bounds of the said tract (TR#A: 282).

4 Sep 1709: James Carroll certified that to prevent an argument betw. Daniel and Dennis Crowley,

he has divided (*), and the land nearest Smith's Addition is to belong to Daniel (TR#A: 15).

CROWLEY'S (FIRST) VENTURE

Dec 1699: 100 a. pat. by Daniel and Dennis Crowley (MPL 30:337, 38:156).
18 Oct 1705: Daniel and Dennis Crowley of BA Co., planters, conv. 100 a. (*), granted by Lord Baltimore to said Daniel and Dennis on 1 June 1700, to Philip Connor of BA Co., planter (RM#HS: 578).
13 July 1734: Thomas Porter and w. Eleanor conv. 100 a. (*) to William Rogers (HWS#M: 107).

CUB HILL

26 March 1690: Surv. for William Burgess, late of AA Co., and bequeathed by him to Nicholas Watkins (TB#D: 3).
5 Sep 1744: Nicholas Watkins of AA Co. conv. 500 a. (*) to Maj. Thomas Sheredine and Thomas Slight. NW's w. Margaret cons. (TB#D: 3).
3 Nov 1748: Thos. Sligh and Thomas Sheredine conv. 200 a. (*) to John Lynch. Sophia w. of Thos. Sligh, and Tabitha w. of Thomas Sheredine cons. (TR#C: 173).
1750: John Lynch owned 200 a. (*) (1750 DB: 89).

CUCKOLDMAKER'S HALL

28 Feb 1733: 50 a. pat. to Bloyce Wright (MPL PL#8: 798, AM#1: 228).
1750: owned by heirs of Thomas Wright (1750 DB).

CUCKOLDMAKER'S HAZARD

20 Jan 1720: Surv. for John Boring.
20 May 1725: 300 a. pat. to John Boring (MPL PL#6:175, IL#A: 455).
12 March 1763: Avarilla Boring, widow, conv. to Nicholas Britton her right of dower, 1/3 interest in Boring's Gift, Boring's Forest, and (*) (B#L: 116).
27 July 1765: Absolom Boring and w. Ann to Charles, John and Charles Ridgely, Jr., (land betw. Gunpowder Falls and Jones Falls. Signed by Absalom Boreing (B#O: 331).

CUCKOLDMAKER'S PALACE

1 June 1700: Surv. (IS#L: 318).
5 March 1732: Samuel Maccubbin of BA Co. and w. Mary conv. 100 a. (*), 98 a. Murphy's Pleasure, surv. 10 Jan 1705, and 52 a. The Addition, surv. 10 Jan 1705, to John Parrish (IS#L: 318).

CULLEN'S PARK

22 Oct 1724: Pat. to Thomas Cullen (IS#I: 163).
7 Aug 1728: Thomas Cullen and w. (Catherine?) conv. 150 a. (*) to John Cooper (IS#I: 163).

CULLIN'S DEAR PURCHASE
(Pt. MARGARET'S MOUNT)

1 Nov 1724; Thomas Cullin of BA Co., shoemaker, conv. 100 a. (*) to John Miles of BA Co., carpenter, and w. Mary (IS#H: 86).

CULLIN'S LOT (pt. of TOLLEY'S PURCHASE)

16 April 1725: Date of cert. of surv. for (*) (IS#L: 181).
15 Jan 1731: Thomas Tolley, Sr., of BA, Gent., conv. (*) to s. Thomas, Jr.; if he dies s.p., then to second s. Walter; if he d. s.p., then to 3rd s. James (IS#L: 181).

CULVER'S ENTRANCE

6 June 1765: Benjamin Culver conv. 100 a. (*) to his dau. Elizabeth Barnes and her husband James Barnes (B#O: 241, 282).

CUMBERLAND

10 Sep 1737: Thomas Sligh and w. Sophia conv. 100 a. (*) to Edward Corbin (HWS#M: 16).
7 July 1740: Phillis Wilkinson for love she bears her s. Jethro Lynch Wilkinson, conv. him 100 a. (*). Robert Wilkinson is a witness (HWS#1-A: 398).
10 April 1747: Edward Corbin and w. Jane conv. 58 a. (*) to their s. William Wilkinson Corbin (TB#E: 547).
4 Jan 1749/50: Edward Corbin of BA Co. conv. 100 a. pt. (*) to Thomas Sligh. EC's w. Jane cons. (TR#C: 363).
4 Jan 1749/50: Edward Corbin of BA Co. and w. Jane conv. 50 a. (*) to Edward Corbin, Jr. (TR#C: 365).

CURGAFURGUS (See CARRICKFERGUS)

CURTIS' NECK

2 April 1662: 200 a. surv. for Paul Kinsey and later held by William Slade (MRR: 103).

DAILY INCOME

c1763/4: owned by Peter Gosnell, Jr. (AHAL).

DAIRY (THE)

1750: Henry Stevenson owned 100 a. (1750 DB).

DALEY'S DISCOVERY

14 Nov 1743: Capt. John Smith of CV Co., merchant, in exch. for 636 a., 66 per. of Hall's Craft in CV Co., conv. to Walter Smith of the Freshes of the Patuxent, s. and heir of Walter Smith, dec., the following tracts: 300 a. pt. (*), 700 a. The Groves, and 424 a. pt. Addition to Poor Jamaica Man's Plague (TB#C: 416).

DALLAM'S SELF PRESERVATION

17 July 1750: William Dallam of BA Co. conv. 300 a., pt. of (*) to Godfrey Walters. The tract had been pat. by said WD on 7 Dec 1747 (TR#D: 9).

DAN

17 April 1697: 80 a. surv. for Col. Thomas Richardson (TR#A: 257).

20 Oct 1713: Francis Whitehead and w. Elizabeth conv. 50 a. (*), 100 a. Emanuel's Hope, 100 a. Emanuel's Rest, and 300 a. Oglesby's Chance, to William Tibbs of BA Co., clerk (TR#A: 257).

1722: Patent of Tibbs United Inheritance granted to Rev. William Tibbs; tract made up of 77 a. (*) and other lands (MPL CE#1, 430).

DANBY HILLS

10 Nov 1727: Ackn. division of land, 350 a. (*) which George Burgess of AA Co. sold to John Bayly of AA Co. on 11 Oct 16--, and which John Bayly conv. to his sons Thomas and John, who now divide it (IS#I: 26).

DANIEL'S ... (See DARNALL'S ...)

DANIEL'S SYLVANIA
(See DARNALL'S SYLVANIA)

DANIEL'S GIFT

4 Nov 1713: Daniel Stanbrough of BA Co., for love he bears his bro. Thomas conv. him (*), being pt. of a larger tract called Strife (TR#A: 252).

DANIEL'S HOPE

28 Oct 1685: Daniel Lawrence, tailor, conv. 100 a. (*) to Thomas Lightfoot (RM#HS: 182).

DANIEL'S LOT

4 Sep 1733: Sarah Ruff, widow, conv. tract to her s. Richard Ruff (IS#L: 425).

1750: Daniel Preston owned 25 a. (1750 DB: 52).

DANIEL'S NECK

8 April 1663: 150 a. surv. for Thomas O'Daniel on the eastern shore of Gunpowder R.; later held by the orphans of William Westbury; still later by Francis Dallahide for Westbury's orphans (MRR: 36).

13 Aug 1666: John Lee conv. 20 a. of Thomas O'Daniel's land to Richard Adams (IR#PP: 55).

5 Nov 1684: William Horne and w. Mary conv. to John Hall two tracts: 67 a. Hornisham, pat. 18 June 1681 to said Horne; and 2nd, ⅓ pt. of three pts. of Daniel's Nest, estimated at $16\frac{1}{2}$ a., which Horne holds as dowry of his w. Mary, said land having come to her by inheritance) RM#HS: 101).

27 July 1686: Thomas Thurcall and w. Jane, dau. of Thomas O'Daniel, conv. ⅓ of (*) to William Westbury (RM#HS: 188).

17 Nov 1686: John Hall conv. 50 a. Hornesham and $16\frac{1}{2}$ a. Daniel's Nest to William Westbury (RM#HS: 206).

4 June 1695: Margaret Oless, now w. of Robert Oless of Gunpowder Hundred, cooper, and formerly the relict of William Westbury, deeded to dau. E. Westbury, spinster, all that property belonging to Margaret, being ⅓ of Daniel's Nest. If E. Westbury should die without heirs, the land was to go to Margaret's next sister (RM#HS: 466).

30 March 1703: Elizabeth Westbury conv. to Simon Pearson and his heirs her right and interest to Hornesham and (*) (HW#2: 274).

3 Aug 1703: Simon Pearson conv. 50 a. of (*) and 50 a. of Hornesham to Francis Dallahide (HW#2: 275).

8 March 1710: John Butteram and w. Elizabeth, and William Bond and w. Mary, conv. to Simon Pearson, weaver, their interest in lands formerly belonging to Thomas [O']Daniel and William Westbury, said Elizabeth being heirs of thereof (TR#A: 63).

6 April 1713: Francis Dallahide mortgaged Daniel's Nest [sic], Hornesham, 100 a. pt. Wandsworth and 200 a. Watertown to William Bladen of Annapolis; mortgage to run until; 20 march 1713/4 (TR#A: 227).

8 June 1723: Francis Dallahide, eld. s., and heir of Francis Dallahide, dec., conv. 50 a. (*) to James Maxwell (IS#G: 160).

1750: James Maxwell owned 50 a. (*) (1750 DB: 25).

DANIEL'S NEGLECT

Orig. surv. for Robert West.

8 Aug 1733: Robert West of BA Co. conv. 75 a. (*) to Josias Middlemore (IS#L: 423).

DANIEL'S NEST (See DANIEL'S NECK)

DANIEL'S TOWN

8 Feb 1724/5: George Grover, Sr., conv. 50 a. (*) to his s. George Grover, Jr. (IS#H: 18).

DANIEL'S WHIMSEY

15 Nov 1712: John Cole conv. pt. of (*), which contains in all 200 a. by cert. of surv. to s. Joseph Cole (TR#A: 362).

30 Aug 1725: 200 a. pat. by John Cole (TB#A: 66).

21 Jan 1726: John Cole conv. 100 a., pt. (*) to John Gardner of Bear Creek; also pt. of Happy Be Lucky, taken up by Cole on 4 Dec 1696, and pt.

of Haphazard, taken up by Cole on 20 Feb 1714. JC's w. Dinah cons. (IS#H: 340).
1 March 1734: John Cole, Sr., conv. 100 a., being half of (*), to s. John Cole, Jr. (*).
18 Oct 1737: John Cole, Sr., and John Cole, Jr., with cons. of latter's w. Mary, conv. pt. (*) to John Ensor (HWS#1-A: 25).
14 Jan 1741: Luke Trotten and William Hamilton, execs. of John Gardiner, conv. pt. (*) to Alexander Lawson (TB#A: 66).
31 Aug 1764: Anthony Chamness, Gent., of Orange Co., NC, and w. Sarah, conv. 100 a. pt. (*) to Joseph Ensor (B#O: 62, 71).

DANN

1722: William Tibbs pet. to have four tracts: 200 a. Oglesby's Chance (laid out for George Oglesby), 100 a. Emanuel's Hope (in 1684 laid out for Emanuel Ceeley (Celly), 100 a. Emanuel's Rest, and 77 a. (*), resurv. and any vacant land added. He is now granted one entire tract called Tibb's United Inheritance, beginning on the s. side of a branch of Middle R., cont. 640 a. (MPL CE#I, 430).

DARLEY HALL

3 Nov 1697: Capt. John Oldton of BA Co., conv. 300 a. (*) to John Ensor (IR#AM: 104).

DARNALL'S

1 June 1727: Henry Darnall conv. ½ of Affinity, ½ of 1000 a. called (*) and ½ of 500 a. Darnall's Sylvania, to John Digges of PG Co. (IS#I: 69).
11 Nov 1734: John Digges of PG Co. conv. ½ of Affinity, ½ of 1000 a. called (*) and ½ of 500 a. Darnall's Sylvania, to Samuel Hyde, exec. of John Hyde of London, merchant (HWS#M: 198).

DARNALL'S CAMP (1693)

26 July 1693: Cert. of surv. for 200 a. by Thomas Richardson; poss. for Michael Judd or Edward Felkes (RM#HS: 423).

DARNALL'S SYLVANIA

1 June 1727: Henry Darnall conv. ½ of Affinity, ½ of 1000 a. called Darnall's and ½ of 500 a. Darnall's Sylvania, to John Digges of PG Co. (IS#I: 69).
1729: Henry Darnall, Charles Diggs et al. conv. (*) to John Diggs (IS#K: 91).
11 Nov 1734: John Digges of PG Co. conv. ½ of Affinity, ½ of 1000 a. called Darnall's and ½ of 500 a. Darnall's Sylvania, to Samuel Hyde, exec. of John Hyde of London, merchant (HWS#M: 198).

DAUGHADAY'S PURCHASE

8 Oct 1761: Richard Chenoweth of BA Co. conv. 201 a. (*), being pt. of Chenoweth's Adventure, to John Daughaday, blacksmith. RC's w. Keziah cons. (B#I: 337).

DAVID'S FANCY

22 June 1671: 100 a. surv. for David Williams on n. side of Patapsco; later owned by Thomas or William Cromwell, and later by Thomas Cromwell (MRR: 99).
15 April 1679: John Arthern (Ardern) conv. 100 a. (*) at head of Howard's Branch to Rowland Thornborough, being the same land formerly pat. to David Williams. JA and w. Sarah ackn. to grantee before George Wells and Henry Haslewood (IR#PP: 32).
5 July 1680: Rowland Thornborough and w. Ann conv. 100 a. (*) to William Cromwell (IR#PP: 50).
29 Nov 1727: Thomas Cromwell conv. (*), now in possession of Jacob Giles, s. of John Giles, dec., to Capt. John Cromwell of AA Co. TC's w. Eleanor cons. (IS#I: 47).
10 June 1736: Mrs. Hannah Worthington, late widow and extx. of Capt. John Cromwell, conv. (*), and Oliver's Range to John Moale of BA Co. (IS#IK: 444).

DAVIS' LOT

10 Jan 1667/8: (*) pat. to William Davis (RM#HS: 127).
14 March 1680/1: William Davis made a will leaving (*) to John Homewood and Robert Davidge, both of AA Co. (RM#HS: 127).
28 Sep 1681: Robert Davidge of AA Co. made a will leaving (*) to his w. Providence (RM#HS: 127).
11 March 1684/5: John Reynolds, planter of AA Co., and w. Providence, relict and extx. of Robert Davidge, dec., conv. 200 a. (*) to John Bennett (RM#HS: 127).
30 May 1695: John Bennett ackn. sale of 200 a. (*) to John Conway, being the same land sold by John Reynolds and w. Providence to John Bennett (RM#HS: 470).
9 May 1698: Joseph Conway with cons. of w. Jane, conv. 200 a. (*) to Alexander Lumley (TR#RA: 279).

DAY'S PRIVILEGE

2 June 1756: John Day conv. 6+3/4 a. (*) to Thomas Dawney (BB#I: 541).

DEAN'S RIDGE

7 Oct 1754: Abraham Vaughn, Jr., assigned to Joseph Bosley (*), which was leased in 1742 to Vaughan by Benjamin Tasker (BB#I: 324).

DEAR BIT

Feb 1704: 665 a. surv. for William Farfarr; 17 Feb 1705: 665 a. pat. to William Farfar (MPL CD#4: 210).

5 March 1705: William Farfarr and w. Johanna conv. 219 a. pt. (*) to Nicholas Fitzsimmons (IR#AM: 37).

26 Feb 1712: William Farfarr of Back R. and w. Eleanor, conv. 256 a. pt. (*), now called Barrett's Rest, to John Barrett of Patapsco R. (TR#A: 219).

3 Sep 1733: Nicholas Corbin and w. Eleanor conv. 125 a. pt. Barrett's Rest, orig. pt. of (*), which John Barrett devised by will of 21 June 1717 to Nicholas Corbin, to Philip Sindall (IS#L: 421).

5 Nov 1734: John Royston and w. Mary conv. 125 a. Barrett's Rest to Thomas Green (HWS#M: 126).

9 April 1743: John Keith and w. Katherine conv. pts. of (*) and Shrewsbury Hall to Francis Rider (TB#C: 241).

20 May 1746: Francis Rider conv. pt. (*) and Shrewsbury to Thomas Green; land was bought by Rider on 9 April 1743 from John Keith (TB#E: 70).

29 March 1755: Nicholas Corbin conv. his claim to (*) to John Ensor, Jr. (BB#I: 373).

DEARING'S INCREASE

22 Nov 1698: John Dearing of London, s. and heir of John Dearing of AA Co., conv. 200 a. (*) to Robert Eagle of AA Co. (HW#2: 3).

6 Nov 1712: Robert Eagle conv. 200 a. (*) to Thomas Hammond (TR#A: 273).

27 May 1735: Lawrence Hammond, s. and devisee of Col. Thomas Hammond, conv. his share of (*) and other lands, which LH had resurv. into Brother's Inheritance, to his bro. William. LH's w. Abarilla cons. (HWS#M: 313).

DEASON'S ADVENTURE

1720: William Deason leased 100 a. of Gunpowder Manor, which he called (*), for the lives of: Samuel age 63 in 1767, William, Jr., age 60 in 1767, and John, age 58 in 1767 (he went to VA about 15 years ago (Slattery: 5).

DEAVER'S ADDITION

2 Nov 1731: John Deaver of, Sr., of BA Co., con. 17 a. (*) to Thomas Deaver of BA, blacksmith; John's w. Johanna cons. (IS#L: 156).

23 Nov 1731: John Deaver of BA conv.pt. (*) to Richard Ruff, bricklayer. Deaver's w. Hannah cons. (IS#L: 176).

DEAVER'S ENDEAVOR

10 June 1706: 133 a. Broken Islands pat. by John Daver (MPL DD#5: 211, PL#2: 131).

30 March 1713: John Deaver, planter, conv. 93 a. pt. (*), being pt. The Broken Islands, to Richard Deaver. The tract was surv. 5 April 1705. JD's w. Hannah cons. (IS#I: 182).

20 Nov 1729: John Deaver conv. 20 a. (?) (*) to Richard Deaver. John's w. Hannah cons. (IS#K: 144).

DEER PARK

11 Nov 1740: Pursuant to will of ..., dated 27 Oct 1736, Woolgist and Joseph Cromwell agreed to divide 110 a., ½ (*) (HWS#1-A:451).

DELAWARE BOTTOM

2 July 1724: Elizabeth Jones, widow, conv. 300 a. (*) to Benjamin Belt of PG Co. (IS#G: 338).

DELPH

15 April 1669: 600 a. surv. for Francis Stockett; later owned by heirs of James Pendall, still later held by Thomas Newson (MRR: 12).

9 July 1669: Francis, Henry, and Katherine Stockett of the Ridge, AA Co., appoint Nathaniel Stiles their atty. to acknowledge sale of (*) and adj. island to Thomas Thurston (IR#PP: 75).

20 Oct 1669: Francis and Henry Stockett and Henry's w. Katherine conv. (*) 600 a. on the w. side of Delph Creek to Thomas Thurston (IR#PP: 75).

3 Dec 1683: Thomas Thurston, for £150 conv. 600 a. (*) to James Fendal of Bright Helmston, Susses, England; land was near Rumley Marsh, and near land of Samuel Goldsmith and John Hatton. TT's w. Mary cons. Seisin was given by turf and twig to grantor's atty. Miles Gibson (i.e., Fendall's atty.) (RM#HS: 63, 64).

29 July 1720: Thomas Brocklesby, of City of Cork, Gent., conv. 700 a. (*) and 1000 a. in CE Co., to Samuel Massey of Cork. Deed states that James Fendall of Bright Helmston, Sussex, mariner, married on 16 Dec 1686 Elizabeth Brocklesby, dau. of Richard Brocklesby of Cork and his w. Loveday; Fendall possessed 700 a. (*) and 1000 a. in CE Co.; Fendall d. leaving widow Elizabeth and a dau. Elizabeth. Dau. Elizabeth d. a minor, and widow Elizabeth d. leaving a will in which she bequeathed all land in MD to her bro. Edward Brocklesby, a minor. EB was sent by his father to MD, and then to Barbados, where he d. while still a minor. After death of Richard and w. Loveday, all land in MD desc. to their s. Thomas who now sells the land. NOTE: Deed was dated 3 Oct 1710, and latter date above is date of acknowledgement in MD (TR#DS: 101).

20 Oct 1720: Ennion Williams conv. cons. of sale of pt. of (*) (720 in all) by Sarah Massey, acquired by will of Samuel Massey, to Aquila Paca (IS#K: 322).

3 Sep 1729: Sarah Massey of Philadelphia, extx. of last will of Samuel Massey, conv. 600 a. Delf and 120 a. Delf's Neglect to Aquila Paca. (Deed conv. detailed descent of property) (IS#K: 114).

DELPH ISLAND

14 July 1662: 115 a. surv. for Henry Stockett on the northerly side of Rumley Creek; later held by Robert Gibson, and later by Capt. Thomas Bale (MRR: 9).

20 Oct 1669: Francis and Henry Stockett and Henry's w. Katherine conv. to Thomas Thurston, merchant, 115 a. on (*); they had appointed Nathaniel Stiles their atty. (IR#PP: 75).

13 Dec 1683: Thomas Thurston conv. 115 a. (*) to Miles Gibson. TT's w. Mary cons. (RM#HS: 66).

20 Aug 1704: Thomas Bale and w. Sarah conv. 115 a. (*), 400 a. Persimmon Point, and 50 a. Port Royal to Thomas Edmonds. Property came to Miles Gibson who d. intestate; land came to Robert Gibson who left it to Sarah Bale (HW#2: 356).

5 Sep 1704: Thomas Edmonds conv. all the above three tracts back to Thomas Bale (HW#2: 358).

11 July 1744: Kemp Plummer of Glouc. Co., VA, conv. 115 a. (*) and other lands, to Thomas White. Plummer was the s. of William Plummer of Glouc. Co., VA, who was the bro. of Ann who m. 1st Anthony Bale, and 2nd Michael Taylor, and who d. s.p. (TB#C, f: 576).

DELPH NEGLECT

1683: Mary Stanesby had a warrant for 250 a. granted to her; she named 120 a. of the land (*), and assigned it to Miles Gibson (RM#HS: 251).

13 March 1683: 120 a. surv. for Miles Gibson on the w. side of Delph Creek; later possessed by the heirs of James Fendall in the Kingdom of England (MRR: 12).

20 April 1688: Miles Gibson of BA Co., assigned 120 a. (*) to James Fendall; w. Ann cons. (RM#HS: 251).

3 Sep 1729: Sarah Massey of Philadelphia, extx. of the LWT of Samuel Massey, conv. 600 a. Delph and 120 a. (*) to Aquila Paca. Deed gives a detailed descent of property (IS#K: 114).

DEMMITT'S DELIGHT

20 March 1720: Ebenezer Cooke of CE Co., Agent for Lord Baltimore, leased to William Demmitt the tract (*) for the lifetimes of William, and his sons William, Jr., and James (TB#E: 541).

17 Sep 1747: William Demmitt, Sr., relinquishes his right to above lease to his s. William, Jr. (TB#E: 544).

DENBIGH

30 July 1682: Andrew Peterson, planter of CE give p/a to John Boring to acknowledge sale of 700 a. (*) to Thomas (?) (IR#AM: 189, 190).

DENCHWORTH

18 July 1679: Pat. to George Yate, Gent., of AA Co. The tract is located at Curtis Creek on the s. side of Patapsco R., bounding on Shore Branch and Spring Branch (RM#HS: 36).

6 Feb 1682/3: George Yate, Gent., of AA Co. conv. 250 a. (*), now held by William Slade, to George Hope (RM#HS: 36).

DENNIS' CHOICE

5 Feb 1698, 300 a. surv. for James Dennis above the head of Bush R.; 100 a. later held by Jeremy Hakes (MRR: 27).

3 Nov 1703: James Dennis of BA Co., planter, conv. 150 a., ½ the tract, to Simon Pearson, weaver (HW#2: 318).

20 March 1706: James Dennis conv. 100 a. to Jeremiah Hakes (RM#HS: 572).

28 March 1707: Simon Pearson conv. 100 a. to William Noble (RM#HS: 543).

20 Feb 1710: William Noble and w. Elizabeth conv. 100 a., being ⅓ of the tract, to John Standiford (TR#A: 156).

6 March 1715: William Noble and w. Elizabeth conv. 100 a., pt. of 300 a., to James Preston (TR#A: 379).

11 March 1720: Jeremiah Hacks of BA Co. conv. 100 a. to James Maxwell, in trust, provided that Maxwell maintains Hacks with sufficient diet, lodging and clothing for the rest of his life (TR#DS: 301).

8 June 1727: James Maxwell conv. 100 a. to James Preston, barber, tract formerly belonging to Jeremiah Hacks, adj. to James Preston's now dwelling plantation (IS#H: 413).

5 Nov 1740: deed of partition betw. James Preston and Daniel Preston, who inher. 300 a. (*) by the last and will and testament of their dec. father James Preston, each s. to have 133 a. (HWS#1-A: 435).

1750: Daniel Preston owned 150 a., pt. of (*) (1750 DB: 52).

DENTON

5 Sep 1699: Richard Taylor and w. Anne of PG Co. conv. 600 a. (*) to William Bladen (HW#2: 9-10).

n.d.: Simon Jackson conv. 50 a. pt. (*) to William Arnold (IS#K: 246).

DENTON'S HOPE
(See BACHELOR'S HOPE)

24 May 1751: William Denton of BA conv. to John Davis of William a $\frac{1}{2}$ moiety of (*) (311 a. in all) and $\frac{1}{2}$ of Bachelor's Meadows. WD's w. Elizabeth cons. (TR#D: 176).

20 April 1761: William Denton and w. Mary conv. pt. (*) to John Davis, s. of Walter (B#I: 100).

DESART

12 May 1696: Cert. of surv. dated (IS#H: 179).

21 July 1724: John Dorsey of BA Co., Gent., conv. 148 a. (*) to Philip Norwood (IS#H: 179).

DESERT OF ARABIA

20 Dec 1729: John Cooper, yeoman, conv. two parcels of ... of Aarabia, 10 a. and 40 a. to Godfrey Hatfield of CH Co. (IS#K: 181).

DEVITION (See DIVISION)

DICKENS(T)ON

3 April 1662: 100 a. surv. for Walter Dickinson; granted 30 June 1663 to WD, and later sold to Charles Gorsuch (TB#A: 222).

30 Oct 1663: Walter Dickeson assigned 120 a. Dickensons Memoranda to Daniel Jones (RM#HS: 7) (Scisco transcribes this 420 a. Dickenston).

19 Aug 1664: Daniel Jones conv. 420 a. to John Dixon (IS#IK: 1).

9 Feb 1679/80: Walter Dickenson of TA Co. conv. to Charles Gorsuch three parcels; first, his share of 1100 a. near the mouth of Patapsco R. formerly laid out for Thomas Thomas and William Batten (North Point?); second the 150 a. tract Upper Spring Neck, near land the grantor formerly bought from Edward Loyd and sold to Abraham Clark; and third the tract Dickinson (9 Feb 1679/80: Walter Dickinson appointed Miles Gibson or James Phillips to acknowledge sale of lands to Charles Gorsuch; 26 May 1680, personal letter from Charles Gorsuch requesting "cousin Gibson" to receive in court acknowledgement from James Phillips an acknowledgement of tract bought from Walter Dickinson and Solomon Thomas, unless the court objects to Gibson because he is an atty. alternate with James Phillips, in which case Gorsuch would like Col. Wells to act for him, and in so doing would oblige his loving uncle) (IR#PP: 48; see also IR#PP: 50).

1 June 1682: Thomas Scudamore and w. Abigail of Back R. conv. to Thomas Long, Gent., 136 a. of 420 a. (*), being the plantation where Long now lives in right of his w. Same day; Scudamore conv. bond to Thomas Long (IR#AM: 187).

28 May 1689: John Hayes of Back R., planter, and w. Abigail, conv. 136 a. to Thomas Long, Gent. (RM#HS: 296).

6 Jan 1699: John Hayes conv. (*) to James Todd (who m. Penelope Scudamore, dau. of John Hayes' w. Abigail by her 1st husband Thomas Scudamore). Hayes' dau. Jane is mentioned in the deed (TR#RA: 418).

31 July 1742: Charles Gorsuch, s. and heir-at-law of John Gorsuch, who was s. and heir-at-law of Charles Gorsuch, dec., conv. 100 a. (*) to Philip Jones, Jr. CG's w. Susanna cons. (TB#A: 222).

DIGGS CHOICE

10 Oct 1724: John Diggs, of PG Co., Gent., conv. 152 a., pt. (*) to George Counce of Conewago, adj. the land of John Morningstar (TB#C: 658).

7 July 1746: John George Counce of BA Co., farmer, conv. 150 a. (*) to his s. John Counts, who in return will provide home and maintenance for JGC and his w. Catherine (JC's mother) (TB#E: 191).

DINHAM'S CHOICE

July 1728; John Hale and w. Elizabeth, of KE Co., conv. 57[?] a. (*) to William Taylor of KE Co. (IS#K. 136).

DISCOVERY

29 Feb 1691/2: James Thompson of BA Co., Gent., and w. Anne conv. 150 a. (*) (on the e. side of Gunpowder R., on the e. side of land formerly taken up by John Collett, called Elk Neck) to John Taylor of BA Co., cooper (RM#HS: 341).

DISMAL SWAMP

10 July 1725: 55 a. pat. to James Bond and James Hill, Jr. (IS#L: 136).

11 Sep 1731: James Bond of BA Co., cooper, conv. his interest in (*) to John Hill (IS#L: 136).

DISPATCH

9 March 1748: John Paca, Jr., conv. 170 a. (*) to Richard Garrison [Garrettson?] of BA Co. (TR#C: 177).

DITTO'S DELIGHT

15 July 1745: William Ditto mortgaged (*), pt. of Bathnia Cambria (which had been leased to said WD for 3 lives), to Henry Morgan and James Richard (TB#D. 247).

DIVIDENTE

1750: Surv. for Wm. Young; 320 a. pat. by Capt. William Young (MPL TI#4: 640).

See Horvath Plat: Owings Mills.

7 Dec 1759: William Young of BA Co. conv. 320 a. (*) to William Demmitt. Young's w. Clare cons. (B#H: 61).

13 April 1761: William Demmitt of Thomas conv. pt. (*) to Thomas Stansbury (B#I: 107).

13 Oct 1767: Tobias and George Stansbury, sons of Tobias Stansbury, conv. pt. (*) to Thomas Owings (B#Q: 142).

DIVIDING (THE)

n.d.: 600 a. pat. to Thomas Edmonds and Jasper Gerin, located at Gering's Creek in Elk R. (IR#PP: 59).

12 June 1665: Thomas Edmonds conv. 300 a., pt. (*), to William Price (IR#PP: 59).

DIVISION (DEVITION)

n.d.: Simon Jackson conv. 50 a. (*) to William Arnold (IS#K: 246).

DIVISION
(Pt. of TURKEY HILLS and STRAWBERRY HILLS)

4 Nov 1708: John Beaven of BA Co. conv. 81 a. (*) to Zachariah Browne. JB's w. Hannah cons. (RM#HS: 624).

20 Sep 1721: William Wood and w. Jane conv. 50 a. (*), pt. of 250 a. in all, to Simeon Jackson (IS#G: 61).

18 May 1721: William Wood and w. Jane conv. 100 a. pt. (*) to Thomas Mitchell (IS#G: 225).

2 June 1725: Joshua Wood and w. Martha conv. 40 a. (*) to Richard Jenkins, with other tracts (IS#H: 105).

1 Dec 1731: Thomas Mitchell and w. Ann conv. 62 a. pt. (*) to Thomas Gilbert (IS#L: 218).

4 Aug 1730: Benjamin Jones conv. 100 a. (*) and other lands to John Browne (IS#L: 1).

4 Aug 1730: John Browne and w. Mary conv. 81 a. (*) and other lands back to Jones (IS#L: 3).

27 Nov 1740: Diana Jones of BA Co., widow of Benjamin Jones, conv. 81 a. (*) and 50 a. (*) to William Bradford, who had orig. bought the lands from BJ on 1 Nov 1738; by his LWT BJ directed his w. to conv. the land to WB (HWS#1-A: 481).

1750: Kent Mitchell owned 100 a. (*) (1750 DB: 81).

26 Nov 1752: Thomas Arnold conv. 50 a. (*) to Samuel McCarty. TA's w. Sarah cons. (TR#D: 478).

DIXON

24 July 1704: James Todd conv. 151 a., pt. (*) to John Oldton (IR#PP: 162).

DIXON'S CHANCE (See DIXON'S CHOICE)

DIXON'S CHOICE (or CHANCE)

8 June 1667: 300 a. surv. for John Dixon in Gunpowder R.; later held by John Richardson, and still later by William Adams (MRR: 59).

1 March 1668/9: John Dixon conv. 300 a. (*) to Richard Ellinsworth (1 Nov 1669: Dixon appointed Richard Thurrell his atty. to acknowledge the sale) (IR#PP: 74).

11 June 1685: Richard Ellinsworth conv. 300 a. (*) to Thomas Richardson (RM#HS: 165).

3 Aug 1697: Thomas Richardson conv. to his s. John two tracts (*) and Long Point (IS#IK: 166).

7 July 1702: John Richardson conv. pt. (*), pt. Long Point, and pt. Taylor's Mount, in all 310 a., to William Adams of CV Co. (HW#2., 144).

22 April 1708: John Richardson of BA Co. conv. 300 a. (*) and 250 a. Taylor's Mount to William Adams of BA Co. (RM#HS: 657).

1 April 1729: Henry Adams of BA Co., carpenter, s. and heir of William Adams of BA Co. (formerly of CV Co.), dec., conv. 310 a. (*), Long Point and Taylor's Point to Thomas Tolley. 310 a. of these tracts had been sold to William Adams on 7 July 1702 (IS#I: 296).

29 March 1742: Robert Emms of Great Yarmouth, Co. Norfolk, clerk, s. and heir of Thomas Emms of Great Yarmouth, dec., conv. 300 a. (*) and 125 a., being $\frac{1}{2}$ of Taylor's Mount, to Edward Day of BA Co., through John Galloway of AA Co., his atty. (TB#C: 9).

30 Nov 1743: Henry Adams of BA Co., planter, conv. quitclaim of 500 a. (*) and 250 a. Taylor's Mount to Edward Day, who now possesses the tracts by virtue of a deed from Robert Emmes of London, merchant (TB#C: 381).

DIXON'S NECK

7 June 1667: 450 a. surv. for John Dixon (MRR: 92).

1 Aug 1671: Jane Dixon conv. the entire 450 a. tract to Joseph Hawkins (IR#PP: 107).

23 March 1671/2: Joseph Hawkins, Gent., of Back R., appointed his kinsman Richard Thurell his atty. to conv. the tract to Thomas Long, if Long surrenders a bill made by Hawkins (G#J:15, TR#RA: 11, 13).

On 6 Aug 1672 Richard Thurrell, planter, as atty. for his kinsman Joseph Hawkins, sold 450 a. (*) to Joseph Sumner and Robert Garrett (C:28). The Rent Rolls for BA Co. state that Sumner and Robert Garrett bought 450 a. of

(*) from John Dixson, but they deserted this province 26 years ago, and the land was uncultivated (MRR: 92).

8 Jan 1743: John Long and w. Eleanor conv. 450 a. to Thomas Stansbury, Jr. (TB#C: 402).

1 Nov 1743: Thomas Stansbury and w. Jane conv. the tract to Thomas Stansbury (TB#C:341).

3 June 1747: Thomas Stansbury and w., Jane conv. 450 a. (*) to s. Thomas (TB#E: 400).

(This tract was the subject of a case in the Prov. Court. See Prov. Court Judgements EI#10#1: 743-746 A summary of the vase is given below).

Dr. Charles Carroll summoned to answer a charge of William "Thrustout", lessee of Thomas Stansbury, Jr. With force and arms, Carroll is said to have ejected "Thrustout" from a tract 450 a., (*), which "Thrustout" had leased from Thomas Stansbury, Jr., for a term not yet passed .... (p. 743).

Thomas Stansbury, Jr., on the 1st of October 1744 at Baltimore leased the land to said William, for a term of ten years (p. 744).

The case was imparled until court of 14 April 1747; a jury was summoned.

Several documents cited:

Patent dated 10 October 1667, to John Dixon, from Proprietary, for 450 a. ... stated that John Dixon of BA Co. has due him 450 a. granted him out of a warrant for 900 a. granted the said Dixon 10 January 1666 ... Dixon was granted 450 a. called (*), on Back R. ....

The said Dixon d. seized of the lands in question as the law requires leaving issue an only child being a dau. who intermarried with a man named --- Skidmore, and had by him an only child, a dau. called Penelope, who intermarried with a certain James Todd, since dec., and the said Penelope d. s.p. under the age of 21 years; and that the said Abigail, after the death of Skidmore, intermarried with a certain Hayes, and had by him issue only one child called Jane, which said Jane is the w. of Thomas Stansbury, and mother of the plaintiff. Abigail never had any ch. but the said Penelope and Jane.

The said Hayes who intermarried with said Abigail did survive Penelope some years and d. siezed in law of the said lands.

Thomas Stansbury and w. Jane, parents of the plaintiff, by deed dated 1 November 1743, conv. the land to said Thomas Stansbury, Jr. (Deed is quoted).

Thomas and Jane are now living, and have an elder son, John, who is also living.

Thomas Long married Jane, widow of said John Dixon, and said Long d. leaving an only s. and the only heir of said Jane, Thomas Long. The said Thomas Long the s. d. leaving his eld. s. John his heir, who on 8 March 1743 conv. to Thomas Stansbury, Jr., tract called (*). John's w. Eleanor cons. (p. 747).

DOCK (THE)

Nov 1700: 150 a. surv. for Samuel Sicklemore (Card Index to Patents).

6 Nov 1702: Samuel Sicklemore conv. 158 a. (*) to Robert Cutcheon. SS's w. Sarah gave cons. (HW#2: 181).

3 March 1702/3: Robert Cutchin and w. Dorothy conv. 158 a. (*) to Sicklemore (HW#2: 213).

14 June 1711: Samuel Sicklemore, Sr., conv. Sicklemore's Dock to Hannah Sicklemore; as well as ... 200 a. pt. of 400 a. ... to Sutton Sicklemore, and Wolves Harbor to Samuel Sicklemore; they bare all to live together until marriage and to teach Thomas Wriothesley to read and write (TR#A: 244).

31 July 1714: Hannah Sicklemore spinster, conv. 150 a (*) to William Demmitt (TR#A: 304).

1727: William Demmett and w. Elizabeth conv. (*) to Nicholas Day (IS#I: 3).

DOGWOOD RIDGE

7 Aug 1693: Hugh Elbert of Kent Island, KE Co., carpenter, deeded 99 a. (*) to William Lofton of BA Co. No w. signs (RM#HS: 482).

3 June 1726: Thomas Loftin of BA Co. conv. 99 a. (*) to Roland Shepherd (IS#H: 247).

DONMURENINTRUM
(See CLARK'S DEMURRER)

DORSEY'S PLAINS

3 Aug 1726: John Dorsey conv. (*), cont. 775 a. by patent, 150 a. Sims Choice, and 100 a. Swanson (the latter two conv. by Vaughn Davies and w. Catherine, dau. of Gideon Skates, dec.) to Daniel Dulany (IS#H: 272).

DOUBLE TROUBLE

18 Dec 1733: granted to Robert Robertson (TR#D: 42).

8 March 1735: Robert Robertson and w. Sarah conv. 159 a. (*) to Samuel Young of AA Co. (HWS#M: 308).

7 Oct 1750: Pollard Keene and w. Mary, and John Keene and w. Elizabeth, conv. (*) to William Savory. The tract had been granted to Robert Robe[rt]son on 18 Dec 1733. He later sold the land to Samuel Young by which means it desc. to said Mary and Elizabeth, daus. of John Young (TR#D: 42).

DOUGHERTY'S (DAUGHTER'S) CHANCE

8 July 1726: 94 a. pat. by Nathaniel Dougherty (MPL PL#6: 449, IL#B: 34).

26 Nov 1729: Nathaniel Daugherty conv. 94 a. (*) and 50 a. Creek Plantation to Gregory Farmer (IS#K: 152).

2 March 1733: Gregory Farmer, Sr., conv. 50 a. Creek Plantation and 10 a. pt. (*), to s. John Farmer (HWS#M: 27).

1750: James Death owned 10 a. (*) (1750 DB).

DRECUT

4 Nov 1673: Henry Eldesy, planter, and w. Parnell conv. 175 a. pt. (*), and also land bought by Eldesley from his late occupant George Harris, dec., late of KE (G#J: 221; TR#RA: 221).

DREWS ENLARGEMENT

13 April 1752: Anthony Drew, house joiner, with cons. of w. Ann, conv. to Joseph Lusby 788 a. (*) (TR#D: 341).

DRISDALE'S ADVENTURE

10 June 1695: Robert Drisdale of BA Co., tailor, and w. Eleanor conv. 123 a. (*) to William Geffes of AA Co., carpenter (RM#HS: 477).

DRISDALE'S DOCK

1750: George York owned 59 a. (1750 DB: 7).

DRISDALE'S (or DRYSDALE'S) HABITATION

18 Sep 1683: 200 a. surv. for Robert Drysdale at a bounded tree of Edward Beedle's land; later poss. by John Fendall; still later poss. by John Fendall and claimed by John Roberts (MRR: 18).

13 Feb 1705: John Roberts and w. Mary conv. to Henry Wriothesley (*), which was granted to Robert Drysdale on 1 June 1685, 200 a., which he left to his s. Thomas Jackson, now dec., who in his will left it to his w. Mary, now w. of John Roberts (IR#AM: 20).

18 Feb 1719: Samuel Sickelmore of BA Co. conv. 200 a. (*) to Roger Matthews (TR#DS: 98).

7 June 1722: Roger Matthews conv. 100 a. pt. (*) to Benjamin Osborne (IS#G: 43).

17 July 1722: Benjamin Osborne and w. Sarah conv. 45 a. to Joshua Wood (IS#G: 91).

7 Nov 1722: Roger Matthews conv. 100 a. pt. (*) to Joshua Wood (IS#G: 82).

2 June 1725: Joshua and Martha Wood conv. 145 a. pt. (*) and other tracts, to Richard Jenkins (IS#H: 105).

DRUNKORD'S HALL

19 Oct 1744: Samuel Merryman, Sr., conv. 308½ a. (*) to his s. Samuel Merryman, Jr. (TB#C: 650).

DUCK COVE

10 Sep 1687: mentioned as bounding Charity's Delight, being pt. of Rebecca's Delight (RM#HS: 283).

20 Oct 1690: Richard Johns and w. Elizabeth of CV Co. conv. 350 a. (*) to William Coale of AA Co.; tract had orig. been laid out for Paul Kensey (IS#IK: 194).

14 June 1697: William Coale of West R., AA Co., and w. Elizabeth, conv. 350 a. (*) to James Murray; deed states "without molestation of heirs of Paul Kinsey or Richard Jones" (TR#RA: 381).

15 Nov 1725: Melchizedek Murray of BA Co., and w. Sophia, conv. (*) to Thomas Hughes, Sr. (IS#H: 206).

DUCK NECK

1 Sep 1742: William Inlose (or Enloes) was in Hyde Co., NC, by 1 Sep 1742 when he sold to William Right [sic] of BA Co. 50 a. of land (unnamed) lying in BA Co. On Middle R., on the neck betw. the said R. and (unnamed) creek. The deed was recorded in Beaufort Co., NC, Land Records. The grantor may have been William Enloes, s. of Abraham and Eliza (N) Enloes of BA Co. Abraham Enloes d. leaving a will dated 24 April 1709, proved 20 July 1709, by which he left (among other bequests to other ch.) 50 a. called (*) to his s. William. Beaufort Co. Deed Book #2 (1728-1743), folios 418-419; Barnes, BCF, p. 204. (The compiler is indebted to Mary H. Disharoon of Washington Co., NC, who found this deed and sent it to the editor of the *Bulletin* of the MD Gen. Soc.)

DULAY'S BEGINNING

1730: John Duly conv. 50 a. (*) to Ford Barnes (IS#K: 312).

DUNDEE

19 June 1705: Andrew Anderson conv. 174 a. (*) (and 66 a. Anderson's Addition, 34 a. Anderson's Camp, and 100 a. Edinborough, pt. of Robert's Choice, to James Crooke (IR#AM: 15). The same day Anderson conv. all his goods and chattels, real and personal, to Crooke (IR#AM: 17).

4 June 1746: Charles Crook of BA Co. conv. 74 a. (*) to Charles Carroll of Annapolis, chirurgeon (TB#E: 149).

DUNKEEL

10 June 1699: John Scott of the Cliffs, CV Co., Gent., and w. Christiana, for love and a consideration, conv. to Gilbert Scott of the same co., bro. of John Scott, 500 a. (*) granted to said

John Scott on 1 June 1689 at head of Bush R. (HW#2: 1).

DUNKIN'S CHANCE

9 March 1712: Patrick Dunkin and w. Mary conv. 100 a. (*) to Charles Rockhold of AA Co. (TR#A: 239).

DURBIN'S CHANCE

7 Aug 1750: John Durbin of BA Co. conv. to John Stump of CE Co., 50 a. pt. Betty's Lot, and 150 a. pt. of Durbin's Chance. JD's w. Mary cons. (TR#D: 16).

DURBIN'S CHOICE

1 June 1722: John Durbin of BA Co. conv. 48 a. pt. (*) to Samuel Hughes (IS#G: 37).

7 Dec 1726: Samuel Hughes and w. Jane conv. 48 a. (*) (called Durbin's Chance) to John Durbin in consideration of 312 a. conv., by John Durbin to Samuel Hughes (IS#H: 318).

DURHAM'S CHOICE

11 July 1728: Thomas Durham of BA conv. 35 a. (*) to Jeremiah Hakes of KE Co. TD's w. Mary cons. (IS#I: 141).

1729: John Hales and w. conv. 35 a. (*) to William Taylor (IS#K: 136).

DUTTON'S DESIRE

See Horvath Plat: Finksburg to Westminster.

31 March 1759: Dutton Lane, Sr., of BA Co. conv. pt. (*) to his dau. Dinah Gosnell (B#G: 401).

15 Aug 1761: Peter Gosnell, Jr., and w. Diana conv. 31 a. and 51 a. (*), formerly laid out for Dutton Lane, to Thomas Lane (B#I: 298).

c1763/4: Dinah Gosnell owned 31 a. (*) (AHAL: 129).

EAGLE'S NEST

1724: 400 a. surv. for John Rowles.

See Horvath Plats: Wards Chapel and Baltimore/Carroll County.

25 Aug 1733: John Rowles of QA Co. and w. Martha conv. 400 a. pt. (*) to Philip Jones of AA Co. (IS#L: 427).

EAGLESTON'S ADDITION

6 Aug 1707: Charles Gorsuch, Sr., conv. to John Eaglestone 3 a. (*), pt. of a larger tract called Willin (RM#HS: 551).

EAGLESTON'S INLET

March 1719: John Francis Holland and w. Jane deed to John Eaglestone, carpenter, 24 a. (*) being pt. of Willin, formerly taken up by Charles Gorsuch (IS#G: 97).

EAST HUMPHREYS

1 March 1661/2: Mary M. Humphreys, widow, conv. 300 a. (*) to her dau. Mary Humphreys; dau. was not yet 16; property was now occupied by Richard Ball, husband of Mary Humphreys (RM#HS: 7).

27 Jan 1665/6: Lancelot Sockwell of Rappahannock Co., VA, by Abraham Clark his atty., conv. 300 a. (*) to Richard Ball of Patapsco. Thomas Humphreys, late of VA, by his will recorded in Lancaster Co., VA, left the tract to Lancelot Sockwell and John Duke, and Duke is now dead leaving Sockwell as sole heir (IR#PP: 54).

30 March 1682: Thomas Everest and w. Hannah, als. Hannah Bale, conv. to Charles Merryman of Corotoman R., VA, 300 a. as pat. to Hannah Bale. On 8 April 1682 Everest appointed John Boring and James Phillips as his atty, (IR#AM: 176).

30 Oct 1745: Merryman Cox of BA Co., and w. Honour, deed 40 a. (*) to Tobias Stansbury (TB#E: 229).

21 Sep 1748: Samuel Smith and w. Elizabeth, Merryman Cox and Jacob Cox sell 40 a. (*) to Tobias Stansbury (TR#C: 92) .

15 Oct 1748: Samuel Smith and w. Elizabeth, Merryman Cox, and Jacob Cox, conv. 40 a. pt. (*) to Tobias Stansbury (TR#C: 93).

EAST LOTHIAN

1749/50: 966 a. surv. for Wm. Hamiton.

See Horvath Plat: Granite.

16 March 1770: Edward Hamilton conv., to Meshack Baker 105 a. (*) and Bald Hills (AL#B: 14).

EASTLAND HILLS

26 March 1720: John Hall of BA Co. and w. Martha conv. 102 a. (*) and pt. Sophia's Dairy to John Durbin (TR#DS: 203).

7 Dec 1726: John Durbin and w. Avarilla conv. 112 a. pt. (*) and Sophia's Dairy, and 200 a. Hathaway's Hazard to Samuel Hughes, except for a parcel of Hathaway's Hazard given by Samuel Bourne (who later sold the land to Durbin) to Charles Whitaker (IS#H: 370).

14 May 1746: Samuel Hughes of BA Co. conv. (*), pt. Sophia's Dairy and Hathaway's Hazard, to Col. John Hall, Jacob Giles, and Isaac Webster (TB#E: 432).

EATON

14 June 1679: 400 a. surv. for John Larkins; located on the w. side of Susquehanna R.; later possessed by James Phillips (MRR: 14).

11 Sep 1679: granted to John Larkin (See 7 Dec 1739 deed below).

4 (---) 1683: John Larkin, innholder, appointed Thomas Hedge his atty. to acknowledge conv. of 400 a. (*) to James Phillips. 4 June 1684: John Larkin, innholder of AA Co., conv. to James Phillips, innholder, 400 a. (*) on the w. side of Susquehanna R. (RM#HS: 99).

7 Dec 1739: James Phillips of BA Co., Gent., conv. 400 a. (*) (which John Larkin had conv. to his grandfather James Phillips on 4 June 1684) to Thomas White. JP' w. Sarah cons. (HWS#1-A [betw. 310 and 318]).

EBDEN'S REST

7 Aug 1723: James Ebden, s. and heir of William Ebden of BA Co., dec., conv. 100 a. (*), which desc. to sd. James from his father, to George Buchanan (IS#G: 186).

4 June 1724: George Buchanan of BA Co., chirurgeon, conv. 100 a. (*) to Robert Robertson, except for pt. that was taken away by an elder surv. (IS#G: 325).

EBENEZER'S LOT

30 Aug 1726: Ebenezer Blakiston of KE Co. conv. 200 a. (*) to John Stokes (IS#H: 310).

15 Oct 1731: John Stokes of BA Co., Gent., conv. 200 a. (*) and other tracts to Philip Smith of London, merchant. JS's w. Susanna cons. (IS#L: 172).

25 May 1737: Philip Smith of London, now living in AA Co., s. and heir of Philip Smith, late of London, conv. 200 a. (*) and other lands to Jacob Giles (IS#IK: 432).

EBENEZER'S PARK (1684)

16 April 1684: 200 a. surv. for Ebenezer Blackiston at the head of Salt Peter Creek (MRR: 28, 42).

March 17(??): Ebenezer Blackiston and w. Sarah of KE Co. conv. 200 a. (*) to John Jones of KE Co. (TR#A: 538).

10 March 1731: John Jones of BA Co. conv. 50 a. (*) to Bartholomew Millhuse of BA Co. JJ's w. Margaret cons. (IS#L: 287).

10 March 1731: John Jones conv. pt. (*) to Ralph Woodall, JJ's w. Margaret cons. (IS#L: 288).

2 Aug 1749: Joseph Wright and w. Jane conv. (*) to William Andrew (TR#C: 282).

EDEN'S ADDITION

11 June 1685: 100 a. surv. for Adam Birchall (Burchall); later belonging to the orphans of said Birchall, and later held by Samuel Brown (MRR: 21).

13 Nov 1704: Thomas Burchell of BA Co., conv. 100 a. (*) to Cadwallader Jones (IR#PP: 134).

12 Dec 1707: Samuel Brown of BA Co. conv. 100 a. (*) to William Norris of BA Co.; Samuel's w. Mary cons. (RM#HS: 592).

2 May 1720: William Norris made his will leaving his entire estate to his daus. Mary, b. 1704, m. Henry Millen, and Elizabeth, b. 1713 (Barnes, BCF: 474).

1750: George Lester owned 100 a. (1750 DB: 48).

EDINBOROUGH
(Pt. ROBERTS' CHOICE, q.v.)

EDINBOROUGH (See also CALEDONIA)

28 July 1696: John Roberts conv. 100 a. (*), pt Roberts Choice to Andrew Anderson (IS#IK: 14).

7 Sep 1697: Andrew Anderson conv. 100 a. (*) to Michael Cunnyworth. Mary Anderson made her mark. (IS#IK:199, 201).

19 June 1705: Andrew Anderson conv. 174 a. Dundee (and 66 a. Anderson's Addition, 34 a. Anderson's Camp, and 100 a. (*), pt. of Robert's Choice, to James Crooke (IR#AM: 15). The same day Anderson conv. all his goods and chattels, real and personal, to Crooke (IR#AM: 17).

19 Nov 1708: Alexander Gardener conv. 100 a. (*) to James Crook (TR#A: 65).

8 June 1743: Alexander McComas and w. Hannah conv. 100 a. (*) to Josias Middlemore (TB#C: 244).

EDMOND'S CAMP

10 Sep 1698: 200 a. pat. by Edmund Hensley (MPL 38:121).

27 March 1698/9: Edmond Hansley grants p/a to Francis Dallahide to conv. (*); on 6 Nov 1704: FD conv. 200 a. (*) to William Wright (IR#AM: 1).

25 June 1723: William Wright and w. Gillian conv. 100 a. (*) to Samuel Durham (IS#G: 177).

8 Aug 1723: William Wright and w. Gwilthin conv. 100 a. (*) to Edmund Hayes (IS#G: 240).

10 Aug 1723: Edmund Hayes mortgaged 100 a. (*) to Josias Middlemore; mortgage to run until 10 Nov 1727 (IS#G: 201).

Sep 1729: Edmund Hayes and w. Mary conv. (*) to Thomas Pycraft of BA Co., tailor (IS#K: 97).

c1754: Samuel Durham owned pt. (*); Bilbury Hall; Durham's First Addition to D'o; D'o Second Addition to D'o; D'o Third Addition to D'o; pt. Edwin's Contrivance, and Friend's Advice (IBC: 63).

EDWARDS AND WILLS VALLEYS AND HILLS

1703: 786 a. surv. for Edward Stevenson (Stevenson Gen.).

c1704: Edward Stevenson petitions concerning the boundary trees of (*) and Friend's Discovery (HW#2: 342).

2 March 1735: Edward Stevenson conv. 290 a. (*) to his bro. Richard King Stevenson (HWS#M: 386). The same day he conv. 290 a. (*) to his bro. John Stevenson (HWS#M: 388).

1750: John Stevenson owned 290 a., pt. (*); Richard King Stevenson owned 290 a., pt. (*) (called Edward and William) (1750 DB).

EDWARDS DELIGHT

9 Feb 1761: Edward Parrish conv. 4 a. pt. (*) to Edward Stocksdale (B#I: 25).

EDWARDS' ENLARGEMENT

1 June 1714: Moses Edwards conv. to Henry Thompson, 50 a. pt. (*). No w. (TR#A: 288).

5 Feb 1717/8: Moses Edward, with cons. of w. Alice, conv. 10 a. pt. (*) to the vestrymen and churchwardens of St. Paul's Parish (IS#I: 193).

11 July 1745: Richard Rutter of BA Co., ordinary keeper, leased (*) to William Lyon of BA Co., surgeon (TB#D: 242).

1 Oct 1748: John Edwards, s. and heir of Moses Edwards of BA Co., conv. 50 a. (*) to Richard Rutter, heir at law of Henry Thompson; ME conv. the tract to Henry Thompson on 1 June 1714, but the indenture omitted one course; now JE makes another deed to RR to make good the title. JE's w. Mary cons. (TR#C: 141).

31 Oct 1749: John Edwards of BA Co. conv. 899 a. Wilkinson's Folly, Edwards Lot and (*) (except for that pt. which Moses Edwards, father of John, sold to Thomas Rutter and Jonathan Hanson and 2 a. to St., Paul's Parish, and Huntington, laid out for 135 a. JE's w. Mary cons. (TR#C: 320).

1 Sep 1750: Richard Rutter conv. 40 a., pt. (*), to James Cawley of London, mariner. RR's w. Mary cons. (TR#D: 53).

EDWARDS' LOT

9 July 1686: A 300 a. tract surv. for William York; later held by Mark Swift (MRR: 53).

4 July 1699: Mary, late w. of James Frissell, dec., released her right of dower to (*), and Hathaway's Trust to William and Oliver York, sons of William York (TR#RA: 391).

8 Aug 1699: William and Oliver York of BA Co., planters, conv. 300 a. (*) to Mark Swift of BA Co., merchant (TR#RA: 392).

13 May 1703: Mark Swift and w. Elizabeth give p/a to Henry Wriothesley to conv. (*) to ... (grantee not named) (HW#2: 368).

1 June 1714: Moses Edwards conv. 50 a. pt. (*) to Thomas Rutter (TR#A: 286).

23 Jan 1721: Thomas Rooter (Rutter) of BA Co., planter, conv. 50 a. of (*), pt. of a larger tract, to Jonathan Hanson, millwright; Rutter's w. Hester cons. (RM#HS: 671).

15 June 1723: Elizabeth York of CE Co. conv. 300 a. (*) to Abraham Taylor (IS#G: 200).

6 July 1723: John Dawney and w. Elizabeth, dau. of Mark Swift, release 300 a. (*) to Abraham Taylor (IS#G: 205).

6 July 1723: In exch. for 196 a. Pitchcraft, 75 a. Polecat Ridge, and 100 a. pt. Wansworth, Dr. George Buchanan conv. to Abraham Taylor 100 a. pt. (*), resurv. 10 July 1686. The title to Edwards Lot currently rests in Mark Swift who is not yet of age (IS#G: 184).

18 Aug 1724: Mark Swift conv. 300 a. (*) to George Buchanan (*) (IS#G: 369).

2 Sep 1724: George Buchanan of BA Co., chirurgeon, conv. 100 a. pt. of 300 a. (*), to Roger Matthews; tract is in Land of Nod Forest on Bynum's Run (IS#G: 377).

21 July 1738: George Buchanan and w. Eleanor conv. 200 a. pt. (*) (in all 300 a.) and 50 a. United Lot, to Roger Matthews; deed includes GB's 7 year lease on (*), to Robert Collins expiring Nov 1742 (HWS#1-A: 98).

31 Oct 1749: John Edwards of BA Co. conv. 899 a. Wilkinson's Folly, (*) and Edwards Enlargement (except for that pt. which Moses Edwards, father of John, sold to Thomas Rutter and Jonathan Hanson and 2 a. to St., Paul's Parish, and Huntington, laid out for 135 a. JE's w. Mary cons. (TR#C: 320).

50 a. held by Jonathan Hanson, 4 wh. inhabs. (1783 TL).

EDWIN'S CONTRIVANCE

c1754: Samuel Durham owned pt. Edmund's Camp; Bilbury Hall; Durham's First Addition to D'o; D'o Second Addition to D'o; D'o Third Addition to D'o; pt. Edwin's Contrivance, and Friend's Advice (IBC: 63).

EGYPT

10 March 1737: Joseph Thurman conv. 75 a. (*) to Henry Austin (HWS#1-A: 56).

30 Aug 1740: Henry Oyston and w. Jane conv. 75 a. (*) to Francis Rider (HWS#1-A: 430).

15 July 1749: Francis Rider of BA Co. conv. 75 a. (*) to Richard Carter (TR#C: 226).

EIGHTRUPP (See AITRUPP)

29 Dec 1664: 500 a. surv. for Thomas Griffith on the w. side of Susquehanna R.; given by Griffith to one Henry Hazlewood who was his pt.ner; sold by the execs. of Hazlewood to Richard Perkins and William Loftin; later possessed: 468 a.

Richard Perkins and 32 a. Daniel Johnson. Land was escheated (MRR: 25; TB#E: 619).

16 Aug 1701: William Lofton conv. 200 a. (*) to Daniel Johnson (RM#HS: 661).

9 Nov 1701: William Lofton conv. bond he will conv. 180 a. formerly taken up by Thomas Griffith to Richard Perkins (IR#AM: 19).

2 March 1702: Richard Perkins of BA Co., cooper, and w. Mary conv. 32 a. (*) to Daniel Johnson; Mary did not sign but is mentioned as giving cons. (HW#2: 213).

25 March 1724/5: Thomas Griffith of SM Co., Gent., conv. p/a to William Cummings of AA Co., merchant, to take possession of 500 a. (*) and 150 a. Mount Ararat in CE Co., formerly owned by TG's father, Thomas Griffith, dec., and to lease them (IS#H: 139).

13 Nov 1732: Pat. to Richard, William, and Elisha Perkins for 423 a. The three bros. agreed on a division, and had the same recorded. Elisha Perkins d., and on 28 Jan 1741 William conv. his share to Richard (TB#E: 619).

23 Oct 1739: Elisha Perkins of Orange Co., VA, conv. bond he will conv. 94 a. pt. (*) to Jonathan Jones (TR#D: 111).

28 Nov 1741: Richard Perkins conv. 121 a. pt. (*) to William Perkins; on 13 Nov 1732 Lord Baltimore granted 423 a. escheat land to Richard and William Perkins and their bro. Elisha, who on 26 Aug 1728 (before the patent was made) agreed to divide the land. Elisha is now dec. The deed mentions a parcel of (*) sold by the Perkins' father to Daniel Johnson (TB#A: 123).

16 Dec 1742: Richard Perkins leased pt. (*) to Thomas Gallyhampton for 10 years (TB#C: 181).

1 Aug 1746: Richard Perkins of BA Co. conv. pt. (*) to Thomas White. RP's w. Mary cons. (TB#E: 137).

19 Nov 1747: Richard Perkins of BA Co. conv. 208 a. pt. (*) to Col. Thomas White. Perkins' w. Mary cons. (TB#E: 619).

16 Jan 1750/1: Jonathan Jones assigned his right to the land to the land to Jacob Giles (TR#D: 111).

13 Oct 1752: Daniel Sullivan and w. Winifred conv. 115 a. pt. (*) to Robert Brierly (TR#D: 434).

ELBURTON

2 Nov 1703: Thomas Thurston of BA Co., planter, s. and heir of Col. Thomas Thurston, dec., conv. (*) to James Empson of CV Co. (HW#2: 307).

5 Aug 1712: Thomas Thurston of BA Co., s. and heir of Thomas Thurston, conv. 500 a. (*), being ½ of the tract, to Lawrence Draper. Tract was surv. for Thomas Thurston, Sr., on 15 Aug 1683, pat. 1 June 1685; other half of the tract has already been sold to Edward Batson late of CV Co. (sic) (TR#A: 196).

9 Oct 1717: Lawrence Draper of BA Co., planter, conv. 250 a. pt. (*) to Ephraim Gover of CV Co. LD's w. Mary cons. (TR#A: 525).

9 Oct 1717: Lawrence Draper of BA Co. conv. 250 a. pt. (*) to Samuel Gover of AA Co. LD's w. Mary cons. (TR#A: 530).

25 Feb 1724/5: Ephraim Gover conv. 50 a. (*), being pt. of 250 a. purch. from LD, to Samuel Griffith, Jr. (IS#H: 91).

19 Sep 1725: Ephraim Gover of CV Co. and w. Mary conv. to William Allnut also of CV Co., 200 a. pt. (*). Tract was bought from Lawrence Draper (IS#H: 83).

1729: Elizabeth Whiteacre conv. 250 a. pt. (*) to Francis Taylor (IS#K: 109).

6 March 1733: Samuel Griffith, Jr., conv. 50 a. (*) to Samuel Gover, Sr. of AA Co.; 250 a. had been bought from Lawrence Draper, and SG had already sold 200 a. to William Allnut (HWS#M: 89).

24 Nov 1735: Francis Taylor of BA Co., planter, and w. Elizabeth, conv. 200 a. pt. (*) to Jacob Giles (HWS#M: 339).

25 March 1737: Gregory Farmer and w. Rachel conv. 100 a. pt. (*) to Jacob Giles (IS#IK: 371). Miller suggests that Rachel was the widow of James Empson.

9 Dec 1743: John Hawkins and w. Rebecca conv. 100 a. pt. (*) to Jacob Giles (TB#C, f: 396).

20 Nov 1744: William Allnut and w. Mary, and James Allnut, of CV Co., planter, conv. 200 a. pt. (*) to Ephraim Gover, Jr., of BA Co. (TB#C, f: 681).

ELFORD FIELDS

10 June 1684: 500 a. surv. for William Blackiston, located on a ridge near James Run and adj. to Abbotts Forest (MRR:16).

ELIJAH'S LOT

See Horvath Plat: Old Hampstead.

1 Sep 1768: Jacob Cox conv. 50 a. (*) to Benjamin Wheeler. JC's w. Elizabeth cons. (B#Q: 601).

ELINOR'S RESERVE

2 June 1674: Mary Harmer, widow, conv. 150 a. (*) to John Johnson and Robert Benger (G#J: 242).

ELISHA'S LOT

9 Jan 1721: Elisha Perkins of BA Co. conv. 50 a. (*) to John Cooper, weaver. Margery Perkins cons., but she is not called w. (IS#G: 123).

ELIZABETH ANN'S PLEASANT HILLS

21 June 1757: Thomas Broad and w. Ann of BA Co. conv. 242 a. (*) and other lands to John Ensor, Sr., and to Abraham Ensor (B#G: 9).

25 Oct 1757: Thomas Broad, John Ensor, and Abraham Ensor assign 242 a. (*) to Henry Cross. No wives joined. The land was orig. leased to Thomas Broad (B#G: 55).

ELIZABETH'S CHOICE

3 Aug 1726: Josias Hendon conv. 100 a. (*) to his father-in-law James Isham. JH's w. Elizabeth cons. (IS#H: 262).

5 Oct 1736: James Isham of BA Co., innholder, conv. 100 a. (*) and 50 a. the Neglect, to John Hatton, tailor (TB#A: 83). (This is actually the bond for conveyance).

3 March 1741: James Isham conv. the above two tracts to John Hatton; deed mentions bond had been dated 5 Oct 1736 (TB#A: 85).

7 May 1745: John Hatton, taylor, conv. 100 a. (*), 27 a. Moorfields, and 50 a. Neglect, to William Dallam. JH's w. Sarah cons. (TB#D, f: 142).

ELIZABETH FRENCH'S LOT

23 Oct 1728: 100 a. surv. for Michael French (IS#L: 102).

20 March 1730: Michael French of BA Co., conv. 50 a. pt. (*) to Stephen Onion of CE Co. (IS#L: 102).

ELIZABETH'S DELIGHT

30 Nov 1741: Surv. for William Sinclair (C: 18: cites BA Unpat. Cert. #475).

ELIZABETH'S FANCY

8 July 1749: Richard Jones of BA Co. conv. 100 a. (*) to Samuel Owings. RJ's w. Hannah cons. (TR#C: 238).

ELIZABETH'S PURCHASE

2 Dec 1745; John Hollowan of BA Co., and w. Elizabeth conv. 100 a. (*) to John Macoll [Mackall?] of CV Co. (TB#D: 392).

20 Nov 1746: James Mackall of CV Co. [planter conv. 100 a. (*) and 30 a. Cope or Hope (surv. for Edward Cox) to William Wilson. JM's w. Martha cons. (TB#E: 289).

ELIZABETH'S ROCK
See also BORING'S PASSAGE

1754: 25 a. pat. by James Boring and w. Sarah (MPL BC&GS#2: 18).

11 Aug 1787: James Boreing of BA Co. and w. Sarah sold to Thomas Cockey Deye (WG#AA: 429).

ELK NECK

19 --- 1664: 300 a. pat. (RM#HS: 11-13).

7 Nov 1664: John Collett agrees with Hendrick Enloes and John Alkemore for sale of 300 a. (*) at Gunpowder R. (RM#HS: 11-13).

27 Dec 1718: William Marshall and w. Mary conv. 600 a. (*) to John Presbury (son of James) and his w. Martha. The tract had been surv. 20 Oct 1667 for John Collett (TR#RA: 477).

ELLEDGES FARM

16 Oct 1731: 50 a. surv. for Joseph Elledge (IS#IK: 308).

20 Oct 1738: Joseph Elledge and w. Elizabeth of BA Co., conv. 50 a. (*) to Joseph Murray (IS#IK: 308).

ELLEDGES FARM, ADDITION TO

31 May 1755: Josephus Murray, Sr., and w. Ruth conv. 66 a., pt. (*), to Samuel Hooker, Sr. (BB#I: 395).

12 June 1767: Josephus Murray, for love and affection, conv. 398 a. pt. (*) to his s. John, who is to hold the land immediately after the death of said Josephus (B#Q: 174).

ELLEDGE'S FOLLY

3 May 1745: Christopher Gist conv. 50 a. (*) and 50 a. Gist's Meadow to William Cromwell (TB#D: 99).

1783: Joseph Osborne held 50 a. in Pipe Creek hundred (1783 TL).

ELLEDGE'S GROVE

1750: Joseph Bosley owned 30 a. of (*); John Merryman owned 50 a. of (*) (1750 DB).

ELLIOTT'S DELIGHT

30 Sep 1736: Benjamin Tasker of Annapolis, Agent and Receiver General of Lord Baltimore, leased 100 a. (*) to George Elliott for the lifetimes of said GE, Ann Elliott, and Susanna Westwood (HWS#M: 66).

ELLIOTT'S SUCCESS

1746: Benjamin Tasker leased 100 a. (*) to George Elliott for 99 years (TB#D: 178).

ELLIOTT'S TENTS

4 Nov 1743: Thomas Elliott conv. 50 a. (*) to William Dallam (TB#C: 360, 426).

ELLIS'S CHOICE

11 Oct 1721: John Tydings and w. Mary conv. 210 a. (*) to Richard Colegate of BA Co., merchant (TR#A: 200).

ELY O'CARROLL

1695/96: 1000 a. surv. for Charles Carroll.

See Horvath Plat: Green Spring Valley.

17 Sep 1745: Charles Carroll of Annapolis, leased 117 a., pt. (*) to William Harvey for lives of said WH, Margaret Harvey, and Thomas Harvey (TB#D: 340).

ELZEY'S GROVE

13 Dec 1726: John Elzey conv. 80 a. (*) to Joseph Bosley. JE's w. Bridget cons. (IS#H: 304).

26 Aug 1748: Joseph Bosley conv. 50 a. (*) to John Merryman, jr. JB's w. Ann cons. (TR#C: 76).

EMANUEL'S HOPE

21 Feb 1687/8: Emanuel Ceely conv. 100 a. (*), adj. to Oglesby's Chance, to Edward Dowse (RM#HS: 265).

20 Oct 1713: Francis Whitehead and w. Elizabeth conv. to William Tibbs of BA Co., clerk, 50 a. Dann, 100 a. (*), 100 a. Emanuel's Rest, and 300 a. Oglesby's Chance (TR#A: 357).

1722: William Tibbs pet. to have four tracts: 200 a. Oglesby's Chance (laid out for George Oglesby), 100 a. (*) (in 1684 laid out for Emanuel Celly), 100 a. Emanuel's Rest, and 77 a. Dann, resurv. and any vacant land added. he is now granted one entire tract called Tibb's United Inheritance, beginning on the s. side of a branch of Middle R., cont. 640 a. (MPL CE#I: 430).

10 Oct 1724: Oliver Harriott, John Legate, Elizabeth Whitehead, Elizabeth Whitehead, Jr., and Francis Whitehead, release their interest in (*) to William Tibbs (IS#H: 13).

EMANUEL'S REST

5 Aug 1684: date of cert. of surv. to Emanuel Ceeley (TR#RA: 292).

4 Sep 1698: Emanuel Ceely and w. Sarah conv. 100 a. (*) to Francis Whitehead. Wife did not sign or acknowledge (TR#RA: 292).

20 Oct 1713: Francis Whitehead and w. Elizabeth conv. to William Tibbs of BA Co., clerk, 50 a. Dann, 100 a. Emanuel's Hope, 100 a. Emanuel's Rest. amd 300 a. Oglesby's Chance (TR#A: 357).

1722: William Tibbs pet. to have four tracts: 200 a. Oglesby's Chance (laid out for George Oglesby), 100 a. Emanuel's Hope (in 1684 laid out for Emanuel Celly), 100 a. (*), and 77 a. Dann, resurv. and any vacant land added. he is now granted one entire tract called Tibb's United Inheritance, beginning on the s. side of a branch of Middle R., cont. 640 a. (MPL CE#I: 430).

EMM'S DELIGHT

10 Aug 1730: Henry Donahue, s. and heir of Henry Donahue of BA Co., dec., conv. 114 a., being ½ of (*) to Thomas Pycraft. HD's w. Rachel cons. The deed mentions a division of land made with the grantor's bro. Roger Donahue (IS#L: 19).

5 April 1743: Roger Donahue conv. 168 a., pt. (*) to Robert Briarly. RD's w. Elizabeth cons. The deed mentions half the tract to be enjoyed by his mother for life, and also mentioned RD's bro. Henry Donahue (TB#C: 213).

END (THE)

3 Aug 1743: Thomas Bond conv. 90 a. (*) to Edward Norris (TB#C: 297).

ENLARGED LOT

9 Nov 1745: William Bond and w. Elizabeth conv. 535 a. (*) and 100 a. Philemon's Lot, to Abraham Raven (TB#D: 402).

2 Jan 1748: Abraham Raven makes deed of gift of 535 a. (*) to his dau. Elizabeth Risteau (TR#C: 182).

ENLARGEMENT (THE) (1665)

27 Feb 1665: 200 a. tract surv. for George Goldsmith lying in Swan Creek on the s. side adj. Proctor's Hall now in possession of John Walsh/Walston? (MRR: 7).

4 Jan 1686/7: George Gouldsmith and w. Martha conv. 200 a. (*) and 200 a. Proctor's Hall to John Walston, Gent. (RM#HS: 212).

15 May 1718: Mary Wells of BA Co., widow, conv. to John Hall 11 a. Woodpecker Hall, being pt. of (*) formerly taken up by George Goldsmith, Sr. (TR#RA: 439).

2 April 1736: Bennett Garrett and w. Avarilla, dau. of John Walson, conv. 200 a. (*) and 200 a. Proctor's Hall to Mary Marshall and George Presbury. Deed also corrected a deficiency in 109 a. deed for Rayly (HWS#M: 424).

ENLARGEMENT (THE) (1704)

1704: 144 a. surv. for Edward Stevenson; pat. 10 Jan 1706 (MPL DD#5: 204, and PL#2: 288).

1804: Mordecai Stevenson, formerly of BA Co., now of Green Co., PA, conv. to Nicholas Brice his interest in (*) and Labyrinth (WG#80: 368).

ENLARGEMENT (THE) (1706)

10 Jan 1706: 128 a. pat. by John Whitaker (MPL CD#4: 235).

6 March 1722: Peter Whitacre and w. Frances conv. 64 a. ½ of (*) to William Bradford (IS#G: 120).

2 June 1724: Abraham Whiteacre of BA Co., planter, conv. 32 a. being ½ of (*) to William Bradford, schoolmaster (IS#G: 329).

2 June 1724: Abraham Whiteacre conv. 32 a. (*) to John McComas (IS#G: 332).
9 June 1726: William Bradford and w. Elizabeth conv. 20 a. pt. (*) to John McComas in return for 20 a. pt. Come By Chance (IS#H: 244).

ENLOES

15 Oct 1670: 100 a. surv. for Abraham Inloes on the n. side of Back R.; later possessed by John Boring (MRR: 94).

ENLOES COVE

1 April 1700: Abraham Enloes of BA Co., conv. 150 a. (*) to William Holland (HW#2: 27).

ENLOES REST

1750: Anthony Enloes owned 62 a. (*) (1750 DB).
1763/4: Anthony Enloes' heirs owned 195 a. (*) (AHAL: 17).

ENSOR'S CHOICE

7 July 1731: John Ensor of BA co., conv. 100 a. (*) to Thomas Gorsuch. No w. cons. (IS#L: 145).
1750: Thomas Gorsuch conv. 100 a. (*) to his s. John Gorsuch (TR#D: 279).

ENVELL CHASE

17 May 1696: 230 a. surv. for Thomas Norris (TB#E: 73).
4 June 1746: John Norris, only s. and heir of above Thomas, of BA Co., conv. 230 a. (*) to William Bennett of BA Co., carpenter. JN's w. Ann cons. (TB#E: 73).
10 Oct 1746: William Bennett conv. 230 a. (*) to Stephen Onion, ironmaster. WB's w. Hannah cons. NB: The deed stated that ½ a. was reserved to John Norris for use as a rolling house [a building used for metal bars and sheets were rolled out from iron] (TB#E: 214).

ESCAPE

1757: 300 a. surv. for Robert Gilcresh.
See Horvath Plat: Wards Chapel.
1762: Robert Gilchrist conv. to Wm. Bouren 58 a. pt. of (*) (B#K: 442).

ESSEX (or ESSEX NECK)

18 June 1687: Michael Judd conv. (*), which he had recently surv., and adj. to Locust Neck, to Edward Hensley of BA Co., planter. Jane Judd signed (RM#HS: 260).
1 Aug 1693 (or 1698): Edmund Hensley and w. Sarah conv. 100 a. (*), formerly belonging to Michael Judd, to William Osborn (here called Essex) (IR#AM: 72).
3 June 1718: Charles Miles of BA Co., planter, conv. 100 a. (*) to Benjamin Hanson (TR#RA: 469).
6 March 1727: Benjamin Hanson conv. 100 a. (*) to William Byfoot. BH's w. Sarah cons. (IS#I: 52).
6 Aug 1728: William Byfoot conv. 100 a. (*) to Benjamin Hanson (IS#I: 242).

EVANS' BEGINNING

19 July 1739: Job Evans conv. 100 a. (*), pt. of Fox Hall, to John Evans. JE's w. Mary cons. (HWS#1-A: 251).
30 Oct 1747: John Evans, with cons. of w. Catherine, conv. 100 a. (*) to Joseph England (TB#E: 580).

EVERLY HILL

29 Dec 1694: 394 a. surv. for Thomas Preston in the woods above the head of Bush R. on the e. side of Winter's Run (MRR: 62).
4 Dec 1718: James Preston conv. 356 a., formerly taken up by Thomas Preston of BA Co., dec., on the n. side of Winter's Run, adj. Poplar Neck and the land of Miles Gibson, to Thomas Preston. JP's w. Elizabeth cons. (TR#RA: 533).
4 March 1718[/19]: Thomas Preston conv. 356 a. of the tract, pat. to Thomas Preston on 6 Nov., 1695, to John Norris, of AA Co., planter (TR#RA: 519).
9 Nov 1724: John Norris, Sr., of AA Co., conv. 170 a. of the land to his s. Benjamin Norris. JN's w. Mary cons. (IS#H: 35).
22 Feb 1742: Thomas Norris conv. 178 a., pt. of the tract, to Benjamin Norris. TN's w. Avarilla cons. (TB#C: 190).

EVE'S DOWRY

29 Sep 1712: Richard Shipley conv. (*), being the same tract known as Adam The First, to James Barnes. RS' w. Susannah cons. (TR#A: 210).
18 April 1713: James Barnes and w. Keturah mortgaged 114 a. (*), being pt. of 500 a. Adam the First, to John Brice, merchant. Adam the First had been pat. to Adam Shipley, whose s. Richard sold (*) to James and Keturah for a dwelling plantation (TR#A: 242).

EWEN'S CONTRIVANCE

Aug 1698: 691 a. surv. for Jno. Ewens (Card Index to Patents).
1 March 1703; John Ewings of BA Co. conv. 400 a. (*) and 210 a. Chilberry Hall to John Brice of AA Co. John Swinyard, now in poss. of Chilberry Hall to be allowed to remain there for three years (HW#2: 312).
14 March 1704: John Brice paid 29 shillings for alienation of 361 a. (*) and 194 a. Chilberry Hall.

On 19 May 1704 John Ewings have a receipt (HW#2: 373).

28 Nov 1744: John Brice of Annapolis, Gent., heir-at-law to John Brice conv. 400 a. (*) to Samuel Durham. JB's w. Sarah cons. (TB#D: 23).

EWING'S LUCK

10 Jan 1705: Granted to Joshua Ewings; after the death of John Ewings, the land desc. to his only dau. Darcas Ewing who m. the afsd. Edward Mead and had one s. James Mead (TB#E: 188).

6 Nov 1746: Edward Mead and his s. James Mead conv. 100 a. (*) to Nicholas Maccubbin (TB#E: 188).

12 July 1750: Nicholas Maccubbin of Annapolis, merchant, conv. to Lemuel Howard 262 a. (*), orig. granted to John Ewing for 600 a., but found to contain only 262 a. NM's w. Mary Clare cons. (TR#C: 543).

EXECUTOR'S MANAGEMENT

1750: William Sinclair owned 50 a. pt. (*); Ketura, widow of Thomas Price, owned 200 a. pt. (*). (1750 DB).

EXPECTATION (1683)

15 May 1683: 500 a. surv. for Thomas Lightfoot on the n. branch of Gunpowder R.; later possessed by James Sanders (MRR: 73).

9 April 1685: Thomas Lightfoot, surveyor, conv. 500 a. James' Forest to James Sanders of AA Co., the tract being pt. of 1000 and 500 a. tracts both called (*). TL's w. Rebecca also signs (RM#HS: 121).

EXPECTATION (1683)

15 May 1683: A 500 a. tract surv. for Thomas Lightfoot on the n. branch of Gunpowder R.; later held by James Sanders of AA Co. (MRR: 73).

16 Sep 1683: A 1000 a. tract surv. for Thomas Lightfoot (MRR: 73).

16 Sep 1683: 1000 a. surv. for Thomas Lightfoot above Gunpowder R. (MRR: 73).

9 April 1685: Thomas Lightfoot, surveyor, conv. to James Sanders, planter, of AA Co., 500 a. tract James Forest, being pt. of two tracts, one 500 a., and 1000 a. tract, both called (*); land adjoins Leaf's Forrest, Belt's Prosperity, and Nangemie. Rebecca Lightfoot sign with grantor (RM#HS: 121).

29 April 1685: Thomas Lightfoot, surveyor, conv. to Edward Carter of AA Co. 500 a. Carter's Rest, being pt. of two tracts of 500 a. and 1000 a. both called (*). Rebecca Lightfoot also sign (RM#HS: 125).

29 April 1685: Thomas Lightfoot, surveyor, conv. to Richard Walsh, planter, 200 a. Richards' Hope, being pt. of 1000 a. and 500 a. tracts called (*). TL's w. Rebecca signs (RM#HS: 124).

EXPECTATION (1683)

25 Sep 1683: 350 a. surv. for Peter Ellis in the woods above the head of Mosquito Creek; later possessed: 100 a. William Stevens; 200 a. Samuel Jackson; 50 a. Tobias Emerson (MRR: 17).

24 March 1702: John Ellis conv. to Cadwallader Jones 100 a. called Cadwallader, being pt. of (*) (IR#PP: 132).

21 March 1702/3: John Ellis conv. 50 a. (*), now called Bedlam to Miles Hannes (HW#2: 287).

10 March 1704: Thomas Morris of BA Co., and w. Eliza conv. to William Stevens 100 a. pt. (*), now called Morris' Folly (IR#PP: 146).

17 March 1704: John Ellis conv. 100 a. (*) being the eastern most half of the land, to Samuel Jackson (IR#AM: 7).

30 June 1705: Cadwallader Jones conv. 100 a. Cadwallader, pt. of (*) to William Norris of BA Co., carpenter. CJ's w. Mary cons. (IR#PP: 173).

28 Dec 1705: William Norris and w. Sarah conv. 100 a. Cadwallader, pt. of Expectation to Samuel Jackson (IR#AM: 18).

3 Feb 1706: Miles Hannes of BA Co., planter, conv. 50 a. pt. (*), called Bedlam to Tobias Emminson (RM#HS: 541).

2 March 1708: Tobias Emminson of BA Co., conv. 50 a. Bedlam, pt. (*) back to Miles Hannes (RM#HS: 648).

2 March 1720: Thomas Morris with cons. of w. Mary conv. to Edward Parks 100 a. (*), adj. The Grove; land was formerly held by William Stevens of KE Co. (RM#HS: 678, 679).

13 May 1721: Oliver Hickinbotham of KE Co., capenter, conv. p/a to Edward Hall of BA Co. to sell his interest in (*) and the interest of the heirs of William Stevens, to Thomas Morris, tracts (*) and The Grove (RM#HS: 679).

16 Nov 1728: Edward Parks conv. bond to Simon Jackson he will make over to him 100 a. pt. of a larger tract called (*) (HWS#1-A: 9).

EXPECTATION (1706)

10 June 1706: 406 a. pat. to Thomas Preston (MPL DD#5: 197, and PL#2: 111).

29 May 1711: Thomas Preston of BA Co., planter, conv. to Sarah Skates of BA Co., widow, 135 a. (*) and 95 a. Tower Hill (TR#A: 165).

15 June 1711: James Preston of BA Co., conv. 135 a., being ⅓ of (*) (a 406 a. tract granted to Thomas Preston, father of James) to Thomas Barton of BA Co. (TR#A: 139).

1 June 1714: Thomas Preston of BA Co. conv. 134 a. (*) to Peter Carroll (TR#A: 300).

19 Feb 1716: Thomas Preston of BA Co. conv. 100 a., the remainder of (*) (pt. of 406 a. granted to grantor's father Thomas Preston, Sr.) to John Norris of BA Co. (TR#A: 471).

5 Nov 1741: Thomas Preston conv. 135 a. of (*), being pt. of a 406 a. tract, to John Barton. The deed mentions a bond formerly sold by James Preston, bro. of said Thomas, to Thomas Barton, father of said John. TP's w. Elizabeth cons. (TB#A: 89).

7 March 1743: John Barton conv. to Thomas Elliott 135 a. formerly belonging to his father Thomas Barton, dec. (evidently pt. of a tract owned by Peter Carroll and John Norris). JB's w. Anna cons. (TB#C: 426).

6 Aug 1746: Thomas Elliott conv. 135 a. pt. (*) (bought by Thomas Barton from Thomas Preston) to William Bennett of BA Co., carpenter. Deed states that Abigail Barton should live her life in the old dwelling house, and Thomas Elliott reserves ½ a. for a burying place where Thomas Barton is buried. TE's w. Ann cons. (TB#E: 198).

6 Oct 1746: James Preston of KE Co., s. and heir of Thomas Preston, dec., conv. to Stephen Onion, ironmaster, tract (*), orig. granted to Thomas Preston "the Elder?" grandfather of said James (TB#E: 240).

10 Oct 1746: William Bennett conv. 135 a. pt. (*) to Stephen Onion. Deed states that James Preston had no right to sell it to Thomas Preston to sell it to Thomas Barton; Thomas Preston sold it to Thomas Elliott who sold it to William Bennett for 135⅓ a., except of a ½ a. burying ground where Thomas Barton is buried; Abigail Barton, widow of Thomas, has the right to use the old dwelling house for life (TB#E: 217).

8 March 1748: John Norris of BA Co. conv. to Stephen Onion any iron ore that may be found on (*) or Norris' Venture, now known as Norris' Choice (TR#C: 197).

18 Aug 1748: John Norris of BA Co. conv. to James Norris, after dec. of said John and his w. Ann, parents of said James, pt (*), orig. granted to Thomas Preston, and Norris' Venture. JN's w. Ann cons. (TR#C: 36).

1750: Peter Carroll owned 135 a. (*) and John Norris owned 100 a. (1750 DB).

EXPECTATION (unplaced tracts)

3 March 1742: Rowland Kimble, with cons. of w. Hannah, conv. 100 a. (*) to their s. Samuel; if Samuel d., the land was to go to their s. John, and if he d., to the youngest bro. living (TR#C: 172).

3 March 1742: Rowland Kimble, with cons. of w. Hannah, conv. 50 a. pt. (*) to s. John; if he dies the land is to go to s. Stephen, and if he dies, to the ygst. bro. then living (TB#C: 186).

FALL HILL

100 a. pat. by Arthur Taylor (IR#PP: 83).

2 Aug 1670: Taylor sold it to Richard Winley; also 125 a. being ½ of Taylor's Mount which John Taylor bought from Benjamin Reid; Arthur's w. Margaret cons. (IR#PP: 83).

20 Feb 1670/1 Richard Winley sold (*) to Robert Gates; Winley's w. Mary, "spinster," gave cons., and on 22 Feb 1670/1 gave p/a to John Waterton to acknowledge her cons. (IR#PP: 97).

28 April 1695: Robert Gates by his LWT devised 50 a. to Sarah Spinks and 50 a. to Thomas Litton, Sr. (TB#E: 675).

2 April 1728: Heathcote Pickett ackn. he has sold 50 a. (*) to Benjamin Jones (IS#J: 78).

4 March 1732: Heathcote Pickett and Benjamin Jones conv. 50 a. (*) to Mary Tolley, extx. of Thomas Tolley, dec., and to James Tolley, s. and heir of dec.; land was lately in poss. of William Pickett who devised it to his s. Heathcote (IS#L: 354).

23 Feb 1747: Thomas Litton, s. and heir of Thomas Litton, the Elder, dec., conv. 50 a. (*) (which Robert Gates devised to grantor's father), to Nicholas Ruxton Gay. Litton's w. Ann cons. (TB#E: 675).

20 Aug 1748: Nicholas Ruxton Gay conv. 50 a. (*), (and two other tracts, Litton's Improvement and Speedwell, which Thoams Litton sold to NRG on 3 Feb 1747), to Walter Tolley (TR#C: 69).

FALLS (THE)

29 May 1688: Michael Judd and w. Jane conv. 16 a. (*) to John Fuller. The tract was orig. called Reignall's Rest (RM#HS: 258).

FALMOUTH

1 May 1672: 200 a. pat. by William Salsbury (TR#RA:122).

2 Aug 1673: William Salsbury, planter, and w. Sarah conv. 200 a. (*) (called FAWMOUTH in deed) to William Morgan and William Welsh, on Worton Creek (TR#RA: 122).

FANCY (THE) (See BORING'S FANCY)

1719: 50 a. surv. for James Boring (Index to MPL).

1724 (or 1734): James Boring patents (*) (MPL, EI#8: 288).
11 March 1724: James Boring of BA Co. conv. to James Spicer pt. (*); Boring's w. Jane cons. (IS#H: 49).
18 Feb 1725: James Boring, John Boring and w. Presotia, and William Buckner, conv. (*) to John Spicer (IS#H: 218).
7 July 1746: Juliatha Spicer, widow and extx. of John Spicer conv. 50 a. (*), pat. to James Boring, to Charles Ridgely (TB#E: 169).

FAREALL

4 Aug 1673: John George, planter, conv. 200 a. (*) to Thomas Rumsey; land on w. side of Torson's Creek (TR#RA:109; G#J:149).
3 June 1674: Thomas Rumsey conv. 200 a. (*) to John West (G#J:239).

FARFARR'S FARM

5 Aug 1735: Thomas Harris conv. 100 a. (*) to his grandson William Johnson, s. of William (HWS#M: 281).

FARMER'S FARM

2 March 1708: John Miles conv. 50 a. of (*) and Margaret's Mount to Gregory Farmer (R#HS, 647).
30 Oct 1712: Miles made another deed to Farmer, correcting errors in the first deed after Farmer complained about the errors (TR#A: 124; RM#HS: 647).
27 Nov 1712: Gregory Farmer renounced the previous conveyance because of mistakes in bounds, so Miles made another deed (RM#HS: 647).
3 May 1726: William Brashar and w. Jane conv. 10 a., (*), and 56 a., pt. of Margaret's Mount, to Richard Wells (IS#H: 266).
11 Aug 1730: Richard Wells conv. 10 a. of (*) and 56 a. Margaret's Mount to Robert Hawkins (IS#L: 6).
12 April 1751: Gregory Farmer of BA Co., conv. 40 a., pt. of a 50 a. tract (*) to his s. Samuel (TR#D: 121).

FATHER-IN-LAW'S BOUNTY

15 Sep 1716: John and Mary Miles conv. 62 a. (*), being ½ of Margaret's Mount, to Thomas Litton (TR#A: 449).

FATHER'S REQUEST

7 Aug 1742: Ignatius Gardiner and Richard Gardiner of CH Co. conv. 534 a. (*) to John Lyon of CH Co. IG's w. Ann cons. (TB#A: 244).

FELK'S FOREST

2 Dec 1688: 200 a. surv. for Edward Felkes on the n. side of Back R., and later held by one Harebottle for the orphans of Henry Francis; still later possessed by Hew Merriday (MRR: 64).
17 Nov 1692: Edward Felkes and w. Eleanor conv. 200 a. (*) to Henry Francis (RM#HS: 370).
22 Oct 1740: John Young and w. Eliza of VA, conv. 200 a. (*) to Joseph Thomas (HWS#1-A: 441).

FELK'S RANGE

14 Aug 1688: 200 a. surv. for Edward Felkes on the southwest branch of Gunpowder R., and later possessed by Edward Felkes; still later possessed by Ann Felkes (MRR: 64).
19 June 1738: Edward Pigg of Spottsylvania Co., VA, conv. 200 a. (*) as well as 150 a. Black Wolf Neck and 200 a. Good Hope to Samuel Maxwell (HWS#1-A: 104).
13 Oct 1738: Samuel Maxwell of BA Co., conv. 200 a. (*) and other tracts as above, to Buckler Partridge of BA Co., surgeon (HWS#1-A: 184).
14 June 1740: Samuel Maxwell conv. pt. 200 a. (*) and pt. 150 a. Black Wolf Neck to Walter James. SM's w. Jane cons. (HES#1-A: 396).

FELLOWSHIP (1696)

12 June 1696: 200 a. surv. for John Oldton; later possessed by Edward Stevenson (MRR: 109).
See Horvath Plat: Ruxton and Riderwood.
2 Sep 1702: John Oulton conv. 200 a. (*) to Edward Stevenson, merchant. JO's w. Mary cons. (HW#2: 169).
1750: Edward Stevenson owned 200 a. (1750 DB).
9 June 1760: Edward Stevenson made a will leaving (*) to his sons Henry and Joshua (BAWB 2: 64).

FELLOWSHIP

(May be more than one tract)

11 June 1726: Luke Raven, Sr., conv. 300 a. (*) to s. Abraham and all heirs male of his body; failing heirs, land to pass to other male heirs of grantor (IS#H: 268).
2 June 1773: William Cromwell and w. Elizabeth conv. (*), Gay's Good Fellowship, and Venture Not to dau. Catherine Risteau (AL#G: 400).

FELLOWSHIP, ADDITION TO

2 March 1735: Edward Stevenson conv. 202 a. (*) to his bro. Henry Stevenson. (HWS#M: 384).

FELLOWSHIP, RESURVEY ON

1745: 394 a. surv. for Abraham Raven.
See PW Plat H.

FELL'S FOREST

23 Aug 1740: William Wright made a will leaving 200 a. (*) to his sons Abraham and Isaac (MCW#VIII: 103).

FELL'S FOREEST

1745/62: 500 A. surv. for Edw. Fell.

See Horvath Plats: Randallstown and Granite.

29 May 1767: Thomas Bond and Ann Fell, extx. of Edward Fell, conv. (*) to Susanna Bond, relict of William Bond and her dau. Catherine Bond (B#P: 565).

FERRY POINT

6 Nov 1731: Jacob Giles agreed to lease 45 a. (*), now in possession of John Giles, to Thomas Woodward, cooper (IS#L: 218).

FERRY'S RANGE

15 Nov 1697: 280 a. surv. for John Ferry; later 110 a. in poss. of John Shields, and 170 a. in poss. of James Boaring (MRR).

24 Aug 1704: John Boreing and w. Mary conv. 100 a. to Henry Shields (HW#2: 360).

13 Jan 1707: John Boring of BA Co. and w. Sarah sell 189 a. to Alexander Lawson 109 a. (HWS#1-A: 48).

18 Feb 1725: John Boring and w. Pretiosa, and James Boring and w. Jane conv. 50 a. Boring's Pasture, 50 a. Boring's Range, and 80 a. Swan Harbor, and 189 a. pt. Ferry Range to William Buckner (IS#H: 218).

30 Aug 1735: Thomas Buckner of VA conv. 189 a. pt. (*) to John Boring of BA Co. (HWS#M: 294).

6 Oct 1747: Solomon Shields conv. bond he will conv. pt. (*) to William Barney (BB#I: 10).

19 Oct 1761: Philip Shields, s. and heir of Solomon Shields, dec., with cons. of (Philip's) w. Rachel, conv. 50 a. pt. of (*) (which had been conv. to Henry Shields, grandfather of Philip) to Jacob Sindall (B#I: 385).

FEWGATES FORK

14 Sep 1683: 300 a. surv. for (N) Fewgate on a branch of Swan Creek; later Fewgate was noted as having run away into VA, and no heirs having appeared (MRR: 17).

FEW'S INDUSTRY

10 Feb 1745: Benjamin Tasker, Agent for the Lord Proprietary, leased to William Few 30 a. (*), pt. of His Lordship's Reserve (TR#C: 202).

17 June 1749: William Few conv. 30 a. (*) to Donn Connelly (TR#C: 219).

FILIAL CARE

12 July 1739: 50 a. pat. to William Andrews (MPL EI#5: 353, EI#6: 73).

30 Sep 1742: William Ambrose [Andrews?], innholder, and w. Mary conv. 50 a. (*) to William Bond (TB#C F: 177).

1750 Capt. William Bond owns 50 a. (*) (1750 DB: 76).

FINCHES (THE) (Pt. of COLE'S HARBOR)

25 June 1709: John Ensor of BA Co. conv. bond to Grace Ramsey, widow of BA Co., he will conv. to her 100 a. (*), pt. of tract formerly belonging to John Cole (TR#A: 120).

25 April 1710: Richard Owens of BA Co., merchant, gave p/a to John Hurst to conv. 100 a. (*) to Henry Knowles (TR#A: 111).

30 Dec 1710: Henry Knowles, with cons. of w. Katherine, conv. 100 a. (*) (pt. of Cole's Harbor), to Nicholas Rogers (TR#A: 114).

FINEGAL

20 Oct 1740: Michael Taylor of PG Co., Gent., prisoner in PG Co. Jail, conv. 675 a. Finegal (which was granted to Taylor by a special warrant of escheat), 200 a. Scrutiny Conveniency (pt. of Elizabeth's Delight) (in PG Co.), 260 a. Skipton in Craven, and 380 a. Scrutiny to John Hepburn, High Sheriff of PG Co. (TB#E: 374).

FITCH'S CHOICE

10 April 1773: William Fitch of BA Co., conv. 133 a., pt. (*) to Richard Fowler. WF's w. Sarah cons. (AL#G: 159).

FOLLY

13 April 1670: Joseph Langley conv. to Joseph Hopkins, Gent., 250 a., pt. (*) which was 400 a. in all, and taken up by Richard Bennett, dec. (IR#PP: 83).

FOOD PLENTY

25 April 1717: 160 a. pat. to William Baker (MPL FF#7: 176, PL#4: 298).

See KN Plat WO; Horvath Plat: Granite.

21 Feb 1742: William Baker of BA Co. conv. 150 a. (*) to George Buchanan. WB's w. Ann cons. (TB#C, 248).

FORBEARANCE

23 Aug 1726: George Yate of BA Co. conv. 144 a. (*) and 400 a. Yates Contrivance to Col. Thomas Cockey. The land desc. to the grantor by virtue of his being the eld. s. and heir of his father George, per the latter's will, or by the deaths of his younger bros. before they reached the age of 21 (IS#H: 281).

FORBEARANCE, ADDITION TO

1 Oct 1737: Emanuel Teale, with cons. of w. Katherine, conv. 54 a. (*) to John Moale (HWS#1-A: 21).

20 March 1758: Emanuel Teale conv. 54 a. (*) to Edward Norwood (B#G: 140).

FORBERRY NECK

11 Nov 1694: John Bevans of Gunpowder R. and w. Sarah conv. 210 a. Midsummer Hill and 180 a. (*) to Frances Dallahide and w. Providence of AA Co. (RM#HS: 442).

14 June 1741: Barnet Bond of BA Co., mariner, conv. 201 a. Midsummer Hill and 180 a. (*) to William Bond (HWS#1-A: 514).

FORD'S CHOICE (Pt. SELSED)

See Horvath Plat: Ruxton and Riderwood.

22 Jan 1718: John Boring of BA Co. conv. 202 a. pt. Selsed, now called Ford's Chance, to Thomas Ford. JB's w. Pretiosa cons. (TR#RA: 524).

20 May 1745: John Boring of BA Conv. 202 a. *, now called (*), to Thomas Ford. JB's w. Sarah cons. (TB#D: 298-299).

FORD'S FANCY

4 April 1747: Thomas Ford, Sr., of BA Co., conv. 60 a. (*) to Alexander Lawson (TB#E: 520).

FORD'S FOLLY

1 May 1762: Thomas Ford assigned the lease of (*) to Benjamin Barney (B#H: 129).

19 Nov 1763: Thomas Ford conv. (*) to William Lux of Baltimore Town (B#M: 111).

FOREST (THE) (1672)

16 Sep 1672: 100 a. surv. for Charles Gorsuch on the w. side of Back R., and later possessed by Isaac Sampson (MRR: 91).

15 April 1679: Charles Gorsuch of TA Co. conv. to Thomas James 100 a (*) on w. side of Back R. 8 Feb 1678/9: Sarah Gorsuch conv. letter of atty. to cousin Miles Gibson to acknowledge sale of 80 a. to John Boren and 100 a. to Thomas James (IR#PP: 30, 31).

25 July 1687: Thomas James conv. 100 a. (*) to Richard Sampson. Sarah James cons. (RM#HS: 277).

8 Feb 1728/9: Isaac Sampson conv. to Luke Stansbury 100 a. (*), 100 a. Sampson's Addition, and 26½ a. Sampson's Angle (IS#I: 284).

5 June 1733: Luke Stansbury, merchant, with cons. of w. Jane, conv. to Samuel Maxfield 100 a. (*), 100 a. Sampson's Addition, and 26½ a. Sampson's Angle (IS#L: 376).

FOREST (THE) (1678)

23 March 1678: 1000 a. surv. for Thomas Taylor on the n. side of Patapsco R.; later 900 a. possessed by William Chew and 900 a. by Col. Edward Dorsey (MRR: 74).

See PW Plat G.

FOREST (THE)

16 April 1687; William Deane appointed Robert Benjer his atty. to recover debts and give receipts (RM#HS: 230).

7 June 1687: Edward Douse and w. Elizabeth, and Emanuel Ceely and w. Sarah conv. to William Deane of KE Co., 200 a. (*) at head of Saltpeter Creek. Douse and Ceely gave bond to William Deane they would perform the covenants (RM#HS: 233).

10 Sep 1741: William Worthington conv. (*) to Benjamin Long and Neal Haile (TB#A: 1).

9 March 1746: Benjamin Long conv. to Joseph Taylor and Sarah Fell pt. (*), orig. granted to Long and Haile (TB#E: 410).

FORK (THE)

4 Sep 1683: 150 a. surv. for James Phillips, on e. side of Bush R.; now in poss. of Edward Weildy (MRR: 9).

23 March 1699: James Phillips and w. Bethia conv. 150 a. (*) to Edward Weildy (IS#IK: 258).

29 Oct 1725: John Powell and w. Phillis conv. 150 a. (*) to Solomon Armstrong (IS#H: betw. 196 and 200).

3 June 1731: John Powell of BA Co., tailor, makes good the deed to Solomon Armstrong dated 29 Oct 1725 (IS#L: 108).

3 June 1731: Solomon Armstrong and w. Mary conv. 150 a. (*) to Thomas White. Tract was granted to James Phillips, dec.; transferred on 23 March 1699 by James Phillips, Jr. (now also dec.) s. of James, to Edward Wild, who by his LWT it decended to Phillis Temple who m. John Powell (IS#L: 110).

FORSEBERRY NECK

10 July 1676: 180 a. surv. for William Ebden on s. side of Gunpowder R.; later possessed by Francis Dallahide, the later by Thomas Frisby of CE Co. (MRR: 35).

1 Aug 1683: William Ebden and w. Elizabeth conv. 47½ a. (*) to William Galloway (IR#AM: 89).

11 Nov 1694: John Bevens and w. Sarah conv. 180 a. (*) and 210 a. Midsummer Hill to Francis Dallahide and w. Providence of AA Co. (RM#HS: 442).

3 April 1734: Peregrine Frisby conv. 180 a. (*) and 210 a. Midsummer Hill to William Bond (HWS#M: 43).

14 June 1741: Barnet Bond of BA Co. conv. mariner, conv. 180 a. (*) and 201 a. Midsummer Hill to William Bond (HWS#1-A: 514).

1750: Capt. William Bond owned 180 a. (*), as well as other lands (1750 DB: 76).

FORTUNE

12 Sep 1685: Thomas Lightfoot conv. 300 a. (*) and 100 a. Winlies Forest to Benjamin Williams (RM#HS: 156).

9 May 1717: Benjamin Williams of AA Co., with cons. of w. Margaret, conv. 295 a. (*) and 100 a. Windleys Forest to Edward Ward of AA Co. (TR#A: 457).

FORTUNE (1715)

10 Dec 1715: 295 a. surv. (TB#C: 668).

9 Jan 1744: Lemuel Howard and w. Ann conv. 295 a. (*) and 50 a. pt. Windley's Forest to Stephen Onion (TB#C: 668).

FOSTER'S NECK
(Also called GOLDSMITH'S NECK)

24 Feb 1661: Tract pat. by Matthew Goldsmith and Edward Foster, who later conv. it to Richard Winley and James Phillips (IR#PP: 56; RM#HS: 553).

8 Nov 1666: Richard Winley and James Phillips conv. to Francis Trippas 200 a. at (*) in Gunpowder R., not far from John Taylor's plantation (IR#PP: 62).

5 June 1707: John Boone and w. Jane conv. 200 a. (*) to John Ewings (RM#HS: 553).

20 Nov 1708: John Ewing and w. Elizabeth conv. 200 a. (*) and 14 a. Arthur's Delay to John Roberts (RM#HS: 616).

FOUNTAIN OF FRIENDSHIP

22 July 1749: George Turnbull, carpenter, conv. 40 a. (*) to Richard Jack. GT's w. Grace cons. (TR#C: 248).

FOWLER'S CHANCE

5 Jan 1696/7: 98 a. surv. for Joshua Fowler near Bush R. (MRR#II: 316).

2 June 1718: Joseph Fowler conv. 98 a. (*) to Samuel Hughes (MRR#II; TR#RA: 413).

5 March 1720: Samuel Hughes and w. Jane conv. (*) to Joshua Fowler (MRR#II; IS#G: 20).

12 Feb 1731/2: James Fowler, 2nd s. of Joshua Fowler, late of BA Co., dec., and eld. bro. of Joshua Fowler, Jr., conv. 98 a. (*) to Thomas White. James' w. Margaret cons. (IS#L: 188).

FOX HALL (c1670)
(See EVANS' BEGINNING)

19 Oct 1670: Richard Whitton, planter, conv. 50 a. (*) to John Masters, at Gunpowder R.; adj. land taken up by William Wegnall (IR#PP: 90).

7 Feb 1673/4: John Masters, planter, of Gunpowder R., conv. 50 a. (*) to John Waterton; tract was pat. by Richard Whitton and sold by him to Masters. Seisin given by twig and turf on 10 Feb 1673/4. 3 March 1673/4 Sheriff Thomas Carleton received 1 shilling for alienation from Dr. John Waterton. 7 Feb 1673/4: John Masters appointed John Rudge his atty. to acknowledge sale of land (G#J: 228).

4 June 1706: Thomas Reed and Thomas Ridge of Newport, Isle of Wight, Southampton, England, execs. of John Waterton, conv. 50 a. (*) to William Peckett (IR#AM: 43).

6 Aug 1723: George Reade, atty. for Thomas Reade and Thomas Rudge of Newport, Isle of Wight, conv. 50 a. (*) to John Dorsey (IS#G: 179).

25 Nov 1726: John Dorsey of BA Co., Gent., conv. 50 a. (*), 50 a. Wee Bitt, and 200 a. Wignall's Rest, to James Durham (IS#H: 284).

2 April 1728: Heathcote Pickett conv. 50 a. (*) and $6\frac{1}{4}$ a. Waterton's Neglect to his sister Elizabeth now w. of Benjamin Jones. Tracts had been in poss. of William Pickett who devised them to his sons William and Heathcote (IS#J: 64).

3 March 1735: Benjamin Jones conv. 50 a. (*) and $6\frac{1}{4}$ a. Waterton's Neglect to Thomas Franklin. No w. (HWS#M: 409).

14 May 1745: Thomas Franklin conv. 46 a. pt. (*) to John Hammond Dorsey (TB#D: 368).

FOX HALL (1695)

10 Nov 1695: 200 a. in BA Co. pat. by Stephen Benson of TA Co. (MPL 34:80, 40:66).

FOX HALL (1724)

10 July 1724: 100 a. pat. by Thomas Taylor (MPL PL#6: 306, IL#A: 193).

19 May 1724: Thomas Taylor and w. Elizabeth conv. to Philip Smith: 100 a. Fox Hall, 100 a. Rich Level, and 50 a. Cold Comfort (IS#G: 318).

FOX HALL (Unplaced)

8 April 1712: George Hadaway, Sr., of KE Co., and w. Sarah conv. 200 a. (*) to John Bond of London, mariner. On 12 April 1717 Sarah Hadaway gave p/a to Nicholas Lurty, to acknowledge sale TR#A: 187).

19 March 1727/8: John Bond of London, mariner, by Christopher Randall, Sr., his atty., conv. 500 a. (*) to Job Evans (*) (IS#I: 202).

FRANCIS CHOICE

5 March 1699: Francis Dallahide and w. Sarah of BA Co., for 5000 lbs. tob., conv. 200 a. (*) to Thomas Cockey of AA Co. (HW#2: 10).

FRANCIS' DELIGHT

Nov 1716: 100 a. surv. for John Mackeldory (Card Index to Patents).

21 Oct 1718: Pat. to said JM (IS#H: 153).

20 July 1725: John Muckeldory of BA Co. conv. 100 a. (*) to Benjamin Wheeler. JM's w. Frances cons. (IS#H: 153).

7 June 1732: Benjamin Wheeler conv. (*) to Thomas Bond. BW's w. Elizabeth cons. (IS#I, 241).

24 July 1746: Thomas Bond conv. (*) and other lands to s. Thomas Bond, Jr. (TB#E: 112).

26 Nov 1751: Thomas Bond conv. to Edward Mattingly 100 a. (*), 210 a. Bond's Choice, 109 a. Bond's Beginnings, 122 a. Good Neighbor, and 56 a. pt. Bond's Fortune. TB's w. (unnamed) cons. (TR#D: 257).

FRANCIS' FREEDOM

1697: 1000 a. surv. for Samuel Young.

See PW Plat G.

FRANKFORT

1750: Thomas Brasher owned 54 a. (1750 DB).

FRANKLIN'S BEGINNING AND NANCY'S ENDING

6 March 1728/9: Thomas Franklin conv. 120 a. (*) to John Standiford (IS#K: 4).

FRANKLIN'S CHANCE

1730: Thomas Franklin conv. 100 a. (*) to John Summer (IS#K: 308).

FRANKLIN'S GIFT

7 June 1732: Thomas Franklin conv. 100 a. (*) being pt. of Long Crandon in the Hill, taken up by TF, to John Rutledge (IS#L: 252).

9 Sep 1747: John Rutledge and w. Jane conv. 100 a. (*) to John Wilmot, Jr. (TB#E: 560).

FRANKLIN'S PURCHASE

28 Oct 1748: Charles Carroll conv. Luke's Good Will, 111 a., and Parishes Neglect, 58 a., and (*), 685 a. (TR#C: 115).

7 Feb 1752: Thomas Stansbury, Jr., conv. to Edmund Stansbury 44 a. Franklin's Purchase. TS' Jr.'s w. Hannah cons. (TR#D: 280).

FRATERNITY

6 Nov 1739: John Hall and w. Hannah conv. 152 a. (*) to Thomas White (HWS#1-A: 301).

Dec 1739: Thomas White, with cons. of w. Sophia, conv. 152 a. (*) (granted to John Hall), and 93 a. pt. Leafe, Jr., to James Phillips (HWS#1-A: 338).

FRAZIER'S ROCK RIDGE

26 May 1743: leased by Benjamin Tasker to John Frazier (TB#E: 14).

5 March 1745: John Frazier leased (*) to Charles Bosley (TB#E: 14).

FREEBORNE'S PROGRESS

13 May 1723: Robert Ridgely of BA Co., conv. 520 a., being $\frac{1}{2}$ of 1040 a. (*) to Thomas Wainwright; tract had been laid out for Thomas Freeborne of AA Co., dec. RR's w. Sarah cons. (IS#G: 155).

FREE GIFT

150 a. surv. for Resurvey from Samuel's Hope.

See Horvath Plat: Ruxton and Riderwood.

28 Feb 1718/9: Thomas Hooker and w. Eleanor, conv. 150 a. (*), being pt. of Samuel's Hope, to s. Samuel (TR#RA: 528).

FREELAND'S MOUNT

2 Aug 1715: George Freeland and w. Mary conv. 50 a. (*) to William Jenkins (TR#A: 343).

2 Aug 1715: George Freeland and w. Mary conv. 75 a. Johnson's Folly, being pt. of (*), to Thomas Johnson (TR#A: 345).

1 March 1719: George Freeland and w. Mary conv. 38 a. pt. 300 a. (*) to Thomas Johnson (TR#DS: 165).

3 March 1719: John Freeland conv. 150 a. (*) to George Freeland (TR#DS: 168).

16 Feb 1724: George Freeland of CE Co., planter, conv. 100 a. pt. (*) to Thomas Johnson of BA Co., sawyer (IS#H: 47).

16 Feb 1724: George Freeland of CE Co., planter, conv. 50 a. (*) to Richard Touchstone, weaver (IS#H: 44).

16 Feb 1724: Richard Touchstone conv. 50 a. (*) to Alexander Urquhart (IS#H: 51).

5 March 1760: William Urquhart conv. 50 a. (*) to Thomas Allender, hammerman (B#H: 114).

FREEMAN'S MOUNT

17 June 1749: Benjamin Goodwin of BA Co. conv. 50 a. (*) to Thomas Allender, hammerman (TR#C: 265).

FRENCH PLANTATION

22 Jan 1673: 100 a. surv. for Peter Fewcate at head of Cat Hole Creek; later possessed by Thomas Cord (MRR: 10).

1 April 1727: Thomas Cord conv. bond to Abraham Cord he will let Abraham occupy the designated pt. of Cord's Purchase, French Plantation, and

Peter's Addition, which they inher. from their father Thomas Cord, and which they have divided (IS#H: 402).

1 April 1727: Abraham Cord conv. bond to Thoams Cord he will guarantee the right of TC to occupy the specified half of land bequeathed them by their father Thomas Cord (IS#I: 58).

2 Nov 1743: Abraham Cord leased pt. Cord's Purchase, pt. (*), 19 a. Ten Pound Purchase, and pt. (*) to Abraham Taylor (TB#C: 365).

FRENCHES BEDFORD

2 Aug 1749: Benjamin Wheeler conv. 45 a. (*) to John Bull. BW's w. Elizabeth cons. (TR#C: 253).

FRENCHMAN'S REPOSE

Sep 1717: Surv. for Lewis Demoss (Card Index to Patents).

6 Nov 1735: Lewis Demoss, Jr., late of BA Co., conv. 69 a. (*) to William Grafton (HWS#M: 330).

FRIENDLY PURCHASE

1744/45: Surv. for Dorsey Peddicoat.

See Horvath Plat: Granite.

30 March 1751: Dorsey Peddicord and w. Sarah, conv. 140 a. (*) to John Randall, shipwright (TR#D: 132).

FRIEND'S ADVICE

c1754: Samuel Durham owned pt. Edmund's Camp; Bilbury Hall; Durham's First Addition to D'o; D'o Second Addition to D'o; D'o Third Addition to Do'o; pt. Edwin's Contrivance, and Friend's Advice (IBC: 63).

FRIEND'S DELIGHT

3 March 1747: Dutton Land conv. 1 a. (*), pt. of Pork Hall, to Samuel Hooker and Thomas Matthews (TB#E: 672).

FRIENDS DISCOVERY (1694)

13 June 1694: 1000 a. surv. for Job Evans on a ridge by a branch of the Herring Run; later possessed by Francis Mauldin; still later possessed by Francis Mauldin (MRR: 81; MPL B#23:313, 314).

25 Feb 1699: Job Evans conv. 1000 a. (*) to Francis Mauldin (TR#DS: 51).

c1704: Undated petition of Edward Stevenson concerning boundary trees of (*) and other lands (HW#2: 342).

14 Jan 1710: Francis Mauldin made a will leaving 1000 a. (*) to his sons William and James (MCW#III: 187).

25 July 1719: William Mauldin of CV Co. conv. 500 a. (*) to Gerard Hopkins of AA Co. (TR#DS: 51).

25 July 1719: James Mauldin of CV Co., Gent., conv. 500 a. (*) to Nathaniel Giles (TR#DS: 79).

7 Oct 1721: Nathaniel Giles conv. bond to Gerard Hopkins to divide (*), which they purch. from William and James Mauldin; same date the actual agreement to divide was made (RM#HS: 672, 673).

Dec 1722: Nathan(iel) Giles conv. 200 a., being "half" of the portion he bought from James Mauldin, to Gerard Hopkins (IS#G: 64).

5 Nov 1736: Nathaniel and John Giles of BA Co. conv. 390 a. (*) to Thomas Taylor. JG's w. Sarah cons. (IS#IK: 424).

14 June 1737: Thomas Taylor of BA Co. conv. 400 a. Bachelor's Fancy, being pt. of Friend's Discovery, to Henry Morgan (HWS#1-A: 20).

27 Sep 1746: Henry Morgan mortgaged 390 a. (*) and other lands to Christopher Grindall (TB#E: 182).

FRIENDS DISCOVERY (1703)

c1703: 500 a. pat. to Richard Colegate (MPL WD:493).

5 Nov 1737: George and Patience Elliott conv. 500 a. (*) to Benjamin Wheeler (HWS#1-A: 35).

25 Nov 1740: Benj. Wheeler, Sr., conv. 500 a. (*), granted 20 May 1705 to Col. Richard Colegate, to Benjamin Colegate (HWS#1-A: 453).

FRIENDS DISCOVERY (1737)

c1737: 100 a. surv. for or pat. to Lewis Igoe (MPL EI#5:218 and EI#2:665).

See Horvath Plats: Green Spring Valley and Owings Mills.

FRIENDS' ENLARGEMENT

16 Oct 1705: Thomas Hammond and w. Rebecca give p/a to Francis Dallahide to acknowledge their conv. of 100 a. (*) to John Webster, being pt. of Best Endeavor (IR#PP: 195).

FRIENDSHIP (THE) (1670)

20 Dec 1670: 100 a. surv. for Robert Benjer and Thomas Pert on the northeast side of the Falls of the Northwest Branch; later possessed by Alexander Graves who was reported to have run away (MRR: 110).

c1671: 100 a. pat. to Robert Benjer and Thomas Pert (MPL 16:157, 253).

FRIENDSHIP (1684)

10 May 1684: 600 a. surv. for William Harris on the w. side of Susquehanna R., adj. land called

Canaan; later supposed to belong to the heirs of Harris (MRR: 17).

20 July 1738: John Dorrumple and w. Eleanor of CV Co. conv. 200 a. pt. (*) to Benjamin Ellt of CV Co.; Eleanor is dau. of William Harris of CV Co. who owned 600 a. (*) and left 200 a. to dau. Eleanor, and 400 a. (*) to s. William and then to Richard Harris (HWS#1-A: 123).

24 April 1750: George Howard of CV Co. conv. 200 a. (*) to Jacob Giles of BA Co., Gent. William Harris of CV Co., d. owning (*), which he left by will to his dau. Elinor who later m. John Derumple. Derumple sold the land on 20 July 1738 to Benjamin Elt. Now GH conv. all 200 a. GH's w. Margaret cons. (TR#D: 1).

FRIENDSHIP (1685)

7 May 1685: 400 a. surv. for Michael Judd on the n. side of Gunpowder; later poss. by William Hicks (MRR: 55).

FRIENDSHIP (1692)

10 Oct 1691: Cert. of surv., for 400 a. (*) laid out by Thomas Richardson; possessed by Michael Judd (RM#HS: 423).

6 June 1693: Michael Judd and w. Jane conv. 200 a. pt. (*) to William Hicks (RM#HS: 373).

24 Feb 1696: Michael Judd and w. Jane conv. 200 a., residue of (*) to William Hicks (IS#IK: 373).

27 Dec 1719: James Hicks of BA Co. conv. 100 a. (*) (which he had inher. from his father William) to John Chapman (TR#DS: 38).

9 Aug 1722: Nehemiah Hicks of BA Co. conv. to John Rattenbury, s. of John (*) (which NH had inher. from his father William, late of Gunpowder Neck, dec.) (IS#G: 29).

14 March 1723: John Chapman of BA Co. conv. 100 a. pt. (*) (which James Hicks sold to JC in 1719) to George Buchanan. JC's w. Ann cons. (IS#G: 280).

3 March 1724: Henry Hicks, s. of William, conv. 100 a. (*), which he inher. from his father, to George Buchanan (IS#H: 56).

1 May 1724: George Buchanan conv. 100 a. pt. (*) to Benjamin Jones (IS#G: 309).

3 Aug 1726: George Buchanan conv. another 100 a. (*) to Benjamin Jones. GB's w. Eleanor cons. (IS#H: 277).

1729: Benjamin Jones conv. 200 a. pt. (*) to William and John Copeland (IS#K: 249).

14 May 1730: William Hicks of KE Co. on DE, eld. s. of William Hicks, dec., conv. 400 a. (*) (100 a. of which is free of encumbrances) to Eric Erickson (IS#K: 296).

15 July 1732: Erick Erickson of BA Co., carpenter, conv. 400 a. (*) to William and John Copeland. EE's w. Mary cons. The deed stated that Michael Judd surv. the tract on 7 May 1689; MJ later conv. it to William Hicks, who conv. it to his sons James, Nehemiah, and Henry, all of whom are dead, and William, who sold it to EE on 14 May 1730 (IS#L: 284).

5 June 1734: George Buchanan conv. bond he will save Benjamin Jones harmless from his sale of ½ of (*) to William and John Copeland (HWS#M: 77).

19 Oct 1749: William Copeland of BA Co. conv. to John Timmons, weaver, 400 a. (*), orig. on 7 May 1689 granted to Michael Judd, who conv. it to William Hicks, who devised it by will to his sons William, James, Nehemiah, and Henry; the tract devolved upon the eld s. William Hicks, who on 14 May 1730 sold it to Erick Erickson, who on 15 July 1732 sold it to William and John Copeland. WC's w. Jane cons. (TR#C: 284).

FRIENDSHIP (1697)

15 June 1697: 1000 a. surv. for Robert Lockwood, on a point on the e. side of Bush R.; later poss. by John Wilson of AA Co.; still later held by the heirs of John Wilson (MRR: 15).

28 Oct 1687: Robert Lockwood, planter of AA Co., conv. 1000 a. (*) to John Wilson; deed states the tract had been pat. 1 July 1685 [sic]; Lockwood's w. Elizabeth cons. (RM#HS: 242).

9 May 1718: William Wilson conv. 300 a. (*) to James Lee; w. Rachel cons. (TR#RA: 511).

23 Jan 1722: William Wilson, guardian and heir of John Wilson, both of AA Co., conv. (*) to William Holland, except for 300 a. sold to James [Lee] (IS#G: 176).

5 Sep 1732: James Lee, Sr., conv. 300 a. (*) to Isaac Webster (IS#L: 296).

13 Feb, 1745: Capt. William Holland of CV Co., Gent., conv. upper pt. of 700 a. pt. (*) to Isaac Webster; tract was bought by Col. William Holland from William Wilson, and devised by Wm. Holland to his s. Francis Holland, against whom an (exeat?) was filed by afsd. Capt. William Holland (TB#E: 28).

22 Feb 1745: Francis Holland, s. of Francis, grants title to (*), and Creed's Beginning and Miles' Forest, to quiet the title of William Holland to Isaac Webster. FH's w. Cordelia cons. (TB#E: 25).

FRIENDSHIP (1727)

1727: 250 a. surv. for Thomas Bond et al. (BA Cert. 562).

FRIENDSHIP (1733)

1733: 600 a. granted to William Rogers (Penniman and Waring Land Grants in MDG 13:27; MPL AM#1: 356; EI#1: 58).

See Horvath Plat: Green Spring Valley.
4 Sep 1734: Edward Stevenson and William Rogers conv. 50 a. pt. (*), orig, granted to William Rogers, to John Osborn (HWS#M: 120).
4 Sep 1734: same grantors conv. 130 a., pt. (*), to John Bond of Peter (HWS#M: 121).
20 April 1737: William Rogers and w. Sarah conv. 120 a. pt. (*) to Thomas Gorsuch (IS#IK: 402).
10 Dec 1738: William Rogers of BA Co., innkeeper, and w. Sarah, conv. 100 a. pt. (*) to Samuel Underwood (HWS#1-A: 344).
7 March 1739: William Rogers, innkeeper, conv. 90 a. pt. (*) to John Chilcoat (HWS#1-A: 361).
7 Jan 1744: John Chilcoat of BA Co. conv. 90 a. (*) and other land to John Pindall (TB#D: 29).
12 March 1746: William Rogers of BA Co., innholder, conv. 105 a. pt. (*) to Samuel Fort. WR's w. Sarah cons. (TB#E: 381).
30 Aug 1746: John Osborn and Edward and Susanna Stevenson conv. 50 a. (*) to James Kelley (TB#E: 208).
6 Nov 1752: Edward Choate and w. Elizabeth, dau. of Samuel Underwood, conv. 50 a. (*) to John Ford (TR#D: 451).
24 Oct 1753: Mary Underwood, widow of Samuel, Samuel Underwood, s. of Samuel, and Elizabeth, dau. of Samuel and now w. of Edward Choate, Jr., conv. pt. (*) to John Ford (BB#I: 145).

FRIENDSHIP (1746)

1746: 120 a. surv. for Benjamin Wheeler (BA Cert. 559).

FRIENDSHIP (1747)

1747: 50 a. surv. for or pat. to William Roberts (MPL LG#C: 697, and BT&BY#3: 270).

FRIENDSHIP (1752)

1752: 1913 a. surv. for Andrew Scott (BA Cert. 561).

FRIENDSHIP (1753)

c1753: 50 a. surv. for or pat. to Thomas Story (MPL GS#1:246, Y&S#8:643).

FRIENDSHIP. (Pt. of DARLEY HALL)

15 Dec 1713: John Ensor conv. (*), pt. of a larger tract called Darley Hall, to Richard Taylor (TR#A: 277).

FRIENDSHIP
(unplaced tracts named Friendship)

4 Nov 1731: John Fuller of BA Co. conv. 180 a. (*) to James Isham (IS#L: 161).
4 Aug 1757: John Travis, with cons. of w. Nancy, conv. 400 a. (*) to Thomas Sligh (B#G: 27).
24 June 1783: Thomas Story of BA Co. conv. to Richard Richards 50 a. (*) and Story's Addition (WG#O: 129).

FRIENDSHIP ADDITION

5 Sep 1732: James Lee conv. (*) to Isaac Webster (IS#L: 297).

FRIENDSHIP, ADDITION TO

1703: 202 a. surv. for Edward Stevenson (Stevenson Gen.)
A tract of this name is shown on PW Plat W.
2 March 1735: Edward Stevenson conv. 202 a. (*) to his bro. Henry Stevenson (HWS#M: 384).
1750: Henry Stevenson owned 202 a. (1750 DB:)

FRIENDSHIP, ADDITION TO

4 Aug 1750: John Robertson of BA Co. conv. 26 a. (*) to Susanna Bramwell, widow and extx. of Samuel Fort. JR's w. Elizabeth cons. (TR#C: 532).

FRIZZELL'S PURCHASE

1701: Lewis Duvall conv. 53 a. Frizzell's Purchase (pt. of Middle Plantation) to James Frizzell (AALR WT#1: 184-187).

FROGMORTON

27 March 1694: Hendrick Cornelius and w. Eliza of Middle R.,m give p/a to William Wright to alienate tract (*) to Samuel Smith of Biddeford, Co. Devon (RM#HS: 430).
23 April 1694: HC and w. Elizabeth conv. 53 a. (*) to Samuel Smith (RM#HS: 515).

FRUGALITY

See Horvath Plat: Old Hampstead.
9 Sep 1758: Richard Richards, yeoman, conv. 50 a. (*) to John Deane (B#G: 233).

FULLER'S FOREST

20 March 1720: Ebenezer Cooke of CE Co., Gent., leased (*) to John Fuller for the lifetimes of John Fuller and his sons Henry and Nehemia (RM#HS: 668).

FULLER'S OUTLET

11 Jan 1665: 100 a. surv. for John Fuller; later held by William Wright (MRR: 68).
20 May 1688: John Fuller and w. Easter of BA Co. conv. 100 a. (*) to Robert Benger, cordwainer (RM#HS: 276).
6 Nov 1691: Robert Benger and w. Deborah of BA Co., conv. (*) to William Wright (RM#HS: 333).
9 June 1738: Solomon Wright of BA Co. conv. (*) to William Wright (HWS#1-A: 81).

23 Aug 1740: William Wright made a will leaving 100 a. (*) to his s. William (MCW#VIII: 103).
4 March 1756: William Wright conv. 100 a. (*) to William Andrew (BB#I: 553).

GALLIER'S BAY

24 March 1665: 100 a. surv. for Joseph Gallion on the s. side of Bush R. in Erbie Creek; later sold to Edward Gunnell, who left it to his bro. George, who sold it to James Mills, who sold it to James Phillips; now in the possession of John Hall (MRR: 30).
6 Feb 1676/7: Joseph Gallion, planter, and w. Sarah, for 4500 lbs. tobacco, conv. 100 a. (*) to Edward Gunnell at Heart's Creek, s. side of Bush R. Gallion's w. Sarah gave her cons. to the sale (IR#PP: 4).
4 April 1682: James Phillips, innholder, and w. Susannah conv. 100 a. (*) to Cornelius Boyce, cooper; tract was on Earle creek on the s. side of Bush R., The tract would revert to the grantor if the grantee did not pay the purchase price. Susannah Phillips gave cons. before Capt. Henry Johnson. On the same day, Phillips conv. bond for the performance of the covenants (IR#AM: 165).
2 July 1685: George Gunnell of Allemack Co., NC, conv. to James Mills 100 a. Galliarbe, formerly belonging to Joseph Gallion, and sold by him to Edward Gunnell, bro. of the grantor (RM#HS: 175).
6 June 1687: James Mills conv. to James Phillips his interest in the 100 a. tract Galliarbe, which formerly belonged to Joseph Gallion, and later to said George Gunnell (RM#HS: 227).
12 Dec 1691: George Gunnell, chirurgeon, heir and admin. of Edward Gunnell, conv. to Cornelius Boyce 100 a. Gallard's Bay, which was once sold by Joseph Gallion to Edward Gunnell, dec. (RM#HS: 336).
2 Sep 1696: Cornelius Boyce, s. and heir of Cornelius Boyce, late of BA Co., dec., conv. 100 a. (*) (which George Gunnell had conv. to Cornelius Boyce, Sr.) to Michael Judd (IS#IK: 129).
6 Aug 1700: James Phillips and w. Bethia conv. 100 a. (*) to John Hall (HW#2: 18).
8 June 1710 (?): John Hall and w. Martha conv. 100 a. (*) and 150 a. Bushey Wood to James Maxwell (TR#DS: 86).

GALLION'S ADDITION

13 Dec 1732: John Gallion of BA, planter, eld. s. of JG, dec., conv. to James, Thomas, Solomon, Samuel, Henry, and Joseph Gallion, all devisees of JG, dec., their share of the lands, including (*), devised to them by the said JG (IS#L: 324).

GALLION'S HAZARD

13 Dec 1732: John Gallion of BA, planter, eld. s. of JG, dec., conv. to James, Thomas, Solomon, Samuel, Henry, and Joseph Gallion, all devisees of JG, dec., their share of the lands, including (*), devised to them by the said JG (IS#L: 324).

GALLOWAY'S ENLARGEMENT

24 May 1743: William Galloway made a will leaving (*) to his s. Moses and 132 a. (*) to his s. William (BCF).
1750: Moses Galloway owned 80 a., pt. (*); the heirs of William Galloway owned 356 a. pt. (*) (1750 DB).
c1754: Moses Galloway owned (*) (IBC: 66).
1763/4: Moses Galloway owned 436 a. (AHAL: 74).

GALLOW'S BAY (See GALLIER'S BAY)

GARDEN

3 Dec 1684: Thomas Lightfoot, Gent., conv. to George Yate, Gent., 118 a., pt. of (*), about a mile from the w. side of the Susquehanna R., adj. to Stockett's Choice, The Levill, and Bedell's Pasture (RM#HS: 117).

GARDEN OF EDEN

May 1685: 150 a. surv. for Adam Birchall; later held by the orphans of said Birchall (MRR: 20).
18 June 1685: Surv. for (?) (Cert. of Surv.: See TR#A: 311).
21 Oct 1704: Thomas Burchfield (Birchall?) conv. 150 a. (*) to Roger Matthews (HW#2: 373).
3 Nov 1714: Roger Matthews conv., 150 a. (*) to Peter Lester (TR#A: 311).
1750: George Lester owned 150 a. (1750 DB).

GARDEN SPOT

20 March 1741: 10 a. surv. for Sarah Glaspin on n. side of Deer Creek (BA Unpat. Cert. 575).

GARDESON (See JURDISTON)

GARDINER'S FARM

28 March 1750: Hyde Hoxton of PG Co. conv. 100 a. (*) to Edward Lee of BA Co. (TR#C: 507).

GARDNER'S ADDITION

16 March 1731/2: John Gardiner of AA Co. conv. (*) and Boddy's Adventure to his dau. Susanna Walker (PCLR PL#8: 89).
14 Oct 1743: Luke Trotten and William Hamilton, execs. of John Gardner, conv. 60 a. (*), 80 a. Gunworth, 200 a. pt. Honderton (?), and 300 a. Timber Neck to Sabritt Sollers (TB#C: 327).

GARDNER'S FARM

1716/18: 100 a. surv. for Christopher Gardner.
See Horvath Plat: Randallstown.

4 May 1727: Christopher Gardner and w. Sibrah, conv. 100 a. (*) to Hyde Hoxton of BA Co. (IS#H: 422).

GARDNER'S MILL

10 April 1727: Richard Thacker of BA Co. conv. 100 a. (*), 367 a. Long Discovery, and 320 a. Thacker's Chance to Thomas Cockey (IS#H: 358).

GARRART

22 Sep 1750: George Atkinson, exec. of Capt. Christopher Grindall, conv. 100 a., pt. of (*), and 60 a. Hooker's Addition, to Joseph Bosley (TR#D: 97).

GARRISON'S NEGLECT

10 Sep 1746: Samuel Howell and Sarah Durbin entered into a [prenuptial?] agreement; he would conv. to her the following tracts: (*), Howell's Contrivance, Johnsons's Bed, Johnson's Rest, Joshua Wood's Mistake, and Lofton's Neglect. He also conv. her a child's portion of his estate, for her and any heirs she has by him; if she d. without heirs by him, the above tracts would be divided among his male heirs; she relinquished her dower right to ⅓ of his estate (TB#E: 177).

GARTRELL'S REST

30 July 1698: Anthony Johnson conv. 100 a. (*) to John Gartrell of AA Co. (TR#RA: 332).

GASH'S NEGLECT

5 March 1723: John Stokes, Gent., conv. 64 a. (*) to Archibald Buchanan (IS#G: 234).

5 Oct 1730: Archibald Buchanan conv. 64 a. (*) and 386 a. Martin's Rest to James Donaldson and to John Copson. AB's w. Ann cons. (IS#K: 316, 324).

26 Jan 1730/1: James Donaldson of Annapolis, conv. 64 a. (*) and 380 a. Martin's Rest to William Smith (IS#L: 44).

18 March 1730/1: Buchanan grants quitclaim of 64 a. (*) and 386 a. Martin's Rest to William Smith, who purch. the tracts from James Donaldson (IS#L: 117).

GASH'S PURCHASE

(Pt. New Westwood, surv. for Robert West)

7 April 1740: Robert West conv. 100 a. (*) to Thomas Gash (HWS#1-A: 411).

29 June 1751: Thomas Gash conv. 60 a., pt. (*) to Edward Wakeman. TG's w. Johannah cons. (TR#D: 245).

24 Feb 1754: Thomas Gash and w. Johanna conv. 50 a. (*) to Bennett O'Neal, s. of Henry O'Neal, dec. (BB#I: 159).

GASSAWAY'S RIDGE

1679: 500 a. for Nicholas Gassaway; On PW Plat G

17 April 1744: Thomas Gassaway, Gent., conv. 500 a. (*) to Edward Sprigg, III; Gassaway's w. Sarah cons. (TB#C: 467).

GATES CLOSE

5 June 1684: 30 a. (*) surv. for Thomas Richardson; later held by John Fuller (MRR: 48).

20 July 1685 (1686?): Richardson conv. 30 a. (*) to Robert Gates; tract had been pat. in 1685; on 20 July 1686 Richardson gave bond to Gates (RM#HS: 199).

5 Nov 1691: Robert Gates conv. 30 a. (*) to John Fuller. No w. mentioned (RM#HS, 335).

1 March 1692: John Fuller and w. (?) conv. 30 a. (*) to Thomas Heath (RM#HS: 345).

8 Nov 1695: Thomas Heath of BA Co., and w. Sarah conv. 30 a. (*) to John Fuller (RM#HS: 496).

GAY'S ENLARGEMENT

1 Dec 1750: Nicholas Ruxton Gay conv. all of (*), granted to said Gay for 640 a., to Thomas Harrison (TR#D: 82).

GAY'S INSPECTION

1764: Isaac Risteau conv. 100 a. (*) to Samuel Stansbury (B#N: 15).

GENERAL'S POINT

19 March 1693/4: George Hadaway of TA Co., and w. Sarah conv. 150 a. (*) to Thomas Jones. The tract had been laid out for George Langford, and had recently been in the tenure of Roland Hadaway, predecessor of said grantor (RM#HS: 412).

15 Oct 1694: Thomas Jones of TA Co. conv. 150 a. (*) to Jonas Bowen (RM#HS: 445).

GEORGE'S ADDITION

21 Nov 1746: George Ogg, with cons. of w. Mary, conv. ½ pt. of (*), George's Beginning, and Rich Level to John Metcalf (TB#E: 282).

28 Feb 1746: John Metcalfe, with cons. of w. Mary conv. to Rachel Bailey, 170 a. being ½ pt. of (*), George's Beginning, and Rich Level, 100 a. Mary's Meadows, and 100 a. Metcalf's Addition. (TB#E: 315).

GEORGE'S BEGINNING

1738: Surv. for George Ogg.
See Horvath Plat: Green Spring Valley.

23 Sep 1745: George Ogg of BA Co., with cons. of w. Mary, conv. 40 a. (*) and pt. Addition to Rich Level to John Risteau (TB#D: 331).

27 Aug 1746: John Risteau conv. 170 a. (*) and Addition to his dau. Catherine and her husband Thomas Cockey; if Catherine d. land to go to her eld. child; if Catherine d. s.p., the land was to go to TC (TB#E: 276).

21 Nov 1746: George Ogg, with cons. of w. Mary, conv. ½ pt. of George's Addition, (*), and Rich Level to John Metcalf (TB#E: 282).

28 Feb 1746: John Metcalfe, with cons. of w. Mary conv. to Rachel Bailey, 170 a. being ½ pt. of George's Addition, (*), and Rich Level, 100 a. Mary's Meadows, and 100 a. Metcalf's Addition. (TB#E: 315).

GEORGE'S FANCY

30 March 1719: John Ashman, with cons. of w. Constant, conv. 100 a. (*) to Lancelot Todd (TR#RA: 541).

GEORGE'S HALL

30 Sep 1732: Thomas Williamson, with cons. of w. Sarah, conv. 11 a. (*) to Bennett Garrett (IS#L: 323).

GEORGE'S HILL

150 a. surv. 20 Oct 1667 for George Collett on Gunpowder R. on the e. side of the R. near Foster's Creek; 20 a. later held by Thomas Preston, and 130 a. held by the orphans of William Lewis. (MRR: 60).

2 March 1671/2: John Collett, Gent., conv. 150 a. to James Ives (G#J: 73; TR#RA: 53).

5 June 1677: James Ives and w. Martha conv. 150 a. at Foster's Creek, formerly taken up by John Collett, to Arthur Taylor (IR#PP: 11).

6 Dec 1681: Arthur Taylor conv. 25 a. to Thomas Preston; land is described as being on n. side of Gunpowder R., on a neck betw. Elk Creek and Thomas Cook's land (IR#AM: 149).

7 June 1693: John Taylor conv. 53.5 a. to Samuel Sickelmore (RM#HS: 387).

7 Jan 1694: Samuel Sickelmore and w. Martha conv. 53.5 to John Taylor (RM#HS: 450).

27 Jan 1694: John Taylor of BA Co., planter, conv. to John Evins, boatwright, the land now or lately held by Samuel Sickelmore (RM#HS: 447).

8 Sep 1697: John Ewings of BA Co., boatwright, conv. 53 a. to William Lewis (IS#IK: 207).

6 June 1723: Thomas Tolley and w. Mary conv. 53 a. to John Merriken (IS#G: 175).

27 Oct 1726: John Taylor conv. pt. Spring Neck, pt. of a larger tract called (*) to Joshua Merriken; (*) was taken up by Arthur Taylor, father of the said John (IS#H: 336).

6 Nov 1726: Joshua Merriken made his will leaving (*) to his s. Hugh and to an unborn child (if a s. to be named Joshua (MCW#VI: 11).

9 Aug 1744: Amos Garrett conv. 11 a., pt. (*), to Jacob and Martha Combest (TB#C: 550).

1750: Robert Dutton owned 130 a. (1750 DB: 50).

GEORGE'S PARK

1703: 400 a. surv. for Thomas Carpenter.

See Horvath Plat: Randallstown.

10 Feb 1703: Thomas Carpenter of AA Co., merchant, conv. 400 a. (*) to George Miller of AA Co., planter (TR#A: 309).

10 March 1747: Christopher Randall conv. 133 a. (*), 150 a. Jeopardy, and 75 a. Randall's Meadows to Rachel Bailey of BA Co., widow (TB#E: 696).

29 May 1747: Joseph Miller and w. Comfort, and William Miller and w. Johanna, conv. 133 a. pt. (*) to Christopher Randall (TB#E: 396).

24 March 1750: William Miller mortgaged 50 a. (*) to Charles Ridgely (TR#D: 155).

24 March 1750: Joseph Miller mortgaged 59 a. (*) to Charles Ridgely (TR#D: 157).

GERAR (See HOOKER'S FARM)

2 Nov 1726: Thomas Hooker and w. Eleanor of BA Co., sell to Samuel Hooker all that pt. of (*) called Hooker's Farm, orig. surv. for the said Thomas Hooker (IS#H: 287).

17 June 1730: Thomas Hooker of BA Co., planter, conv. to Penelope Deye, Gentlewoman, 280 a., the residue of (*). TH's w. Eleanor cons. (IS#K: 301).

GIBSON'S MARSH

3 Sep 1683: 200 a. surv. for Miles Gibson on Rumley Creek, adj. Delph Island; later held by Robert Gibson, and later by Capt. Thomas Bale (MRR: 9).

17 July 1744: Kemp Plummer of Glouc. Co., VA, conv. (*) and other lands to Thomas White. deed stated that Ann Bale was the residuary legatee by Anthony Bale's will, and she m. Michael Taylor, and d. a femme covert s.p. The land desc. to Kemp Plummer, s. of William Plummer of Glouc. Co., VA, who was bro. and heir at law to Ann Taylor (TB#C: 576).

GIBSON'S PARK

19 Sep 1683: 800 a. surv. for Miles Gibson on the s. most branch of Bush R.; later held by Robert Gibson, and still later 500 a. by Anthony Bale, 200 a. by George Wells, and 100 a. by Capt. Thomas Bale (MRR: 9).

10 Sep 1684: Pat. to Miles Gibson who d. intestate and land desc. to his s. Robert Gibson who left

100 a. to Joseph Compton and the rest to his w. Mary (See TR#A: 129).

7 Feb 1709: Joseph Compton of BA Co. conv., 100 a. pt. Gibson's Park and Good Luck to Aquila Paca. JC's w. Margaret cons. (RM#HS: 657).

9 Dec 1710: George Wells and w. Mary conv. 700 a. (*) to Aquila Paca (TR#A: 129).

GIBSON'S RIDGE (1683)

19 Sep 1683: 500 a. granted to Miles Gibson; later possessed by Robert Gibson and later by Thomas Bale (364 a.) and Henry Rhodes (136 a.) (MRR: 9; see also TB#C: 576).

30 Aug 1702: Robert Gibson of BA Co. conv. 500 a. (*) to Thomas Bale (HW#2: 205).

6 March 1733: Henry Rhodes and w. Ann conv. 50 a. pt. (*) to Edward Sanders (HWS#M: 182).

25 June 1737: Henry Rhodes conv. 180 a. pt. (*) to John Parker; tract had orig. been purch. by the grantor's father, Henry; this conveyance was made in exch. for 214 a. Parker's Folly and 224 a. Parker's Choice (IS#IK: 474).

2 March 1738: John Parker conv. 180 a. (*) to Thomas Bond (HWS#1-A: 193).

17 July 1744: Kemp Plummer of Glouc. Co., VA, conv. pt. (*) which was not sold by Anthony Bale or his bro. Thomas, and other lands to Thomas White. The deed stated that Ann Bale was the residuary legatee by Anthony Bale's will, and she m. Michael Taylor, and d. a femme covert s.p. The land desc. to Kemp Plummer, s. of William Plummer of Glouc. Co., VA, who was bro. and heir at law to Ann Taylor (TB#C: 576).

14 May 1745: Col. Thomas White conv. 300 a. pt. (*) to Benjamin Norris (TB#D: 159).

GILBERT'S ADDITION

28 June 1740: Michael Gilbert, s. and heir of Garvice Gilbert, dec., conv. Gilbert's Addition and pt. Gilbert's Outlet to his bro. Samuel Gilbert. MG's w. Mary cons. (HWS#1-A: 422).

27 Sep 1744: Samuel Gilbert of BA Co. conv. 50 a. Gilbert's Addition and 75 a. Gilbert's Outlet to Thomas Mitchell. SG's w. Martha cons. (TB#C: 645).

GILBERT'S ADVENTURE

1 Dec 1731: Thomas Gilbert conv. 150 a. (*) to Thomas Mitchell. TG's w. Elizabeth cons. (IS#L: 193).

GILBERT'S CHANCE

17 Sep 1735: Garvas Gilbert conv. 60 a. pt. Clark's Tobacco, 40 a. pt. Gilbert's Chance, and 145 a., pt. Hall's Pipe, to his s. Michael Gilbert. GG's w. Mary cons. (HWS#M: 302).

GILBERT'S OUTLET

28 June 1740; Michael Gilbert, s. and heir of Garvice Gilbert of BA Co., conv. 125 a., pt. Low's Lot and pt. Gilbert's Outlet to his bro. Garvice. MG's w. Mary cons. (HWS#1-A: 413).

28 June 1740: Michael Gilbert, s. and heir of Garvice Gilbert, dec., conv. Gilbert's Addition and pt. Gilbert's Outlet to his bro. Samuel Gilbert. MG's w. Mary cons. (HWS#1-A: 422).

27 Sep 1744: Samuel Gilbert of BA Co. conv. 50 a. Gilbert's Addition and 75 a. Gilbert's Outlet to Thomas Mitchell. SG's w. Martha cons. (TB#C: 645).

17 March 1747: Garvice Gilbert conv. 125 a. pt. Low's Lot and Gilbert's Outlet to Thomas Downs. GG's w. Elizabeth cons. (TB#E: 711).

GILBERT'S PIPE

12 March 1760: Michael Gilbert and w. Mary conv. 666 a. pt. (*) to William Cox (B#H: 201).

14 Jan 1768: William Cox conv. 666 a. (*) to Jacob Giles. WC's w. Mary cons. (B#Q: 297).

GILES AND WEBSTER'S DISCOVERY

25 March 1737: Isaac Webster and Jacob Giles conv. 195 a. pt. (*) to Thomas Johnson of Deer Creek (IS#IK: 399).

25 March 1737: Isaac Webster and Jacob Giles conv. all of (*) not already sold to Thomas Johnson to Thomas Renshaw. IW's w. Margaret cons. (IS#IK: 413).

2 Nov 1743: Thomas Johnson conv. 98 a. (*) to Joseph Johnson. TJ's w. Mary cons. (TB#C: 345).

2 Nov 1743: Thomas Johnson conv,. another 98 a. (*) to William Elletts (TB#C: 375).

6 March 1744: Thomas Renshaw, Sr., conv. Donmurenintrum and Giles and Webster's Discovery, in all 250 a. to his s. Thomas Renshaw, Jr. (TB#D: 47).

29 April 1751: Thomas Renshaw of BA Co. conv. 11 a. pt. (*) to Samuel Webb, tanner and currier. TR's w. Frances cons. (TR#D: 205).

GILLINGHAM

6 Aug 1684: 400 a. surv. for Col. Henry Jowles; later held by Amos Garrett (MRR: 48).

4 April 1700: Col. Henry Jowles of SM Co. conv. 400 a. (*) to Amos Garrett of BC, merchant (HW#2: 223).

GILL'S FANCY

26 March 1729: Stephen Gill conv. 100 a. (*) to William Parrish. SG's w. Elizabeth cons. (IS#K: 9).

1 Jan 1730: William Parrish conv. 100 a. (*) and other land to George Walker. WP's w. Susannah cons. (IS#L: 90).

GIST'S INSPECTION

14 March 1743: Christopher Gist mortgaged 100 a. Counterscarpe, 83 a. Milford, Gist's Inspection, 500 a. Joshua's Lot, 50 a. Gist's Meadows, and 2 lots in Baltimore Town (TB#D: 438).

28 July 1746: James Richard, atty. for Stephen Theodore Jannsen, conv. 100 a. Counterscarpe, 83 a. Milford, Gist's Inspection, 500 a. Joshua's Lot, 50 a. Gist's Meadows, and 2 lots in Baltimore Town to William Cromwell and Tobias Stansbury, who have paid the mortgages (TB#D: 438).

GIST'S INSPECTION, ADDITION TO

14 March 1743: Christopher Gist mortgaged 100 a. Counterscarpe, 83 a. Milford, Gist's Inspection, 500 a. Joshua's Lot, 50 a. Gist's Meadows, and 2 lots in Baltimore Town (TB#D: 438).

28 March 1746: James Richard, atty. for Stephen Theodore Jannsen, conv. 100 a. Counterscarpe, 83 a. Milford, Gist's Inspection, 500 a. Joshua's Lot, 50 a. Gist's Meadows, and 2 lots in Baltimore Town to William Cromwell and Tobias Stansbury, who have paid the mortgages (TB#D: 438).

GIST'S MEADOWS

1741/43: 50 a. surv. for Richard Gist.

See Horvath Plats: Owings Mills and Green Spring Valley.

14 March 1743: Christopher Gist mortgaged 100 a. Counterscarpe, 83 a. Milford, Gist's Inspection, 500 a. Joshua's Lot, 50 a. Gist's Meadows, and 2 lots in Baltimore Town (TB#D: 438).

3 May 1745: Christopher Gist conv. 50 a. Elledges Folly and 50 a. (*) to William Cromwell (TB#D: 99).

28 March 1746: James Richard, atty. for Stephen Theodore Jannsen, conv. 100 a. Counterscarpe, 83 a. Milford, Gist's Inspection, 500 a. Joshua's Lot, 50 a. Gist's Meadows, and 2 lots in Baltimore Town to William Cromwell and Tobias Stansbury, who have paid the mortgages (TB#D: 438).

GIST'S REST

21 Feb 1693: Thomas Hammond of BA Co., Gent., and w. Rebecca, late widow, relict, and legatee of Thomas Lightfoot, conv. to Richard Gist, s. and heir of Christopher, 125 a. Gist's Rest (100 a. now in possession of John Beecher and his w. who was the late relict and widow of Christopher Gist (RM#HS: 417).

10 Sep 1705: Richard Gist conv. to Richard Cromwell the land which Thomas Hammond and w. Rebecca conv. to said Richard: 125 a. Gist's Rest, and another 100 a. adj., in all 225 a., now called Rebecca's Delight. RG's w. Zipporah cons. (IR#PP: 192).

GIST'S SEARCH

1725: 400 a. granted to Richard Gist.

26 Sep 1730: Richard Gist of BA Co. conv. 76 a. pt. (*) to Richard Bond (*) (IS#L: 43).

6 March 1731: Richard Gist of BA Co. conv. 284 a. pt. (*) to his s. Nathaniel (IS#L: 201).

2 July 1737: Richard Bond of BA Co. conv. 50 a. pt. (*) to Peter Bond. RB's w. Mary cons. (IS#IK: 465).

28 Feb 1738: Nathaniel Gist of BA Co., p., conv. 101 a. pt. (*) to James Kelly; NG's w. Mary cons. (HWS#1-A: 191).

18 May 1741: Nathaniel Gist conv. pt. (*) to John Ford, 108 a.. NG's w. Mary cons. (HWS#1-A: 511).

28 Sep 1744: John Ford conv. pt. Gist's Search to James Kelly. JF's w. Ruth cons. (TB#C: 574).

3 Oct 1744: Nathaniel Gist, with cons. of w. Mary, conv. 77 a., pt. (*) to John Chilcoat (TB#C: 647).

7 Jan 1744/5: John Chilcoat of BA Co. conv. 90 a. pt. Friendship and 77 a. pt. (*) to John Pindall (TB#D: 29).

GITTINGS CHOICE

7 March 1726/7: Ebenezer Cooke of MD, Gent., leased 450 a. (*) to Thomas Gittings, the lease to run for the lifetimes of Thomas, his w. Elizabeth and dau. Margaret (IS#H: 344).

c1750: Thomas Gittings of BA Co. made a deed of gift to his son-in-law John Chamberlaine of 258 a., pt. of three tracts in His Lordship's Manor, leased to Gittings by the Proprietary's Agent: 155 a. pt. Gittings Choice, 26 a. no name, and 78(?) a. no name (TR#C: 489).

GLEBE (THE)

1 Sep 1702: Col. John Thomas of BA Co. conv. 123¾ a. (*), pt. of Good Luck, to the vestrymen and church wardens of St. Paul's Parish. The same day Jane Thomas gave p/a to Richard Colegate to acknowledge the sale (HW#2: 171).

GOD'S PROVIDENCE

14 July 1676: 200 a. formerly called Puddle Wharf, surv. for John Tillard on the southwest side of Bush R., adj. a tract formerly laid out for Francis Trippas called Bridewell Dock; these two parcels were later surv. into one tract and possessed as follows: 160 a., held by Charles Adams, and 140 a. held by Richard Tilliard; still later called Sarah's Delight and (*), comprising 280 a. in all; and held as follows: 160 a. Thomas Chamberlain, and 120 a. by Richard Tilyard (MRR: 63).

3 Nov 1698: John Tilyard of KE Co. conv. 140 a. (*) to Charles Adams; Tilyard's w. Mary

empowered her father George Green to acknowledge the deed (TR#RA: 308).

16 Nov 1703: Charles Adams conv. 140 a. (*) to Thomas Chamberlain. Adams also conv. 20 a. Adam's Addition (might have also been called Prospect) to Chamberlaine (HW#2: 350).

2 Oct 1713: Thomas Chamberlaine conv. 20 a. (*) (may be Adam's Addition), to Charles Carroll of Annapolis (TR#A: 399).

9 Aug 1716: Thomas Chamberlain and w. Mary conv. 20 a. Adams' Addition and 140 a. (*) to Richard King, being the property mortgaged to him on 2 Oct 1713 (TR#A: 402).

23 May 1728: John Tilliard of KE Co., carpenter, conv. pt. of (*) to George Debruler. JT's w. Mary cons. (IS#I: fols. 172, 175).

8 Nov 1732: John Powell of BA Co., planter, conv.100 a. being ½ of (*) to Thomas Denbow (IS#L: 303).

1750: William York owned pt. Good Providence [(*)] (1750 DB: 71).

27 April 1754: Thomas Phillibrown, Jr., of Devonshire St., London, cooper, and Thomas Wright of Cullum Street, woolen draper, and w. Elizabeth, being the heirs of Richard King of BA Co., conv. 147 a. (*) to William York (BB#I: 295).

GOLDEN FOREST

1746: Surv.

See KN Plat WO; See Horvath Plat: Granite.

GOLDEN FOREST, ADDITION TO

See KN Plat WO; Horvath Plat: Granite.

GOLDEN MINE

8 March 1754: Francis Ingram of BA Co. conv. 1095 a. (*) to John Buck (BB#I: 183).

GOLDSMITH'S ENLARGEMENT

17 June 1663: 90 a. surv. for George Goldsmith; later held by John Hall for George's orphans; still later 70 a. held by George Wells (MRR: 4).

GOLDSMITH'S HALL

15 July 1658: 800 a. surv. for Samuel Goldsmith; later held by orphans of Col. George Wells (MRR: 7).

7 Oct 1667: Maj. Samuel Goldsmith, Gent., conv. to George Wells, 3rd s. of Richard Wells of Herring Creek, AA Co., half of all the donor's estate after his death, said Wells about to marry donor's youngest dau. Blanch (IS#IK: 25).

13 Feb 1726/7: John Smithers of KE Co., Gent., eld. s. of Blanch Smithers, (dau. of Col. George Wells and sister and coheir of George Wells, Jr.) conv. his interest in the following tracts to John Stokes: 800 a. (*), 24 a. Matthews Neglect, 400 a. Planter's Delight, 200 a. Timber Proof, and 81 a. Watson's Addition (some of which were resurv. into 1150 a. Coheir's Lot) (IS#H: 385).

GOLDSMITH'S NECK

5 June 1707: John Boone and w. Jane conv. 200 a. (*) to John Ewings. Tract was orig. taken up by Matthew Goldsmith and Edward Foster by patent dated 24 Feb 1661; conv. by Matthew Goldsmith to Richard Winley to James Phillips, who in turn sold it to Francis Trippols, whose only heir was the above named Jane Boone (RM#HS: 553).

20 Nov 1708: John Ewings and w. Elizabeth conv. 200 a. (*) (also called Foster's Neck), plus 14 a. Arthur's Delay, to John Roberts (RM#HS: 616).

22 Nov 1742: Stephen Roberts, s. and devisee of John Roberts of BA Co., dec., conv. his interest in 200 a. (*) and other lands which had been devised to him by his father, to John Roberts, another s. and devisee of John Roberts (TB#C: 219).

GOLDSMITH'S REST

3 July 1682: 630: Surv. for George Goldsmith with a s. course; cert. of resruvey returned and now in occupation of John Hall for the orphans of George Goldsmith; later still poss. by George Wells (MRR: 6).

July 1728: Mary Marshall of BA Co. conv. 28 a. pt. (*) to Joshua Wood (IS#I: 199).

GOOD ENDEAVOR (1686)

15 Oct 1686: 500 a. surv. for Robert Gelly on the e. side of Bush R. (MRR: 29).

GOOD ENDEAVOR (1689)

1 May 1689: 40 a. surv. for Charles Gorsuch by Thomas Richardson, Deputy Surveyor, on the w. side of Patapsco on the n. side of Bear Creek; later possessed by John Cooper and still later by Nicholas Rogers (MRR: 108; RM#HS: 384).

18 March 1727/8: John Copper of BA Co. conv. 40 a. (*) to John Francis Holland. Joseph Gostwick, age 78, deposed that he lived in the house where John Copper was born, and that JC is 21 years of age (IS#I: 107).

GOOD ENDEAVOR (1695)

29 July 1695: 139 a. surv. for James Dennis in the woods on the e. side of the Little Falls; later possessed by William Noble (MRR: 55).

2 March 1702/3: James Dennis ackn. he had sold 139 a. (*) to William Noble (HW#2: 29).

[Notes by George Archer state that land was escheated after Dennis d. intestate and land was granted to Stephen Onion in 1744.]

GOOD HOPE (1683)

19 Sep 1683: 200 a. surv. for James Banister on the e. side of Bush R., adj. East Land Wells formerly taken up by one Ogburn Banister; his heirs carried out of the province "15 years ago and not returned" (MRR: 19).

GOOD HOPE (1696)

8 Aug 1696: 200 a. surv. for Edward Felks, on the s. side of the main falls of Gunpowder R.; later possessed by Ann Felks (MRR: 45).

19 June 1738: Edward Pigg of Spottsylvania Co., VA, conv. 200 a. (*) (12 Aug 1696 granted to Edward Felks), and other lands, to Samuel Maxwell (HWS#1-A: 104).

13 Oct 1738: Samuel Maxwell of BA Co. conv. 200 a. (*) to Buckler Partridge of BA Co., surgeon (HWS#1-A: 184).

1 Dec 1738: Samuel Maxwell of BA Co., conv. 200 a. (*) to William Wright; SM's w. Jane cons. (HWS#1-A: 152).

GOOD LUCK (1684)

11 Aug 1684: 200 a. surv. for John Thomas. Later, 100 a. held by John Thomas and 100 a. held by the vestrymen of St. Paul's Parish (See also The Glebe) (MRR: 74).

GOOD LUCK

7 Feb 1709: Joseph Compton of BA Co. conv., 100 a. pt. Gibson's Park and Good Luck to Aquila Paca. JC's w. Margaret cons. (RM#HS: 657).

GOOD LUCK (1724)

10 Sep 1724: Thomas Johnson pat. 100 a. Good Luck.

6 March 1733: Thomas Johnson of the Land of Nod, conv. 100 a. Good Luck and 100 a. Bear Range to John Poteet. Johnson's w. Alice cons. (HWS#M: 30).

1750: John Poteet owned 100 a. Good Luck (1750 DB).

7 March 1753: James Poteet conv. to his bro. John Poteet, Jr., 100 a. Good Luck. James' w. Elizabeth cons. (TR#D: 544).

5 Nov 1760: John Poteet of BA Co. conv. to Evan Evans 100 a. Good Luck. John's w. Ruth cons. (B#I: 105).

GOOD LUCK

4 Nov 1750: Thomas Sheredine, Sabrett Sollers, William Lynch, and Thomas Franklin conv. to Dobiny [Daubeny] Buckler Partridge, the Glebe Land of St. Paul's Parish, being pt. of a larger tract called (*) (TR#D: 48).

GOOD NEIGHBOR

26 Nov 1751: Thomas Bond conv. to Edward Mattingly 100 a. Francis Delight, 210 a. Bond's Choice, 109a. Bond's Beginnings, 122 a. (*), and 56 a. pt. Bond's Fortune. TB's w. (unnamed) cons. (TR#D: 257).

GOOD NEIGHBORHOOD

20 May 1720: Surv. for John Mackeldory and Robert Clark (IS#L: 241).

6 June 1722: John Muckelroy of BA Co., conv. 122 a. (*). His w. Frances cons. (RM#HS: 681).

7 June 1722: Robert Clark, with cons. of w. Selina, conv. 122 a. (*) to John Muckleroy (RM#HS: 682).

20 July 1725: John Muckeldory and w. Frances conv. 244 a. pt. (*) and 100 a. Francis' Delight, to Benjamin Wheeler (IS#H: 153).

7 June 1732: Benjamin Wheeler, with cons. of w. Elizabeth, conv. (*) and Francis Delight to Thomas Bond (IS#L: 241).

24 July 1746: Thomas Bond of BA Co., conv. 216 a. Bond's Choice, 100 a. Francis' Delight and 122 a. (*) to his s. Thomas Bond, Jr. (TB#E: 112).

GOOD NEIGHBORHOOD ENLARGED

24 Nov 1732: granted to Samuel Young, and was composed of tracts Good Neighborhood, granted 1 June 1700 to Samuel Young, and vacant land. Samuel Young by his LWT left the tract equally to his granddaughter Mary and Elizabeth, daus. of his s. John (TR#C: 469).

7 June 1746: Pollard Keene and John Keene make a deed of partition (TB#E: 88).

19 June 1750: John Keene of BA, and w. Elizabeth, youngest dau. of Dr. John Young of SM Co., conv. to Mary Keene, w. of Pollard Keene and eld. dau. of John Young, their share of (*), bequeathed to them by their grandfather Samuel Young by his will dated 22 Jan 1732 (TR#C: 469).

19 June 1750: Pollard Keene and w. Mary conv. to John and Elizabeth Keene .... (TR#C: 475).

GOOD SPEED

16 Jan 1760: Michael Taylor of BA Co. conv. 100 a. (*), formerly owned by Abraham Taylor, to Andrew Lendrum, clerk, of BA Co. Michael stated that he believed he was born before 14 Nov 1738 (B#H: 71).

GOODMANS ADVENTURE

13 May 1678: 250 a. surv. for Edward Goodman on Swan Creek; Goodman was killed by Indians and no heirs appear (MRR: 13).

GOODWILL (Pt. BURMAN'S FOREST)

17 Oct 1722: Ebenezer Blackiston and w. Sarah of KE co., conv. 100 a. (*) to Edward Peregoy (TR#A: 412).

GOODWILL (1749)

See Horvath Plat: Reisterstown.

1749: 91 a. granted to William Gosnell (AL#A: 601).

20 April 1765: William Gosnell, with cons. of w. Sarah, conv. 31 a. (*) to John Ford (B#O: 166).

30 Dec 1769: William and Sarah Gosnell conv. 60 a. (*) to John Clark (AL#A: 601).

GOODWILL

1750: Richard King Stevenson owned 200 a. (1750 DB).

GOODWILL

1750: John Day of Edward owned 42 a. (1750 DB: 80).

27 Nov 1752: John Day of Edward, with cons. of w. Philizanna, conv. 42 a. (*) to Mary Jackson, Sr., and her daus. Mary Jackson, Jr., and Elizabeth Jackson (TR#D: 509).

27 Nov 1752: John Day of Edward conv. 42 a. (*) to Mary Jackson, Sr., and her daus. Mary Jackson, Jr., and Elizabeth Jackson; Day's w. Philizanna cons. (TR#D: 509).

GOODWILL PURCHASED AGAIN

3 Aug 1726: Thomas Bond, with cons. of w. Ann conv. 1500 a. (*) to Joseph Galloway of AA Co. (IS#H: 274).

1750: Joseph Galloway owned 1500 a. (*) (1750 DB).

c1754: Heirs of Joseph Galloway owned (*) (IBC: 72).

GOODWILL SURVEYED

21 Dec 1767: Aquila Carr conv. 60 a. (*) to John Naylor of BA Co. (B#Q: 532).

GOOSE HARBOR (1679)

5 Oct 1679: 41 a. surv. for Rowland Thornbury on the s. side of Gunpowder R.; later held by Joseph Wells for the orphans of said Thornbury (MRR: 109).

GOOSE HARBOR

5 Dec ---; 200 a. a. surv. for Rowland Thornbury on the s. side of Back R.; later held by Joseph Wells for the orphans of said Thornbury (MRR: 110).

25 Feb 1716: John Thornborough late of BA Co., now of Lancaster Co., VA, conv. 200 a. (*) to Nicholas Haile of BA Co. Haile agrees to pay the land rent for the last 15 years (TR#RA: 446).

21 April 1739: Roger [Robert?] Burgin of BA Co., conv. 80 a. pt. (*) to Philip Burgin (HWS#1-A: 204).

2 June 1739: Robert Burgin conv. 120 a. pt. (*) to Benjamin Bowen of John, except for 80 a. formerly conv. to Philip Burgin (HWS#1-A: 246).

21 Jan 1744/5: Philip Burgin gave bond he would conv. to Francis Rider a parcel called Goose Harbour, 80 a., lying on the s. side of Bread and Cheese Creek. On 4 Dec 1750 Rebecca Burgin, widow of Philip Burgin, gave bond she would conv. to said Rider her right of dower in tract (*) (BACT 1: 31, 33).

GOOSEBERRY NECK

May 1673: 100 a. surv. for William Ebden (MRR: 87).

3 April 1676: William and Jane Ebden conv. (*), in Deep Creek in Back R., to Jonas Bowen (IR#PP: 8).

GORE (THE)

3 Feb 1724: Joshua and John Dorsey of Elk Ridge conv. 135 a. (*) (pat. to Joshua and John Dorsey on 21 Feb 1722) to Caleb Dorsey (IS#H: 41).

GORSUCH'S FOLLY

3 Jan 1721/2: John Gorsuch of BA Co. and w. Elizabeth, conv. 114 a. (*) to Alexander Grant (RM#HS: 669).

GORSUCH'S VENTURE

25 March 1749: John Gorsuch, s. and heir of Charles Gorsuch, conv. 150 a. (*) (surv. for Chas. Gorsuch on 20 Feb 1723), to Charles Carroll, JG's w. Mary cons. (TR#C: 170).

GOSHAN

27 Feb 1733: 100 a. pat. by John Bowen (MPL PL#8: 804, AM31: 133).

See Horvath Plat: Reisterstown.

12 Jan 1744: John Bowen [Bowers?] of BA Co. conv. 100 a. (*) to Robert Holliday, surgeon. JB's w. Lelly cons. (TB#D: 7).

GOSNELL'S ADVENTURE

1684: 199 a. pat. to William Gosnell, who sold it to Maurice Baker. Baker left it in his will to James Smith, who "has runaway out of the province." The title to the land was confirmed by Act of Assembly on 4 Nov 1724 to William Anderson (IS#H: 2).

22 June 1721: James Smith of AA Co. gave bond he would conv. 199 a. (*) to William Anderson when Anderson has paid (IS#H: 1).

11 Dec 172-: William Anderson assigned the bond to John Hammond (IS#H: 1).

1 Dec 1724: William Anderson, with cons. of w. Mary, conv. 199 a. (*) to John Hammond, Sr. (IS#H: 2).

GOSNELL'S PLEASANT PASTURES

25 May 1767: John Gosnell, s. and heir of William Gosnell, conv. (*) to Zebediah Gosnell. JG's w. Sarah cons. (B#P: 700).

GOSNELL'S PURCHASE

27 Feb 1767: Peter Gosnell, with cons. of w. Ann, conv. to John Botts two contiguous tracts on the Great Falls of the Patapsco: 90 a. Absolom's Place and 10 a. (*) (B#P: 482).

GOSNELL'S RANGE

13 Dec 1729: Morris Gosnell of BA Co., with cons. of w. Susanna, conv. 50 a. (*) to Edward Stocksdale (IS#K: 220).

GOSTWICK'S CHOICE

5 Feb 1728/9: Thomas Gostwick, s. and heir of Joseph Gostwick, late of BA Co., dec., with cons. of his w. Elizabeth, conv. 197 a. (*) to Thomas Stansbury (IS#I: 287).

GRAFTON'S GIFT

23 Oct 1723: Surv. (prob. for William Grafton) (IS#H: 381).

1726: William Grafton conv. 100 a. of the tract to his friend John Constant and w. Susanna for life; then to their dau. Susanna; then to John Constant, Jr.; Grafton also conv. 50 a. to John and Susanna's dau. Sarah, w. of Thomas Brashiers (IS#H: 381).

4 August 1742: Thomas Brazier and w. Sarah conv. 40 a. of the tract to William Grafton (TB#A: 231).

5 June 1745: William Donahoe and w. Susanna conv. $50\frac{1}{2}$ a., pt. of Grafton's Gift, to William Grafton (TB#D: 134).

10 May 1751: William Brasher and w. Ann conv. 100 a. to William Grafton (TR#D: 139) [This William is almost certainly a s. of Thomas and Sarah (Constance) Brashier/Brazier-RWB.]

GRAVE (THE)

30 June 1734: 210 a. pat. to William Smith (TB#C: 288).

3 Aug 1743: William Smith of CE Co. conv. (*) to Henry Charlton. WS' w. Rachel cons. (TB#C: 288).

GRAVELLY HILLS

3 March 1758: John Wood, s. and heir of Joshua Wood of Lower Spesutia Hundred, conv. 50 a. pt. (*) to Thomas White (B#G: 118).

GRAY'S LOT

5 March 1700: Edward Smith and w. Elizabeth conv. 160 a. (*) and 45 a. Smith's Addition to Richard Banks (HW#2: 11).

GRAY'S LUCK

20 June 1757: Thomas Roles, late of AA co., now of Fairfax Co., VA, conv. pt. (*), 163 a. to Nicholas Maccubbin (AALR BB#2: 44).

GREAT MEADOW

12 Sep 1740: Andrew Macgill conv. 100 a. (*) to John and Christian Piggsler (TB#C: 334).

4 Aug 1746: John and Christian Pigglser, farmers, conv. pt. (*) to Peter Lemmon (TB#E: 121).

GREAT OAKS

2 July 1649: 200 a. pat. to Josias Fendall (IR#PP: 86).

20 May 1669: Josias Fendall conv. 2000 a. (*) at Fendall's Creek on s. side of Bacon Bay, to John Vanheek, Gent. (IR#PP: 86). On the same day, Fendall and his w. Mary posted bond they would guarantee the title of (*) (IR#PP: 86).

7 Oct 1670: Josias Fendall, Gent., of CH Co. appoints Capt. Thomas Howell his atty. to give seisin of (*) to John Vanheek or his atty. (IR#PP: 86).

GREEN OAK

16 April 1663: Nathaniel and Mary Utie of Spesutia, conv. (*) at Sassafras R. to Richard Bennett, Jr. (IR#PP: 63).

GREEN SPRING

20 May 1734: Samuel Owings and Christopher Randall agree to divide (*); the deed mentions Hannah Randall's LWT, her gift to Urath Randall, and Urath's marriage to Samuel Owings (HWS#M: 80).

28 May 1734: Christopher Randall conv. 100 a. (*) to ... (HWS#M: 65).

15 Sep 1741: Benjamin Wheeler conv. 30 a. (*) to his s. Thomas, but latter is not to have possession of the 30 a. until after the grantor's death. Thomas Wheeler's w. Elizabeth cons. (HWS#1-A: 546).

GREEN SPRING TRAVERSE
(See PRICHARD'S PURCHASE)

See Horvath Plat: Green Spring Valley.

18 Aug 1722: Richard Gist of BA Co. and w. Zepporah conv. to Christopher Choate Choate's Fancy, being pt. of (*), and pt. of Street's Adventure (IS#G: 111).

5 Sep 1728: Richard Gist conv. 350 a. pt. (*), Addition to Green Spring Traverse; and one other tract to Christopher Gist (IS#I: 196).
28 May 1742: Christopher Choate, Sr., and Christopher Choate, Jr., conv. 108 a., pt. (*) and pt. Choate's Adventure, to Nathaniel Gist. Flora, w. of [one of the] Christopher Choate[s], cons. (TB#A: 155).

GREEN SPRING TRAVERSE, ADDITION TO
5 Sep 1728: See Green Spring Traverse (above).

GREEN'S CHANCE
2 Nov 1726: Lewis Pottee, Jr., and w. Catherine, one of the daus. and coheirs of Matthew Green, dec., and one of the granddaughters and grantees of Jane Boon of BA Co., conv. to Thomas Cole 1/3 of pt. Levy's Tribe, pt. of (*), and pt. Choice Trippas (IS#H: 290).
8 March 1732: William Hill of BA Co., and w. Martha, dau. and coheir of Matthew Green, and also one of the granddaughters of Jane Boone, sell to Thomas Coale pt. of Choice Trippas, (*), and Levy's Tribe (IS#L: 326).
23 Aug 1794: John Boring and w. Sarah conv. 2¾ a. (*) to Ezekiel Boring (WG#PP: 347).
23 Aug 1794: John Boring conv. to George Keller of Manheim Twp., York Co., PA, 19¼ a. pt. (*): 128 a. George's Meadows; and 13 a. Anything at All. JB's w. Sarah cons. (WB#PP: 238).

GREEN'S DESIRE
2 Aug 1760: George Green, with cons. of w. Ann, conv. 50 a. (*) to Oliver Matthews (B#H: 312).

GREEN'S LOT. (Pt. of BURMAN'S FOREST)
17 Oct: 1716: Ebenezer Blackistone and w. Sarah of KE Co. conv. 48 a. (*) to Robert Green (TR#A: 416).
18 March 1763: John Green of BA conv. 80 a. (*) on Mount Ararat, and Green's Palace: to Isaac Green (B#L: 122).

GREEN'S PALACE
8 March 1727; William Cox and w. Mary conv. 50 a. (*) to John Green (IS#H: 364).
7 March 1731: William Cox, with cons. of w. Mary, conv. (50?) a. (*) to John Green for 1000 lbs. tobacco (IS#L: 195).
1745: Jacob Wright leased 157 a. of Gunpowder Manor called (*) for the lives of Ezekiel Wright (age 39 in 1767) and Solomon Watkins Wright (age 40 in 1767) (Slattery, Gunpowder Manor, p. 10).
18 March 1763: John Green of BA conv. (*) and 80 a. Green's Lot on Mount Ararat, to Isaac Green (B#L: 122).

GREEN'S PURCHASE
3 April 1728: Henry Pergeoy and w. Amey conv. 50 a. (*), pt. of a larger tract called Success, on the s. side of Back R., to Robert Green (IS#I: 128).

GREEN'S RANGE
1729: Ann Cowdry conv. (*) to Thomas Coale (IS#K: 193).

GREENFIELD'S PURCHASE
1 June 1724: William Greenfield of BA Co., conv. pt. (*) and pt. Hazlewood's Retirement to Joshua Woods. Greenfield's w. Elizabeth cons. (IS#H: 175).
5 Aug 1731: William Greenfield conv. to Joshua Wood pt. of (*) and pt. Hazlewood's Retirement (IS#L: 119).

GREER'S DISCOVERY
24 Jan 1720: 92 a. surv. for John Greer (MRR#I; MSA: 249).
2 March 1747: John Greer of BA conv. 92 a. (*) to Mark Guishard (MRR#I; TB#E: 689).

GREER'S IMPROVEMENT
24 Jan 1720: 50 a. surv. for John Greer (MRR#I; MSA: 248).
5 April 1748: John Greer conv. (*) to Mark Guishard (MRR#I: 248; TB#E 715).
8 June 1748: Mark Guishard conv. 50 a. (*) and 100 a. Greer's Park to Thomas Starkey. MG's w. Dinah cons. (TR#C: 20; MRR#I: 248, stated he conv. this to John Starkey).

GREER'S PARK
3 Feb 1718: 100 a. surv. for John Greer on the Great Falls of the Gunpowder (MRR#I; MSA: 230).
6 March 1732: Tract pat. to John Greer (Ibid.).
5 April 1748: John Greer conv. 100 a. (*) to Mark Guishard (Ibid.; TB#E: 715).
8 June 1748: Mark Guishard conv. 100 a. (*) and 58 a. Greer's Improvement to Thomas Starkey. Mark's w. Dinah cons. (TR#C: 20).

GRESHAM COLLEGE
1 June 1685: 500 a. pat. to John Gresham (TB#E: 43).
18 June 1729: Solomon Wooding [Wooden] of BA and w. Sarah conv. (*) to William McComas (IS#K: 31).
10 Oct 1733; Richard Gresham of KE Co., conv.500 a. (*) to Solomon Wooden. RG's w. Martha cons. (HWS#M: 35).
8 March 1745: Solomon Wooden of AA Co., and w. Sarah conv. 195 a., pt. (*), to William McComas (TB#E: 38).

24 March 1745: Solomon Wooden and w. Sarah conv. 165 a., pt. (*) to Daniel McComas (TB#E: 43).

GREYHOUND FOREST

3 Dec 1762: Greenbury Wilson of BA Co. conv. 250 a. (*) to Warner Gosnell (AL#F: 436).

23 Aug 1773: Warner Gosnell of BA Co., with cons. of w. Sarah, conv. 250 a. (*) to James French (AL#H: 36).

GRIMES' CHOICE

10 Sep 1724: Pat. to Nicholas Grimes (TB#C: 168).

15 Nov 1731: Nicholas Grimes, formerly of BA Co., now of Prince William Co., VA, conv. 50 a. (*) to Thomas Worthington of AA Co. (PCLR PL#8: 61).

20 April 1738: William [sic] Worthington conv. (*) to Basil Dorsey (TB#C: 168).

3 Feb 1742: Basil Dorsey, with cons. of w. Sarah, conv. 50 a. (*) to William Ricks (TB#C: 168).

22 Feb 1752: Benjamin Martin conv. to Charles Pierpoint (*) and other livestock (TR#D: 283).

GROOM'S CHANCE

300 a. pat. to Moses Groome, father of Moses Groome, Jr., and of Rebecca Saunders (TB#D: 338).

4 June 1745: Robert Saunders of AA Co. and w. Rebecca conv. (*) to s. Darby Lux [sic] (TB#D: 338).

6 June 1764: Joshua Bond leased 100 a. (*) except for land already leased to Samuel Talby and William Hugins, to George Cowen (B#N: 327).

GROSS' OUTLET

3 Aug 1743: Anthony Asher conv. 50 a. (*) and 75 a. Haphazard to George Presbury (TB#C: 301).

GROVE (THE) (c1670)

11 May 1670: Richard Low, Gent., conv. to John Gilbert and Abraham Wild merchants, the 1000 a. tract bought from Philip Calvert, also adj. tract of 600 a. tract Haslemore, both tracts on s. side of Elk R. (IR#PP: 85).

1 Nov 1670: John Gilbert, merchant, conv. to Abraham Wild, 1600 a. including 1000 a. (*) and 600 a. Haslemore (G#J: 21; TR#RA: 15).

GROVE (THE) (1671)

3 Jan 1671: 250 a. surv. for John Tarkinton at the head of Mosquito Creek; Palmer dead and all his heirs here; land is held by his widow for right of her thirds; later held by Miles Hennis, who paid the rent (MRR: 11).

3 Aug 1674: John Tarkinton and w. Florence conv. to William Palmer two adj. parcels of land; 250 a. (*), pat. 1 May 1672, and 250 a. Woodland; on 4 Aug 1674 Sheriff Samuel Boston has received ten shillings from Palmer for alienation (G#J: 276).

10 Feb 1708: John Palmer of Towcester in Co. North'ton, bro. and heir of William Palmer, late of MD, dec., gave p/a to John Davison of CE Co., surgeon, to recover 600 a. Palmer's Forest, 250 a. (*), 500 a. Palmer's Point, 300 a. Swan Harbor, and 500 a. Towcester or Tolchester in CE Co., from John Hall of James Presbury (TR#A: 126). 10 Feb 1708: John Watson and Richard Hutchins certified that John Palmer is the s. of William and Dorothy Palmer, and eld. bro. of William Palmer, who they heard d. in MD. Charles Palmer, Vicar, Wm. Clark and Thomas Kingston depose that they know JW and RH and they believe JP to be the eld. s. of W. and DP.

1 Sep 1720: William Mathew of Martin, Co. Surrey, through his atty. Richard Bennett and Thomas Bordley, both of AA Co., conv. 250 a. (*), 600 a. Palmer's Forest, 500 a. Palmer's Point, and 100 a. Tunnington to Josias Middlemore of BA Co., chirurgeon (TR#DS: 216).

GROVE (THE) (1683)

Sep 1683: 1150 a. surv. for Richard Jones (or Johns) on the w. branch of Bush R. (MRR: 44).

GROVE(S) (THE)

11 May 1670: Richard Low, Gent., conv. to John Gilbert and Abraham Wild, merchants, 1000 a., Grove, bought from Philip Calvert, and 600 a. Haslemore, both tracts being on the s. side of Elk R. (IR#PP: 85).

1 Nov 1670: John Gilbert conv. to Abraham Wild, merchant, 1600 a. embracing (*) and an adj. 600 a. tract Haslemore (G#J: 21; TR#RA: 15).

20 March 1741: Samuel Hyde of London, merchant, exec. of LWT of John Hyde of London, conv. 120 a. (*) to Jacob Bull (TB#A: 192).

14 Nov 1743: Capt. John Smith of CV Co., merchant, in exch. for 636 a., 66 per. of Hall's Craft in CV Co., conv. to Walter Smith of the Freshes of the Patuxent, s. and heir of Walter Smith, dec., the following tracts: 300 a. pt. Daley's Discovery, 700 a. (*), and 424 a. pt. Addition to Poor Jamaica Man's Plague (TB#C: 416).

1761: Edward Cockey conv. 50 a. pt. (*) to Loveless Gorsuch (B#Q: 371).

GUNNELL'S DEVOTION

12 April 1680: 60 a. surv. for George Gunnell, near the mouth of Rumley Creek; "it appears to be no such land, Gunnell dead" (MRR: 29).

GUNNER'S RANGE

10 Oct 1707: 250 a. pat. by James Crook (MPL DD#5: 434 PL#2: 249).

See PW Plat H; Horvath Plat: Ruxton and Riderwood.

21 Nov 1751: Walter Dallas, with cons. of w. Cloe, conv. to Samuel Gott, Gunner's Range, 250 a. (TR#D: 297).

24 April 1752: Samuel Gott, with cons. of w. Rachel, conv. to William Towson, blacksmith, 73 a. pt. (*) (TR#D: 348).

GUNPOWDER ISLANDS

20 June 1733: Bloyce Wright made a will leaving (*) (may have been called Carvell's Island or Phillips Island) to his eld. s. Thomas (MCW#VII: 232).

1 Sep 1741: Bloyce Wright conv. 150 a. (which he inher. from his father Bloyce Wright), to Abraham Jarrett. BW's w. Sarah cons. (HWS#1-A: 560).

GUNPOWDER MANOR

2 March 1737: Benjamin Tasker, Agent for Lord Baltimore, leased to Thomas Gittings 153 a. pt. (*), for the lives of Susannah, Thomas and James Gittings, ch. of Thomas Gittings (HWS#1-A: 390).

GUNSON'S NECK

13 April 1703: William Loney of BA Co. and w. Jane conv. 200 a. (*) and 100 a. Hamstead's Marsh to Anthony Drew; tracts were formerly possessed by Thomas Overton and at his death passed to his dau. Jane Loney (HW#2: 220).

GUNWORTH

31 July 1661: 81 a. surv. for Walter Dixson; on n. side of Patapsco R., adj. land of William Clapham; later possessed by Francis Petitie "no heirs;" land uncultivated; a later rent roll reads 80 a. sold to Francis Poteet "supposed to be an alien," who left a dau. (MRR: 91-92).

17 Aug 1663: Walter Dickeson assigns to Richard Bale [sic] the tract Gunworth, location not stated (RM#HS: 4).

3 Jan 1667: Richard Ball, with cons. of w. Mary conv. 80 a. of land on the n. side of Patapsco R., adj. the land of William Clapham, to Francis Poteet (IR#PP: 63).

14 Oct 1743: Luke Trotten and William Hamilton, execs. of John Gardner, conv. 60 a. Gardner's Addition, 80 a. (*), 200 a. pt. Honderton (?), and 300 a. Timber Neck to Sabritt Sollers (TB#C: 327).

28 Feb 1758: Sabrett Sollers conv. 52 a. (*) to Josias Bowen (B#G: 146).

GURSHES

20 April 1705: Richard Owen of BA Co. conv. p/a to John Hurst to conv. 100 a. (*) to Mrs. Katherine Scutt, but she is not be paid with a certain bill of exch. drawn by RO on a certain John Owen of London (TR#A: 71).

GUTTERIDGE'S ADDITION

20 Dec 1690: Robert Burman conv. to James Dryden 150 a. (*), 100 a. The Cross, and 120 a. Burhan's Industry (IR#AM: 113).

4 July 1731: John Moale conv. back to Christopher Randall Kinsey's Choice and Guttrick's Addition, any excess acreage above 40 a. orig. conv. by Randall on 20 Jan 1729 (See IS#K: 165). Excess occurred due to errors in bounds. JM's w. Rachel cons. (IS#L: 163).

26 July 1731: Christopher Randall, Jr., conv. 70 a. of (*) and Kinsey's Choice to John Moale. CR's w. Catherine cons. (IS#L: 148).

4 Dec 1735: John Moale conv. (*) and Kinsey's Choice back to Christopher Randall who sold them to JM on 26 July 1731; orig. deed stated the tracts contained 70 a. but they did not. The purpose of this deed was to conv. tracts back to CR who was to resurv. them and then conv. back to JM with proper metes and bounds (HWS#M: 353).

HAB NAB AT A VENTURE

30 June 1688: 350 a. surv. for Thomas Durbin and later held by his orphans; c1707 150 a. were held by his orphans and 200 a. held by John Eaglestone (MRR: 76).

6 May 1689: Pat. to Thomas Durbin (TB#A: betw. 74 and 80).

7 March 1703: Christopher Durbin conv. pt. (*) to John Eagleston (HW#2: 315).

1 June 1703: Durbin conv. another parcel (*) to John Eagleston (HW#2: 252).

22 May 1705: Durbin and w. Mary conv. pt. (*) (150 a. acc. to TB#A: see below). to John Gardner (IR#PP: 183).

1 June 1716: John Eagleston conv. two parcels, 154 a. and 46 a. of (*) to Nicholas Rogers. Eagleston's w. Mary cons. (TR#A: 396).

4 Nov 1730: Josias Hendon and w. Margaret conv. 100 a. (*) to John Sergeant (IS#L: 30).

14 Jan 1741: Luke Trotten and William Hamilton conv. 150 a. (*) to Dr. George Buchanan (TB#A: betw. 74 and 80).

4 April 1741: John Sergeant of BA Co. conv. 100 a. (*) to Christopher Duke (HWS#1-A: 453).
28 Jan 1752: Elinor Buchanan, widow of Dr. George Buchanan, released to her s. Lloyd Buchanan tract (*) (TR#D: 307).

HABERSTON

1693: John Arden of BA Co. conv. 50 a. pt. Bachelor's Delight and (*) to Richard Thompson of BA co. (RM#HS: 437).

HAILE'S ADVENTURE

2 May 1689: 56 a. surv. for Nicholas Haile; later poss. by Edward Stevenson. (MRR: 96).
13 July 1728: Nicholas Haile conv. 56 a. (*) to Edward Stevenson. NH's w. Frances cons. (IS#I: 244).

HAILE'S ADVENTURE (B)

7 July 1748: Nicholas Haile, Jr., conv. 100 a. (?) to Dutton Lane. NH's w. Ruth cons. (TR#C: 45).
1750: Dutton Lane owned 100 a. (*) (1750 DB).

HAILE'S DISCOVERY

31 Oct 1724: Henry Sater and w. Mary conv. 100 a. (*) to Benjamin Knight (IS#H: 25).
17 June 1745: Sarah Knight of BA Co., widow, conv. 100 a. (*) and 85 a. pt. Knight's Addition, to Sarah Boring (TB#D: 253).
19 Feb 1753: Sarah Boreing conv. (*) to Wm. Askew of Annapolis (BB#I: 218).
5 Oct 1761: William Askew, with cons. of w. Keziah, conv. 100 a. (*) and 85 a. Knights Addition, to Alexander Stewart (B#I: 427).

HAILE'S FELLOWSHIP

1695: Surv. for N. Haile.
See Hosvath Plat: Ruxton and Riderwood.
6 April 1745: Nicholas Hailes conv. 100 a. pt. (*) to Christopher Grindall of London, mariner (TB#D: 83).
30 March 1747: Christopher Grindall conv. 100 a. (*) to Nicholas Haile (TB#E: 486).
30 March 1747: Nicholas Haile conv. 100 a. (*) to Charles Ridgely (TB#E: 487).

HAILE'S FOLLY

19 Feb 1702: Nicholas Haile surv. 100 a. (*) (Card Index to Patents).
28 Aug 1742: Charles and Millicent Merryman, and Richard Miller Cole and w. Sabina, in exch. for 100 a. Boring's Gift, conv. 100 a.(*) to John Boring, Jr., for the lifetimes of John Boring, Jr., John Boring, Sr., and the latter's w. Sarah (TB#C: 18).
1750: held by the heirs of John Boring (1750 DB).

HAILE'S FOREST

6 April 1745: Nicholas Hailes conv. 100 a. pt. (*) to Christopher Grindall of London, mariner (TB#D: 83).
28 March 1747: Nicholas Haile of BA Co. conv.100 a. (*) to Christopher Grindall of London, mariner (TB#E: 347).
1750: George Atkinson conv. 100 a. (*) to Nehemiah Hicks (TR#D: 56).
1 Oct 1750: George Atkinson of Annapolis, exec. of the will of Capt. Christopher Grindall, conv. 100 a. (*) to Nehemiah Hicks (TR#D: 56).

HAILE'S LONG GROVE

6 April 1745: Nicholas Haile conv. 200 a. pt. (*) to Christopher Grindall of London, mariner, but only for the remainder of the 99 year lease (TB#D: 83).
28 March 1747: Nicholas Haile of BA Co. conv. 200 a. (*) to Christopher Grindall of London, mariner (TB#E: 347).

HAIL'S PARK

7 Aug 1746: Benjamin Tasker leased 92 a. (*) to Matthew Hail for 99 years (AL#I: 52).
2 April 1750: Matthew Hail assigns his lease of (*), pt. of His Lordship's Reserve Lands, to Jacob Cox (TR#C: 399).
(date not shown): Jacob Cox assigned the lease to James Bosley (AL#I: 52).
20 Jan 1774: James Bosley assigns (*) to Daniel Rees for the remainder of the lease (AL#I: 52).

HAIL'S PLAINS

23 Sep 1732: Sylvanus or Sylvester Jones conv. 100 a. (*) to John Risteau (IS#L: 283).

HAINES (or HAMES) POINT

7 March 1681: William Hames(?) conv. (*) to George Ogleby (RM#HS: 92).
5 Aug 1684: George Ogleby of BA Co., tailor, conv. (*) to Thomas James, planter. GO's w. Johannah cons. (RM#HS: 92).
20 June 1696: Thomas James of Chester Co., PA, house carpenter,conv. 64 a. (*) to his son-in-law Giles Stevens (RM#HS: 529).

HALL'S ADDITION

10 Sep 1722: Henry Hall, Sr., conv. 100 a. (*) to Henry Hall, Jr. HH's w. Elizabeth signed (IS#G: 86).

HALL'S APPROACH

28 May 1742: William Hall and w. Mary conv. 50 a. (*) to Christopher Choate (TB#A: 152).

14 June 1743: Christopher Shoat conv. 50 a. (*) (which he bought from William Hall), to Henry Morgan (TB#C: 257).

27 July 1745: William Hall and Christopher Choate conv. 50 a. (*) to Amon Butler. WH's w. Mary and CC's w. Flora cons. (TB#D: 282).

2 Aug 1745: Christopher Choate of BA Co., conv. 50 a. (*) to Amon Butler, s. of Henry Butler, innkeeper (TB#D: 281).

HALL'S (HELL'S?) LOT

24 Nov 1715: Robert Brown, of AA Co., Gent., conv. 300 a. (*) to William and John Bond. RB's w. Catherine cons. (TR#A: 365).

HALL'S PALACE

11 Oct 1710: Henry Hall and w. Elizabeth conv. 300 a. (*) to Amos Garrett (TR#A: 105).

19 Sep 1711: Henry Hall of BA Co., planter, and w. Elizabeth, conv. 300 a. (*) to Amos Garrett (TR#A: 163).

HALL'S PARK

Nov 1734: 1152 a. pat. to Col. Edward Hall as a resurv. on Andrew's Conquest, being 480 a. which Hall had purch. in 1719, and 300 a. claimed as escheat land for want of heirs of Nicholas Rogier, als. Rogers (TB#C: 531).

9 July 1744: Avarilla Hall, widow and extx. of Col. Edward Hall sold land to Col. John Hall (TB#C: 531).

23 Oct 1744: John Hall, with cons. of w. Hannah, agreed to conv. 50 a. (*) to Francis Bucknall, in exch. for 50 a. being ½ of Conquest. If Bucknall d. s.p., land would go to his sister Mary as limited by the will of Thomas Bucknall (TB#C: 653).

1 Nov 1744: Francis Bucknall, with cons. of w. Blanche, conv. 50 a. (*) to John Hampton and Daniel Pologe (TB#C: 660).

HALL'S PIPE

28 July 1718: John Hall conv. 145 a. (*) to John Clark. JH's w. Martha cons. (TR#DS: 26).

17 March 1718: John Clark conv. 145 a. (*) and 100 a. Clark's Tob..., to Lawrence Draper. JC's w. Elizabeth cons. (TR#RA: 515).

7 Oct 1727: Lawrence Draper conv. 145 a. (*) and other land to Garvas Gilbert. LD's w. Mary cons. (IS#H: betw. f. 20 and 26).

17 Sep 1735: Garvas Gilbert conv. 60 a. pt. Clark's Tobacco, 40 a. pt. Gilbert's Chance, and 145 a., pt. Hall's Pipe, to his s. Michael Gilbert. GG's w. Mary cons. (HWS#M: 302).

HALL'S PLAINS

3 Nov 1702: John Hall of BA Co. conv. 100 a. pt. (*) to Richard Owens of Herring Creek, AA Co. (HW#2: 187).

March 1704/5: Richard Owings of BA Co., merchant, conv. 100 a. (*) to John Cotter, Dr. of Physic (IR#PP: 151).

4 June 1705: John Cotter, Dr. of Physic, conv. 100 a. (*) to Edward Jones (IR#PP: 154).

1 Nov 1715: John Hall and w. Martha conv. 200 a. pt. (*) to Obadiah Pritchard (TR#A: 356).

25 March 1740: Samuel, Obadiah, and James Pritchard, sons of Obadiah Pritchard, agreed to divide 300 a. (*), 50 a. Obadiah's Venture and 25 a. Margaret's Purchase. James' will have the last two tracts completely, and enough of (*) to make it equal (HWS#1-A: 408).

5 Aug 1741: Obadiah Pritchard, s. of Obadiah, dec., conv. his share of (*) to Edward Wakeman, physician. His w. Elizabeth cons. Deed mentions grantor's bros. Samuel and James (TB#A: 36).

1 May 1745: Samuel Pritchard and w. Isabella conv. 93 a. pt. (*) to Henry Baker of CV Co. (TB#D: 151).

HALL'S PURCHASE

20 Sep 1742: John Hall, s. of Edward Hall who was a s. and heir of John Hall dec., conv. Hall's Purchase (a resurv. of all of the land bought of the Kimballs), 50 a. Mascall's Humor, 400 a. Taylor's Good Hap, and 470 a. Timber Neck, to John Hall, one of the sons and devisees of John Hall (TB#C: 13).

HALL'S RICH (or RIDGE) NECK

19 Dec 1699: 400 a. surv. for John Hall and w. Martha on a ridge near a branch of Deer Creek (MRR: 10).

19 Sep 1747: Col. John Hall of BA Co. conv. 110 a. pt. (*) to John Hall, s. of Col. Edward Hall; Col. JH's w. Hannah cons.; deed mentioned a judgment recorded in Prov. Court (TB#E: 549).

5 Nov 1747: Thomas White conv. pt. (*) to John Hall, s. of Col. Edward Hall (TB#E: 582).

15 Aug 1748: John Hall of Cranberry, s. of Edward (who was s. and heir of John Hall and w. Martha), deeds to Thomas White all (*), orig. granted to afsd. John and Martha Hall for 620 a. Grantor's w. Bethia cons. (TR#C: 118).

HALL'S RIDGE

1 April 1693: John Hall conv. 28 a. Hall's Ridge, pt. of a warrant for 640 a., to his dau.-in-law Isabella Hooper. If she d. without lawfully begotten heirs, land to go to her sister Ann Collier. If Ann d. without legitimate heirs, land would revert to John Hall; if Hall bought 31 a. Waterton's Angle,

formerly belonging to John Waterton, (and gave it to Isabella) she was to give her sister Ann an equal amount of above 218 a. (HW#2: 122).

1 April 1748: Isaac Jackson conv. 50 a. (*) to Benj. Legoe, Jr. (TB#E: 704).

8 March 1749: Mary Jackson, widow of Isaac Jackson, conv. 250 a. (*) to Benjamin Lego, Jr. (TR#C: 393).

HAMMOND'S ADDITION

29 a. orig. granted to Thomas Hammond (HWS#M: 313).

27 May 1735: Lawrence Hammond, s. and devisee of Col. Thomas Hammond, conv. his share of Dearing's Increase, 200 a. Health, and 100 a. Spring Point, which LH had resurv. into Brother's Kindness, in all 371 a., to his bro. William Hammond. LH's w. Abarilla cons. (HWS#M: 313).

HAMMOND'S HOPE

13 May 1678: 300 a. surv. for James Hammond who d. without heirs; land was liable to an escheat (MRR: 5).

1730: Christopher Gist conv. 300 a. (*) to Edward Hall (IS#K: 266).

26 Feb 1733: Edward Hall, Gent., gave bond to Robert Courtney he would make over the tract Hammond's Hope (HWS#M: 30).

4 Sep 1733:: Edward Hall and w. Avarilla conv. 300 a. (*) to Robert Courtney (HWS#M: 18).

3 March 1742: Robert Courtney conv. 100 a. (*) to his s. John Courtney (TB#C: 171).

3 March 1742: Robert Courtney conv. 100 a. (*) to his s. Jonas Courtney (TB#C: 174).

3 June 1743: Robert and Hannah Courtney conv. 100 a. (*) to Daniel Johnson of Newcastle Co., DE (TB#C: 293).

8 Aug 1748: John Courtney of BA Co. deeds to Col. Thomas White, late of BA Co., now of Philadelphia, 100 a., the middle pt. of (*), orig. surv. for James Hammond on 13 May 1678; granted to Christian Geist by patent of escheat on 27 Aug 1727; on 21 May 1730: Geist sold it to Edward Hall (IS#K: 266); on 4 Sep 1733 EH sold it to Robert Courtney, father of John (HWS#M: 18); on 3 March 1742 RC gave the middle pt. to his s., the afsd. John Courtney. JC's w. Usaan Courtney cons. (TR#C: 27).

11 Aug 1748: Daniel Johnson was conv. parts of (*) by various persons, and now conv. the tract to Thomas White. DJ's w. Lavinia cons. The deed stated that Christian Geist conv. the land to Robert Courtney (TR#C: 32).

HAMMOND'S PURCHASE

4 June 1747: William Hammond conv. 377 a. Brother's Inheritance (except 148½ a. now called Hammond's Purchase), 109¼ a. Hammond's Purchase Resurv. (except for 19½ a. sold to Benjamin Tasker) and 100 a. Hammond's Struggle (except for 11 a. taken away) to Charles Carroll. WH's w. Sarah cons. (TB#E: 448).

HAMMOND'S PURCHASE RESURVEYED

4 June 1747: William Hammond conv. 377 a. Brother's Inheritance (except 148½ a. now called Hammond's Purchase), 109¼ a. Hammond's Purchase Resurveyed (except for 19½ a. sold to Benjamin Tasker) and 100 a. Hammond's Struggle (except for 11 a. taken away) to Charles Carroll. WH's w. Sarah cons. (TB#E: 448).

HAMMOND'S RICH LAND (or NECK)

1740: 100 a. surv. for Laurence Hammond.
See Horvath Plat: Randallstown.

1 March 1744: Lawrence Hammond conv. 100 a. (*) to William Arnold. LH's w. Abarilla cons. (TB#D: 55).

4 Aug 1750: William Arnold mortgaged 100 a. (*) to Charles Ridgely (TR#C: 529).

1754: William Arnold conv. 100 a. (*) to William Black (BB#I: 155).

HAMMOND'S STRUGGLE

4 June 1747: William Hammond conv. 377 a. Brother's Inheritance (except 148½ a. now called Hammond's Purchase), 109¼ a. Hammond's Purchase Resurveyed (except for 19½ a. sold to Benjamin Tasker) and 100 a. Hammond's Struggle (except for 11 a. taken away) to Charles Carroll. WH's w. Sarah cons. (TB#E: 448).

HAMPTON COURT

15 Oct 1725: Dutton Lane gave bond he will conv. quitclaim for (*) to Richard Lane (IS#K: 192).

30 Aug 1740: William Merryman conv. 50 a. pt. (*) to James Boreing. WM's w. Margaret cons. (HWS#1-A: 462).

11 July 1746: William Merryman and James Boreing conv. 100 a. (*) to Charles Ridgely. WM's w. Margaret cons. (TB#E: 166).

HAMPTON COURT

1747: 316 a. surv. for Charles Ridgely.
See PW Plat H.

HAMSTEAD MARSH

12 March 1665/6: John Brown, merchant of Salem, New England, conv. 100 a. (*) to Thomas Overton (IS#IK: 6).

13 April 1703: William Loney of BA Co. and w. Jane conv. 100 a. (*) to Anthony Drew; tract was formerly possessed by Thomas Overton and at his death desc. to his dau. Jane Loney (HW#2: 220).

HANETTS FANCY

1739: Samuel Watkins conv, 196 a. (*) to William Bond (IS#K: 259).

HANNAH'S LOT

15 Dec 1733: William Wheeler and w. Constant conv. (*) to Thomas Wheeler (HWS#M: 24).

16 Jan 1747: Thomas Wheeler conv. 100 a. (*) to Charles Ridgely. TW's w. Ann cons. (TB#E: 660).

HANSON'S IMPROVEMENT

9 June 1711: Charles Carroll conv. 31 a. (*), pt. of Cole's Harbor, to Jonathan Hanson (TR#A: 138).

HANSON'S WOOD LOT

11 Oct 1732: Jonathan Hanson conv. 150 a. (*) to his sister Mary Hanson (IS#L: 394).

HAPHAZARD (1682)

11 May 1682: 100 a. surv. for John Bevan on s. side of Gunpowder R., adj. Harwood's Lion, later poss.: 30 a. Capt. Harwood, 70 a. Edward Jones; still later 36 a. by Richard Harwood and 64 a. by Edward Jones (MRR: 41).

6 June 1688: John Bevan and w. Julian conv. 36 a. (*), adj. to Harwood's Lion, to Richard Harwood (RM#HS: betw. 271-276).

25 April 1693: John Bevan and w. Sarah conv. 70 a. (*) to John Fuller (RM#HS: 372).

6 March 1693/4: Hester Fuller, w. of John Fuller, conv. 70 a. (*) to Edward Jones (HW#2: 373).

1695: John Bevan and w. conv. 36 a. (*) to Richard Harwood (RM#HS: 273?).

4 May 1721: Sylvanus Jones conv. 75 a. pt. (*) to Anthony Asher (TR#DS: 316).

4 Nov 1742: Giles Stevens and w. Alce conv. 28 a. Hap Hazard and 64 a. Horn Point to Joseph Thomas (TB#C: 60).

3 Aug 1743: Anthony Asher conv. 50 a. Gross' Outlet and 75 a. Haphazard to George Presbury (TB#C: 301).

HAPHAZARD (1714)

20 Feb 1714: 300 a. pat. to John Cole (TB#A: 66).

21 Jan 1726: John Cole conv. to John Gardner of Bear Creek; also pt. of Happy Be Lucky, taken up by Cole on 4 Dec 1696, and pt. of Haphazard, taken up by Cole on 20 Feb 1714. JC's w. Dinah cons. (IS#H: 340).

14 Jan 1741: Luke Trotten and William Hamilton, execs. of LWT of John Gardner, dec., conv. 200 a. Daniel's Whimsey, 300 a. Haphazard and 126 a. Happy Be Lucky to Alexander Lawson; John Cole sold pt. of Daniel's Whimsey and the last two tracts to John Gardner (TB#A: 66).

HAPPY BE LUCKY

20 July 1726: 126 a. pat. by John Cole (TB#A: 66).

21 Jan 1726: John Cole conv. to John Gardner of Bear Creek; also pt. of Happy Be Lucky, taken up by Cole on 4 Dec 1696, and pt. of Haphazard, taken up by Cole on 20 Feb 1714. JC's w. Dinah cons. (IS#H: 340).

14 Jan 1741: Luke Trotten and William Hamilton, execs. of LWT of John Gardner, dec., conv. 200 a. Daniel's Whimsey, 300 a. Haphazard and 126 a. Happy Be Lucky to Alexander Lawson; John Cole sold pt. of Daniel's Whimsey and the last two tracts to John Gardner (TB#A: 66).

HAPPY CHANCE (or CHOICE)

8 June 1723: James Frizzell, s. of James Frizzell, dec., conv. 331 a. (*) to Henry Wetherall (IS#G: 191; IS#H: 35).

HAPPY HARBOR

10 April 1671: 400 a. pat. to Richard Leake (G#J: 92; TR#RA: 65).

5 Aug 1671: Richard Leake, tailor and w. Gwilthin conv. 400 a. (N) at Duck Creek on Sassafras R., to Henry Penington, planter (G#J: 92; TR#RA: 65).

HARBOROUGH

18 Aug 1663: 350 a. surv. for Paul Kinsey; later held by the orphans of James Greeneff (MRR: 102).

23 Jan 1685/6: Richard Johns and w. Elizabeth, of CV Co., conv. 500 a. Harborow and 150 a. White Oak Spring to Thomas Lightfoot (RM#HS: 172).

6 April 1687: Thomas Lightfoot, Gent., conv. to James Greeniff, planter, 350 a. (*). TL's w. Rebecca cons. 25 April 1687: Lightfoot gave bond to Greeniff for performances of covenants. 20 April 1687: Thomas and Rebecca appoint Thomas Scudamore their atty. to conv. land (RM#HS: 227).

14 Jan 1701: James Greeneff of AA Co. (s. of "John" Greeneff, dec. (sic) who was conv. tract by Thomas Lightfoot on 25 April 1687), (in another place grantor is called s. of James), conv. 300 a. "Half of the tract" (*) to John Howard of AA Co., Gent. (HW#2: 163).

9 May 1719: William Orrick of BA Co. and w. Hannah conv. 10-12 a. (*) to Francis Ouchterlony (TR#RA: 539).

HARD SCUFFLE

1752: 34 a. surv. for Teago Tracey as pt. of His Lordship's Reserved Land (BA Co. Unpat. Cert. # 662).

HARE'S GREEN (See HART'S GREEN)

HARGIN

2 Oct 1685: George Thompson of SM Co., Gent., conv. 375 a. (*) to Richard Tydings of AA Co. (RM#HS: 164).

HARMAN (See HARMER)

HARMER'S (HARMAN'S) HOPE

100 a. resurv. by Daniel Scott as pt. of Scott's Improvement (q.v.) (TB#E: 534).

HARMER'S (HARMAN'S) TOWN

30 Aug 1688: Thomas Stockett, s. and heir apparent of Thomas Stockett late of AA Co., dec., conv. (*) and another 200 a. at Point Comfort to Jacob Loton of CE Co. (RM#HS: 294).

7 Oct 1713: Jacob Loton of CE Co., joiner, conv. his filial portion of (*), due him by the LWT of his father Jacob Loton, to John Stokes; land was purch. by elder John Loton from Thomas Stockett and is free of charges except for a mortgage which JS is to pay (TR#A: 244).

24 Nov 1713: John Loton, s. of John Loton, dec., conv. his filial portion of (*) to John Stokes; land is free and clear (TR#A: 250).

15 March 1714: Mary Loton, spinster, conv. her filial portion of (*) to John Stokes; deed stated her father purch. it from Thomas Stockett and then left it to her by her LWT (TR#A: 324).

11 Nov 1736: George Stokes, s. of John Stokes, with cons. of George's w. Susanna, conv. (*) (which had been devised to him by his father John Stokes) and Montserada (which John Stokes purch. from Edward Parrish) to Humphrey Wells Stokes, in exch. for 2/3 of Coheir's Lot (IS#IK: 334).

HARMER'S HOPE

Orig. surv. for Godfrey Harmer and Oliver Sprye and sold to John Shadwell, Sr. (IS#G: 352).

1 Aug 1670: Godfrey Harmer, merchant, and w. Mary, conv. 100 a. (*), on s. side of Salt Peter Creek in Gunpowder R., to John Shadwell (IR#PP: 84).

21 July 1724: John Jones of BA Co., and w. Margaret, dau. and sole heir of a certain John Shadwell, the Younger, conv. to Daniel Scott, the Younger, s. of Daniel Scott, the Elder, 490 a., comprised of the following tracts: Chestnut Neck and Stanharkat (both orig. surv. for John Shadwell, Sr.), and (*) and Hunting Creek (both orig. surv. for Godfrey Harmer and Oliver Sprye and sold to John Shadwell, Sr., grandfather of said Margaret Jones) (IS#G: 352).

HARMER'S (HARMOND'S) (S)WANTOWN

15 April 1658: 200 a. surv. for Godfey Harmer and James Robertson near Swan Creek; now possessed by James Phillips, supposed to belong to orphan of Edward Boothby (MRR: 15).

200 a. pat. by Godfrey Harmer and James Robertson (TR#A: 91).

8 June 1710: James Maxwell, Gent., with cons. of w. Ann, conv. (*) to John Hall (TR#A: 91).

HARMOND (See HARMER)

HARRIOTT'S FANCY

7 June 1721: Oliver Harriott and w. Susanna conv. 196 a. (*) to Samuel Watkins (TR#RA: 318).

1730: Samuel Watkins, with cons. of w. Mary, conv. (*) to William Bond (IS#K: 259).

HARRIS' CHOICE

6 June 1692: Peter Bond and w. Alice conv. 200 a. of (*) and 140 a. Prosperity to Thomas Hedge of BA Co. (RM#HS: 227).

HARRIS'S DELIGHT

4 June 1735: John Harris, BA Co. shoemaker, and w. Dorothy, conv. 100 a. Harris' Delight to William (or John Poteet: the clerk seems to have made an error) Putteet, planter (HWS#M: 224).

6 Aug 1755: John Poteet, s. of William, conv. to Henry Green 100 a. Harris' Delight. John's w. Elizabeth cons. (BB#I: 428). (The dates fit for him to be the s. of William who m. Jane Stewart in 1733; John's w. could be Elizabeth Ryley).

HARRIS' TRUST

25 May 1685: William Harris conv. 300 a. (*) at Bynam's Branch to Thomas Hedge (deed includes bond and letter of atty.) (RM#HS: 141).

6 April 1705: Peter Bond conv. 100 a. (*) to Thomas Bond; the land was devised by Peter Bond of BA Co., dec., to his sons Thomas, William, and John as tenants in life; he conv. 100 a. to John Bond and 100 a. to William Bond (IR#PP: 176, 177, 179).

HARRYMAN'S DESIRE

29 Oct 1786: Benjamin and Dorcas Buck conv. $42\frac{1}{2}$ a. (*) to John Hatton (WG#Y: 29).

HARRYMAN'S LANDING

14 May 1745: George Harryman of BA Co., with cons. of w. Ann, conv. 50 a. Harryman's Landing,

100 a. Harryman's Range and 19 a. K... (granted 20 May 1725 to J. Rivess) to Charles Carroll of Annapolis, chirurgeon (TB#D: 155).

HARRYMAN'S PASTURE

21 March 1747; Samuel Harryman, with cons. of w. Comfort, conv. 42 a. (*) to William Smith of BA Co., cordwainer (TB#E: 713).

HARRYMAN'S RANGE

20 Aug 1734: Cert. of surv. (See TR#C: 383).
14 May 1745: George Harryman granted release (or confirmation) of his title to 100 a. (*) to Charles Carroll of Annapolis, chirurgeon (TR#C: 383).
14 May 1745: George Harryman of BA Co., with cons. of w. Ann, conv. 50 a. Harryman's Landing, 100 a. (*) and 19 a. K... (granted 20 May 1725 to J. Rivess) to Charles Carroll of Annapolis, chirurgeon (TB#D: 155).

HART'S (or HARE'S) GREEN

Orig. pat by Edward Mumford, and later held by Robert Lynch for the orphans of Samuel Greenwood (MRR: 90).
4 Dec 1688: Edward Mumford, with cons. of w. Ann, conv. 35 a. (*) and 15 a. other land to Samuel Greenwood (RM#HS: 320).
2 June 1714: Samuel Greenwood, s. and heir of Samuel Greenwood, conv. 35 a. (*) to Robuck Lynch (TR#A: 295).
17 March 1730: Joseph Crouch of AA Co., and w. Mary (formerly w. of Robuck Lynch) conv. Hart's Green, Jones' Inheritance, and Polar Ridge (formerly taken up by John Martin) to William Lynch (IS#L: 114).
1750: William Lynch owned 19 a. (*); Robert Lynch owned 19 a. (*) (1750 DB).

HASLE PARK

3 Nov 1675: Henry Haslewood, Gent., and w. Elizabeth conv. to Rutgertson Garretts, planter, 75 a. (*) G#J: 335).
4 Nov 1675: Rutgertson Garretts planter conv. 75 a. (*) adj. to Woodpecker's Hall, to Dennis English (IR#PP: 20).
27 Feb 1705: John English, s. and heir of Dennis English, late of BA Co., dec., conv. 75 a. (*) to Aquila Paca (RM#HS: 555).
8 March 1715: Aquila Paca, Gent., conv. 75 a. (*) to George Wells and w. Mary (TR#A: 394).

HASLEMORE

11 May 1670: Richard Low, Gent., conv. to John Gilbert and Abraham Wild, merchants, 1000 a., Grove, bought from Philip Calvert, and 600 a. Haslemore, both tracts being on s. side of Elk R. (IR#PP: 85).
1 Nov 1670: John Gilbert conv. to Abraham Wild, merchant, 1600 a. embracing The Grove and adj. 600 a. tract (*) (G#J: 21; TR#RA: 15).

HASLEWOOD'S RETIREMENT

Jan 1676: Henry Haslewood and w. Elizabeth conv. (*) to John Ireland (IR#PP: 10).
8 Aug 1701: James Ives of BA Co. conv. 50 a. (*) to Thomas Greenfield; the land was taken up by Henry Haslewood and left to James Ives by the LWT of Henry Haslewood, Jr. (HW#2: 281).
7 Aug 1703: James Ives made another deed to secure Greenfield's title to (*) (HW#2: 282).
1 June 1724: William Greenfield of BA Co., conv. pt. (*) and pt. Greenfield's Purchase to Joshua Woods. WG's w. Elizabeth cons. (IS#H: 175).
5 Aug 1731: William Greenfield of BA Co. conv. pts. of Greenfield's Purchase and Hazlewood's Retirement to Joshua Wood (IS#L: 119).

HATHAWAY'S HAZARD

28 Jan 1716: Humphrey Jones conv. 200 a. (*) to Samuel Brown who may have the land after decease of Humphrey's w. Mary; Brown to seat himself on the plantation this year (TR#A: 435).
29 March 1720: Samuel Brown and w. Mary conv. 100 a. pt. (*) to John Durbin except for a small plot at the beginning tree of the tract, 10 perches x 25 perches, which we give to Charles Whitaker forever (TR#DS: 200).
20 July 1725: Samuel Brown and w. Mary conv. 200 a. (*) to John Durbin except for the 10 x 25 perches parcel given to Charles Whitaker (IS#H: 156).
7 Dec 1726: John Durbin and w. Avarilla conv. 112 a. pt. Eastland Hills and Sophia's Dairy, and 200 a. Hathaway's Hazard to Samuel Hughes, except for a parcel of Hathaway's Hazard given by Samuel Bourne (who later sold the land to Durbin) to Charles Whitaker (IS#H: 370).
30 July 1742: John Whitemore and w. Mary conv. 30 a. pt. Jones Addition and 10 a., 25 perches, pt. (*) to John Hughes, with the exception of land deeded by John Durbin to John Hughes (TB#C: 287).
3 Aug 1743: Samuel Hughes conv. 174 a. pt. (*) to s. John Hughes (TB#C: 291).
14 May 1746: Samuel Hughes of BA Co. conv. Eastland Hills, pt. Sophia's Dairy and (*), to Col. John Hall, Jacob Giles, and Isaac Webster (TB#E: 432).

HATHAWAY'S TRUST

28 March 1685: 150 a. surv. for John Hathaway on e. side of the southwest branch of the Bush R.;

now in poss. of Mark Rifle; later held by John Gresham (MRR: 50).
3 June 1691: John Hathaway conv. 150 a. (*) to William Yorks, Sr. (IR#AM: 80).
4 July 1699: Mary, late w. of James Frissell, dec., released her right of dower to Edwards Lot and (*) to William and Oliver York, sons of William (TR#RA: 391).
8 Aug 1699: William and Oliver York conv. 150 a. (*) to Mark Swift (TR#RA: 388).
29 May 1703: Mark Swift and w. Elizabeth, through their atty. Richard Colegate, conv. 150 a. (*) to John Gresham, Sr., of AA Co. (HW#2: 298).
22 March 1749: Richard Gresham of KE Co. conv. 150 a. (*) to Thomas Harrison (TR#C: 438).
3 March 1749/50: Richard Gresham grants release to Thomas Harrison. RG's w. Martha cons. (TR#C: 439).

HAWKINS CHANGE

9 Dec 1743: John Hawkins, with cons. of w., Rebecca, conv. 100 a. Hawkins Change to Michael Hodgkins (TB#C: 399).

HAWKINS CHOICE

19 July 1725: Nathan Rigbie, with cons. of w. Cassandra, conv. 100 a. (*) to John Hawkins (IS#K: 174).
22 March 1736: John Hawkins and w. Rebecca conv. 100 a. (*) to Joseph Hopkins of BA Co., Gent. (IS#IK: 395).

HAWKINS DESIRE

22 Dec 1742: Augustine Hawkins of BA Co. planter conv. 50 a. being ½ of (*) to John Hawkins (TB#C 180).
6 June 1743: John Hawkins conv. 100 a. (*) to James Gardner (TB#C: 242).
6 Jan 1747: James Gardiner mortgaged 100 a. (*) to Darby Lux (TB#E: 654).
1750: James Gardner owned 100 a. (*) and 50 a. Liverpool (1750 DB).
1763/4: 100 a. owned by James Gardner who "lives near Baltimore Town" (AHAL: 39).

HAY DOWN

15 Sep 1665: 300 a. pat. by Henry Downes (G#J: 144; TR#RA: 103).
(date not given): Henry Downes and w. Bridget of KE Co., conv. 300 a. (*) at Elk R. to Obadiah Judkins (G#J: 137; TR#RA: 102.
27 May 1673: Obadiah Judkins and w. Jane of TA Co., conv. to John Hillen 300 a. (*) on s. side of Capt. John's Creek on s. side of Elk R. (G#J: 144; TR#RA: 99-103).

2 Nov 1710: Henry Ward of CE Co. conv. 250 a. Montserado to Edward Parrish in exch. for 300 a. (*) (TR#A: 463).

HAZARD (1681)
(See also HARWOOD'S HAZARD)

24 June 1681: 100 a. surv. for John Yeo; later regranted to Thomas Preble; still later possessed by Mary Preble for Thomas' orphans; Archibald Buchanan had m. the widow (MRR: 21).

HAZARD (1682)

29 Sep 1682: 100 a. pat. by Francis Fry (MPL 25:1, 30:67).
Orig. surv. for Francis Fry who d. s.p., and land was escheated. John Copson, als. Weaver, had it resurv. as 495 a. Hazard Enlarged. Copson, als. Weaver, d. recently leaving a dau. Mary, w. of Jacob Rogers (TB#E: 202).
14 Aug 1747; Jacob Rogers and w. Mary of Great Britain, through their attys. Col. Thomas Colvill, Peter Bayard, and Robert Carmichael, all of CE Co., conv. 100 a. (*) to Amos Garrett (TB#E: 202).

HAZARD (1693)

8 Nov 1693: 200 a. surv. for Thomas Greenfield on the branches of Swan Creek; later possessed by the orphans of said Greenfield (MRR: 22).
10 Dec 1695: Pat. to Thomas Greenfield (IS#H: 161).
8 Jan 1704/5: Thomas Greenfield made a will leaving 200 a. (*) to his dau. Mary Drunkord, dau. Sarah, and s. Thomas, and dau. Jane (MCW#III: 53).
2 Oct 1715: Edward Murphy and w. Jane of CE Co. conv. their interest in 200 a. (*) to Thomas Mitchell; Jane was dau. of Thomas Greenfield (TR#A: 376).
29 Aug 1724: William Greenfield and w. Elizabeth conv. their interest in (*) to Patrick Ruark. Deed stated that William's bro. Thomas and sister Sarah have d. (IS#H: 161).
29 Aug 1724: William Greenfield conv. 100 a., being ½ of Hazard (pat. 10 Dec 1695 to Thomas Greenfield, father of the grantor) to Patrick Ruark. Tract was surv. by the grantor's father who by his LWT devised the land to William's bro. Thomas and sisters Mary, Jane, and Sarah. Thomas and Sarah d. and their share came to William as heir of their father (IS#H: 161).
1729: Patrick Ruark conv. 150 a. pt. (*) to William Vestale (IS#K: 292).
5 March 1728: John Debruler of St. John's Parish, and w. Mary, dau. and devisee of Thomas Greenfield, late of St. George's Parish, dec., conv. 50 a. pt. Hazard (200 a. granted to Thomas

Greenfield on 10 Dec 1695) to Patrick Ruark of St. George's Parish, labourer (IS#I: 266).

1 May 1730: Patrick Ruark of BA Co. conv. 150 a., 3 pts. of (*) to William Vestall of CE Co., carpenter (IS#K: 292) (MRR#II: 326).

27 Dec 1736: William Vestall of Orange Co., VA, conv. 150 a. pt. (*) to Joseph Hall of Oxford Twp., Philadelphia Co.; tract was pat. 10 Dec 1695 to Thomas Greenfield who left it to his ch. Thomas, Mary, Jane, and Sarah; by death of said ch., ½ of the tract desc. to William Greenfield, heir-at-law of Thomas; William conv. tract to Patrick Ruark, who conv. it to said Vestall (IS#IK: 319) (MRR#II: 136).

1 May 1739: Thomas Mitchell, with cons. of w. Ann, conv. to Thomas White 50 a. pt. Hazard (pt. of 250 a. pat. to Thomas Greenfield (HWS#1-A: 208).

HAZARD (unplaced tracts named Hazard)

6 Nov 1718: Michael Rutledge and w. Hannah conv. 50 a. (*) to Thomas Hindes (TR#RA: 472).

5 June 1727: Michael Rutledge of BA Co. deeds to John Harryman pt. Hazard 50 a. when it was made over to Rutledge it was called Purchase. MR's w. Hannah cons. (IS#H: 403).

HAZARD ENLARGED

495 a. granted to John Copson, als. Weaver, who d. leaving an only dau. Mary, w. of Jacob Rogers (TR#C: 453).

16 March 1748: Jacob Rogers and w. Mary of Bedford, Great Britain, conv. to Amos Garrett the tract (*) (TR#C: 453).

HEA(L)TH (THE)

200 a. orig. granted to Charles Gorsuch.

28 Sep 1674: Charles Gorsuch conv. 200 a. (*) to William Wheatley and 100 a. Spring Point.

24 Nov 1674: Charles Gorsuch, Gent., gave p/a to Thomas Long to acknowledge sale of 200 a. (*) 2 March 1674/5: Capt. Thomas Long as atty. for Gorsuch ackn. the sale in court (G#J: 290).

8 May 1692: Nicholas Smith of London, mariner, conv. 200 a. (*) and 100 a. Spring Point to John Hammond of AA Co. (RM#HS: 474).

20 Nov 1694: John Conaway of Ratcliffe, Stepney Parish, Middlesex, mariner, gave p/a to Nicholas Smith to take poss. of 200 a. (*) and Spring Point (RM#HS: 476).

27 May 1735: Lawrence Hammond, s. and devisee of Col. Thomas Hammond, conv. his share of Dearing's Increase, 200 a. Health, and 100 a. Spring Point, which LH had resurv. into Brother's Kindness, in all 371 a., to his bro. William Hammond. LH's w. Abarilla cons. (HWS#M: 313).

HEATH'S ADDITION

11 Dec 1684: George Holland of TA Co. pledges 200 a. (*) and 650 a. Holland, to James Phillips, innholder (RM#HS: 134).

3 Aug 1697: Thomas Heath and w. Sarah conv. 115 a. (*), 50 a. Blocksedge, and 50 a. Hughs' Island to Henry Matthews (IS#IK: 154).

8 March 1731: Thomas Cross and w. Sarah conv. to Henry Weatherall ½ of Mathews Double Purchase, als. (*), 140 a. (IS#L: 198).

HEATHCOTE'S COTTAGE

22 March 1678: 500 a. surv. for Nathaniel Heathcote of AA Co. (IS#L: 202).

11 Dec 1727: John Dorsey of CE Co., carpenter, and w. Sylvia, relict of John Heathcote of CE Co., true and legal heir of Nathaniel Heathcote of AA Co., conv. 500 a. (*) to John Baldwin and William Rumsey (IS#I: 82).

8 March 1731: Heathcote Pickett conv. 500 a. (*) to Joseph Thomas. HP's w. Mary cons. (IS#L: 202).

4 Feb 1741: Joseph Thomas (and w. Dorcas), conv. 500 a. (*) to George Browne and William Young (TB#A: 70).

22 March 1743/4: Sarah Heathcote, spinster, sole heiress of John Heathcote of CE Co., conv. 500 a. (*) to John Baldwin of CE Co., Gent. (TB#C: 471).

11 June 1747: John Baldwin (and w. Mary) of CE Co., conv. 500 a. (*) and 200 a. Thompson's Choice to Stephen Onion, iron master. (*) was surv. for Nathaniel Heathcote who d., and the land desc. to John Heathcote, his brother's s., who d. in KE Co.; land desc. to his s. John who m. in CE Co., and had a dau. Sarah, who conv. it to John Baldwin (TB#E: 502).

HECTOR'S CHANCE

10 April 1719: 300 a. surv. for Hector McLane (Card Index to Patents).

1736: John Stinchcomb gave bond to John McClaine to carry out agreement they made to divide (*) which Hector McLane devised to his s. John and dau. Katherine now w. of JS (HWS#M: 382; see also HWS#M: 122 for another bond).

30 June 1744: John Maclain conv. 150 a., being ½ of (*) to John Stinchcomb. JM's w. Margaret cons. (TB#C: 544).

HECTOR'S FANCY

2 Aug 1743: William Hopkins and w. Rachel conv. 60 a. (*) to William Jenkins (TB#C: 296).

8 April 1745: William Jenkins of BA Co., planter, conv. 60 a. pt. (*) to Charles Ridgely (TB#D: 88).

HECTOR'S HOPYARD

9 Nov 1695: 300 a. pat. by Hector McClane (MPL 34: 109, 40: 69).

See Horvath Plat: Ruxton and Riderwood.

28 March 1702: James Carroll conv. 200 a. pt. (*) to Hector Maclane (HW#2: 132).

12 Feb 1728: James Carroll of Fingaul, All Hallows Parish, made a will leaving Hopyard to Edward Tully and to Michael Tully's two sons and their heirs (MCW#VI: 133).

14 June 1742: Edward and Michael Tully, sons of Michael Tully, dec., conv. tract Hopyard, bequeathed them by their kinsman James Carroll of AA Co., to Jacob Young of BA Co. (TB#A: 184).

9 March 1746: Jacob Young deeds to John Bosley 19 a. The Hopyard (Hector's Hopyard?), JY's w. Eleanor cons. (TB#E: 532).

1750: Michael Tully owns 100 a. (Hunter's?) Hopyard.

14 Sep 1751: Jacob Young of BA Co. conv. to Ann Fishpaw 100 a. Hopyard, adj. Thomas Hooker's land; Jacob's w. Eleanor cons. (TR#D, f: 224).

23 May 1761: William Murray, s. and heir of Jabez Murray, dec., conv. pt. (*) to McLane and Jabez Bailey, heirs of George Bailey, dec. (B#I: 171).

Aug 1765: Edward Tulley has a land commission to investigate the boundaries of Hector's Hopyard, 100 a. Commission convened on 1st Tuesday in Nov 1765. Deponents included: Joseph Murray, of FR Co., age c60, s. of Morgan Murray, dec., Absolom Barney, age 43, Samuel Wheeler, age not given, mentions Jabez Murray, 28 or 30 years ago, now dec., William Govane, age 49, Jacob Young, age 55 (B#P: 297).

HELLMORE

9 Jan 1735: Thomas Carpenter of Alphington, near Exeter, formerly of MD, conv. 300 a. (*) to Capt. John Cockey (HWS#M: 420).

HELLMORE'S ADDITION

See Horvath Plat: Green Spring Valley.

9 Jan 1735: Thomas Carpenter of Alphington, near Exeter, formerly of MD, conv. 170 a. (*) to Capt. John Cockey (HWS#M: 420).

HEMLEY

1 March 1669: Gabriel Brown conv. 150 a. (*) to Humphrey Nicholls (IR#PP: 78).

HENDON'S HOPE

10 Nov 1732: Edward Day conv. 100 a. now called Hendon's Hope, pt. of 300 a. tract Avarilla's Garden, to Richard Hendon (IS#L: 305).

HENDRICKSON

3 Aug 1668: Hendrick Hendrickson planter, and w. Juniber, conv. 50 a. (*) to William Howard (IR#PP. 69).

HENLEY'S REPOSE

27 Oct 1766: Clement Green of BA Co. assigned a lease for 125 a., pt. Henly's Repose, to Thomas Poteet, for 99 years (B#P: 354).

HENRY'S DELIGHT IN AMY'S GARDEN

18 April 1749: Henry Perrigoe, Sr., conv. 20 a., pt. (*), to Thomas Sligh (TR#C: 217).

HENRY'S LOT

11 May 1761: Henry Peregoy conv. (*) to Richard Chenoweth. HP's w. Alice cons. (B#I: 134).

HENRY'S PLEASURE

23 Nov 1748: Henry Thomas and w. Jane conv. 50 a. (*) to Samuel Forwood (BB#I: 348).

HEN'S ROOST

2 Oct 1667: Pat. to Thomas Pryor (IR#PP: 114).

1 March 1671/2: Thomas Pryor, planter, conv. to Matthew Adams, $\frac{1}{2}$ of 200 a. (*) at Herring Creek on e. side of Sassafras R. TP's w. Margaret cons. (IR#PP: 114).

HERBERT'S CARE, ADDITION TO

May 1703: 50 a. surv. for Elinor Herbert (Card Index to Patents).

HEREFORD (also HARRIFORD)

6 Aug 1719: James Isham and w. Mary [my notes show w. Elizabeth cons.] conv. 179 a. to John Poteet (TR#DS: 45).

15 May 1734: John Powell and w. Elizabeth, relict and widow of John Poteet, Sr., dec., conv. 179 a. (*) to John Poteet, Jr. (HWS#M: 55).

15 May 1734: John Poteet, Jr., and w. Ann conv. 179 a. (*) to Thomas Miles (HWS#M: 53).

26 Nov 1751: Thomas Miles of BA Co., and w. Catherine conv. 179 a. to Clement Mattingly of AA Co. (TR#D: 255).

HERKEMIL

17 Nov 1686: John Hall conv. 50 a. (*) to William Westbury (RM#HS: 206).

HEROD'S CAMP

20 May 1737: Benjamin Hammond and w. Margaret give bond to Cornelius Howard to warrant the title to (*), which was among those lands conv. by BH and w. Margaret to Mordecai Hammond and which Mordecai conv. to CH on 18 Feb 1736 (IS#IK: 440).

HERRINGTON'S INHERITANCE

7 Nov 1718: Cornelius Herrington of BA Co. conv. 50 a. to Jeremiah Downes. CH's w. Elizabeth cons. (TR#RA: 509).
6 Sep 1721: Jeremiah Downes of BA Co. conv. 50 a. (*) to Henry Wetherall (RM#HS: 659).
8 Sep 1726: Henry Wetherall and w. Elinor conv. 50 a. (*) to David Carlisle (IS#H: 303).

HEWS ISLAND
(See HUGHES' ISLAND)

HICCORY BOTTOM

Pat. by 1747, for Michael Huff, 90 a. (MPL TI#1: 316, TI#3: 287).

HICKORY BOTTOM

Surv. by 1744, for John Gill, 150 a., cert. in BA Cert. # 697.

HICKORY HOLLOW

7 June 1758: John Litton assigns 30 a. (*) to James Clarke (B#G: 61).

HICKORY LEVEL(Pt. RICHARDSON'S OUTLET)

3 Aug 1697: Thomas Richardson conv. (*), pt. of 830 a. pat. as Richardson's Outlet, to his s. James (IS#IK: 164).

HICKORY RIDGE

June 1707: 30 a. surv. for Robert Morris (Card Index to Patents).

HICKS ADVENTURE

Surv. by 1719 for Nehemiah Hicks. 100 a. BA Cert. #699.
Pat. by 1734, for Nehemiah Hicks, 100 a. (cert. in MPL EI#3:341, patent in MPL EI#1:359).
3 March 1730/1: Nehemiah Hicks conv. 100 a. (*) to Henry Hicks. NH's w. Phillis cons. (IS#L: 63).
12 Oct 1751: William Robinson, with cons. of w. Temperance, conv. to Laban Ogg 100 a. Hicks Adventure, and 82 a. Bond's Forest (TR#D: 250).
1765: David Malsby conv. 100 a. pt. (*) and 100 a. pt. Bond's Forest to Charles Baker (B#C: 225).

HILLENS HAPHAZARD

22 Sep 1750: Stephen Price conv. pt. (*) to Abraham Raven. SP's w. Rebecca cons. (TR#D: 58).

HILL'S CAMP

1684: 1000 a. pat. to Clement Hill, (cert. in MPL 22:47; patent in MPL IB&IL#C: 131).

HILL'S FOREST

1684: 1000 a. for Richard Hill; On PW Plat G.

HINES' DESIRE

6 March 1744: Thomas Hines of St. Paul's Parish, conv. 100 a. Bachelor's Ridge and 16 a. (*) and 16 a. Hines Desire to Edward Fell, the sale to take effect after the death of said Hines and his w. Elizabeth (TB#D: 20 (or 70).
31 May 1763: Edward Fell, s. of William Fell, dec., conv. 100 a. Bachelor's Ridge and 16 a. (*) to Richard Fowler (B#L: 235).

HIS LORDSHIPS RESERVE LAND

12 Feb 1755: Randle Ramsey of Brookshire Co., VA, appointed his friend John Demoss his atty. to conv. 80 a. (*) to William Few (B#K: 20).

HITCHCOCK'S FOLLY
(Pt. ROBERTS' FOREST)

1 April 1712: Elizabeth Roberts, widow of John, conv. 250 a. (*), orig. called Roberts' Forest, to George Hitchcock, school-master (TR#A: 184).

HITCHCOCK'S FORTUNE

16 March 1702: William Hitchcock conv. 100 a. (*) to Edward Reynolds of CV Co., in exch. for 262 a. Turkey Hill (HW#2: 201).

HOBBS CHOICE

5 June 1745: Lemuel Howard of BA Co. conv. 100 a. (*) to John Dorrumple, the assignment of a 99 year lease made by Benjamin Tasker, Agent for Lord Baltimore, to LH (TB#D: 234).

HOBSON'S CHOICE (c1710)

By 1710: 100 a. pat. to Hugh Jones, (cert. in MPL DD: 659; patent in MPL DD#5: 660 and PL#3: 276).

HOBSON'S CHOICE (1744)

1744: 19 a. surv. for Thomas Foy; (BA Cert. 716).

HOBSON'S CHOICE

23 Feb 1748: Joshua Wood of BA Co. conv. (*), granted to Joshua Wood, father of the grantor, and other tracts (Benjamin's Choice and Woods' Choice), to Abraham Taylor (TR#C: 157).
15 Sep 1758: Michael Taylor leased 50 a. (*) to William and Jacob Osborn (B#G: 285).

HOCKLEY

See Horvath Plat: Elkridge.
23 June 1669: 100 a. surv. for William Ebden; later held by Col. Edward Dorsey (MRR: 101).
5 Sep 1688: William Ebden, Michael Judd and w. Jane, conv. 6 a. (*) to Edward Lunn, adj. Foster's Fancy (RM#HS: 287).
5 Oct 1698: Edward Lunn of AA Co., conv. 100 a. to Edmund Talbott; tract had been assigned by

George Yate to William Ebden, and conv., by Ebden and Michael Judd to Lunn (TR#RA: 323).

HOG NECK (1670)

12 Aug 1670: 150 a. pat. to Nathaniel Stiles (G#J: 53).
1 March 1671/2: Nathaniel Stiles, Gent., conv. (*), on s. side of Bush R., to Lodowick Williams (G#J: 53).
9 May 1685: Thomas Richardson, and w. Rachel conv. 150 a. (*) to Michael Judd; tract had been taken up by Nathaniel Stiles, sold to Lodowick Williams, who sold it to John Towers, now dec., who left it to his w. Rachel, now w. of the Thomas Richardson (RM#HS: 216).
9 Nov 1715: Edward Williams, s. and heir of Lodowick Williams, conv. Hog Neck and Mates Affinity to Richard Colegate (see HWS#M: 325).
10 May 1732: Richard Colegate, s. and heir of Richard Colegate, conv. (*) and Mates Affinity to Robert Robertson (See HWS#M: 325).
5 Nov 1735: Robert Robertson conv. 150 a. pt. (*) and Mates Affinity to Matthew Beck. RR's w. Sarah cons. (HWS#M: 325).
14 April 1750: Elijah Beck conv. to James Preston parcels of (*) and Mates Addition (TR#C: 526).

HOG NECK (1684)

15 Nov 1684: 50 a. surv. for Edward Reeves; later possessed by John Savory; still later taken away by an elder surv. (MRR: 21).
3 Nov 1685: Edward Reeves, conv. 50 a. (*) to George Coningham; included is a cert. of surv. from Thomas Lightfoot giving the metes and bounds, also a bond dated 3 Nov 1685, from Reeves to Coningham (RM#HS: 162).
24 March 1685/6: George Coningham, cooper, pledges to William Osborne 50 a. (*) and livestock, against loss by Osbourne (RM#HS: 171).
4 March 1723: John Savory conv. 50 a. (*) to Rowland Shepherd (IS#G: 238).

HOG POINT

7 Dec 1676: 40 a. surv. for Thomas Preston on n. side of Gunpowder R., adjacent a parcel of land formerly laid out for Arthur Taylor (MRR: 61).
17 July 1680: Pat. by Thomas Preston (See TR#RA: 439).
6 Aug 1718: James Preston and w. Elizabeth conv. 50 a. of Hog Point, pat. 17 July 1680 to Thomas Preston, father of said James, to John Cameron (TR#RA: 439).
1750: Heirs of John Cameron owned 40 a. Hog Point (1750 DB).

HOG RANGE

1762: Robert Gilchrest conv. 50 a. to Wm. Bourne (B#K: 442).

HOGG'S NORTON

17 March 1711: Elizabeth Roberts of BA Co. conv. to John Cross 100 a. Hogg's Norton, being pt. of a larger tract called Roberts Choice (TR#A: 179).
1 Nov 1726: John Cross conv. Hoggs Norton, being pt. of a larger tract called Roberts' Forest [sic] to James Moore (IS#H: 288).
6 Feb 1728/9: James Moore of BA Co., cordwainer, conv. 100 a. Hoggs Norton, being pt. of Roberts' Forest, to John Wilmot (IS#K: 1).
14 Feb 1733: James Moore of BA Co., cordwainer, conv. 188? a. Hoggs Norton and 11 a. Shoemaker Lot to Thomas Woodward, cooper (HWS#M: 38).
26 Sep 1741: James Moore executes another deed for 188 a. Hoggs Norton to Thomas Woodward in order to secure title (TB#A: 27).
2 Nov 1741: Thomas Woodward, cooper, mortgaged. 180 a. Hoggs Norton and 11 a., 90 perches of Shoemakers Lot to John Ensor. TW's w. Mary cons. (TB#A: 92).
25 Nov 1746: John Ensor granted to Mary Woodward a release of mortgage made by Thomas Edward on Hoggs Norton and Shoemaker's Lot (TB#E: 278).

HOG'S ISLAND

21 April 1759: Richard Richards sold 50 a. (*) to Luke Tipton (B#G: 382).

HOLLAND

11 Dec 1684: George Holland of TA Co. pledged 650 a. Holland, and 200 a. Heath's Adventure to James Phillips (RM#HS: 134).

HOLLAND'S ADVENTURE

7 Nov 1705: Francis Watkins conv. 200 a. (*) to Robert Cutchin (IR#AM: 9).
4 March 1725/6: Robert Cutchin conv. 20 a. pt. (*) to James Maxwell (IS#H: 227).
31 Jan 1732: Robert Cutchin conv. (*) and Wolf's Neck to Brian Taylor (IS#L: 332).
8 March 1743: Winifred Cutchin, widow of Robert, conv. (*) and Wolf's Harbor to Stephen Onion of Gunpowder Iron Works. Cutchin had previously conv. land to Brian Taylor, but Winifred had not conv. her ⅓ dower rights (TB#C: 427).

HOLLAND'S CHOICE

9 Nov 1719: Thomas Holland of PG Co., and w. Margaret conv. 120 a. pt. (*) to Elizabeth Foster of PG Co., widow (TR#DS: 247).

16 July 1724: Richard Gott and w. Sarah conv. 120 a. pt. (*) (in all 580 a.) to Jacob Holland (IS#G: 3431).

HOLLAND'S LOT

13 March 1717: Thomas Woodfield of AA Co., and w. Eliza (lately Eliza Gott, dau. and devisee of Anthony Holland of AA Co.), conv. 100 a. (*), out of 580 a. in all, to Thomas McNamara of Annapolis (TR#A: 544).

HOLLAND'S LOT

19 May 1725: Samuel Young of AA Co. conv. 400 a. Holland's Lot and 500 a. New Stadt to his s. Joseph Young of KE Co.; Samuel had purch. land from Thomas Francis (Holland?) on 1 Jan 1696/7 (IS#H: 122).

HOLLAND'S PARK

14 Oct 1683: Surv. (See HW#2: 277).

2 Aug 1703: Thomas Larkin of AA Co., Gent., conv. 150 a. (*) to John Ford; 3 Aug 1703: Larkin gave p/a to Henry Wriothesley to execute deed (HW#2: 277).

HOLLAND'S PURCHASE (1686)

1686: 22 a. surv. for William Holland (MPL 22:216).

HOLLAND'S PURCHASE (1686)

1686: 300 a. pat. to John Natt (MPL IB&IL#C: 242).

HOLLIS' DESIRE

5 Nov 1724: William Hollis conv. 150 a. pt. (*) to his nephew William Osborne, s. of grantor's sister Avarilla and her husband William Osborne (IS#H: 28).

HOLLIS REFUGE AND UNION (1737)

1737: 270 a. surv. for William Hollis (BA Cert. 724).

HOLLIS REFUGE AND UNION (1750)

1750: 90 a. surv. for William Hollis (BA Cert. # 1663).

HOLLY NECK

17 Nov 1664: 475 a. surv. for Richard Wells and later held by the orphans of Col. Wells (MRR: 7).

HOLMWOOD (See HOMEWOOD)

HOMER

7 Aug 1741: James Isham, Sr., and James Isham, Jr., with cons. of latter's w. Ann, conv. 103 a. Homer and 193 a. pt. Isham's Second Addition, to Stephen Onion (TB#A: 2).

HOMLEY

1 March 1669/70: Gabriel Browne, conv. 150 a. (*), where Browne lately dwelt, near Laramore's Branch on s. side of Elk R., to Humphrey Nichols, planter (IR#PP: 78).

HOMEWOOD (HOLMWOOD?)

1 April 1693: Sarah Hall, w. of John, conv. 100 a. (*) to her dau. Isabella Hooper; if Isabella d. under age the land to go to her sister Ann Collier, then to John Burley, s. of Stephen Burley, late of Severn (HW#2: 38).

HONDERTON (HONDERYON?)

14 Oct 1743: Luke Trotten and William Hamilton, execs. of John Gardner, conv. 60 a. Gardner's Addition, 80 a. Gunworth, 200 a. pt. Honderton (?), and 300 a. Timber Neck to Sabritt Sollers (TB#C: 327).

HOOKER'S ADDITION

17 Aug 1726; Samuel Hooker of BA Co. conv. 100 a. Hooker's Addition and 100 a. Hooker's Farm, pt. of Gerar, to Nicholas Haile (IS#IK: 282).

28 March 1747: Nicholas Haile conv. 100 a. Hooker's Farm (part of Gerar), 60 a. Hooker's Addition, 100 a. Hailes' Forest, 200 a. Haile's Long Grove, 80 a. pt. Taylor's Discovery, 50 a. Smallwood, to Christopher Grindall of London, mariner (TB#E: 347).

22 Sep 1750: George Atkinson, exec. of Capt. Christopher Grindall, conv. 100 a., pt. of Garrar, and 60 a. Hooker's Addition, to Joseph Bosley (TR#D: 97).

HOOKER'S CHANCE (may be in AA Co.)

7 Nov 1732: Thomas Hooker, with cons. of w. Eleanor, conv. 150 a. (*) to Robert North (IS#L: 301).

HOOKER'S ENLARGEMENT

17 Aug 1756: Samuel Hooker conv. 250 a. (*) and 150 a. Point Lookout to his s. Thomas (BB#I: 579).

HOOKER'S FARM (See also GERAR)

17 Aug 1726; Samuel Hooker of BA Co. conv. 100 a. Hooker's Addition and 100 a. Hooker's Farm, pt. of Gerar, to Nicholas Haile (IS#IK: 282).

6 April 1745: Nicholas Haile conv. 100 a. (*) (part of Gerar), 60 a. Addition to Hooker's Farm, 100 a. Hailes' Forest, 100 a. pt. of Haile's Fellowship, 80 a. pt. Taylor's Discovery, 50 a. Smallwood, 200 a. Hailes Discovery, 200 a. Shadrack's Lot, and 200 a. Meshack's Garden, to Christopher Grindall of London, mariner (TB#E: 83).

28 March 1747: Nicholas Haile conv. 100 a. Hooker's Farm (pt. of Gerar), 60 a. Hooker's Addition, 100 a. Hailes' Forest, 200 a. Haile's Long Grove, 80 a. pt. Taylor's Discovery, 50 a. Smallwood, to Christopher Grindall of London, mariner (TB#E: 347).

HOOKER'S FARM, ADDITION TO

6 April 1745: Nicholas Haile conv. 100 a. Hooker's Farm (pt. of Gerar), 60 a. (*), 100 a. Hailes' Forest, 100 a. pt. of Haile's Fellowship, 80 a. pt. Taylor's Discovery, 50 a. Smallwood, 200 a. Hailes Discovery, 200 a. Shadrack's Lot, and 200 a. Meshack's Garden, to Christopher Grindall of London, mariner (TB#E: 83).

HOOKER'S MEADOWS

7 June 1763: Richard Hooker of BA Co., conv. 84 a., pt. (*) to Jonathan Griffith (B#L: 275).

HOOKER'S PROSPERITY

20 Dec 1706: 114 a. pat. by William Wheeler (MPL DD#5: 241, PL#2: 48).

See Horvath Plat: Ruxton and Riderwood.

13 Feb 1746: Wason Wheeler conv. 56½ a. (*) to Charles Ridgely (TB#E: 298).

HOOKER'S RIDGE

9 March 1748: Richard Hooker of BA Co. deeded to William Wheeler 100 a. (*) and 70 a. Tipton's Adventure. RH's w. Martha cons. (TR#C: 163).

HOOPER'S ISLAND

1 June 1669: Mary Gouldsmith conv. 75 a. on (*), on s. side of Gunpowder R., to Capt. Thomas Todd (IR#PP: 72).

7 March 1733/4: Samuel Chew gave to Richard Jones of BA Co., a receipt for 190 a. Denton, 80 a. Walker's Neck, 100 a. (*), 330 a. North Point, 546 a. Old Road, 120 a. Industry, 1000 a. Shawan Hunting Ground, 50 a. Thorold's Nest, 100 a. Luke's Privilege, and 100 a. Bagford (HWS#M: 193).

HOPE? (or COPE)

30 a. surv. for Edward Cox (TB#E: 289).

20 Nov 1746: James Mackall of CV Co. [planter conv. 100 a. (*) and 30 a. Cope or Hope (surv. for Edward Cox) to William Wilson. JM's w. Martha cons. (TB#E: 289).

HOPE (THE) (See THE LEVEL)

1704: 200 a. surv. for Henry Butler.

See Horvath Plat: Pikesville.

6 May 1711: Henry Butler conv. 200 a. (*), of which 100 a., The Level, is ½, to Richard Jones of BA Co. (TR#A: 193).

1 May 1775: Mary Butler, widow and relict of Absalom Butler, conv. release of dower to tract called (*), to William Butler of BA Co., innholder (AL#H: 461).

28 Jan 1778: William Butler, with cons. of w. Sarah, conv. 200 a. (*) to Edward Stevenson of FR Co. (WG#B: 301).

HOPE'S ADDITION

8 July 1743: Thomas Williamson, with cons. of w. Eliz. conv. (*) and Williamson's Hope, in all 89 a., to Samuel Griffith (TB#C: 272).

HOPE'S LOT

9 Aug 1695: 200 a. surv. for George Hope (B).

See Horvath Plat: Elkridge.

HOPEFUL MARSH

16 July 1684: 55 a. surv. for John Hall on n. side of Gunpowder R. and later possessed by William Lenox (MRR: 49).

5 Oct 1686: John Hall conv. 55 a. (*) to William Lenox (RM#HS. 194).

8 Aug 1739: James Lennox of BA Co., planter, with cons. of w. Mary, conv. 55 a. (*) to John Hall. Tract was originally taken up by John Hall, dec., who sold it to William Lenox, and land desc. to James Lennox (HWS#1-A: 263).

HOPEWELL (1662)

20 July 1662: 50 a. surv. for Oliver Spry; later possessed by James Maxwell (MRR: 37).

HOPEWELL (1676)

8 June 1676: 185 a. surv. for Thomas Long on s. side of Middle R.; later possessed by William Barker for the orphans of Francis Watkins (MRR: 77).

7 June 1681: Thomas Long, for natural affection and through the intercession of his w., conv. to Francis Watkins the 185 a. tract Hopewell, said Watkins having m. Christiana Wrighs (?) or Waites, dau. of Long's w. (IR#AM: 121).

28 May 1707: Francis Watkins of BA Co., planter, conv. (*), Bettor Hope, and Surplus, to James Crooke (RM#HS, 559).

HOPEWELL (1676)

7 Dec 1676: 60 a. surv. for Thomas Preston on n. side of Gunpowder R.; later held 41 a. by John Rawlins, and the rest by Abra. Taylor (MRR: 61).

2 June 1703: Thomas Preston conv. 41 a. to John Rawlings (IR#AM: 64).

4 Aug 1703: John Rawlings, of BA Co., and w. Dorothy, conv. 40 a. to John Armstrong (HW#2: 285).

2 Feb 1704: John Armstrong of BA Co. conv. 60½ a., pt. Collett's Neck, and 41 a. Hopewell (formerly in poss. of Michael Judd); to Abraham Taylor, blacksmith. JA's w. Mary cons. (IR#PP: 143).

10 April 1707: Abraham Taylor conv. to Gaen Stevenson, of Chester Co., PA, 41 a. pt. Hopewell, and 76.5 a. Collett's Neglect, lately in possession of John Armstrong (RM#HS: 536).

1 March 1708: Abraham Taylor of BA Co., blacksmith, and w. Jane, conv. 41 a., Hopewell and 76.5 a. Collett's Neglect to William Howard (RM#HS: 637).

HOPEWELL (1681)

10 March 1681: 15 a. surv. for Edward Mumford on n. side of Patapsco R. in Blockhouse Creek; later possessed by Nicholas Fitzsimmons for the orphans of Heathcote [Pickett] (MRR: 93).

1 June 1686: Edward Mumford conv. 15 a. (*) to Charles Gorsuch, on s. side of Sparrow's Creek; 2 June 1686: Charles Gorsuch certifies he will not trouble Edward Mumford (RM#HS: 181).

4 Aug 1691: Charles Gorsuch and w. Ann conv. 15 a. (*), 58 a. Sparrow's Nest, and 156 a. Walltown to Joseph Heathcote of AA Co. (IR#AM: 107).

HOPEWELL (1687)

15 Jan 1686/7: 381¼ a. surv. for James Cullen on the n. side of Patapsco R.; later possessed by William Bladen (MRR: 75).

HOPEWELL (1687)

4 June 1687: 204 a. surv. for William Standiford on Seneca Ridge; later possessed by the execs. of Edward Boothby (MRR: 53).

4 June 1696: Israel Skelton and w. Mary conv. 204 a. (*) to Edward Boothby (RM#HS: 527).

HOPEWELL (1687)

1 Sep 1687: 60 a. surv. for Robert Benger on n. side of Sterling Creek; later possessed by Michael Rutledge (MRR: 68).

8 June 1698: Robert Benger and w. Deborah conv. 60 a. (*) to Michael Rutledge (IS#IK: 235).

HOPEWELL (unplaced)

1691: Mary Adams conv. 45 a. (*) to her son-in-law Richard Adams; also 40 a. Middle Olive's to same Adams; also 100 a. Island Point (IR#AM: 88).

2 Aug 1699: Walter Bosley and w. Mary, conv. 45 a. (*) to Charles Whitehead of AA Co. (TR#RA, f: 378).

15 Jan 1700: John Shaw of CE Co. conv. to Alexander Graves of BA co., 100 a. (*), 100 a. being ½ of Salisbury Plains, 70 a. Witherington, 80 a. Shadwell's Range and 100 a. Smith's Range (HW#2: 53).

8 Nov 1721: Joseph Elledge of BA Co. conv. 50 a. (*) to Herbert Pritchard of BA Co. JE's w. Elizabeth cons. (RM#HS: 661).

25 May 1722: Josias Middlemore of BA Co., and w. Frances, conv. 200 a. (*) to James Isham of BA Co., innholder (IS#G: 75).

1729: John Norrington conv. 76 a. (*) to William Davis (IS#K: 25).

4 June 1742: James Isham, Sr., and James Isham, Jr., of BA Co., blacksmith conv. 50 a. pt. (*) to Charles Mathias Boulton. JI's w. Mary cons. (TB#A: 204).

17 Sep 1742: James Isham, Sr., and James Isham, Jr., (and latter's w. Mary), conv. 154 a. pt. (*), 100 a. pt. Isham's Second Addition, 27 a. Isham's Addition, and 50 a. Seneca Ridge, to Stephen Onion (TB#C: 45).

6 May 1745: Charles Mathias Bolton of BA Co., with cons. of w. Anne, conv. 50 a. (*), bought from James Isham, to William Andrew of BA Co., innholder (TB#D: 288).

6 Sep 1745: John Norrington of BA Co., planter, conv. 76 a. (*) to Abraham Jarrett of BA Co., cordwainer (TB#D: 358).

1750: William Andrew conv. 50 a. (*) to Joseph Buckley (TR#D: 538).

HOPEWELL MARSH

(See also HOPEFUL MARSH)

11 June 1667: 50 a. surv. for Oliver Spry; later possessed by James Maxwell (MRR: 37).

HOPFORD

Jan 1716: 100 a. surv. for Jno. McKenzie (MRR).

HORN POINT

6 May 1688: 64 a. surv. for William Horn in one of the forks of Salt Peter Creek; later possessed by Giles Stephenson (Stephens?); still later poss. by Giles Stephens (MRR: 66).

7 May 1681/2: William and w. Mary of Gunpowder R., cooper, conv. to George Ogleby, tailor, 64 a. (*); tract was pat. 12 July 1679; same date: Horne gave bond to Oglesby he will perform the covenants (IR#AM: 159).

5 Aug 1684: George Ogleby, tailor, and w. Johanna, conv. 64 a. (*) to Thomas James, planter; ackn. 5 Aug Court by grantor and w. before John Boreing (RM#HS: 92).

11 June 1724: Samuel Stevens, planter, conv. 64 a. (*) to Giles Stevens (IS#G: 335).

4 Nov 1742: Giles Stevens and w. Alce conv. 28 a. HapHazard and 64 a. (*) to Joseph Thomas (TB#C: 60).

HORNER

30 Oct 1686; John Collett and Mary Goldsmith conv. 150 a. (*), at Goldsmith Branch, s. side of Captain John's Creek, Elk R., to Robert Morgan, planter (IR#PP: 70).

HORNE'S POINT

6 May 1688: 64 a. surv. for William Horn in one of the forks of Salt Peter Creek; later possessed by Giles Stephenson (Stephens?); still later possessed by Giles Stephens (MRR: 66).

7 May 1681/2: William and w. Mary of Gunpowder R., cooper, conv. to George Ogleby, tailor, 64 a. (*); tract was pat. 12 July 1679; same date, Horne gave bond to Oglesby he will perform the covenants (IR#AM: 159).

5 Aug 1684: George Ogleby, tailor, and w. Johanna, conv. 64 a. (*) to Thomas James, planter; ackn. 5 Aug Court by grantor and w. before John Boreing (RM#HS: 92).

11 June 1724: Samuel Stevens, planter, conv. 64 a. (*) to Giles Stevens (IS#G: 335).

HORNISHAM

18 June 1681: A 50 a. tract surv. for William Horn on e. side of Gunpowder R., adj, to the land called Daniels Neck; later belonging to the orphans of William Westbury; still later possessed by Francis Dallahide (MRR: 36).

5 Nov 1684: William Horne and w. Mary conv. to John Hall two tracts: 67 a. Hornisham, pat. 18 June 1681 to said Horne; and 2nd, ⅓ pt. of three parts of Daniel's Nest, estimated at 16½ a., which Horne held as dowry of his w. Mary, said land having come to her by inheritance) RM#HS: 101).

17 Nov 1686: John Hall conv. 50 a. Hornesham and 16½ a. Daniel's Nest to William Westbury (RM#HS: 206).

30 March 1703: Elizabeth Westbury conv. to Simon Pearson and heirs, her right and interest in Hornesham and Daniels Neck (Nest?) (HW#2: 274).

3 Aug 1703: Simon Pearson, weaver, conv. to Francis Dallahide, 50 a. Daniels Neck, and 50 a. Hornisham (HW#2: 275).

8 March 1710: John Butteram and w. Elizabeth, and William Bond and w. Mary, conv. to Simon Pearson, weaver, their interest in lands formerly belonging to Thomas [O']Daniel and William Westbury, said Elizabeth and Mary being heirs of thereof (TR#A: 63).

6 April 1713: Francis Dallahide mortgaged Daniel's Nest [sic], Hornesham, 100 a. pt. Wandsworth and 200 a. Watertown to William Bladen of Annapolis; mortgage to run until 20 March 1713/4 (TR#A: 227).

8 June 1723: Francis Dallahide, eld. s. and heir of FD, late of BA Co., dec., conv. 50 a. Daniel's Neck, 50 a. Hornisham, and 100 a. Wansworth, 200 a. in all (latter surv. for William Orchard) (IS#G: 160).

HORSE RANGE

10 May 1689: 200 a. surv. for Thomas Richardson on n. side of Back R. (RM#HS: 386).

6 June 1693: Thomas Richardson, with cons. of w. Rachel, conv. 200 a. (*) to Nicholas Day (RM#HS: 376).

4 Nov 1720: Joshua Merriken, boatwright, with cons. of w. Dinah, conv. 100 a. pt. (*) to Alexander McComas; deed states that Thomas Richardson took up the tract [and pat. it] on 10 Nov 1695, and sold it to] Nicholas Day, whose LWT left it to his daus. Elizabeth and Dinah (TR#DS: 251).

HORTON'S FORTUNE

25 Nov 1670: 100 a. surv. for Edward Horton and later owned by Hugh Jones (MRR: 85).

4 Nov 1673: EH conv. 100 a. (*) to Thomas Byworth (G#J: 216).

HOWARD'S ADDITION

3 Aug 1719: Otho Holland of AA Co., with cons. of w. Mary (late w. of Charles Howard of AA Co.) and Thomas Howard, conv. 50 a. (*) and 100 a. pt. Roper's Increase (300 a. pat. to Thomas Roper), to Pleasance Dorsey of BA Co. (TR#DS: 157).

4 Aug 1749: Capt. John Dorsey, Jr., sold 200 a. Roper's Increase and 150 a. Howard's Addition to John Taylor. JD's w. Elizabeth cons. (TR#C: 268).

HOWARD'S ADVENTURE

17 Aug 1743: Everard Taylor of CV Co. conv. pt. (*), and pt. Wolf's Harbour to Stephen Onion (TB#C: 318).

HOWARD'S CHANCE

30 June 1716: Orlando Griffith of AA co. conv. 100 a., being the upper half of (*) to John Gill; tract was bequeathed to OG by the LWT, dated 30 Dec 1695 of John Howard (TR#A 517).

2 Oct 1724: Joseph Howard of AA Co., with cons. of w. Margery, conv. 200 a. (*) to John Swynward (IS#G: 391).

HOWARD'S FANCY

1722/31: Surv. for Edmond Howard.
See Horvath Plats: Green Spring Valley and Owings Mills.

19 Aug 1732: Joshua Howard of BA Co., conv. 200 a. (*) to his s. Edmond Howard. JH's w. Joanna cons. (IS#L: 278).

HOWARD'S FOREST

10 Jan 1705: 200 a. pat. by William Howard (TR#DS: 60, 294).

4 Nov 1719: William Burney [Barney?] and w. Martha, relict and sole extx. of William Howard, conv. 100 a., being ½ of (*) to Abraham Taylor (TR#DS: 60).

8 March 1720: Abraham Taylor and w. Dinah conv. 100 a., being the s. half of (*) to John Webster (TR#DS: 294).

HOWARD'S HARBOR

8 Aug 1743: John Howard of AA Co. and w. Mary conv. 63 a. pt. (*) to Henry Garrett (TB#C: 207).

8 Aug 1743: JH and w. Mary conv. 124 a. (*) to John Bull (TB#C: 313).

8 Aug 1743: JH conv. 95 a. pt. (*) to Richard Ruff (TB#C: 315).

9 Aug 1745: Henry Garrett and w. Mary, dau. and devisee of Isaac Butterworth, conv. to Col. Thomas White the following parcels: 63 a. 70 p. pt. (*), 150 a. Isaac's Addition (surv. 18 Oct 1723 and pat. 6 May 1728), and 270 a. Isaac's Englargement (surv. 10 March 1719 and pat. 6 May 1728) (TR#D: 300).

HOWARD'S INHERITANCE

15 May 1735: Joshua Howard certified he had places a stone at the beginning point of (*) (HWS#M: 236).

HOWARD'S RANGE

7 Oct 1702: John Howard of AA Co., with cons. of w. Katherine, conv. 240 a. (*) to Anthony Johnson (HW#2: 254).

8 Aug 1722: Catherine Johnson of BA Co., widow, conv. 15 a. pt. (*), and 5 a. The Plantation, to Peter Besson of BA Co., chirurgeon (IS#G: 35).

27 Nov 1751: John Paca, with cons. of w. Elizabeth, conv. to Thomas White 321 a. (*) (TR#D: 260).

HOWELL'S CONTRIVANCE

10 Sep 1746: Samuel Howell and Sarah Durbin entered into a [prenuptial?] agreement; he conv. to her the following tracts: Garrison's Neglect, Howell's Contrivance, Johnsons's Bed, Johnson's Rest, Joshua Wood's Mistake, and Lofton's Neglect. He also gave her a child's portion of his estate, for her and any heirs she has by him; if she d. without heirs by him, the above tracts would be divided among his male heirs; she relinquished her dower right to ⅓ of his estate (TB#E: 177).

HOWELL'S NECK

30 July 1671: 100 a. surv. for Howell Powell (MPL 5: 16).

HOWELL'S POINT
(Later called POWELL'S POINT)

30 Aug 1701: Mary Ruxton, widow of Nathaniel Ruxton, late of BA Co., dec., conv. to Richard Colegate (70?) a. of Howell's Point and 100 a. Ruxton's Range (HW#2: 89).

3 Sep 1701: John Gay and w. Frances of BA Co. conv. to Richard Colegate 70 a. of Howell's Point on n. side of Patapsco at Clapham's Creek, and 100 a. Ruxton's Range adjacent the land of Nicholas Ruxton (HW#2: 90).

HUDSON'S FOREST (1688)

27 Dec 1688: Matthew Hudson made his will leaving Burman's Forest on s. side of Back R., and H... [Hudson's Forest?] on the same side of said river to his w. Jane during her life, reserving 100 a. Jonas' Range for Joseph Perego. Ebenezer Blackstone was exec. (MCW#IV: 239, cites RM#HS: 345).

3 June 1693: Cert. of surv. by Thomas Richardson: states that by virtue of a warrant for 400 a. to Michael Hastings, assigned to Edward Boothby, and assigned by Boothby to Thomas Richardson, and 200 a. assigned by Richardson to Matthew Hudson, and by virtue of a warrant dated 20 Dec 1688 for 300 a. to Edward Boothby, there is now laid out a parcel called Hudson's Forest on s. side Back R., 268 a. adj. Burman's Forest; the land is now in possession of Richard Sampson (RM#HS: 422).

HUGHES CABIN

25 Sep 1747: Samuel Hughes leased (*) to Roger Perryman for 99 years, SH had leased the land from Benjamin Tasker on 18 July 1746, for 222 a. (TB#E: 629).

HUGHES CHANCE

10 Aug 1669: 150 a. surv. as Chance for Joseph Hughes; 150 a. on w. side of Bush R.; later poss. by Thomas Preston who m. heiress of Hughes (MRR: 62).

-- June 1727: Thomas Cross pet. the court that he poss. Hughes Chance, laid out for Joseph Hughes 1 Aug 1669; he held this land in right of his w. Sarah (BALC, HWS#3: 15).

2 April 1728: Thomas Cross of BA Co., cordwainer, and w. Sarah conv. to James Standiford 50 a. pt. (*) (IS#I: 77).

Nov 1728: James Standiford conv. 50 a. pt. (*) to William [illegible]; James' w. Mary cons. (IS#I: 222).
9 March 1731: Catherine Whayland, dau. of Henry Matthew, conv. 50 a. (*) to Thomas Lego; by LWT Henry Matthews devised 100 a. (*) to dau. Sarah Matthews, and 50 a. to dau. Catherine (IS#L: 208).
5 June 1734: Thomas Cross conv. 10 a. out of 50 a. he is entitled to, to William Rhodes; pt. of 150 a. (*); w. Sarah cons. (HWS#M: 67).
8 Aug 1734: William Rhodes conv. 60 a. (*) to Theophilus Jones and w. Elizabeth; Rhodes bought 50 a. from Thomas League (who bought it from Patrick Whayland and w. Catherine, who inher. it from her father Henry (Matthews), and 10 a. from Thomas Cross who m. Sarah, dau. of Henry (Matthews?); William's w. Mary cons. (HWS#M: 90).

HUGHES' CHOICE

2 Oct 1716: 200 a. surv. for Samuel Hughes near deer Creek (MRR#II: 485).
2 June 1718: Hughes deeds 100 a. (*) to Joshua Fowler (MRR#II: 485).
25 March 1720: Fowler conv. 100 a. back to Hughes (TR#DS: 180). (See also TR#RA: 460).
7 Dec 1726: Samuel Hughes and w. Jane conv. 200 a. (*) to John Durbin in consideration of 312 a. conv., by John Durbin to Samuel Hughes (IS#H: 318).
22 Sep 1743: mentioned in will of John Durbin.
25 Nov 1751: Daniel Durbin conv. to Thomas Durbin, (sons of John Durbin, who by his LWT bequeathed to them Hughes Adventure), his share of (*) (TR#D: 252).

HUGHES' ENLARGEMENT

30 April 1722: Samuel Hughes of BA Co. conv. 100 a. (*) to Solomon Armstrong. Samuel's w. Jane is mentioned in the text. The deed was signed by Solomon and Mary Armstrong (RM#HS: 684).
7 Dec 1726: Samuel Hughes and w. Jane conv. 200 a. (*) to John Durbin in consideration of 312 a. conv., by John Durbin to Samuel Hughes (IS#H: 318).
22 Sep 1743: John Durbin in his LWT left (*) to his s. William (TR#D: 301).
10 Feb 1752: WIlliam Durbin conv. to James Pritchard 25 a. pt. (*) (TR#D: 301).

HUGHES ISLAND

3 June 1673: Joseph Hughes gave bond he would pay Thomas Heath for the land he recently bought, or would reconvey the land to Heath (IS#IK: 44, 45).
3 Aug 1697: Thomas Heath, with cons. of w. Sarah, conv. (*), and other tracts, adj. land of Joseph Hughes to Henry Matthews (IS#IK: 154).

HUNTING CREEK

Orig. surv. for Godfrey Harmer and Oliver Sprye and sold to John Shadwell, Sr. (IS#G: 352).
21 July 1724: John Jones of BA Co., and w. Margaret, dau. and sole heir of a certain John Shadwell, the Younger, conv. to Daniel Scott, the Younger, s. of Daniel Scott, the Elder, 490 a., comprised of the following tracts: Chestnut Neck and Stanharkat (both orig. surv. for John Shadwell, Sr.), and Harmer's Hope and (*) (both orig. surv. for Godfrey Harmer and Oliver Sprye and sold to John Shadwell, Sr., grandfather of said Margaret Jones) (IS#G: 352).

HUNTING NECK (1668)

25 April 1668: 300 a. surv. for Thomas Cole and William Hollis on e. side of Bush R. at the head of Hunting Creek; later possessed by George Smith for the orphans of Daniel Peverell; still later possessed by David Thomas for the orphans of Peverell (MRR: 12).
1 July 1675: 300 a. pat. to William Hollis and Thomas Cole (IR#PP: 40).
1 Aug 1679: William Hollis of BA Co., with cons. of w. Elizabeth, and Charles Gorsuch of TA Co., conv. to Miles Gibson 300 a. (*) (IR#PP: 40).
6 July 1680: Miles Gibson conv. 300 a. (*) to Daniel Peverell. Thomas Hedge, clerk of the court, certified that MG's w. Ann also cons. (IR#PP: 50).
By c1707 George Smith held 300 a. (*) and 100 a. Mates Angle for the orphans of Daniel Peverell. Later David Thomas held both tracts (MRR: 12).
4 Sep 1733: Sarah Ruff, widow, and dau. and heiress of Daniel Peverell, conv. 300 a. (*), granted 31 July 1675 to Francis [sic] Cole, to her s. David Ruff (IS#L: 426).

HUNTING NORTH (See HUNTING WORTH)

HUNTING QUARTER

23 Feb 1739: Thomas Carr, with cons. of w. Elizabeth, conv. 50 a. (*) to Oliver Harriott and w. Susannah (HWS#1-A: 349). Harriott and his w. conv. the tract to their dau. Susannah (HWS#1-A: 350).
23 Feb 1739: TC, with cons. of w. Elizabeth, conv. 67 a. pt. (*) to William Coine (HWS#1-A: 334).
6 March 1748; William Quine and w. Martha conv. 8 a. pt. (*) to William Grover.

HUNTING WORTH (NORTH)

17 Aug 1659: 150 a. surv. for Abraham Holdman on e. side of Bush R., and now in poss. of Samuel Browne. 100 a. held by James Phillips; 50 a. held by Samuel Brown (MRR: 10).

5 June 1683: Abraham Holman, planter, s. of Abraham Holman of Bush R., dec., conv. to James Collier 150 a. "Hausing Worth" (as abstracted by Sisco) at Hunting Creek; it being pat. 15 Feb 1659/60. No w. cons. (RM#HS: 55).

13 Feb 1687: Edward Collier, of Philadelphia, feltmaker, conv. 150 a. (*) to Samuel Brown; land was sold to James Collier in June 1683; James Collier, now dec., and land desc. to Edward Collier of Philadelphia (RM#HS: 263).

16 Feb 1701: Samuel Browne and w. Mary conv. 100 a. (*) to James Phillips (HW#2: 117).

23 Jan 1719: James Brown of BA Co., conv. 50 a. pt. (*), 190 a. Brown's Chance, and 200 a. pt. James Addition to James Phillips (TR#DS: 109). On 18 Feb 1719: Samuel Brown conv. to James Phillips his interest in the above three tracts, except for a lease to David Thomas (TR#DS: 111).

HUNTINGTON

20 June 1688: 1000 a. surv. (RM#HS: 478).

8 July 1695: Tobias Starnborough and w. Sarah conv. 136 a. to Richard Thompson (RM#HS: 478).

1 June 1714: Henry Thomson of BA Co. conv. 136 a. (*), on the n. side of Jones' Falls, on the first great branch of the Falls, to Moses Edwards (TR#A: 290).

12 July 1717: John Gorsuch of BA Co., planter conv. 146 a. of (*) to Capt. Colegate. Gorsuch's w. Eliza cons. (TR#A: 508).

10 Oct 1747: Benjamin Colegate leased all the cultivated land in Huntington, Powell's Point, and Ruckston's Range to William Hammond for 14 years (TB#E: 612).

31 Oct 1749: John Edwards of BA Co. conv. 899 a. Wilkinson's Folly, Edwards Lot and Edwards Enlargement, except for that pt. which Moses Edwards, father of John, sold to Thomas Rutter and Jonathan Hanson and 2 a. to St. Paul's Parish, and Huntington, laid out for 135 a. JE's w. Mary cons. (TR#C: 320).

31 Oct 1749: Charles Ridgely of BA Co., Gent., leased 20 a. pt. (*) to Elizabeth Price (TR#C: 302).

HURD'S CAMP

16 Aug 1669: 100 a. sur. (TB#C: 351).

1 Nov 1700: Pat. to William Talbot (TB#C: 351).

See Horvath Plat: Green Spring Valley.

17 June 1743: Benjamin Hammond and w. Margaret, dau. and heir at law to William Talbot, conv. 100 a. (*) to Cornelius Howard (TB#C: 351).

28 Oct 1743: Josephus Murray conv. 100 a., pt. Counterscarpe and Hurd's Camp, to his dau. Jemima Ashman (TB#C: 340).

HURST'S MARCH

29 Oct 1753: Bennett Hurst conv. his lease to 45 a. (*) to William Rogers (BB#I: 94).

25 Oct 1770: Resurv. into PITT (q.v.).

HUTCHINS' BEGINNING

7 Aug 1745: Thomas and Nicholas Hutchins, execs. of the LWT of their father, Thomas Hutchins, dec., conv. 70 a. (*) to Thomas Franklin (TR#D: 405).

7 April 1750: John Hutchins of BA Co. conv. 100 a. (*) to Thomas Gittings. JH's w. Elizabeth cons. (TR#C: 451).

HUTCHINS' LOT

8 June 1757: Nicholas Hutchins conv. (*) to Roger Boyce (B#G: 86).

HUTCHINS' NEGLECT

8 June 1757: Nicholas Hutchins conv. 166 a. (*) to Roger Boyce (B#G: 86).

ILL WILL

Aug 1739: Richard Taylor of Goochland Co., VA, deposed that about 5 years ago (*) and Roberts Choice were resurv. into Taylor's Range (HWS#1-A: 279).

IMBLE'S UNION

22 Sep 1743: mentioned in will of John Durbin.

IMPROVED VENTURE

1750: James Pritchard owned 50 a. (*) (1750 DB).

17 Jan 1774: Daniel Durbin made a will, proved 23 March 1774. In his will he left to his dau. Avarilla Durbin (to be extx.), and to have 50 a. Obadiah's Venture and 50 a. Improved Venture conv. by James Richards; Charles Gilbert to have 3-4 a. of Improved Venture (Morgan, HCW: 17, cites HCW AJ#2: 134).

INDIAN RANGE

4 March 1672/3: Richard Leake, tailor, and w. Gwilthin, conv. 300 a. (*) at the head of the western branch of Back Creek in Sassafras R., to Hanse Peterson and James Watson (G#J: 120; TR#RA: 85).

INDUSTRY

7 March 1733/4: Samuel Chew conv. to Richard Jones of BA Co., a receipt for 190 a. Denton, 80

a. Walker's Neck, 100 a. Hooper's Island, 330 a. North Point, 546 a. Old Road, 120 a. (*), 1000 a. Shawan Hunting Ground, 50 a. Thorold's Nest, 100 a. Luke's Privilege, and 100 a. Bagford (HWS#M: 193).

INHERITANCE

7 March 1701: Robert West and w. Sarah of BA Co. conv. 50 a., pt. (*), to Walter Murrough; tract formerly (belonging to?) Robert Yates, and may be pt. Fall Hill (HW#2: 194).

20 Feb 1709: John Morrow, s. of Walter, conv. 50 a. (*) to William Pickett (TR#A: 41).

10 June 1709: William Pickett made a codicil to his will leaving (*) to his s. Heathcote (BCF: 505).

INLOES

18 Aug 1736: Selah Barton conv. 100 a. (*) to Thomas Stansbury. SB's w. Comfort cons. (IS#IK: 273).

INLOES LOYNE

15 Oct 1670: 100 a. surv. for Abraham Inloes (MRR).

5 Nov 1679: Hendrick Inloes conv. 100 a. (*) to John Boring. HI's w. Christian cons. (IR#PP: 44).

17 June 1710: Thomas Boring and John Boring of BA Co. conv. 100 a. (*) to Selah Dorman on n. side of Back R. (TR#A: 82).

INTENT (THE)

2 Feb 1708: Surv. for Joseph Hawkins (Cert. of Surv.).

25 March 1717: Joseph Hawkins of BA Co. conv. 100 a. (*) to John Hawkins, Jr., of AA Co. Jos. Hawkins' w. Elizabeth cons. (TR#RA: 465).

INTEREST

17 Oct 1716: Ebenezer Blackstone and w. Sarah of KE Co., conv. 97 a. (*), being pt. of Burman's Forest, to Joseph Peregoy (TR#A: 413).

IPSWICH

May 1705: 400 a. surv. for Samuel Sickelmore (Card Index to Patents).

ISAAC WRIGHT'S RANGE

1750: heirs of Isaac Wright owned 50 a. (*) (1750 DB).

ISAAC'S ADDITION

10 Oct 1723: Surv. for Isaac Butterworth (MRR#II: 539).

9 Aug 1745: Henry Garrett and w. Mary (dau. and devisee of Isaac Butterworth conv. to Col. Thomas White the following parcels: 63 a. 70 p. pt. Howard's Harbour), 150 a. (*) (surv. 18 Oct 1723 and pat. 6 May 1728), and 270 a. Isaac's Englargement (surv. 10 March 1719 and pat. 6 May 1728) (TR#D: 300).

ISAAC'S DELIGHT

24 Jan 1744: Isaac Webster conv. 81 a. (*), in two parcels of 46 a. and 35 a.) to Isaac Bullock of Chester Co., PA. IW's w. Margaret cons. (TB#D: 10).

23 May 1749: Isaac Bullock of Chester Co., PA conv. to Ralph Pile of Chester Co., PA, tanner, 46 a. (*) and 35 a. (*), lying together. IB's w. Margery cons. (TR#C: 190).

ISAAC'S ENLARGEMENT

6 Aug 1735: Isaac Webster of BA Co., planter, conv. 135 a. (*) to Nathaniel Giles of BA Co., planter. IW's w. Margaret cons. (HWS#M: 291).

4 Aug 1742: Nathaniel Giles of BA Co. conv., 135 a. (*) to David Thomas (TB#A: 226).

9 Aug 1745: Henry Garrett and w. Mary (dau. and devisee of Isaac Butterworth conv. to Col. Thomas White the following parcels: 63 a. 70 p. pt. Howard's Harbour), 150 a. Isaac's Addition (surv. 18 Oct 1723 and pat. 6 May 1728), and 270 a. (*) (surv. 10 March 1719 and pat. 6 May 1728) (TR#D: 300).

ISAAC'S INHERITANCE

7 Nov 1745: Isaac Butterworth conv. 200 a., pt. (*) to James Lee. IB's w. Jane cons. (TB#C: 640).

11 Jan 1745: Isaac Butterworth conv. 200 a. pt. (*) to Isaac Webster. IB's w. Jane cons. (TB#E: 22).

ISHAM'S GARDEN

3 Aug 1726: James Isham of BA Co. conv. 170 a. (*) to his son-in-law Josias Hendon and his s. William. JI's w. Elizabeth cons. (IS#H: 261).

ISHAM'S SECOND ADDITION

7 Aug 1741: James Isham, Sr., and James Isham, Jr., with cons. of latter's w. Ann, conv. 103 a. Homer and 193 a. pt. Isham's Second Addition, to Stephen Onion (TB#A: 2).

25 Sep 1741: James Isham, Sr., and Stephen Onion agree on a division of (*) (TB#A: 5).

ISLAND (THE)

Feb --- [illegible]: John [Lee] and William Boulton conv. 150 a. on Lee Island, to John Waterton (IS#IK: 20).

3 March 1665/6: John Lee signs cert. that he and William Boulton have conv. 130 a. (*) to John Waterton; earlier deed was defective (IS#IK: 20).

9 May 1666; John Waterton of Bush R. conv. 150 a. on Lee Island, which he bought from John Lee and William Boulton, to James Phillips (IR#PP: 56).
1750: The heirs of Thomas Wright owned 150 a. (*) (1750 DB: 16).

ISLAND POINT
1691: Mary Adams conv. to Richard Adams (IR#AM: 88).

ISLES OF CAPREA
(orig. surv. for John Crockett)
8 Oct 1748: Mary Dorsey and her husband Eli Dorsey of AA Co., conv. to John Greeneff Howard (*), which desc. from John Crockett, the orig. grantee, to his s. and heir at law John Crockett, Jr. He d. intestate and the land passed to his sisters Mary Dorsey and Hannah Crockett (TR#C: 104).
31 Aug 1751: Bazil Dorsey and w. Hannah conv. 656 a. Isle of Caprea to Thomas Bond. Land was property of John Crockett, then of John Crockett, Jr., who d. without heirs, leaving two sisters, Mary, and aforesaid Hannah w. of Bazil Dorsey. The sisters divided the property and Mary got the 656 a. (TR#D: 180).
5 Sep 1751: Ely Dorsey sold residue of Isle of Caprea to Thomas Miles (TR#D: 188).

IVENTON
1 May 1672: Pat. to James Ives (G#J: 325).
9 March 1674/5: James Ives, merchant, and w. Martha, conv. 100 a. (*) to William Palmer (G#J: 325).
1 March 1708: Richard Smithers of BA Co., Gent., conv. 100 a. (*) to Archibald Buchanan of BA Co., tailor; land was orig. granted to James Ives, Sr., on 1 May 1672, and conv. to Smithers by James Ives his s. and heir (RM#HS: 642).

JACK'S DOUBLE PURCHASE (Pt. SELSED)
3 Dec 1710: Francis Thornbury of BA Co. conv. 200 a. (*) to John Vickory; deed mentions that Roland Thornborough left his youngest s. 300 a. Selsed (TR#A: 95).
2 March 1735: Richard King Stevenson conv. 120 a. (*) (also known as Jack's Double Purchase) to George Buchanan; tract desc. to grantor by the death of Richard Stevenson Vickory in pursuance of the will of Vickory's father (HWS#1-A: 32).
30 Oct 1737: Richard King Stevenson conv. 150 a. (*), which desc. to him by the will of Richard Stevenson Vickory's father, to George Buchanan, and which formerly belonged to Richard Stevenson Vickory. RKS' w. Rachel cons. (HWS#M: 32).
12 Aug 1739: Richard Stevenson Vickory conv. 100 a. (*) to George Buchanan of BA Co., surgeon, and will defend the sale against all except the heirs of Roland Thornborough who took up Selsed (HWS#M: 258).
30 Aug 1740: Richard King Stevenson conv. 50 a. (*) to his cousins John and Jonathan Plowman (HWS#1-A: 438).
30 March 1747: Ann Plowman, Jonathan Plowman and John Plowman conv. 50 a. of Selsed, called (*), to Thomas Ford. Eliza, w. of Jonathan Plowman, relinquished her right of dower (TB#E: 386).

JACK'S PEACOCK
3 Feb 1724/5: Thomas Jack and w. Mary conv. (*) to John Taylor (IS#H: 7).

JACKSON'S ADVENTURE
6 Dec 1718: Samuel Jackson leased (*) to Miles Hannis and w. Elizabeth Hannis for their lifetimes (TR#RA: 506).

JACKSON'S CHANCE
11 July 1709: John and James (?) Jackson conv. 150 a. (*) to Nicholas Besson. Sarah w. of James cons. (TR#A: 10).
10 Oct 1730: James Jackson conv. 100 a. (*) to John Jones (IS#L: 27).

JACKSON'S OUTLET (Pt. of CARTER'S REST)
19 Nov 1731: Mary Foster conv. 100 a. (*), (being pt. of Carter's Rest, 400 a., orig. purch. by Robert Jones from Col. Nathaniel Utie), to James Taylor (IS#L: 165).
19 Oct 1734: James Taylor conv. 30 a. pt. (*) (100 a. in all), to Rowland Kemble. JT's w. Mary cons. (HWS#M: 155).

JACKSON'S PURCHASE
c1754: Samuel Durbin, Jr., owned Jackson's Purchase (IBC: 68).

JACOB'S CHASE (or JACOB'S CHOICE)
21 May 1684: Jacob Jenifer conv. to Thomas Long, Gent., 733 a. (*) at Burchen Run at head of Back R. (RM#HS: 78).
5 Sep 1706: Thomas Long and w. Susanna deed to James Crooke, 733 a. (*) (RM#HS: 544).
23 April 1725: James Crooke of AA Co., conv. 778 a. (*) to Daniel Dulany of Annapolis (IS#H: 99).

JACOB'S DELIGHT
20 March 1754: Jacob Rowles conv. (*) to John Chapman (BB#I: 301).

JACOB'S INHERITANCE

10 May 1722: William Wright, who took up the tract, conv. it to his s. William (IS#G: 28).

23 Aug 1740: William Wright made his will leaving the tract to his s. William (MCW#VIII: 103).

JACOB'S LOT

7 March 1743: Jacob Morris, for love and affection, conv. 50 a. (*) to Thomas Rutter, s. of Henry (TB#C: 428).

16 July 1749: Morris, now of AA Co., conv. tract to Thomas Rutter again (Morris calls Rutter kinsman) (TR#C: 482 or 492).

16 July 1750: Thomas Rutter of Henry was conv. 300 a. Jacob's Lot by his kinsman Jacob Morris of AA Co., formerly of BA Co. Morris calls Rutter kinsman (TR#C: 492).

JACOB'S PASTURE

2 Aug 1755: Jacob Shilling, Jr., blacksmith, conv. 14 a. pt. (*) to Richard Richards (BB#I: 423).

JACOB'S SQUARE

17 Oct 1714: 110 a. surv. for Jacob Bull; pat. 10 Sep 1716 (MRR#II: 289).

JACOB'S STRUGGLE

5 March 1745: Jacob Cox of BA Co. conv. 47 a. (*) to Charles Bosley. JC's w. Elizabeth cons. (TB#E: 12).

JAMAICA

27 July 1723: Surv. for John Taylor (IS#H: 333).

16 Nov 1726: John Taylor of Gunpowder R., conv. 150 a. (*) to Robert Love (IS#H: 333).

4 Nov 1730: Robert Love conv. 43 a. pt. of 150 a. (*) to Thomas Johnson; Love's w. Sarah cons. (IS#L: 49).

2 Nov 1737: Robert and Sarah Love conv. residue of 150 a. (*) to Sutton Sickelmore (HWS#M: 54).

8 March 1744/5: Sutton Sickelmore and w. Constance conv. 107 a. pt. (*) to William Young (TB#D: 67).

JAMES' ADDITION

16 Feb 1701: James Phillips of BA Co., Gent., and w. Bethia, conv. 200 a. pt. 630 a. (*) to Samuel Browne (HW#2: 138).

23 Jan 1719: James Brown of BA Co., conv. 50 a. pt. Hunting North, 190 a. Brown's Chance, and 200 a. pt. (*) to James Phillips (TR#DS: 109).

18 Feb 1719: Samuel Brown conv. to James Phillips his interest in the above three tracts, except for a lease to David Thomas (TR#DS: 111).

3 Nov 1742: James Phillips leased 100 a. pt. (*) and pt. Brown's Chance, to Amos Garrett (TR#C: 33).

JAMES' CHOICE

7 March 1809/10: Simon Pearson of BA Co., weaver, conv. 50 a. (*), pt. of a 300 a. tract, to Thomas Barton, planter, and James Preston, barber. Eme Person signed (TR#A: 52).

JAMES FARME

18 July 1730: 50 a. pat. (TB#E: 435).

28 March 1746: Sarah Roberts or Robinson or Robertson and John Carter conv. 50 a. (*) to James Richard (TB#E: 435).

JAMES' FORECAST

Nov 1686: 500 a. surv. for Thomas James; later held by Giles Stevens (MPL 22: 289, and NS#2: 507).

20 June 1696: Thomas James of Chester Co., PA, house carpenter, conv. 50 a. (*) to his son-in-law Giles Stevens. MJ signed as atty. for her husband (RM#HS: 530).

JAMES' FOREST

9 April 1685: Thomas Lightfoot, surveyor, conv. 500 a. James' Forest to James Sanders of AA Co., the tract being pt. of 1000 and 500 a. tracts both called Expectation. W. Rebecca also signs (RM#HS: 121).

JAMES' FOREST

Surv. for Thomas James (TB#A: 146).

5 March 1741: Samuel Stevens and w. Martha sell 50 a. to Joseph Thomas (TB#A: 146).

JAMES' GIFT

19 June 1747: John and William Montgomery of New London Twp., PA, conv. 150 a. (*) to David Maxfield. WM's w. Fortune cons. (TB#E: 459).

JAMES' LOT

28 Oct., 1739: Henry Darnall of Portland Manor, AA Co. leased 100 a. James' Lot, being pt. of Land of Promise, to William James for 20 years (HWS#1-A: 363).

JAMES' MEADOWS

1702/6: 200 a. pat. to Thady Tracey.

See PW Plat H; Horvath Plat: Ruxton and Riderwood.

9 Sep 1709: Teague Tracey of BA Co., cooper, conv. 100 a. pt. of (*), on Briton Ridge, to Mordecai Price of AA Co., planter. TT's w. Mary signed (TR#A: 146).

29 March 1745/6: James Tracey of Craven Co., NC, appoints John Ensor of Patapsco Parish, his atty. to acknowledge deed to John Cole, Jr., for James Meadow and Teague's Park (TB#D: 248).

JAMES' MISTAKE

15 Oct 1743: John Baker of Patapsco conv. 50 a. (*) to William Hill or Fell (TB#C: 338).

JAMES' PARK (1678)

30 May 1678: 200 a. surv. for Thomas James on s. side of Middle R.; later possessed by George Grover; still later by Jno. Ewings (MRR: 68).

7 Nov 1699: Thomas James of Newcastle Co., PA, carpenter, conv. 200 a. (*) to George Grover of BA Co., plasterer; TJ's w. Mary cons. (TR#RA: 413).

2 March 1709: John Ewings of BA Co., Gent., conv. 200 a. (*) and 100 a. Addition to James Park to John Willis. JE's w. Elizabeth cons. (RM#HS: 646).

5 June 1734: John Wheeler of BA Co. and w. Margaret conv. 200 a. (*), and other lands, to Abraham Burkholder of Conestoga, Lancaster Co., PA (HWS#M: 58).

31 Jan 1742: Walter James conv. 200 a. (*) to Thomas Sligh; WJ's w. Elizabeth cons. (TB#C: 100).

JAMES PARK (1681)

23 April 1681: 1175 a. surv. for James Phillips on e. side of Bush R. (MRR: 29).

July 1718: James Phillips for love of the Protestant Religion, conv. 2 a. pt. (*) where St. George's Church now stands, to ... (TR#RA: 484).

7 Dec 1739: James Phillips of BA Co., s. and heir of Col. James Phillips of BA Co., dec., conv. 500 a. pt. James' Park and pt. Benjamin's Choice, to his sister Johanna, w. of Jacob Giles (HWS#1-A: 310).

JAMES PARK (1683)

28 Dec 1683: 500 a. surv. for James Ellis; later possessed by the orphans of said Ellis; and later by Mary Ellis (MRR: 48).

10 May 1685: Pat. to James Ellis (TB#C: 367).

17 Nov. 1743: Samuel Lockwood, planter, conv. 500 a. (*) to John Bond, tanner. SL's w. Elinor cons. (TB#C: 367).

19 Sep 1745: John Bond conv. 26 a. (*) to William Dallam and George Brown. JB's w. Aliceanna cons. (TB#D: 308).

19 Sep 1746: William Dallam conv. 26 a. and 34 a. of James' Park and 16 a. Owner's Landing to Thomas Harrison (TB#E: 249).

19 Sep 1746: George Browne of Joppa conv. $\frac{1}{4}$ of James Park and Owners Landing to Thomas Harrison (TB#E: 253).

JAMES' PARK, ADDITION TO

2 March 1709: John Ewings of BA Co., Gent., conv. 200 a. (*) and 100 a. Addition to James Park to John Willis. JE's w. Elizabeth cons. (RM#HS: 646).

JAMES' PASTURE

Aug 1687: 136 a. surv. for Thomas James; later possessed by William Tolfare for orphans of William Barton; still later possessed by Lewis Barton (MRR: 69).

11 May 1688: Thomas James of BA Co. planter conv. 136 a. (*) to Lewis Barton. Sarah James cons. (RM#HS: 498).

29 Nov 1709: Lewis Barton conv. 136 a. (*) to Andrew Anderson (TR#A: 35).

25 April 1713: Andrew Anderson of Back R. conv. 136 a. (*) to John Fitzredmond. AA's w. Elizabeth cons. (TR#A: 223).

JAMES TOWN

5 Aug 1723: George Reade, atty. for Thomas Ridge and Thomas Reade of Newport, Isle of Wight, conv. 150 a. James Town, and 50 a. Walter Town, to George Groome (IS#G: 160).

JENIFER'S DELIGHT (1681)
(See also SHOEMAKER'S HALL)

11 Oct 1681: 250 a. warrant issued to Thomas Taylor of CH Co.; the warrant was purch. by Henry Bonner who conv. it on 23 Nov 1682 to John Roberts (RM#HS: 428).

5 Sep 1694: John Roberts and w. Eleanor conv. 250 a. (*) to John Gay (RM#HS: 428).

25 June 1696: John Gay, cordwainer, with cons. of w. Frances, conv. to Thomas Weekes 100 a. Shoemaker's Hall, being pt. of (*) which JG purch. from John Roberts (RM#HS: 531).

JENIFER'S DELIGHT (1683)

1683: Pat. to Jacob Jenifer (RM#HS: 89).

15 June 1684: Maj. Thomas Long, atty. for Jacob Jenifer, conv. to Thomas Tench, merchant of London, 200 a. (*) on the n. side of Swan Creek, as pat. in 1683 to Jenifer (Deed and Letter of Atty. in RM#HS: 39).

JENIFER'S KINDNESS

6 March 1682/3: Robert Benger, shoemaker, and w. Katherine, conv. 150 a. Oliver's Reserve and 30 a. Jenifers Kindness, to Daniel Scott (RM#HS: 33).

3 Aug 1703: Daniel Scott and w. Jane conv. 150 A. Oliver's Reserve and 30 a. Jenifer's Kindness to William Galloway (HW#2: 334).

JENKINS RANGE

17 Nov 1750: Francis Jenkins conv. 247 a. (*) to Jacob Giles (TR#D: 112).

29 April 1752: Jacob Giles conv. back to Francis Jenkins 247 a. (*) (TR#D: 327).

29 April 1752: Francis Jenkins conv. 147 a., pt. (*), to John Rigdon (TR#D: 321).

29 April 1752: Francis Jenkins conv. 100 a., pt. (*), to James Billingslea (TR#D: 323).

JEOPARDY

19 April 1720: Surv. (HWS# 1-A, 210).

See Horvath Plat: Randallstown.

31 March 1739: Daniel Rawlings, with cons. of w. Mary, conv. 150 a. pt. (*) and pt. Addition to Jeopardy to Christopher Randall (HWS#1-A: 210).

10 March 1747: Christopher Randall conv. 133 a. George's Park, 150 a. (*), and 75 a. Randall's Meadows to Rachel Bailey of BA Co., widow (TB#E: 696).

JEOPARDY, ADDITION TO

18 April 1726: Surv. (HWS#1-A: 210). 9 June 1727; 100 a. pat. to Daniel Rawlings (MPL PL#6: 556, IL#A: 717).

See Horvath Plat: Randallstown.

31 March 1739: Daniel Rawlings, with cons. of w. Mary, conv. 150 a. pt. Jeopardy and pt. Addition to Jeopardy to Christopher Randall (HWS#1-A: 210).

JERICOE (JERICHO)

5 Oct 1702: Cert. of surv. granted to Jacob Regnier of AA Co.; JP, of Lincolns' Inn, Barrister, now res. of NY [pat. 20 May 1705 to JR: MPL WD: 403 and DD#5: 147]. By his LWT dated 6 Nov 1714 he left all his estate in America, England, or wherever to his w. Elizabeth. Elizabeth Regnier, extx. of Jacob Regnier, by her LWT dated 2 July 1715 left her entire estate in America, Great Britain, etc., to her mother Joanna Markham and bro.-in-law Daniel Regnier of London, Gent. (TR#RA: 543).

6 April 1719: Joanna Markham of NY, widow, and Daniel Regnier of NY, Gent., conv. 1000 a. (*) to John Hall of Cranberry (TR#RA: 543).

John Hall purch. 1000 a. pt. (*) from the heirs of Jacob Regnier (TB#A: 63).

17 Dec 1741: Edward Hall, s. of John Hall, dec., conv. pt. (*), pt. Cranberry Hall, and pt. Sophia's Dairy, to his bro. Parker Hall (TB#A: 63).

JERUSALEM

20 May 1687: 318 a. surv. for Nicholas Hemstead and John Valley on the north side of the Little Falls of Gunpowder R.; later possessed by Enoch Spinks. Later edition says John Walley; still later possessed by Henry Wriothesley (MRR: 53).

8 March 1702: Enoch Spinks conv. 318 a. (*) to Henry Wriothesley (HW#2: 161).

1 April 1720: Esther Brown of CE Co., widow, conv. 318 a. (*) to Joshua Cockway [Cockey]; tract was sold by Roger Matthews, atty. for Ann Wriothesley, to William Brown, dec., husband of Esther (TR#DS: 161).

8 Aug 1722: Sarah Cockway [Cockey], widow, conv. 159 a. $\frac{1}{2}$ (*) to Sarah Hanson; if Sarah d. then to grandson John Hanson; if John d., then to Sarah Cockway's grandson Benjamin Hanson (IS#G: 182).

8 Aug 1746: Sutton Sickelmore conv. 200 a. Ann's Delight and 318 a. (*) to Stephen Onion (TB#E: 159).

JERUSALEM, RESURVEY ON

318 a. orig. granted to Nicholas Hempstead and John Walley (TR#C: 199).

21 Aug 1745: Sarah Tayman conv. (*) to William Dallam; also conv. by ST as Sarah Cockey to her granddaughter Sarah Hanson, now w. of John Garrettson (TB#D: 311).

10 March 1748: William Dallam conv. to Stephen Onion tract (*) which Tayman purch. from Sarah Tayman (TR#C: 199).

JOB'S ADDITION

5 June 1745: Leonard Decosse of BA Co. conv. 225 a. (*) to Jane Bourdillon of BA Co., widow (TB#D: 114).

22 Dec 1746: Jane Bourdillon conv. 225 a. (*) to Charles Ridgely, being same land JB had mortgaged from Leonard Decausse on 5 June 1745 (TB#E: 292).

29 Jan 1746/7: Leonard Decauss conv. (*) to Charles Ridgely (TB#E: 293).

JOB'S BEGINNING

6 July 1728: Job Evans of BA Co. conv. 55 a. (*) to John Moale. JE's w. Mary cons. (IS#I: 134).

JOHN AND ISAACS ENLARGEMENT

25 June 1703: 562 a. granted to Isaac Butterworth (MPL CD#4: 160).

JOHN AND ISAACS LOT

26 March 1714: 189 a. surv. for Isaac Butterworth (MRR#II: 518).

JOHN'S AND ISAAC'S LOT

11 Nov 1742: John Webster of BA Co. conv., 200 a. pt. (*) to Samuel Gilbert (TB#C: 68).

JOHNS BARRENS ENLARGED

20 Dec 1771: 477 a. surv. for Abraham Jarrett (C:18).

JOHNS BEGINNINGS (1729)

5 May 1729: 200 a. pat. to John Muckeldory (MPL PL#7: 208; IL#B: 58).

5 Sep 1732: John Muckeldory of BA Co. conv. 200 a. pt. (*) to John Long of CE Co. (IS#L: 280).

JOHNS BEGINNINGS

1729: Thomas Harris conv. 50 a. (*) to John Gregory (IS#K: 205).

8 July 1738: John Rogers conv. 40 a. John's Beginning and 50 a. Michael's Beginning to Thomas Sligh (HWS#1-A: 89).

JOHN'S CHANCE

20 April 1748: 1603 a. pat. to John Hammond of Charles of AA Co. (TR#C: 232).

See Horvath Plat: Wards Chapel.

22 July 1749: John Hammond of Charles, of AA Co., conv. 400 a. pt. (*) to Abel Brown of AA Co., Gent. JH's w. Anne cons. (TR#C: 232).

JOHN'S DELIGHT

7 Jan 1700: Henry Hedge and w. Mary conv. 100 a. (*) to John Boon (TR#RA: 39).

JOHN'S FAVOUR

30 Jan 1744: Joseph Cornelius of BA Co., carpenter, conv. 100 a. (*) to Thomas Sheredine (TB#D: 12). [This may have been a mortgage]

18 Feb 1745: Thomas Sheredine, merchant, assigned mortgage of (*) (which Joseph Cornelius and w. Elizabeth mortgaged to TS on 13 Jan 1744) to William Fell (TB#E: 19).

JOHNS FOREST

2 March 1750: Surv. for Richard Rhodes, Jr. (C:18: cites BA Unpat. Cert. 811).

JOHN'S HABITATION

29 June 1683: 200 a. surv. for John Linager (TB#E: 537).

24 March 1746: George Linager of KE Co., planter, conv. 200 a. (*) to dau. Sarah, now w. of James Power of CE Co., carpenter. Deed stated that the tract originally belonged to John Linegar, father of George (the eld. s.), and JL had three other ch.: 2 daus. who d., in MD, and a s. who went to remote parts and not having been heard from in a long time, is presumed dead (TB#E: 537).

JOHN'S INTEREST (1683)

12 May 1683: 150 a. surv. for Michael Judd on w. side of Bush R.; later possessed by Elizabeth Ebden for the orphans of William Ebden; later poss. by John Nicholson's orphans (MRR: 42).

(by) 1 Jan 1691: Michael Judd and w. Jane conv. 150 a. (*) to William Ebden, the "natural s." of said Jane (RM#HS: 340).

JOHN'S INTEREST (1686)

14 May 1686: 200 a. surv. for Michael Judd on w. side of Back R., and later possessed by Abraham Delapp; later possessed by James Isum for Delapp's orphans; Jeremiah Downes married the heir (MRR: 43; IS#IK: 219).

3 Aug 1692: Michael Judd and w. Jane conv. 200 a. (*) to Robert Oulesse (RM#HS: 354).

3 March 1697/8: Robert Olesse and w. Margaret conv. 200 a. (*) to Abraham Delapp (IS#IK: 219).

30 Dec 1708: Nicholas Herbert and w. Sarah conv. (*) to James Isham (TR#A: 1).

JOHN'S INTEREST (Pt. of TODD'S RANGE)

7 June 1699: Cert. of surv. dated for (*), pt. of Todd's Range (HW#2: 155).

12 June 1699: James Todd of BA Co. conv. 50 a. (*), pt. of Todd's Range, to John Harryman (TR#RA: 397).

7 July 1702: John Harryman and w. Elinor conv. 50 a. (*) to Michael Young (HW#2: 155).

3 Aug 1725: Richard Marchant of BA Co., weaver, and w. Mary, conv. 50 a. (*) to Samuel Harryman (IS#H: 150).

JOHN'S INTEREST

4 March 1723: Lewis Nowell [sic] and w. Jane conv. Aberly Lodge, 100 a. Crow Perches and two parcels of John's Interest to Henry Wetherall (IS#G: 277).

1729: Thomas Downs conv. 200 a. (*) to Henry Wetherall (IS#K: 19).

JOHN'S LAVOUR

1750: held by heirs of John Boring (1750 DB).

JOHN'S LEVEL or LOT(?)

1 April 1737: John Hathaway of AA Co., carpenter, conv., 50 a. (*) to Samuel Shipley of AA Co. (IS#IK: 382).

19 Oct 1744: Samuel Shipley conv. 50 a. John's Lot, to John Hood. SS' w. Martha cons. (TB#D: 1).

JOHNSON

(See JOHNSTON)

JOHNSON'S ADDITION

4 Nov 1730: Robert Love conv. 43 a. (*) to Thomas Johnson. RL's w. Sarah cons. (IS#L: 69).

JOHNSON'S BED

16 April 1684: 268 a. surv. for John Johnson (IS#IK: 177).

30 Aug 1697: John Johnson and w. Ann conv. 328 a., parts of (*) (168 a.) and 150 a. Johnson's Rest, to Thomas Freeborne (IS#IK: 177).

13 June 1720: Jane Thomas have p/a to Thomas Tolley to divide parcels of (*) and Johnson's Rest, where her bro. Richard Freeborne lately lived. At his death then lands desc. to her four sisters: Eliz. Garrison, Mary Tolley, Jane Thomas, and Priscilla Freeborne (RM#HS: 661).

10 Nov 1722: Thomas Tolley and w. Mary, and Jane Thomas conv. to Samuel Howell the lands (Johnson's Bed and Johnson's Rest) which desc. to them after the death of Richard Freeborne (IS#G: 115).

20 Oct 1739; Eliz. Garrettson, widow, conv. her share of Johnson's Bed and Johnson's Rest to Samuel Howell (HWS#1-A: 292).

10 Sep 1746: Samuel Howell and Sarah Durbin enter into a [prenuptial?] agreement; he conv. to her the following tracts: Garrison's Neglect, Howell's Contrivance, Johnsons's Bed, Johnson's Rest, Joshua Wood's Mistake, and Lofton's Neglect. He also conv. her a child's portion of his estate, for her and any heirs she has by him;; is she d. without heirs by him, the above tracts will be divided among his male heirs; she relinquishes her dower right to ⅓ of his estate (TB#E: 177).

JOHNSON'S CHANCE

27 April 1763: Thomas Johnson conv. 200 a. (*) to William Crooks late of Bucks Co., PA (B#L: 268).

JOHNSON'S DELAY

7 Aug 1741: John Stokes, s. and devisee of John Stokes, dec., conv. (*), als. Shrewsbury, to Jacob Giles (HWS#1-A: 538).

JOHNSON'S DOCK

4 Aug 1694: James Todd of BA Co., Gent., conv. 250 a. to Stephen Johnson of AA Co., shipwright (RM#HS: 398).

-- Jan 1699: Stephen Johnson of BA Co., shipwright, and w. Ann conv. 250 a. (*) to Robert Johnson of BA Co., shipwright (TR#RA: 416).

29 April 1703: Robert Johnson, s. and heir of Stephen Johnson of BA Co., dec., and Robert's w. Hannah conv. 250 a.(*) to George Eager (HW#2: 251).

22 June 1704: James Todd of BA Co., planter, conv. 250 a. parts Johnson's Dock, Powell's Pumpkin Patch, and pt. Todds' Range, to Robert Johnson of AA Co., shipwright (HW#2: 344).

JOHNSON'S FOLLY

See Horvath Plat: Elkridge.

2 Aug 1715: George Freeland and w. Mary conv. 75 a. Johnson's Folly, being pt. of Freeland's Mount, to Thomas Johnson (TR#A: 345).

JOHNSON'S ISLAND

27 Oct 1731: Richard Touchstone, with Thomas Cresap, William Cannon, Edward Evans, Robert Cannon, conv. 60 a. (*), the next largest island to Palmer's Island. Sophia, w. of Robert Cannon and Rachel w. of Edward Evans cons. (IS#L: 214).

4 Aug 1736: William Cannon, with cons. of w. Frances, conv. a 1/6 moiety of (*) to Stephen Onion (HWS#M: 430).

9 Aug 1739: Thomas Cresap and w. Hannah conv. (*), left to Hannah by her father Daniel Johnson, to Stephen Onion, Ironmaster (HWS#1-A: 291).

JOHNSON'S RANGE

22 June 1750: Matthew Johnson of Annapolis, cordwainer, conv. 100 a. Johnson's Range to Emmanuel Teale. MJ's w. Sarah cons. (TR#C: 513).

JOHNSON'S REST

10 Sep 1662: 150 a. surv. for John Johnson in the woods above Swan Creek; later 100 a. poss. by William Lofton and Richard Perkins, and 50 a. in poss. of Thomas Freeborne. Later Rent Rolls give date of surv. as 1683 (MRR: 28).

30 Aug 1697: John Johnson and w. Ann conv. 328 a., parts of Johnsons Bed (168 a.) and 150 a. (*), to Thomas Freeborne (IS#IK: 177).

13 June 1720: Jane Thomas have p/a to Thomas Tolley to divide parcels of Johnson's Bed and (*), where her bro. Richard Freeborne lately lived. At his death then lands desc. to her four sisters: Eliz. Garrison, Mary Tolley, Jane Thomas, and Priscilla Freeborne (RM#HS: 661).

8 Sep 1720: Richard Perkins conv. 100 a. pt. (*) to Thomas Lofton (TR#DS: 279).

8 Sep 1720: Thomas Lofton conv. 100 a. (*) to Nathaniel Daughtie (Daugherty?) (TR#DS: 281).

10 Nov 1722: Thomas Tolley and w. Mary, and Jane Thomas conv. to Samuel Howell the lands (Johnson's Bed and Johnson's Rest) which desc. to them after the death of Richard Freeborne (IS#G: 115).

27 Nov 1729: Nathaniel Dougherty of CE Co. conv. 100 a. (*) to John Poloke (IS#K: 161).

20 Oct 1739; Eliz. Garrettson, widow, conv. her share of Johnson's Bed and Johnson's Rest to Samuel Howell (HWS#1-A: 292).

10 Sep 1746: Samuel Howell and Sarah Durbin entered into a [prenuptial?] agreement; he conv. to her the following tracts: Garrison's Neglect, Howell's Contrivance, Johnsons's Bed, Johnson's Rest, Joshua Wood's Mistake, and Lofton's Neglect. He also gave her a child's portion of his estate, for her and any heirs she might have by him; if she d. without heirs by him, the above tracts would be divided among his male heirs; she relinquished her dower right to ⅓ of his estate (TB#E: 177).
19 Aug 1747: James Gallion and w. Phoebe, Solomon Gallion and w. Martha, and James Lowe and w. Mary, conv. 100 a. (*) to John Pogue (TB#E: 568, 570).
31 May 1750: John Pogue and w. Sarah conv. (*) and Brotherly Love to Jacob Giles (TR#D: 3).
22 June 1750: Matthew Johnson and w. Sarah conv. 100 a. (*) to Emanuel Teale; Johnsons were of AA Co. (TR#C: 513).

JOHNSTON (or JOHNSON)
4 Feb 1659: Tract was pat. by John Dickenson (IR#PP: 45).
22 Dec 1662: John Dickenson assigned the land to his bro. Walter Dickenson (IR#PP: 45).
13 Oct 1676: Walter Dickenson of TA Co. conv. 200 a. (*) to Thomas Durbin; land located on e. side of Dickenson's Branch on e. side of Welshman's Creek, on n. side of Patapasco. Sarah Dickenson signed with the grantor. On 16 March 1676/7 Dickenson and his w. authorize Michael [sic] Gibson to act as atty. (IR#PP: 15).
23 Nov 1679: John Dickenson, bro. of Walter, confirms the sale of (*) to Thomas Durbin (IR#PP: 45).
25 April 1708: Christopher Durbin conv. 200 a. (*) to John Brice of AA Co., along with 18 a. Thomas' Addition. Durbin's w. Mary is mentioned in the deed but did not give her cons. privately (RM#HS: 604).
19 Feb 1732: John Brice of AA Co., Gent., with the cons. of Madame Sarah Brice, conv. 200 a. (*) to Philip Jones, Jr., and other tracts (IS#L: 364).
3 March 1739: Philip Jones, Jr., conv. 40 a. pt. (*) to Jacob Rowles. PJ's w. Ann cons. (HWS#1-A: 378).
3 July 1746: Philip Jones, Jr., conv. 40 a. pt. (*) to Jacob Rowles. PJ's w. Ann cons. (TB#E: 194).
22 July 1746: Jacob Rowles of BA Co. conv. 40 a. pt. (*) to Philip Jones, Jr. (TB#E: 133).

JOLLY QUARTER (THE)
(See JOSHUA'S DELIGHT)

JONATHAN'S INHERITANCE
7 July 1725: 100 a. in CE Co. pat. to Jonathan Jones (MPL PL#6, 252, IL#A: 523).
5 Aug 1741: Jonathan Jones of Chester Co., PA, carpenter, conv. (*) to William Smith of Lancaster Co., PA. Gwin Carmack relinquishes her right of dower (HWS#1-A: 522).

JONES ADDITION (1676)
11 July 1676: 79 a. surv. for Thomas Jones on the n. side of Gunpowder R.; later the land granted to John Yeo (MRR: 31).
11 July 1676: 79 a. surv. for Thomas Jones; later granted to John Yeo (MRR: 31).
4 April 1683: Robert Jones, heir of Thomas Jones conv. 73 a. (*) plus York's Hope to John Yeo, who on 5 June 1683 authorized Peter Ellis to receive transfer from Jones' atty. Edward Beedle (RM#HS: 53).

JONES ADDITION (1696)
20 July 1696: 100 a. surv. for Humphrey Jones near the head of Bush R. (MRR: 26).
27 March 1716: Humphrey Jones conv. (*) to grandch. William and Mary Kemble, ch. of William and Mary Kemble (TR#A: 389).
5 March 1727/8: Charles Whitaker and w. Mary conv. to John Powell 70 a. (*) IS#I: 95).
5 March 1727/8: Charles Whitaker and w. Mary conv. 70 a. (*) to Samuel Hughes, except land excepted by John Durbin who sold it to CW (IS#I: 152).
6 April 1731: John Powell, ropemaker, with cons. of w. Phillis, conv. 70 a. pt. (*) to Sherwood Lee (IS#L: 97).
30 Nov 1737; Sherwood Lee, with cons. of w. Eleanor, conv. 70 a. (*) to Josias Middlemore (HWS#1-A: 39).
30 July 1742: John Whitemore and w. Mary conv. 30 a. pt. (*) and 10 a., 25 perches, pt. Hathaway's Hazard to John Hughes, with the exception of land deeded by John Durbin to John Hughes (TB#C: 287).
16 June 1748: John Hughes conv. 100 a. (*) and 200 a. Ah Ha At a Venture to Thomas White (TB#E: 725).

JONES' ADDITION (Unplaced)
31 March 1739: William Norton and w. Ann conv. 50 a. Jones Addition and 40 a. Norton's Addition to William Lynch (HWS#A-1, 218).

JONES' ADVENTURE
10 Dec 1715: 200 a. pat. to Capt. Philip Jones of AA Co. (MPL EE#6: 310, CE#1: 360).
See KN Plat WO, Horvath Plat: Granite.

27 July 1731: Philip Jones of AA Co. conv. 200 a. (*) to John Moale; Jones orig. sold the land to Moale on 14 March 1720, but the land wasn't pat. until 26 May 1721 (IS#L: 150).

26 June 1741: William Holland of CV Co., conv. 1000 a. Bachelor's Good Luck and 50 a. pt. (*) to Henry Chew; WH's w. Anne cons. (TB#A: 17).

13 Feb 1741/2: Henry Chew of BA Co., Gent., conv. pt. (*) and pt. Bachelor's Good Luck, in all about 100 a., to Joseph Chew (TB#A: 100).

20 March 1754: Jacob Rowles conv. 100 a. (*) and other lands to David Rowles (BB#I: 302).

JONES' ANGLE

24 July 1704: James Todd conv. 28 a. Jones Angle and 1 a. 16 perches Leakins to John Oldton, Gent. (IR#PP: 165).

JONES CHANCE

c1700: John Thomas held 100 a. for the orphans of John Kemp (MRR: 87).

4 Nov 1744: Jacob Jones, with cons. of w. Elizabeth, conv. 74 a. (*) to Isaac Hardin.

3 Dec 1745: John Jones conv. (*) to Salathiel, Absolom and Aquila Galloway, land which his father William Jones had promised to conv. to grantees' father William Galloway (TB#D: 387).

14 Dec 1645: Zachariah Gray and w. Rebecca conv. 20 a. (*) to Sabrett Sollers (TB#E: 16).

1750: Heirs of William Galloway owned 50 a. (*) (1750 DB).

c1754: Moses Galloway owned (*) (IBC: 66).

1763/4: Moses Galloway owned 50 a. (*) (AHAL: 74).

JONES' FARM

1729/30: 50 a. surv. for John Jones.

See Horvath Plat: Pikesville.

7 Nov 1739: John Jones conv. 50 a. (*) to Sarah Dorsett, widow (HWS#1-A: 301, 307).

13 Oct 1748: James Richard, merchant, mortgaged 50 a. (*), 150 a. North Carolina, and 646 a. Carolina Felix to Charles Ridgely and Joseph Taylor, exec. of William Fell (TR#C: 82).

JONES' GIFT

8 June 1738: Edward Evans, with cons. of w. Rachel, conv. 150 a. (*) to Nathaniel Porter (HWS#1-A: 75).

25 Jan 1744: Nathaniel Porter, with cons. of w. Sarah, conv. 150 a. (*) to John and William Montgomery of PA (TB#D: 14).

JONES (JOHN'S) INHERITANCE (1667)

5 Sep 1667: 150 a. surv. for John Jones on Patapsco R.; later held by Charles Merryman for the orphans of John Boring (MRR: 93).

5 March 1705: John Boring and w. Mary conv. land taken up by grantor's father, John Boring, to Robuck Lynch (IR#AM: 49).

10 May 1707: John Boring of BA Co., planter, conv. 74 a. Norton's Lot, being pt. of a greater tract called Jones His Inheritance, to John Norton. John's w. Mary cons. (RM#HS: 612).

17 March 1730: Joseph Crouch of AA Co., and w. Mary (formerly w. of Robuck Lynch) conv. Hart's Green, (*), and Polar Ridge (formerly taken up by John Martin) to William Lynch (IS#L: 114).

JONES' INHERITANCE (1683)

28 Sep 1683: 1000 a. surv. for Robert Jones on the head of Gunpowder R.; Jones reported to be dead (MRR: 44).

JONES' INHERITANCE

9 March 1722: Theophilus Jones conv. 126 a. pt. 500 a. (*) to Stephen Onion and Thomas Russell of CE Co.; (*) is a resurv. on Cadwallader and St. Jones (IS#G: 184).

JONES MISTAKE

1750: Greenbury Dorsey, et al., released (*) to John Baker (TR#D: 368).

18 July 1752: John Baker and w. Margaret conv. pt. (*) to John Hawkins (TR#D: 371).

JONES' NEGLECT

5 April 1760: William Demmitt, s. of Thomas, with cons. of w. Sophia, conv. 50 a. (*) to William Holmes (B#H: 160).

JONES RANGE

8 Dec 1679: David Jones conv. 380 a. (*), at Denton Creek on n. side of the Patapsco, to Charles Gorsuch of TA Co. Anna Jones signed with the grantor (IR#PP: 47).

9 Dec 1679: Charles and Sarah Gorsuch appoint their cousin Miles Gibson their atty. to acknowledge their sale of (*) back to David Jones (IS#IK: 59).

19 Sep 1716: John Bowen and w. Mary conv. pt. (*) to Edward Corbin (TR#A: 439).

10 Sep 1739; Edward Corbin and w. Jane conv. 50 a. pt. (*) and pt. Corbin's Rest, to Thomas Sligh (HWS#M: 13).

20 July 1746: Thomas Sligh, with cons. of w. Sophia, conv. 150 a. Corbin's Rest, 48 a. Rider's Industry, and 50 a. pt. (*) to Peter Dowell (TB#E: 196).

17 Nov 1748: Peter Dowell conv. 23 a., pt. (*) and Rider's Industry, to Samuel Bowen (TR#C: 146).

JONES' VENTURE

2 May 1721: Cadwallader Jones conv. 50 a., ½ of (*), to Thomas Phelps (TR#DS: 330).

24 Nov 1724; Cadwallader Jones conv. 50 a. (*) to Col. William Holland of AA Co., merchant (IS#H: 71).

20 April 1762: Avington Phelps of Roan Co., NC, and David McIlvain (or McSwain) conv. 50 a., ½ of (*) to Edward Morgan (B#K: 720.

JOSEPH'S FAVOR

3 Oct 1726: Surv. for Joseph Beasman, but pat. on 8 May 1727 to Samuel Peele (MPL PL#6: 554, IL#A: 687).

29 Aug 1741: William Beasman, s. and heir of Joseph Beasman, dec., conv. 100 a. pt. (*) to Elizabeth Beasman, widow and relict of Joseph. William's w. Ruth cons. (TB#A: 8).

1759: William Peale's exec. conv. 100 a. (*) to Reese Bowen (B#H: 16).

JOSHUA WOOD'S MISTAKE

10 Sep 1746: Samuel Howell and Sarah Durbin enter into a [prenuptial?] agreement; he conv. to her the following tracts: Garrison's Neglect, Howell's Contrivance, Johnsons's Bed, Johnson's Rest, Joshua Wood's Mistake, and Lofton's Neglect. He also conv. her a child's portion of his estate, for her and any heirs she has by him;; is she d. without heirs by him, the above tracts will be divided among his male heirs; she relinquishes her dower right to ⅓ of his estate (TB#E: 177).

JOSHUA'S ADDITION

4 Dec 1725; Joshua Sewell, with cons. of w. Mary, conv. 250 a. (*), Joshua's Folly, and 100 a. Joshua's Grove to Thomas Cockey (IS#H: 212).

JOSHUA'S DELIGHT

29 June 1724; Joshua Sewell and w. Mary conv. 136 a. (*) formerly called The Jolly Quarter, to Thomas Wainwright (IS#G: 295).

JOSHUA'S EXPECTATION

29 June 1724: Joshua Sewell and w. Mary conv. 77 a. (*) to Thomas Wainwright (IS#G: 288).

JOSHUA'S FOLLY

4 Dec 1725; Joshua Sewell, with cons. of w. Mary, conv. 250 a. Joshua's Addition, (*), and 100 a. Joshua's Grove to Thomas Cockey (IS#H: 212).

JOSHUA'S GROVE

4 Dec 1725; Joshua Sewell, with cons. of w. Mary, conv. 250 a. Joshua's Addition, Joshua's Folly, and 100 a. (*) to Thomas Cockey (IS#H: 212).

JOSHUA'S LOT

21 Jan 1726/7: John Dorsey mortgaged 200 a. Collinbourne and (?) a. Joshua's Lot (mortgage to run until 1 July 1727) to Richard Snowden of AA Co., merchant (IS#H: 353).

14 June 1742: Richard Snowden of AA Co. conv. 500 a. (*) to Christopher Gist (TR#A: 181).

14 March 1743: Christopher Gist mortgaged 100 a. Counterscarpe, 83 a. Milford, Gist's Inspection, 500 a. Joshua's Lot, 50 a. Gist's Meadows, and 2 lots in Baltimore Town (TB#D: 438).

28 March 1746: James Richard, atty. for Stephen Theodore Jannsen, conv. 100 a. Counterscarpe, 83 a. Milford, Gist's Inspection, 500 a. Joshua's Lot, 50 a. Gist's Meadows, and 2 lots in Baltimore Town to William Cromwell and Tobias Stansbury, who have paid the mortgage (TB#D: 438).

JOSHUA'S LOT, ADDITION TO

6 Aug 1754: Tobias Stansbury, with cons. of w. Mary, conv. 97 a. (*), on the n. side of the Western Run of Gunpowder, to Josephus Murray (BB#I: 275).

JOSIE'S ANGLE

6 March 1706: John Oldton, Gent., conv. 24 a. 24 perches (*) to Aquila Paca (IR#AM: 55).

JUDD'S ADDITION

20 Feb 1688, 28 a. surv. for Michael Judd lying betw. Gunpowder and Bush river, now in the possession of Thomas Preston (MRR: 62).

JULLCAN BAY

30 Sep 1712: James Maxwell, for natural love, conv. 100 a. (*) to his son-in-law Spry Godfrey Gundry (TR#A: 207).

JUMPER'S DELIGHT
(See SHOEMAKER'S HALL)

JURDISTAN (also called GARDESON)

8 Feb 1688: 299 a. surv. for John Thomas in the woods betw. Patapsco R. and Back R.; later John Thomas poss. 249 a. and Joseph Wells poss. 50 a. (MRR: 86)

13 April 1695: John Thomas conv. 50 a. Wells' Lot, being pt. of (*) to James Wells, in consideration that Thomas be excused from teaching said Wells to read and write (RM#HS: 460).

29 Nov 1737: John Thomas conv. 299 a. (*) (except for the 50 a. which John Thomas, late of BA Co., dec., conv. to James Wells) to William Tweedie (HWS # 1-A, 40).

9 Sep 1738: William Tweedie of BA Co., merchant, mortgaged 299 a. (*), surv. 28 Feb 1688 [sic], to

William Cumming of Annapolis (HWS#1-A: 146).
31 Jan 1743: Robert Burgin conv. 50 a. (*), formerly taken up by John Thomas, to William Chetwynd, Samuel and Osgood G...(?), Thomas Russell, merchant, Mrs. Mary Wrightwick, John Price and Capt. Law. Washington (TB#C: 400).
16 March 1746/7: William Cummings of Annapolis, Gent., conv. to Sir Nicholas Hackett Carew, Bart., Osgood Gaa [?], and Thomas Russell and Co. of Great Britain the tract (*), which was forfeit under terms of the mortgage made 9 Sep 1738 by William Tweedie (TB#E: 425).

K......

20 May 1725: granted to J. Rivess (TB#D: 155).
14 May 1745: George Harryman of BA Co., with cons. of w. Ann, conv. 50 a. Harryman's Landing, 100 a. Harryman's Range and 19 a. K... (granted 20 May 1725 to J. Rivess) to Charles Carroll of Annapolis, chirurgeon (TB#D: 155).

KEMP'S ADDITION

1 Dec 1686: John Kemp made a will leaving (*) to his s. Richard and Parker's Heaven to his w. Sarah. He also named his dau. Mary (MCW#II: 11).
c1700: John Thomas held 100 a. (*) for John Kemp's orphans (MRR: 85).
10 May 1708: Richard Kemp and Mary w. of John Boring conv. 100 a. (*) and 100 a. Parker's Heaven to Nicholas Rogers (RM#HS: 587).

KENDALL'S DELIGHT

13 Jan 1702: Daniel Kendall and w. Johanna deed 250 a., being ½ of 500 a. (*) to John Brice (HW#2: 203).

KEY'S INDUSTRY

10 Oct 1753: John Keys conv. 50 a. (*) to Stephen Onion, ironmaster; land had been surv. for Keys in 1745 (BB#I: 80).

KIDDERMINSTER

9 March 1704; Simon Pearson and w. Emma conv. 100 a. (*) to John Roberts (IR#PP: 189).
11 March 1708: John Roberts conv. 100 a. (*) to George Rigdon (TR#A: 54).

KINDERTON

26 May 1670: William Clapham, Sr., conv. (through his atty. Thomas Todd) to Richard Ball 50 a. on Patapsco R. The deed states that Walter Dickenson by his bond of 22 Nov,. 1659 agreed to take up 500 a. and to build two houses thereon, and to deliver a patent of the premises to Clapham, but failed to do so, whereupon Clapham on 20 Oct 1668 made Ball the assignee of the bond, and Dickenson then agreed to deliver the patent already recorded in the name of Clapham to Ball, before 1 March 1669/70 (IR#PP: 83).
12 May 1681: Thomas Everest and w. Hannah of Patapsco R., conv. to John Thomas 100 a. at Clapham's Point, being pt. of 500 a. pat. to William Clapham, and sold by him on 26 May 1670 to Richard Ball, whose dau. and heir Hannah is m. to Everest (IR#AM: 135).
12 May 1681: Thomas Everest and w. Hannah conv. to Nathaniel Hinchman 100 a. of (*), being pt. of 500 a. pat. to William (Chapman: sic) ... (IR#AM: 140).
12 May 1681: Thomas Everest and w. Hannah conv. 100 a. (*) to John Kemp ... above history recited again (IR#AM: 143).

KINDNESS

3 Sep 1701: John Richardson conv. 234 a. (*) to Capt. John Oulton, Gent. (HW#2: 86). 3 Sep 1701: Thomas Richardson, father of above named John Richardson conv. bond to John Oulton he will carry out terms of the conveyance; JR had 234 a. due him, and assigned them to TR, but patent was made out in name of John Richardson (HW#2: 88).
5 Aug 1730: John Lenox and w. Elizabeth conv. 268 a. (*) to Edward Evans (IS#L: 12).

KINGS ADVENTURE

8 May 1767: Edmond Baxter and w. Susannah, widow of William King, conv. to Andrew Buchanan, King's Adventure, and Susannah's Addition to King's Adventure, in all 20 a., being Susannah's ⅓ dower) (B#P: 567).

KINGS ADVENTURE, SUSANNAH'S ADDITION TO

8 May 1767: Edmond Baxter and w. Susannah, widow of William King, conv. to Andrew Buchanan, King's Adventure, and Susannah's Addition to King's Adventure, in all 20 a., being Susannah's ⅓ dower (B#P: 567).

KING'S INCREASE

24 June 1724: Pat. to Thomas Knight who sold it to Isaac Butterworth who sold it to Samuel Hughes (HWS#M: 412).
19 June 1736: Samuel Hughes conv. 100 a. (*) to Gregory Farmer. SH's w. Jane cons. (HWS#M: 412).

KINGSBERRY

4 Aug 1698: Charles Calvert, Lord Baltimore, grants 124 a. (*) to Henry King (HW#2: 58).

10 Nov 1724: William King and w. Susanna conv. 124 a. (*) and 500 a. Maiden's Hill to Thomas Sheredine (IS#H: 14).

KINGSBERRY RESURVEYED

470 a. orig. surv. for Thomas Sheredine (HWS#M: 146).

9 March 1733: Samuel Chew and Philip Thomas gave receipt for following tracts to Thomas Sheredine: 473 a. Kingsbury Resurveyed, 250 a. Long Point, 500 a. Mason's Oate, 187 a. The Plains, 100 a. Rogers Road, and 150 a. Sheredine's Bottom (HWS#M: 19).

20 Nov 1734: Thomas Sheredine conv. 470 a. (*) and 150 a. Sheredine's Bottom to William Chittum of Beddington, Co. Surrey, and John Whittiwicks of Craden, Surrey, and to the Principio Iron Co. TS' w. Tabitha cons. (HWS#M: 146).

KINSEY'S CHOICE

4 July 1731: John Moale conv. back to Christopher Randall any excess acreage above 40 a. orig. conv. by Randall to Moale on 20 Jan 1729 (IS#K: 165); excess occurred due to errors in bounds. JM's w. Rachel cons. (IS#L: 163).

26 July 1731: Christopher Randall, Jr., conv. 70 a. (*) to John Moale. CR's w. Catherine cons. (IS#L: 148).

4 Dec 1735: John Moale conv. (*) back to Randall in order for him to correct any errors in metes and bounds (HWS#M: 353).

KNAVERY DISCOVERED
(Pt. WILLIAMSON'S PURCHASE)

1 Sep 1709: John Frizzell, now of BA Co., conv. Williamson's Purchase, being pt. of Knavery Discovered, to Patrick Duncan (TR#A: 30).

On the same day Patrick Dunkin conv. 50 a. of that tract to Thomas Williamson (TR#A: 38).

27 June 1713: John Frizzell conv. 150 a. pt. of Knavery Detected, to William Pumphrey. JF's w. Elizabeth cons. (TR#DS: 143).

3 Oct 1721: Frizzell and w. Elizabeth sold pt. of the tract to William Forest (RM#HS: 664).

KNAVERY PREVENTED

3 May 1700: 400 a. surv. (RM#HS: 579).

27 Dec 1707: John Selby of AA Co., planter, and George Valentine of AA Co., innholder, conv. 400 a. (*) to Jacob Regnier of NY. Selby's w. Hester cons. (RM#HS: 579).

KNAVERY (or KNAVES) PREVENTED

3 April 1735: Joshua Wood, yeoman, conv. $14\frac{1}{2}$ a. pt. (*) to Samuel Howell. JW's w. Mary cons. (HWS#M: 185).

25 Aug 1739: Joshua Wood, carpenter, conv. 18 a. (*), orig. taken up by JW, to William Robinson. JW's w. Mary cons. (HWS#1-A: 276).

KNAVES INSPECTION

1 Sep 1741: John Roberts conv. 50 a. (*) to Capt. Henry Morgan. JR's w. Ann cons. (HWS#1-A: 564).

27 Sep 1746: Henry Morgan, merchant, mortgaged 50 a. (*) to Christopher Grindall (TB#E: 182).

KNIGHT'S ADDITION

17 June 1745: Sarah Knight, widow, conv. 85 a. (*), 100 a. Hailes Discovery, to Sarah Boring (TB#D: 253).

8 Feb 1748: William Knight conv. 50 a. (*) to Benjamin Long (TR#C: 264).

1753: Sarah Boring conv. (*) to William Askew (BB#I: 218).

2 Oct 1761: Benjamin Long conv. 50 a. (*) to John Daughaday, blacksmith (BB#I: 340).

5 Oct 1761: William Askew, with cons. of w. Keziah, conv. 100 a. Hailes Discovery and 85 a. (*) to Alexander Stewart (B#I: 427).

KNIGHT'S INCREASE

24 June 1728: 100 a. pat. to Thomas Knight (IS#L: 61).

5 Feb 1727/8: Thomas Knight, schoolmaster, conv. 100 a. (*) to Isaac Butterworth. TK's w. Susanna cons. (IS#J, 133).

1 March 1730/1: Isaac Butterworth, with cons. of w. Jane, conv. 100 a. (*) to Samuel Hughes (IS#L: 61).

(date not given): Samuel Hughes conv. 50 a. (*) to Gregory Farmer: mentioned in TB#E: 573).

28 July 1739: Gregory Farmer, Jr., conv. 100 a. (*) to Samuel Hughes. Tract was granted 24 June 1728 to Thomas Knight who sold it to Isaac Butterworth who sold it to SH on 1 March 1730. GF's w. Rachel cons. (HWS#1-A: 267).

7 May 1747: Samuel Hughes conv. 50 a. (*) to John Haven, schoolmaster (TB#E: 440).

3 Sep 1747: Samuel Hughes conv. 50 a. (*) to George Bolts (TB#E: 573).

2 April 1754: John Haven of NC, schoolmaster, conv. (*) to John Wyatt. JH's w. Elizabeth cons. (BB#I: 203).

KNIGHTON'S FANCY

9 March 1709: Thomas Knighton and w. Dorothy conv. 100 a. (*) to Nicholas Fitzsimmons (TR#A: 46).

LAMBERT'S MARSH

23 March 1665: 100 a. surv. for William Orchard on e. side of Bush R.; later possessed by James

Phillips, and still later by Thomas Hanson (MRR: 14).

1 March 1703/4: James Phillips of BA, Gent., and w. Bethia, conv. 100 a. of a tract in possession of JP, and adjacent to Covent Garden, to Thomas Hanson (IR#PP: 118).

18 March 1703/4: Thomas Hanson granted to (?) a release of interest in "aforesaid land" (grantee and name of tract not specified) (HW#2: 322).

LAND IN KIND

1720: granted to Benjamin Price; 1732: Pat. (?) for Benjamin Price. The tract is located on s. side of Gunpowder Falls, on e. side of a run descending into Beaver dam Run, adjacent Taylor's Hall. (See MHM 25:337; see also PW Plat H).

17 June 1738: Benjamin Price of BA conv. 150 a. (*) to Thomas Taylor. BP's w. Elizabeth cons. (HWS#1-A: 95).

26 July 1738: Thomas Taylor of BA Co. conv. 150 a. (*) to George Buchanan (HWS#1-A: 95).

LAND IS ALL
(also LANDISELL)

1652: it was surv. this date. The cert. mentions Broad (now Bear) Creek (MHM 25:334).

11 June 1694: William Hollis and w. Mary, dau. of Abraham Clark and his w. Sarah, conv. (*), which formerly belonged to Hollis' w. Mary, to William Wilkinson (RM#HS: 401).

27 March 1722: Edward Corbin and w. Jane of BA Co. conv. 425 a. (*) and 50 a. Wilkinson's Spring to Tamar Wilkinson (IS#G:6).

22 May 1758: Edward Corbin and w. Jane conv. to Robert Wilkinson (*) which they had already conv. to his mother, Tamar Wilkinson (in IS#G: 6) (B#G, 157).

LAND OF GOSHEN

10 June 1705: 320 a. pat. by John Israel (MPL DD#2: 929 PL#2: 106).

See Horvath Plat: Elkridge.

20 July 1710: John Israel and w. Barbara conv. (*) to Amos Garrett of AA Co. (TR#A: 97).

LAND OF PROMISE (1684)

5 Oct 1683: 2000 a. pat. by Col. Henry Darnall (MPL 25:48, 32:600 MRR: 17 gives date of surv. as 10 Sep 1684, but MRR: 44 gives date of surv. as 28 Sep 1683). Tract was located on n. side of s. branch of Gunpowder, adjacent to a manor owned by Lord Baltimore; adj. land taken up by Thomas Griffin.

28 Oct 1739: Henry Darnall of Portland Manor, AA Co. leased 100 a. James' Lot, being pt. of Land of Promise, to William James for 20 years (HWS#1-A: 363).

LAND OF PROMISE (1723)

21 Feb 1723: 200 a. pat. by Obadiah Pritchard (MPL PL#%: 155, IL#A: 42).

1 March 1724: Obadiah Pritchard of BA Co., carpenter, conv. 200 a. (*) to Charles Anderson of BA Co., carpenter (IS#H: 59).

14 Oct 1732: Charles Anderson leased 200 a. (*) to James Morgan and Elizabeth Walker for 12 years (IS#L: 294).

8 March 1738: Charles Anderson conv. 200 a. (*), which Anderson bought from Obadiah Pritchard in 1724, to Jacob Bull. CA's w. Grace cons. (HWS# 1-A: 187).

LAND OF PROMISE
(Unplaced tracts of this name)

21 Oct 1742: John Taylor of the Parish of Christ Church, Middlesex, England, and Margaret Higginson of St. Mary's Whitechapel, Middlesex., dau. and only heir of John Taylor, conv. 712 a., pt. (*) to Jacob Giles, as per deed to Giles, by John Galloway, atty. for John Taylor (TB#C:246).

LANDELLO

10 Oct 1707: Granted to David Thomas, who by his LWT bequeathed the land to his sons David and Henry; s. David d.

21 July 1750: Henry Thomas, with cons. of w. Jane, conv. 62 a. (*) to John Atkinson (TR#C: 534).

LANDING (THE)

20 Jan 1741: John Boreing for love he bears his son-in-law Dutton Lane conv. to him 100 a. (*) (TB#A:66).

2 Jan 1741 [sic]: Dutton Lane conv. 100 a. (*) to Thomas Sligh. DL's w. Dianah cons. (TB#A:109).

1 Oct 1741: Samuel Underwood of BA, s. and heir-at-law of Samuel Underwood, dec., who was s. and heir-at-law of Thomas Underwood of AA Co., for love, good will and affection, conv. 100 a. including (*) to his kinsman, Thomas Cockey (TB#C:17).

LANE'S TRIANGLE

1695: Surv. for Dutton Lane.

See Horvath Plat: Ruxton and Riderwood.

14 Feb 1746: Dutton and Samuel Lane conv. pt. (*) to Charles Ridgely. DL's w. Dinah and SL's w. Kane cons. (TB#E:300).

8 Dec 1747: Dutton Lane conv. 100 a. (*) to Charles Ridgely. DL's w. Dinah cons. (TB#E:658).

LANE'S VENTURE

14 Feb 1746: Dutton and Samuel Lane conv. 75 A., pt. (*), to Charles Ridgely. DL's w. Dinah and SL's w. Jane cons. (TB#E:300).

LANGLEYS FOREST

10 March 1683: 356 a. surv. for Robert Langley, who d. without heirs (MRR: 16).

LANGLEY'S HABITATION

30 Aug 1659: 300 a. surv. for Thomas Overton on w. side of Spesuty Creek; later held by John Kemball and later by John Hall (MRR: 8).

5 April 1687: John Langley, s. and heir apparent of Robert Langley, late of BA, dec., conv. 300 a. (*) to Robert Kemball of CE Co. (RM#HS:252).

LAST (THE)

1666: Pat. to John James on s. side of Charm Creek.

3 Aug 1668: John James, Gent., conv. 200,a. (*) on Charm Creek, to Charles James, merchant (IR#PP: 68).

3 Sep 1672: Charles James, Gent., conv. 200 a. (*), formerly taken up by John James, to Thomas Middlefield, carpenter (G#J: 8; TR#RA: 1).

LAWRENCE'S PASTURE

1683: 150 a. surv. for Lawrence Richardson, on s. side of a branch of Gunpowder R., commonly called Back R., by the side of Windley's Branch (MRR; MHM 20:273).

10 May 1685: granted [patented?] to Lawrence Richardson.

27 Feb 1720: Thomas Richardson of BA Co. conv. 150 a. (*) to William Bond (TR#DS: 206).

LEAFE'S CHANCE

[Leafe's Chance is adjacent to Heathcoate's Cottage, Gassaway's Ridge, William the Conqueror, and Clarkson's Hope. It has been divided into John's Delight or Boone's Delight; pt. was later resurv. into Onion's Prospect Hills and pt. was called Selby's Hope: MHM 15:118n, 120; 20:279; 53:244n.]

10 July 1678: 375 a. surv. for Francis Leafe betw. the Falls of Gunpowder R.; later 125 a., possessed by William Lennox, 100 a. by John Boone and 150 a. by Charles Hewitt; still later, 125 a. by William Lenox, 100 a. Thomas Hutchins, and 150 a. by Edward Selby (MRR: 62; see also PW Plat G).

13 June 1685: Francis Leafe, bricklayer of CV Co., conv. 375 a. (*) to William Ramsey. His w. Sarah ackn. the sale (RM#HS: 148).

5 June 1694: John Ramsey conv. 150 a. to Thomas Ramsey (RM#HS: 395).

2 June 1696: Charles Ramsey and w. Elizabeth conv. 100 a. to Edward Jones (RM#HS: 513).

2 June 1696: Edward Jones, with cons. of w. S(?), conv. (*) to John Campbell (RM#HS: 518, 606).

7 Sep 1696: John Ramsey conv. p/a to his bro. Charles to ackn. sale of 125 a. pt. (*), now called pt. William the Conqueror, to William Lennox (IS#IK: 176).

16 Oct 1696: Charles Ramsey and w. Elizabeth conv. 150 a. (*) to William Lennox (IS#IK: 169).

5 Nov 1696: Thomas Bevan and w. Elizabeth conv. 150 a. (*) to Nicholas Day (IS#IK: 120).

29 Feb 1703/4: Charles Ramsey and w. Elizabeth conv. 150 a. Selby's Hope, being pt. (*) to Edward Selby; tract was sold by Francis Leafe to William Ramsey who gave pt. of (*) to his s. Charles (HW#2: 320).

16 May 1706: William Lenox and w. Ann conv. 170 a. pt. (*), being pt. William the Conqueror, to William Robinson (i.e., 120 a. (*) and 50 a. pt. William the Conqueror) (RM#HS: 606).

24 Jan 1730: Charles Baker and w. Providence conv. 1/5 of (*) and 1/5 of William the Conqueror, 125 a. in all, to Josias Hendon (IS#L: 35).

5 March 1744: George York and w. Elinor conv. to Joseph and James Mead Selby's Hope, pt. (*), and anything due the grantors by the death of James Hackett, father of E. York (TB#D: 49).

5 March 1745: George Presbury and w. Isabella conv., to Stephen Onion pt. (*) and pt. William the Conqueror, which William and Ann Lenox sold to William Robinson, father of said Isabella (TB#E: 34).

3 Dec 1745: Hannah Hendon and Mary Bosworth (daus. and coheirs of William Robinson) and Mary's husband John Bosworth conv. 170 a. being $\frac{1}{2}$ of (*) and $\frac{1}{2}$ of William the Conqueror to Stephen Onion, ironmaster (TB#D: 428).

13 July 1750: Joshua Cross of AA Co. conv. to Robert Adair land in BA Co., 150 a. Selby's Hope, pt. of Leaf's Chance (Fol. 170).

7 June 1753: Isham Hendon, s. of Josias, conv. to Stephen Onion his interest in (*) and William the Conqueror. IH's w. Keziah cons. (BB#I: 8).

LEAFE'S FOREST

18 May 1679: granted by patent to Francis Leafe (TR#RA: 395).

13 June 1685: Francis Leafe, bricklayer of CV Co., conv. 200 a. (*) to Joseph Owen, tailor. FL's w. Sarah cons. (RM#HS: 146).

10 Nov 1698: Joseph Owen of AA Co., tailor, conv. (*) to John Martin of CH Co., boatwright (TR#RA: 395).

LEAFE'S FOREST, ADDITION TO

20 June 1707: John Martin conv. 306 a. (*) to William Crouch of AA Co. (RM#HS: 547).

8 Sep 1707: William Crouch conv. bond to John Martin, boatwright, for conv. of 300 a. (*) (RM#HS: 537).

LEAFE JUNIOR

14 June 1699: 256 a. surv. for Francis Leafe of CV Co. (RM#HS: 424).

1729: John Dew and Rachel Hutchinson conv. 252 a. (*) to Samuel Griffith (IS#K: 71).

22 March 1730: John West of PG Co., joiner, and w. Ann, lately Ann Dews, conv. ⅓ of 258 a. (*) and ⅓ 100 a. of Polecat Neck, to Thomas White (IS#L: 88).

3 April 1735: Samuel Griffith and Thomas White each owning ⅓ of the tract, agree to a deed of partition (HWS#M: 179).

LEAKINS (Pt. THURRELL'S NECK)

24 July 1704: James Todd conv. 28 a. Jones Angle and 1 a., 16 perches Leakins to John Oldton, Gent. (IR#PP: 165).

24 July 1704: John Oldton conv. an orchard called (*), pt. of (Thurrell's Neck), 1 a., 16 p., to John Harryman. JO's w. Mary cons. (IR#PP: 159).

Dec 1739: Thomas White and w. Sophia conv. 93 a. pt. (*) to James Phillips (HWS#1-A: 338).

LEE'S ISLAND

1664: Surv. for John Lee; 1746: resurv. as Carroll's Island, and in 1770 resurv. as Clonlisk Carroll's Island (MHM 25:363).

16 June 1719: James Phillips, with cons. of w. Joanna, conv. 150 a. (*) And 200 a. Phillips' Addition to Blois Wright (TR#DS: 32).

LEE'S RANGE

Feb 1713: 90 a. surv. for Francis Lee; pat. 10 Dec 1714 (MPL EE#6: 228, and RY#1: 360).

LENEY (THE)

7 Nov 1671: John Cock, Ann Cock, and Andrew Peterson conv. to William Ward 300 a. (*), near the head of Back Creek on the n. side of Sassafras R. (IR#PP: 109).

LENNOX' ADVENTURE

6 March 1705/6: Richard Lennox and w. Mary conv. 200 a. (*), and 218 a. Maiden's Choice, (orig. granted to Mary Richardson, now Mary Lennox), to Nicholas Fitzsimmons (IR#AM: 40).

1 April 1725: Nicholas Fitzsimmons conv. 200 a. (*) and 215 a. Maiden's Choice to Richard Lenox, who with w. Mary, had earlier conv. the tract to NF (IS#H: 73).

LETTERKENNY

1726: 329 a. for Edward Coyle; pat. 10 June 1727 (MPL PL#6: 523, and IL#A: 733).

1 Sep 1736: Eliz. Coyle, Clement Mattingly, and Anna Burton Mattingly conv. 329 a. (*) to Charles Carroll of Annapolis (TB#C: 474).

6 April 1744: Charles Carroll of Annapolis conv. 329 a. (*) to Dr. George Buchanan (TB#C: 474).

LEVEL (THE) (See THE HOPE)

19 July 1688: 100 a. surv. for Solomon Jones (MRR: 75).

28 Oct 1717: Richard Jones, with cons. of w. Ann, conv. 100 a. The Level to Henry Butler (TR#A: 532).

2 Oct 1725: William Jones of SM Co., and w. Mary, and William Langley and w. Elizabeth, dau. of Solomon Jones, conv. 200 a. (*) to John Gardner (IS#H: 183).

14 Jan 1741: Luke Trotten and William Hamilton conv. 350 a. parts of The Level and 150 a. Hab Nab at a Venture, to Dr. George Buchanan (TB#A: betw. 74 and 80).

LEVEL BOTTOM

Surv. for Peter Ellis (TB#E: 157).

19 May 1746: Charles Jones (son and sole heir of Mary Jones, dau. of Peter Ellis and sister of John Ellis, dec.) conv. 50 a. (*) to Rowland Kimble (TB#E: 157).

4 Aug 1746: William Hall, weaver, and w. Mary, conv. 50 a. (*) to William Cross (TB#E: 155).

10 Jan 1756: William Cross and w. Anne conv. 23 a. Cross's Lot and 50 a. Level Bottom to Samuel Lane (BB#I: 493; See MHM 15:346).

LEVEL UNION

8 Jan 1761: Nicholas Orrick conv. 33½ a. (*) to Christopher Randall (B#H, 539).

LEVEL'S ADDITION (THE)

28 Nov 1726: Thomas Plummer of PG Co., and w. Elizabeth, conv. 118 a. (*) to Samuel Howell (IS#H: 299).

LEVY'S TRIBE

4 July 1672: 100 a. surv. for Christopher Topley (Talpey?) and Levy Wharfe; on s. side of Bush R.; later possessed by Samuel Durham; still later possessed by Matthew Green (Interlined by John Durham) (MRR: 60).

20 July 1673: Pat. to Tapley and Wharfe.

1 July 1679: Christopher Tapley boatwright conv. 100 a. to John Durham undated clerk's minute that Christopher Tapley petitions for Thomas Cannon to deliver to Tapley a certain patent for land (IS#IK: 67).

1 March 1705: John Boone of BA Co. and w. Jane sell (*) to Matthew Green; Tapley sold it to John Durham who left it to his s. Samuel Durham who left it to John Boone (IR#AM: 60).
2 Nov 1726: Lewis Puttee and w. Katherine, dau. and coheir of Matthew Green, and granddaughter of Jane Boone, conv. to Thomas Coale, pt. of (*), Choice Trippas, and Green's Chance (IS#H: 290).
1729: Ann Cowdry conv. (*) to Thomas Coale (IS#K: 193).
1729: Erick Erickson conv. two 50 a. parcels of (*) to Thomas Coale (IS#K: 210, 274).
8 April 1730: Robert Smith d. owning two parcels of land, one of which was Levy's Tribe; Smith d. leaving the land to his w. Mary now the w. of Erick Erickson; they sell the land to Thomas Coale (IS#K: 210).
8 March 1732: William Hill of BA Co., and w. Martha, dau. and coheir of Matthew Green, and also one of the granddaughters of Jane Boone, sell to Thomas Coale pt. of (*), Choice Trippas, and Green's Chance (IS#L: 326).
6 March 1733/4: Eric Erickson and w. Mary, release their right to (*) to Thomas Cole. (This deed confirms an earlier deed.) (HWS#M: 32).

LEVY'S TRIBE, ADDITION TO

14 April 1681: Surv. for John Durham the Elder, who left it to his s. Samuel, who left it to his bro. John, who was the father of Samuel Durham, the grantor below (IS#H: 406).
9 Jan 1726: Samuel Durham, with cons. of (unnamed) w., conv. pt. (*) to Thomas Coale (IS#H: 406).

LEWIS CHANCE
(Pt. of HIS LORDSHIP'S RESERVE)

31 May 1748: Nathan Rigbie leased 40 a. (*) to Richard Wells (TB#E: 718).

LEWIS REFUGE

3 Oct 1760: John Long conv. 113 a. (*) to John Struthers (B#H: 113).

LIDECAN

15 April 1746: Patrick Lynch and William Lynch make a deed of partition (TB#E: 85).
1750: William Lynch owned 29½ a. (*) (1750 DB).

LIMERICK

5 Nov 1695 [sic]: 100 a. surv. for John Bevins; later possessed by Marcus Tench [sic] [Lynch] who left the country some 12 years ago; still later poss. by Robuck Lynch (MRR: 65).
1 March 1685/6: John Bevan, planter, and w. Julyan conv. (*) to Marcus Lynch of Galloway, Ireland (RM#HS: 173).
6 Aug 1728: Patrick, William, and Mary Lynch, ch. of Robuck Lynch, conv. (*), which their father had inher. from his kinsman Marcus Lynch, to John Bevan, Jr. (IS#I: 160).
4 Aug 1743: John Bevans conv. 100 a. (*) to William Bond (TB#C: 302).
1750: Capt. William Bond owned 100 a. (*) (1750 DB: 76).

LINES TENT (See LYNES TENTS)

LINGAN

1716: Surv. for Thomas Harp; located on Ben's Run in 2nd District (MHM 25: 340).

LITCHFIELD CITY

9 May 1738: Francis Hinckley conv. 60 a. (*) to William Worthington (HWS#1-A: 65).
6 May 1740: William Worthington of AA Co. conv. 60 a. (*), orig. surv. for Francis Hinkley, to John Wilmot. WW's w. Hannah cons. (HWS#1-A: 418).

LITCHFIELD'S CITY

1747: 192 a. for John Williams; on PW Plat H.

LITTLE BRITAIN

1 Sep 1696: Pat. to George Green of KE Co. (IS#I: 106).
23 May 1728: John Tilyard (acc. to a later deed in TB#E: 322, he was a grandson of said Green) of KE Co., conv. 116 a. pt. (*) to John Debruler. JT's w., unnamed, cons. (IS#I: 106).
1 Feb 1728/9: John Debruler made a will leaving to w. Mary (*), which he had recently bought from John Tilyard (IS#I: 316).
5 March 1746: John Debruler conv. 116 a. pt. (*) to Stephen Onion. Deed traces descent of property from Green to Tilyard to Debruler. Conveyance is made on the condition that Debruler and "his now w." may occupy the property for life (TB#E: 322).
1757: James Allen conv. 103 a. (*) to John Love (B#G: 30).

LITTLE DRAYTON

3 Sep 1672: Charles James conv. 100 a. (*) on w. side of Cherne Creek, to Thomas Middlefield (G#J: 8; TR#A: 1).

LITTLE MARLEY

27 Sep 1684: 200 a. surv. for Miles [i.e., Michael] Judd on a neck betw. Bush and Gunpowder Rivers; sold to John Hathaway who bequeathed it to George Smith (MRR: 32).
9 Feb 1684/5: Michael Judd, shipwright on Gunpowder R., conv. 200 a. to John Hathaway.

Jane Judd also signed. Bond was dated the same day (RM#HS: 137).

3 Oct 1690: John Hathaway assigned his interest on the within named patent (Little Marloe) to Michael Judd (IR#AM: 66).

LITTLE MARSHES

17 June 1698: Edmund Hansley (Hemsley?) conv. 100 a. (*) to Michael Judd (IS#IK: 246).

LITTLE MEATH

1716: 200 a. pat. to Edward Tully (MPL EE#6: 316).

LITTLE ROOM

31 Aug 1743: 100 a. pat. by Norton Groves Baker (MPL LG#B: 752, LG#E: 154).

See Horvath Plat: Randallstown.

8 Oct 1744: Norton Groves Baker, schoolmaster, conv. (*) plus household furniture and livestock to William Fell (TB#C: 649).

LITTLE SCOTLAND

3 June 1723: James Durham conv. 100 a. to Timothy Keon (IS#G: 323).

LITTLETON

14 May 1684: 600 a. surv. for Thomas Thurston on e. side of Bush R.; later 452 a. held by Robert Love and 182 a. by Stephen Gill; still later described as 632 a., with 180 a. held by Stephen Gill and 452 a. by John Israel (MRR: 59).

8 June 1687: Thomas Thurston of Bush R., for love, good will and affection, conv. to Stephen Gill, s. of Stephen Gill, late of Severn R., 182 a. (*) (RM#HS: 226).

8 Aug 1705: Thomas Thurston conv. 450 a. (*) to John Rattenbury, Gent., and to John Israel, factor (IR#PP: 181).

23 May 1710: Stephen Gill of AA Co. conv. 182 a. (*) to John McComas, s. of Daniel, 182 a. pt. (*) in exch. for 98 a. Brown's Chance, on s. side Severn R. (TR#A: 78).

20 July 1710: John Israel and w. Barbara conv. to Amos Garrett of AA Co., 632 a. Littleton (granted to Thomas Thurston on 14 May 1684) and 100 a. Robins Camp (granted to Robert Rogers on 24 April 1700) (TR#A: 97).

5 Aug 1712: John Rattenbury, chirurgeon, and w. Margaret, conv. 226 a. (*) to Amos Garrett; deed states that the tract was pat. by Thomas Thurston on 14 May 1684; his heir Thomas, Jr., conv. 425 a. to Rattenbury and John Israel on 8 Aug 1705, and now Rattenbury conv. his half to Garrett TR#A: 204).

27 Nov 1712: John McComas conv. 90 s. (*) to William McComas (TR#A: 202).

4 Nov 1714: John McComas conv. 92 a. pt. (*) to John Norrington, being the upper pt. of 182 a. which Thomas Thurston conv., to Stephen Gill of AA Co. (TR#A: 30).

1729: William Davis conv. 92 a. (*) to John Norrington (IS#K: 28).

18 Aug 1748: William Davis conv. 92 a. (*) to Thomas Harrison. WD's w. Elizabeth cons. (TR#C: 50).

2 Aug 1762: Thomas White of Philadelphia, formerly of BA Co., conv. 982 a (*) to James McComas (B#K: 271).

LITTLEWORTH

3 March 1725/6: John Dorsey, atty. for Hezekiah and Elizabeth Clark of AA Co., conv. (*), 100 a. Love Point, and 200 a. Tracey's Level, to Thomas Tolley (IS#H: 225).

6 April 1730: Thomas Tolley, Gent., and w. Mary, conv. 100 a. (*) to Robert Devinish of KE Co. (IS#K: 289).

5 Sep 1732: James Lee, Sr., conv. (*) to Isaac Webster (IS#L: 298).

1750: Michael Tully owned 200 a. (1750 DB).

LITTON'S ADVENTURE

Pat. to John Miles (TR#DS: 284).

2 Nov 1720: John Miles w. Mary conv. 60 a., being $\frac{1}{2}$ of (*) to Thomas Litton (TR#DS: 284).

LITTON'S IMPROVEMENT

20 Aug 1748: Nicholas Ruxton Gay conv. 41 a. (*) and other land to Walter Tolley (TR#C: 69).

LIVERPOOL

1750: James Gardner owned 50 a. (*) and 100 a. Hawkins Desire (1750 DB: 43).

1 Nov 1750: James Gardner, schoolmaster, conv. 50 a. (*) to William Fell (TR#D: 46).

LLOYDS POINT

1729: Solomon Sparrow conv. 45 a. (*) to Richard Galloway (IS#K: 44).

LOCASKEEK

10 June 1732: William Byfoot conv. 100 a. (*) to Henry Wetherall (IS#L: 290).

LOCKWOOD'S ADVENTURE

8 May 1679: Pat. to Robert Lockwood of AA Co. (See RM#HS: 40).

10 Jan 1681/2: Robert Lockwood conv. 400 a. (*) to Ralph Cooper, mariner, of Stepbunheath, Middlesex, England. Lockwood's w. (not named) cons. Lockwood appointed Francis Watkins and John Cromwell his attys. to give seisin (RM#HS: 40).

LOCUST NECK

16 May 1685: Jane Claridge, widow, for love and affection, and because of her intended marriage to John Wright, conv. him 100 a. (*), effective at her death, as deeded on 2 Nov 1669 (RM#HS: 136).

21 Feb 1687/8: John Wright of BA Co., planter, conv. 100 a. (*) on Bush R. to James Phillips (RM#HS: 247).

4 Sep 1688: James Phillips, innholder, conv. 100 a. (*) to William Osborne; JP's w. Susannah cons. (RM#HS: 285).

3 June 1718: Charles Miles conv. 100 a. (*) to Benjamin Hanson (TR#RA: 467).

6 March 1727: Benj. Hanson of BA Co. and w. Sarah conv. (*) to William Byfoot (IS#I: 55).

LOCUST NECK (1744)

1744: 50 a. surv. for Henry Morgan; later included in 810 a. resurv. called Drumqu'hasle (MHM 52:202).

27 Sep 1746: Henry Morgan, merchant, mortgaged 50 a. (*) and other lands to Christopher Grindall (TB#E: 182).

LODGE

1658: Surv. for Patrick Forest; located on n. side of a back branch of Back R.; lies on Brown's Creek in Back R. (MHM, 25:326; 30:326).

LODOWICK'S RIDGE

Undated clerk's minute that Lodwick Williams assigns his 200 a. tract (*) to William Palmer, who is atty. for Robert Jones, Samuel Hatton, and for Arthur Carleton (admin. of Thomas Carleton) (IS#IK: 55).

19 Nov 1715: Edward Williams of Paspotank R. in Sawyer's Creek, NC, conv. 100 a. where Matthew Green's widow and Robert Smith, shoemaker, dwell, 200 a. Lodowick's Ridge, 150 a. Matt's Addition, 100 a. Thomson's Fortune, 300 a. United Friendship, and 150 a. Williams' Fortune, and all other lands in MD belonging to Williams by right of inheritance, to Richard Colegate, merchant (TR#A: 373).

LODWICK'S REFUSE

50 a. surv. 7 Dec 1667 (or 1676) for Thomas Preston on n. side of Gunpowder R. (MRR: 611).

LOFTON'S NEGLECT

10 Sep 1746: Samuel Howell and Sarah Durbin enter into a [prenuptial?] agreement; he conv. to her the following tracts: Garrison's Neglect, Howell's Contrivance, Johnsons's Bed, Johnson's Rest, Joshua Wood's Mistake, and Lofton's Neglect. He also conv. her a child's portion of his estate, for her and any heirs she had by him;; is she d. without heirs by him, the above tracts would be divided among his male heirs; she relinquishes her dower right to ⅓ of his estate (TB#E: 177).

LOGSDON'S ADDITION

See Horvath Plat: Pikesville.

19 Sep 1726: William Logsdon conv. 97½ a. Pleasant Green, being pt. of Logsdon's Addition, to his dau. Ann Durbin, and the heirs of her body. WL's w. Honour cons. (IS#H: 338).

22 Sep 1730: William Logsdon and w. Honour conv. 150 a. pt. (*) and 100 a. Bedford, to Matthew Coulter, tailor (IS#L: 46).

29 May 1742: Matthew Coulter, tailor, conv. 152½ a. (*) and 240 a. Bedford to Thomas Bond (TB#A: 169).

25 July 1747: Thomas Bond conv. 100 a., pt. Bedford Resurveyed and pt. Logsdon's Addition to Patrick and Eliz. Gray. TB's w. Phebe cons. (TB#E: 494).

25 July 1747: Thomas Bond, tavernkeeper, conv. 62½ a. Bedford Resurveyed and 37½ a. (Logsdon's Addition?) to Benjamin Bond. TB's w. Phebe cons. (TB#E: 494).

7 April 1757: William Shrider and w. Susannah conv. 100 a. Logsdon's Addition and Bedford Resurveyed to Thomas Johnson (B#G: 162).

LONDON

1729; William Binney? conv. release of 100 a. (*) to William Denton and w. (IS#K:197).

11 June 1743: John Jamison conv. 130 a. Burney's Purchase, 100 a. London, and 100 a. Pitchcraft and Polecat Ridge, to Samuel Howell. JJ's w., unnamed, cons. (TB#C: 258).

18 Aug 1748: Samuel Howell conv. 100 a. London and 130 a. Barney's Purchase to William Savory. SH's w. Sarah cons. (TR#C: 43).

LONG ACRES

1730: John Owings conv. 159 a. (*) to Richard Owings (IS#K: 239).

15 March 1730: Richard Owings conv. 106 a. (*) to Henry Owings. RO's w. Sarah cons. (IS#L: 94).

LONG AIRE

1 Nov 1709: Edward Smith and w. Bridget conv., 54 a. (*) to William Smith (TR#A: 19).

LONG CRANDON

7 June 1732: Thomas Franklin conv. pt. (*) to Joseph Peregoy, Jr., s. of Henry Peregoy (IS#L: 239).

LONG CRANDON IN THE HILL

7 June 1732: Thomas Franklin conv. 100 a. Franklin's Gift, being pt. of Long Crandon in the Hill, taken up by TF, to John Rutledge (IS#L: 252).

LONG DISCOVERY

10 April 1727: Richard Thacker of BA Co. conv. 100 a. Gardner's Mill, 367 a. (*), and 320 a. Thacker's Chance to Thomas Cockey (IS#H: 358).

LONG ISLAND

1720: 100 a. surv. for Samuel Stansbury on s. side of Great Falls of Gunpowder (MHM, 9:78).

LONG ISLAND ADDITION

22 May 1764: Samuel Stansbury conv. (*) to Isaac Risteau. (B#H: 344).

LONG ISLAND POINT

31 Oct 1671: A 100 a. tract surv. for William Poultney on n. side of Patapsco R.; later 50 a. possessed by Thomas Stone, and 50 a. by John Broad; still later 50 a. possessed by the above two, but "Thos Hodge (possessed) the whole as I am informed" (MRR: 84; Tract was on the site of Fell's Point: See MHM 16: 116n).

2 March 1685/6: Edward Mumford planter conv. 100 a. Long Island Point to Thomas Stone and Dennis Garrett; same day: Mumford conv. bond to Stone and Garrett he will perform the covenants in the deed (RM#HS: 166).

1 March 1691/2: Thomas Stone conv. to Barbara Garrett and her heirs the above tract; Stone mentioned the love and affection he had for Dennis Garrett, dec., and for his ch. begotten by said Barbara (RM#HS: 341).

29 June 1704: Thomas Stone conv. 50 a. to Richard Owens; Christian Stone signs (IR#PP: 119).

2 Feb 1704/5: Richard Owens conv. 50 a. to Thomas Hedge; tract was formerly conv. by Edward Mumford to Dennis Garrett and Thomas Stone, and conv. by Stone to Owens (IR#PP: 168).

1 Sep 1730: Barbara Broad and Frances Haile conv. 100 a. Long Island Point to Nicholas Haile (IS#L: 26).

7 June 1734: Nicholas Haile conv. 50 a. being $\frac{1}{2}$ of (*) to William Fell; tract was orig. surv. for George Yates (HWS#M: 125).

22 May 1764: Samuel Stansbury conv. (*) to Isaac Risteau. (B#H: 344).

LONG LOOKED FOR (Pt. of WARRINGTON)

31 May 1695: John Hill conv. 50 a. (*) to James Cowdrey and w. Martha (RM#HS: 464).

LONG POINT (1682)

16 June 1682: 250 a. surv. for David Jones on w. side of a branch of Back R.; later possessed by Richard Cromwell (MRR: 101).

1 Nov 1728; John Cromwell of AA Co. conv. 250 a. (*) to Thomas Sheredine. JC's w. Hannah cons. (IS#H: 239).

9 March 1733: Samuel Chew and Philip Thomas gave receipt for following tracts to Thomas Sheredine: 473 a. Kingsbury Resurveyed, 250 a. Long Point, 500 a. Mason's Oate, 187 a. The Plains, 100 a. Rogers Road, and 150 a. Sheredine's Bottom (HWS#M: 19).

20 Nov 1734: Thomas Sheredine and w. Tabitha conv. 250 a. (*) to William Chettum, Esq., of Beddington, Surrey, John Whittiwicks of Craden, Surrey, and to the Principio Iron Works Company (HWS#M: 146).

LONG PORT (1683)

15 June 1683: 111 a. tract surv. for Major Thomas Long adjacent to tract granted to said Long called Hopewell; 60 a. later held by Edward Jones for the orphans of Richard Enoch, and 50 a. in possession of Johanna Bumbridge; still later "all dead - none claims" (MRR: 69).

4 Aug 1684: Thomas Long, Gent., and w. Jane of Back R., conv. to Richard Enoch and Francis Freeman, planters of same place, 111 a., adj. tract Hopewell; on 5 Aug Long ackn. sale, and John Boring certified Long's w.'s cons. (RM#HS: 95).

4 Aug 1684: Long conv. bond to Enoch and Freeman (RM#HS: 94).

17 March 1691: Christopher Bembridge conv. 111 a. Long Port, adj. to Hopewell, formerly taken up by Maj. Thomas Long, to Francis Watkins (RM#HS: 611).

LONG POINT (1687)

1 Sep 1687: 150 a. surv. for Thomas Richardson; later possessed by John Richardson, and still later by James Crooke (MRR: 58).

3 Aug 1697: Thomas Richardson, for love and affection, conv. (*) and Dixon's Chance to his s. John (IS#IK: 166).

7 July 1702: John Richardson conv. to William Adams of Calvert Co. parts of (*), Dixon's Chance, and Taylor's Mount (HW#2: 144).

1 April 1729: Henry Adams, carpenter, s. of William Adams, formerly of CV Co., conv. to Thomas Tolley 310 a. of the three parcels conv. to WA by John Richardson on 7 July 1702 (IS#I: 296).

1732: Thomas Tolley leaves pt. of (*) to his s. Walter (MCW#VI: 233).

24 Oct 1741: James Lennox conv. 150 a. pt. (*) (pat. 10 Aug 1684 by Thomas Richardson) to

Edward Day, innholder. JL's w. Mary cons. (TB#A: 9).

2 July 1743: James Lenox conv. 150 a. (*) to Stephen Onion. JL's w. Mary cons. (TB#C 304-306).

LONG POINT (1694)

10 Nov 1694: 50 a. surv. for John Ferry; later possessed by Thomas Boring (MRR).

16 Feb 1710/11: Thomas Boring conv. p/a to John Norton to conv. (*) and Come By Chance to John Boring (TR#A: 135).

14 July 1715: John Boring conv. 50 a. (*) to George Pickett (TR#A: 383).

LONG REACH

28 May 1713: Benjamin Dorsey conv. 100 a. of the land deeded by Col. Edward Dorsey to his s., the said Benjamin, poss. (*) to Joshua Dorsey (TR#A: 338).

31 May 1715: Benjamin Dorsey conv. 200 a. (*) to Thomas Worthington (TR#A: 341).

LONG TRACT

2 Aug 1737: 150 a. pat. by John Boring (MPL EI#2: 619, and EI#5: 210).

6 Sep 1739: John Boring, with cons. of w. Sarah, conv. pt. of 150 a. (*) to Stephen Price, s. and heir apparent of Stephen Price (HWS#1-A: 290).

LONG VALLEY

3 March 1747: Samuel Whipps and w. Mary conv. (*) to William Gosnell (TB#E: 670).

4 Nov 1758: William Gosnell, Jr., with cons. of w. Sarah, conv. (*) to Benjamin Williams (B#G: 280).

12 Sep 1767: Adam Shipley, s. of Charles, with cons. of (Adam's) w. Ann and Margaret, relict of Charles Shipley, conv. 50 a. (*) to Dr. John Stevenson (B#Q: 38).

LONG'S ADDITION

21 Nov 1734: Thomas Sheredine, with cons. of w. Tabitha, conv. 150 a. (*) to John Mahorne (HWS#M: 175).

5 March 1741: John Mahone left 100 a. (*) to his youngest dau. Isabel (MWB 22:533).

19 Jan 1750: Dr. Charles Carroll conv. 144 a. Long's Addition to Tobias Stansbury, Jr. (TR#D: 99).

LONGLAND'S PURCHASE

3 Aug 1705: John Hayes conv. p/a to w. Elizabeth to make over (*) to Richard Longland; also to sell another 209 a. of land (IR#AM: 15).

5 Sep 1705: John Hayes and w. Elizabeth conv. 100 a (*), pt. of Privilege, to Richard Longland (IR#PP: 187).

25 Feb 1728/9: George Insull and w. Alice conv. 100 a. (*), pt. Privilege, to Thomas Sheredine (IS#I: 251).

25 Nov 1731: Thomas Sheredine and w. Tabitha conv. 100 a. Longland Purchase, pt. Privilege, to Thomas Sligh (IS#L: 279).

LONGWORTH

Originally taken up by Thomas Long.

4 March 1736: James Lenox, with cons. of w. Mary, conv. 123 a. (*) to Francis Brown (IS#IK: 369).

LORD BALTIMORE'S GIFT

(See also MY LADY'S MANOR)

31 Aug 1731: Thomas Brerewood, Jr., of Horton, Co. Bucks., and his w., the Hon. Charlotte, dau. and devisee of the LWT of the Rt. Hon. Margaret, Baroness of Baltimore, conv. 10,000 a. (*) to Thomas Brerewood, Sr., of Horton, to sell the above land to satisfy the debts of Thomas Brerewood, Jr. The deed mentioned the patent of 10 Sep 1713 (IS#L: 222, 229, 231).

LOT (THE)

1710: 105 a. pat. to Luke Stansbury (MHM 9:77).

25 April 1713: John Fitzredmond conv. 100 a. to Andrew Anderson (TR#A: 268).

7 June 1715: Andrew Anderson and w. Elizabeth conv. 100 a. (*) to George Newport, blacksmith (TR#A: 349).

LOVE POINT

20 July 1673: 100 a. pat. to Richard Sims, on n. side of e. branch of Gunpowder.

7 Nov 1682: Richard Sims conv. 100 a. (*) on the n. side of the western branch of Gunpowder, to Lawrence Richardson (Deed and Bond RM#HS: betw. 53 and 55).

17 Dec 1691: Richard Taylor and w. Anne conv. 100 a. (*) to Thomas Richardson.

2 Nov 1720: Thomas Richardson conv. 100 a. (*) to Hezekiah Clark.

3 March 1725/6: John Dorsey, atty. for Hezekiah and Elizabeth Clark of AA Co., conv. Littleworth, 100 a. Love Point, and 200 a. Tracey's Level, to Thomas Tolley (IS#H: 225).

LOVELESS' ADDITION

1731: 100 a. pat. to Thomas Gorsuch. [The tract is located on Hillen Road, adjacent to Ensor's Choice]. (MPL EI#3:80, 298).

1750: Thomas Gorsuch conv. (*) (as "Lovely's Addition") to Thomas Gorsuch (TR#D: 278).

14 Feb 1752: Thomas Gorsuch gave his s. Thomas 100 a. (*) (TR#D: 278).
1759: Resurv. with Ensor's Choice into 160 a. Gorsuch's Regulation by Thomas and John Gorsuch (MPL BC#12: 318).

LOW LANDS
7 March 1687: 33 a. surv. for Hendrick Inloes betw. the mouth of Middle R. and Seneca Creek (MRR: 67).
1750: Anthony Enloes owned 33 a. (*) (1750 DB).
1763/4: Anthony Enloes' heirs owned 33 a. (*) (Aquila Hall's Assessment Ledger, Fol. 17).
1775: Abraham Enloes conv. 33 a. (*) to Thomas Brown (abst. in TE Gen. Coll.).
1778: Abraham Enloes conv. 33 a. (*) to William Godsgrace (abst. in Thomas Enloes Gen. Coll., MHS).

LOW NECK
9 July 1710: Richard Guest [Gist], with cons. of w. Zipporah, conv. 100 a. (*) to Joseph Conway of AA Co., carpenter. Guest had formerly sold the land to John Summerland, but never made it over to him, and Summerland never paid for it, but Summerland sold the land to Henry Hilliard of AA Co., who exch. the land with John Conway for a plantation in AA Co. (TR#A: 177).

LOW'S LOT
Nov 1705: 100 a. surv. for William Low (Lough) (Card Index to Patents, MSA).
4 Nov 1707: William Lowe and w. Rebecca conv. 100 a. (*) to Garvis Gilbert (RM#HS: 561).
28 June 1740; Michael Gilbert, s. and heir of Garvice Gilbert of BA Co., conv. 125 a., pt. Low's Lot and pt. Gilbert's Outlet to his bro. Garvice. MG's w. Mary cons. (HWS#1-A: 413).
17 March 1747: Garvice Gilbert conv. 125 a. pt. Low's Lot and Gilbert's Outlet to Thomas Downs. GG's w. Elizabeth cons. (TB#E: 711).

LOW'S RANGE (Now WHITEHEAD'S FOLLY)
5 Aug 1735: James Low and w. Mary conv. 50 a. (*), now Whitehead's Folly, to Robert Whitehead (HWS#M: 278).
7 Nov 1735: James Low of BA Co., conv. 50 a. pt. (*), 200 a. tract in all, to Robert Whitehead. James' w. Mary cons. (HWS#1-A: 142).
22 March 1743: Robert Whitehead mortgaged 100 a. (*) (surv. 6 April 1731) to Robert North (TB#C: 459, 563).
11 Sep 1751: Alexander Lawson, exec. of Capt. Robert North, conv. (*) to Benjamin Cross of BA Co. (TR#D: 272).
2 April 1764: Benjamin Cross, with cons. of w. Elizabeth, conv. 50 a. (*) to John Cross (B#N: 47).
2 April 1764: Benjamin and Elizabeth Cross conv. 50 a. (*) to William Cross (B#N: 50).
24 Oct 1765: John Cross, with cons. of w. Philizanna, conv. (*) to George Myers (B#O: 552).

LOW'S THICKET
6 March 1728/9: William Low, with cons. of w. Sarah, conv. 100 a. (*) to Thomas Franklin (IS#J: 274).

LOWERY'S LOT
See Horvath Plat: Winfield to Eldersburg.
2 Sep 1767: James Lowery, with cons. of w. Aperilla, conv. 50 a. (*) to John Gosnell (B#Q: 230).

LOYDS TRUST
22 May 1734: Lloyd Harris, Gent., conv. 200 a. Loyd's Trust and 200 a. Martin's Rest to Dr. George Buchanan (HWS#M: 63).

LUCKY ADVENTURE
April 1720: 250 a. surv. for Daniel Rawlings (Rent Rolls).
See KN Plat WO, and Horvath Plat: Randallstown.

LUCKY HOLE
16 Jan 1727: Charles Mackarty of AA Co. conv. 100 a. (*) to John Conaway (IS#G: 248).

LUDLOW'S LOT
28 Feb 1669/70: Francis Johnson, of AA Co., conv. 200 a. (*), formerly granted to Robert Loyd, chirurgeon of AA Co., and assigned by him to said Johnson, to John Larkin (IR#PP: 78).

LUFFMAN'S DUE (in AA Co.)
26 Oct 1690: William Luffman, late of Severn in AA C., conv. 131 a. (*) to John Hurst (HW#2: 239).

LUKE'S ... (Pt. of MY LADY'S MANOR)
7 June 1739; Thomas Brerewood conv. 100 a. (*) to Luke Wiley (HWS#1-A: 236).

LUKE'S ADDITION
13 May 1728: Pat. to Luke Stansbury.
31 July 1746: John Hall and w. Bethia conv. to Abraham Raven 100 a. Coxes Fancy, 15 a. Luke's Addition, and pt. Richardson's Neglect, to Abraham Raven (TB#E: 126).

LUKE'S ADVENTURE

30 May 1687: 317 a. pat. to Luke Raven, on the n. side of Middle R., adj. 77 a. Triangle, at the head of Cove Creek (MPL 22: 309, NS#2: 516).

1765: Luke Raven conv. 200 a. (*) to Nicholas Merryman (B#O: 576).

LUKE'S GARDEN

11 June 1726: Luke Raven conv. 317 a. (*), The Outlet and 100 a. The Triangle to his eld. s. Luke Raven (IS#H: 271).

LUKE'S GOODWILL

28 Oct 1748: Charles Carroll conv. 111 a. (*), originally granted to Col. John Smith, and Parishes Neglect, 58 a., and Franklin's Purchase, 685 a. (TR#C: 115).

LUKE'S PRIVILEGE

7 March 1733/4: Samuel Chew conv. to Richard Jones of BA Co., a receipt for 190 a. Denton, 80 a. Walker's Neck, 100 a. Hooper's Island, 330 a. North Point, 546 a. Old Road, 120 a. Industry, 1000 a. Shawan Hunting Ground, 50 a. Thorold's Nest, 100 a. (*), and 100 a. Bagford (HWS#M: 193).

LUNN'S LOT

5 June 1688: Edward Lunn of Severn R. conv. 200 a. (*), on n. side of Patapsco R., to George Eager (RM#HS: 253).

LURGAN

21 Oct 1717: 100 a. pat. by Thomas Earp (MPL FF#7: 206, PL#4: 36).

See KN Plat WO and Horvath Plat: Granite.

27 Nov 1728: John Earp of Stafford Co., VA and Joseph Earp of AA Co. gave p/a to William Parrish to conv. 100 a. and McLain's Friendship to Charles Wells (IS#I: 254, 258).

LYDICAM (See LIDECAN)

LYMERE TENT

1750: William Allen and Co. grants release of two tracts, 20 a. (*), to Alexander Lawson and Co. (TR#D: 118).

LYNE'S ADDITION

10 Nov 1749: George Rock, merchant, mortgaged to Stephen Onion and Alex Lawson Lyne's Tent and (*), which were conv. to George Rock by Thomas Bladen (TR#C: 343).

19 Dec 1749: George Rock granted to Stephen Onion and Alex. Lawson a release on land previously mortgaged (TR#C: 355).

2 April 1750: Stephen Onion, Alexander Lawson of BC and George Rock of CE Co. conv. 600 a. (*) and 100 a. Lyne's Tents to Thomas White of Philadelphia, and Thomas Harrison (TR#C: 443).

17 April 1750: George Rock of CE Co., with cons. of w., Mary, granted release of his share of both tracts to Thomas White and Thomas Harrison (TR#C: 448).

LYNES' TENT (Also LYON'S TENTS)

11 May 1684: 1000 a. surv. for Philip Lines on w. side of Susquehanna R. (MRR: 16).

12 June 1723: Thomas Bladen of London, Gent., by Benjamin Tasker, his atty., leased 100 a. pt. (*) to John Belcher for lifetimes of John, Mary, and Ruth Belcher, or for 21 years (IS#G: 217).

13 Aug 1723: Thomas Bladen leased 150 a. pt. (*) to Daniel Collett for lifetimes of Daniel, Ruth, and Moses Collett (IS#G: 221).

28 Feb 1739: Bladen, through his atty. Benjamin Tasker, leased 100 a. pt. (*) to James Crowe for lifetimes of James and Hannah Crow and Ruth Beliken (HWS#1-A: 399).

7 April 1747: George Rock of CE Co. leased 100 a. pt. of (*) to Samuel Scarlett for lifetimes of Scarlett and his w. Ruth (TB#E: 390).

10 Nov 1749: George Rock, merchant, mortgaged to Stephen Onion and Alex Lawson (*) and Lyne's Addition, which were conv. to George Rock by Thomas Bladen (TR#C: 343).

13 Dec 1749: Samuel Fisher conv. 100 a. (*), which Samuel Ogle granted to SF on 2 March 1748, to George Rock (TR#C: 353).

19 Dec 1749: George Rock grants to Stephen Onion and Alex. Lawson a release on land previously mortgaged (TR#C: 355).

2 April 1750: Stephen Onion, Alexander Lawson and George Rock of Cecil Co. conv. 600 a. Lyne's Addition and 100 a. (*) to Thomas White of Philadelphia, and Thomas Harrison (TR#C: 443).

17 April 1750: George Rock of Cecil Co., grants release of his share of both tracts to Thomas White and Thomas Harrison. GR's w. Mary cons. (TR#C: 448).

LYNN

8 Nov 1671: John James, Gent., conv. to Charles Nicholetts, minister of God's word, 150 a. (*) (IR#PP: 111).

5 March 1671/2: Charles Nicholetts, Minister of God's Word and w. Justice conv. 150 a. (*) to John James (G#J: 68;1 TR#RA: 50).

LYN'S ADDITION

1750: William Allen and Co. granted release of two tracts, 20 a. (*), to Alexander Lawson and Co. (TR#D: 118).

MACEDON(IA)

1 May 1723: Alexander McComas, Gent., and w. Elizabeth conv. 100 a. (*) to John Norris (IS#G: 168).

7 Nov 1746: John Norris conv. 100 a. (*) to Thomas Norris (TB#E: 234).

MACHAIL'S (MICHAEL'S) CHANCE

1724: 100 a. for Michael Byrnes; On PW Plat D.

MAGILL'S CHOICE

15 Oct 1747: Andrew Magill conv. 50 a. (*), and 150 a. unnamed to Thomas Parke (TB#E: 554).

MAIDEN'S BOWER

1 May (or March) 1715: 300 a. (*) surv. for Isaac Butterworth (MRR#II: 482; TB#A: 196).

25 April 1717: 300 a. pat. to Isaac Butterworth (TB#A: 196).

17 May 1728: Isaac Butterworth made his will leaving (*) to his dau. Hannah (TB#A: 196).

15 May 1742: Daniel Scott and w. Hannah, dau. and devisee of Isaac Butterworth, conv. 300 a. (*) to John Paca (TB#A: 196).

1762: Joseph Henley conv. 36 a. pt. (*) to Constance Daughaday (B#K: 438).

MAIDEN'S BOWER SECURED

25 Aug 1748: John Paca conv. 54 a. (*) to Henry Beach(?). JP's w. Elizabeth cons. (TR#C: 60).

MAIDEN'S CHOICE

17 Aug 1673: 450 a. surv. for Thomas Cole, and later held by the s. of Charles Gorsuch (MRR: 110). The tract lies w. of Gwynns Falls and s. of present Frederick Road; includes the land now included in Loudon Park Cemetery. (Marye, MHM, 16: 113n; also MHM, 9: 73).

8 Dec 1679: Charles Gorsuch of TA Co. conv. to David Jones 1200 a. in three parcels which had been inher. by his w. Sarah under the will of Thomas Cole: 650 a. Cole's Harbour; 450 a. Maiden's Choice; and 200 a. Maryebon (formerly laid out for George Hixon of BA or AA Co. (IR#PP: 46).

1 Aug 1682: Sarah Gorsuch, w. of Charles, and dau. and sole heir of Thomas Cole, stated that her cons. to the sale of 1200 a. to David Jones. She now gave her cons. (IR#AM: 185).

6 March 1705/6: Richard Lennox and w. Mary conv. 200 a. Lennox's Adventure, and 218 a. Maiden's Choice, (orig. granted to Mary Richardson, now Mary Lennox, to Nicholas Fitzsimmons (IR#AM: 40).

11 March 1708: John Gorsuch, carpenter, and Thomas Gorsuch conv. 450 a. (*) to Thomas Cromwell (RM#HS: 651).

1 April 1725: Nicholas Fitzsimmons conv. 200 a. Lennox Adventure, and 215 a. Maiden's Choice to Richard Lennox, who with w. Mary, had earlier conv. the tracts to NF. (IS#H: 73).

29 Nov 1727: Thomas Cromwell conv. 225 a. being ½ (*) to Henry Wright (IS#I: 48).

MAIDEN'S CHOICE (1694)

Nov 1694: 218 a. surv. for Mary Richardson (MRR: 101).

MAIDEN'S DAIRY

20 Feb 1695: 248 a. surv. for Thomas Hooker on n. side of Patapsco on Hunting Ridge; later possessed by Richard Cromwell (MRR: 97).

See PW Plat B, Horvath Plat: Elkridge.

20 May 1701: Thomas Hooker conv. 248 a. (*) to John Yeakley. TH's w. Sarah cons. (HW#2: 66).

MAIDEN'S HILL

10 Nov 1724: William King and w. Susanna conv. 124 a. Kingsberry and 500 a. (*) to Thomas Sheredine (IS#H: 14).

MAIDEN'S MOUNT

17 May 1722: Robert West leased 400 a. (*) to Nicholas Roach, Philip Syng, and Michael Webster for 99 years (IS#G: 131).

18 Feb 1722/3: Robert West Sr. planter conv. pt. (*) and Paradise, now called West's Addition to dau. Constant Barnes and the heirs of her body (IS#G: 94).

22 April 1727: Robert West conv. pt. (*) to s. John and his male heirs; if John d. without heirs, land to go to s. Enoch; if Enoch d. without heirs, land to go to the name of West provided he be a poor man and have no land and be a Protestant (IS#H: 393).

22 April 1727: Robert West conv. pt. (*) to his dau. Sarah Cook and her male heirs; if she d. without heirs, land to go to her sister Priscilla West (IS#H: 395).

22 April 1727: Robert West, Sr., conv. pt. (*) to s. Jonathan and his male heirs; if he d. without heirs, land to go to dau. Mary; and if she d. without heirs, then land to pass as in the deed on folio 393 (IS#H: 397).

8 Nov 1733: Robert West, Sr., conv. pt. (*) and pt. Paradice, now called West's Addition to his dau. Comfort Barnes; if she d. s.p., then after the dec. of her husband Job Barnes, lands to go to grantor's s. Enoch West (HWS#M: 9).

22 April 1727: Robert West conv. pt. (*) to s. John and his male heirs; if John dies without heirs land to go to s. Enoch; if Enoch dies without heirs, land to go to the name of West provided he be a

poor man and have no land and be a protestant (IS#H: 393).

22 April 1727: Robert West conv. pt. (*) to his dau. Sarah Cook and her male heirs; if she dies without heirs land to go to her sister Priscilla West (IS#H: 395).

22 April 1727: Robert West, Sr., conv. pt. (*) to s. Jonathan and his male heirs; if he dies without heirs land to go to dau. Mary, and if she dies without heirs, then land to pass as in the deed on folio 393 (IS#H: 397).

MAIDEN'S OUT

----: 500 a. granted to Henry King

20 Nov 1734: Thomas Sheredine conv. (*) to William Chettum, Esq., of Beddington, Surrey and John Whittiwicks of Craden, Surrey, and the Company of the Principio Iron Works. TS' w. Tabitha cons. (HWS#M: 146).

MAIDEN'S OUTLET

24 Dec 1730: Patrick Lynch, who m. Martha, dau. of Jonas Bowen, and Zachariah Gray who m. Rebecca, dau. of Jonas Bowen, submit to arbitration by Thomas Sheredine and John Eaglestone, to divide the lands that Jonas Bowen devised to his daus.: 155 a. Maidens Outlet (orig. laid out for 31 a., and now only 20 a.) and pt. Willen (originally laid out for 168 a.). Lynch is to have 82 a. Willen, and Gray is to have 73 a. Willen and 20 a. Maidens Outlet (MWS#M: 464).

MAJOR'S CHOICE (1694)

19 July 1694: 140 a. surv. for John Thomas on the n. side of Patapsco R., adj. Ruxton's Range (MRR: 77).

4 March 1698/9: Col. John Thomas of BA Co. conv. 140 a. (*) to Robert Burgan (TR#RA: 341).

15 May 1701: Robert Burgan makes a will leaving half of (*) to eld. s. John, and half to s. Robert (MCW#2: 228).

23 Aug 1707: Robert Burgan, planter, conv. 140 a. (*) to Jacob Morris (RM#HS: 608).

MAJOR'S CHOICE (1695)

13 April 1695: 553 a. surv. for James Maxwell above the head of Bush R. on Bynum's Branch (MRR: 38).

4 Jan 1727: James Maxwell, Gent., left (*) at the Land of Nodd to his s. Asahel (MCW#VI: 64).

2 April 1729: Asael Maxwell left (*) to his sister Ann and his heirs, unless Asael and his w. should have a child (MCW#VI: 120).

MAJOR'S CHOICE

4 Sep 1714: Amos Garrett, Merchant of Annapolis, left 200 a. of this tract to his nephew Garrett Woodward, with instructions to make it over to Sarah, widow of Samuel Norwood if she fulfilled certain conditions (MCW#VI: 55).

22 June 1728: Henry Enlows of KE Co., with cons. of w. Mary, conv. ...jor's Choice, originally taken up by Hendrick Enlows, to Josias Middlemore and w. Frances (IS#I: 219).

MARGARET'S CHOICE

4 Nov 1742: Edward Fell, merchant, conv. 26 a. (*) to Stephen Onion, ironmaster (TB#C: 48).

MARGARET'S DELIGHT

20 Oct 1715: Robert Parker conv. 26 a. Margarets Delight to Mary Scutt, devisee of Henry Knowles, dec. (TR#A: 370).

7 July 1720: William Douglas and w. Mary conv. 26 a. (*) to Tobias Emison (TR#DS: 338).

1729: George Goodwin and w. conv. 26 a. (*) to Edward Fell (IS#K: 103).

MARGARET'S MOUNT

10 Oct 1704: Pat. to John Miles (IS#H: 266).

2 March 1708: John Miles conv. 50 a. Farmer's Farm, pt. of Margaret's Mount, to Gregory Farmer (RM#HS: 647).

30 Oct 1712: John Miles again conv. 50 a. of Farmer's Farm, pt. of Margaret's Mount, to Gregory Farmer; this deed corrected mistakes in the deed of 2 March 1708 (TR#A: 124).

27 Nov 1712: Gregory Farmer renounced the deed of 2 March 1708 because of mistakes in the boundaries; Miles then ackn. another conveyance (RM#HS: 647).

3 March 1713: John Miles, carpenter, and w. Mary, conv. 100 a., pt. of Margaret's Mount, to Thomas Cullin, shoemaker (TR#A: 265).

3 Aug 1715: John Miles and w. Mary conv. 100 a. of the land to Robert Hawkins (TR#A: 354).

15 Sep 1716: John and Mary Miles conv. 62 a. of Father-In-Law's Bounty, being one half of Margaret's Mount, to Thomas Litton (TR#A: 449).

7 Aug 1722: John Miles conv. pt. of Margaret's Mount, pat. to John Miles on 10 Oct 1704, to William Brashier (IS#G: 40).

3 May 1726: William Brashar and w. Jane, conv. 56 a. of Margaret's Mount and 10 a. Farmer's Farm to Richard Wells (IS#H: 266).

11 Aug 1730: Richard Wells conv. 56 a. of Margaret's Mount and 10 a. Farmer's Farm to Robert Hawkins (IS#L: 6).

7 March 1754: Samuel Smith of Deer Creek conv. 104 a. of Margaret's Mount to Richard Dallam, (BB#I: 183).

MARGARET'S PURCHASE

25 --- 1738: James Prichard and w. Elizabeth conv. 25 a. (*) to Michael Eastwood (HWS#1-A: 83).

25 March 1740: Samuel, Obadiah, and James Pritchard, sons of Obadiah Pritchard, agree to divide 300 a. Hall's Plains, 50 a. Obadiah's Venture and 25 as. Margaret's Purchase. James will have the last two tracts completely, and enough of Hall's Plains to make it equal (HWS#1-A: 408).

13 June 1759 Thomas Wilkinson and w. Hannah conv. to Benjamin Culver, 25 a. (*), originally laid out in 1724 for Obadiah Pritchett (B#G: 468).

MARIANA

14 Oct 1747: John Crockett agrees to lease 100 a. pt. (*) to David Copeland (TR#C: 133).

MARKEFELD (See also PETER'S FIELDS)

10 Nov 1660: Marcus Severson conv. 100 a. (*) at Sassafras R. to Abraham Coston [sic] (RM#HS: 1).

15 June 1670/1 [sic]: Abraham Coffen and w. Joyce conv. to John Gilbert 100 a. (*) at Veale Quarter Creek. and also 50 a. Peterfield (IR#PP: 108).

MARSH (MARSHES) (THE)

26 May 1674: Richard Leake, planter, and w. Gwenlean conv. 200 a. (*) to Thomas Warde (G#J: 261).

29 Jan 1744: Christopher Sheppard leased 50 a. pt. (*) to Gabriel Brown. Sarah Sheppard signed (TB#C: 266).

7 Nov 1753: Christopher Sheppard conv. to John Atkinson 100 a. (*), granted to Joshua Wood (conv. by his s. and heir at law Joshua Wood to Rowland Sheppard, father of said Christopher), and 10 a. Natty's Island (BB#I: 115).

MARSH'S VICTORY

1724: 200 a. on s. side of Gwynn's Falls granted to John Marsh.

4 May 1751: Richard Marsh, s. of John Marsh, dec., conv. (*) to Charles Carroll (TR#D: 165).

MARSHALL'S HOPE (Pt. THE PASSAGE)

3 Nov 1696: Michael Gormacon conv. 100 a. (*), pt. of Passage, to Isaac Marshall (IS#IK: 100).

MARSHALL'S REST

11 Aug 1707: Thomas Hooker, with cons. of w. Sarah, conv. 230 a. (*) to Nicholas Fitzsimmons, cordwainer. Tract had been escheated 4 June 1679 for non-payment of taxes; resold to George Yates of AA Co. who then conv. it to Thomas Hooker, Jr. (RM#HS: 58).

MARTIN

1662: 100 a. surv. for John Martin on s. side of Back R. (MRR).

MARTINS ADDITION

10 Jan 1706: 100 a. pat. by John Martin (MPL DD#5: 202, PL#2: 299).

See Horvath Plat: Ruxton and Riderwood.

1 Sep 1710: John Martin, with cons. of w. Eleanor, conv. 100 a. (*) and Martinton to William Cole of AA Co. (TR#A: 108).

4 Nov 1741: Thomas Coale, with cons. of w. Mary, conv. to William Coale of AA Co. following tracts: Young Man's Adventure, (*) and Martinton (TB#A: 22).

MARTINS CHOICE

1 April 1725: Richard Lenox conv. 418 a. (*) to Thomas Hatchman, innholder (IS#H: 77).

MARTIN'S FAVOUR

Feb 1708: 100 a. surv. for James Sweeny (Rent Rolls).

MARTIN'S NEST

13 July 1724; 200 a. pat. by William Murphy (MPL PL#6:56, IL#A: 332).

See Horvath Plat: Randallstown.

1 Aug 1727: William Murphy and w. Elizabeth conv. 200 a. (*), originally resurv. for Benj. Martin, dec.) to George Buchanan (IS#I: 15).

3 Nov 1742: Dr. George Buchanan conv. 200 a. (*) to Edward Thomas (TB#C: 35).

15 Feb 1744: Edward Thomas conv. 200 a. (*) to William Fell (TB#D: 18).

MARTINS REST

15 July 1688: 196 a. surv. for Lodwick Martin; located near the mouth of Susquehanna; later possessed by James Phillips for the orphan of Edward Boothby (MRR: 15, 20).

4 April 1697: Lodowick Martin and w. Mary conv. (*) to Edward Boothby (IS#L: 140).

12 Nov 1717: Frances Boothby, spinster, conv. 136 a. (*) to Archibald Buchanan (TR#A: 502).

26 Jan 1730/1: James Donaldson of Annapolis, merchant, conv. 380 a. (*) and 60 a. Gash's Neglect to William Smith (IS#L: 44).

18 March 1730/1: Archibald Buchanan grants quitclaim on 386 a. (*) and 64 a. Gash's Neglect to William Smith, who purch. the tracts from James Donaldson (IS#L: 117).

5 July 1732: George Buchanan of BA Co., chirurgeon conv. (*) to Lloyd Harris. GB'S w. Eleanor cons. (IS#L: 275).

MARTIN'S REST

10 Sep 1724: 386 a. pat. by Archibald Buchanan (MPL PL#5:703; IL#A: 486).

1730: Archibald Buchanan mortgaged 64 a. Gasher's Neglect and 386 a. (*) to James Donaldson, and to John Copson (IS#K: 316, 324).

18 March 1730/1: Archibald Buchanan grants quitclaim on 386 a. (*) and 64 a. Gash's Neglect to William Smith, who purch. the tracts from James Donaldson (IS#L: 117).

22 May 1734: Lloyd Harris, Gent., conv. 200 a. Loyd's Trust and 200 a. (*) to Dr. George Buchanan (HWS#M: 63).

MARTINTON (MARTINSON)

1662: 100 a. surv. for John Martin on s. side of Back R. within the mouth of Gunpowder R. (MHM 21:339).

9 Dec 1684: John Martin, by his atty Thomas Scudamore, conv. 100 a. (*), which had been granted to his father John Martin, to John Boring (RM#HS: 115).

3 April 1685: John Martin of AA Co. through his atty. James Phillips, conv. 100 a. (*) to Joseph Sadler of KE Co.; but if any of the land should overlap the portion lately sold to John Boring, Sadler is not to trouble said Boring (RM#HS: 169).

27 Feb 1693/4: Joseph Sudler/Sadler, with cons. of w. Cecily, conv. 100 a. (*) to John Arden (RM#HS: 426).

1 Sep 1710: John Martin, with cons. of w. Eleanor, conv. 100 a. Martins Addition and Martinton to William Cole of AA Co. (TR#A: 108).

4 Nov 1741: Thomas Coale, with cons. of w. Mary, conv. to William Coale of AA Co. following tracts: Young Man's Adventure, Martin's Addition and (*), granted to John Martin (TB#A: 22).

12 May 1743: William Coale conv. 10 a. (*) to Nicholas Haile (TB#C: 249).

MARTINSON, RESURVEY ON
(See TRIPLE UNION)

MARY'S ADVENTURE

7 Aug 1741: Mary Jarman, widow of Robert Jarman, conv. 47 a. (*) to William Galloway (HWS#1-A: 540).

24 May 1743: William Galloway made a will leaving (*) to his s. Moses (BCF).

1750: Moses Galloway owned 47 a. (*) (1750 DB).

c1754: Moses Galloway owned (*) (IBC: 66).

1763/4: Moses Galloway owned 47 a. (*) (AHAL: 74).

MARY'S DELIGHT

4 Aug 1725: Thomas Gudgeon (Cutchin) conv. 100 a. (*) to Cadwallader Jones (IS#H: 141).

7 June 1732: Edmund Hayes, [Jr.?], with cons. of w. Mary, conv. 100 a. (*) to Abraham Jarrett (IS#L: 247).

MARY'S DELIGHT
(Pt. HIS LORDSHIP'S RESERVE)

7 March 1744: Joseph Butler, Sr., assigned the lease to Thomas Baker Rigdon (TB#D: 21).

MARY'S GOOD HOPE

15 April 1734: Thomas Price conv. 50 a. to William Sinkler (HWS#M: 61).

MARY'S LOT

22 Aug 1736: John Paca, with cons. of w. Elizabeth, conv. (*) to Mary Galloway; deed mentioned Paca's sister Susannah Galloway (IS#IK: 269).

MARY'S MEADOWS

15 Aug 1729: 300 a. pat. to Mary Hanson (MPL PL#7: 220; IL#B: 46).

12 Oct 1745: Mary Walker, widow, formerly Mary Hanson, conv. (*) to her dau. Mary Hanson (TB#D: 363).

28 Feb 1746: John Metcalfe, with cons. of w. Mary conv. to Rachel Bailey, 170 a. being ½ pt. of George's Addition, George's Beginning, and Rich Level, 100 a. (*) and 100 a. Metcalf's Addition (TB#E: 315).

MARY'S PLAINS

1 Jan 1730: William Parrish, with cons. of w. Susannah, conv. 100 a. Gill's Fancy, Mary's Plains, and 150 a. pt. Talbot's Plains (part of 628 a. taken up by Edmund Talbot who devised it to his s. John, whose w. Mary had it resuryeved as Mary's Plains), to George Walker (IS#L: 39).

MARY'S PROMISE

14 Feb 1745: Benjamin Tasker leased 25 a. to Edward Sheppard for 99 years (TR#C: 378).

7 March 1749: Edward Sheppard conv. to William Walker 25 a. Mary's Promise, which on 14 Feb 1745 was leased to ES for 99 years (TR#C: 378).

MARYEBON

8 Dec 1679: Charles Gorsuch of TA Co. conv. to David Jones 1200 a. in three parcels which had been inher. by his w. Sarah under the will of Thomas Cole: 650 a. Cole's Harbour; 450 a. Maiden's Choice; and 200 a. Maryebon (formerly laid out for George Hixon of BA or AA Co. (IR#PP: 46).

1 Aug 1682: Sarah Gorsuch, w. of Charles, and dau. and sole heir of Thomas Cole, stated that her cons. to the sale of 1200 a. to David Jones. She now gave her cons. (IR#AM: 185).

MASCALL'S HAVEN

11 Oct 1670: 100 a. tract was surv. for Richard Mascall, and a patent was granted in the name of James Wells. The tract was later possessed by Jonathan Neale, and still later by Robert Judd (MRR: 105).

1 Nov 1698: John Wells of BA Co. conv. 100 a. (*) to Jonathan Neale of BA Co.; tract was located on s. side of Patapsco R., and was surv. for Robert Mascall (TR#RA: 303).

MASCALL'S HOPE

1 Nov 1677: John Boring, by Anthony Demondidier his atty., conv. 100 a. (*) on n. side of Curtis Creek, to William Cromwell (IR#PP: 17).

MASCALL'S HUMOR

6 Nov 1673: 50 a. surv. for Andrew Bennett at the head of Mosquito Creek; later held by Thomas Jackson; still later by John Hall (MRR: 11).

12 Nov 1677: Benjamin Bennett, planter, assigned 50 a. (*) to Edward Jackson (IR#PP: 15).

17 Dec 1704: Thomas Jackson made a will leaving (*) to his w. Mary (RM#HS: 655).

24 Jan 1705: John Roberts, Gent., and w. Mary, conv. 50 a. (*) (which Thomas Jackson had left to his w. Mary, now w. of John Roberts) to John Hall (IR#AM: 23).

8 June 1709: See RM#HS: 655.

20 Sep 1742: John Hall, s. of Edward Hall who was a s. and heir of John Hall dec., conv. Hall's Purchase (a resurv. of all of the land bought of the Kimballs), 50 a. Mascall's Humor, 400 a. Taylor's Good Hap, and 470 a. Timber Neck, to John Hall, one of the sons and devisees of John Hall (TB#C: 13).

MASON'S OATE

9 March 1733: Samuel Chew and Philip Thomas gave receipt for following tracts to Thomas Sheredine: 473 a. Kingsbury Resurveyed, 250 a. Long Point, 500 a. Mason's Oate, 187 a. The Plains, 100 a. Rogers Road, and 150 a. Sheredine's Bottom (HWS#M: 19).

MATE'S AFFINITY (1683)

1 March 1683: 200 a. surv. for Emanuel Ceeley and Edward Dowse on a branch of Gunpowder R. called Salt Peter Creek; later possessed by Edward Boothby's orphans (MRR: 25, 59).

10 June 1698: Emanuel Ceely, with cons. of w. Sarah, conv. 200 a. to Edward Boothby (TR#RA: 345).

7 May 1745: Dr. Josias Middlemore conv. 200 a. (*) to his kinsman William Dallam (TB#D: 146).

MATE'S AFFINITY

Surv. for 150 a. for Lodowick Williams (HWS#M: 325).

9 Nov 1715: Edward Williams, s. and heir of Lodowick Williams, conv. Hog Neck and (*) to Richard Colegate (HWS#M: 325).

10 May 1732: Richard Colegate, s. and heir of Richard Colegate, conv. Hog Neck and (*) to Robert Robertson (HWS#M: 325).

5 Nov 1735: Robert Robertson conv. 150 a. pt. Hog Neck and (*) to Matthew Beck. RR's w. Sarah cons. (HWS#M: 325).

14 April 1750: Elijah Beck conv. to James Preston parcels of Hogs Neck and Mates Addition [sic; almost certainly (*)] (TR#C: 526).

8 Aug 1750: William Dallam, merchant, conv. to John Hatton, planter, 98 a. Caswell's Venture and 200 a. (*) (TR#D: 71).

MATE'S ANGLE

12 Nov 1668: Surv. for William Osburn and John Lee; located on the eastern side of Bush R. at the northward bounds of Lambert's Marsh; later possessed by George Smith; still later possessed by Daniel Thomas for George Smith's orphans (MRR: 12).

2 June 1673: William Osborne, through Eusebius Beale his atty. conv. 100 a. (*) on e. side of Bush R., about 5 miles up, to Anthony Brispoe (TR#RA: 102, 103).

By c1707 George Smith held 300 a. Hunting Neck and 100 a. Mates Angle for the orphans of Daniel Peverell. Later David Thomas held both tracts (MRR: 12).

2 Feb 1716; William Smith, s. and heir of George Smith, conv. 100 a. (*) to James Phillips. Note that Hannah, now w. of David Thomas, cons. (TR#A: 477).

MATE'S NECK

6 Nov 1694: Thomas Hedge conv. (*), 46 a. Broad Street, and Common Garden to s. Henry Hedge (RM#HS: 435).

24 June 1724: Salem Hedge of Salem Co., West Jersey, through Thomas Sheredine, his atty., conv. 180 a. (*), 100 a. Broad Street and pt. Common Garden to Roger Matthews (IS#G: 358).

MATELIONSET

1 Oct 1742: Samuel Underwood, s. and heir-at-law of Samuel Underwood, dec., who was s. and heir of Thomas Underwood of AA Co., dec., conv. to his kinsman Thomas Cockey 100 a. including The Landing, (*), and Middle Neck (TB#C: 17).

MATSONS LOT

3 April 1682: 10 a. in BA Co. pat. to Andrew Matson of CE Co., planter (MPL 24: 499 and 31: 515).

8 Feb 1688/9: Andrew Mattson and w. Jane conv. to Mark Richardson 200 a. Rayley and 10 a. (*), formerly laid out for Elias Robinson (RM#HS: 318).

2 March 1712: James Phillips and w. Bethia conv. 10 a. Matson's Lot and 200 a. Rayley to John Webster; both tracts had formerly been in possession of Andrew Matson who conv. them to Mark Richardson; said Richardson by his LWT bequeathed them to his w. Susanna and after her death to his dau-in-law Bethia Phillips (TR#A: 241).

12 March 1716: James Phillips of BA Co., Gent., conv. 10 a. Matson's Lot, and 200 a. Rayley to Francis Holland; tracts had formerly been possessed by Francis Holland, late of BA Co., dec., and sold by James Phillips and w. Bethia to John Webster (TR#A: 475).

28 May 1725: Francis Holland of BA Co., Gent., conv. 10 a. Matson's Lot, and 200 a. Rayley to John Stokes (IS#H: 128).

7 Feb 1726: John Stokes of BA Co., Gent., conv. this tract, 10 a. and 200 a. Rayley to Rev. Stephen Wilkinson minister and the vestrymen of St. George's Parish (IS#H: 433).

MATTHEWS ADDITION

2 Sep 1742: Thomas Matthews, with cons. of w. Sarah, conv. 30 a. pt. (*), 100 a. Matthews Farm, and 50 a. Matthews Meadow, to Charles Gorsuch (TB#C: 97).

24 Sep 1746: John Gorsuch conv. 200 a. (*), 100 a. Matthews' Farm and 50 a. Matthews' Meadows to his bro. William Gorsuch (TB#E: 186).

MATTHEWS CHANCE (1722)

7 Sep 1718: Tract was surv.

20 July 1722: 100 a. pat. by Thomas Matthews (MPL FF: 373, and CE#I: 412).

11 July 1741: Thomas Matthews, with cons. of w. Sarah, conv. 100 a. (*) to John Mackonicken, cooper (HWS#1-A: 516).

27 March 1747: John Maconiken conv. 100 a. (*) to James Russell, James Wardrop, James Johnson and Alexander Lawson (TB#E: 5170.

MATTHEWS CHANCE (1728)

25 May 1728: 114 a. pat. to Roger Matthews (MPL PL#6: 625; IL#B: 210).

26 Nov 1731: Roger Matthews conv. 114 a. (*) to James Rutter (IS#L: 217).

30 Sep 1732: James Rutter, cooper, conv. 114 a. (*) to John Watkins (IS#L: 314).

MATTHEWS DOUBLE PURCHASE

8 March 1731: Thomas Cross, with cons. of w. Sarah, conv. 140 a., ½ of (*), als. Heaths Addition, to Henry Wetherall (IS#L: 198).

24 Nov 1731: William Rhoades and w. Mary, dau. of Henry Matthews, conv. ½ of (*) to William Smith (IS#L: 185).

MATTHEWS' FARM
(Pt. of ADDITION TO POOR
JAMAICA MAN'S PLAGUE)

2 Sep 1742: Thomas Matthews, with cons. of w. Sarah, conv. 30 a. pt. Matthews Addition, 100 a. Matthews Farm, and 50 a. Matthews Meadow, to Charles Gorsuch (TB#C: 97).

24 Sep 1746: John Gorsuch conv. 200 a. Matthews Addition, 100 a. (*) and 50 a. Matthews' Meadows to his bro. William Gorsuch (TB#E: 186).

MATTHEWS' FOREST

See Horvath Plat: Reisterstown.

17 Feb 1740: 150 a. pat. by Thomas Matthews (MPL EI#5: 430, and EI#6: 157).

22 June 1742: Thomas Matthews, with cons. of w. Sarah, conv. 50 a. pt. (*) to John Clossey (HWS#1-A: 544).

13 Feb 1743/4: John Clausey and w. Mary conv. 50 a. (*) to William Watson (TB#C: 422).

16 Oct 1745: Thomas Matthews and w. Sarah conv. 50 a. of (*) to Richard Pinkham (TB#D: 327).

25 Feb 1747: Thomas Matthews and w. Sarah, conv. 50 a. (*) to Charles Ridgely (TB#E: 642).

1 Dec 1762: William Watson, with cons. of w. Elizabeth, conv. (*) to Samuel Mannon (B#L: 88).

MATTHEWS FRAME

17 Feb 1723/4: Jonathan Tipton, Sr., and w. Mary conv. 100 a. (*) to Thomas Matthews (IS#G: 307).

MATTHEWS' MEADOWS

2 Sep 1742: Thomas Matthews, with cons. of w. Sarah, conv. 30 a. pt. Matthews Addition, 100 a. Matthews Farm, and 50 a. (*) to Charles Gorsuch (TB#C: 97).

24 Sep 1746: John Gorsuch conv. 200 a. Matthews Addition, 100 a. Matthews' Farm and 50 a. (*) to his bro. William Gorsuch (TB#E: 186).

MATTHEWS NEGLECT

13 Feb 1726/7: John Smithers of KE Co., Gent., eld. s. of Blanch Smithers, (dau. of Col. George Wells and sister and coheir of George Wells, Jr.) conv. his interest in the following tracts to John Stokes: 800 a. Goldsmith's Hall, 24 a. Matthews Neglect, 400 a. Planter's Delight, 200 a. Timber Proof, and 81 a. Watson's Addition (some of which were resurv. into 1150 a. Coheir's Lot) (IS#H: 385).

MATTHEWS NEIGHBORS

4 March 1742: Daniel Scott, Sr., conv. 200 a. (*) to Jarvice Gilbert (TB#C: 187).
26 Jan 1748: Garvis Gilbert, with cons. of w. Elizabeth, conv. pt. (*), cont. 231 a. in all (TR#C: 210).
1750: Bernard Preston owned 123 a., pt. of the tract (1750 DB: 96).
26 Sep 1766: Preston Gilbert of Bedford Co., VA, s. and heir of Garvis Gilbert, late of BA Co., dec., conv. 89 a. (*) to Thomas Gash (B#O: 328).

MATT'S ADDITION

19 Nov 1715: Edward Williams of Paspotank R. in Sawyer's Creek, NC, conv. 100 a. where Matthew Green's widow and Robert Smith, shoemaker, dwell, 200 a. Lodowick's Ridge, 150 a. Matt's Addition, 100 a. Thomson's Fortune, 300 a. United Friendship, and 150 a. Williams' Fortune, and all other lands in MD belonging to Williams by right of inheritance, to Richard Colegate, merchant (TR#A: 373).

MATTSON'S LOT

13 April 1682: 10 a. surv. for Andrew Mattson on s. side of Swan Creek; later held by Mark Richardson, and then by Thomas Wainwright (MRR: 6).
8 Feb 1688/9: Andrew Mattson and w. Jane conv. 200 a. Rayley and 10 a. Matson's Lot, formerly laid out for Elias Robertson, to Mark Richardson (RM#HS,. 318).
2 March 1712: James Phillips and w. Bethia, conv., 200 a. Rayley and 10 a., Mattson's Lot to John Webster; both tracts were sold by Andrew Mattson to Mark Richardson who bequeathed them by his will, after the death of his w. Susanna, to his dau.-in-law Bethia Phillips (TR#A: 241).
12 March 1716: James Phillips, conv. both tracts to Francis Holland, even though the deed states that both tracts had earlier been sold by Phillips and his w. to John Webster (TR#A: 475).
28 May 1725: Francis Holland conv. both tracts to John Stokes (IS#H: 128).
28 May 1725: Francis Holland conv. 10 a. Mattsons Lot and 200 a. Rayley to Francis Holland (IS#H: 170).
7 Feb 1726: John Stokes, Gent., conv. both tracts to Rev. Stephen Wilkinson, minister, and the vestrymen of St. George's Parish (IS#H: 433).

MAXWELL

9 June 1737: Samuel Maxwell conv. 240 a. (*), surv. on 20 Dec 1735, to William Maccubbin (IS#IK: 446).

MAXWELL'S CONCLUSION

8 Aug 1750: Joseph Maxwell, only surviving s. of Samuel Maxwell, and bro. of James Maxwell, dec., conv. to Nicholas Ruxton Gay, 100 a. Spring Neck and 100 a. Maxwell's Hope (TR#C: 555).

MAXWELL'S HABITATION
(Pt. THE FOREST and ADDITION, q.v.)

24 Nov 1737: 240 a. pat. to Samuel Maxwell (MPL EI#2: 650, and EI#5: 228).
8 June 1737: James Maxwell conv. 50 a. pt. (*) to Nicholas Gostwick (IS#IK: betw. 454 and 461).
1 Dec 1738: Nicholas Goswtick, with cons. of w. Avarilla, conv. 50 a. (*) to Samuel Maxwell (HWS#1-A: 157).
17 March 1738: Samuel Maxwell, with cons. of w. Jane, conv. 240 a. (*), made up of The Forest and Addition, to William Maccubbin (HWS#1-A: 248).

MAYNOR'S BEGINNING

19 da., 8 mo, 1744: Henry Maynor and w. Susanna conv. (*) to Dennis Garrett Cole (TB#C: 651).

MAYNOR'S PRIVILEGE

3 Aug 1731: William Maynor and w. Martha, conv. 80 a. (*) to John Ensor (IS#L: 152).

McCOMAS' MANOR

6 Sep 1753: William McComas of Wm., deeded to John Poteet, Jr., 100 a. (of a 200 a. tract), pt. McComas' Manor (BB#I: 61).
3 Oct 1767: John Poteet assigns lease for 100 a. McComas' Manor to Aquila McComas. No w. was required to sign an assignment of a lease (B#Q: 413).

McLANE'S FRIENDSHIP

1719: 50 a. pat. by John Earp (MPL IL#A: 456).
See Horvath Plat: Granite.

1728: John and Joseph Earp of AA Co. conv. 100 a. and McLain's Friendship to Charles Wells (IS#I: 254, 258).

27 Nov 1728: John Earp of Stafford Co., VA, gave p/a to William Parrish to acknowledge Earp's conv. of 50 a. (*) to Charles Wells (IS#J, 258, 259).

6 Oct 1754: Charles Wells conv. 50 a. (*) to James Chilcoat. CW's w. Sarah cons. (BB#I: 143).

7 March 1760: James Chilcoat conv. 50 a. (*) to John Stevenson (B#H: 125).

3 July 1762: Charles Wells and w. Sarah, and James Chilcoat conv. 50 a. (*) to George Zimmerman (B#K: 212).

McLANE'S HILLS

5 Oct 1753: John Maclan conv. 74 a. pt. McLane's Hills and Addition to Maclanes Hills to Solomon Stocksdale. JM's w. Margaret cons. (BB#I: 139).

McLANE'S HILLS, ADDITION TO

5 Oct 1753: John Maclane conv. 74 a. pt. McLane's Hills and Addition to MacLane's Hills to Solomon Stocksdale. JM's w. Margaret cons. (BB#I: 139).

1756: John McLain conv. 100 a. Addition to McClains Hills to Thomas Porter (BB#I: 527; Emison).

28 Aug 1762: Edward Stocksdale conv. pt. (*) to Thomas Stocksdale (B#K: 281).

1768: Thomas Porter conv. to Richard Porter 100 a. (*) (B#Q: 257).

McLANE'S HOPE

8 April 1698: Hector McLane conv. (*) to James Murray in exch. for 100 a. Athol (IS#IK: 254).

MEADOW (THE)

15 Sep 1741: Benjamin Wheeler conv., 10 a. (*) and 10 a. pt. St. Omer's to dau. Charity, w. of Benjamin Colegate (HW#S#1-A, 57).

MEADOW LAND

10 Nov 1730: laid out for Stephen Onion (MHM 16:130n).

10 Aug 1750: Stephen Onion conv. (*) to Agnes Porter, widow. Her s. Alexander Porter is mentioned in the deed (TR#C: 557).

MELINDA

1706: 400 a. surv. for William Talbot (Penniman and Waring).

16 July 1738: Benjamin Hammond and w. Margaret conv. 400 a. (*) to Matthew Coulter (HWS#1-A: 128).

30 June 1739: Matthew Coulter, tailor, conv. 400 a. (*) to William Hammond, Gent. (HWS#1-A: 256).

MERRIKEN'S PURCHASE

18 May 1710: Joshua Merriken, s. of Hugh, conv. (*) to John Brice of AA Co., merchant; tract had been purch. [by Hugh Merriken?] from Thomas Lightfoot on 6 Nov 1686. Merriken also sold Point Lookout. (TR#A: 79).

MERITON'S LOT

11 Oct 1684: 500 s. pat. to John Meriton (RM#HS: 189).

9 Feb 1685/6: John Meriton, Gent., of AA Co., conv. 500 a. (*) to John Sellman of AA Co. (RM#HS: 189).

MERRYMAN'S ADDITION

1695: 120 a. pat. by Charles Merryman; lies partially in Guilford (MHM 51:14n).

2 Nov 1714: Charles Merryman, Sr., carpenter, conv. 120 a. (*) to his second s. John Merryman (TR#A: 320).

MERRYMAN'S ADVENTURE

29 Oct 1737: Samuel Merryman conv. 50 a. pt. (*) to his friend Lewis Buffking for life (HWS#M: 30).

31 March 1739: Levin Buffking, schoolmaster, conv. 50 a. pt. (*) to Thomas Stains, carpenter (HWS#1-A: 203).

25 Nov 1746: Samuel Merryman conv. 100 a. of (*) to John Price, Sr. (TB#E: 246, 261).

23 Oct 1748: John Price conv. 100 a. pt. (*) to John Chilcoat. JP's w. Hannah cons. (TR#C: 86).

MERRYMAN'S BEGINNING

1704: 246 a. surv. for Charles Merryman (MHM 10:182; 58:230).

11 July 1746: William Merryman and Charles Merryman conv. (*) to Charles Ridgely. Millicent Merryman w. of (?) Merryman cons. (TB#E: 161).

MERRYMAN'S CHOICE

12 July 1743: Benjamin Tasker leased 88 a. called (*) to Charles Merryman (TB#E: 483).

23 March 1746: Charles Merryman leased (*) to George Haile (TB#E: 483).

MERRYMAN'S DELIGHT

24 May 1742: John Merryman, Sr., conv. 150 a. (*) to Moses Merryman (TB#C: 32).

MERRYMAN'S GROTTO

See Horvath Plat: Old Hampstead.

5 May 1750: William Merryman and w. Margaret conv., 50 a. (*) to Jabez Murray (TR#D: 14).

23 June 1764: William Murray and w. Diana conv. 7 a. Merryman's Grotto and 68 a. pt. Murray's Ridge to Wheeler Murray (B#N: 243).

MERRYMAN'S LOT

24 June 1688; 210 a. surv.; 1689: Pat. to Charles Merryman and Nich's Hale (MHM 51: 14, 54: 346, 353, 354).

2 Nov 1714; Charles Merryman, carpenter, conv. 105 a. pt. (*) to his second s. John Merryman (TR#A: 320).

MERRYMAN'S PASTURE

1704: 200 a. surv. for Charles Merryman (MHM 10: 179).

1705: 200 a. pat.

2 Nov 1714: Charles Merryman conv. 200 a. (*) to his youngest s. Samuel Merryman (TR#A: 321).

MERRYMAN'S PURCHASE
(Originally pt. of BROAD'S IMPROVEMENT)

21 July 1724: Thomas Broad, with cons. of w. Ann, conv. 102 a. (*) to John Merryman (IS#H: 159).

22 March 1738: John Merryman conv. 102 a. (*) to Thomas Broad (HWS#1-A: 197).

MESHACK'S GARDEN

6 April 1745: Nicholas Haile conv. 100 a. Hooker's Farm (part of Gerar), 60 a. Addition to Hooker's Farm, 100 a. Hailes' Forest, 100 a. pt. of Haile's Fellowship, 80 a. pt. Taylor's Discovery, 50 a. Smallwood, 200 a. Hailes Discovery, 200 a. Shadrack's Lot, and 200 a. Meshack's Garden, to Christopher Grindall of London, mariner (TB#E: 83).

METCALFE'S ADDITION

28 Feb 1746: John Metcalfe, with cons. of w. Mary conv. to Rachel Bailey, 170 a. being ½ pt. of George's Addition, George's Beginning, and Rich Level, 100 a. Mary's Meadows, and 100 a. (*) (TB#E: 315).

19 Aug 1768: Thomas Metcalfe of FR Co., s. and heir at law of John Metcalfe, conv. 100 a. (*) to William Lyon (B#Q: 643).

METON'S REVOLUTION

5 Nov 1753: Samuel Shipley, with cons. of w. Martha, conv. 225 a. (*) to Cornelius Howard (BB#I: 91).

MICHAEL'S BEGINNING

3 March 1719: Michael Byrne conv. 50 a. (*) to John Rogers. MB's w. Sarah is mentioned (TR#DS: 182).

8 July 1738: John Rogers conv. 40 a. John's Beginning and 50 a. Michael's Beginning to Thomas Sligh (HWS#1-A: 89).

MICHAEL'S CHANCE

2 May 1721: Michael Byrne conv. 100 a. to John Ingram. MB's w. Sarah cons. (TR#DS: 310).

MIDDLE JENIFER

Nov 1683: Jacob Jennifer, for love and affection makes deed of gift of 97 a. (*) on n. side of Middle R. to Otho Holland of AA Co. (RM#HS: 62).

13 Jan 1684/5: Otho Holland conv. 97 a. (*) to John Skinner, planter of AA Co. OH's w. Mehitable cons. (RM#HS: 152).

4 Feb 1688: John Skinner of AA Co. conv. 987 a. (*) to John Sillman (RM#HS: 249).

1750: Richard Clark owned 97 a. pt. (*) (1750 DB).

MIDDLE NECK

1 Oct 1742: Samuel Underwood, s. and heir-at-law of Samuel Underwood, dec., who was s. and heir of Thomas Underwood of AA Co., dec., conv. to his kinsman Thomas Cockey 100 a. including The Landing, Matelionset, and (*) (TB#C: 17).

MIDDLE OLLEYS

1691: Mary Adams gave 40 a. (*) and 45 a. Hopewell to her son-in-law Richard Adams (IR#AM: 88).

MIDDLE RIDGE

1707: 200 a. surv. for William Talbot.

25 June 1737: Moredecai Hammond conv. 100 a., being ½ of (*) to Peter Bond. MH's w. Frances cons. (IS#IK: 503).

25 June 1737: Mordecai Hammond conv. 100 a. being ½ of (*) to Richard Bond. MH's w. Frances cons. (IS#IK: 506).

28 July 1737: Benjamin Hammond and w. Margaret give bond to (Peter Bond?) to guarantee title to 100 a. (*) sold Bond by Mordecai Hammond (IS#IK: 505).

MIDDLEMORE'S RANGE

29 Aug 1765: Isaac Hersey of New Castle Co., PA, and w. Henrietta, formerly Holland, legatee of Frances Middlemore, conv. (*) to Gregory Barnes (B#O: 418).

MIDSUMMER HILL

17 June 1689: 200 a. surv. for Edward Boothby by Thomas Richardson, Deputy Surveyor (RM#HS: 385).

18 July 1689: 201 a. surv. for John Bevan on n. side of Salt Peter Creek; later poss. by Francis Dallahide (MRR: 65).

11 Nov 1694: John Bevans of Gunpowder R. and w. Sarah conv. 210 a. (*) and 180 a. Forberry Neck to Frances Dallahide and w. Providence of AA Co. (RM#HS: 442).

14 June 1741: Barnet Bond, mariner, conv. 201 a. (*) and 180 a. Forberry Neck to William Bond (HWS#1-A: 514).

1750: Capt. William Bond listed as owning 246 a. (*) (1750 DB: 76).

MILE END (MILLEND)

5 July 1672: 100 a. surv. for Miles Gibson; located in Rumley Creek; later possessed by Roger Matthews (MRR: 13).

MILES

7 Aug 1733: Thomas Miles as s. and devisee of John Miles, dec., conv. to Mary Miles, widow of John Miles and to John Miles Youngblood .... Deed mentions tract Miles which JM gave to MM for her life and then to JMY. Thomas Miles' w. Catherine cons. (IS#L: 419).

MILES' ADDITION

6 Oct 1695: 200 a. surv. for John Miles (MRR: 5). This may be the same tract mentioned below:

16 Dec 1695: date of cert. of surv. (IS#L: 328).

11 Nov 1732: William Cook and w. Hannah conv., 200 a. (*) to Roger Matthews (IS#L: 328).

8 Aug 1733: Roger Matthews and w. Elizabeth conv. 200 a. (*), pat. 1 Oct 1695, to Edward Wakeman (IS#L: 411).

MILES DEFENSE

12 Oct 1750: Thomas Miles conv. (*) (leased from Benjamin Tasker) to James Billingsley (TR#D: 28).

MILES END

2 Aug 1681: Miles Gibson, Gent., conv. 100 a. (*) and other land (100 a. unnamed, and 140 a. Common Garden) to Thomas Hedge, Gent. (IR#AM: 162).

6 March 1682/3: Thomas Hedge, Gent., conv. 100 a. (*) to Roger Matthews (RM#HS: 31).

MILES' FOREST

2 Nov 1703: John Miles, carpenter, conv. 200 a. (*) to Bennett Creed of CV Co. (HW#2: 305).

10 Oct 1709: Bennett Creed of CV Co. leased 200 a. (*) to William Holland for 2000 years (TR#A: 92).

13 Feb 1745: William Holland of CV Co., surviving exec. of William Holland, assigned mortgage of 200 a. (*) and 225 a. Creed's Beginning to Isaac Webster (TB#E: 20).

22 Feb 1745: Francis Holland, s. of Francis, granted title to (*) to quiet title of deed from William Holland to Isaac Webster. FH's w. Cordelia cons. (TB#E: 25).

MILES HILL

22 Dec 1720: Thomas Nusum conv. 100 a. (*) to Samuel Hughes (IS#G: 95).

5 March 1727/8: Samuel Hughes conv., 100 a. (*) to Charles Whitaker. SH's w. Jane cons. (IS#I: 92).

29 Aug 1751: John Whiteacre, with cons. of w. Mary, conv. to Robert Patterson, two tracts of land: (*), 100 a., and Whiteacre's Ridge, 75 a. (TR#D: 249).

MILES' IMPROVEMENT (1719)

8 Dec 1719: 100 a. surv. for John Miles (HWS#1-A: 148).

3 Nov 1736: John Miles Youngblood and w. Mary conv. 100 a. (*) to Jacob Giles (IS#IK: 297).

23 Oct 1738: John Miles Youngblood of AA Co. and w. Mary conv. 100 a. (*) to Richard Dallam. (HWS#1-A: 148).

MILES IMPROVEMENT (1739)

9 May 1739: 40 a. pat. to Thomas Miles (TB#E: 652).

6 Nov 1747: William Bond conv. (*) and 100 a. Tower Hill to Thomas Bond, Jr. (TB#E: 652).

MILLEND (See MILE END)

MIL(L)FORD

1728/29: Surv. for Richard Gist.

See Horvath Plat: Pikesville.

14 March 1743: Christopher Gist mortgaged 100 a. Counterscarpe, 83 a. Milford, Gist's Inspection, 500 a. Joshua's Lot, 50 a. Gist's Meadows, and 2 lots in Baltimore Town (TB#D: 438).

28 March 1746: James Richard, atty. for Stephen Theodore Jannsen, conv. 100 a. Counterscarpe, 83 a. Milford, Gist's Inspection, 500 a. Joshua's Lot, 50 a. Gist's Meadows, and 2 lots in Baltimore Town to William Cromwell and Tobias Stansbury, who have paid the mortgages (TB#D: 438).

4 Sep 1750: Tobias Stansbury received tract Milford from Christopher Gist, now of VA, s. of Richard Gist (TR#D: 94).

31 Oct 1750: Tobias Stansbury conv. to Thomas Price, planter, and John (Boons?), cooper, 83 a. Milford, which had been conv. to Stansbury by Christopher Gist. TS' w. Mary cons. (TR#D: 36).

21 Sep 1751: Thomas Bond conv. pt. Milford, 83 a., to Samuel Stock [or Hooke]. TB's w. Phoebe cons. (TR#D: 290).

11 June 1753: Samuel Hooke of Baltimore Town conv. 83 a. (*) to Edward and John Haw. SH' w. Catherine cons. (BB#I: 15).

MILL HAVEN

10 Dec 1684: Thomas Lightfoot, Gent., of AA Co. conv. to Anthony Ruley, currier of same co., 100 a. (*) on the Middle Branch and n. side of Patapsco R. 27 Oct 1684: Lightfoot, surveyor, assigns to Anthony Ruley, 100 a. (*) (RM#HS: 144).

25 June 1685: Charles Gorsuch, planter, and w. Sarah conv., to Thomas Lightfoot 50 a. (*) and 50 a. Whetstone Point (Could this have been actually 1683 and transcribed inaccurately as 1685?) (RM#HS: 143).

11 April 1686: Anthony Ruly conv. 100 a. (*) to John Mercer. Johanna Ruly signs with the grantor (RM#HS: 176).

13 April 1686: Thomas Lightfoot, Gent., grants a quitclaim deed for 100 a. (*) to John Mercer (RM#HS: 175).

30 Sep 1707: John Mercer, late of AA Co., by virtue of p/a to Joseph Hill, Gent., conv. 100 a. (*) to Jabez Pierpoint of AA Co. (RM#HS: 598).

MILLER'S CHOICE

10 Sep 1743: Luke Trotten and William Hamilton, execs. of John Gardner, conv. 25 a. (*) and 100 a. Betty's Choice to John Bosley (TB#C: 404).

MILLERS PURCHASE
(See WITH'S ADVENTURE)

2 Sep 1729: Henry Peregoy and w. Amey conv. 50 a., residue of Success, now called Miller's Purchase, to John Miller, planter (IS#K: 174).

1 June 1731: John Miller and w. May conv. Success (orig. held by Henry Peregoy and now called With's Adventure) to George With (IS#L: 125).

MILLFORD (See MILFORD)

MINERS ADVENTURE

22 May 1717: 200 a. taken up by Col. William Holland of AA Co., on n. side of Deer Creek. It lies betw. Ady and Cherry Hill (C:14-15).

MINTO

See Horvath Plat: Granite.

17 March 1749: George Turnbull, carpenter, conv. 50 a. (*) to John Hurd. GT's w. Grace cons. (TR#C: 459).

MISTAKE (THE)

9 June 1744: William Lewis conv. 100 a. (*) and 50 a. The Addition to Andrew Scriber of PA. WL's w. Ruth cons. (TB#C: 634).

MOALE'S SUCCESS

1729: John Boone conv. (*) to Edward Hall (IS#K:15).018 ??

June 1729; William Byfoot makes deed of gift to Moses Byfoot (1S#K: 18).

MOLLY AND SALLY'S DELIGHT

28 July 1730: Jonathan Tipton, Sr., conv. 100 a., pt. (*) to Jonathan Tipton, Jr. (IS#L: 25).

10 Dec 1735: Jonathan Tipton conv. ½ of (*) to his granddaughter Mary Tipton; he had conv. the other half to JT, Jr., on 28 July 1730 (HWS#M: 360).

22 June 1747: Jonathan Tipton conv. 100 a. pt. (*) to John Stevenson. JT's w. Juliatha cons. (TB#E: 461).

27 Aug 1749: Henry Morgan of BA conv. 100 a. (*) to Thomas Sligh; land had been the dwelling plantation of the late Jonathan Tipton, Jr. (TR#C: 272).

1750: John Stevenson owned 100 a. pt. (*) (1750 DB).

MOLLY'S GARDEN

10 July 1725: 50 a. pat. to William Mainer (MPL PL#6: 257, and IL#A: 523).

1729: William Mainer conv. 50 a. (*) to Edward Talby (IS#K: 58).

18 Feb 1741: Thomas Baxter and w. Mary Ann of New Castle Co., PA, conv. 50 a. (*) to Valentine Carback (TB#A: 118).

MOLLY'S INDUSTRY

8 July 1747: Thomas Logsdon conv. 100 a. (*) to John Cryder. TL's w. Mary cons. (TB#E: 462).

MONMOUTH GREEN

2 March 1695: John Carrington of BA and w. Katherine, conv. 100 a. (*) to David Mackelfresh of AA Co., mariner (RM#HS: 521).

MONTSERADA

2 Nov 1710: Henry Ward of CE Co. conv. 250 a. (*) to Edward Parrish in exch. for 300 a. Haydowne (TR#A: 463).

27 June 1717: Edward Parrish of AA Co., cooper, conv. to John Stokes, Gent., 250 a. (*), pat. for 550 a. (TR#A: 463).

11 Nov 1736: George Stokes, s. of John Stokes, with cons. of George's w. Susanna, conv. (*) (which had been devised to him by his father John Stokes) and Montserada (which John

Stokes purch. from Edward Parrish) to Humphrey Wells Stokes, in exch. for 2/3 of Coheir's Lot (IS#IK: 334).

1 April 1745: Mary Stokes, widow and admx. of Humphrey Wells Stokes conv. 250 a. pt. (*) to Col. Thomas White (TB#D: 78).

MOOREFIELDS

19 May 1676: Thomas Thurston, in consideration of marriage made by his dau. Ann to Miles Gibson conv. to MG 600 a. in Talbot County embracing tracts Coles Banks and Moorefields (G#J: 330).

MOORES FIELDS

12 Jan 1697: Thomas Staly of BA, Gent., conv. 50 a. (*) being the easternmost half, to his son-in-law James Durham (HW#2: 50).

5 June 1728: James Armstrong of BA, conv. 82½ a., being ½ of (*) to John Armstrong (IS#I: 206).

3 March 1739: John Armstrong, planter, conv. 82 ½ a. (*), being ½ of (*), to John Hatton of BA, tailor; mentions land conv. on 5 June 1728 (HWS#1-A: 233).

5 April 1739: John Hatton conv. 60 a., the eastern pt. of (*), to Robert Scott, cordwainer. The tract was originally granted to Thomas Staley for 165 a., and pat. 6 May 1689; pt. was resurv. for Robert Scott on a warrant for escheat, now in Scott's occupancy and possession (HWS#1-A: 253).

7 May 1745: John Hatton, tailor, conv. 27 a. pt. Moorefields, and 50 a. the Neglect to William Dallam. JH's w. Sarah cons. (TB#D: 142).

MOORE'S MANOR

15 April 1749: Benj. Tasker, Agent for Lord Baltimore, leased to James Moore 200 a. (*); the lease to run for the lives of James Moore, Jr.'s, ch.: Rezin and Mary (TR#C: 411).

MOORE'S PARK

1730: Heathcote Pickett and w. conv. 50 a. (*) to James Moore (IS#K: 271).

17 May 1735: James Moore conv. 50 a. Moore's Park, being pt. of Roberts' Forest, to John Wilmot (HWS#M: 276).

MOORTON

19 Feb 1669/70: Richard Leake conv. 600 a. (*) on e. side of Herring Creek on s. side of Sassafras R., to John Larkin (IR#PP: 77).

MORGAN'S DELIGHT

12 June 1694: Surv. for James Murray who devised if to his s. Morgan (HWS#1-A: 502).

15 Jan 1717: Morgan Murray, with cons. of w. Sarah, conv. 150 a. pt. (*) to widow Mary Stevenson (TB#E: 512).

16 Jan 1717: Mary Stevenson, widow, conv. 150 a. pt. (*) to dau. Elizabeth Barney. Appended to the deed is an Act of the Assembly authorizing William Barney, s. of Elizabeth Barney, to have the deed recorded (TB#E: 512).

24 May 1741: Joseph Murray, s. of Morgan, mortgaged 150 a. of (*) to George Buchanan (HWS#1-A: 502).

13 Oct 1744: Joseph Murray, with cons. of w. Jemima, conv. 150 a. (*) to William Rogers (TB#C: 656).

22 Jan 1747: Jabez Murray, with cons. of w. Mary, conv. 40 a. pt. (*) to William Rogers (TB#E: 639).

23 Jan 1747: Jabez Murray of BA, carpenter, conv. 50 a. Samuel's Industry, pt. of Morgan's Delight, to Samuel Wheeler. JM's w. Mary cons. (TB#E: 663).

2 Oct 1747: Jabez Murray and Joseph Murray agreed to divide the land which James Murray left to his sons Morgan and Jabez. Morgan is now dec. leaving a s. Joseph (TB#E: 556).

26 July 1748; William Barney, with cons. of w. Frances, conv. 128 a. (*) to William Rogers (TR#C: 71).

20 March 1754: Jabez Murray conv. 40 a. Morgan's Delight (orig. granted to James Murray for 500 a. on 10 Nov 1695) to William Rogers (BB#I: 201).

30 May 1754: Jabez Murray and w. Mary conv. 110 a. pt. (*) to Benjamin Bowen als. Cox (TR#A: 252).

MORGAN'S DEVICE (or DESIRE)

1752: Thomas Bishop and w. conv. 75 a. (*) to David Morgan (TR#D: 487).

MORGAN'S TENT RESURVEYED

1754: George Ogg conv. 238 a. Morgan's Tent Resurveyed, 30 a. Plumb Tree Bottom, and 60 a. Mount Pleasant to Lovelace Gorsuch (BB#I: 458).

17 Sep 1755: George Ogg conv. 132 a. pt. (*) to Luke Chapman (BB#I: 453).

MORLEY'S CHOICE

22 Nov 1693: Robert Proctor of AA Co. conv. 300 a. (*) to George Norman; the deed mentioned Proctor's w. Rachel (RM#HS: 425).

MORNING CHOICE

15 March 1695: 400 a. surv. for John Scott (B).

MORRIS' LOT

4 Nov 1713: Thomas Morris conv. 31 a. (*) to Rowland Kemble (TR#A: 256).

MOSQUITO PROOF

22 Dec 1672: A 250 a. tract surv. for James Ives in Mosquito Creek later 200 a. possessed by James Ives, and 50 a. sold to John Sheeles and now in poss. of Elizabeth Sheeles his widow; still later held by John Hall (MRR: 25).

15 Nov 1697: James Ives of BA Co. sold 50 a. to John Shields (IS#IK: 230).

4 March 1703/4: James Ives of BA Co., made a will (proved 13 March 1703/4) leaving Mosquito Proof to John Kimble and heirs (MCW#III: 31).

28 Dec 1708: John Hall conv. 102½ a., being pt. of 250 a., to John Stokes (RM#HS: 631).

29 Dec 1708: John Stokes the Elder conv. to John Stokes the Younger 102½ a. Mosquito Proof, which John Hall sold to Stokes; also 125 a. Beaver Neck which James Ives left by will to Susanna w. of John Stokes (RM#HS: 632).

22 March 1710: John Hall of BA Co. conv. 68 a. Cord's Purchase, a pt. of Mosquito Proof, to Thomas Cord (may be two separate tracts) (TR#A: 100).

17 March 1718: John Stokes and w. Susanna conv. 125 a. Beaver Neck, and 102½ a. Mosquito Proof to John Clarke of BA Co. (TR#RA: 422).

2 Nov 1723: John Clarke conv. 125 a. Beaver Neck and 102 a. (*) to John Hall (deed traces descent of property from Bernard Utie who devised to Henry Haslewood, Sr., who devised to Henry Jr., who devised it to James Ives, who devised to Susanna Wells now w. of John Stokes and sold by them to John Clark (IS#G: 212).

MOTHER'S CARE

12 July 1703: 500 a. pat.; on PW PLat H (TB#C: 395).

18 Nov 1743: Richard Johns of CV Co. conv. 500 a. (*) to Daniel Dulany. RJ's w. Margaret cons. (TB#C: 395).

MOTT'S ADDITION

July 1731: William Buckner and w. Patience conv. 150 a. (*), 100 a. Thompson's Fortune and 150 a. William's Fortune to Robert Robertson (IS#L: 149).

MOULD'S SUCCESS

10 June 1681: John Mould surv. 400 a. (*) on w. side of Swan Creek; later held by Henry Borne; still later held 198 a. by Lawrence Draper, and 100 a. by John Cottrell; 102 a. taken away by an elder surv. (MRR: 15).

1 Aug 1693: Barbara Mould spinster conv. to Thomas Kerkjoy of BA Co. 133⅓ of tract, the middle third, which came to Barbara by descent from her father John, who surv. the land (IR#AM: 99).

4 July 1694: Peter Fucatt and w. Frances (one of the daus. of John Mould) conv. 133⅓ a., the lowermost third of the land to Edward Boothby (RM#HS: 419).

3 Aug 1694: Thomas Kerksick and w. Sarah conv. to Edward Boothby the 133⅓ a. of (*) they bought from Barbara Mould (RW#HS: 420).

26 March 1694: John Dunkin and w. Ann (dau. of John Mould) grant p/a to William Galloway to conv. 133⅓ a. of tract to Michael Judd, innholder (RM#HS: 422).

27 Sep 1698: Edward Boothby of BA Co., Gent., conv. 400 a. (*) to William Bourne of BA Co., carpenter. EB's w. Elizabeth cons. (TR#RA: 297).

27 Dec 1698: Edward Boothby conv. to tract to William Borne (HW#2: 289).

1 Sep 1701: Henry Borne conv. 100 a. (*), now Cotterels Purchase to John Cotterell (HW#2: 140).

31 Oct 1702: Henry Borne of BA Co., s. of William, conv. 198 a. of tract (all that is left of 400 a. after a portion is taken away by elder survs.) to Lawrence Draper (HW#2: 289).

17 March 1717: Lawrence Draper, s. of Capt. Lawrence Draper, conv. 198 a. (*) to John Stokes; deed traces ownership from Edward Boothby to William Bourne to Henry Bourne who found that tract contained only 298 a., of 400 a., and conv. 100 a. to John Cottrell, and 198 a. to Capt. Lawrence Draper. LD's w. Mary cons. (TR#A: 541).

4 Nov 1725: John Stokes of BA Co. conv. 400 a. (*) to dau. Frances and her husband Aquila Paca, and to the heirs of her body (IS#H: 200).

3 June 1729: John Borne conv. pt. Mould's Success to Edward Hall; grantor is now John Borne or Boreing of CE Co., tract was owned by William Borne or Boreing, then by his Henry, and then by Henry's s. John, the grantor (IS#K: 15).

9 July 1744: Avarilla Hall, widow and extx. of Edward Hall conv. 30 to 40 a. (*) to Col. John Hall; deed states that John Borne s. and heir of Henry Borne sold the land to Edward Hall, whose will left it to widow Avarilla (TB#C: 531).

1750: John Paca, Jr. owns 198 a. (1750 DB: 75).

MOUNT ARARAT

25 March 1724/5: Thomas Griffith of SM Co., Gent., gave p/a to William Cummings of AA Co., merchant, to take possession of (*), 150 a. in CE Co., and 500 a. of Eightrupp (formerly owned by Thomas Griffith's father, Thomas Griffith, dec.) and to lease them (IS#H: 139).

MOUNT GILBOA

See Horvath Plat: Elkridge.

5 Aug 1707: Hon. John Dorsey conv. (*), taken up by John Dorsey in 1706, to Richard Colegate, in consideration that Colegate has m. the dau. of Eleanor Herbert, who is now Rebecca Colegate (RM#HS: 569).

MOUNT HAYES

2 July 1695: 317 a. surv. for John Hayes on n. side of Back R. (MRR: 54).

11 Nov 1719: John Hayes conv. 370 [sic] a. (*) to Thomas Harris, with the agreement that the dower rights of Hayes' w. Mary Ann be excepted; on 1 Dec 1719 Hayes gave p/a to Mary Ann to acknowledge the sale of said 370 a. (TR#DS: fols. 12-13).

8 June 1737: Thomas Stansbury conv. 50 a. pt. (*) to Luke Stansbury and Tobias Stansbury, Jr. (IS#IK: f. 442).

27 Jan 1750; 1440 a. of Stansbury's Inheritance, comprising pt. (*) and Priviledge, pat. by Tobias Stansbury (MPL BY#1: 564 and BY#2: 339).

1750: Tobias Stansbury owned 50 a. (1750 DB).

c1754: Thomas Harris' widow paid rent on 266 a., pt. (*) and Priviledge (IBC: 41).

MOUNT HAZARD (Pt. ADDITION TO POOR JAMAICA MAN'S PLAGUE)

1 Jan 1730: Jonathan Tipton and w. Mary conv. 100 a. pt. (*) to Ann Attwood of AA Co., widow of Henry Atwood, and to Jane Atwood, minor, heir apparent to Henry Attwood (IS#L: 152).

MOUNT ORGAN

See Horvath Plat: Green Spring Valley.

11 May 1707: Matthew Organ of BA conv. 350 a. (*) to Christopher Randall. MO's w. Catherine cons. (RM#HS: 595).

31 Aug 1717: Christopher Randall conv. 350 a. (*) to John Newman. CR's w. Ann cons. (TR#A: 499).

14 May 1735: Rebecca Newman, widow of John, conv. pt. (*) to John Simkins (HWS#M: 216).

14 May 1735: Rebecca Newman, widow of John, conv. pt. (*) to Charles Motherby on condition he take care of her for life (HWS#M: 219).

28 Feb 1749: 28 Feb 1742: Lawrence Hammond and w. Avarilla conv. 50 a. pt. (*) and pt. Simkins Addition, left to Avarilla by her father John Simkins), to John Hawkins (TB#C: 169).

20 July 1749: John Simkins of BA conv. 25 a. Mount Organ and 35 a. Addition to Simkins Repose to John Hawkins. JS's w. Mary cons. (TR#C: 229).

2 Nov 1751: John Hawkins, with cons. of w. Mary, conv. 50 a. being pt. of Mount Organ and Addition to Simpkins Repose to John Shermadine (TR#D: 294; see also following deed on f. 296).

c1765/6: John Shelmerdine owns pt. (*) (AHAL).

MOUNT PLEASANT

1754: George Ogg conv. 238 a. Morgan's Tent Resurveyed, 30 a. Plumb Tree Bottom, and 60 a. (*) to Lovelace Gorsuch (BB#I: 458).

MOUNT PLEASANT

1704: Taken up by Nicholas Haile (See MHM 58:231).

1763/4: William Green owns 75 a. pt. (*), and 25 a. Addition to (*) (Sheriff Aquila Hall's Assessment Book, 3).

MOUNT PLEASANT

18 March 1746: Benjamin Barnes and w. Martha conv. 60 a. (*) to Robert Gilcresh (TB#E: 3320.

MOUNT PLEASANT, ADDITION TO

1763/4: William Green owns 75 a. pt. (*), and 25 a. Addition to Mount Pleasant (Sheriff Aquila Hall's Assessment Book, 3).

See MHM 58: 231.

MOUNT YEO

9 June 1683: 400 a. surv. for John Yeo; located on w. side of Susquehanna at the mouth of Deer Creek; Yeo is dead and his heirs live in the w. of England (MRR: 16).

MOUNTAIN (See COLE'S MOUNTAIN)

14 Sep 1741: Benjamin Hammond and w. Margaret conv. 50 a., $\frac{1}{2}$ (*), to Charles Robertson (TB#A: 25).

25 Aug 1742: Charles Robertson conv. 50 a. (*) to William Hamilton of Benjamin (TB#C: 40).

4 March 1747: Benjamin Hammond conv. 50 a. (*) to his s. William Hammond (TB#E: 674).

22 Oct 1747: Thomas Johnson conv. 10 a. pt. (*) to James Lee (TB#E: 576).

MOUNTENY

15 Nov 1750: John Colegate and Thomas Colegate conv. 300 a. including parts of Cole's Harbor and Mounteny (which Richard Colegate left to his sons) to Thomas Sheredine and Thomas Sligh. TC's w. Cassandra cons. (TR#D: 61).

MOUNTENY'S NECK

1662: Surv. for Alexander Mounteny, adj, to Cole's Addition (See MHM 15:118).

22 March 1685/6: Samuel Wheeler and w. Ann of CE Co. conv. 200 a. (*) to David Jones; SW and w. had appointed Thomas Lightfoot their atty. (RM#HS: 180).

3 March 1701: James Todd of BA conv. 160 a. pt. Mounteny's Neck and ... ½ a., Cole's Harbor, purch. by James Todd, to John Hurst (HW#2: 123).
13 Oct 1702: John Hurst of BA and w. Hannah conv. 135 ½ a. Cole's Harbor and 164 ½ a. Mounteny's Neck (formerly belonging to Alexander Mounteny), to Richard Colegate (HW#2: 196).
19 March 1749: John Hurst of BA conv. to Thomas Sheredine and Thomas Sligh: a) 135 a. Cole's Harbor, and b) 164 a. [Mountney's Neck?] formerly belonging to Alexander Mounteny and purch. by James Todd (TR#C: 419).

MULBERRY MOULD
19 June 1666: Briant O'Mely conv. 200 a. (*) on s. side of Bohemia R., to James Magriges (IR#PP: 57).

MULBERRY POINT
14 Dec 1708: John Campbell conv. 200 a. at head of Bush R. to Eleanor Campbell (TR#A: 71).
4 June 1713: Eleanor Campbell conv. 100 a. being ½ of (*) to her s. John Roberts (TR#A: 222).
13 Nov 1738: John Roberts als. Campbell conv. 200 a. (*) to Richard Caswell (HWS#1-A: 143).
22 March 1745: Richard Caswell, Gent., conv. 200 a. (*) to William Dallam (TB#E: 32).
6 Nov 1747: William Dallam, with cons. of w. Elizabeth, conv. 200 a. (*) to William Andrew, innholder (TB#E: 680).

MURDOCK'S (MURDAGH'S) CHANCE
3 Dec 1748: Daniel Murdoch conv. 100 a. (*) to Henry O'Neale (TR#C: 134).

MURPHY'S ADDITION
15 Dec 1704: 52 a. surv. for Patrick Murphy (Rent Rolls).
4 May 1726: Patrick Murphy, with cons. of w. Sarah, conv. 250 a. comprised of (*) and Murphy's Delight, to George Buchanan (IS#H: 237).

MURPHY'S ADVENTURE
March 1706: 250 a. surv. for William Murphy (Rent Rolls).

MURPHY'S DELIGHT
See KN Plat WO, and Horvath Plat: Granite.
4 May 1726: Patrick Murphy, with cons. of w. Sarah conv. 250 a. comprised of Murphy's Addition and (*), to George Buchanan (IS#H: 237).

MURPHY'S HAZARD
(Pt. ADDITION TO POOR
JAMAICA MAN'S PLAGUE)
31 May 1722: John Tipton and w. Mary conv. 114 a. (*), to Edward Murphy (IS#G: 46).
23 Dec 1723: Edward Murphy conv. 114 a. (*) to William Tipton (IS#G: 305).

MURPHY'S HAZARD (1734)
10 June 1734: 100 a. pat. to John Murphy (MPL EI#1: 513, and EI#3: 334).
12 Jan 1732 [sic]: John Murphy conv. 50 a. pt. of 100 a. (*) to John Thomas (IS#L: 320).
[date not given]: Timothy Murphy, s. and heir of John Murphy, dec., conv. 100 a. (*) to Aquila Hall. TM's w. Elizabeth cons. (B#H: 85).

MURPHY'S PLEASURE
Dec 1704: 98 a. surv. for Patrick Murphy (Rent Rolls).
5 March 1732; Samuel Maccubbin and w. Mary conv. 100 a. Cuckoldmaker's Palace, 98 a. (*), surv. 10 Jan 1705, and 52 a. The Addition, surv. 10 Jan 1705, to John Parrish (IS#L: 318).

MURPHY'S RETIREMENT
6 Sep 1749: William Murphy conv. 50 a. (*) to Philip Edelman of Lancaster Co., PA . Wm's w. Rachel cons.

MURRAY'S DESIRE
8 Dec 1749: Thomas Brothers of BA conv. 141 a. (*), as shown by cert. of surv. dated 15 Jan 1747, to Thomas Sheredine (TR#C: 361).

MURRAY'S MEADOWS
See Horvath Plat: Green Spring Valley.
27 March 1729: Melchizedek Murray of AA Co., with cons. of w. Sophia, conv. 100 a. (*) to William Handcock of AA Co. (IS#I: 319).
30 July 1745: William Hancock of AA Co., with cons. of w. Jane, conv. 100 a. (*) to John Metcalfe (TB#D: 268).
17 Dec 1745: John Metcalfe mortgaged 100 a. (*) to Thomas Norris (TB#D: 414).

MURRAY'S NEST
23 Feb 1715: Josephus Murray conv. 44 a. (*) to John McCarty (TR#A: 387).

MURRAY'S POINT
9 March 1722: Hannah Randall, widow, conv. to Christopher Randall, Gent., a 25 x 16 lot and house and Hannah Randall's land called (*) (IS#G: 100).
6 Jan 1723: Hannah Randall, widow, conv. 68 a. (*) to John Moale (IS#G: 236).

MURRAY'S RIDGE

23 June 1764: William Murray and w. Diana conv. 7 a. Merryman's Grotto and 68 a. pt. (*) to Wheeler Murray (B#N: 243).

1 April 1765: William Murray, with cons. of w. Dinah, conv. 53 a. (*) to John Foster (B#O: 145).

MY LADY'S MANOR

Shown on PW Plats AS and AT.

30 March 1739: Thomas Brerewood, formerly of Horton, England, now of BA Co., conv. 413 a. Woodcot, pt. (*) to William Brerewood of SO Co., MD; William was to pay his father, Francis Brerewood (HWS#1-A: 231).

7 June 1739: Thomas Brerewood conv. 100 a. to Thomas Anderson (HWS#1-A: 238).

5 June 1740: TB leased 200 a. to William Dallam for lives of WD, w. Elizabeth and s. Jonas (HWS#1-A: 428).

15 Nov 1740: 75 a. pt. surv. by John Bond, to John Strawbridge for lives of s. John, Jr., c2, dau. Eliza, 7, and dau. Mary, c5 (TB#C: 106).

15 Nov 1740: 100 a. leased to Daniel Pocock for lives of Susanna, 50, s. John, c14, s. Abel c7 (TB#C: 21).

7 Aug 1741: 122 a. to Edward Mortimer for lives of EM, w. Eleanor, and Easter Bray, dau. of Eleanor (HWS#1-A: 536).

7 Nov 1741: William Dallam released his 200 a. back to TB (TB#A: 47).

3 Feb 1742: TB leased 32⅔ a. to Martin Bacon as before; for same lives and rent (TB#C: 145).

15 Feb 1742: 95 a. to Henry Taylor for lives of HT, c32, Luke Wiley of Luke, c3, and Martha Wiley of Luke, c12 (TB#C: 151).

16 Feb 1742: 72 a. to William Armstrong for lives of WA, 27, w. Eliza, c26, and dau. Temperance, c6 (TB#C: 159).

16 Feb 1742: 28 a. to John Sharp for lives of JS, 29, w. Elizabeth, 32 and Nath. Shepperd of Wm (TB#C: 133).

16 Feb 1742: 100 a. plus 52½ a. to Benjamin Anderson for lives of BA, 33; w. Sarah, c35, and s. William, c14 (TB#C: 124).

22 Feb 1742: 195 a. to William Wright for lives of WW, c26, w. Sarah, c23, and dau. Mary, c4 mos. (TB#C: 211).

22 Feb 1742: 67½ a. to Luke Wiley, plus 37½ a. for same lives as before (TB#C: 143).

22 Feb 1742: 205 a. to Thomas Oakley for lives of TO, 30, w. Prudence c27, plus an addtional 23½ a. and 17½ a. for lives of above two plus JO, Jr., 1 (TB#C: 135).

8 July 1742: 75 a. to Luke Wiley for lives of LW, c36, LW, Jr., 3, and s. Walter, age c3 mos. (TB#C: 24).

26 July 1742: 172 a. (in 97 and 75 a. parcels) to William Roe for lives of WR 38, s. William, Jr., 6, and dau. Ann, c8 (both parcels had orig. been laid out for Aquila Carr (TB#C: 218).

15 Oct 1742: 150 a. to Thomas Marshall for lives of TM, 34, w. Sarah 22, and s. John, c1 (TB#C: 52).

15 Oct 1742: 99⅓ a. to Martin Bacon for lives of Martin, c26, w. Mary 22, and her s. William Watson, c5 (TB#C: 55).

25 Oct 1742: 106½ a. to Francis Hines for lives of FH 35, w. Frances c23, and s. Samuel, c2 (TB#C: 27).

25 Oct 1742: 123 to William Watkins for lives of WW 22, w. Ann, c28, and bro. John W., c15 (TB#C: 111).

13 Nov 1742: 120 a. to Walter Carr of CV Co., for lives of WC, c46, s. WC, Jr., c8, and s. Seaborn, c10 (TB#C: 79).

25 Nov 1742: 100 a. to James Fugate for lives of JF, c66, s. James als. Peter, c15 and s. James c13 (TB#C: 108).

25 Nov 1742: 55½ a. to John Higgins, Jr., for lives of JH, Jr., 22, w. Mary c17, and a bro. Daniel, c9 (TB#C: 115).

25 Nov 1742: 105 a. to Nathaniel Shepherd of BA Co.; NS 70, w. Elizabeth, 50, and s. John (by w. Elizabeth), c30; (TB#C: 85).

25 Nov 1742: To John Frizzell of AA Co., s. Gale, c19, s. Nathan, c12, and dau. Susanna, c15 (TB#C: 138).

25 Nov 1742: 108¾ to Charles Prosser, w. Mary, c30, dau. Eliza., c4, and dau. Sarah, c2 (TB#C: 141).

25 Nov 1742: 90 a. to Moses Collett, sd. MC, c24, Daniel Collett, c18, and William Anderson of Benjamin, c14 (TB#C: 127).

25 Nov 1742: 61¼ a. to Peter Knowles for PK, c26, w. Mary, c19, and s. Peter c1 (TB#C: 130).

25 Nov 1742: 100½ a. to Samuel Deason, for s. William, c5, dau. Jemima, c2, and dau. Mary, c2 (TB#C: 156).

25 Nov 1742: 70⅝ a. to Thomas Anderson, for TA, c41, William Wiley of Luke, c10, and Benjamin Anderson of Benjamin, c11 (TB#C: 118).

25 Nov 1742: 109 a. to John Armstrong, for JA 61, w. Rebecca 43, and s. Henry, c23, plus another 25 a. (TB#C: 146).

25 Nov 1742: 66½ a. to James Marsh for JM, c34, w. Margaret 23, and s. James, Jr. (TB#C: 149).

25 Nov 1742: 125 a. to Edmund Deason for Ed, c22, w. Eliz, c17, and dau Rebecca, c2mos (TB#C: 154).

25 Nov 1742: 33⅛ and 76¾ a. to Edward Mortimer, for EM, c39, w. Eleanor, c39 and Hester Bray, c18 (TB#C: 206).

25 Nov 1742: 100 a. to Jacob Frizzell of AA Co. for Jacob Frizzell, c21, Abraham Frizzell, Jr., c20, and Ann Taylor (TB#C: 82).

11 Dec 1742: 140½ a. to William Slade for lives of WS c26, w. Eliz. c20, and dau. Margaret c2 (TB#C: 199).

11 Dec 1742: 150 a. to Thomas Slade of AA Co., for lives of sd. TS c25, Anne Besson c18 and Margaret Slade c1. (TB#C: 209).

14 Dec 1742: 118 a. to Jacob Bull for lives of s. Isaac c15, s. Samuel c17, and s. Edmund c13 (TB#C: 121).

18 Jan 1743: 57½ a. to Gale Frizzell for lives of Susannah c20, John, Jr., s. of John c18, and William Blizard, s. of Elizabeth c12 (TB#C: 443).

20 Jan 1743: 106½ a. formerly held by Thomas Franklin to Edward Mortimer for lives of EM c38, w. Eleanor c39 and Hester Bray c18 (TB#C: 445).

10 Feb 1743: 100 a. to James Maydwell for lives of JM 29, Eliza Ady Garrison c22, and her s. Job Garrison c2 (TB#C: 447).

15 Feb 1743: An additional 52¾ a. to Daniel Pocock for lives of Daniel's w. c53, s. John c17, and s. Abel c10 (TB#C: 450).

16 Feb 1743: 100 a. to Israel Standiford for lives of sd. IS c23, w. Cassandra c17, and Benjamin Anderson c11 (TB#C: 432).

26 March 1743: 28½ a. to William Slade for lives as above (TB#C: 201).

30 March 1743: 30 a. to John Wiley for lives of JW, JR. c15, s. Benjamin c7, and s. Abel c5 (TB#C: 201).

12 April 1743: Nathaniel Shepherd assigns to his w. Elizabeth and ch. his lease to pt. (*); mentions ch. John, Temperance, Tesia, and Elizabeth (TB#C: 265).

12 April 1743: 96⅓ a. to William Hunt for lives of WH c33, w. Eliz. c24, and dau. Sarah c4 (TB#C: 231).

21 April 1743: 75 a. to John Fuller of Thos., for lives of JF c28, w. Ruth c25, s. Thomas c3 (TB#C: 233).

25 April 1743: 175 and 2/5 a. to Michael Connolly for lives of MC 30, s. Henry c3, and dau. Bridget c3 (TB#C: 228).

27 April 1743: 110 a. to John Huggins for lives of JH c43, s. John, Jr. c21, and s. William c12 (TB#C: 235).

15 July 1743: 131¼ a. to John Grimes for lives of JG 36, w. Mary c35, and dau. Mary c8 (TB#C: 284).

15 Nov 1743: 102½ a. to John Tyler for lives of JT c44, dau. Tirla c6, and dau. Eliz c4 (TB#C: 431).

15 Nov 1743: 61¼ a. to Jonathan Ady for lives of JA c24, w. Rebecca c17, and dau. Rachel c14 days (TB#C: 433).

15 Nov 1743: 75 a. to Thomas Wilmouth for lives of TW c31, s. Thomas c4, and dau. Mary c2 (TB#C: 436).

15 Nov 1743: 50 a. formerly leased to Aquila Carr plus 32 a. additional land to John Hooper for lives of JH c44, Mary Fugate now Mary Knowles c20, and Ann Fugate dau. of James c7 (TB#C: 440).

15 Nov 1743: 70½ a. to John Spenceley for lives of JS c24, w. Jane c24, and dau. Elizabeth age 6 weeks (TB#C: 438).

30 Dec 1743: 40½ a. to John Fuller of Thos. for lives of JF c29, w. Ruth c26 and s. Thomas c4 (TB#C: 552).

2 Jan 1744: 112 a. to Andrew Rowland for lives of AR c27, w. Margaret c23 and dau. Frances c3 (TB#D, f: 221).

30 Jan 1744: 82½ a. to John Hooper (orig. leased to Hooper, pt. of which was laid out for ---Carr, 50 a.; and additional 32½ a.; JH flung up the lease and requested TB transfer the lease to Thomas Fisher, who has absconded; this lease returned the land to John Hooper for lives of JH c45, Mary Fugate (now Knowler) c21, and Ann Fugate, dau. of James, c8 (TB#C: 225).

12 April 1744: Thomas Brerewood leased to John Barton 72¼ a., being pt. of My Lady's Manor, the lease to run for lifetimes of John Barton, age 29, his w. Ann, age c20, and Jemima Barton, age c16 mos. (TB#C: 516).

12 April 1744: 100 a. to John Bourne for lives of JB c28, dau. Mary Davis c23, and John Anderson c4 (TB#C: 502).

12 April 1744: 100 a. to Edward Haley for lives of EH c37, dau. Mary c5, and dau. Ann c4 (TB#C: 505).

12 April 1744: 70½ a. plus 60 a. to John Spencely for lives of JS c24, w. Jane c24, and dau. Eliz. c6 mos. (TB#C: 509).

12 April 1744: 108¾ a. to Charles Prosser for lives of his w. Mary c31, dau. Eliz. c5, and dau. Sarah c3 (TB#C: 492).

12 April 1744: 95 a. to William Wright was leased land on 22 Feb 1742, and now relinquishes all but 95 a.; lease of 95 a. for lives of WW c27, w. Sarah c24, dau. Mary c18 mos. (TB#C: 513).

24 April 1744: 177 a. to William Row for lives of WR c40, s. WR, Jr. c8, and dau. Ann c10 (TB#C: 488).

1 May 1744: 100 a. (relinquished by William Wright) to Francis Hines for lives of FH c39, w. Frances c23, and s. Samuel c4; also an additional 50 a. (TB#C: 556).

21 Aug 1744: 100 a. (orig. leased on 12 April 1744 to Edwd. Hayley, who the lease to said Paul Garron) for lives of PG c35, s. John c12, and s. James c9 (TB#C: 583).

1 Sep 1744: 50 a. plus another 50 a. to William Harman, for lives of WH c36, w. Sarah, and her ch. Edward Powell c3 (TB#C: 587).
1 Sep 1744: 50 a. adj. his old tract to Thomas Slade for lives of TS c26, Ann Besson of A. A. Co. c19, and Mary Slade c2 (TB#C: 540).
3 Sep 1744: 100 a. formerly leased to John Bourne who surrendered the land for use by William Bull for lives of WB c25, w. Martha c24, and dau. Eleanor c3 (TB#C: 593).
10 Sep 1744: 139 a. to Benjamin Coale for lives of BC c29, w. Margaret c25, and BC, Jr. c½ yr. (TB#C: 596).
25 Sep 1744: 112 a. to Nicholas Seavers and John Wood for lives of NS c38, JW c50, Eliz. Seaver c33, Lidia Seaver c10, Prudence Seaver c5, and Ann Wood c44 (TB#C: 616).
1 Oct 1744: 32½ a. formerly leased to John Hooper, who relinquished to Thomas Fisher for lives of TF c34, Martha Harding c24, and Martha Terry c40 (TB#C: 620).
5 Oct 1744: 108 a. to John Rockhold for lives of JR c33, s. Jacob R. c4, s. John R., Jr. c2 (TB#C: 623).
2 Nov 1744: 95 a. (being pt. of 190 a. formerly leased to William Wright on 12 April 1744) to John Rockhold for lives of JR c33, s. Jacob 4, and s. JR, Jr. c2 (TB#C: 626).
15 Dec 1744: 39 a. to Thomas Beamsley for lives of TB c40, Mary B. c32, and Sarah Deason, dau. of Samuel, age c4 (TB#C: 365).
20 Dec. 1744: 100 a. to Edward Haley for lives of EG c38, dau. Mary c6, and dau. Ann, age (not given) (TB#C: 176).
10 March 1745: 75 a. to John Christeson (formerly in poss. of Thos. Wilmouth, then in poss. of John Richardson) for lives of JC c22, w. Margaret c19, and Thomas Hamilton c16 (TB#C: 371).
10 April 1745: 100 a. (formerly surv. for Francis Hines who has "flung up" the said lease) plus 50 a. to Paul Garron for lives of PG c40, s. James c3 mos., and dau. Mary c5 (TB#D: 165).
12 July 1745: John Huggins, Jr., mortgaged two lots (leased 25 Nov 1742 and 27 April 1743 to John Huggins, Sr., now dec.) to Thomas Brerewood (TB#D: 279).
3 Dec 1745: Jonathan Ady, cooper, mortgaged 61 a. pt. (*) to John Ridgely (TB#D: 407).
10 Dec 1745: 83⅓ a. to Samuel Talbie for lives of ST c35, w. Eliz. c23, and s. Zephaniah c3 (TB#C: 217).
16 Dec 1745: John Shewbridge mortgaged 70 a. pt. (*) to Charles Ridgely (TB#D: 417).
10 March 1746: Michael Conely assigned a lease for 175 a. of (*) to James Richard (TB#E: 336).
1 Sep 1746: 139 a. formerly surv. for Benjamin Coale, who has run away; now leased to John Crockett for lives of JC c30, w. Ann c30, and Ann Row dau. of Wm. Row, c8 (TB#C: 368).
10 Oct 1746: 112 a. to Jonathan Ady (land had formerly been leased to Nicholas Seaver and John; Wood has absconded, and Seaver surrendered the lease to TB; TB grants new lease to Jonathan Ady for lives of JA c27, w. Rebecca c22, dau. Rachel c3 (TB#E: 356).

NANJEMOY

2 Oct 1685: George Thompson of SM Co. conv. 375 a. (*) to Richard Tydings(?) of AA Co. (RM#HS: 164).
25 June 1719: Robert Crump and w. Eliza of QA Co. conv. 375 a., being ½ of (*) to Philip Thomas of AA Co. (TR#DS: 47).
27 Dec 1726: Michael Pasquinet of Bath Co., NC, and w. Charity give p/a to loving cousin John Belt, to sell (*); p/a proved in AA Co. on 26 Aug 1727 by oath of John Peddicort, Jr., who was in NC in Dec 1726 (IS#I: 36).
12 Feb 1727: Michael Pasquinet of Bath Co., NC, and w. Charity, dau. and devisee of Richard Tydings, Sr., conv. 375 a. (*) to John Belt, Jr., by John Belt, Sr., their atty. (IS#I: 61).
3 Oct 1748: Philip Thomas of AA Co. deeded a moiety of (*), 187½ a. to Thomas Harrison (TR#C: 99).
4 Oct 1748: Philip Thomas of AA Co. deeded a moiety of (*), 187½ a. to Thomas Harrison. PT's w. Ann cons. (TR#C: 89).
12 Dec 1750: Charity Sellman, dau. of Richard Tydings of AA Co., conv. 375 a. (*) to Thomas Harrison (TR#DS: 107).

NARROW NECK

4 Feb 1697: William Hollis and w. Mary conv. 100 a. (*) to John Hall (IS#IK: 214).
5 March 1727: William Byfoot and w. Sarah conv. 50 a. (*) to Benjamin Hanson in exch. for 100 a. Essex and 100 a. Locust Neck (IS#I: 50).
5 March 1744: Thomas Donovan and w. Frances conv. to John Hanson s. of Benjamin their share of (*). Deed states that John Hall of Bush R. d. owning 100 a. (*), which desc. to his two daughters and coheirs: Sarah (who m. William Byfoot and conv., her share to Benjamin Hanson, dec.), and Frances, who m. Thomas Donavin; the latter now conv. their share to John Hanson (TB#D: 51).

NARROWS (THE) (1678)

22 March 1678: 100 a. surv. by George Yates on Patapsco R. on n. side of Stony Creek; assigned to Francis Leafe; later possessed by William McCarty (MRR: 103).

9 Sep 1679: Pat. to Francis Leafe, bricklayer, of CV Co. (RM#HS: 22).
29 Dec 1680: Francis Leafe and w. Sarah conv. (*) to Jenkin Smith (RM#HS: 22).
24 Dec 1684: Jenkin Smith, planter of CV Co. conv. 100 a. (*) to Richard Robeson or Robinson. JS' w. Ann cons. (RM#HS: 222).

NARROWS (THE) (1695)

11 Sep 1695: 77 a. surv. for James Maxwell on n. side of Gunpowder (MRR: 55).

NASH'S REST

24 Oct 1661: A 200 a. tract surv. for John Collett; later possessed by William Dennis (MRR: 93).
2 March 1662/3: John Collett conv. 200 a. (*) to Abraham Clarke, on n. side of the Patapsco R. (RM#HS: 2,7,20).
2 March 1662/3: John Collett conv. 200 a. (*) to Abraham Clarke a second time. By an appendant deed, 7 March 1662/3, Abraham Clarke shipwright, conv. his interest to Thomas Montross (RM#HS: 8).
13 April 1664: Thomas Montross conv. his interest to John Robinson of Mockjack Bay, VA (RM#HS: 8).
23 April 1664: John Robinson conv. his interest to Nicholas Rackstone of Mockjack Bay, VA (RM#HS: 8).
3 May 1674: Nicholas Ruxstone and w. Alice conv. 200 a. (*) to Thomas Jones, boatwright; deed states land was pat. 3 June 1663 by John Collett (G#J: 280; TR#RA: ...).
3 May 1674: Alice, w. of Nicholas Ruxton appoints Richard Ball her atty. to conv. 200 a. to Thomas Jones. (G#J: 281).
24 May 1735: John Gray and w. Anne of AA Co., conv. 200 a. (*) to Zachariah Gray (HWS#M: 298).

NATHAN'S DESIRE

18 Aug 1764: Nathan Chapman conv. 25 a. Nathan's Desire and 50 a. Buck's Forest to Francis Brothers. NC's w. Rebecca cons. (B#N: 318).

NATHAN'S FOREST

30 June 1730: 100 a. pat. by Thomas Gorsuch (MPL PL#8: 41; IL#B: 263).
See Horvath Plat: Reisterstown.
2 April 1737: Thomas Gorsuch conv. 100 a. (*) to William Rogers (IS#IK: 421).

NATTYS ISLAND

7 Nov 1753: Christopher Sheppard conv. to John Atkinson 100 a. The Marsh (granted to Joshua Wood, conv. by his s. and heir-at-law Joshua Wood to Rowland Sheppard, father of said Christopher), and 10 a. (*) (BB#I: 115).

NECESSITY

19 Nov 1747: Richard Rhodes and w. Magdalena, and James Amos and his w. Hannah, conv. 100 a. (*) to Robert Collins (TB#E: 601).
2 Nov 1748: Richard Rhodes and James Amos conv. 100 a. (*) to Robert Collins (TR#C: 107).

NEGLECT

-- March 1707: 100 a. surv. for John Chaffinch; 10 May 1709: Pat. to Chaffinch (MPL DD#5: 550, PL#3: 120).
5 Oct 1736: James Isham of BA Co. innholder conv. 50 a. (*) to John Hatton of BA Co., tailor (TB#A: 83).
3 March 1741: James Isham actually conv. 50 a. (*) to John Hatton. the document of 5 Oct 1736 was a bond for conveyance (TB#A: 85).
7 May 1745: John Hatton, tailor, conv. 27 a. pt. Moorefields, and 50 a. the Neglect to William Dallam. JH's w. Sarah cons. (TB#D: 142).

NEIGHBOR'S GOOD WILL

3 Sep 1738: William Allein, with cons. of w. Mary, conv. 80 a. (*) to John Prible (HWS#1-A: 273).

NEIGHBORHOOD

6 Sep 1733: Charles Carroll of Annapolis conv. (*) pt. of 6000 a. with other tracts to Jacob Giles and Isaac Webster (HWS#M: 12).
10 March 1735: Isac Webster (and w. Margaret) and Isaac Giles (and w. Hannah) conv. 754 a. (*) to Michael Webster (HWS#M: 394).
10 March 1735: Michael Webster and w. Elizabeth conv. 372 a. including ½ of (*) to Henry Jones of Chester Co., PA. (HWS#M: 397).
3 Aug 1737: Michael Webster and w. Elizabeth conv. 50 a. pt. (*) to John Farmer (HWS#M: 12).
13 Aug 1737: Michael Webster of BA Co. and w. Elizabeth sell pt. (*) to Joseph Wilson (HWS#1-A, folio 3).

NEIGHBORHOOD

1750: James Death owned pt. (*) (1750 DB).

NEIGHBORLY KINDNESS

3 Sep 1747: Charles Carroll of Annapolis conv. 100 a. (*) to Frederick Cryder (TB#E: 636).

NEIGHBOR'S AFFINITY

5 Nov 1703: Samuel Sicklemore and w. Sarah conv. 400 a. of (*) to William Jones of Upper End of Cliffs, CV Co. (HW#2: 302).

29 Nov 1709: Samuel Sicklemore conv. ½ of 400 a. (*) to Benjamin Braine of London; tract was granted to Samuel Sicklemore by Lord Baltimore on 1 June 1701; Sarah Sicklemore signed as atty.-in-fact for Samuel Sicklemore. (TR#A: 22).
14 June 1711: Samuel Sicklemore, Sr., conv. 200 a., pt. 400 a. Neighbor's Affinity to s. Sutton Sicklemore; other tracts to other ch.; they are all to live together until they marry, and to teach Thomas Wriothesley Sicklemore to read and write (see also Sicklemore's Dock and Wolves' Harbor (TR#A: 244).
7 Aug 1723: Sutton Sicklemore conv. 300(?) (may be 200 a.) ½ of Neighbor's Affinity (deeded to him by his father) to George ... (IS#G: 187).
1729: George Read conv. 150 a. pt. (*) to John Gardiner (IS#K: 234).
4 June 1747: Samuel Hart of AA Co., conv. ½ of (*) and 150 a. being ½ of Body's Adventure, to Dr. James Walker of AA Co., and Dr. William Lyon of BA Co., and gave p/a to JW and WL to pay his debts in property (TB#E: 402).
26 Aug 1749: Samuel Harte and w. Catherine, and Elizabeth Gardner, all of AA Co., conv. to Thomas Harrison, ½ of (*) which was laid out for Samuel Sickelmore, sold by his s. Sutton to George Reade, who sold it to John Gardiner, father of the said Catherine and Elizabeth (TR#C: 296).
1750: John Gardner owns 200 a. pt. (*) (1750 DB: 93).
4 May 1751: Jacob Jones, s. and heir of Benjamin Jones who was bro. and heir of William Jones of CV Co., conv. 235 a. pt. Neighbor's Affinity (400 a. in all) to Thomas Harrison. JJ's w. Rachel cons. Deed refers to HW#2: 302 (TR#D: 136).

NEVE'S CHOICE

4 Aug 1668: Robert Neife, planter, conv. 250 a. (*) to William Pearce on e. side of Fendall's Creek; Elizabeth Neife signed with grantor (IR#PP: 63).
1 Nov 1670: William Pearce, planter, and w. Isabell conv. 150 a. (*) to Fendall's Creek, to Thomas Weymouth and John Powell (IR#PP: 91).
1 Nov 1670: William Pearce, planter, and w. Isabel conv. 100 a. (*) to Philip Macanady (IR#PP: 92).
5 March 1672: Philip Macanaday, planter, conv. 100 a. (*) to Richard Adams. Dorothy Macanaday signed with grantor (TR#RA: 35).
5 Aug 1672: John Powell, planter, conv. to Thomas Weymouth, 75 a. being ½ 150 a. (*) bought by Powell and Weymouht from William Pearce (TR#RA: 52).

NEW GERMANY

16 Feb 1761: Philip Adleman, conv. pt. (*) to Philip Baker. PA's w. Margaret cons. (B#H: 515).
30 March (1763?): Philip Baker, conv. 178 a. pt. (*) to Avarilla Boring. PB's w. Luriana cons. (B#L: 141).

NEW PARKE

25 Sep 1683: 150 a. surv. for John Yeo near a place called The Level; bequeathed by Yeo to Garrett Garrettson (MRR: 8).
29 Dec 1683: John Yeo, Gent., for love and affection, conv. to his son-in-law Garrett Fitzgarret (effective at grantor's decease), 150 a. (*); deed mentioned the grantee's mother, Somelia Yeo (RM#HS: 62).
7 March 1738: George Garrettson, s. and heir of Garrett Garrettson, conv. 75 a., ½ of (*) to his bro. James Garrettson (HWS#1-A: 196).
6 Nov 1740; George Garrettson, s. and heir of Garrett Garrettson, conv. 75 a., ½ of (*) to his bro. John Garrettson (HWS#1-A: 445).

NEW STADT

19 May 1725: Samuel Young of AA Co. conv. 400 a. Holland's Lot and 500 a. (*) to his s. Joseph Young of KE Co.; Samuel had purch. land from Thomas Francisa (Holland?) on 1 Jan 1696/7 (IS#H: 122).

NEW TOWN

18 April 1723: John Baldwin of CE Co., Gent., conv. 200 a. (*) to John Giles (IS#G: 196).
5 Jan 1731/2: Nathaniel Giles, mariner, conv. 200 a. (*) to John Stewart of AA Co. (IS#L: 197).

NEW WESTWOOD

22 Nov 1750: Josias Middlemore, practitioner in Physick, conv. (*) and Westwood to Ephraim Andrew. JM's w. Frances cons. (TR#D: 239).
29 June 1751: Thomas Gash, conv. to Edward Wakeman 60 a. being pt. of (*) and Gash's Purchase. TG's w. Johanna cons. (TR#D: 245)

NEW YEAR'S GIFT

15 June 1711: Charles Carroll of AA Co. conv. 1300 a. (*) to James Carroll (TR#A: 166).

NEW YEAR'S PURCHASE

25 Feb 1684: 500 a. pat. to Richard Tydings (MPL 25: 34, 31: 521).
5 Feb 1683: 500 a. surv. for Richard Tydings who bequeathed it to his daus. Pretiosa (m. Dutton Lane; she sold her half to Thomas Hooker and

Richard Gist on 15 Jan 1708; Gist sold tract to Philip Dowell, who m. Mary Tydings) (TB#E: 522).

3 April 1704: John Hall signed a statement that Dutton Lane is a debtor on 19 years rent for New Year's Purchase (HW#2: 73).

15 Jan 1708/9: Dutton Lane and w. Pretiosa sold their moiety of 250 a. (being ½ of the 500 a.) New Year's Purchase to Thomas Hooker and Richard Guest (RM#HS: 634).

5 April 1717: Philip Dowell and w. Mary conv. ½ of (*) to sons John and Luke Dowell of AA Co.; land was left by LWT of Richard Tydings to his daughter Mary, now w. of Philip Dowell (TR#A: 436).

12 Oct 1722: Thomas Hooker and Richard Guest sold pt. of (*) to Philip Dowell; they had been conv. the land by Dutton Lane who had married Pretiosa Tydings, daughter of Richard Tydings. Wives Eleanor Hooker and Zipporah Gist cons. (IS#G: 68).

4 April 1747: John Dowell, with cons. of w. Susanna, Luke Dowell, with cons. of w. Ann, and Philip Dowell, with cons. of w. Mary, all of CV Co., conv. (*) to Alex. Lawson and Co. (TB#E: 522).

NEWSAM'S MEADOWS

20 March 1736: William Smith agreed to conv. to Helen Newsam 254 a. Benjamin's Choice (granted to Thomas Hedge); in exch. for 200 a. Contrivance, and 50 a. Newsam's Meadow (HWS#1-A: 299).

NO MAN (or NO NAME)

30 Dec 1698: Giles Stevens and w. Rebecca conv. 120 a. (*) to Joseph Peake; land was originally laid out for Giles Stevens, father of the grantor (TR#RA: 320).

3 Jan 1698/9: Joseph Peake conv. his interest in (*) to his w. Jane (TR#RA: 322).

July 1731: Benjamin Knight and w. Jane conv. 120 a. (*) to Robert Robertson (IS#L: 167).

13 Dec 1732: James Gallion conv. 50 a. (*) to John Gallion (IS#L: 346).

NOBLE'S CRAFT

31 May 1748: Nathan Rigbie, Jr., leased 52 a. (*), pt. of His Lordship's Reserve, to John Gray (TB#E: 721).

NOBLE'S DESIRE

7 Nov 1717: William Noble and w. Elizabeth conv. 92 a. Noble's Desire and Turkey Range to John Walker of BA Co. (TR#A: 61).

5 Nov 1719: John Walker conv. Noble's Desire and Turkey Range to Henry Wetherall referred to in deed below.

2 March 1719/20: Henry Wriothesley conv. above two tracts to Simon Pearson in exch. for 200 a. Pearson's Outlet (RM#HS: 660).

7 April 1720: John Walker and w. Mary conv. 92 a. Noble's Desire and Turkey Range to Simon Pearson (TR#DS: 173).

21 May 1722: (See RM#HW: 683): Simon Pearson, of BA Co., weaver, again conv. Pearson's Outlet, 200 a. to Henry Wetherall, in exch. for Henry Wetherall's parts of Noble's Desire, and Turkey Range, conv. to HW by John Walker on 5 Nov 1719; Simon's w. Sarah cons. (RM#HS: 683).

7 Aug 1730: Simon Pearson conv. to William Buckner all of Noble's Desire, all of Turkey Range, and all of Pearsons Enlargement (IS#L: 13).

7 Feb 1732: Thomas Buckner of VA conv. to Simon Pearson three tracts: Turkey Range, pt. of Noble's Desire, and all of Pearson's Enlargement, which Pearson had conv. to Thomas' bro. William Buckner (who d. leaving a widow Patience, now w. of George Elliott; Patience Elliott relinquishes her right of dower (IS#L: 328).

22 Feb 1736: Simon Pearson of BA Co., by virtue of an Act of Assembly, assigned to Edward Hall, late Sheriff of BA Co., three parcels: pt. Turkey Range, (*), and Pearsons' Privilege (IS#IK: 351).

19 June 1738: Edward Hall, Esq., formerly Sheriff of BA Co. conv. 148 a. pt. of Turkey Range, (*), and Pearsons' Privilege, to Beviss Spain [Pain] (HWS#1-A: 86).

17 March 1746: Land Commission: Thomas Bond deposed that William Noble in his life time showed him the beginning place (TB#E: 352).

22 July 1748: Bevis Pain mortgaged 148 a. pt. (*) to George and John Rigdon (TR#C: 189).

17 Aug 1754: William Noble of Augusta Co., VA, s. and heir of William Noble of BA Co., dec., conv. parts of Noble's Desire and Turkey Range to William Dallam (BB#I: 297).

NONE SO GOOD IN FINLAND (or FIRM LAND)

3 March 1668/9: John Cock conv. 200 a. (*) to Edmund Webb (IR#PP: 69).

4 March 1688/9: Bartlett Hendrickson conv. 200 a. (*) to John Cocke (IR#PP: 72, 259).

30 Nov 1669: Edmund Webb of AA Co., by Capt. Thomas Howell, his atty., conv. 200 a. (*) to Thomas King (IR#PP: 82).

NORBERRY

14 Jan 1680/1: James Thompson, smith, stated he had received 2 years' rent by Michael Judd for

180 a. (*) and 300 a. Colletts Neglect (RM#HS: 61).

NORRAM

8 Dec 1684: 37 a. surv. for Robert Owlas (Rent Rolls).

NORRIS' ADDITION

10 Dec 1747: Benjamin Norris conv. 100 a. (*) to his dau. Elizabeth and her husband James Hughes (TB#E: 637).

NORRIS' CHANCE

13 July 1743: 100 a. pat. by Thomas Norris (MPL LG#B: 696, LG#E: 137).

See Horvath Plat: Green Spring Valley.

7 May 1753: Thomas Norris and w. Avarilla conv. pt. of (*) to Dr. John Stevenson (TR#D: 550).

NORRIS'S VENTURE

8 March 1746: John Norris conv. Stephen Onion any iron ore that may be found in (*) or Expectation (TR#C: 197).

18 Aug 1748: John Norris, with cons. of w. Ann, conv. 50 a. (*), orig. granted to John Norris, conv. 50 a. (N) and pt. Expectation, to their s. James; deed to be effective after decease of said John and Ann (TR#C: 36).

NORTH CAROLINA

1745: 950 a. surv. for James Richards.

See Horvath Plat: Pikesville.

13 Oct 1748: James Richard, merchant, mortgaged 50 a. Jones Farm, 150 a. (*) and 646 a. Carolina Felix to Charles Ridgely and Joseph Taylor, exec. of William Fell (TR#C: 82).

NORTH HUNDRED

9 Dec 1684: John Martin to John Boring. On s. side of Back R. near Papapsco (RM#HS: 115).

NORTH POINT

31 Jan 1679/80: Solomon Thomas of CV, s. and heir of Thomas Thomas, conv. to Charles Gorsuch his share of 1100 a. called North Point (Deed, bond and letter of atty., IR#PP: 48).

9 Feb 1679/80: Walter Dickenson of TA Co. conv. to Charles Gorsuch: a) his share of 1100 a. laid out for Thomas Thomas and William Batten; b) 150 a. Upper Spring Neck; and c) Dickenson. (IR#PP: 58).

7 March 1733/4: Samuel Chew gave to Richard Jones of BA Co., a receipt for 190 a. Denton, 80 a. Walker's Neck, 100 a. Hooper's Island, 330 a. (*), 546 a. Old Road, 120 a. Industry, 1000 a. Shawan Hunting Ground, 50 a. Thorold's Nest, 100 a. Luke's Privilege, and 100 a. Bagford (HWS#M: 193).

NORTH YARMOUTH

14 Sep 1683: A 200 a. tract of surv. for James Fugate at the head of Swan Creek now in possession of Robert Gibson; later held by Thomas Brown (MRR: 9).

1 May 1686: James Fugett leased 200 a. to Miles Gibson of BA Co., Gent. (HW#2: 136).

5 May 1686: James Fugett and w. Dorothy conv. 200 a. to Miles Gibson, as well as some cattle (some of which fomerly belonged to James Ives, dec.); also a servant named Thomas Wallingford (RM#HS: 186).

1 April 1702: Robert Gibson, s. and heir of Miles Gibson, assigned his interest in above tract to Thomas Browne; tract was mortgaged (HW#2: 137).

24 Jan 1707/8: Thomas Browne of BA Co. left (*) jointly to Edward Swan and Bartholomew Welch (MCW#III: 114).

-- July 1711: Edward Swan of BA Co., tailor, conv. to William Cook his interest in ½ of (*), left him by virtue by will of Thomas Browne of BA Co., dec. (TR#A: 156).

5 May 1734: Thomas Browne and w. Sarah gave bond for conv. of (*) to Samuel Howell of BA Co., innholder (HW#WM, f: 134).

7 June 1743: Thomas Browne conv. 100 a. pt. (*) to Daniel Johnson of Newcastle Co., DE, assignee of Robert ... assignee of Samuel Howell who was the purchaser of the land from Thomas Browne. Browne's w. Sarah cons. (TB#C: 276).

NORTHAMPTON

3 March 1742: Stephen Wilkinson conv. 100 a. (*) on draft of Brice's Run, to Thomas Harrison (TB#C: 174).

NORTHAMPTON (1750)

2 April 1745: Anne Hill of PG Co., Gentlewoman, and sons Clement and Henry Hill conv. 1500 a. (*) to Charles Ridgely. Mary w. of Clement Hill, and Mary Ann w. of Henry Hill, cons. (TB#D: 94).

1758: 1962 a. for Charles Ridgely; on PW Plat H.

NORTHSTEAD

1769: Taken up; on KN Plat WO.

NORTHWICK

6 May 1680: Maj. Thomas Long and w. Jane of Back R. conv. 200 a. (of 450 a. pat. to Thomas Long) ...Wick on Middle R., 200 a. to Thomas Gibson (IR#PP: 51).

3 June 1682: Thomas Long and w. Jane conv. 100 a. (*) to Thomas Peart (Deed and bond, IR#AM: 170).

6 June 1682: Thomas Long and w. Jane conv. 100 a. of 450 a. (*) to Thomas Gibson of CH Co. (IR#AM: 183).

29 Oct 1745: John Long, s. and heir of Thomas Long, dec., conv. (part?) of 457 a. (*) to Christopher Duke; pt. of the tract desc. to the grantor by the death of said Thomas Long TB#E: 8).

13 Oct 1752: William Guy of CH Co., and w. Elizabeth, only dau. of Jno., Gibson, s. of Thomas who was s. of Thomas, conv. 100 a. (Northwick), to Tobias Stansbury (TR#D: 516).

NORTON'S ADDITION
(Pt. BACHELOR'S DELIGHT)

6 June 1710: Samuel Arden conv. 41 a. (*) to John Norton (TR#A: 67).

31 March 1739: William Norton and w. Ann conv. 50 a. Jones Addition and 40 a. (*) to William Lynch (HWS#A-1, 218).

NORTON'S LOT (Pt. JONES INHERITANCE)

10 May 1707: John Boring, conv. parcel called (*), pt. of a larger tract called Jones' Inheritance to John Norton. JB's w. Mary cons. (RM#HS: 612).

NORWICH (See OLD'S REST)

9 Aug 1750: Nicholas Hutchins, conv. ⅓ pt. of 100 a. (*) to Isaac Raven. NH's w. Elizabeth cons. (TR#D: 85).

NORWOOD'S DELIGHT

10 July 1725: 100 a. pat. by Samuel Norwood (MPL PL#6: 318, IL#A: 557).

See Horvath Plat: Granite.

1729: Samuel Norwood conv. 100 a. (*) to William Peddicord (IS#K: 244).

NORWOOD'S DISCOVERY

3 Feb 1724: The estate of Edward Norwood included 100 a. (*) and 100 a. Ruth's Lot; it was distributed by Sheriff of William Smith to Thomas Worthington. The deed mentioned an Act of Assembly passed 20 Feb 1724 to discharge said Edward Norwood from debt and to deliver him from gaol (IS#G: 410, 412).

NOTCH POINT

29 April 1669: Ralph Williams, merchant from Bristol, conv. to Thomas Todd, merchant, 330 a. (*) at Wignall's Creek; said tract was taken up by William Batten, and sold to Walter Dickenson, who sold it to Williams (IR#PP: 71).

NOTLEY'S ISLAND

22 April 1700: William Loney and w. Jane conv. 100 a. (*), surv. 16 Nov 1668, and 100 a. Penny Come Quick to Robert Gibson; the tracts were left by Overton to Jane, his sole heir, now w. of Loney (HW#2: 54).

10 July 1701: Robert Gibson conv. (*) and Penny Come Quick to Roger Matthews (HW#2: 81).

NOVA SCOTIA

9 June 1684: 1500 a. pat. to Thomas Sterling of CV Co., Gent. (MPL 25: 92, 33:64).

1500 a. surv. for Thomas Sterling, who by his LWT left 500 a., pt. of (*), to William Derumple, who d. and land desc. to his s. John, who also d. and land desc. to his (John's) s. John.

25 April 1746: Christian Adair of KE Co., widow of Alexander Adair of KE Co., conv. 500 a. pt. (*) to Robert Adair of Baltimore County (TB#E: 55).

-----1748: Robert and Christian Adair conv. 1000 a. (*) to Col. John Hall et al. (TR#C: 297).

12 Dec 1748: John Derumple of CV Co. conv. 500 a. pt. (*) to John Bond; the tract was originally laid out for Thomas Sterling, who left it to his bro. William Derumple who left it to his s. John, who left it to his s. John, the present grantor (TR#C: 465).

11 Oct 1749: Christian Adair, widow, extx. of Dr. Alexander Adair, and only heir of Thomas Sterling of KE Co., dec. (who first took up said tract), and Robert Adair, s. of Alexander and Christian, conv. 100 a., pt. of (*), Col. John Hall, Jacob Giles, and Isaac Webster (TR#C: 297).

12 Dec 1749: John Derumple (s. of John of William) conv. to John Bond 500 a. (*). (TR#C: 465).

OAKHAMPTON

18 March 1747: 440 a. pat. by Charles Ridgely (MPL TI#1: 312, TI#3: 300). The tract is adj. to Northampton (MHM 43:97).

See PW PLat H.

OAKINGTON

5 Sep 1659: 800 a. surv. for Col. Nathaniel Utie; 500 a. sold to Edward Beedle and later held by Thomas Browne; 300 a. in poss. of Garrett Garrettson (MRR: 8).

15 Feb 1659/60: 800 a. (*) pat. to Nathaniel Utie (IS#IK: 80).

6 April 1668: Nathaniel Utie and w. Elizabeth conv. 500 a., pt. of 800 a. (*) to Edward Beedell (IR#PP: 68).

2 March 1672/3: Nathaniel Utie, Gent., conv. 300 a. (*) to Rutten Garrett on n. side of Swan Creek (G#J: 104; TR#RA: 74).

30 Dec 1696: John Hall and w. Martha, and Mary Utie (said Martha and Mary being the daus. and coheirs of Edward Bedell, late of BA Co., dec.), deed 500 a. (*) to Thomas Brown (IS#IK: 80).

OBADIAH'S VENTURE

25 March 1740: Samuel, Obadiah, and James Pritchard, sons of Obadiah Pritchard, agree to divide 300 a. Hall's Plains, 50 a. (*) and 25 a. Margaret's Purchase. James was to have the last two tracts completely, and enough of Hall's Plains to make it equal (HWS#1-A: 408).

1750: James Pritchard owned 50 a. (*) (1750 DB).

17 Jan 1774: Daniel Durbin made a will, proved 23 March 1774. In his will he left to his dau. Avarilla Durbin (to be extx.), 50 a. (*) and 50 a. Improved Venture conv. by James Richards (Morgan, HA Co. Wills: 17, cites HA Co. Wills, AJ#2: 134).

OBLONG

20 June 1687: 150 a. surv. for Hendrick Inloes on the S. side of Middle R.; later possessed by William Holland (MRR: 67).

4 Aug 1702: Hendrick Enloes and w. Christiana conv. 150 a. pt. (*) to William Holland of BA Co. (HW#2: 150).

8 Nov 1751: John Bond conv. 84 a. (*) to Charles Baker. JB's w. Aliceanna cons. (TR#D: 233).

OGG KING OF BASHAN

7 Sep 1721: Henry Weatherall conv. 400 a., being half of Ogg King of Bashan, Pearson's Outlet and Weatherall's Last Addition, to John Roberts of BA Co. (TR#DS: 304).

8 March 1723: Thomas Bond of BA Co. conv. 200 a. pt. (*) to Henry Weatherall. TB's w. Ann cons. (IS#G: 189).

9 March 1726/7: John Roberts conv. 200 a., pt. (*), Pearson's Outlet, and Weatherall's Last Addition to Edmund Talbott. JR's w. Mary cons. (IS#H: 313).

9 March 1732: John Taylor and w. Mary conv. 200 a. Bond's Gift and (*) to William Talbott for the life of said Mary Taylor, formerly the w. of Edward [sic] Talbott (IS#L: 392).

2 April 1740: William Talbott and w. Mary conv. 100 a. pt. of (*), Pearson's Outlet, and pt. Weatherall's Last Addition, to John Chocke (HWS#1-A: 376).

OGG'S BASHAN

4 Aug 1706: Surv. for George Ogg (IS#IK: 310).

13 Oct 1736: George Ogg of BA Co. conv. 150 a. (*) to John Eaglestone (IS#IK: 310).

16 Sep 1738: John Eaglestone conv. 150 a. (*) to George Ogg. JE's w. Mary cons. (HWS#1-A: 118).

OGLESBY'S CHANCE

31 Oct 1687: George Oglesby, tailor, conv. 200 a. (*) to Edward Dowse. Johanna Oglesby signed with the grantor. (Deed and bond, RM#HS: betw. 188 and 240).

1696: Thomas Jones and w. Mary (formerly Harrison, who was mentioned in the will of Edward Dowse), conv. (*) to Francis Whitehead (RM#HS: 524).

20 Oct 1713: Francis Whitehead and w. Elizabeth conv. to William Tibbs of BA Co., clerk, 50 a. Dann, 100 a. Emanuel's Hope, 100 a. Emanuel's Rest. and 300 a. (*) (TR#A: 357).

1722: William Tibbs pet. to have four tracts: 200 a. (*) (laid out for George Oglesby), 100 a. Emanuel's Hope (in 1684 laid out for Emanuel Celly), 100 a. Emanuel's Rest, and 77 a. Dann, resurv. and any vacant land added. he is now granted one entire tract called Tibb's United Inheritance, beginning on the s. side of a branch of Middle R., cont. 640 a. (MPL CE#I: 430).

OGLESBY'S MOUNT

28 March 1691: George Ogsleby and w. Johanna conv. 46 a. (*), and 4 a. adj. land to George Goldsmith (IR#AM: 84).

OLD MAN'S FOLLY

10 May 1709: granted to John Leatherwood.

16 Jan 1717: Samuel Leatherwood, conv. 100 a. to Pleasance Dorsey. SL's w. Johanna cons. (TR#A: 547).

OLD PLANTATION

11 March 1731: Mary Marshall conv. (*) to John Stokes (IS#L: 204).

10 June 1733: Susanna Stokes, widow of John, conv. (*), which desc. to her from her father George Wells, to her s. John Stokes (IS#L: 418).

OLD ROAD

-- Dec 1683: Agreement: Whereas Capt. Thomas Todd of BA Co., dec., purch. from Thomas Powell of TA Co. 270 a., being ¼ of 1100 a. formerly taken up by William Batten and Thomas Thomas, and Charles Gorsuch purch. of Solomon Thomas, s. and heir of Thomas Thomas, ½ of the 1100 a. of Walter Dickeson; this document is to certify that: Thomas Todd of Gloucester Co., VA, s. and heir the Thomas Todd, dec., and Charles Gorsuch have agreed that TT should have the said ¼ of the 1100 a. ... and CG to have the land on e. side of Denton Creek (RM#HS: 175). [The articles by J. Hall Pleasants on the Gorsuch Family states that Gorsuch and Todd purch. this land jointly in 1679; See *Gen. of VA Families from the VA Mag. of Hist. and Biog.*, III: 384].

2 June 1685: Charles Gorsuch, planter, with cons. of w. Sarah conv. to Robert Burman, merchant of London, 120 a. on e. side of the Old Road Creek, being pt. of 1100 a. formerly taken up by William Batten and Thomas Thomas. Joseph Burman is grantee's atty. (RM#HS: 134).

7 March 1733/4: Samuel Chew gave to Richard Jones of BA Co., a receipt for 190 a. Denton, 80 a. Walker's Neck, 100 a. Hooper's Island, 330 a. North Point, 546 a. (*), 120 a. Industry, 1000 a. Shawan Hunting Ground, 50 a. Thorold's Nest, 100 a. Luke's Privilege, and 100 a. Bagford (HWS#M: 193).

OLD'S REST
(Pt. NORWICH)

21 Nov 1727: Henry Enlows of KE Co., cordwainer, conv. 100 a. (*) to Samuel Goodwin; land had formerly been taken up by Thomas Long, dec., who sold it to Thomas Peart. Mary Enlows cons. (IS#I: 290).

OLDTON'S FELLOWSHIP

1696: laid out for John Oldton on Little Britain Ridge, near the head of Herring Run, not far s.east of Towson (MHM 16: 115n).

OLDTON'S (OULTON'S) GARRISON (1696)

13 May 1696: 940 a. surv. for John Oldton on n. side of Patapsco R. in the woods pt. of Rangers' Forest; later 163 a. poss. by William Talbot, and the residue by the orphans of James Murray (MRR: 84. MRR: 98 gives the acreage as 340 a.).

See Horvath Plat: Green Spring Valley.

-----1699: John Oldton conv. 396 a. to Thomas Cromwell and James Murray. Oldton's w. Anne is mentioned in the deed (RM#HS: 365).

10 May 1700: Thomas Cromwell conv. his half of (*) to James Murray. Deed states that tract was granted by Lord Baltimore to John Oldton on 1 June 1696, and sold by sd. Oldton to Cromwell and Murray on 1 Aug 1699 (HWS# 1-A: 101).

4 Aug 1701: James Morray and w. Jemima of BA Co. conv. 163 a. (*) to William Talbot; land adjoins tract (Ely?) O'Carroll (HW#2: 103).

18 March 1736: Benjamin Hammond conv. all his interest in Credentia and 163 a. pt. (*), which he held in right of his w. Margaret, a dau. of William Talbot, to John Risteau, who m. Catherine, widow of said WT. (IS#IK: 377).

25 July 1747: Josephus Murray conv. 439 a. Counterscarpe and 340 a. (*) to Richard Croxall. JM's w. Ruth cons. Zipporah Gist granted a quitclaim on the two tracts to Josephus Murray (TB#E: 464, 468).

1 Sep 1750: Josephus Murray grants a release of Counterscarpe and (*) to Richard Croxall, which Murray had earlier sold to Gist; the terms being that Zeporah Gist shall live at Brother's Good Will (TR#D: 13).

OLIVE YARD

12 June 1733: Thomas Stone and w. Elizabeth conv. 100 a. (*) to Philip Jones, Jr. (IS#L: 399).

OLIVER'S RANGE

29 Oct 1724: John Cromwell, conv. 183 a. (*) to John Giles. JC's w. Hannah cons. (IS#G: 395).

10 June 1736: Mrs. Hannah Worthington, late widow and extx. of Capt. John Cromwell, conv. Oliver's Range to John Moale of BA Co. (IS#IK: 444).

OLIVER'S RESERVE

10 June 1667: 150 a. surv. for Oliver Sprye; later held by Daniel Scott, and still later held by James Durham for William Galloway's orphans (MRR: 67).

2 June 1674: Mary Harmar, widow, conv. 150 a. (*) to Robert Benger and John Johnson, being the same land formerly taken up by Oliver Spry, dec., and then by the grantor's dec. husband Godfrey Harmer (G#J: 242).

31 May 1681: Robert Benger of Gunpowder R. gave bond to Thomas Harris he will conv. to Harris before 10 Dec 1682, 150 a. (*) (IR#AM: 134).

6 March 1682/3: Robert Benger, shoemaker, and w. Katherine, conv. 150 a. (*) and 30 a. Jenifers Kindness, to Daniel Scott (RM#HS: 33).

3 Aug 1703: Daniel Scott and w. Jane conv. 150 A. Oliver's Reserve and 30 a. Jenifer's Kindness to William Galloway (HW#2: 334).

ONION'S INHERITANCE

1746: A Resurv. of Windley's Forest and other tracts; the cert. mentioned Cat Creek (MHM 25: 364).

ONION'S INTEREST

(Includes lands formerly pat. as Beals Purchase and Roper's Range)

2 June 1735: 240 a. pat. to Christopher Randall.

5 Dec 1735: Christopher Randall, conv. (*) to Stephen Onion. CR's w. Catherine cons. (HWS#M: 343).

ORANGE

22 May 1742: Alexander Lawson on behalf of Benjamin Tasker and the Baltimore Iron Works, leased 100 a. pt. (*) to Jasper Hall for 21 years (TB#A: 161).

ORCHARD'S NECK

10 March 1663/4: William Orchard conv. 150 a. (*) to James Browne (RM#HS: 6).

6 Jan 1667/8: James Browne, merchant of Salem, New England, conv. to ... G... (*) on e. side of the Bay, formerly pat. to William Galloway (IR#PP: 63).

ORGAN'S FANCY

[date not given]: Matthew Organ, formerly of BA Co., now of Prince William Co., VA, conv. 100 a. (*) to others (PCLR PL#8: 388).

OSBORNE'S LOT

24 May 1721: Frances Wilson of CV Co., widow, and Thomas Wilson of PG Co., Gent., conv. 500 a. (*) to Josiah Wilson of PG Co., Gent. TW's w. Priscilla cons. (TR#DS: 333).

10 Nov 1744: Henry Wilson of PG Co., conv. 200 a., pt. (*) (in all a 500 a. tract) to Thomas Bond. Wilson's w. Ann cons. Wilson was the s. and heir of Josiah Wilson of PG Co., dec.; Josiah was the grantee of Frances Willson, widow, and Thomas Willson of PG Co. (TB#C: 678).

OUTLET

11 June 1726: Luke Raven conv. 317 a. Luke's Garden, (*), and 100 a. The Triangle to his eld. s. Luke Raven (IS#H: 271).

OUTQUARTER (THE)

10 Nov 1709: granted to James Carroll.

14 Dec 1732: Charles Carroll, John Digges, and Charles Carroll, chirurgeon, acting execs. of James Carroll of AA Co., dec., conv. 200 a. pt. (*) to Thomas Shea (IS#L: 330).

OVERLOOKED

30 March 1724: William Baker mortgaged 150 a. (*) to John Furley. The tract was granted by warrant dated 9 Dec 1719 to Maurice Baker, and assigned 25 Feb 1719/20 to Owen Williams who assigned it on 25 Feb to William Baker (IS#G: 251).

1752: Resurv. by John Stinchcomb as Stinchcomb's Hills.

OVERTON

4 Nov 1673: Rowland Williams, planter, by John Walston, his atty., conv. 300 a. (*) at the mouth of Spesutia Creek, to James Ives (G#J: 254).

OWINGS' ADDITION

See Horvath Plat: Elkridge.

3 Nov 1729: Richard Owings and w. Sarah conv. (*) to Richard's sister Ruth Norwood (IS#K: 237).

30 Sep 1731: Richard Owings, s. of Richard, dec., conv. (*) and Owings's Adventure to William Richardson. RO's w. Sarah cons. (IS#L: 130).

24 May 1732: Richard Owings and w. Sarah, conv. 32 a. (*) to Ruth Norwood, spinster, for her natural life (IS#L: 238).

OWINGS' ADVENTURE

10 Oct 1694: 450 a. surv. for Richard Owings on the w. side of Patapsco R., on n. side of Col. Taylor's land. Later possessed by 22 a. said Owings, and 225 a. Col. Edward Dorsey (MRR: 108).

See Horvath Plat: Elkridge.

13 Aug 1704: Richard Owings conv. (*) to Col. Edward Dorsey (HW#2: 354).

1 June 1708: Richard Owings of BA Co., carpenter, conv. 100 a. pt. (*) to Richard Acton, planter. RO's w. Rachel cons. (RM#HS: 590).

10 June 1728: Francis and Edward Dorsey conv. pt. (*) to Charles Dorsey, in exch. for United Friendship (bequeathed by Col. Edward Dorsey to his sons Francis, Edward, and Charles Dorsey) (IS#I: 139).

1729: Richard Owings and w. by deed of gift conv. (*) to Ruth Norwood (IS#K: 113).

1730: Richard Owings and w. conv. pt. (*) and pt. Owings Addition to Ruth Norwood (IS#K: 237).

14 Sep 1731: Amos Woodward of Annapolis conv. 450 a. (*) to William Richardson; tract had been conv. to AW by Richard Owings on 4 June 1729 (IS#L: 127).

30 Sep 1731: Richard Owings, s. of Richard, dec., conv. Owings' Addition and (*) to William Richardson. RO's w. Sarah cons. (IS#L: 130).

27 Nov 1732: Philip Hammond and Co., merchants, conv. 225 a. being ½ of (*) to William Richardson of AA Co.; being same land which Charles Dorsey mortgaged to PH on 26 Nov 1729. This may be an assignment of mortgage rather than a conveyance (IS#L: 339).

20 Dec 1732: Francis and Edward Dorsey granted a quitclaim to Charles Dorsey on all land bequeathed by Col. Edward Dorsey to his sons Charles, Lewis, Francis, and Edward. Lewis has

d.; one of these tracts was (*) (IS#L: 340).

21 Dec 1732: Charles Dorsey of BA Co., planter, conv. or mortgaged (*) to William Richardson; w. Ann cons.; tract was pat. 10 Nov 1695 by Richard Owings, and sold by him on 30 Aug 1704 to Edward Dorsey (IS#L: 342).

OWINGS' (OWEN'S) OUTLAND PLAINS

1724: Surv. for Richard Owings.

See Horvath Plats: Sykesville and Wards Chapel and Eldersburg.

1730: Richard Owings conv. 470 a. (*) to William Smith (IS#K: 268).

5 Nov 1747: John Paca and w. Elizabeth conv. 400 a. (*) to Abell Brown of AA Co. (TB#E: 584).

OWNER'S LANDING

14 May 1745: Thomas Franklin conv. 46 a. pt. Fox Hall, 32 a. Owners' Landing, and $6\frac{1}{4}$ a. Waterton's Neglect, to John Hammond Dorsey (TB#D: 368).

19 Sep 1746: William Dallam conv. 26 a. and 34 a. of James' Park and 16 a. Owner's Landing to Thomas Harrison (TB#E: 249).

19 Sep 1746: George Browne of Joppa conv. $\frac{1}{4}$ of James Park and Owners Landing to Thomas Harrison (TB#E: 253).

OXELL'S NECK

18 Jan 1663/4: William Stanley, soapboiler, conv. 300 a. (*) to Oxelle Stille. 12 Feb 1663/4: Stille conv. (*) to William Fisher (IS#IK: 8).

OXFORD

16 Feb 1680/1: warrant for 200 a. issued (IR#AM: 155).

12 April 1681: 65 a. surv. for Michael Judd on e. side of Gunpowder R., at Elk creek; Judd ran away and his s. would not claim it; land was later sold to Cornelius Boyce who d. without heirs and late possessed by Thomas Kitten (MRR: 73).

2 Aug 1681: Michael Judd and w. Jane conv. 65 a. on the s. side of Elk Creek to Henry Lawrence; covered by a 200 a. warrant issued last 16 feb (IR#AM: 155).

6 June 1683: Henry Lawrence and w. Elizabeth conv. 65 a. at Elk Creek to Cornelius Boyce (RM#HS: 47).

22 Dec 1697: Cornelius Boyce conv. 65 a. (*), pat. 10 Aug 1694, to Theophilus Kitten (TR#RA: 311).

1 April 1723: Edward Kitten and w. Mary, conv. 65 a. (*) to ... (IS#G: 137).

PACA'S DELIGHT

1750: Joseph Galloway owned 304 a. (*) (1750 DB).

PADANANUM

5 June 1734: John Wheeler and w. Margaret conv. 110 a. (*) to Abraham Burkholder of Conestoga, Lancaster Co., PA (HWS#M: 58).

PAINTERS HALLS (or HILLS)

16 June 1731: Cert. of surv. (HWS#M: 59).

24 Jan 1737: John Parrish conv. 100 a. (*) to Christopher Cole (HWS#M: 59).

PALMER'S FOREST

9 Sep 1673: 600 a. surv. for William Palmer; later, land liable to escheat; still later, no rent paid for 20 years (MRR: 12, 32).

10 Feb 1708: John Palmer of Towcester in Co. North'ton, England, bro. and heir of William Palmer, late of MD, dec., gave p/a to John Davison of CE Co., surgeon to recover 600 a. (*), 250 a. The Grove, 500 a. Palmer's Point, 300 a. Swan Harbor, and 500 a. Towcester or Tolchester in CE Co., from John Hall of James Presbury (TR#A: 126).

14 Feb 1708: Richard Hutchins of Towcester, Co. Northampton, testified that he saw the p/a signed as well as the two following certs. (TR#A: 128).

10 Feb 1708: Cert. of John Watson and Richard Hutchins stated that John Palmer of Towcester, Northampton, was the eld. s. of William and Dorothy Palmer, and eld. bro. of William Palmer, who was heard to have d. in MD (TR#A: 129).

10 Feb 1708: Cert. of Charles Palmer, Vicar, and William Clark and Thomas Kingston, churchwardens that they knew Watson and Hutchins and they believed John Palmer to be eld. s. of William and Dorothy and the eld. bro. of William Palmer, dec. (TR#A: 129).

1 Sep 1720: William Mathew of Martin, Co. Surrey, England, through his atty. Richard Bennett and Thomas Bordley, both of AA Co., conv. 250 a. The Grove, 600 a. (*), 500 a. Palmer's Point, and 100 a. Tunington to Josias Middlemore of BA Co., chirurgeon (TR#DS: 216).

PALMER'S POINT

23 June 1675: 500 a. surv. for William Palmer on the w. side of Swan Creek; Palmer dead; land is liable to escheat (MRR: 13).

10 Feb 1708: John Palmer of Towcester in Co. North'ton, bro. and heir of William Palmer, late of MD, dec., gave p/a to John Davison of CE Co., surgeon to recover 600 a. Palmer's Forest, 250 a. The Grove, 500 a. (*), 300 a. Swan Harbor, and 500 a. Towcester or Tolchester in CE Co., from John Hall of James Presbury (TR#A: 126).

1 Sep 1720: William Mathew of Martin, Co. Surrey, through his atty. Richard Bennett and Thomas Bordley, both of AA Co., conv. 250 a. The Grove,

600 a. Palmer's Forest, 500 a. (*), and 100 a. Tunington to Josias Middlemore of BA Co., chirurgeon (TR#DS: 216).

PANTHER'S RIDGE

27 Jan 1752: William Knight conv. pt. (*) to his s. Benjamin (TR#D: 277).

25 Feb 1754: Benjamin Knight and Jabez Murray, carpenters, conv. 50 a. (*), formerly surv. for William Knight, to John Daughady, blacksmith. Benjamin's w. Elizabeth cons. (BB#I: 175).

PANTHERS RIDGE

25 Feb 1754: Benjamin Knight and Jabez Murray, carpenters, sell to John Daughaday, blacksmith, 50 a. Panther's Ridge, formerly surv. for William Knight. Benjamin's w. Elizabeth cons. (BB#I: 175).

PARADISE (1673)

5 May 1673: 300 a. in Back R. surv. for Giles Stevens ...; sold to Theophilus Hackett, who had since d.; "no heirs;" later purch. by Mr. James from the heirs of Hackett; later held by James Heath (MRR: 111).

27 Feb 1673/4: Giles Stevens conv. 33 a. to Richard Bennett (IR#RA: 178) (100:117) (G#J: 233) (TR#RA: --).

10 Feb 1684/5: Elizabeth Bolton of AA Co., widow of Richard Bennett, conv. Theophilus Hacket 300 a. (*) (RM#HS: 110).

PARADISE (1687)

8 June 1687: 1000 a. surv. for Thomas Lightfoot on the w. side of Susquehanna R. (MRR: 29).

PARADISE (1695)

10 Nov 1695: granted to Robert Mason of SM Co. (TR#C: 258).

4 July 1735: Thomas Lee of Westmoreland Co., VA conv. 490 a. (*) to Robert Mason of SM Co., being the same land which Matthew Mason, father of Robert, made over to Lee (TR#C: 2546).

27 Sep 1738: Patent of Confirmation granted to Jonathan Seale of SM Co. (TR#C: 258).

9 March 1749: Jonathan Seale of SM Co. conv. (*) to Col. Thomas White. JS' w. Mary cons. (TR#C: 258).

PARADISE (now called WEST'S ADDITION)

8 March 1720: John Hammond of BA Co. planter, conv. 100 a. West Addition, pt. (*), to Robert West (TR#DS: 297).

14 Nov 1721: John Hammond conv. 200 a. to John Lone or Love (prob. Lowe) of CE Co. (IS#G: 79).

18 Feb 1722/3: Robert West, Sr., planter conv. pt. Maiden's Mount, and (*), now called West's Addition, 100 a. to dau. Constant Barnes (IS#G: 94).

4 July 1724: Matthew Mason of SM Co., conv. 490 a. (*) to Thomas Lee of Westmoreland Co., VA, pat. by his father Richard Mason, and divided by his LWT: Matthew's w. Mary cons. (IS#G: 405).

27 Sep 1728: John Hammond of CE Co. conv. 400 a., being ½ (*) to Alexander McCanless (IS#I, betw.: 224 and 230).

4 March 1730: John Hammond of CE Co., conv. 100 a. pt. (*) to William Cannon (IS#L: 84).

8 Nov 1733: Robert West, Sr., conv. pt. Maiden's Mount and pt. (*), now called West's Addition to his dau. Comfort Barnes; if she d. s.p., then after the dec. of her husband Job Barnes, lands were to go to grantor's s. Enoch West (HWS#M: 9).

4 June 1734: John White and Priscilla his w. conv. 50 a. pt. (*) to Nathan Rigbie (HWS#M: 76).

6 June 1734: John Lowe of BA Co., and w. Elizabeth conv. 50 a. (*) to John White (HWS#M: 71).

8 Aug 1734: John Lowe of BA Co., and w. Elizabeth conv. 50 a. (*) to William Cannon (HWS#M: 92).

8 Aug 1734: William Cannon and w. Frances conv. 50 a. (*) to John Lowe (HWS#M: 95).

21 March 1736: John Lowe of BA Co. and w. Elizabeth conv. 150 a. pt. (*) to Edward Stapleton (IS#IK: 405).

PARADISE ORIGINAL

1695: Granted to Robert Mason and later held by John Mason of SM Co. (MRR: 21).

25 Sep 1736: Robert Mason, of SM Co., grandson of the original patentee, with cons. of w. Susannah, conv. (*) to Jonathan Seall (IS#IK: 286).

PARAN

15 Oct 1726: Henry Owings conv. 150 a. Paran and 200 a. Plains of Paran, to Christopher Randall, Sr., as security for loan (IS#H,292).

PARK

11 Nov 1738: 50 a. pat. by John Tye (MPL EI#2: 834; EI#3: 526).

30 March 1741: John Tye of BA Co., with cons. of w. Preciosa, conv. 50 a. (*), to Richard Clark (HWS#1-A: 492).

15 Oct 1765: Henry Clark and w. Rachel conv. 35 a. (*) to Edward Stocksdale (B#O: 461).

PARKER'S CHANCE

15 June 1683: 550 a. surv. for George Parker on the w. side of the Susquahanna R.; later held by the orphans of the said Parker, and still later by Capt. Thomas Gray (MRR: 16).

17 June 1703: George Buxton of CV Co. conv. 500 a. of the land to George Young, Jr., also of CV Co. (IR#AM: 26).

2 March 1705: George Young, the Younger, conv. the 550 a. to Thomas Gray of CV Co. Young's w. Mary cons. (IR#AM: 30).

8 Aug 1728: John Moale, atty., for Jonathan Forwood of London, England, conv. 175 a., being ½ of the tract, to Antil Deaver. The tract had formerly been owned by Thomas Gray, formerly of Maryland, who sold the tract to John Goodwin of London, on 13 May 1707; about 1711 Goodwin became bankrupt, and empowered Forwood to collect all of his (Goodwin's debts) (IS#I: 178).

12 Oct 1728: John Moale, atty. for Jonathan Forwood of London, as above, conv. 275 a., ½ of the tract, to Richard Brashar. The land had been bought by William Brashar, who d. before the land could be made over to him. William Brashar d. leaving a widow Jane, and an infant s. Richard (prob. the present purchaser) (IS#I: 224).

5 June 1734: Antil Deaver and w. Sarah conv. 275 a., ½ the tract, to Nathan Rigbie (HWS#M: 74).

19 April 1743: Richard Brashier conv. 275 a., being ½ the tract to Nathan Rigbie. No w. signed the deed (TB#C: 217).

PARKER'S CHOICE

25 June 1737: John Parker conv. 224 a. (*) and 214 a. Parker's Folly to Henry Rhodes in exch. for 180 a. pt. Gibson's Ridge (IS#IK: 474).

28 Sep 1745: Henry Rhodes of BA Co., cooper, conv. 224 a. (*) to Henry Phillips of KE Co. (TB#D: 322).

22 July 1749: Henry Phillips of KE Co., conv. (*) to John Atkinson, being the same land which HP purch. from Henry Rhodes. HP's w. Mary cons. (TR#C: 245).

PARKER'S FOLLY

12 Sep 1695: 214 a. surv. for John Parker on n. side Bush R., against Abbey Island Marshes, in mouth of Jeffrey's Neck; later held by the orphans of said Parker (MRR: 21-22).

25 June 1737: John Parker conv. the tract to Henry Rhodes. The deed stated that Lord Baltimore granted the tract to John Parker and granted another tract called Parker's Choice for 224 a. to John Parker. William Parker d. a minor, and now John Parker, s. of aforesaid John, conv. the 438 a. (both tracts) to Henry Rhodes, cooper, in exch. for 180 a., the remainder of 230 a. Gibson's Ridge, which said Henry Rhodes' father, Henry, purch. from Thomas Bale (IS#IK: 472-474).

PARKER'S HEAVEN

1 Dec 1686: John Kemp made a will leaving Kemp's Addition to his s. Richard and (*) to his w. Sarah. He also named his dau. Mary (MCW#II: 11).

10 May 1708: Richard Kemp and Mary w. of John Boring conv. 100 a. Kemp's Addition and 100 a. (*) to Nicholas Rogers (RM#HS: 587).

PARKER'S INCREASE

19 July 1726: Thomas Croker, with cons. of w. Frances, conv. 112½ a. (*), being ½ of the tract, to Hugh Merclin? (IS#H: 259).

PARKER'S LOT

7 June 1734: Edgar Tippen and w. Mary conv. 176 a. (*) to William Snelson (HWS#M: 72).

21 Aug 1746: John Parker, s. and heir of John Parker, dec., conv. 176 a. (*) to Abraham Snelson, s. of William Snelson, dec. The deed stated that John Parker, Sr., sold the tract to Edward Tipper on 6 Jan 1719; on 7 June 1734, Edward Tipper sold the tract to William Snelson, s. and heir of Abraham Snelson, dec. William Snelson left the tract to his s. Abraham but directed William Hollis, his exec., to search the title. Hollis found that the original deed from, Parker to Tipper had never been recorded (TB#E: 174).

PARKER'S PALACE

16 Oct 1695: 500 a. surv. for Robert Parker on n. side of Hunting Ridge, adj. to Scutt's Morning Choice. 250 a. later held by Robert Parker, and 250 a. held by Elizabeth Griffith or Griffin of AA Co. (MRR: 82).

6 Aug 1700: Robert Parker and w. Margaret conv. the upper half of the 500 a. tract (*) to Philip Griffin of AA Co. (HWS#1-A: 20).

13 June 1716: Robert Parker conv. 50 a. (*) to Nicholas Rogers and Christopher Randall (TR#A: 422).

21 Nov 1730: Henry Lewis and w. Caturah, dau. of Robert Parker who was granted (*), conv. 250 a. of said tract to George Buchanan (IS#L: 50).

28 June 1736: George Buchanan, surgeon, conv. 200 a. pt. (*) to Rev. Joseph Hooper, minister of the Gospel. GB's w. Eleanor cons. (IS#IK: 365).

21 June 1740: George Buchanan conv. 50 a. pt. (*) formerly in poss. of William Teal, who sold to GB, to John Baker. GB's w. Eleanor cons. (HWS#1-A: 420).

17 April 1749: John Baker of BA Co., planter, mortgaged 50 a. (*) to Charles Ridgely (TR#C: 185).

PARRISH'S FEAR

8 Jan 1730: Ann Puntany, widow of William Puntany, late of BA Co., planter, conv. 113 a. (*) to John Gill, s. of Stephen Gill. The deed stated that this was pt. of the tract devised by Edward Parrish of AA Co. to his dau. Ann Parrish, and the same land which William Puntany, husband of said Ann, promised to conv. to Stephen Gill (IS#L: 90).

31 July 1742: John Gill of BA Co., conv. 113 a. pt. (*) to Mayberry Helm (TB#A: 190).

PARRISH'S FOREST

8 July 1737: 200 a. pat. by John Parrish, Jr. (MPL PL#8: 804, AM#1: 225).

See Horvath Plat: Baltimore/Carroll Co.

19 July 1739: John Parrish, with cons. of w. Elizabeth, conv. 100 a. pt. (*) to Edward Parrish (HWS#1-A: 257).

PARRISHES' NEGLECT

28 Oct 1748: Charles Carroll conv. 50 a. (*), granted to Charles Carroll by escheat patent, 24 Oct 1746, 111 a. Luke's Good Will and 685 a. Franklin's Purchase. CC's w. Anne cons. (TR#C: 115).

PARRISH's OVERSIGHT

1729: George Buchanan conv. 117 a. (*) to William Rogers (IS#K: 23).

PARRISH'S RANGE

-----Lies across western pt. of Baltimore City and its suburbs e. of Gwynn's Falls, and on Gwinn's Run (MHM,15: 225).

5 Oct 1678: 3000 a. surv. for Edward Parrish on n. side of Patapsco, on the fall of Middle Branch; later 1400 a. poss. by Edward Parrish; 300 a. in poss. of John Wooden of AA Co., and 300 a. possessed by George Hogg (Ogg?) in AA Co.; still later 1330 a. poss. by Edward Parrish, and 370 a. poss. by John Wooding (MRR: 82).

25 Aug 1693: Edward Parrish of AA Co., planter, conv. 300 a. (*) to George Ogg; tract was pat. to Edward Parish, father of grantor. EP's w. Mary cons. (IR#AM: 76).

15 Oct 1697: Edward Parrish of AA Co. conv. 300 a. (*) to John Wooden of AA Co., carpenter. Mary Parrish cons. (RM#HS: 510).

26 June 1700: Edward Parrish conv. to John Wooden (pt.?) of (*) to John Wooden. EP's w. Mary cons. (PCLR (TL#S: 325)

30 Nov 1727: Edward Parrish of AA Co., granted quitclaim on 80 a. (*) to his uncle William Parrish who had been given the land by his bro. Edward Parrish, Sr. EP's w. Rachel cons. (IS#I: 86).

31 March 1729: William Parrish of BA Co. conv. 75 a. pt. (*) to Stephen Gill. WP's w. Susan cons. (IS#I: 301).

13 Sep 1735: John Wooden conv. 100 a. (*) to his s. Solomon Wooden. JW's w. Elizabeth cons. 300 a. of land had been conv. to JW by Edward Parrish on 15 Oct 1697; 70 a. conv. to JW by Edward Parrish on 26 June 1700 (HWS#M: 319).

16 Sep 1738: John Wilmot of AA Co., conv. 300 a. pt. (*), sold by Edward Parrish of AA Co., to George Ogg on 26 Aug 1697 to John Wooden; JW's w. Hannah cons. (HWS#1-A: 110).

1 Sep 1739: Edward Parrish of AA Co., and John Parrish conv. 50 a. pt. (*) to William Rogers (HWS#1-A: 275).

22 Aug 1747: John Gill, with cons. of w. Mary, conv. 75 a. pt. (*) to William Puntany (TB#E: 528).

14 Feb 1752: John Wooden, Sr., with cons. of w. Mary, conv. by deed of gift to his s. John Wooden, Jr., 100 a. (*). The same day he conv. to his s. Solomon 120 a. (*) (TR#D: 274, 275).

4 March 1754: John Wooden and w. Mary conv. 150 a. (*) to their s. William, and 120 a. (*) to their s. Solomon (BB#I: 171).

17 June 1758: John Gill conv. to William Ponteny 75 a. pt. (*) (B#G: 179).

PARTNERSHIP

13 Nov 1749: Edward Norwood, planter, mortgaged 256 a. Bachelor's Fear and 44 a. (*), to Edward Dorsey (TR#C: 336).

PARTRIDGE'S CHANCE

3 Dec 1725: Thomas Matthews and w. Sarah conv. 165 a. Thomas' Adventure, pat. 19 July 1688 to Col. John Thomas, and now called (*), to Buckler Partridge of Bristol, merchant (IS#H: 208).

PARTRIDGE'S FOREST

2 June 1735: John Boreing of BA Co., conv. pt. of Selsed, known as (*) to Buckler Partridge (HWS#1-A: 221).

PASSAGE

3 Nov 1696: See Marshal's Hope (IS#IK: 100).

PATRICK'S MEADOW

Nov 1726: Patrick Ruark conv. 50 a. (*) to William Robinson (IS#L: 390).

PAUL'S NECK

10 April 1672: 200 a. surv. for Paul Kinsey; later poss. by John Lockett for Richard Gwiun's orphans (MRR: 107).

10 June 1685: James Kyle, cooper and planter of AA Co., in consideration of lands conv. to him, now conv. to Richard Gwinn his interest in 200 a. (*), which was pat. on 29 June 1663 [sic] to Paul Kinsey who d. intestate without a w., but leaving a s. who d. an infant, and the land desc. to Elizabeth w. of Richard Johns of CV Co.; said Johns and w. conv. it to Richard Gwinn and JK on 23 March 1681/2 (RM#HS: 154).

PAY MY DEBTS

(date not given): George Buck of Bideford, Co. Devon, England, s. and heir of John Buck (late of same place, dec.) by his w. Judith Pawley, dau. of William Pawley of same place, appointed Thomas Lovering of Tavistock, Co. Devon, England, his atty. to sell (*) (B#K: 202).

PEARCE'S FOLLY

1716: (?) a. surv. for William Pearce (on PW Plat H).

6 Nov 1720: 100 a. pat. to William Pearce (HWS#1-A: 220).

15 Oct 1737: William Pearce, of BA Co., tailor, and w. Mary, conv. 100 a. (*) to Dr. George Buchanan (HWS#M: 34).

11 May 1739: William Pearce of BA Co. and John Pearce of AA Co., conv. 100 a. (*), which was bequeathed to them by the will of their father, William Pearce, to Dr. George Buchanan (HWS#1-A: 220).

PEARMAN'S HOPE

10 Nov 1702: John Chadwell of BA Co. conv. 100 a. (*) (or Shearman's Hope) to Daniel Scott (HW#2: 213).

PEARSON'S ENLARGEMENT

7 Aug 1730: Simon Pearson conv. (*) and other tracts to William Buckner (IS#L: 13).

7 Feb 1732: Thomas Buckner of VA conv. (*) and other lands back to Simon Pearson, who had conv. them to William Buckner, dec. George Elliott and w. Patience, widow of William, relinquishing her right of dower (IS#L: 328).

PEARSON'S LODGE

12 March 1714: Simon Pearson, weaver, conv. to Andrew Thompson 100 a. (*), adj. Emm's Delight (TR#A: 298).

10 March 1747: Andrew Thompson of BA Co. conv., 60 a., pt. (*), to John Thompson. AT's w. Elizabeth cons. (TB#E: 692).

PEARSON'S OUTLET

2 March 1719/20: Simon Pearson conv. (*) to Henry Wriothesley in exch. for Noble's Desire and Turkey Range (RM#HS: 660).

7 Sep 1721: Henry Weatheral conv. 400 a., being ½ of (*), Ogg King of Bashan, and Weatherall's Last Addition to John Roberts (TR#DS: 304).

21 May 1722: Simon Pearson of BA Co., weaver, and w. Sarah again exch. 200 a. (*) to Henry Weatherall in exch. for HW's pts. of Noble's Desire and Turkey Range (RM#HS: 683).

9 March 1726/7: John Roberts conv. 200 a. (*) pt. Ogg King of Bashan, (*), and Weatherall's Last Addition to Edmund Talbott. JR's w. Mary cons. (IS#H: 313).

2 April 1740: William Talbott and w. Mary, conv. 100 a., pts. of (*), Ogg King of Bashan, and Wetherall's Last Addition, to John Chocke (HWS#1-A: 376).

4 Aug 1757: James Talbott conv. to Samuel Day 50 a. (*) and Weatherall's Last Addition (B#G: 45).

3 April 1762: Samuel Day and w. Sarah conv. 50 a. (*) and Wetherall's Last Addition to Robert Patterson (B#K: 49).

PEARSON'S PARK

24 Aug 1698: 300 a. surv. for Simon Pearson, above the head of Bush R.; later held by Henry Wriothesley (MRR: 27).

3 May 1699: Simon Pearson conv. 300 a. (*) to Samuel Standiford (TR#RA: 352).

4 March 1702: Simon Pearson and w. Em conv. 200 a. pt. (*) to Henry Wriothesley (HW#2: 120).

25 Aug 1714: Ann Wriothesley, of BA Co., widow, conv. 300 a. (*) and 400 a. Rochester, to Roger Matthews. (*) was pat. 24 Aug 1698 (TR#A: 313.

PEARSON'S RANGE

29 April 1709: Tract was surv. for Simon Pearson (TR#A: 331).

24 Jan 1714: Simon Pearson of BA Co., weaver, conv. 230 a. (*) to Benjamin Wheeler of PG Co. (TR#A: 331).

1 Sep 1730: Benjamin Wheeler mortgaged pt. Pearson's Range and pt. Three Sisters, to Josias Middlemore (IS#L: betw. 14 and 18).

15 Sep 1741: Benjamin Wheeler conv. 350 a. pt. (*) and Wheeler and Clark's Contrivance to s. Ignatius Wheeler. The deed mentioned BW's daus. Eliza, Mary, and Ann. The same day he conv. 315 a. of (*) to his s. Leonard (HWS#1-A: 549, 551).

PEARSON'S PRIVILEGE

22 Feb 1736: Simon Pearson of BA Co., by virtue of an Act of Assembly, assigned to Edward Hall,

late Sheriff of BA Co., three parcels: pt. Turkey Range, Noble's Desire, and (*) (IS#IK: 351).
19 June 1738: Edward Hall, Esq., formerly Sheriff of BA Co. conv. 148 a. pt. of Turkey Range, Noble's Desire, and (*), to Beviss Spain (HWS#1-A: 86).

PEDDICORD'S (PETTICOURT'S) ADDITION
1720: Surv. for John Petticoat; on Ben's Run in the 2nd Dist. BA Co. (MHM 25: 340).
See KN Plat WO and Horvath's Plat Granite.
23 July 1723: 150 a. pat. to John Pettycourt (MPL PL#5:403, IL#A: 779).

PEDDICORD'S (PETTICOURT'S) BENEFIT
Shown on KN Plat WO.

PEDDICORDS LOT
20 Nov 1762: Dorsey Petticot, with cons. of w. Sarah, conv. 150 a. (*) to Morris Baker (B#K: 488).

PEDDICORD'S (PEDDICORT'S) WISH
26 Oct 1724: Cert. of surv. (IS#H: 234).
See Horvath Plat: Granite.
1 Oct 1725: John Peddicoart gave bond he would conv. (*) to Zachariah Baker for a debt of £5 (IS#H: 203).
8 July 1726: 100 a. pat. by John Pettycourt, Jr. (MPL PL#6: 504, IL#B: 65).
15 July 1726: John Peddicort conv. 100 a. (*) to William Peddicort (IS#H: 234).

PEDDICORT (See PEDDICORD)

PEMBLICOE (See PIMLICO)

PENCE'S ENCOURAGEMENT
12 Dec 1727: John Digges, with cons. of w. Eleanor, of PG Co. conv. 1000 a. (*) to John Hyde of London, merchant IS#I: 70).

PENNY COME QUICK
13 Oct 1665: Surv.
22 April 1700: William Loney and w. Jane conv. 100 a. Notley's Island and 100 a. (*) to Robert Gibson; the tracts were left by Overton to Jane, his sole heir, now w. of Loney (HW#2: 54).
10 July 1701: Robert Gibson conv. Notley's Island and (*) to Roger Matthews (HW#2: 81).

PERKINSON
15 Dec 1683: Thomas Lightfoot, Deputy Surveyor, certified he had laid out 100 a. (*), at head of Musketa Creek, bounded by The Grove, Mascall's Humor, and Beaver Neck, for Richard Perkins, cooper (RM#HS: 62).

PERKINGTON
20 Oct 1703: Thomas Edmonds conv. 100 a. (*) to Thomas Morris (HW#2: 293).
3 Jan 1708: Thomas Morris and w. Mary conv. 100 a. (*) to Rowland Kimble (RM#HS: 627).

PERSIMMON POINT
1 Aug 1658: 400 a. surv. for James Rigby on n. side of Rumley Creek; later held by Robert Gibson, and later by Capt. Thomas Bale (MRR: 8).
11 March 1678/9: Samuel Hatton, Gent, with cons. of w. Elizabeth, of TA Co., conv. 400 a. (*) to Miles Gibson (Deed and letter of atty. in IR#PP: 32).
20 Aug 1704: Thomas Bale, with cons. of w. Sarah, conv. 400 a. (*), 50 a. Port Royal, and 115 a. Delfe Island to Thomas Edmonds. The property had been owned by Miles Gibson who d. intestate; it was inher. by Robert Gibson who left the land to the said Sarah Bale (HW#2: 356).
5 Sep 1704: Thomas Edmonds conv. all the lands back to Thomas Bale (HW#2: 358).
17 July 1744: Kemp Plummer of Glouc. Co., VA, conv. (*) and other lands to Thomas White. The deed stated that Ann Bale was the residuary legatee by Anthony Bale's will, and she m. Michael Taylor, and d. a femme covert s.p. The land desc. to Kemp Plummer, s. of William Plummer of Glouc. Co., VA, who was bro. and heir-at-law to Ann Taylor (TB#C: 576).

PETERFIELD
15 June 1670/1: Abraham Coffen and w. Joyce conv. (50?) a. of 200 a. (*) to John Gilbert (MHM 27:126).

PETER'S ADDITION
29 Nov 1685: 100 a. surv. for Peter Fewcate; later held by Thomas Cord (MRR: 11).
29 Dec 1685: 100 a. pat. to Peter Fucatt (MPL 25:244, 30:306).
16 Oct 1686: Peter Fucatt, planter, mortgaged to John Walston, carpenter, for 6 years, the 100 a. lately occupied by Fucatt and the 100 a. adj. (RM#HS: 208).
6 Jan 1690: Peter Fuckett and. w. Frances of BA Co. conv. 100 a. (*) and 100 a. French Plantation to Thomas Cord (RM#HS: 329).
1 April 1727: Thomas Cord gave bond to Abraham Cord he will let Abraham occupy the designated pt. of Cord's Purchase, French Plantation, and (*), which they inher. from their father Thomas Cord, and which they have divided (IS#H: 402).
1 April 1727: Abraham Cord gave bond to Thomas Cord he will guarantee the right of TC to occupy the specified half of land bequeathed them by their father Thomas Cord (IS#I: 58).

2 Nov 1743: Abraham Cord leased pt. Cord's Purchase, pt. French Plantation, 19 a. Ten Pound Purchase, and pt. French Plantation to Abraham Taylor (TB#C: 365).

PETER'S DISCOVERY

1765: Thomas Stevens conv. (*) to Thomas Gorsuch, Jr. (B#O: 574).

PETER'S FIELDS (CE Co.)
(See MARKEFELD)

1658: 200 a. pat. to Peter Jacobson (MPL Q: 264).

10 Nov 1660: Peter Jacobson conv. to Marcus Severson 75 a. of 200 a. of (*) (RM#HS: 1).

15 June 1670/1 [sic]: Abraham Coffen and w. Joyce conv. to John Gilbert 100 a. Markefeld at Veale Quarter Creek, and also 50 a. (*) (IR#PP: 108).

PETER'S FOREST

1 March 1688/9: John Arden of BA Co., planter, with cons. of w. Sarah, conv. 50 a. pt. (*) to John Watts of BA Co. (RM#HS: 295).

PETER'S PURCHASE

7 Aug 1762: Peter Shipley of BA Co., conv. 100 a. (*) to Absolom and Adam Shipley (PCLR DD#2: 87).

PETTICOAT, PETTICOART
(See PEDDICORD)

PHANTASCO

17 Feb 1704: 100 a. surv. for Edward Boarman (Card Index).

10 Jan 1706: 100 a. pat. by Edward Boarman (MPL CD#4: 267).

15 April 1728; Thomas Howard of BA Co., and w. Catherine, conv. 100 a. (*) to Sylvanus Pumphrey. The land was granted to Edward Boarman on 10 Jan 1702 [sic]. By his LWT dated 10 Feb 1704 EB left the land to William Johnson, s. and heir of Catherine Johnson when he should attain age of 21; if he d., land was to go to his mother, now the w. of Thomas Howard (IS#G: 273).

PHILEMON'S LOT

9 Nov 1745: William Bond and w. Elizabeth conv. 535 a. The Enlarged Lot and 100 a. (*) to Abraham Raven (TB#D: 0402).

PHILLIPS ADDITION (1669)

27 April 1668: Taken up by James Phillips (See MHM 20:25; 21:293; 25:363).

24 Oct 1669: 200 a. surv. for James Phillips in Gunpowder R. on the w. side of Lees Island; later poss. by Jno. Carwell (MRR: 32).

16 June 1719; James Phillips, with cons. of w. Joanna, conv. 150 a. Lee's Island and 200 a. (*) to Blois Wright (TR#DS: 32).

1729: Samuel Thomas conv. 200 a. (*) to Robert North (IS#K: 75).

PHILLIPS ADDITION (1672)

18 May 1672: 200 a. surv. for Philip Thomas on n. side of Patapsco R.; later poss. by Samuel Thomas and later by Thomas Roberts for ST (MRR: 89).

PHILLIPS CHOICE (See PHILLS CHOICE)

PHILLIPS FANCY

10 Aug 1684: Granted to William Cromwell, Sr., who bequeathed the land to his s. William, Jr. (HW#2: 68).

26 Dec 1701: William Cromwell, Jr., of BA Co., Gent., conv. 60 a. (*) to Thomas Crooker. "M. C." gave cons. (HW#2: 68).

PHILLIPS ISLAND

20 June 1733: Bloyce Wright made a will leaving the tract to his eld. s. Thomas (MCW#VII: 232).

1 Sep 1741: William Wright, with cons. of w. Sarah, conv. to Abraham Jarrett 150 a. Swallow Fork, and (*), which he inher. from his father (HWS#1-A: 560).

PHILLIPS PURCHASE

15 July 1683: 2000 a. surv. for James Phillips on the w. side of Susquehanna R., adj. Ann's Lot; later poss. by Thomas Tench (MRR: 16).

7 June 1687: James Phillips, innholder, conv. 1000 a. (*) to Thomas Tench of AA Co. Susanna Phillips signed with grantor. Same date: James Phillips gave bond for performance of covenants. James and w. Susanna ackn. in court (RM#HS: 231).

7 Nov 1700: James Phillips, Gent., s. and heir of James Phillips, dec., and w. Rachel, conv. $\frac{1}{2}$ of (*), 1000 a., to Thomas Tench (HW#2: 42).

-- Sep 1728: Nathan Rigbie of AA Co., and w. Cassandra conv. 500 a. pt. (*), to Gerard Hopkins (IS#I: 230).

15 Oct 1729: Nathan Rigbie and w. Cassandra conv. 200 a. pt. (*) to Thomas Jones (IS#K: 169).

15 Oct 1729: Nathan Rigbie and w. Cassandra sell 200 a. pt. (*) to Thomas Jones (IS#K: 169).

8 June 1731: Nathaniel Rigbie of AA Co., and w. Cassandra conv. 200 a. pt. (*) to Henry Cole (IS#L: 143).

29 Sep 1737: Nathaniel Rigbie of BA Co., merchant, conv. $3\frac{1}{2}$ a. pt. (*) to the Quakers (HWS#M: 17).

7 Nov 1741: Thomas Wells conv. 200 a. pt. of (*) (in all pt. of a 2000 a., tract called Wells Lot), to Charles Worthington (TB#A: 55).
7 Nov 1741: Henry Coale, with cons. of w. More conv. 200 a. pt. (*) to Charles Worthington (TB#A: 52).

PHILLIPS SWAMP

15 July 1672: 100 a. surv. for James Phillips at the head of Rumley Creek (MRR: 14).
27 July 1738: James Phillips of BA Co., Gent., conv. 100 a. (*) to Samuel Griffith (HWS#1-A: 159).
7 Dec 1739: JP, with cons. of w. Sarah, conv. 100 a. (*) to Samuel Griffith (HWS#1-A: 342).

PHILLS (PHILLIPS) CHOICE

29 Sep 1667: A 100 a. tract surv. for John Collier in Bush R.; belonging to the orphans of John Wood (MRR: 31).
13 May 1670: John Collier, Gent., of Bush R., conv. to Richard Adams and William Robinson, planters, 100 a. (*), on southwest side of Bush R. Ann Collier cons. (IR#PP: 82).
29 July 1683: Edward Reeves gave bond he ackn. and records in open court a deed of gift to Elizabeth Swanson, sole dau. of Edward Swanson, 100 a. (*). Reeves gave the bond to Richard Adams who assigned the bond on 5 Sep 1688 to John Wood who m. the said Elizabeth Swanson (IR#AM:67).
6 Aug 1683: Richard Adams and w. Catherine of CE Co., conv. to Edward Reeves, planter, 100 a. (*), including 50 a. formerly deeded by Adams and w. on 7 Nov 1671 to Henrietta Robinson, relict of William Robinson co partner with Adams in the 100 a., and now w. of Reeves. Catherine Adams, w. of RA, cons. before Johnson (RM#HS: 58).
5 Sep 1683: Richard Adams assigned 100 a. (*) to John Wood (IR#AM: 67).
10 Oct 1683: Edward Reeves gave bond to Richard Adams he will record deed of gift of 100 a. (*), to Elizabeth Swanson, sole dau. of Edward Swanson (IR#AM: 67).
16 July 1724: Edward Smith mortgaged to Josias Middlemore and John Crockett 100 a. (*) lately called Smith's Purchase, and 77 a. Smith's Discovery (IS#G: 344).

PICKETT'S VENTURE

8 March 1731: Heathcote Pickett and w. Mary, conv. 100 a. (*), being ½ of the tract, pt. of a larger tract called Dorsey's Discovery, to Joseph Thomas (IS#L: 199).

PIERPONT'S DISCOVERY

10 Dec 1720: Surv. for Charles Pierpoint (IS#G: 291).
15 May 1724: Charles Pierpoint of BA Co., with cons. of w. Sydney, conv. 73 a. (*) to Thomas Wainwright (IS#G: 291).

PILGRIM'S REST

2 March 1743; Amos Pilgrim and w. Rachel leased 100 a. (*) to Skipwith Coale (TB#C: 423).

PIMLICO (also PEMBLICO)

1699: 800 a. surv. for John Oldton and Thomas Hedge; later owned by Thomas McNamara; located on or about the site of Pimlico Race Course in BA Co. (MHM 16:114n, 119n).
See Horvath Plat: Pikesville.

PIMLICO

10 April 1725: 192 a. (Pemlico) granted to William Lowe (TB#C: 15).
18 Sep 1742: William Lowe, with cons. of w. Sarah, conv. (*) to Walter Tolley (TB#C: 15).

PISTOL THICKET

20 Oct 1716; Richard Lenox, with cons. of w. Mary, conv. 100 a. (*) to John Harryman (TR#A: 491).

PISTOLE

18 Nov 1728: 150 a. granted to Moses Rawlings (TB#C: 63).
10 Aug 1742: Vachel Denton of AA Co., Gent., conv. 75 a., ½ of (*) and 75 a., ½ of Addition to Pistole, to Nathaniel Stinchcomb (TB#C: 63).

PISTOLE, ADDITION TO

10 Aug 1742: Vachel Denton of AA Co., Gent., conv. 75 a., ½ of Pistole and 75 a., ½ of (*), to Nathaniel Stinchcomb (TB#C: 63).

PITCHCRAFT

112 a. surv. 29 December 1694 for Thomas Preston on n. side of Bush R. near Tillier's Creek; later held by Robert Shaw (MRR: 62).
20 Feb 1701: Thomas Preston, Sr., and w. Mary, conv. 112 a. to Robert Shaw (HW#2: 130).
6 July 1723: Abraham Taylor conv. 196 a. (*), which Taylor had resurv. on 23 March 1719, plus other lands, to Dr. George Buchanan (IS#G: 184, 196).
2 April 1728: Abraham Taylor conv. 100 a., pt. (*) and Polecat Ridge, to William Burney (IS#J: 100).
20 April 1733: Abraham Taylor conv. 100 a., pts. of (*) and Polecat Ridge to William Burney, annulling previous deed made 2 April 1728, and correcting the boundaries (IS#L: 370).

20 April 1733: Abraham Taylor conv. 170 a., pts. of (*) and Polecat Ridge to John Fling of KE Co. (IS#L: 357).

21 July 1736: John Fling of KE Co. made a will leaving his est. in BA Co. (being pts. of (*) and Polecat Ridge) to his w. Mary, for the use and maintenance of his ch. (MCW#VII: 191).

11 June 1743: John Jamison conv. 100 a. (*) and Polecat Ridge, 100 a. London, and 130 a. Burney's Purchase to Samuel Howell; Jamison's w., unnamed, cons. (TB#C: 258).

PITT

25 Oct 1770: Surv. for Benjamin Rogers. This was a Resurv. on Rogers Reserve and Hurst's March (C:19: cites BA Pat. Cert. #3859). It was advertised for sale in the Maryland Journal of 27 Nov 1786 ad 12 Feb 1787).

PLAINS (THE)

2 July 1688: Laid out by cert. of surv. (IS#IK: 188).

3 June 1696: James Todd of BA Co., Gent., and w. Elizabeth conv. (*) to Henry King of BA Co. (IS#IK: 188).

16 June 1726: William King conv. 187 a. (*) to Thomas Sheredine (IS#H: 279).

1729: Samuel Thomas conv. 300 a. (*) to Robert North (IS#K: 75).

9 March 1733: Samuel Chew and Philip Thomas gave receipt for following tracts to Thomas Sheredine: 473 a. Kingsbury Resurv., 250 a. Long Point, 500 a. Mason's Oate, 187 a. (*), 100 a. Rogers Road, and 150 a. Sheredine's Bottom (HWS#M: 19).

20 Nov 1734: Thomas Sheredine took the 187 a. tract surv. for James Todd and resurv. it into 259 a. TS and w. Tabitha conv. (*) to William Chettum of Beddington, Co. Surrey, and John Whittiwicks of the parish of Craden, Surrey, and the Company of the Pricipio Ironworks (HWS#M: 146).

14 May 1744: Robert North conv. 300 a. (*) which he had purch. from Samuel Thomas on 23 Aug 1729, to Patrick Lynch. Madam Frances North gave her cons. (TB#C: 525).

---- 1750: Patrick Lynch owned 300 a. (*) (1750 DB: 25).

PLAINS OF PARAN

15 Oct 1726: Henry Owings conv. 150 a. Paran and 200 a. (*), to Christopher Randall, Sr., as security for loan (IS#H: 292).

PLANTATION

8 Aug 1722: Catherine Johnson of BA Co., widow, conv. 15 a. pt. Howard's Range, and 5 a. (*), to Peter Besson of BA Co., chirurgeon (IS#G: 35).

PLANTER'S DELIGHT (See STONY POINT)

15 July 1658: 600 a. surv. for John Hawkins and Thomas Goldsmith and later held by the orphans of Col. George Wells (MRR: 5).

----- 1661: Thomas Goldsmith assigned remainder of tract to Edward Carter (RM#HS: 1).

----- 1662: John Collett conv. 200 a. of tract (RM#HS: 2).

28 Feb 1670/1: Richard Wells and w. Sophia of AA Co., conv. to their bro. George Wells of BA Co., 300 a. (*), bought 20 May 1661 from George Goldsmith, and adj. land of Samuel Goldsmith. Grantors give possession by affixing a silver six pence to the seals of the deed. 28 Feb 1670/1: Richard Wells and w. Sophia appoint Thomas Salmon their atty. (IR#PP: 95).

7 Aug 1694: George Utie and w. Mary conv. ½ of (*) (formerly laid out for John Hawkins and Thomas Goldsmith, and which desc. to George Utie) to George Wells in exch. for 400 a. Benjamin's Choice (RM#HS: 407).

4 April 1725: Richard Smithers of BA Co., Gent., conv. 250 a. Stony Point, being pt. Planter's Delight and pt. Colletts Point (formerly occupied by Col. George Wells, dec.) to John Stokes, adj. the land bequeathed by Col. George Wells to dau. Frances and s. George (IS#H: 124).

13 Feb 1726/7: John Smithers of KE Co., Gent., eld. s. of Blanch Smithers, (dau. of Col. George Wells and sister and coheir of George Wells, Jr.) conv. his interest in the following tracts to John Stokes: 800 a. Goldsmith's Hall, 24 a. Matthews Neglect, 400 a. (*), 200 a. Timber Proof, and 81 a. Watson's Addition (some of which were resurv. into 1150 a. Coheir's Lot) (IS#H: 385).

PLANTER'S LEAVE

1 Oct 1745: John Bosley, with cons. of w. Hannah, conv. 100 a. (*) to Samuel Tipton (TB#D: 361).

PLANTER'S PARADICE

1658: Surv. for Thomas Cornwallis (MHM 25:326).

29 Nov 1679: 829 a. surv. for William Cornwallis on w. side of northwest branch of Back R.; Cornwallis is dead; no heirs; land later poss. by Steven Bentley (MRR: 34).

1 Oct 1715: Isaac Simon of BA Co. and w. Deborah conv. 104 a. (*) to Ephraim Gover of CV Co. (TR#A: 342).

24 Feb 1724/5: Ephraim Gover of CV Co., conv. 104 a. (*) to Samuel Griffith. Tract had been bought from Isaac Simons (IS#H: 92).

14 April 1736: George Simmons of BA Co., s. of Isaac of AA Co.; conv. 94 a. (*) to Isaac Webster. 106 a. has already been sold. Tract was granted and surv. for Isaac Simmons for 200 a. GS's w. Elizabeth cons. (IS#IK: 293).

13 Aug 1737: Samuel Griffith conv. 104 a. (*) to James Lee. SG's w. Mary cons. (HWS#1-A: 4).

29 Sep 1738: Isaac Webster of BA Co. conv. 150 a. (*) to James Lee; IW's w. Margaret cons. (HWS#1-A: 135).

20 Nov 1741: John Ross, Gent., and Charles Carroll, chirurgeon of Annapolis, conv. 829 a. (*) to Luke Stansbury; they purch. the tract from Andrew Caldwell of KE Co., on Delaware Bay. This deed gives the descent of property from original patentee (TB#A: 94).

23 June 1742: William Demond of CH Co. and w. Mary conv. 200 a. (Miller says poss. pt. of (*)) to Thomas Hargues of PG Co. (TB#A: 163).

28 June 1742: Thomas Hargues of PG Co., carpenter, conv. 200 a. (*) to Edward Evans of BA Co., carpenter (TB#A: 166).

PLASTERER'S HALL

7 July 1683: 100 a. pat. for John Nicholson (MPL 25:92 and 22:109); later held by Henry Carter.

1 March 1698: John Nicholson of AA Co., with cons. of w. Rebecca, conv. 100 a. (*) to Henry Carter of BA Co., glazier (TR#RA: 410).

PLEASANT GARDEN

8 Aug 1739: Capt. Thomas Cresap conv. 200 a. pt. Bond's Manor and 150 a. (*) to Jacob Mires. TC's w. Hannah cons. (HWS#1-A: 243).

11 Oct 1754: George Green, with cons. of w. Sarah, conv. 50 a. (not already conv. by Green's father to Charles Bosley) to said Bosley (BB#I: 325).

PLEASANT GREEN (1722)

July 1722: 100 a. surv. for Morto McDowell (Card Index).

26 Sep 17030: Morto McDowell, with cons. of w. Eleanor, conv. 100 a. (*) to Richard Gist (IS#L: 38).

26 March 1742: Christopher Gist, with cons. of w. Sarah, conv. 100 a. (*), on the w. side of North Run, to his sister Jemima Seabrook (TB#A: 132).

4 Sep 1749: Charles Carroll of Annapolis Surgeon, conv. 100 a. (*) to William Seabrook (TR#C: 280).

PLEASANT GREEN
(Pt. LOGSDON'S ADDITION,
surv. for William Logsdon)

19 Sep 1726: William Logsdon conv. 97½ a. (*), being pt. of Logsdon's Addition, to his dau. Ann Durbin, and the heirs of her body. WL's w. Honour cons. (IS#H: 338).

27 Oct 1737: Samuel Durbin conv. 97½ a. (*) to William Mattingly. SD's w. Ann cons. (HWS#M: 24).

PLEASANT LEVELS

1758: Benjamin Arnold conv. 50 a. (*) to Andrew Appenhymer (B#G: 191).

PLEASANT SPRING

20 Aug 1749: 235 a. surv. for Benjamin Wells (WHC, App. 1: 2).

PLEASANT VALLEY

3 July 1746: Jacob Clawson conv. 50 a. pt. (*) to Thomas Sheredine (TB#E: 99).

PLUMB PARK

7 June 1671: William Palmer, Gent., conv. pt. (*) on the s. side of Sassafras R., to Richard Boyer and Francis Robinson (IR#PP: 101).

PLUMB POINT

13 April 1665: Walter Machanellin conv. 100 a. pt. (*) in Bush R., to William Orchard (IS#IK: 7).

1 March 1702: James Phillips of BA Co., with cons. of w. Bethia, conv. 100 a. (*) to Henry Matthews (HW#2: 310).

28 May 1748: Catherine Whayland, widow of Henry Wayland and her s. Henry conv. 100 a. (*) to Edward Brusbanks. HW's w. Rebecca cons. (TR#C: 25).

PLUMB TREE BOTTOM

1754: George Ogg conv. 238 a. Morgan's Tent Resurv., 30 a. (*), and 60 a. Mount Pleasant to Lovelace Gorsuch (BB#I: 458).

POCASON

20 April 1673: 100 a. surv. for James Phillips at the head of Rumley Creek (MRR: 14).

1 Aug 1721: James Phillips of BA Co., Gent., with cons. of w. Bethia, conv. 100 a. (*) to Thomas Handson of AA Co. (HW#2: 72).

POINT (THE) (Pt. of WARRINGTON)

4 March 1725/6: John Hill, mariner, s. of John Hill, conv. 100 a. (*) to James Maxwell (IS#K: 228, 229

29 May 1732: Christopher Divers conv. (*), formerly John Hill's Point, to William Hill (IS#L: 260).

POINT LOOKOUT

10 Nov 1695: 40 a. in AA Co. pat. by Hugh Merriken (MPL 40:116).

18 May 1710: Joshua Merriken, s. of Hugh, dec., with cons. of JM's w. Elizabeth, conv. $40\frac{1}{2}$ a. (*) to John Brice (TR#A: 79).

17 Aug 1756: Samuel Hooker conv. 150 a. (*) and 250 a. Hooker's Enlargement to his s. Thomas (BB#I: 579).

POLAR RIDGE

Formerly taken up by John Martin (IS#L: 114).

5 March 1705: John Boring of BA Co., planter, with cons. of w. Mary, conv. 100 a. (*) to Robuck Lynch (IR#AM: 53).

17 March 1730: Joseph Crouch of AA Co., and w. Mary (formerly w. of Robuck Lynch) conv. Hart's Green, Jones' Inheritance, and (*) (formerly taken up by John Martin) to William Lynch (IS#L: 114).

POLE ALMANAC NECK

26 Oct 1667: Surv. for William Davis (MRR: 1005).

9 Aug 1684: John Hawkins, of AA Co., eld. s. of John Hawkins of AA Co., dec., stated that his father took up (*) and sold 100 a. to Henry Constable (RM#HS: 1003).

POLECAT NECK

100 a. surv. for Henry Bowes (TB#C: 358).

22 March 1730: John, of PG Co., joiner, with cons. of w. Ann, lately Ann Dews, conv. ⅓ of 100 a. (*) and ⅓ of 258 a. Leafe Junior to Thomas White of BA Co., Gent. (IS#L: 88).

3 Nov 1743: Thomas White conv. 33 a., ⅓ of (*) and 300 a. White Hall, to Stephen Onion (TB#C: 358).

POLECAT RIDGE (1680)

28 June 1680: 150 a. pat. to James Phillips (MPL 28: 7).

3 Aug 1703: James Phillips conv. (*) to James Gallion. JP's w. Bethia cons. (HW#2: 284).

6 July 1723: Abraham Taylor conv. to George Buchanan following tracts: 75 a. (*) lately conv. to AT by John Gallion; deed also mentions Edwards' Lot, Pitchcraft, and 100 a. Wansworth (q.q.v.) (IS#G: 184).

2 April 1728: Abraham Taylor conv. 100 a. Pitchcraft and (*) to William Burney; tracts are adj. Burney's tract London (IS#J: 100).

1 Nov 1732 (?): James Gallion conv. (*) to Abraham Taylor. Tract was surv. 20 or 29 Nov 1679 (IS#L: 316).

20 April 1733: Abraham Taylor conv. pt. (*) to John Fling of KE Co. (IS#L: 357).

20 April 1733: Abraham Taylor conv. (*) to William Burney; Taylor annulled the deed made 2 April 1733, and rectified the boundaries (IS#L: 370).

11 Feb 1733/4: William Burney conv. (*) to John Jamison (HWS#M: 21).

21 July 1736: John Fling of KE Co. left pt. (*) and Pitchcraft to his w. Mary for the use and maintenance of ch. Jonathan, Joseph, John, and Ann (MCW#VII: 191).

11 June 1743: John Jamison conv. 130 a. Burney's Purchase, 100 a. London, and 100 a. Pitchcraft and (*), to Samuel Howell. JJ's w., unnamed, cons. (TB#C: 258).

POLECAT RIDGE

28 June 1680: 150 a. pat. by James Phillips (MPL 28: 7).

30 May 1692: Edmund Hansley of Back River, and w. Sarah, conv. 100 a. (*) to Edward Scott (RM#HS: 353).

3 Aug 1703: James Phillips conv. (*) to James Gallion. JP's w. Bethia cons. (HW#2: 284).

6 July 1723: Abraham Taylor conv. to George Buchanan the following tracts: 75 a. (*) lately conv. to AT by John Gallion; deed also mentions Edwards' Lot, Pitchcraft, and 100 a. Wansworth (q.v.) (IS#G: 184).

2 April 1728: Abraham Taylor conv. 100 a. Pitchcraft and (*) to William Burney; tracts are adj. Burney's tract London (IS#J: 100).

1 Nov 1732(?): James Gallion conv. (*) to Abraham Taylor. Tract was surv. 20 or 29 Nov 1679 (IS#L: 316).

See also entries under Pitchcraft for following dates: 20 April 1733, 11 Feb 1733/4, 21 July 1736, and 11 June 1743.

POOLE ISLAND

7 Jan 1659: granted to Robert Morris (Sr.) (TR#A: 166).

14 March 1706: John Morris, London, merchant, bro. and heir of Robert Morris, who was the eld. s. of Robert Morris, (Sr.), mariner, of London, also dec., conv. 200 a. (*) to John Carvil (TR#A: 166).

PORK FOREST

23 Aug 1755: John Love conv. 100 a. (*) to Charles Baker (BB#I: 438).

POOR JAMAICA MAN'S PLAGUE

8 Aug 1717: John Boreing of BA Co. conv. to Jonathan Tipton 250 a. pt. of Selsed, now called (*) (TR#A: 417).

2 Dec 1725: Jonathan Tipton conv. 600 a. pt. (*), pt. Selside, pt. Port Royal, and pt. Addition to Port Royal, to Thomas Cockey of AA Co. JT's w. Mary cons. (IS#H: 210).

-- Nov 1728: Jonathan Tipton conv. pt. (*) and pt. Port Royal to John Smith of CV Co. JT's w. Mary cons. (IS#I: 236).
-- June 1734: Jonathan Tipton makes a deed to correct errors in earlier deed of 1 June 1728 to John Smith of CV Co. JT's w. Mary cons. (HWS#M: 123).
6 July 1745: Matthew Haile and w. Rebecca conv. 150 a. pt. (*) to Richardson Stansbury (TB#D: 291).

POOR JAMAICA MAN'S PLAGUE, ADDITION TO
(See MOUNT HAZARD, SELSED, SMITH'S PLAINS)

5 Aug 1733: Jonathan Tipton conv. 30 a. pt. (*) to James Chilcoat (HWS#M: 103).
19 Sep 1738; Jonathan Tipton conv. 150 a. pt. (*) to Mathew Hale (HWS#1-A: 120).
14 Nov 1743: Capt. John Smith of CV Co., merchant, in exch. for 636 a., 66 perch. of Hall's Craft in CV Co., conv. to Walter Smith of the Freshes of the Patuxent, s. and heir of Walter Smith, dec., the following tracts: 300 a. pt. Daley's Discovery, 700 a. The Groves, and 424 a. pt. (*) (TB#C: 416).
9 July 1747: Jonathan Tipton conv. 50 a. pt. Port Royal and pt. (*) to Thomas Sheredine (TB#E: 610).
20 June 1748: James Chilcoat conv. 30 a. pt. (*) to Alexander Lawson. JC's w. Elizabeth cons. (TR#C: 493).
20 June 1750: James Chilcoate, with cons. of w. Elizabeth. conv. to Alexander Lawson, Merchant, 30 a. (*) (TR#C: 493).

POOR MAN'S BEGINNING

Aug 1708: John Hall conv. 78 a. (*) to Robert West (RM#HS: 453).

POPLAR NECK (c1666)

4 March 1666: William Fisher of VA, chirurgeon, and w. Frances conv. 1400 a. to Henry Ward (IR#PP: 61).

POPLAR NECK (1672)

16 Jan 1672: 100 a. surv. for Tobias Sternbridge on n. side of Patapsco R. on the s. side of Bear Creek (MRR: 90).

POPLAR NECK (1683)

20 Sep 1683: 1000 a. surv. for Mark Richardson at the head of Bush R.; later poss. by William Nicholson (MRR: 6). (See MHM 16: 140n for notes on location).
16 Nov 1703: Mark Richardson of BA Co., Gent., conv. 1000 a. (*) to William Nicholson (HW#2: 301).
5 Aug 1704: Cert. of Resurv. of (*) for William Nicholson of AA Co. (HW#2: 366).
31 Dec 1736: Richard Dorsey of AA Co., Gent., and w. Elizabeth sell 1000 a. (*) to Thomas Bond; tract was pat. 10 Sep 1664 to Mark Richardson, sold by him on 10 Nov 1703 to William Nicholson who devised it by his will to his s. William Nicholson, Jr., former husband of Elizabeth Dorsey; WN, Jr., by his will 28 Dec 1731, appointed his w. Elizabeth extx. to sell (*) to the highest bidder (IS#IK: 372).
8 Nov 1752: Thomas Bond conv. ½ of (*) to his s. Jacob. No w. joins (TR#D: 463 (Hayward).
25 April 1763: William Stansbury, s. and heir-at-law of Daniel Stansbury, dec., conv. to Richard Stansbury, another s. of said Daniel, 100 a. pt. (*). WS's w. Elizabeth cons. (B#L: 350).

POPLAR RIDGE

----- 1706: John Boring conv. 100 a. to Robuck Lynch (IR#AM: 53).

POPLAR SPRING GARDEN

18 March 1718: granted to John Petticoat (TR#DS: 185).
29 March 1720: John Petticoat of BA Co., with cons. of w. Sarah, conv. 120 a. (*) to Pleasance Dorsey (TR#DA: 185).

PORK FOREST

3 March 1725/6: Robert Love of BA Co. conv. 100 a. (*) to Charles Baker, Jr. (IS#H: 231).
9 March 1731: Robert Love made a new deed to ratify earlier sale of (*) to Charles Baker, Jr., original deed of 3 March 1725 contained mistakes (IS#L: 209).

PORK HALL

27 July 1745: John Bowen, with cons. of w. Lilly, conv. 100 a. (*) to Dutton Lane (TB#D: 263).
3 March 1747: Dutton Lane conv. 1 a. Friends Delight, pt. of (*), to Samuel Hooker and Thomas Matthews (TB#E: 672).

PORK HILL

10 Oct 1707: 100 a. in AA Co. pat. to David Mackelfresh (MPL DD#5: 420, PL#2: 205).
1 March 1745: Matthew Baker, ironmaster, lately of New England, conv. 100 a. (*) to William Bond (TB#E: 129).
1750: Capt. William Bond owned 100 a. (*) (1750 DB: 76).
6 Nov 1751: William Bond. conv. 100 a. (*) to Robert Collins. No w. signed (TR#D: 221: FSH).

PORKE POINT

14 April 1667: 100 a. surv. for James Phillips on e. side of Bush R. (MRR: 13).

3 March 1667/9: James Phillips conv. 100 a. (*) on e. side of Bush R., and pat. to said Phillips, to Thomas Thurston (IR#PP: 66).

9 Feb 1684/5: Thomas Thurston conv. 100 a. (*) to James Phillips, innholder (Deed and bond, RM#HS: 118).

28 Aug 1742: James Phillips leased (*) to Roger Perryman for 10 years (TB#C: 3).

PORT ROYAL (See STRIFE)

5 Jan 1671: 50 a. surv. for John Desjardin in Rumley Creek; later held by Robert Gibson, and later by Capt. Thomas Bale (MRR: 7).

1 May 1672: 50 a. pat. to John Desjardine (G#J: 126; TR#RA: 89).

3 June 1672: John Desjardines, Gent., conv. 50 a. (*) at Port Royal Creek in Rumley Creek, to John Rogers, merchant of Bristol (G#J: 126; TR#RA: 89).

6 Oct 1677: John Rogers, merchant of Bristol, appointed Joseph Sanders, merchant of Bristol, his atty. to conv. (*) to Miles Gibson. On 30 April 1678 Saunders conv. the tract to Gibson (IR#PP: 21, 22).

20 Aug 1704: Thomas Bale, with cons. of w. Sarah, conv. 400 a. Persimmon Point, 50 a. (*), and 115 a. Delfe Island to Thomas Edmonds. The property had been owned by Miles Gibson who d. intestate; it was inher. by Robert Gibson who left the land to the said Sarah Bale (HW#2: 356).

5 Sep 1704: Thomas Edmonds conv. all the lands back to Thomas Bale (HW#2: 358).

2 Dec 1725: Jonathan Tipton, with cons. of w. Mary, conv. pt. (*) to Thomas Cockey of AA Co., Gent (IS#H: 210).

1 Nov 1728: Jonathan Tipton, with w. Mary, conv. pt. (*) to John Smith of CV Co., Gent (IS#I: 236).

7 June 1734: JT, with cons. of w. Mary, made a deed to correct errors in deed of 1 Nov 1728 to John Smith (HWS#M: 123).

17 July 1744: Kemp Plummer of Gloucester Co., VA, conv. (*) and other lands to Thomas White. Deed states that Ann Bale was the residuary legatee by Anthony Bale's will, and she m. Michael Taylor, and d. a femme covert s.p. The land desc. to Kemp Plummer, s. of William Plummer of Gloucester Co., VA, who was bro. and heir-at-law to Ann Taylor (TB#C: 576).

9 July 1747: Jonathan Tipton conv. 50 a. pt. (*) and pt. Addition to Poor Jamaica Man's Plague to Thomas Sheredine (TB#E: 610).

PORT ROYAL PURCHASE

13 April 1680: 100 a. surv. for Miles Gibson, and later held by Robert Gibson, and later by Capt. Thomas Bale (MRR: 8).

17 July 1744: Kemp Plummer of Gloucester Co., VA, conv. (*) and other lands to Thomas White. Deed states that Ann Bale was the residuary legatee by Anthony Bale's will, and she m. Michael Taylor, and d. a femme covert s.p. The land desc. to Kemp Plummer, s. of William Plummer of Gloucester Co., VA, who was bro. and heir-at-law to Ann Taylor (TB#C: 576).

PORTER'S DESIRE

1768: Thomas Porter conv. 80¾ a. (*) to Adam Shipley (B#Q: 358).

POWELL

1659: Surv. for Thomas Powell; cert. named Bear Creek (MHM 25:334).

4 July 1733: Peter Galloway and w. Elizabeth conv. 300 a. (*), als. Howell, to Richard Galloway of AA Co., Gent. Tract had been surv. 29 July 1659 for Howell Powell (IS#L: 402).

POWELL'S CHOICE

7 Aug 1733: John Powell conv. 100 a. pt. (*) to Jacob Bull. Powell's w. Elizabeth cons. (IS#I: 408).

5 March 1734: Jacob Bull conv. to William Deal 100 a. pt. (*), surv. 22 April 1728 for John Powell. JB's w. Rachel cons. (HWS#M: 207).

15 Aug 1741: William Deal and w. Elizabeth conv. 100 a. pt. (*) to John Taylor (TB#A: 49).

POWELL'S GREEN SPRING

10 July 1724: 300 a. pat. to James Powell (MPL PL#5: 629, IL#A: 202).

See Horvath Plat: Granite.

21 Jan 1724/5: James Powell of BA Co., Gent., with cons. of w. Rebecca, execs. of Richard Colegate, conv. 300 a. (*) and 740 a. Rebecca's Lot (being the land where Richard Colegate lived and left to his w. Rebecca), to Lance Todd (IS#H: 9).

3 Nov 1740: James Powell of BA co., conv. (*) to Charles Ridgely (HWS#1-A: 437).

20 Sep 1743: JP again conv. 300 a. (*) to Charles Ridgely (TB#C: 325).

POWELL'S INHERITANCE

9 Sep 1682: 125 a. then in AA Co., granted to John and James Powell (MPL 24: 464, 30: 236).

15 Aug 1726: Joseph Powell conv. 125 a. (*) to his bro. Richard Jacks, s. of Thomas and Elizabeth Jacks. (John?) Powell d. intestate, and his s. and heir John, by his LWT bequeathed the land, after the death of his mother Elizabeth Jacks, to his bro., the said Joseph Powell (IS#H: 276).

POWELL'S NECK

6 Nov 1663: Howell Powell conv. to Philip Stevenson 100 a. Powell's Neck, location not stated (RM#HS: 7).

POWELL'S POINT (1661)

8 Aug 1661: 70 a. surv. for Howell Powell on n. side of Patapsco R., near Clephas' Creek; later poss. by Mary Ruxton for Nathaniel Ruxton's orphans (MRR: 86).

10 Aug 1662: Howell Powell conv. land to William Lewis and w. Constant (RM#HS: 10).

10 Aug 1662: William Lewis conv. land to Richard Carter or Collett (RM#HS: 10).

21 (?) 1667: Howell Powell conv. 70 a. on n. side of R., betw. Robert Gorsuch's land and the next creek eastward, to Warner Shudall. Elizabeth Powell gave her cons. (IR#PP: 2).

5 March 1667/8: Warner Shudall and w. Ann conv. to Nicholas Ruxton (Rixton?) 60 a. on n. side of Patapsco R., betw. Richard Gorsuch's land and the next creek eastward (IR#PP: 67). (Newspaper article erroneously gave 1687 as the year.)

30 Aug 1701: Mary Ruxton, widow of Nathaniel Ruxton, late of BA Co., dec., conv. to Richard Colegate (70?) a. of (*) and 100 a. Ruxton's Range (HW#2: 89).

3 Sep 1701: John Gay and w. Frances of BA Co. conv. to Richard Colegate 70 a. of (*) on n. side of Patapsco at Clapham's Creek, and 100 a. Ruxton's Range adj. the land of Nicholas Ruxton (HW#2: 90).

10 Oct 1747: Benjamin Colegate leased all the cultivated land in Huntington, (*), and Ruckston's (Ruxton's) Range to William Hammond for 14 years (TB#E: 612).

POWELL'S POINT (1667?)

9 July 1667: 100 a. surv. for Thomas Powell on the n. side of Patapsco R.; later poss. by Robert Johnson (MRR: 95). (This date might have been transcribed incorrectly--RWB.)

17 Aug 1664: Thomas Powell conv. to Thomas Todd of Gloucester Co., VA, 100 a. with houses thereon at or near and e. of Walnut Neck, on n. side of Patapsco R., as pat. to Powell (IR#PP: 66).

17 Aug 1664: Thomas Todd of Gloucester Co., VA, conv. to sons Robert and John Todd three tracts on Patapsco R., bought from Thomas Powell on this date. 6 July 1668: Thomas Todd of Gloucester Co., VA, appoints Richard Ball his atty. to take ackn. of land belonging to Todd (IR#PP: 66).

22 Feb 1667/8: Thomas Powell of TA Co. appoints Samuel Collett his atty. to ackn. sale of land in Patapsco R. to Thomas Todd of VA (IR#PP: 67).

POWELL'S PUMPKIN PATCH

22 June 1704: James Todd of BA Co., conv. Johnson's Dock, (*), and pt. Todd's Range, 250 a. in all, to Robert Johnson of AA Co., shipwright (HW#2: 344).

PRESTON'S CHANCE

16 Jan 1748/9: Bernard Preston of BA Co. conv. 100 a. (*) to James Preston (TR#C: 204).

PRESTON'S DECEIT

July 1738: Charles Baker conv. pts. of (*) to sons Lemuel and Indimeon. CB's w. Avarilla cons. (BCF: 20).

1740: Lemuel Baker conv. pt. (*) to Thomas Durbin (BCF: 21).

(no date): Indimeon Baker sold pt. (*) to Jonathan Hughes (BCF: 21).

1750: Thomas Durbin owned 50 a. (*) (1750 DB: 53).

c1754: Thomas Durbin owned pt. (*) and Chance (IBC: 60).

2 Sep 1766: Thomas Durbin conv. land inher. from his father, Thomas Durbin, dec., including (*) which Lemuel Baker derived from his father Charles Baker, and sold to the afsd. Thomas Durbin, Sr. (PCLR DD#4: 132).

PRESTON'S LUCK

50 a. surv. "no time" for Thomas Preston in a small creek called Cooke's Creek on e. side of Gunpowder R. (MRR: 61).

2 March 1702: Thomas Preston of BA Co., planter, and w. Mary conv. 200 a. pt. (*) to Isaac Baker (HW#2: 199).

15 July 1737: John Baker of BA Co. conv. 200 a. (*) to Rebecca Puttee, w. of Peter Puttee (IS#IK: 516).

15 April 1741: Rebecca Potee conv. the tract (surv. for Thomas Preston) to her dau. Elizabeth Potee, who agrees not to have any right to the land while her mother is living (HWS#1-A: 484).

1750: Rebecca Potee owned 200 a. pt. (*) (1750 DB).

PRICE'S GOOD WILL

1 Jan 1730: Mordecai Price, with cons. of w. Elizabeth, conv. 200 a. (*) to Aquila Carr (IS#L: 71).

5 July 1760: Moredecai Price, eld. s. and heir-at-law to Mordecai Price, late of BA Co., dec., conv. (*) to Thomas Cole, Jr., who m. Sarah, dau. of sd. Mordecai Price, dec. (B#H: 264).

28 June 1760: Aquila Carr of BA Co. conv. pt. (*) to Thomas Cole, Jr. (B#H: 267).

PRICHARD'S PURCHASE
(Pt. GREEN SPRING TRAVERSE)

23 June 1721; Richard Gist, with cons. of w. Zipporah, conv. 100 a. (*), pt. of Green Spring Traverse, to Herbert Prichard (RM#HS: 666).

PRIVILEGE (1670)
(Also LONGLAND'S PRIVILEGE)

13 Sep 1670: 250 a. surv. for Richard Ball; later possessed by Nathaniel Stinchcomb (MRR: 95).

20 Nov 1703: Nathaniel Stinchcomb gave bond to Thomas Long he would make over to him 250 a. (*) (TR#A: 119).

6 Oct 1758: John Stinchcomb conv. to John Long that tract called (*) which Nathaniel Stinchcomb, father of said John, gave bond to Thomas Long, father of afsd. JL for conveyance in 1703 (B#G: 240).

PRIVILEGE (or BENGER'S PRIVILEGE) (1679)

1679: 108 a. surv. for Robert Benger (MHM 25:340).

PRIVILEGE (1709)
(See MOUNT HAYES)

There are two tracts by this name; one is on the s. side of Back R., not in the Back River Lower Hundred.

10 May 1709: 407 a. in BA Co. pat. to James Hayes [sic] who resurv. the tract after purchasing it from Thomas Richardson (MPL DD#5: 546, PL#3: 139).

10 May 1709: 407 a. granted to John Hayes who by his LWT dated 9 Jan 1726/7 left it to Thomas Stansbury (IS#IK: 278).

18 Aug 1736: Thomas Stansbury and w. Jane conv. 407 a. (*) to Thomas Sligh (IS#IK: 278).

27 Jan 1750: 1440 a. of Stansbury's Inheritance, comprising pt. (*) and "Priviledge," pat. by Tobias Stansbury (MPL BY#1: 564, BY#2: 339).

PRIVILEGE (unidentified)

9 Dec 1701: Abraham Taylor conv. 50 a. (*), pt. of a larger tract called Ayer's Addition, to his son-in-law John Courckin (HW#2: 114).

5 Sep 1705: John Hayes and w. Elizabeth conv. 100 a. Longland's Privilege, pt. of (*), to Richard Longland (IR#PP: 187).

15 Oct 1709: Richard Longland of BA Co., made a will leaving (*) to his unborn child (MCW#III: 160).

25 Feb 1728/9: George Insull and w. Alice conv. 100 a. Longland's Privilege, pt. of (*) to Thomas Sheredine (IS#I: 251).

25 Nov 1731: Thomas Sheredine conv. 100 a. (*) to Thomas Sligh; TS's w. Tabitha cons. (IS#L: 279).

5 June 1745: Richard Harriott conv. 50 a. (*) to Henry Adams; RH's w. Mary cons. (TB#D: 130).

1750: Henry Adams owned 50 a. (*) (1750 DB).

PRIVILEGE, ADDITION TO

5 March 1702: Mark Swift, with cons. of w. Elizabeth, conv. 24 a. (*) to Abraham Taylor (HW#2: 128).

5 Aug 1703: Enoch Spinks and John Cutchin conv. 64 a. including Arress's Addition and (*) to James Crook (HW#2: 265).

PROCTOR'S HALL
(Not PRATER'S or PRATHER'S HALL)

30 Aug 1659: Nathaniel Proctor and George Gouldsmith had surv. for them 200 a. on the s. side of Swan Creed (on the westside of the Chesapeake Bay) (MPL 4: 265). The tract was later held by William Osbourne for the orphans of John Walsh or John Walston (MRR: 6).

-- April 1666: George Gouldsmith made his will (proved 20 July 1666), leaving Prater's Hall (actually (*)) on Swan Creek, and 500 a. of Surveyor's Point, on Gunpowder R., to his dau. Mary. (He also named a s. George) (MCW#I: 35).

4 Jan 1686/7: George Gouldsmith, Gent., and w. Martha conv. to John Walston, Gent., two tracts on the s. side of Swan Creek: 200 a. (*), and 200 a. The Enlargement, adj. the land granted to Gouldsmith and Proctor (RM#HS: 212).

2 April 1736: Arabella, dau. of John Walston, dec., and now w. of Bennett Garrett, joined by her husband, conv. to Mary Marshall and George Presbury 200 a. (*) and 200 a. The Enlargement; the deed also corrected a deficiency of 109 a. in a tract called Rayly (HWS#M: 424).

PROGRESS

2 Nov 1754: John Whips of AA Co. conv. pt. (*) to Benjamin Whips of BA Co. (BB#I: 334).

6 Nov 1758: John Whips of AA Co. conv. 100 a. pt. (*) to Edward Dorsey of John (B#G: 256).

PROSPECT (1672)

19 May 1672: 80 a. surv. for Charles Gorsuch on the w. side of Back R.; later held by orphans of William Boring; still later held by James Boring (MRR: 94).

10 June 1673: Charles Gorsuch conv., 86 a. (*), near the head of Bear Creek, to Roger Sedwell; same day, gave Thomas Long p/a to ackn. sale of 86 a. to Sedwell (G#J: 212, TR#A: ?).

20 July 1695: Selah Dorman and w. Jane conv. 80 a. (*) to George Chancey; deed states tract was orig. granted to Charles Gorsuch in 1672 and later sold to Roger Sedwell (RM#HS: 507).

12 June 1698: George Chancey of Patapsco R. conv. 80 a. (*) to Tobias Starnborough; deed states that Chancey bought it from Selah Dorman who m. the heir of Roger Sedwell (TR#RA: 412).

25 April 1763: William Stansbury, s. and heir-at-law of late Daniel Stansbury, dec., conv. 80 a. (*) to Daniel Stansbury; WS'. w. Elizabeth cons. (B#L: 353).

PROSPECT (1687)

13 Aug 1687: 60 a surv. for Robert Benjer on one of the branches of Back R.; poss. by Mr. Watkins and still later by William Farfarr (MRR: 79).

9 March (16?)99: Robert Benger and w. Deborah, late of BA Co., innholder, conv. 60 a. (*) to William Farfarr (TR#RA: 359).

PROSPECT

116 a. orig. surv. for Thomas Preston.

8 May 1710: Thomas Preston, Jr., of BA Co., conv. 243 a. (*) to William Hamilton and Peter Bond; tract is at head of Winter's Run, adj. Timber Hill (TR#A: 77).

6 Nov 1716: Peter Bond and William Hamilton conv. 243 a. (*) to John Norris of AA Co.; PB's w. Eleanor cons. (TR#A: 410).

9 Nov 1724: John Norris, Sr., of AA Co., conv. 116 a. (*) to s. Edward; JN's w. Mary cons. (IS#H: 35).

PROSPECT

16 Nov 1703: Charles Adams conv. 20 a. (*) to Thomas Chamberlain (HW#2: 348).

2 Oct 1713: Thomas Chamberlain, Gent., conv. 20 a. (*) to Charles Carroll of Annapolis (TR#A: 399).

PROSPERITY

20 Sep 1664: A 140 a. tract surv. for Thomas Lightfoot on the w. side of Bush R., at a point at the mouth of the Middle Branch, of said r.; later poss. by Aquila Pace (MRR: 32).

11 Dec 1691: Rebecca Lightfoot, widow, conv. 140 a. to Peter Bond (RM#HS: 351).

6 June 1692: Peter Bond and w. Alice conv. 200 a. of Harris' Trust and 140 a. (*) to Thomas Hedge of BA Co. (RM#HS: 227).

1 Nov 1692: Peter Bond and w. Alice conv. 140 a. to Thomas Hedge, who on the same day conv. it back to PB (did Hedge conv. Bond another tract?) (RM#HS: 363).

8 Aug 1694: Thomas Hedge and w. Ann conv. 145 a. to John Hall of BA Co. (RM#HS: 414).

3 March 1708: John Hall of BA Co. conv. 140 a. to Aquila Paca (RM#HS: 576).

PROVIDENCE

3 May 1745: John Henthorne and w. Margaret conv. 100 a. (*) to James Henthorne and 272 a. to Matthias Smiser (TB#C: 688, 690).

26 April 1746: James Henthorne and w. Mary., conv. 100 a. (*) to Jacob Hook, weaver (TB#E: 49).

PURCHASE

5 June 1727: Michael Rutledge, with cons. of w. Hannah, of BA Co. conv. to John Harryman 50 a., pt. Hazard, which when it was made over to said MR was called (*) (IS#H: 403).

QUARTER (THE)

20 April 1720: Mrs. Sarah Brice, widow and extx. of John Brice of AA Co., conv. (*) and The Tanyard to Edward Teall (who m. Hannah, widow and admx. of Nathaniel Stinchcomb). The deed also mentioned Benj. and George Nelthorpe (TR#DS: 209).

RACHEL'S DELIGHT (1725)

4 June 1725: Surv. for John Muckeldory (HWS#M: 4).

5 Aug 1730: John Muckeldory of BA Co., planter, conv. 50 a., $\frac{1}{2}$ of (*), to Francis Freeman. JM's w. Frances cons. (IS#L: 8).

9 Nov 1733: Francis Freeman conv. 50 a., $\frac{1}{2}$ of (*), to Abraham Jarrett, cordwainer. FF's w. Elizabeth cons. (HWS#M: 4).

12 March 1733/4: Samuel Chew and Philip Thomas give Abraham Jarrett a receipt for an alienation

fine on (*) which Francis Freeman conv. to Jarrett (HWS#M: 81).

3 March 1741: Abraham Jarrett and w. Elinor, and Francis Freeman, conv. 100 a. (*) to Patrick Vance (TB#A: 113).

5 Aug 1741: Avinton Phelps (who m. Rachel Muckeldory on 23 April 1730 in St. George's Parish), now of Orange Co., VA, and w. Rachel, conv. 50 a. (*) to Henry Thomas (HWS#1-A: 519).

23 July 1747: Andrew Vance conv. 100 a. pt. (*) to Robert Bryerly (TB#E: 490).

RACHEL'S DELIGHT (1728)

28 Nov 1728: Tract surv. for William Deale (HWS#M: 203).

5 March 1734: William Deale of BA Co. conv. 100 a. (*) being pt. of Aston and Deale's Chance, to Henry Donahue. WD's w. Eleanor cons. (HWS#M: 203).

27 March 1742: Henry Donahue and w. Rachel conv. 1009 a. (*) to Benjamin Wheeler (TB#A: 134).

RADINGE (REDINGE)

3 Aug 1674: Stephen Whyte (White), and w. Ann conv. 100 a. pt. (*) on the s. side of Patapsco R., to Joseph Symons (G#J: 286).

RADNIDGE

8 June 1710: Christopher Cox, innholder, and w. Mary, conv. 160 a. (*) to Stephen White (TR#A: 75).

RAMA

28 April 1687: 100 a. surv. for Samuel Sickelmore; later held by John Parker for the orphans of Thomas Smith, and later by the orphans of TS (MRR: 69).

6 June 1693: Samuel Sickelmore and w. Sarah conv. 100 a. (*) to Thomas Smith (RM#HS: 382).

RANDALL'S FANCY

1728: 100 a. pat. to Christopher Randall (Card Index to Patents).

1752: 170 a. pat. to John Randall (Card Index to Patents).

RANDALL'S MEADOWS

30 Aug 1743: 75 a. pat. by Christopher Randall (MPL LG#B: 757, LG#E: 148).

See Horvath Plat: Randallstown.

10 March 1747: Christopher Randall conv. 133 a. George's Park, 150 a. Jeopardy, and 75 a. (*) to Rachel Bailey of BA Co., widow (TB#E: 696).

RANDALLS RETIREMENT

25 Sep 1760: Randall Ramsey conv. 80 a. (*) to Archibald Akin (B#K: 21).

RANGE (THE) (1685)

22 Dec 1685: 240 a. surv. for Henry Constable on the s. side of r.; later poss. by the heir of Rigby (MRR: 108).

RANGE (THE) (1686)

11 Nov 1686: 200 a. surv. for Edward Dowse and Emanuel Ceely at the head of Salt Peter Creek; later poss. by William Dane (MRR: 59).

RANGE (THE)

24 Feb 1686/7: Charles Gorsuch and w. Sarah of Patapsco R., for 14,000 pounds of tobacco, conv. to Roger Newman of London, 260 a. (*) at Denton Creek (RM#HS: 220). Same day: CG gave bond he will fulfill the covenants. Same day Sarah Gorsuch appoints John Boring her atty. to ackn. conveyance of 260 a. (RM#HS: 220).

RANGE (THE) (1705)

13 Jan 1705: Lord Baltimore granted 200 a. (*) to Robert Hewett (TR#A: 174).

24 Dec 1711: Robert Hewett of AA Co., and w. Elizabeth conv. to Amos Garrett of AA Co. 200 a. (*). Hewett gave p/a to Wornall Hunt or any of the attys. of the Prov. or County Court to ackn. the above deed (TR#A: 174).

RANGER'S LODGE

10 Aug 1684: 550 (or 500) a. pat. to David Jones (RM#HS: 205).

17 Nov 1686: David Jones, planter, conv. 550 a. (*) to John ... (RM#HS: 205).

9 Nov 1739: George Stokes and w. Susanna and James Philips make an agreement concerning conv. of (*) to Isaac Webster (TB#A: 40).

14 Sep 1741: Susannah, widow of George Stokes, and James Phillips (her bro.: they are ch. of Col. James Phillips, dec.), conv. 500 a. (*) to Isaac Webster (TB#A: 42).

RANTER'S RIDGE

19 Nov 1718: Joshua Brown of BA Co., planter, gave quitclaim deed for 207½ a., being the lower half of (*), to Amos Garrett. Tract was formerly owned by Thomas Brown of BA Co., who made a will on 22 March 1715, naming three sons: Thomas (heir-at-law), John, and Joshua (TR#RA: 479).

20 Nov 1718: Amos Garrett of AA Co., conv. 100 a. (*) to Joshua Brown (TR#RA: 497).

RATTLESNAKE NECK

8 Feb 1719: Nathan Rigbie of AA Co. conv., 300 a. (*) to Robert Boone and James Moss of BA Co. (TR#RA: 537).

RATTLESNAKE RIDGE

1739: Surv. for Edw. Richards.

See Horvath Plat: Old Hampstead.

19 July 1765: Richard Richards and w. Sarah conv. 33¾ a. pt. (*) and 16¼ a. pt. Transilvania to Andrew Stigar and Peter Earp, Sr. (B#O: 338).

RAVEN'S OUTLET

24 Dec 1726: Luke Raven conv. 125 a. (*) to his s., Luke Raven (IS#H: 388).

RAVEN'S REFUSE

n.d.: on PW Plat H.

RAYLEY

9 Aug 1659: 200 a. surv. for James Robinson; later held by Mark Richardson and still later by Thomas Wainwright (MRR: 6).

5 March 1683/4: Elias Robertson of CE Co., conv. 200 a. (*) to Andrew Mattson, carpenter; tract is on n. side of Swan Creek, as described in a deed to James Robertson of CE Co., dec. (RM#HS: 87).

8 Feb 1688/9: Andrew Mattson and w. Jane conv. 200 a. (*) and 10 a. Mattson's Lot, formerly laid out for Elias Robertson, to Mark Richardson (RM#HS: 318).

2 March 1712: James Phillips and w. Bethia, conv., 200 a. (*) and 10 a., Mattson's Lot to John Webster; both tracts were sold by Andrew Mattson to Mark Richardson who bequeathed them by his will, after the death of his w. Susanna, to his dau.-in-law Bethia Phillips (TR#A: 241).

12 March 1716: James Phillips of BA Co., conv. both tracts to Francis Holland, even though the deed states that both tracts had earlier been sold by Phillips and his w. to John Webster (TR#A: 475).

28 May 1725: Francis Holland conv. both tracts to John Stokes (IS#H: 128).

28 May 1725: Francis Holland conv. 10 a. Mattsons Lot and 200 a. (*) to Francis Holland (IS#H: 170).

7 Feb 1726: John Stokes of BA Co., Gent., conv. both tracts to Rev. Stephen Wilkinson, minister, and the vestrymen of St. George's Parish (IS#H: 433).

2 April 1736: Bennett Garrett and w. Arabella, dau. of John Walston, conv. land to Mary Marshall and George Presbury. Deed also corrects a deficiency of 109 a. in (*) (HWS#M: 424).

REBECCA'S DELIGHT

7 Aug 1688 Rebecca Lightfoot, widow of Thomas conv., 32 a. (*) to Christopher Gist (RM#HS: 279).

10 Sep 1705: Richard Gist conv. to Richard Cromwell the land which Thomas Hammond and w. Rebecca conv. to said Richard: 125 a. Gist's Rest, and another 100 a. adj., in all 225 a., now called (*). RG's w. Zipporah cons. (IR#PP: 192).

REBECCA'S LOT

Granted to Rebecca Herbert (IS#H: 9).

21 Jan 1724/5: James Powell of BA Co., Gent., with cons. of w. Rebecca, execs. of Richard Colegate, conv. 300 a. Powell's Green Spring, and 740 a. (*) (being the land where Richard Colegate lived and left to his w. Rebecca), to Lance Todd (IS#H: 9).

10 Nov 1732: Archibald Rollo and w. Rebecca execute another deed for 100 a. (*) to John Norris. The first deed was made 3 March 1730 but not recorded in time (IS#L: 307).

1 Sep 1747: John Norris and w. Ann conv. 100 a. (*) to Stephen Onion (TB#E: 539).

RED BUDD POINT

7 April 1671: Joseph Heves conv. 100 a. (*) on the southwest side of Bush R. to Thomas Heath, planter (IR#PP: 103).

RED MONK

26 Aug 1730: John Roberts conv. 11 a. to Thomas Humphries (IS#L: 14).

RED OAK LAND

18 April 1763: Patrick Irons of BA Co., yeoman, conv. 2 a. (*) on e. side of a small branch desc. into a n. fork of Patapsco Falls, to Richard Richards (B#L: 144).

REDINGE (See RADINGE)

REEVES

2 Jan 1749: Edward Norwood leased to Francis Petty all of tract (*), adj. Toms' Range and near the head of Clapper's Creek, for 21 years (TR#C: 506).

REEVES NECK

July 1725: Edward Cox, with cons. of w. Jane,. conv. 50 a.(*) to William Reeves (IS#H: 144).

REFUGE

10 Jan 1707: 239 a. pat. to Luke Raven (MPL DD#5: 197, and PL#2: 114). Pt. of this tract lies n. of Northampton on Peterson's Run and Pot Spring Run, a branch of the former. It became Northampton Iron Works (MHM 47:99).

21 April 1741: Luke Raven, with cons. of w. Sarah, conv. 239 a(*) to his loving bros. and sisters, viz: Solomon Hillen and w. Elizabeth, and Samuel Griffith and w. Mary (HWS#1-A: 490).

REGULATION

1745: 505 a. for Thomas Carr.

See PW Plat H.

8 Sep 1759: Joseph Taylor, exec. of Thomas Carr, conv. 505 a. (*) to Benjamin Bowen (B#H: 1).

RELYE

9 Aug 1659: 200 a. surv. for James Robinson (MRR: 6).

REPULTA
(Also known as STOCKETT'S CHOICE)

24 Sep 1663: 300 a. pat. to Henry Stockett.

13 Dec 1670: Henry Stockett, Gent., of AA Co. conv. 300 a. (*) to Thomas Ford, planter, of Herring Creek; tract was pat. 24 Sep 1663 to Stockett. On 11 Jan 1670/1 Henry and Katherine Stockett appoint Nathaniel Stiles their atty. (IR#PP: 115).

30 Aug 1719: John Bagby and w. Mary of CV Co. conv. 150 a. ½ of (*) to Samuel Gover of AA Co.; deed stated that Henry Stockett sold the land to Thomas Ford on 13 Dec 1670; Ford d. intestate and land went to his s. James, whose LWT of 28 July 1702, left it to bro. John and sister Elizabeth Ford; John d. intestate and his share went to his dau. Mary, now w. of JB (TR#DS: 147).

27 May 1732: Webber Clarke of BA Co., carpenter, conv. pt. (*) to Ephraim Gover. WC's w. Mary cons. Mentioned deed of gift 8 July 1706 to WC from his mother and father ... and Elizabeth Clark (IS#L: 249).

23 Oct 1735: Elizabeth Norton conv. 200 a. (*) to her s. Ford Barnes (HWS#M: 323).

15 March 1737/8: Ephraim Gover of AA Co. conv. 50 a. (*) to Samuel Gover (HWS#1-A: 88).

30 March 1744: William Scrivener and w. Elizabeth, and John Carr and w. Lewsey of AA Co., coheirs of John Clark, s. of Matthew Clark of BA Co., and son-in-law of MC's w. Elizabeth, sister of James Ford, late of AA Co., conv. pt.(*), no acreage stated, to Samuel Gover (TB#C: 565).

RESERVE (THE)

30 Aug 1735: Emanuel Teal, with cons. of w. Katherine, conv. 200 a. (*) to Edmond Howard (HWS#M: 283).

RESOLUTION

n.d.: 180 a. for Abraham Scott; on PW Plat E.

RICH LAND

19 Feb 1711; Thomas Randall conv. 100 a. (*) to George Ogg. TR's w. Hannah cons. (TR#A: 176).

RICH LEVEL (1668)

20 June 1668: 200 a. pat. to Charles Gorsuch (IR#PP: 104).

1 Feb 1669/70: Charles Gorsuch conv. 200 a. (*), 50 a. Gold Comfort, to Thomas Roper of South R., AA Co. Loveless Gorsuch also signed (IR#PP: 104).

1 Nov 1675: Thomas Roper conv. 100 a. (*), 50 a. Cold Comfort, and 145 a. Roper's Range to Anthony Demondidier. W. Mary Roper released dower (G#J: 316).

-- Nov 1675: Thomas Roper gave bond to Anthony Demondidier (G#J: 316-321).

7 Sep 1698: Anthony Demondidier of BA Co., and Mary his now w. conv. 100 a. (*), 145 a. Roper's Range, and 50 a. Cold Comfort, to Margaret Kiersted of CV Co., widow, and her s. Hance Kiersted (HW#2: 33).

6 Sep 1699: Additional deed conv. tracts to Samuel Sicklemore and Henry Wriothesley in trust for above M. K. and H. K. (HW#2: 29).

19 May 1724: Thomas Taylor and w. Elizabeth conv. 100 a. (*), 100 a. Fox Hall, and 50 a. Cold Comfort, to Philip Smith (IS#G: 318).

RICH LEVEL (1679)

24 March 1679: 800 a. surv. for George Yates at the end of the w. line of Henry Stockett; later poss. by Thomas Plummer of PG Co.; still later poss. by Col. Henry Darnall of PG Co. (MRR: 28).

1 June 1703: Nicholas Brent of Stafford Co., VA, conv. 600 a. pt. (*) to Col. Henry Darnall of PG Co. (HW#2: 262).

26 Aug 1703: Thomas Plummer and w. Mary conv. 200 a. (*) to Col. Henry Darnall; deed stated that the land was granted to George Yates on 29 Jan 1680; on 10 Dec 1682 George Yate sold 600 a. to Henry Brent of CV Co.; George Yate then d. leaving 200 a. to his dau. Elizabeth, w. of TP (HW#2: 309).

RICH LEVEL (1702)

1702: 100 a. pat. by Andrew Hurd (MPL DD#5: 63; see also MWS#1 220).

RICH LEVEL (Pt. SPRING GARDEN)

14 May 1753: John Thomas, with cons. of w. Sarah, only dau. and heir-at-law of Hill Savage, conv. (*) orig. granted to John Roberts as 150 a. known as Spring Garden (TR#D: 548).

RICH NECK

23 July 1674: Thomas Long, Gent., with cons. of w. Jane, of Back River, conv. 74 a. (*), on the s. side of Middle R., to John Leakins (G#J: 308).

5 April 1731: John Parrish, with cons. of w. Catherine, conv. 138 a. (*) to Charles Ridgely (IS#L: 80).

RICH (NECK?) LEVEL

1 Feb 1669/70: Charles Gorsuch, planter, conv. 50 a. Cold Comfort and 100 a. (*) to Thomas Roper. Lovelace Gorsuch also signs the deed (IR#PP: 104).

1 Nov 1675: Thomas Roper of AA Co. conv. to Anthony Demondidier also of BA Co. 295 a. in three parcels: 50 a. Cold Comfort, 100 a. (*) (both conv. to Roper on 1 Feb 1669/70), and 145 a. Ropers Range. TR's w. Mary released seisin on 2 Nov 1675 (G#J: 316).

7 Sep 1698: Anthony Demondidier of BA Co. and w. Mary conv. 50 a. Cold Comfort, 100 a. (*), and 145 a. Roper's Range to Margaret Kiersted of CV Co., widow, and her s. Hance Kiersted (HW#2: 33).

6 March 1699: Anthony Demondidier conv. above three tracts to Samuel Sickelmore and Henry Wriothesley in trust for above named Margaret and Hance Kiersted (HW#2: 29).

19 May 1724: Thomas Taylor and w. Elizabeth conv. 50 a. Cold Comfort, 100 a. Fox Hall, and 100 a. (*) to Philip Smith (IS#G: 318).

21 Nov 1746: George Ogg, with cons. of w. Mary, conv. ½ pt. of George's Addition, George's Beginning, and (*) to John Metcalf (TB#E: 282).

28 Feb 1746: John Metcalfe, with cons. of w. Mary conv. to Rachel Bailey, 170 a. being ½ pt. of George's Addition, George's Beginning, and (*), 100 a. Mary's Meadows, and 100 a. Metcalf's Addition. (TB#E: 315).

RICH LEVEL, ADDITION TO

23 Sep 1745: George Ogg of BA Co., with cons. of w. Mary, conv. 40 a. George's Beginnings and pt. (*) to John Risteau (TB#D: 331).

27 Aug 1746: John Risteau conv. 170 a. George's Beginning and Addition (prob. this tract) to his dau. Catherine and her husband Thomas Cockey; if Catherine d. land to go to her eld. child; if Catherine dies s.p., the land was to go to TC (TB#E. 276).

RICH NECK

5 April 1738: John Parrish conv. 138 a. (*) and 189 a. Brotherly Love to Charles Ridgely. JP's w. Catherine cons. (IS#L: 80).

RICH NECK LEVEL (See RICH LEVEL)

RICHARDS' CHANCE

11 Nov 1758: Richard Richards, yeoman, conv. 50 a. (*) to John Mohargo (B#G: 291).

RICHARDS' HOPE

29 April 1685: Thomas Lightfoot, surveyor, conv. to Richard Walsh, planter, 200 a. (*), being pt. of 1000 a. and 500 a. tracts called Expectation. TL's w. Rebecca signs (RM#HS: 124).

20 May 1720: Thomas Welch of BA Co., conv. 200 a. (*) to John Risteau (TR#DS: 184).

2 March 1742: John Risteau conv. 200 a. (*) to his sons Talbot (to have the upper 100 a.) and Isaac Risteau (to have the lower 100 a.) (TB#C: 114).

RICHARDSON

17 Aug 1664: Thomas Powell conv. 300 a. of (*) to Thomas Todd, now of VA, being the same land Powell had formerly bought from Richard Gorsuch (IR#PP: 66).

17 Aug 1664: Thomas Todd of Gloucester Co., VA, conv. to his sons Robert and John Todd three tracts on Patapsco R., including (*), bought this date from Thomas Powell (IR#PP: 66).

22 Feb 1667/8: Thomas Powell of TA Co. appointed Samuel Collett his atty. to ackn. sales of land in Patapsco R. to Thomas Todd of VA, acc. to writings in possession of John Collett (IR#PP: 67).

6 July 1668: Todd appointed Richard Ball of BA Co. his atty. to take ackn. of land belonging to Todd (IR#PP: 66).

4 Sep 1686: Thomas Richardson conv. 100 a. (*) to John Carpenter. Thomas Scudamore ackn. in court on 3 Nov as atty. for Thomas and w. Rachel. Same: Richardson gave bond to Hayes (RM#HS: 201).

2 Nov 1692: John Hayes of BA Co. conv. 100 a. (*) to Arthur Taylor (RM#HS: 360).

5 June 1694: John Taylor of BA Co., planter, conv. 100 a. (*) to John Ewings, boatwright; tract was formerly sold by John Hayes to Arthur Taylor, father of John Taylor, the grantor (RM#HS: 404).

20 Oct 1695: John Ewings of BA Co., boatwright, conv. 100 a. (*) to Patrick Dunkenson of AA Co., planter; JE' w. Elizabeth cons. (RM#HS: 490).

12 June 1702: James Todd of BA Co. conv. 300 a. Black Walnut (the vulgar name of (*)) to Mark Swift (HW#2: 153).

21 May 1703: Mark Swift of BA Co., and w. Elizabeth (through James Crooke, their atty.) conv. 300 a. (*) to John Sheffield of London, merchant (HW#2: 328).

19 June 1735: Benjamin Hammond of AA Co. deeded to Bezaleel Foster 100 a. of (*). BH's w. Margaret cons. (HWS#M: 241).

RICHARDSONS DELIGHT

31 July 1746: John Hall and w. Bethia conv. to Abraham Raven 100 a. Coxes Fancy, 15 a. Luke's Addition, and pt. (*), to Abraham Raven (TB#E: 126).

RICHARDSON'S FOREST

3 Nov 1692: Thomas Richardson conv. 226 a. (*) to Richard Jones (RM#HS: 358).

6 May 1742: Henry Leake of PG Co., with cons. of w. Cassandra, conv. 226 a. (*) to John Harryman (TB#A 144).

RICHARDSON'S LEVEL

1 April 1681: Thomas Richardson and w. Rachel conv. 207 a. (*), on a branch of Saltpeter Creek on the s. side of Gunpowder R., to John Rockhold of AA Co. (IR#AM: 118).

2 June 1747: Reason Rockhold, labourer, conv. 103½ a., being ½ of (*) to William Andrews, Elizabeth Rockhold, mother of RR, approved (TB#E: 420).

4 Nov 1748: Asel Rockhold conv. to William Andrew all his right to ½ of (*) (TR#C: 143).

12 May 1750: John Rockhold of BA Co., laborer, conv. to William Andrew, innholder, all of JR's right to 207 a. (*). JR's w. Elizabeth cons. (TR#C: 432).

RICHARDSON'S NEGLECT

9 May 1724: 400 a. surv. for John Dorsey (TB#A: 149).

5 Aug 1730: John Crockett and w. Mary and Thomas Bond and w. Ann conv. 400 a. (*) to Thomas Dulany (IS#L: 28).

17 Jan 1732: Charles Smith of BA Co. conv. (*) to Luke Stansbury (IS#L: 348).

19 Jan 1741: Thomas Dulany and w. Sarah conv. ½ of (*) to William Andrews (TB#A: 149).

4 Sep 1741: Samuel Smith conv. 57 a. (*) to Buckler Partridge (TB#A: 72).

6 March 1743: William Andrew, innholder, and w. Mary, conv. 200 a. ½ of (*), to Henry Hendrickson (TB#C: 424).

6 Dec 1749: Samuel Smith conv. to Jane Partridge 57 a. (*), except for parcel sold by Charles Smith, father of Samuel, to Luke Stansbury. SS's w. Elizabeth cons. (TR#C: 417).

RICHARDSON'S OUTLET

12 March 1686/7: 808 a. surv. for Thomas Richardson on the s. side of Gunpowder R.; later 100 a. poss. by Walter Morrow; 230 a. poss. by Thomas Sterling in TA Co.; and 478 a. residue in possession of James Richardson of BA Co. (MRR: 62).

3 Nov 1696: Lt. Col. Thomas Richardson and w. Mary conv. to Walter Morrow 100 a. Walter's Hope, pt. of (*), laid out by cert. of surv. 29 Oct 1696 (IS#IK: 88).

3 Aug 1697: Thomas Richardson conv. Hickory Level, pt. of 830 a. pat. as (*), to his s. James (IS#IK: 164).

18 March 1699: Thomas Richardson of BA Co. and w. Susanna conv. Hickory Level orig. called (*), to Thomas Sterling of CV Co. (HW#2: 15).

4 June 1720: Richard Lenox and w. Mary conv. (pt. of?) 808 a. Hickory Level to Thomas Tolley; tract was granted to Col. Thomas Richardson on 10 Nov 1695; deed mentions James Richardson, s. of Col. Thomas and the bro. of Mary Lenox; also mentions a mortgage to John Brice of AA Co., merchant (TR#DS: 212).

2 Sep 1724: Thomas Tolley of BA Co., Gent., and w. Mary, conv. 100 a. Scholar's Plains, pt. of Hickory Level to William Tibbs, Col. John Dorsey, William Hamilton, Capt. John Stokes, Capt. Thomas Sheredine, and Mr. Riger Matthews, Visitors of the BA Co. Free School. TT's w. Mary cons. (IS#G: 374).

29 Dec 1725: Alexander Adair of CV Co., chirurgeon, and w. Christian, conv. 230 a. Sterling's Purchase, which Thomas Sterling bought from Thomas Richardson on 18 March 1699, to Richard Caswell (IS#H: 220).

10 July 1746: William Dallam conv. 230 a. of Sterling's Purchase, being pt. of Hickory Level, to William Andres and Abraham Andrews, s. of William. WD's w. Mary cons. (TB#E: 265).

RICHARDSON'S OUTLET

1756: Surv. for Thomas Richardson, near Indian Wills Cabin Branch (MHM 16:129n).

1760: William Andrew conv. 105 a. pt. (*) to Alexander Lawson and Co. (B#H: 409).

RICHARDSON'S PLAINS

21 July 1686: Thomas Richardson of Gunpowder R., and w. Rachel conv. 100 a. (*), adj. land of Richard Windley and opposite Spring Neck, to William Caine. On 2 Nov 1686 TR's w. Rachel gave p/a to Thomas Scudamore (RM#HS: 203).

RICHARDSON'S PROSPECT

7 Oct 1684: 100 a. (*) was surv. for Thomas Richardson on the s. side of a branch of

Gunpowder R. called Back R.; later poss. by Walter Bosley (MRR: 49).

1 June 1686: Thomas Richardson conv. 100 a. (*) to John Bird. TR's w. Rachel cons. The same day Richardson gave a bond he would perform the covenant in the deed (RM#HS: 178).

25 June 1726: Mary Bosley of BA Co., widow, sold 50 a., being ½ of (*), to Philip Trapnall. The tract was adj. to Arthur's Choice (IS#H: 253).

9 March 1732: Philip Trapnall, Jr., conv. 50 a., ½ of (*) to Richard Caswell. PT's w. Elizabeth cons. (IS#L: 349).

9 Aug 1734: Richard Caswell conv. 50 a. (*) to John Watson. RC's w. Christian cons. (HWS#M: 160).

RICHARDSON'S RESERVE

214 a. orig. granted to Thomas Richardson (TR#C: 194).

10? Aug 1684: 214 a. pat. for Thomas Richardson (TB#C: 664).

26 May 1686: Thomas Richardson and w. Rachel of Gunpowder R., conv. 214 a. (*) to Richard Ellingsworth. Same day, Richardson gave bond to Ellingsworth (RM#HS: 183).

28 April 1719: Richard Ellingsworth of SO Co., and w. Elizabeth, conv. 214 a. (*) to Bloyce Wright of SO Co. (TR#DS: 131).

28 June 1720: Cert. from SO Co., that Bloys Wright of SO Co. bought 214 a. (*) in BA Co., from Richard and Elizabeth Ellingsworth (TR#DS: 114).

9 June 1721: Bloys Wright of BA Co. conv. 214 a. (*) to William Hitchcock, being the land said Wright bought from Richard Ellinsworth (TR#DS: 327).

5 Dec 1744: Asael Hitchcock and Samuel Talbee and w. Elizabeth, and John Barton and w. Ann conv. (*) to Stephen Onion; also 162 a. Turkey Hill, orig. laid out for Samuel Sicklmore (TB#C: 664).

8 March 1748: William Hitchcock conv. to Stephen Onion (*), orig. granted to Thomas Richardson for 214 a., and 162 a. Turkey Hill, orig. granted to Samuel Sickelmore for 262 a. (TR#C: 194).

RIDER'S INDUSTRY

25 Oct 1736: James Rider conv. 48 a. (*) to Henry Oyston. Francis Rider also signed (IS#IK: 266).

30 Aug 1740: Henry Oyston conv. 48 a. Riders Inheritance [sic] to Thomas Sligh (HWS#1-A: 436).

20 July 1746: Thomas Sligh, and w. Sophia, conv. 150 a. Corbin's Rest, 48 a. (*), and 50 a. pt. Jones' Range to Peter Dowell. TS's w. Sophia cons. (TB#E: 196).

17 Nov 1748: Peter Dowell conv. 23 a., pt. Jones Range and (*), to Samuel Bowen (TR#C: 146).

RIDGELY'S CONCLUSION

1755: 1350 a. pat. by Charles Ridgely.

See PW Plat H, and Horvath Plat: Ruxton and Riderwood.

RIDGELY'S DELIGHT

Resurv. on Howard's Timber Neck made by Charles Ridgely; it lay on Ridgely's Cove or Hollow, betw. Mt. Clare and Lunn's Lot, extending irregularly n. to Mulberry St., s. to Hanover Street, and including Columbia Avenue (now Washington Boulevard) (MHM 16:241, 243, 43:97n).

30 May 1748: Charles Ridgely, with cons. of w. Rachel, conv. 260 a. (*) to his s. John Ridgle (TR#C: 18).

RIDGELY'S WHIM

1745: 990 a. pat. by Charles Ridgely; lying partly in Guilford (MHM 51:14n).

RIGBIE'S THICKET

9 Nov 1727: Nathan Rigbie of AA Co. leased 50 a. pt. (*) to Richard Wells, for 21 years (IS#I: 68).

RILEY (Or THE GLEBE LAND)

17 March 1729: Stephen Wilkinson of BA Co., Minister of St. George's Parish, leased 210 a. (*) to Benjamin Hartley of CE Co., the lease to run for the life of SW or his tenure as minister of St. George's Parish (IS#K: 283).

RISTEAU'S SECURITY

25 May 1747: Pat. to Talbot Risteau (TR#C: 186).

19 May 1749: Talbot Risteau, and of w. Mary, conv. 40 a. (*) to John Hall. TR's w. Mary cons. (TR#C: 186).

ROADE RIVER

28 June 1659: Walter Dickson conv. to Thomas Powell of Corotoman, Lancaster Co., VA, the tract (*), 287½ a., being ½ of 575 a. bought from William Battin. (RM#HS: 4, 5) The deed is recorded a second time, and on 10 Dec 1663, Powell conv. his interest to Lawrence Porter and Philip Jones (RM#HS: 6).

17 Aug 1664: Thomas Powell conv. to Thomas Todd of Gloucester Co., VA, 287½ a. bought from Walter Dickson, and which Dickson had bought from William Battin (IR#PP: 66).

17 Aug 1664: Thomas Todd of Gloucester Co., VA, conv. to his sons Robert and John Todd three tracts on Patapsco R., including (*), bought this date from Thomas Powell (IR#PP: 66).

22 Feb 1667/8: Thomas Powell of TA Co. appointed Samuel Collett his atty. to ackn. sales of land in Patapsco R. to Thomas Todd of VA, acc. to

writings in possession of John Collett (IR#PP: 67).

ROBERT AND JOHNS LOT

Jointly taken up by John Muckeldory and Robert Clark (IS#H: 147).

4 Aug 1725: John Muckeldory and w. Frances conv. 156 a., his pt. of (*), to Robert Clark (IS#H: 147).

ROBERTS CAMP

11 Feb 1703/4: Robert Rogers of AA Co., and w. Katherine, conv. 100 a. (*) to John Israel. RR's w. Katherine cons. (HW#2: 317).

ROBERTS CHOICE (1688)
(See EDINBURGH)

27 March 1688: 153 a. surv. for Thomas Roberts betw. Patapsco and Back R. (MRR: 70, 109 give acreage as 159 a.).

28 July 1696: John Roberts conv. 100 a. Edinburgh, pt. of (*), to Andrew Anderson (IS#IK: 114).

7 Sep 1697: Andrew Anderson of BA Co. conv. 100 a. Edinburgh, pt. (*), to Michael Cunnyworth. AA's w. Mary cons. (IS#IK: 199, 201).

17 March 1711: Elizabeth Roberts conv. to John Cross 100 a. Hogg's Norton, being pt. of a larger tract called (*) (TR#A: 179).

28 March 1713: John Roberts, planter, conv. to Richard Taylor of BA Co. two tracts: 464 a. Roberts Forest, also a plantation in AA Co. where Henry Roberts now lives, and which said John inher. from his father John Roberts of AA Co. (Might be a separate tract) (TR#A: 236).

8 Aug 1717: John Roberts of BA Co. conv. 496 a. (*) to Richard Taylor (TR#A: 496).

31 July 1736: Thomas Birchfield and w. Mary conv. 68 a. (*) to Bennett Garrett (HWS#M: 427).

Aug 1739: Richard Taylor of Goochland Co., VA, dep. that about 5 years earlier Ill Will and (*) were resurv. into Taylors Range (HWS#1-A: 279).

30 Aug 1740: Francis Rider of BA Co. and w. Ann conv. 75 a. pt. (*) to Henry Oyston (HWS#1-A: 429).

30 Aug 1740: Francis and Ann conv. 75 a. pt. (*) to Abraham Eaglestone (HWS#1-A: 427).

----- 1745: Amos Garrett conv. (*) to William Daugherty (TB#D: 396).

7 Nov ---- : Amos was s. and heir of Bennett Garrett, dec., conv. 268 a. pt. of two tracts, (*) and Thomas and Mary's Repose, which BG bought from Thomas Burchfield, to William Daugherty (TB#D: 396).

1763: William Daugherty conv. 68 a. pt. (*) to George Daugherty (B#M: 78).

ROBERTS' FOREST

10 Jan 1705: 500 a. pat. to Thomas Roberts (TR#A: 72); on PW Plat H.

6 March 1709: Elizabeth Roberts, widow, owning (*) in her own right by the LWT of Capt. Thomas Roberts, conv. 100 a. of (*), now called Wilmot's Choice to John Wilmot, Jr. (TR#A: 72).

1 April 1712: Elizabeth Roberts, widow of John, conv. 250 a. Hitchcock's Folly, orig. called (*), to George Hitchcock, schoolmaster (TR#A: 184).

1 Nov 1726: John Cross conv. Hoggs Norton, being pt. of a larger tract called (*) [sic] to James Moore (IS#H: 288).

6 Feb 1728/9: James Moore of BA Co., cordwainer, conv. 100 a. Hoggs Norton, being pt. of (*), to John Wilmot (IS#K: 1).

1 Jan 1730: George Hitchcock, miller, conv. 205 a. and 22½ a., parcels of Hitchcock's Folly to William Parrish (IS#L: 54).

14 Feb 1733: James Moore of BA Co., cordwainer, conv. 188? a. Hoggs Norton and 11 a. Shoemaker Lot to Thomas Woodward, cooper (HWS#M: 38).

17 May 1735: James Moore conv. 50 a. Moore's Park, being pt. of (*), to John Wilmot (HWS#M: 276).

2 June 1735: Thomas Francis Roberts, s. and heir-at-law of Thomas Roberts, conv. 500 a. (*) to James Moore (HWS#M: 243).

ROBERTS LOT

3 March 1730: Archibald Rollo, carpenter, and w. Rebecca, conv. 100 a. (*) to John Norris (IS#L: 205).

ROBERTS PARK

10 Nov 1695: 200 a. pat. by Thomas Roberts (MPL 34: 119, 40: 75).

16 Feb 1741: Cert. of division betw. Thomas Francis Roberts and Matthew Hawkins (TB#A: 83).

11 Oct 1745: Thomas Francis Roberts conv. to his sister Elizabeth, w. of Matthew Hawkins, all his right, title, and interest in 83 a. (*). TFR's w. Comfort cons. (TB#D: 374).

11 Oct 1745: Matthew Hawkins and w. Elizabeth conv. 73 a. (*) to Thomas Francis Roberts (TB#D: 376).

11 Oct 1745: Matthew Hawkins and w. Elizabeth conv. 83 a. (*) to Thomas Harrison (TB#D: 378).

11 Oct 1745: Thomas Francis Roberts conv. residue of (*) to Matthew Hawkins (TB#E: 604).

2 Oct 1747: Thomas Francis Roberts conv. 73 a. pt. (*) to Thomas Harrison (TB#E: 604).

ROBESON'S PARK

23 Oct 1745: John Robeson, with cons. of w. Elizabeth, conv. 70 a. (*) to William Lyon, surgeon (TB#D: 315).

ROBIN HOODS FOREST

8 Sep 1683: 150 a. surv. for Robert Jones near the head of Swan Creek; later held by John Hall, and still lated by John Hall (MRR: 18).

22 Oct 1716: John Hall and w. Martha conv. 150 a. (*) to Miles Hannis (TR#A: 522).

26 March 1717: Miles Hannis conv. ⅔ of tract, now called William and Sarah's Inheritance, to William Robinson (TR#A: 450).

27 Aug 1720: William and Elizabeth Hannis conv. 50 a. (*) to Benjamin Osborne (IS#G: 133).

ROBINDALE

10 Nov 1698: 50 a. pat. for Cornelius Harrington (or Herrington) (MPL 38:44).

ROBIN'S CAMP

24 April 1701: 100 a. pat. by Robert Rogers of AA Co. (MPL 34: 352).

See Horvath Plat: Elkridge.

20 July 1710: John Israel and w. Barbara conv. to Amos Garrett of AA Co., 632 a. Littleton (granted to Thomas Thurston on 14 May 1684) and 100 a. (*) (granted to Robert Rogers on 24 April 1700) (TR#A: 97).

5 March 1747: William Woodward of London, goldsmith, Mary Holmes of Newington Butts, Surrey, trustees of Mary Woodward, late of Newington Butts, Benj. Baron and w. Elizabeth, and Sarah McHokon?, widow of Cornelius Kehawn, conv. 100 a. (*) to Emanuel Teal (TR#C: 380).

28 Feb 1751: Emanuel Teal conv. to James Barton 50 a. (*). (TR#D: 92).

10 Nov 1759: Emanuel Teal conv. all the residue of (*). ET's w. Catherine cons. "Banical?" Barton asks that the deed be recorded on 27 Nov 1759 (B#H: 20).

ROBINSONS BEGINNING

2 March 1754: John Robinson conv. 50 a., pt. (*), to Richard King Stevenson (BB#I: 214).

ROBINSON'S CHANCE

8 June 1757: William Robinson assigns to James Barton the lease (said lease to run for 99 years) for 92 a. (*), which Benjamin Tasker leased to said Robinson on 1 May 1746 (B#G: 2).

20 Sep 1796: By virtue of a judgment against James Barton by Robert Amoss, the leasehold property known as (*), containing 92 a., is sold to Robert Amoss as the highest bidder for 5 shillings. Land is located in HA Co. on the Drafts of the Little Falls of Gunpowder (HALR JLG#N: 217).

ROBORARIUM (THE)

13 March 1744/5: Greenbury Dorsey of PG Co., conv. 175 a. to William Murphy (TB#D: 66).

ROCHESTER

29 Sep 1713: Roger Matthews of BA Co. conv. 400 a. (*) to William Brown of CE Co., merchant (TR#A: 261).

25 Aug 1714: Ann Wriothesley, widow, conv. 400 a. (*) to Roger Matthews, pat. 20 Nov 1705 (TR#A: 313).

ROCK POINT

6 June 1702: Pat. to William Demond of AA Co., sold by William Demond (son of George Demond, who was a bro. of the orig. patentee) to Thomas Hargues, who sold it to Edward Evans (TB#E: 474).

5 March 1746: Edward Evans of Lancaster Co., PA, and w. Rachel conv. 200 a. (*) to William Bennett (TB#E: 474).

ROCK WATER

25 March 1737: Isaac Webster conv. 200 a. (*) to George Rigdon. IW's w. Margaret cons. (IS#IK: 371).

ROCKFORD

10 June 1679: 300 a. surv. for Thomas Ford on the w. side of Susquehanna at a bounded poplar tree; later poss. by James Ford and later by his orphans (MRR: 14).

29 March 1721: John and James Ford conv. 300 a. (*) to William Lock (TR#DS: 230).

20 April 1724: William Lock of AA Co., Esq., conv. 300 a. (*) to Thomas Warren of AA Co.; WL had purch. the tract from John and James Ford. WL's w. Sarah cons. (IS#G: 259).

31 Aug 1737: William Warren of London, coffeeman, bro. of Thomas Warren, dec., conv. land to John Galloway, except for the right of dower of the widow of Thomas Warren (IS#IK: 533).

27 May 1738: Jonathan, Lewis, and Thomas Jones, bros. were sons of (---) Jones and his w. Mary who later married Thomas Warren, now dec.; on this date Mary Warren conv. ⅓ of (*) to her s. Thomas Jones (HWS#1-A: 69, 70, 71).

ROGERS CHOICE

4 April 1745: Nicholas Rogers conv. 78 a. (*) to Dr. George Buchanan. Nicholas Tempest Rogers signs as witness (TB#D: 124).

ROGERS RESERVE

25 Oct 1770: Resurv. into PITT (q.v.).

ROGERS ROAD

10 Feb 1695: 100 a. surv. for Roger Reeves lying at the head of Back R. betw. Herring Run and Stoney Run; later held by Jane Royston for John Royston's orphans, and still later held by John Royston's orphans (MRR: 83).

21 Jan 1726/7: William Reeves and w. Elizabeth conv. 100 a. (*) to John Wilmot (IS#H: 327).

14 June 1732: John Wilmot of BA Co. conv. 100 a. (*) to Thomas Sheredine. JW's w. Rachel cons. (IS#L: 300).

9 March 1733: Samuel Chew and Philip Thomas gave receipt for following tracts to Thomas Sheredine: 473 a. Kingsbury Resurv., 250 a. Long Point, 500 a. Mason's Oate, 187 a. The Plains, 100 a. (*), and 150 a. Sheredine's Bottom (HWS#M: 19).

20 Nov 1734: Thomas Sheredine of BA Co. conv. 100 a. (*) to William Chettum, Esq., of Beddington, Co. Surrey, and John Whittiwicks of the parish of Craden, Co. Surrey, and to the Principio Iron Works Company. TS' w. Tabitha cons. (HWS#M: 146).

ROGUE'S RIDGE

20 May 1725: 100 a. pat. by James Wells (MPL PL#6: 288, IL#A: 456).

See Horvath Plat: Green Spring Valley.

29 Aug 1748: James Wells conv. 100 a., all of (*) to Thomas Wells. JW's w. Anne cons. (TR#C: 48).

ROLLO'S ADVENTURE

1750: 52 a. owned by heirs of Archibald Rollo (1750 DB).

1755: James Hicks conv. 52 a. pt. (*) to Charles Baker (BB#I: 637).

14 June 1763: James Yeo and w. Rebecca conv. (*) (which Archibald Rollo had devised to said Rebecca) to William Yoe (B#M: 137).

ROPER'S INCREASE

4 Aug 1749: Capt. John Dorsey, Jr., sold 200 a. (*) and 150 a. Howard's Addition to John Taylor. JD's w. Elizabeth cons. (TR#C: 268).

ROPER'S RANGE

1 Nov 1675: Thomas Roper of AA Co. conv. to Anthony Demondidier also of BA Co. 295 a. in three parcels: 50 a. Cold Comfort, 100 a. Rich Neck Level (both conv. to Roper on 1 Feb 1669/70), and 145 a. (*). TR's w. Mary released seisin on 2 Nov 1675 (G#J: 316).

7 Sep 1698: Anthony Demondidier of BA Co. and w. Mary conv. 50 a. Cold Comfort, 100 a. Rich Level, and 145 a. (*) to Margaret Kiersted of CV Co., widow, and her s. Hance Kiersted (HW#2: 33).

6 March 1699: Anthony Demondidier conv. above three tracts to Samuel Sickelmore and Henry Wriothesley in trust for above named Margaret and Hance Kiersted (HW#2: 29).

19 May 1715: Margaret Gray of CV Co., widow of George Gray, conv. 145 a. (*) to Thomas Randle (TR#A: 334).

3 Aug 1719: Otho Holland of AA Co., with cons. of w. Mary (late w. of Charles Howard or AA Co.) and Thomas Howard, conv. 50 a. Howard's Addition and 100 a. pt. Roper's Increase (300 a. pat. to Thomas Roper), to Pleasance Dorsey of BA Co. (TR#DS: 157).

ROPER'S REST

1 May 1697: 50 a. surv. for Sarah Teale, widow (IS#IK: 229).

14 May 1698: Philip Roper conv. 1560 perches to Sarah Teale (S#IK: 225).

30 March 1699: John Copus conv. 100 a. pt. (*) to his dau.-in-law Alis Teale. JC's w. Sarah Copus is mentioned, but she signed cons. as Sarah Teale (TR#RA: 538).

ROSES GREEN

2 May 1717: 130 a. pat. to Isaac Butterworth, on n. side of Deer Creek. It lies about 5 miles n. of Bel Air (TB#C: 320; C:14).

12 Sep 1743: Jacob Giles and w. Sarah conv. 130 a. (*) to Thomas Wheeler (TB#C: 320).

ROUND ABOUT (1733)

13 Feb 1733: 50 a. pat. to Peter Bond (MPL AM#1: 212, EI#1: 18).

3 July 1737: Peter Bond conv. 50 a. (*) to Richard Bond. PB's w. Susanna cons. (IS#IK: 464).

ROUND ABOUT (1734)

10 June 1734: 50 a. pat. by Teague Tracey (MPL EI#3: 299, EI#4: 192).

4 Nov 1745: Teague Tracey conv. (*) to William Fell, with 50 a. Bought Deer, 84 a. Coale's Contrivance, and 16 a. pt. Coale's Chance (TB#D: 353).

1752: Joseph Taylor et al. conv. (*) (called Roundabout Neighbors), and other tracts mentioned in 1745 deed to Fell, to John Gorsuch (TR#D: 373).

ROUNDABOUT NEIGHBORS

17 April 1746: Richard Bond, with cons. of w. Mary, conv. 100 a., pt. (*), to John Bond (TB#E: 53).

ROWLES CHANCE

17 Oct 1737: Charles Carroll of AA Co. conv. 150 a. (*) to John Hurd (HWS#1-A: 22).

ROYSTON STUDY

6 Aug 1747; John Royston, with cons. of w. Sarah and of Henry Cross and w. Mary (widow of John Royston, dec.), conv. 50 a. (*) to William Bannister, late of Stafford Co., VA, now of BA Co., wood collier (TB#E: 497).

RUFF'S CHANCE

1750: Bernard Preston owned 150 a. (1750 DB: 96).

13 April 1752: Richard Ruff, s. of Richard, with cons. of w. Mary, conv. to his sister Sarah, w. of Barnett Preston, 150 a. pt. (*). The same day he conv. to his sister Mary Ruff 150 a. of (*) (TR#D: 344).

RUFF'S ENLARGEMENT

6 June 1728: John McComas and w. Ann conv. 80 a. (*), orig. known as Come By Chance (pat. 10 Nov 1686 to Thomas Thurston), to Richard Ruff (IS#I: 189).

RUTH'S LOT

3 Feb 1724: The estate of Edward Norwood included 100 a. Norwood's Discovery and 100 a. (*); it was distributed by Sheriff of William Smith to Thomas Worthington. The deed mentioned an Act of Assembly passed 20 Feb 1724 to discharge said Edward Norwood from debt and to deliver him from gaol (IS#C: 410, 412).

RUTLEDGE'S DELIGHT

13 June 1734: Michael Rutledge pat. 50 a. (MPL EI#4: 203).

28 June 1745: William Rutledge, eld. s. and heir of Michael Rutledge (who pat. the land and d. intestate), sold 50 a. to John Jones. Michael's widow Hannah approved (TB#D: 399).

RUTLEDGE'S VENTURE

21 Feb 1722: 50 a. pat. by Michael Rutledge (MPL PL#5: 169).

3 March 1729: Michael Rutledge conv. 50 a., pt. of (*), to John Weeks. No w. seems to have signed (IS#K: 186).

1750 BA Co. debt Books shows Thomas Wicks as owning 50 a. (p. 93).

RUTTER'S LOT

20 Feb 1724: Edward Norwood conv. 100 a. (*) to Thomas Worthington of AA Co., merchant (IS#G: 412).

RUXTON'S RANGE

10 Sep 1679: 100 a. pat. to Nathaniel Ruxton (Card Index to Patents).

30 Aug 1701: Mary Ruxton, widow of Nathaniel Ruxton, late of BA Co., dec., conv. to Richard Colegate (70?) a. of Howell's Point and 100 a. (*) (HW#2: 89).

3 Sep 1701: John Gay and w. Frances of BA Co. conv. to Richard Colegate 70 a. of Howell's Point on n. side of Patapsco at Clapham's Creek, and 100 a. (*) adj. the land of Nicholas Ruxton (HW#2: 90).

10 Oct 1747: Benjamin Colegate leased all the cultivated land in Huntington, Powell's Point, and (*) to William Hammond for 14 years (TB#E: 612).

S...YARD

5 Nov 1734: James Putee conv. 100 a. (*) to John Cawdrick (HWS#M: 132)

ST. ALBANS

20 May 1724: 500 a. pat. by Ann and Hannah Norwood (MPL PL#5: 588; IL#A: 408).

9 Oct 1724: Ann Norwood and Hannah Norwood of AA Co. conv. 500 a. (*) to John Swinyard; tract was surv. for Andrew Wellplay of AA Co. on 2 April 1706; Wellplay left it in his will to Andrew Norwood, bro. of Elizabeth, Ann and Hannah; Andrew agreed to sell it to JS but d. before it could be sold; land was never actually granted to Wellplay or Andrew Norwood so Lord Baltimore granted it to Ann and Hannah Norwood; they were assignees of John Beal and his w. Elizabeth, another of the sisters of Andrew Norwood (IS#G: 387).

7 Feb 1735/6: John Swynyard of BC leases (*) to Edmund Hayes for his life and that of his w. (IS#IK: 360).

6 March 1738: John Swinyard conv. 100 a., pt. (*), to John Stringer of BC (HWS#1-A: 186).

ST. CLEMENT DANES

16 --- 1664: 100 a. surv. for William Osborn in Rumley Creek on the s. side of said creek; later in possession of John Savory, and later held by William Prichard (MRR: 11).

8 May 1666: Richard Leake, tailor, conv. 100 a. (*), betw. Bush R. and Rumley Creek, formerly taken up by William Osborne, to William Orchard, cooper (IR#PP: 56).

15 Feb 1666/7: William Osborne, planter, conv. 100 a. (*), betw. Bush R. and Rumley Creek, adj. Spry's Mashes, taken up by Oliver Spry, to John Bradford (IR#PP: 60).

11 May 1681: George Skipwith and w. Elizabeth of AA Co. conv. 100 a. (*) and 50 a. Clement, on the

w. side of land formerly taken up by William Hollis and by William Osborne, to Edward Reeves. GS appoints James Phillips his atty. to ackn. sale. On 30 April 1681, GS's w. Elizabeth also gave p/a to James Phillips (IR#AM: 125).

3 Feb 1684/5: Edward Reeves, planter, of Rumley Creek, for love and affection, conv. to Elizabeth Sargent pt. of (*). If Elizabeth dies, John Sergent may carry away all stock and increments due to his own efforts (RM#HS: 109).

14 Dec 1702: John Savory and w. Ann conv. 100 a. (*) and 50 a. Cobler to William Pritchett (HW#2: 211).

15 March 1735: Abraham Cord and w. Mary, sister of Joseph Pritchett, lately dec., conv. 100 a. (*) and 100 a. Broad Neck, and 50 a. Clement to John Atkinson, who promises he would maintain Mary Cord for the rest of her life (HWS#M: 401).

17 Feb 1736: Abraham Cord and w. Mary conv. the same three tracts to John Atkinson (IS#IK: 358).

ST. DENIS

11 Sep 1684: 500 a. surv. for Edward Dannis (MHM 20: 190).

1732: resurv. as pt. of Dulany's Park (MHM 20: 190).

ST. GEORGE'S

5 March 1707: George Thompson of SM Co., Gent., conv. to James Heath of AA Co., Gent., 400 a. (*), orig. pat. to George Thompson. GT's w. Ann cons. (RM#HS: 655).

1783 TL: 1228 a. in Middle River Lower Hundred held by Walter Tolley.

ST. GEORGE'S HILL

6 Dec 1681: Arthur Taylor of BC conv. 25 a. (*) to Thomas Preston. AT's w. Frances cons. (IR#AM: 149).

ST. GILES

Nov 1674: 200 a. surv. for Giles Stevens; later held by Giles Stevens, Jr. (Card Index to Patents).

8 Aug 1726: Samuel Stevens conv. 200 a. (*) to James Durham. SS' w. Martha cons. (IS#H: 283).

ST. JONES

4 July 1672: 100 a. surv. for Thomas Jones; later held by Charles Jones; still later held by Edward Smith for Jones' orphans (MRR: 39).

ST. MARTIN'S LUDGATE

20 July 1730: 200 a. surv. for Thomas White.

30 July 1737: Thomas White conv. 100 a. (*) to Thomas Gash. TW's w. Sophia cons. (IS#IK:490).

30 July 1737; White conv. 50 a. (*) to Samuel Howell. TW's w. Sophia cons. (IS#IK: 493).

30 July 1737: White conv. 100 (?) a. (*) to Richard Mitchell, s. of Thomas Mitchell. White's w. Sophia cons. (IS#IK:497).

28 Nov 1737: Thomas Gash and w. Hannah conv. 50 a. (*), 60 a. Beedle's Reserve, and Scotchman's Generosity, to Benjamin Osborne, s. of William (HWS#1-A: 430).

5 Nov 1742: Thomas White conv. 50 a. (*) to Samuel Howell; pt. of which he had conv. to William Osborne, Samuel Howell, and Richard Mitchell (TB#C: 57).

ST. MARY BOW (or BOURNE)

1669: 200 a. laid out for George Hickson (MHM#54: 16).

ST. OMER'S

15 Sep 1741: Benjamin Wheeler conv. 20 a. pt. (*) to his dau. Charity, w. of Benjamin Colegate (HWS#1-A: 557).

15 Sep 1741: Benjamin Wheeler conv. 80 a. (*), with a plantation called Bald Hill, to his dau. Ann Wheeler (HWS#1-A: 558).

16 Dec 1745: James Scott and w. Anne conv. 80 a. (*), except for 20 a. betw. Roses Green and The Meadow, to Thomas Wheeler (TB#D: 432).

SALISBURY PLAIN

20 July 1682: Robert Benger, planter, made deed of gift, for love and affection to Elizabeth Peart, dau. of Thomas Peart, 50 a. pt. (*) (in all 100 a.) (IR#AM: 186).

15 Jan 1700: John Shaw of CE Co. conv. to Alexander Graves of BA Co., 100 a. Hopewell, 100 a. being $\frac{1}{2}$ of (*), 70 a. Witherington, 80 a. Shadwell's Range. and 100 a. Smith's Range (HW#2: 53).

29 March 1725: Henry Enlows of QA Co., conv. 100 a. (*) to Stephen Body. HE's w. Mary cons. (IS#H: 134).

8 March 1726/7: Stephen Body conv. 100 a. (*) to Thomas Rutter. SB's w. (unnamed) cons. (IS#H: 362).

SALLY AND MOLLY'S DELIGHT

1783 TL: Middle River and Back River Upper Hundred; Thomas Gist owned 100 a.; Benjamin Powell owned 108 a.

SALLY'S DELIGHT (Also SARAH'S DELIGHT)

6 Nov 1699: Richard Tilyard conv. $\frac{1}{2}$ of (*) and $\frac{1}{2}$ of his goods to his friend John Hopkins (TR#RA: 409).

13 Oct 1725: John Tilyard of KE Co., carpenter, conv. 80 a. (*) to George Debruler; tract was

formerly laid out for John Tilyard, grandfather of dec., and bequeathed to Richard Tilyard, father of afsd. John Tilyard (Richard is also now dec.) (IS#H: 192).

1750: William York owned pt. (*) (1750 DB: 71).

SALT PETER NECK

2 May 1750: Thomas Jarman of BC conv. to John Denton his moiety or ½ of (*), Bachelor's Hope, and Bachelor's Meadow, lately owned by William Denton, dec. TJ's w. Mary cons. (TR#C: 483).

2 May 1750: John Denton of BC, and w. Rachel, in exch. for 100 a. called Violin, conv. his moiety of Bachelor's Hope, Bachelor's Meadow, and (*), all formerly held by his father William Denton, dec. (TR#C: 510).

1783 TL: 100 a. in Middle River Lower Hundred held by William Andrews.

SALVETON

1 Sep 1666: William Fisher, chiururgeon, conv. 225 a. (*) on the Eastern Shore, to John Brumfield (IR#PP: 57).

SAMPSON

20 June 1663: Oliver Sprye conv. (*) to his dau. Mary, w. of Godfrey Harmer (RM#HS: 4).

1783: 51 a. in Mine Run Hundred held by George Myers.

SAMPSON'S ADDITION

19 July 1688: 101 a. surv. for Richard Sampson; later held by Isaac Sampson (MRR: 97).

8 Feb 1728/9: Isaac Sampson conv. to Luke Stansbury 100 a. The Forest, 100 a. (*), and 26½ a. Sampson's Angle (IS#I: 284).

5 June 1733: Luke Stansbury, merchant, conv. to Samuel Maxfield 100 a. The Forest, 100 a. (*), and 26½ a. Sampson's Angle. LS's w. Jane cons. (IS#L: 376).

1783: William Maccubbin owned 50 a. in Patapsco Lower Hundred (1783 TL).

SAMPSON'S ANGLE

8 Feb 1728/9: Isaac Sampson conv. to Luke Stansbury 100 a. The Forest, 100 a. Sampson's Addition, and 26½ a. (*) (IS#I: 284).

5 June 1733: Luke Stansbury, merchant, conv. to Samuel Maxfield 100 a. The Forest, 100 a. Sampson's Addition, and 26½ a. (*). LS's w. Jane cons. (IS#L: 376).

SAMPSON'S FAVOUR

13 Aug 1709: 50½ a. laid out for Bray Platt Tailor, on s. side of Back R. (Card Index to Patents).

21 April 1739: Bray Platt Tailor (son of Bray Platt Taylor) conv. 50 a. (*) to Thomas Sligh (HWS#1-A: 213).

28 July 1746: Thomas Sligh conv. (*) to Samuel Harryman. Madam Sophia Sligh cons. (TB#E: 135).

SAM'S MEADOWS

1783 TL: 39 a. in Middlesex Hundred held by Samuel Merryman.

SAMUEL'S ADDITION

1783 TL: 8 a. in Middle River and Back River Upper Hundred held by Samuel Cole.

SAMUEL'S CHOICE

30 July 1698: 92 a. surv. for Samuel Sickelmore (RM#HS: 424).

SAMUEL'S DELIGHT

13 Sep 1687: 150 a. surv. for Samuel Sickelmore and later poss. by John Taylor and John Lowe (MRR: 46).

7 Aug 1686: Samuel Sickelmore conv. 150 a. (*) to Arthur Taylor (RM#HS: 192).

6 June 1694:: John Taylor, carpenter, conv. to John Love, 75 a. (*), orig. conv. by Taylor's father Arthur Taylor to JL's father, Robert Love (RM#HS: 393).

12 June 1701: John Taylor conv. 75 a. (*) to Michael Judd and w. Mary in exch. for 100 a. Swanson. JT's w. Jane cons. (HW#2: 108, 111).

9 Nov 1733: Robert Love conv. 75 a. (*) to Stephen Onion, ironmaster, being the same tract orig. surv. for Samuel Sickelmore, who sold it to Arthur Taylor who sold it to John Love, father of Robert, except for that portion sold by JL to James Maxwell and William James (HWS#M: 6).

7 June 1744: Sarah Lowe, dau. of William Temperance Lowe (dau. of William Pickett), conv. 75 a. (*) to Stephen Onion (TB#C: 522).

SAMUEL'S HILLS

3 July 1672: 150 a. surv. for Samuel Hill on the s. side of the w. branch of Bush R.; Hill has d. or runaway, and no heirs are here; land is uncultivated and no rent paid for 20 years; land liable to an escheat (MRR: 34).

4 March 1730: Lawrence Foreacres and w. Rachel, dau. and surviving heiress of William Hill, late of CE Co., dec., conv. 61 a. pt. (*) to John Crockett; deed stated that William Hill was the s. of Samuel Hill, the original grantee (IS#L: 212).

10 March 1730: Lawrence Foreacres and w. Rachel conv. 150 a. (*) to Charles Baker (IS#L: 211).

30 April 1733: Lawrence Foreacres and w. Rachel conv. 51 a., pt. (*), to John Crockett (IS#L: 359).

30 April 1733: Lawrence Foreacres and w. Rachel conv. 50 a., pt. (*), to Henry Weatherall (IS#L: 420).

SAMUEL'S HOPE

15 June 1694: 500 a. surv. for Thomas Hooker (MRR: 97).
See Horvath Plat: Ruxton and Riderwood.
6 Nov 1716: Thomas Hooker of BC, planter, conv. 100 a. Carr's Pleasure, being pt. of (*) to Benjamin Carr (TR#A: 452).
28 Feb 1718/9: Thomas Hooker and w. Eleanor conv. 150 a. Free Gift, being pt. of (*) to their s. Samuel Hooker (TR#RA: 528).
14 Sep 1720: Thomas Hooker and w. Ellinor conv. 500 a. (*) to Benjamin Bowen, reserving 150 a. which TH had made over to his s. Samuel, and 100 a. conv. to Benjamin Carr (TR#DS: 277).
4 Oct 1736: Samuel Hooker of BC conv. 150 a. (*) to Benjamin Carr, being the same land which Thomas Hooker conv. to said SH on 28 Feb 1718/9. SH's w. Sarah cons. (IS#IK: 313).
1763/4: Benjamin Bowen owned 150 a. (*) (Aquila Hall's Assessment List).
1783: Solomon Bowen, Sr., owned 225 a.; 150 a. held by Jonas Bowen, Jr., and 100 a. by Nathan Bowen, in Middle River Upper Hundred (1783 TL).

SAMUEL'S INDUSTRY

23 Jan 1747: Jabez Murray of BC, carpenter, conv. 50 a. (*), pt. of Morgan's Delight, to Samuel Wheeler. JM's w. Mary cons. (TB#E: 663).

SAMUEL'S LOT

5 March 1734: William Delae (?) of BC conv. 100 a. (*) to Samuel Bull. WD's w. Eleanor cons. (HWS#M: 210).
1783 TL: 8 a. in Patapsco Lower Hundred held by Rachel Brock.

SAMUEL'S MEADOWS

1783 TL: Tract in Middle River Lower and Back River Lower Hundred: 106 a. held by Samuel Cookson; 189 a. held by Mordecai Price of M'o; and 375 a. held by Samuel Price.

SAPPEN HILL

30 May 1747: William Lewis conv. 50 a. (*) to Samuel Owings. WL's w. Ruth cons. (TB#E: 446).

SARAH'S DELIGHT (See SALLY'S DELIGHT)

SATER'S ADDITION

1718: 350 a. surv. for Henry Satyr.
See Horvath Plat: Green Spring Valley.
16 Nov 1742: Henry Sater of BC conv. 1 a. (*) to Henry Loveall, pastor, and Thomas West, William Towson, and William Browne, deacons and elders of the General Baptist Congregation (TB#C: 238).
1783 TL: Tract in Middle River Upper and Back River Upper Hundred; 100 a. held by Charles Sater, 150 a. held by Henry Sater, and 100 a. held by Joseph Sater.

SAVER'S DESIRE

1 July 1748: Joseph Butler of BA Co., leases (*), pt. of His Lordship's Reserve, to Thomas James for residue of term of 99 years (TR#C: 293).

SAVIN'S REST (Now in CE Co.)

1668: 200 a. pat. to William Savin (MPL 8: 347).
10 April 1667: William Saven, planter, conv. to Rowland Williams 200 a. on the s. side of St. Austin's Branch in Bohemia R. Elizabeth Saven signs with grantor (IR#PP: 60).
28 March 1670 (/1671?): Rowland Williams (through his atty. James Ives) conv. 200 a. (*) on the s. side of St. Augustine's Branch, to John Tillyard (G#J: 65; TR#RA: 47).

SCHOLAR'S PLAINS

2 Sep 1724: Thomas Tolley of BA Co., Gent., conv. 100 a. (*), pt. of Richardson's Outlet, to Rev. William Tibbs, Col. John Dorsey, Mr. William Hamilton, Capt. John Stones, Capt. Thomas Sheredine, and Mr. Roger Matthews, Visitors of the BA Co. School. TT's w. Mary cons. (IS#G: 374).

SCOTCHMAN'S DESIRE

1719: Surv. for Maurice Baker.
See Horvath Plat: Granite.
17 Oct 1732: Maurice Baker and w. Sarah of BA Co. conv. 100 a. (*) to Francis Dorsey (IS#L: 322).

SCOTCHMAN'S GENEROSITY

28 Nov 1737: Thomas Gash and w. Hannah conv. (*) to Benj. Osborne of Wm. (HWS#1-A: 43).

SCOTT'S CLOSE

2 March 1742: James and Edward Meads conv. 100 a. (*) to Daniel Scott, Sr., who had orig. had the tract surv. and then assigned it to John Ewings, maternal grandfather of James Meads (TB#C: 188).
5 March 1745: Daniel Scott and w. Hannah conv. 100 a. (*) to James Scott (TB#D: 345).

SCOTT'S FOLLY

14 March 1720: John Fairfax of CH Co. and w. Mary, conv. 200 a. (*) to John Miller of CH Co. (TR#DS: 274).

23 June 1726: John Mellor [sic] conv. 200 a. (*) to Nehemiah Mellor (IS#H: 251).

SCOTT'S HOPEWELL

7 Nov 1696: Tract was surv. for Daniel Scott, Sr. (HW#2: 326).

10 April 1704: Daniel Scott, Jr., conv. 246 a. pt. (*) to John Ewings of BA Co., planter. (HW#2: 326).

SCOTT'S IMPROVEMENT

24 Aug 1725: 720 a. pat. to Daniel Scott, Sr., including pt. Chestnut Neck, surv. for John Chadwell for 100 a., later held by DS, Harman's Hope, 100 a., Stanharket, 190 a., and 320 a. vacant land (TB#E: 534).

30 July 1731: 390 a. pat. by Daniel Scott, Sr. (TB#D: 345).

5 March 1745: Daniel Scott, s. of Daniel Scott, Sr., and w. Hannah conv. 390 a. (*) to James Scott (TB#D: 345).

3 June 1747: Daniel Scott of BA Co. conv. (*) to Benjamin Norris and Aquila Scott, to secure a bond for £180 dated 18 May 1747 (TB#E: 405).

3 June 1747: Daniel Scott, Jr., conv. pt. (*) to William Andrews. DS's w. Hannah cons.

SCOTT'S LODGE

6 March 1704: John Chadwell of BA Co., s. and heir of John Chadwell, late of BA Co., dec. conv. 150 a. to be called (*) to Daniel Scott (HW#2: 12).

SCOTT'S REST

7 March 1692/3: Edmund Hansley of BA Co. conv. 100 a. (*) to Edward Scott of BA Co., planter (RM#HS: 365).

SCRUTINY

20 Oct 1740: Michael Taylor of PG Co., Gent., prisoner in PG Co. Jail, conv. 675 a. Finegal (which was granted to Taylor by a special warrant of escheat), 200 a. Scrutiny Conveniency (pt. of Elizabeth's Delight, in PG Co.), 260 a. Skipton in Craven, and 380 a. (*) to John Hepburn, High Sheriff of PG Co. (TB#E: 374).

8 Dec 1746: John Hepburn, of PG Co., formerly High Sheriff, conv. 380 a. (*) and 260 a. Skipton in Craven to Thomas White (TB#E: 375).

SCRUTINY CONVENIENCY
(Pt. ELIZABETH'S DELIGHT)

20 Oct 1740: Michael Taylor of PG Co., Gent., prisoner in PG Co. Jail, conv. 675 a. Finegal (which was granted to Taylor by a special warrant of escheat), 200 a. (*) (pt. of Elizabeth's Delight, in PG Co.), 260 a. Skipton in Craven, and 380 a. Scrutiny to John Hepburn, High Sheriff of PG Co. (TB#E: 374).

SCUDAMORE'S (SKIDMORE'S) LAST

9 May 1687: 130 a. surv. for Thomas Scudamore on Stony Run; on 10 Oct 1704 granted to John Hayes (MRR: 95).

20 Sep 1733: Thomas Stansbury and w. Jane conv. 130 a. (*) to Philip Sindall (IS#I: 431).

1 April 1734: Philip Sindall and w. Elizabeth conv. 130 a. (*) to Charles Thomas of CE Co. (HWS#M: 45).

7 March 1734(/5?): Charles Thomas and w. Ann conv. 130 a. (*) to Thomas Sligh (HWS#M: 213).

10 Sep 1737: Thomas Sligh and w. Sophia conv. 130 a. pt. (*) to Godfrey Gash (HWS#M: 14).

SCUTT'S LEVEL

1702: 500 a. surv. for John Scutt.

See Horvath Plat: Randallstown.

12 June 1745: Archibald Douglas of CE Co., conv. 250 a., pt. (*), to James Paul Heath of CE Co. (TB#D: 240).

SECURITY (THE)

14 Sep 1723: 50 a. surv. (TB#C: 251).

10 July 1725: 50 a. pat. to George Ogg, Jr. (TB#C: 251).

7 May 1743: George Ogg of BA Co.,and w. Mary conv. 50 a. (*) to Cornelius Howard (TB#C: 251).

SEDGELY

10 April 1708: James Phillips of BA Co., Gent., conv. 200 a. (*) to John Webster. JP's w. Bethia cons. (RM#HS: 601).

SELAS POINT

1670: 120 a. surv. for Robert Burman on n. side of Back R. (MRR. This may be a little above Stansbury Point on the w. bank of Back R.).

18 Aug 1736: Selah Barton conv. 120 a. (*) to Thomas Stansbury. SB's w. Comfort cons. (IS#IK: 273).

SELBY'S HOPE

(For notes on its location, see MHM 15:120 and 53:244n).

29 Feb 1703/4: Charles Ramsey and w. Elizabeth conv. 150 a. (*), being pt. of Leafe's Chance to Edward Selby; tract was sold by Francis Leafe to William Ramsey who gave pt. of Leafe's Chance to his s. Charles (HW#2: 320).

5 March 1744: George York and w. Elinor conv. to Joseph and James Mead (*), pt. of Leafe's

Chance, and anything due the grantors by the death of James Hackett, father of E. York (TB#D: 49).

16 July 1748: Stephen Onion, ironmaster, leases pt. (*) to Robert Bishop (TR#C: 137).

13 July 1750: Joshua Cross of AA Co. conv. 150 a. (*), pt. of a larger tract called Leaf's Chance, in BA Co., to Robert Adair (TR#D: 170).

19 June 1751: George York and w. Eleanor, one of the coheirs of Edward Selby, Sr., and of Edward Selby, Jr., conv. (*) to Robert Adair (TR#D: 168).

SELSED

(See PART RIDGE'S FOREST)

31 July 1694: A 900 a. tract surv. for Rowland Thornborough on northeast branch of Jones Falls; later poss. by Thornborough's orphans; still later the notation was made that Thornbury's orphans had gone into VA (MRR: 84).

See Horvath Plat: Ruxton and Riderwood.

25 July 1695: Roland Thornborough made his will (proved 23 June 1696), leaving the 900 a. tract (*) to his sons John, Roland, and Francis. If the three sons d. s.p., the land was to pass to testator's next of kin, the Thornboroughs of Hampsfield, Lancashire, England (MCW#II: 111).

30 Dec 1710: Francis Thornbury of BA Co. conv. 200 a. Jack's Double Purchase to John Vickory; deed stated that Roland Thornborough left 300 a. to his youngest s. at age 21 (TR#A: 95).

8 Aug 1711: John Thornbury of VA, by Thomas Biddison his atty. conv. 350 a. (*) to John Boring (TR#A: 152).

----- 1716: John Thornbury, late of BA Co., now Lancaster Co., VA, conv. 100 a. Buck's Purchase, being pt. of (*), to Nicholas Rogers who agrees to pay the land rents for 16 years back (TR#DS: 260).

22 Sep 1716: John Thornbury and Francis Thornbury, sons and heirs of Roland Thornbury, dec., conv. to John Boring 200 a. pt. of (*), now known as Boring's Delight (TR#RA: 499).

8 Aug 1717: John Boring conv. 250 a. pt. of (*) to Jonathan Tipton; the tract is now called Poor Jamaica Man's Plague (may be a reference to Jonathan Tipton's place of origin) (TR#A: 417).

22 Jan 1718: John Boring of BA Co. and w. Presiota conv. 202 a. pt. of (*) to Thomas Ford; this portion now known as Ford's Chance (TR#RA: 524).

8 March 1732: Francis Thornbury of BA Co. conv. 50 a. pt. (*) to Thomas Tipton (IS#L: 263).

14 Dec 1733: Nicholas Haile and Roland Thornborough conv. to Henry Sater pt. of Bucks Purchase, pt. of (*) (HWS#M: 20).

2 March 1735: Richard King Stevenson conv. 120 a. (*) (also known as Jack's Double Purchase) to George Buchanan; tract desc. to grantor by the death of Richard Stevenson Vickory in pursuance of the will of Vickory's father (HWS#1-A: 32).

2 June 1735: John Boring of BA Co. deeds to Buckler Partridge, pt. of (*), known as Partridge's Forest (HWS#M: 221).

2 Oct 1735: Francis Thornborough conv. 30 a. pt. (*) to Dr. George Buchanan (HWS#M: 380).

20 May 1745: John Boring of BA conv. 202 a. (*), now called Ford's Choice, to Thomas Ford. This was done to correct errors in the deed of 22 Jan 1718. JB's w. Sarah cons. (TB#D: 298-299).

26 March 1747: Nicholas Haile of BA Co., conv. his right to (*) to Thomas Ford (TB#E: 384).

30 March 1747: Ann Plowman, Jonathan Plowman, and John Plowman conv. to Thomas Ford 50 a. of (*) called Jack's Double Purchase. Eliza Plowman, w. of Jonathan Plowman, released her right of dower.

18 Sep 1755: Thomas Tipton of VA, planter, and w. Sarah, conv. 50 a. pt. (*) to Charles Ridgely (BB#I: 506).

26 March 1763: Francis Thornbury, s. and heir of Roland Thornbury, who was s. and heir of Roland Thornbury, dec., conv. pt. (*) to Thomas Cockey. FT's w. Mary cons. (B#L: 118).

27 March 1763: Francis Thornbury and w. Mary conv. 225 a. (*) to Thomas Cockey (B#L: 120).

1 Aug 1764: William Yates of Bedford Co., VA, and w. Ann, dau. of John Thornborough, dec., who was a s. of Roland Thornborough, dec., conv. pt. (*) to Thomas Cockey (B#O: 121).

9 Oct 1764: Thomas Elledge of Bedford Co., VA, and w. Elizabeth, one of the daus. of John Thornbury of BA Co., dec., conv. 100 a. (*) to Benjamin Bowen (B#O: 97, 99).

25 Feb 1765: Francis Thornburgh conv. (*), granted to Francis' grandfather, Roland Thornburgh, to Samuel Norwood (B#O: 53, 55).

17 Aug 1799: James Boring and w. Elizabeth deed to Charles Ridgely of William and CR's w. Ruth, pt. of (*); "Whereas Thomas Boring late of BA Co., dec. in his lifetime was seized in fee simple of pt. of a tract lying in BA Co. aforesaid called (*) and whereas all the right title estate and int. of the said John [sic] Boreing in and to the said tract at the time of his decease desc. to the said James Boring as s. and heir-at-law to said Thomas Boreing and whereas the said James Boreing on the 24th day of May in the year 1764 did contract with a certain Samuel Norwood the father of said Ruth Ridgely to conv. to the said Samuel Norwood or his heirs by a good and lawful conveyance all his the said James Boreings right title interest claim and demand in and to all and every pt. of the said tract of land called (*). ... for 5 shillings Beginning of the said tract of

land called (*) and running thence with the 1st or giving line of the said tract to the end thereof thence to the end of the 4th line of a tract of land called Ford's Choice (being pt. of the said tract of land called (*)) which was sold by a certain John Boring to a certain Thomas Ford thence with the giving line of Ford's Choice to the beginning of said Ford's Choice thence running to the ends of the 1st line of a tract of land Partridges Forrest being pt. of the aforesaid tract of land called (*). Thence with the said 1st line of Partridges reversely to the 1st place of Beginning the same being also the beginning of Partridges Forrest. (Signed: James Boreing; Witnesses: Wm. Gwynn, Jr., Geo. A. Dunke) (WG#59: 360).

SELTON (?)

26 Oct 1690: William Luffman, late of Severn R., AA Co., conv. (*) to John Hurst; deed is for 100 a. in all, and includes Bright's Neck or Nest (HW#2: 240).

SENECA

10 Nov 1695: 50 a. pat. to Cornelius Herrington (MPL 37: 383).

7 Aug 1717: Cornelius Herrington conv. 50 a. (*) to James Isham (TB#D: 90).

12 March 1744/5: Jacob Herrington, s. and heir of Cornelius Herrington, granted quitclaim on deed conv. by his father on 7 Aug 1717 (TB#D: 90).

SENECA (SENEGAR?) RIDGE (1685)

11 June 1685: 100 a. surv. for Thomas Lightfoot on the s. side of Bush R.; no rent paid since it was taken up by Lightfoot, now dead, gave the land to his w., who did not claim the same as his extx. because of Col. Thomas Taylor who claimed a great debt from the estate (MRR: 72).

2 June 1691: William Standiford of Bush R. conv. to Israel Skelton land on (*); WS's w. Mary cons. (IR#AM: 77).

4 March 1717: John Hammond, Jr., conv. 100 a. (*) to Joshua Merriken, boatwright (TR#A: 527).

5 Nov 1718: Joshua Merriken of BA Co., boatwright, conv. 100 a. (*) to Edmond Talbott (TR#RA: 458).

7 March 1726/7: Edmund Talbot conv. 80 a. Talbot's Care and 100 a. Senegar (Seneca?) Ridge to Nathaniel Shepard. ET's w. Mary cons. (IS#H: 366).

6 Sep 1748: William Shepard of BA Co. conv. to Stephen Onion his right to two tracts of land: a) 100 a. (*), surv. for Thomas Lightfoot, and fell by right of heirship to John Hammond, Jr., and then to Joshua Merriken, and sold by him to Edmond Talbot, who sold it to Nathaniel Shepard, father of the grantor; and b) Talbott's Care (q.v.) (TR#C: 65).

SEWELL'S COFFER

17 Aug 1724: Philip Sewell conv. 100 a. (*) to Lancelott Todd. PS's w. Sarah cons. (IS#G: 301).

SEWELL'S CONTRIVANCE

14 April 1727: Joshua Sewell conv. 100 a. (*), and 150 a. Sewell's Hope to Thomas Cockey (IS#H: 355).

SEWELL'S FANCY

1 Aug 1737: William Young of CV Co., Gent., and w. Clare (lately called Clare Tasker), conv. 1000 a. (*) to Roger Boyce, who on the same day, conv. 1000 a. (*) to William Young (IS#IK: 481).

23 Sep 1747: William Young and w. Clare conv. 250 a., pt. (*), to Philip Wilkinson of BA Co., joiner (TB#E: 682).

23 Sep 1747: Philip Wilkinson and w. Rebecca conv. 250 a. pt. (*) to Alexander Lawson and Co. (TB#E: 686).

SEWELL'S FARM

15 Jan 1733: Clare Tasker of CV Co., Gentlewoman, conv. 1000 a. (*) given her by her father Nicholas Sewell to William Diggs of PG Co. and Col. John Smith of CV Co. (HWS#M: 50).

SEWELL'S HOPE

See Horvath Plat: Granite.

14 April 1727: Joshua Sewell conv. 100 a. Sewell's Contrivance and 150 a. (*) to Thomas Cockey (IS#H: 355).

SEWELL'S RELIEF

1744: Surv. for Samuel Sewell and Philip Jones.

See Horvath Plats: Wards Chapel and Baltimore/Carroll Co.

17 May 1750: Samuel Sewell conv. to Andrew Scott of PG Co., Dr. of Physick, 30 a. (*) SS's w. Mary cons. (TR#C: 467).

SHADRACK'S LOT

6 April 1745: Nicholas Haile conv. 100 a. Hooker's Farm (pt. of Gerar), 60 a. Addition to Hooker's Farm, 100 a. Hailes' Forest, 100 a. pt. of Haile's Fellowship, 80 a. pt. Taylor's Discovery, 50 a. Smallwood, 200 a. Hailes Discovery, 200 a. (*), and 200 a. Meshack's Garden, to Christopher Grindall of London, mariner (TB#E: 83).

SHADWELL RANGE

15 Jan 1700: John Shaw of CE Co. conv. to Alexander Graves of BA Co., 100 a. Hopewell, 100 a. being ½ of Salisbury Plains, 70 a.

Witherington, 80 a. (*), and 100 a. Smith's Range (HW#2: 53).

SHAWAN HUNTING GROUND

1714: Surv. for Thomas Todd for 1500 a.; on PW Plat. W-1B.

1 Aug 1737: Thomas Todd of BA Co., and w. Eleanor, conv. 500 a., pt. (*), to Robert North. (IS#IK: 501).

7 March 1733/4: Samuel Chew gave to Richard Jones of BA Co., a receipt for 190 a. Denton, 80 a. Walker's Neck, 100 a. Hooper's Island, 330 a. North Point, 546 a. Old Road, 120 a. Industry, 1000 a. (*), 50 a. Thorold's Nest, 100 a. Luke's Privilege, and 100 a. Bagford (HWS#M: 193).

1750: Basil and Caleb Dorsey held 1000 a. of the land for the heirs of Thomas Todd (1750 DB).

Nov 1757: John Ensor and w. Eleanor (dau. of Thomas and Eleanor (Dorsey) Todd), joined George Risteau and his w. Frances in conveying pt. of (*) to John Cromwell and w. Elizabeth, the said Eleanor, Frances and Elizabeth being daus. of Thomas Todd (B#G: 91, 93, 95).

1783 Tax list of Middle River Upper and Back River Upper Hundreds: 380 a. held by Robert North Carnan, 320 a., held by Thomas Cromwell, 340 a. held by Eleanor Ensor; 290 a. held by John Moale, and 340 a. held by George Risteau (total of 1670 a. in all).

SHAW'S CHOICE

6 June 1688: Christopher Shaw and w. Elizabeth, for love, good will and affection, conv. 30 a. (*) to John Ashes, planter (RM#HS: 211).

SHAW'S DELIGHT

1688: 97 a. surv. for Christopher Shaw on the s. side of Middle R. (MRR).

6 Dec 1742: Robert Boyd and w. Ruth conv. 97 a. pt. (*), 100 a. pt. Shaw's Fancy, and 80 a. Shaw's Privilege, in all 89½ a., to George Harryman. The tracts were left by Christopher Shaw of BA Co., dec., equally to John Ingle and Ruth Bays, now w. of Robert Boyd (TB#C: 223).

15 Oct 1743: John Ingle conv. to George Harryman all the real estate Christopher Shaw left to JI and Ruth Bayes, to GH (TB#C: 382).

1750: George Harryman owned 97 a. (*) (1750 DB).

SHAW'S FANCY

6 Dec 1742: Robert Boyd and w. Ruth conv. 97 a. pt. Shaw's Delight, 100 a. pt. (*), and 80 a. Shaw's Privilege, in all 89½ a., to George Harryman. The tracts were left by Christopher Shaw of BA Co., dec., equally to John Ingle and Ruth Bays, now w. of RB (TB#C: 223).

5 Oct 1743: John Ingle conv. to George Harryman all the real estate Christopher Shaw left to JI and Ruth Bayes, to GH (TB#C: 382).

1750: George Harryman owned 100 a. (*) (1750 DB).

SHAW'S PRIVILEGE

5 Oct 1743: John Ingle conv. to George Harryman all the real estate Christopher Shaw left to JI and Ruth Bayes, to George Harryman (TB#C: 382).

6 Dec 1742: Robert Boyd and w. Ruth conv. 97 a. pt. Shaw's Delight, 100 a. pt. Shaw's Fancy, and 80 a. (*), in all 89½ a., to George Harryman. The tracts were left by Christopher Shaw of BA Co., dec., equally to John Ingle and Ruth Bays, now w. of RB (TB#C: 223).

1750: George Harryman owned 83 a. (*) (1750 DB).

SHEPHERD'S ADVENTURE

1721/2: laid out for Rowland Shepherd. (For notes on location see MHM 16:127n.).

SHEPHERD'S CHOICE

June 1709: 147 a. surv. for Rowland Shepherd (MRR).

SHEPHERD'S PARADICE

1 May 1749: Tract was leased to Edward Shepherd for 99 years (TR#C: 348).

7 Dec 1749: Edward Sheppard assigns to James Morgan 45 a. (*), leased to ES for 99 years on 1 May 1747 (TR#C: 348).

SHEPHERD'S RANGE

3 March 1741: William Shepherd and w. Margaret conv. 100 a. (*) to Benjamin Norris (TB#A: 115).

SHEREDINE'S BOTTOM

9 March 1733: Samuel Chew and Philip Thomas gave receipt for following tracts to Thomas Sheredine: 473 a. Kingsbury Resurv., 250 a. Long Point, 500 a. Mason's Oate, 187 a. The Plains, 100 a. Rogers Road, and 150 a. (*) (HWS#M: 19).

20 Nov 1734: Thomas Sheredine conv. 470 a. (*) and 150 a. (*) to William Chittum of Beddington, Co. Surrey, and John Whittiwicks of Craden, Surrey, and to the Principio Iron Co. TS' w. Tabitha cons. (HWS#M: 146).

SHEREDINE'S DISCOVERY

5 April 1743: 1900 a. surv. for William Chetwynd and Co. (The Principio Co.). The tract lies on e. side of Guilford, mostly e. of York Road, adj. to the Resurv. on Huntington (MHM 54: 354, 356n).

SHEREDINE'S GROVE

13 June 1734: Thomas Sheredine conv. 200 a. (*) to Robert North. TS's w. Tabitha cons. (HWS#M: 106).

SHILLING'S PLEASURE

18 April 1759: Jacob Schilling, Jr., conv. 25 a. (*) to Christopher Vaughan (B#G: 163).

SHIPLEY'S WELL or WILL

18 Oct 1737: Charles Shipley of AA Co., with cons. of w. Margaret, conv. 050(?) a. (*) to Rowland Williams (HWS#M: 26).

28 Sep 1741: Rowland Williams of BA Co., with cons. of w. Elise, conv. 40 a. (*) to Luke Maciore (?) (TB#A: 12).

SHOEMAKER'S HALL

25 June 1696: John Gay, cordwainer conv. to Thomas Weekes 100 a. (*), being pt. of (*) which JG purch. from John Roberts. JG's w. Frances cons. (RM#HS: 531).

SHOEMAKER'S HALL (1707)

12 March 1707: 150 a. surv. for Richard Taylor (MPL PL#6, 14).

See Horvath Plat: Ruxton and Riderwood.

1726/7: John Hillen of BA Co. leaves (*) to his godson Daniel Sheredine (MCW#VI: 28).

SHOEMAKER HALL, ADDITION TO

1724: 150 a. for Joseph Taylor who was assigned the warrant by Solomon Hillen, s. of John.

1726/7: John Hillen leaves 51 a. to his god-dau. Elizabeth Harrett (MCW#VI: 28).

1726/9: Richard Taylor leaves 99 a. (*) to his s. Joseph (MCW#VI: 131).

SHOEMAKER'S LOT

14 Feb 1733: James Moore of BC, cordwainer, conv. 188? a. Hoggs Norton and 11 a. (*) to Thomas Woodward, cooper (HWS#M: 38).

2 Nov 1741: Thomas Woodward, cooper, mortgaged 180 a. Hoggs Norton and 11 a., 90 perches of (*) to John Ensor. TW's w. Mary cons. (TB#A: 92).

25 Nov 1746: John Ensor grants to Mary Woodward a release of mortgage made by Thomas Edward on Hoggs Norton and (*) (TB#E: 278).

SHREWSBURY

210 a. laid out for Capt. Thomas Stockett (RM#HS: 21).

17 Nov 1682: George Davis, carpenter, of AA Co. conv. 210 a. (*), about two miles from the mouth of the Susquehannah R., to Robert Proctor, innholder, of AA Co. (RM#HS: 21).

6 Nov 1705: Francis Watkins conv. 65 a. to William Farfarr (IR#AM: 46).

26 Feb 1708/9: William Farfar of BA Co. conv. pt. (*) to his dau. Christiana Keith; if she d. without heirs land was to pass to her husband Alexander Keith. Johanna Farfarr signed (RM#HS: 636).

16 June 1724: Joseph Johnson conv. 220 a. (*) to John Stokes (IS#G: 272).

15 Oct 1731: John Stokes of BA Co. conv. 220 a. (*), 400 a. Bourne and 200 a. Ebenezer's Lot to Philip Smith of London. JS' w. Susanna cons. (IS#L: 172).

25 May 1737: Philip Smith of London, now living in AA Co, s. and heir of Philip Smith, late of London, and holding his father's p/a to sell, conv. 220 a. (*) and 400 a. Bourne to Jacob Giles (IS#IK: 432).

7 Aug 1741: John Stokes, s. and devisee of John Stokes, dec., conv. Johnson's Delay, als. (*), to Jacob Giles (HWS#1-A: 538).

9 April 1743: John Keith and w. Katherine conv. pts. (*) and Dear Bit to Francis Rider (TB#C: 241).

20 May 1746: Francis Rider conv. pts. of (*) and Dear Bit to Thomas Green (TB#E: 70).

29 Sep 1749: Benj. Tasker, Agent for the Lord Proprietary, leases 215 a. (*) to N. Ruxton Gay (TR#C: 408).

SHURES INHERITANCE

25 Sep 1730: 52 a. surv. (IS#IK: betw. 454-461).

18 June 1737: Nicholas Gostwick, with cons. of w. Avarilla, conv. 52 a. (*) to Samuel Maxwell (IS#IK: betw. 454-461).

1 Dec 1738: Samuel Maxwell, with cons. of w. Jane, conv. 52 a. (*) to Nicholas Gostwick (HWS#1-A: 158).

SICKELMORE'S (or SICKLEMORE'S) DELIGHT

1729: Robert Love conv. 50 a. (*) to Sutton Sickelmore (IS#K: 85).

SICKELMORE'S (or SICKLEMORE'S) DOCK
(See DOCK)

SIDMONS LAST

1783: 137 a. in Back River Lower Hundred owned by Conduce Gatch (1783 TL).

SIDWELL

1667: 50 a. surv. for Roger (N) on s. side of Back R. (MHM 21:194).

20 July 1695: Selah Dorman and w. Jane conv. 50 a. (*) (orig. granted to Roger Sidwell by Lord Baltimore in 1670) to George Chancey (RM#HS: 503).

8 March 1698: George Chancey conv. 50 a. (*) (orig. granted to Roger Sidwell by Lord Baltimore in 1670, and deeded by Selah Dorman and w. Jane, who was the heir of Roger Sidwell, to Chancey), to Thomas Smith and w. Elizabeth (TR#RA: 325).

SIGN OF THE PAINTHER

110 a. in the Fork betw. the Great Falls of Gunpowder R., and the Western Run, and orig. granted to John and Luke Wiley (TR#C: 551).

23 May 1750: John Wiley (one of the orig. grantees), now of York Co., PA, conv. to William Wright (TR#C: 551).

SIMKINS' ADDITION

28 Feb 1749: 28 Feb 1742: Lawrence Hammond and w. Avarilla conv. 50 a. pt. Mount Organ and pt. (*), left to Avarilla by her father John Simkins), to John Hawkins (TB#C: 169).

SIMKIN'S REPOSE

1717: 100 a. surv. for John Simkins.

See Horvath Plats: Green Spring Valley; Pikesville.

SIMKINS' REPOSE, ADDITION TO

1731: 100 a. surv.

See Horvath Plat: Pikesville.

20 July 1749: John Simkins of BC conv. 25 a. Mount Organ and 35 a. (*) to John Hawkins. JS' w. Mary cons. (TR#C: 229).

2 Nov 1751: John Hawkins, with cons. of w. Mary, conv. 50 a. being pt. of Mount Organ and (*) to John Shermadine. JH's w. Mary cons. (TR#D: 294; see also following deed on folio 296).

SIMMONS CHOICE

12 April 1735: Abraham Simmons of AA Co. planter, conv. 100 a., being ½ of (*) (orig. pat. to AS) to James Lee. AS' w. Ellinor cons. (IS#IK: 289).

31 May 1742: Abraham Symonds [sic] conv. 84 a. (*) to his son-in-law William Taylard (TB#A: 173).

31 May 1742: Symonds conv. 100 a. pt. (*) to his son-in-law Edward Morgan of BC (TB#A: 175).

SIMMS CHANCE

1783: 34 a. owned by Annanias Divers in Gunpowder Upper Hundred (1783 TL).

SIMPKINS (See under SIMKINS)

SIM'S CHOICE

28 Nov 1673 or 1683: Surv. (MRR: 43).

See NOTEBOOK.

3 Aug 1726: John Dorsey conv. Dorsey's Plains, cont. 775 a. by patent, 150 a. (*), and 100 a. Swanson (the latter two conv. by Vaughn Davies and w. Catherine, dau. of Gideon Skates, dec.) to Daniel Dulany (IS#H: 272).

SIMMS DISCOVERY

1783: 136 a. held by Capt. John Slaymaker in Middle River and Back River Upper Hundreds (1783 TL).

SIMPSON'S HAZARD

July 1721: 100 a. surv. for William Simpson (Index to Patents).

24 Aug 1726: William Simpson conv. 100 a. (*) to John Stokes (IS#H: 301).

4 Aug 1742: John Stokes of BC conv. 69 a. (*) to Jacob Giles (TB#A: 229).

SIMPSON'S SECOND HAZARD

4 Oct 1730 (or 1736): William Simpson of BA Co., carpenter, conv. 100 a. (*) to Jacob Giles (IS#IK: 304).

SIMS CHOICE

28 Nov 1673: 150 a. surv. for Richard Sims on n. side of, and near the head of Gunpowder R.; later held: Michael Judd, 50 a.; and 100 a. by Enoch Spinkes; still later by Gideon Skaats (MRR: 43).

28 Sep 1674: Tract was pat. (See IR#PP: 43).

2 Nov 1679: Richard Sims, conv. 100 a. (*) to Nicholas Hempstead. Elizabeth Sims gave cons. (IR#PP: 43).

2 Nov 1692: Charles Ramsey conv. 100 a. of 150 a. (*) to Michael Judd. Tract was left by Nicholas Hempstead to John Wolley, now dec., whose widow m. CR (RM#HS: 356).

5 March 1700: Michael Judd conv. 2 a. (*) to John Hall and other inhabitants of BC. MJ's w. Mary cons. (HW#2: 126).

14 June 1701: Michael Judd and w. Mary conv. 50 a. (*) to John Taylor, carpenter (HW#2: 109).

20 May 1702: John Taylor conv. 150 a. [sic] (*) to Gideon Skaats. JT's w. Jane cons. (HW#2: 258).

5 Aug 1702: Enoch Spinks of BC, planter, conv. 100 a. (*) to John Taylor of BC, innholder. Nicholas Hemstead (our grandfather by affinity) bought the tract from Richard Sims. NH left the tract by will to his w. Eliza Hemstead (our grandmother by consanguinity); Spinks is the heir apparent of his grandmother Elizabeth Hemstead (HW#2: 159).

2 Dec 1723: Vaughan Davies of NY City and w. Catherine (only dau. and heir of Gideon Skaats, dec.) conv. to John Dorsey 150 a., (*), 100 a.

Swanson, and 15 a. Addition to Swanson (IS#G: 283).

3 Aug 1726: John Dorsey conv. Dorsy's Plains, cont. 775 a. by patent, 150 a. (*), and 100 a. Swanson (the latter two conv. by Vaughn Davies and w. Catherine, dau. of Gideon Skates, dec.) to Daniel Dulany (IS#H: 272).

SINCLAIR'S CHASE

1783: 55 a. held by George Lytle in Mine Run Hundred (1783 TL).

SINGS RANGE

1783: 67 a. held by William Wheeler of Benjamin in Middle and Back River Upper Hundreds (1783 TL).

SINGS RANGE, ADDITION TO

1783: 88 a. held by William Wheeler of Benjamin in Middle and Back River Upper Hundreds (1783 TL).

SISTER'S DOWRY

1683: 120 a. surv. for Andrew Mattson; later held by Emanuel Smith and still later by Emanuel Smith's orphans (MRR: 17).

18 March 1686/7: Andrew Mattson and w. Jane conv. (*) to Gideon Gamble (RM#HS: 315).

4 March 1699: Gideon Gamble of CE Co. conv. 120 a. (*) to Emanuel Smith. GG's w. Mary cons. (HW#2: 36).

13 June 1722: Thomas Simpson and w. Mary conv. 170 [sic] a. (*) to Joshua Wood (IS#G: 72).

18 May 1725: Joshua Wood conv. 120 a. (*) to Thomas Mitchell; deed stated that the cert. of surv. was dated 12 Oct 1683. JW's w. Martha cons. (IS#H: 120).

SISTER'S HOPE

12 Nov 1695: 200 a. surv. for Francis Watkins; later held by the orphans of Watkins and by Thomas Bedeson (Biddison) (MRR: 55).

29 Sep 1712: Thomas Biddison conv. 100 a. pt. (*) to Francis Watkins (TR#A: 252).

5 Aug 1741: Francis Watkins conv. 100 a. pt. (*) to Jervis Biddison. FW's w. Elizabeth cons. (HWS#1-A: 521).

1743: Thomas Biddison leaves (*) to his s. Jarvis (MCW#VIII: 237).

SKIDMORE'S LAST (See SCUDAMORE'S LAST)

SKIPTON-IN-CRAVEN

20 Oct 1740: Michael Taylor of PG Co., Gent., prisoner in PG Co. Jail, conv. 675 a. Finegal (which was granted to Taylor by a special warrant of escheat), 200 a. Scrutiny Conveniency (pt. of Elizabeth's Delight, in PG Co.), 260 a. (*), and 380 a. Scrutiny to John Hepburn, High Sheriff of PG Co. (TB#E: 374).

8 Dec 1746: John Hepburn, of PG Co., formerly High Sheriff, conv. 380 a. Scrutiny and 260 a. (*) to Thomas White (TB#E: 375).

SLIPE (THE) (See STRIPE, THE)

1 June 1674: George Willson conv. to William Southbee two adj. parcels on the s. side of Sassafras R.: 125 a. Verina, and 50 a. (*) (G#J: 270).

SMALL HOPES

2 June 1671:L William York, planter, conv. 50 a. (*) to John Collett, near mouth of Deep Creek, on eastern side of Gunpowder (IR#PP: 103).

5 Aug 1730: John Elliott conv. 25 a. (*) to Richard Sampson. JE's w. Sarah cons. (IS#L: 5).

1783: 25 a. in Mine Run Hundred owned by George Myers (1783 TL).

SMALL VALLEY

7 Aug 1745: Watkins James of BC conv. $32\frac{1}{2}$ a. (*) to William Ingle. WJ's w. Mary cons. (TB#D: 271).

13 Oct 1746: William Ingle conv. $32\frac{1}{2}$ a. (*) to his s. William Carback, als. William Ingle. The transfer was to take effect after the decease of the grantor and his w. Catherine (TB#E: 221).

1783: Thomas Gillhampton owned 35 a.; Benjamin Stansbury owned 30 a. in Middle River Lower Hundred (1783 TL).

SMALL VALLEY NEAR

1783: 12 a. in Back River Lower Hundred owned by Thomas Biddison, Sr. (1783 TL).

SMALLWOOD

2 March 1744: Thomas Taylor of BC conv. to Nicholas Haile 50 a. (*), and 80 a. Taylor's Discovery (TB#D: 63).

6 April 1745: Nicholas Haile conv. 100 a. Hooker's Farm (pt. of Gerar), 60 a. Addition to Hooker's Farm, 100 a. Hailes' Forest, 100 a. pt. of Haile's Fellowship, 80 a. pt. Taylor's Discovery, 50 a. (*), 200 a. Hailes Discovery, 200 a. Shadrack's Lot, and 200 a. Meshack's Garden, to Christopher Grindall of London, mariner (TB#E: 83).

28 March 1747: Nicholas Haile conv. 100 a. Hooker's Farm (pt. of Gerar), 60 a. Hooker's Addition, 100 a. Hailes' Forest, 200 a. Haile's Long Grove, 80 a. pt. Taylor's Discovery, 50 a. (*), to Christopher Grindall of London, mariner (TB#E: 347).

1783: Edward Hall of Joshua owned 50 a., and Joshua Hall owned 50 a. in Middle River Upper Hundred (1783 TL).

SMALLWOOD, ADDITION TO

1783: 20 a. owned by Joshua Hall in Middle and Back River Upper Hunds. (1783 TL).

SMITH'S ADDITION

6 June 1695: 45 a. surv. for Edward Smith; later held by Richard Banks (MRR: 104).

5 March 1700: Edward Smith and w. Elizabeth, conv. Gray's Lot and 45 a. (*) to Richard Banks (HW#2: 11).

SMITH'S ADDITION
(Pt. BACHELOR'S DELIGHT)

6 June 1710: Samuel Arden, s. and heir of John, conv., 56 a. Smith's Addition, pt. of Bachelor's Delight, to Thomas Smith of BC, planter (TR#A: 69).

SMITH'S BEGINNING

18 March 1688/9: Thomas Richardson assigns a cert. of surv. to Thomas Smith, who lies out (*); tract was later held by Smith's orphans (RM#HS: 422; MRR: 56).

6 June 1693: Thomas Smith and w. Isabella conv. 100 a. (*) to Robert Benger (RM#HS: 381).

SMITH'S CHANCE

3 June 1730: Charles Smith conv. 200 a. (*) to Henry Fitch (IS#K: 310).

1783: David Parlett and Joshua Parlett each own 50 a. in Back River Lower Hundred (1783 TL).

SMITH'S CHOICE

10 Aug 1732: 290 a. pat. by William Smith (See TB#C: 279).

28 May 1743: William Smith of CE Co. conv. (*) to Daniel Ashelman of Humfields, Lancaster Co., PA. WS' w. Rachel cons. (TB#C: 279).

SMITH'S DISCOVERY

16 July 1724 Edward Smith mortgaged (*) to Josias Middlemore and John Crockett (IS#G: 344).

1750: William Andrews owned 77 a. (1750 DB).

SMITH'S FOLLY

25 May 1745: John Bayley of BC conv. 50 a. (*) to Jacob Combest (TB#D: 148).

SMITH'S FOREST

1698: Surv. for Edw. Smith.
See Horvath Plat: Elkridge.

5 March 1700: Edward Smith conv. 212 a. (*) to Joseph Burton. The land was orig. granted on 4 Aug 1698 (HW#2: 49).

26 Nov 1734: Thomas Linthicum, Jr., of AA Co., and w. Sarah, conv. 106 a., pt. (*), to Robert Chapman, Jr. (HWS#M: 153).

23 Dec 1749: Robert Chapman of BC, wheelwright, s. and heir of Robert Chapman, who d. intestate, conv. to Daniel Dulany 100 a. Yates' Forbearance and 106 a. (*). RC's w. Margaret cons. (TR#C: 385).

SMITH'S FORGE

7 April 1703: Mary Clark of BC, widow, conv. 60 a. (*) after her death, to her grandson James Freeman, eld. s. of Richard Freeman of CV Co. (HW#2: 237).

SMITH'S LOT

8 Aug 1717: Edward Smith and w. Bridget conv. 60 a. (*) to Robert Smith cordwainer (TR#A: 480).

1783: 2¾ a. held by Jno. Bacon in Mine Run Hundred (1783 TL).

SMITH'S NECK

9 Sep 1734: Thomas Brerewood, Sr., late of Horton, Bucks, Great Britain, now of BC, conv. 200 a. (*), pt. of My Lord Baltimore's Gift, to Samuel Browne, late of London, now of AA Co. (HWS#M: 104).

SMITH'S PURCHASE

15 Jan 1700: John Shaw of CE Co. conv. to Alexander Graves of BA Co., 100 a. Hopewell, 100 a. being ½ of Salisbury Plains, 70 a. Witherington, 80 a. Shadwell's Range. and 100 a. Smith's Range (HW#2: 53).

SMITH'S RANGE

6 March 1723/4: Edward Smith conv. 120 a. (*) to John Crockett (IS#G: 243).

SOLITUDE

5 Oct 1725: Capt. Thomas Larkin of Annapolis conv. 125 a., being ½ of (*) to Christian Geist (IS#H: 203).

SON'S ADDITION

9 June 1744: Thomas Amos mortgaged 176½ a. (*) and 40 a. Stewart's Neglect to Robert Bishop and Josias Slade (TB#E: 91).

SOPHIA'S DAIRY

26 March 1720: John Hall of BC and w. Martha conv. 102 a. Eastland Hills and pt. (*) to John Durbin (TR#DS: 203).

7 Dec 1726: John Durbin and w. Avarilla conv. 112 a. pt. Eastland Hills and (*), and 200 a. Hathaway's Hazard to Samuel Hughes, except for a parcel of Hathaway's Hazard given by Samuel Bourne (who later sold the land to Durbin) to Charles Whitaker (IS#H: 370).
3 June 1731: John Hall of BA Co., Gent., conv. 813 a. (*) to dau. Sophia in view of her marriage to Thomas White (IS#L: 105).
17 Dec 1741: Edward Hall, s. of John Hall, dec., conv. pt. Jericoe, pt. Cranberry Hall, and pt. (*), to his bro. Parker Hall (TB#A: 63).
14 May 1746: Samuel Hughes of BC conv. Eastland Hills, pt. (*) and Hathaway's Hazard, to Col. John Hall, Jacob Giles, and Isaac Webster (TB#E: 432).

SOUTH CANTON

6 June 1680: 245 a. pat. (IR#AM: 181).
7 March 1681/2: Robert Clarkson of AA Co. conv. 245 a. (*) to Christopher Gist and Richard Cromwell (IR#AM: 181). (For bond and letter of atty. from Robert Clarkson, see IR#AM: 179, 180.)
14 June 1682: Christopher Gist and Richard Cromwell, conv. 84 a., pt. (*), at Curtis Creek and Rumley Marsh Point. CG's w. Edith cons. On 4 Sep 1682 Richard Cromwell appointed "his bro. Christopher Gist" atty. (IR#AM: 193).

SOUTHAMPTON

Aug 1699: 500 a. surv. for Henry Wriothesley; later held by Joshua Cecil of PG Co. (MRR).
27 Oct 1704: Henry Wriothesley of BA Co. conv. 500 a. (*) to Joshua Cecil of PG Co. HW's w. Ann cons. (HW#2: 369).
27 Sep 1749: William Courts of CH Co., s. and heir of John Courts, dec., conv. 500 a. (*) as follows: 125 a. to Roger Donahue, 150 a. to Andrew Thompson, 100 a. to Robert Bryarly, and 175 a. to Simon Dorsey (TR#C: 324).
6 June 1750: Andrew Thompson conv. 150 a. (*) to Alexander Young. AT's w. Elizabeth cons. (TR#C: 462).

SPARROW'S NEST

1562: Cert. of surv. mentioned Broad (now Bear) Creek on Block House Cove, adj. to Walltown and Hopewell (MHM 25:346-7).
4 Aug 1691: Charles Gorsuch conv. 58 a. (*), 15 a. Hopewell, and 156 a. Walltown to Joseph Heathcote of AA Co., planter. CG's w. Ann cons. (IR#AM: 107).
25 June 1711: Solomon Sparrow of AA Co. conv. 50 a. to Charles Gorsuch. SS's w. Sarah cons. (TR#A: 160).
3 Sep 1723: Richard Gott of AA Co., with cons. of w. Sarah, conv. to Richard Galloway, reversion to 50 a. (*) after the death of Sarah Galloway, relict of Solomon Sparrow, by virtue of a devise to Sara Gott in the LWT of Solomon Sparrow (IS#G: 228).
1729: Solomon Sparrow conv. 55 a. (*) to Richard Galloway (IS#K: 44).

SPEEDWELL

20 Aug 1748: Nicholas Ruxton Gay conv. to Walter Tolley all his right to 47 a. (*) and other land (TR#C: 69).
See MHM 53:41.

SPESUTIA ISLAND

25 July ----: 2000 a. surv. for Col. Nathaniel Utie on an island near the western Shore, near the head of the Bay called Bear Point; pat. 9 Aug 1660; now in occupation of John Hall and Mark Richardson for the orphans of George Utie (MRR: 3).

SPRING GARDEN (1685)

8 April 1685: 200 a. surv. for John Yeo; Yeo d. and his heirs live in England (MRR: 20).

SPRING GARDEN (1697)

22 Sep 1697: 127 a. surv. for Samuel Baker, betw. Rumley and Delph Creek; Baker was dead and land was liable to an escheat (MRR: 27).

SPRING GARDEN (1720)

16 Sep 1720: 150 a. pat. by John Roberts (MPL PL#6: 301, CE#1: 324).
See Horvath Plat: Old Hampstead.
20 June 1721: John Roberts and w. Hannah (signed Enor) conv. 150 a. (*) to Hill Savage (RM#HS: 665).
20 June 1721: Hill Savage of BC, and w. Eleanor conv. 150 a. (*) and other household material to Thomas Randall and William Parrish, if the Savages keep harmless and indemnify TR and WP from a certain testamentary bond which the latter two posted on the estate of Peter Bond of BC, dec. (RM#HS: 662).
27 Sep 1726: William Parrish of BC, planter, and w. Susanna, conv. 150 a. (*) to John Norris (IS#H: 331).
14 May 1753: John Thomas and w. Sarah (only dau. and heir of Hill Savage), deed to John Metcalfe 150 a. Rich Level, als. (*), orig. granted to John Roberts under the latter name (TR#D: 548).

SPRING GARDEN (1730)

7 March 1730: Edward Richards of BA Co. conv. (*), pat. in 1730 to Edward Richards. ER's w. Mary cons. (HWS#1-A: 472).

8 March 1740: John Cole, Jr., of BC, conv. 100 a. (*) to Henry Morgan, mariner (HWS#1-A: 473).

17 April 1750: Benjamin Richards conv. (*) to William Stiles. BR's w. Ann cons. (TR#C: 538).

SPRING GARDEN (1733)

26 Jan 1733: 140 a. pat. by Dunkin Coleman and his w. Sarah (MPL AM#1: 244, EI#1: 108).

6 Sep 1734: Dunkin Coleman and w. Sarah conv. 240 a. (*) to John Wood (HWS#M: 158).

1 June 1745: John Wood of BA Co. conv. 140 a. (*) to Dr. Robert Holliday. JW's w. Eborah (Deborah?) cons. (TB#C: 695).

13 Aug 1745: John and Deborah Wood conv. 140 a. (*) to Henry Morgan (TB#D: 372).

SPRING GARDEN (Unplaced)

12 March 1742: John Metcalfe mortgaged 150 a. (*) and 100 a. Addition to Spring Garden to Rachel Bailey, widow (TB#C: 194).

21 Feb 1746: John Metcalfe of BA Co. conv. 100 a. (*) to Rachel Bailey of BA Co., widow. JM's w. Mary cons. (TB#E: 313).

1750: George Lester owned 127 a. (1750 DB).

10 April 1759: Jacob Schilling, Jr., blacksmith, conv. 140 a. (*) to Christopher Vaughn (B#G: 316).

SPRING GARDEN, ADDITION TO

1 Feb 1742: Benjamin Tasker leased 100 a. (*), pt. of Lord Baltimore's Reserve, to Henry Morgan, for 99 years (TB#C: 630).

12 March 1742: John Metcalfe mortgaged 150 a. Spring Garden and 100 a. (*) to Rachel Bailey, widow (TB#C: 194).

SPRING NECK (Pre-1670)

1 Nov 1670: Robert Neve, planter, and w. Elizabeth conv. 150 a. (*), on e. side of Bay, to Nathaniel Stiles (IR#PP: 89).

SPRING NECK (Pre-1678)

7 Jan 1678/9: Arthur Taylor, planter, conv. to Thomas Cooke, planter, 315 a. (*), on n. side of Gunpowder R. AT's w. Frances cons. (IR#PP: 28).

-- Sep 1680: Thomas Cooke conv. to Israel Skelton, planter, 150 a. (*), being pt. of 750 a. covered by warrant of 13 June 1676 to Thomas Taylor, who assigned the warrant on 7 July 1676 to George Yate of AA Co., who assigned 315 a. to Arthur Taylor, who conv. it to Cooke on 7 Jan 1678/9. George Yate, deputy surveyor, gave cert. of surv. for 315 a. (*) laid out for AT (IR#AM: 146).

2 Aug 1703: John Taylor and w. Jane, innholders, conv. 100 a. (*) to Thomas Nevell (HW#2: 273).

20 Feb 1710: John Standiford and w. Margaret conv. 126 a. (*) to William Noble. (Tract was transcribed by Dr. Miller as Spring Week.) (TR#A: 148).

29 April 1717: William Noble and w. Elizabeth conv. 126 a. (*) to Joshua Merriken, boatwright (TR#A: 419).

27 Oct 1726: John Taylor conv. pt. of George's Hill, being pt. of (*), to Joshua Merriken. The land was taken up by Arthur Taylor, father of said John. The new surv. of (*) lies in the older surv. of George's Hill (IS#H: 336).

3 Sep 1745: Thomas Baxter of Bucks Co., PA conv. (100 a.?) (*) to Samuel Maxwell. TB's w. Mary cons. (TB#D: 351).

8 Aug 1750: Joseph Maxwell, only surviving s. of Samuel Maxwell, and bro. of James Maxwell, dec., conv. to Nicholas Ruxton Gay, 100 a. (*) and 100 a. Maxwell's Hope (TR#C: 555).

SPRING NECK (1697)

-- Sep 1697: 126 a. tract surv. for Israel Skelton (MRR: 63-64).

SPRING NECK (or SPRING POINT)

20 Oct 16--: Walter Dickeson conv. 450 a. pt. (*) to Abraham Clarke, shipwright (RM#HS: 3, 6).

SPRING POINT

31 March 1662: A 100 a. tract surv. for Paul Kinsey on the southern branch of Patapsco R.; now in possession of Thomas Hamon (Hammond?) (MRR: 79).

5 Feb 1663: Paul Kinsey and w. Katherin conv. land to William Gwynn (RM#HS: 32).

26 April 1671: Evan Gwin of MD, and John Gwin of VA, planters, conv. to Charles Gorsuch 100 a. called (*), formerly granted to Paul Kinsey, giving warranty for themselves and Thomas Williams of VA. 27 April 1671: John Gwin of VA appoints his bro. Evan Gwin of AA Co. his atty. to ackn. sale of 100 a. to Charles Gorsuch. 27 April 1671: EG of MD, and JG of VA, assigned to CG their interest in land pat. by PK and assigned by him to William Gwinn, dec. (IR#PP: 113).

28 Sep 1674: Charles Gorsuch conv. 100 a. (*) and 200 a. Health, to William Wheatley, mariner, of London (G#J: 290).

8 May 1692: Nicholas Smith of London, mariner, conv. 100 a. (*) and 200 a. The Heath, to John Hammond of AA Co. (RM#HS: 474).

20 Nov 1694: John Conaway of Ratcliffe, Stepney Parish, Co. Middlesex, England, mariner, gave p/a

to Nicholas Smith to take possession of (*) and The Heath (RM#HS: 476).

27 May 1735: Lawrence Hammond, s. and devisee of Col. Thomas Hammond, conv. his share of Dearing's Increase, 200 a. Health, and 100 a. (*), which LH had resurv. into Brother's Kindness, in all 371 a., to his bro. William Hammond. LH's w. Abarilla cons. (HWS#M: 313).

SPRY'S INHERITANCE

12 Feb 1668: 640 a. surv. for Oliver Sprye and later held by the orphans of Henry Johnson (MRR: 5).

1 Aug 1670: Godfrey Harmer, merchant, and w. Mary, conv. 640 a. (*) to John Fallock, at the head of Rumley Creek, on the n. side of Bush R. (IR#PP: 84).

6 Feb 1674/4: John Fallock and w. Jane conv. 640 a. (*) to Miles Gibson (G#J: 223).

7 June 1676: Miles Gibson conv. 640 a. (*) near the head of Rumley Creek, to Samuel Hedge, Gent. (G#J: 312).

1 Aug 1682: Samuel Hedge, Gent., of Fenwick's Colony, West Jersey, conv. 640 a. (*) to Henry Johnson (Deed and Letter of Atty.). SH's w. Anne cons. (RM#HS: 16).

SPRY'S MARSH

5 Sep 1666: William Osborne of Bush R., conv. 350 a. (*), about three miles up Bush R. on e. side, to John Lee (IR#PP: 58).

4 March 1667/8: Oliver Spry conv. 175 perches (*) to William Osborne and John Lee (IR#PP: 67).

10 March 1672/3: John Lee conv. his half of (*) to William Osborne. JL's w. Florence assigned her interest (G#J: 153, TR#A: 111).

STANDIFORD'S CHANCE

1783: Jno. James owned 120 a. (*) in Gunpowder Upper Hundred (1783 TL).

STANDIFORD'S HOPE

1 May 1728: John Halloway of BC deeds 10 a. (*) to Skelton Standiford (IS#I: 208).

STANFORD'S CLAIMED [sic]
(Pt. THE MANOR OF BALTIMORE)

25 Feb 1744/5: Benjamin Tasker and Gov. Thomas Bladen leased 220 a. (*) to William Standiford for lives of WS, w. Christiana and s. Aquila (TB#D: 71).

STANHARKET

Orig. surv. for John Shadwell, Sr. (IS#G: 352).

17 Sep 1701: John Chadwell and w. Mary conv. 190 a. (*) and 100 a. Chestnut Neck to Daniel Scott (HW#2: 95).

21 July 1724: John Jones of BA Co., and w. Margaret, dau. and sole heir of a certain John Shadwell, the Younger, conv. to Daniel Scott, the Younger, s. of Daniel Scott, the Elder, 490 a., comprised of the following tracts: Chestnut Neck and (*) (both orig. surv. for John Shadwell, Sr.), and Harmer's Hope and Hunting Creek (both orig. surv. for Godfrey Harmer and Oliver Sprye and sold to John Shadwell, Sr., grandfather of said Margaret Jones) (IS#G: 352).

190 a. resurv. as pt. of Scott's Improvement (q.v.) (TB#E: 534).

STANSBURY

1724: 268 a. surv. for Thomas Stansbury on w. side of Little Falls of Gunpowder (MHM 9:76).

STANSBURY'S PLAINS

1734: 692 a. surv. for Thomas Stansbury; on PW Plat W-1.

STEIR'S PROGRESS

4 Nov 1701: John Francis Holland and his w. Jane Francis Holland, conv. 240 a. (*) (formerly taken up by Charles Gorsuch and called Aberle), also pt. William, to Sarah Steirs, spinster (HW#2: 96).

STEPHEN'S FOREST

May 1703: 702 a. surv. for Charles Stephens (Card Index to Patents).

STEPNEY

3 Oct 1683: 200 a. surv. for John Miles on e. side of Bush R.; later poss. by Archibald Buchanan (MRR: 5).

18 March 1706/7: John Miles conv. 200 a. (*) to Archibald Buchanan (RM#HS: 545).

22 Dec 1707: Archiblad Buchanan and w. Mary conv. 200 a. (*) to Edward Swan, tailor (RM#HS: 584).

31 Aug 1723: Aquila Hall of BA Co. conv. 200 a. (*) to bro. Parker Hall (IS#G: 216).

STEPP

25 Aug 1690: Amos Nicholls, of CE Co. conv. 400 a. (*) to Thomas Brown (RM#HS: 321).

5 Jan 1702: Thomas Browne conv. 400 a. (*) and a servant man Robert Whisley (for the rest of his term) to his loving s. John Browne (HW#2: 192).

STERLING'S PURCHASE

18 March 1699: Thomas Richardson of BC and w. Susanna conv. (*) orig. called Richardson's Outlet, to Thomas Sterling of CV Co. (HW#2: 15).

29 Dec 1725: Alexander Adair of CV Co., chirurgeon, and w. Christian conv. 230 a. (*) to Richard Caswell (IS#H: 220).

16 Jan 1745: Richard Caswell of BC, Gent., conv. 230 a. (*) and 98 a. Caswell's Venture to William Dallam. RC's w. Christiana cons. (TB#D: 422).

10 July 1746: William Dallam conv. 230 a. (*) to William Andrews and Abraham Andrews, s. of William. WD's w. Mary cons. (TB#E: 265).

STEVENS' HOPE

16 April 1742: Samuel Stevens conv. 150 a. (*) to Andrew Macgill. SS's w. Martha cons. (TB#A: 158).

STEWART'S NEGLECT

9 June 1744: Thomas Amos mortgaged 176½ a. Son's Addition and 40 a. (*) to Robert Bishop and Josias Slade (TB#E: 91).

STEVENSON'S PLAINS

1729: 100 a. pat. by Edward Stevenson (MPL IL#B: 73, PL#7: 117).

25 March 1745: Thomas Brothers conv. 100 a. (*) to Thomas Sheredine (TB#D: 258).

1750: Thomas Brothers owned 100 a. (*) (1750 DB: 36).

28 March 1753: Edward Stevenson and w. Susanna conv. 100 a. (*) to Nathaniel Brothers, at head of Bear's Wallowing Branch (TR#D: 527).

21 March 1761: Nathaniel Brothers pat. 125 a. (*) (Patent Cert. 4668; MSA).

STILLIN

4 March 1666/7: William Fisher, chirurgeon, of VA, and w. Frances, conv. to Henry Ward, mariner, 1400 a. at Poplar Neck on St. Alban's Creek on the s. side of Elk R., including 1000 a. taken up by Fisher, and 300 a. (*) taken up by Oxell Still, and 100 a. formerly taken up by Thomas Cauker (IR#PP: 61).

STINCHCOMB'S DELIGHT

1770 taken up: on KN Plat WO.

STINCHCOMB'S HILLS

11 Feb 1752: Surv. for John Stinchcomb as a Resurv. on Overlookt.

See KN Plat WO; Horvath Plat: Granite.

1 Oct 1760: John Stinchcomb conv. 100 a. (*) on e. side of Morgan's Run, to George Shipley of AA Co. JS's w. Catherine cons. (B#H: 416).

STOAKLEY MANOR

6 Aug 1672: Vinson Elliott (Ellet), boatwright, conv. 550 a. (*) on the main run of a branch of Bush R., to Jeremiah Eaton of KE Co. (G#J: 86; TR#RA: 61).

STOCKSDALE'S ADDITION

1755: Surv. for Edw. Stocksdale.

See Horvath Plat: Reisterstown.

8 May 1760: Edward Stocksdale conv. 67 a. (*) to Nathaniel Davis. ES' w. Catherine cons. (B#H: 184).

STONE HILL

30 Aug 1725: 704 a. pat. by Charles Carroll.

6 Sep 1733: Charles Carroll of Annapolis, chirurgeon, conv. (*) to Jacob Giles and Isaac Webster (HWS#M: 12).

25 March 1737: Isaac Webster and Sarah Giles conv. 352 a., being ½ of (*) to Charles Worthington. IW's w. Margaret cons. (IS#IK: 390).

25 March 1737: Isaac Webster and w. Margaret and Jacob Giles conv. 352 a. (*) to Skipwith Coale (IS#IK: 408).

4 March 1760: James Carey conv. 51 a. (*) to George Cole. JC's w. Ann cons. (B#H: 111).

STONE HILLS

30 Sep 1734: 81 a. surv. for Col. John Smith; pat. 30 Oct 1736 (TB#E: 423; MPL EI#2: 462; EI#5: 114).

7 April 1747: John Smith of CV Co., Gent., conv. 81 a. (*) to Thomas Sheredine. JS's w. Mary cons. (TB#E: 423).

STONES (THE)

May 1705: 400 a. surv. for Thomas Rowles; pat. 10 Jan 1705 (MPL CD#4: 268).

STONES ADVENTURE

7 July 1743: 100 a. pat.

12 July 1743: Henry Stone and w. Constant conv. (*) to William Fell (TB#C: 282).

STONE'S ADVENTURE RESURVEYED

1706: 372 a. for William Fell; on PW Plat H.

STONES DELIGHT

3 Oct 1714: Surv. for Richard Taylor; 98 a. of this is included in Drumqu'hasle. (For location see MHM#58: 227).

7 April 1716: Surv. for Richard Taylor, Jr., adj. land formerly surv. for Job Evans, on Western Run and a branch of Herring Run; pat. 25 April 1717 for 100 a. (MPL FF#7: 180, PL#4: 3).

1721: Richard Taylor, Jr., conv. (*) on Little Britain Ridge to William Lyell. RT's w. Mary cons. (IS#G: 402).

16 April 1723: Richard Taylor, Jr., now of Stafford Co., VA, gave p/a to his father, Richard Taylor, to sell (*), RT, Jr.'s, w. Mary agreed (IS#G: 400).
8 June 1727: William Lyell conv. 100 a. (*) to Richard Huett (IS#I: 9).
15 Jan 1742: Samuel Tipton conv. 100 a. (*) and Lot 19 in Joppa Town to Henry Morgan, mariner. ST's w. Mary cons. (TB#C: 166).

STONES RANGE

1695: 194 a. surv. for Thomas Stone on the w. side of the main run of Back R., beginning at a Spanish oak of John Broad (MRR).
26 Nov 1709: Thomas Stone conv. 174 a. (*) to George Cole. TS's w. Christian cons. (TR#A: 25).

STONEY HILL
(See THE WIDOW'S CHOICE)

19 Oct 1765: Thomas Stansbury, Jr., conv. $61\frac{1}{2}$ a., (*), now called The Widow's Choice, to Reuben Boring (B#O: 608).

STONEY RIDGE (1703)

20 June 1703: 1290 a. surv. (TR#A: 360).
2 March 1713: Aquila Paca conv. 108 a., pt. (*) to Timothy Keen. AP's w. Martha cons. (TR#A: 360).
20 Sep 1756: Timothy Keene conv. 108 a. (*) to James Armstrong. TK's w. Anne cons. (BB#I: 673).

STONEY RIDGE

Pat. to Richard Deaver (TB#E: 615).
5 Feb 1741: Richard Deaver conv. 100 a. (*) and 50 a. Addition to Stony Ridge to Roger Perryman of CE Co. (TB#A: 80).
1 Oct 1747: Roger Perryman conv. 100 a. (*) and 50 a. Addition to Stoney Ridge to William Morton. RP's w. Martha cons. (TB#E: 615).

STONEY RIDGE, ADDITION TO

Pat. to Richard Deaver (TB#E: 615).
5 Feb 1741: Richard Deaver conv. 50 a. (*) and 100 a. Stoney Ridge to Charles Perryman (TB#A: 80).
1 Oct 1747: Roger Perryman conv. 100 a. Stoney Ridge and 50 a. (*) to William Morton. RP's w. Martha cons. (TB#E: 615).

STONY POINT
(Pt. PLANTER'S DELIGHT and
Pt. COLLETT'S POINT)

5 Sep 1724: Richard Smithers, Gent., conv. 220 a. (*) to his s. John Smithers, who will take possession after the death of Richard (IS#G: 381).
4 April 1725: Richard Smithers, Gent., conv. 250 a. (*), adj. the land bequeathed by Col. George Wells to his dau. Frances and s. George, to John Stokes (IS#H: 124).
13 Feb 1726/7: John Smithers of KE Co., s. of Richard of BA Co., have deed for 250 a. (*) to John Stokes to quiet title, since RS had already conv. land to Stokes and then conv. it to his s. JS. The deed stated that George Wells devised the tracts to his daus. Susanna and Mary (IS#H: 382).

STONY RUN HILLS

March 1719: 50 a. surv. for Thomas Hughes; pat. 10 July 1724 (MPL PL#5: 88; IL#A: 197).
15 May 1725: Thomas Hughs, carpenter, leased 50 a. to Benj. Belt of PG Co. for 99 years (IS#H: 94).

STOP LYING

1 Jan 1710: Anthony Drew and w. Margaret conv. 400 a. (*) to Richard King (TR#A: 103).
6 Jan 1710: Richard King conv. 400 a. Stopp (?) to Anthony Drew (TR#A: 104).

STOOP (or STOPP) (THE)

24 March 1679: 118 a. surv. for George Yates by Born Branch; later poss. by Thomas Brown, and later by John Brown (MRR: 9).
3 Sep 1684: George Yate, Gent., and w. Mary, of AA Co., conv. 118 a. (*), lying betw. Capt. Thomas Stockett's tracts Bourn and his tract Harmer's Town, to Thomas Lightfoot, Gent. (RM#HS: 140).
27 June 1741: Thomas Brown, s. and heir of John Brown, dec., conv. (*) or Stop Lying to his bro. Augustus Brown (HWS#1-A: 528).
2 March 1744/5: Augustus Brown of Lancaster Co., PA, conv. 124 a. (*) to Jacob Giles (TB#D: 35).

STOUT

1702/04: Surv. for Thomas Bale.
See Horvath Plat: Elkridge.
10 May 1704: Thomas Bale of BA Co., merchant, conv. 200 a. pt. (*), in all 529 a., to John Whips, Jr. TB's w. Sarah cons. (IR#PP: 137).
5 Nov 1717: Anthony Bale of BA Co. conv. 329 a., residue of 529 a., to Thomas Randall (TR#A: 513).
25 July 1724: John Whips and w. Margaret, mortgaged tract (*) to Philip Smith of London (IS#G: 348).
19 Jan 1733: John Whips conv. to Richard Gist 200 a. pt. of (*), which Whips bought from Thomas Bale. JW's w. Margaret cons. (HWS#M: 26).

-- Nov 1754: Roger Randall and w. Rachel conv. 429 a. pt. (*), to William Williams, iron founder, and w. Mary (BB#I: 336).

10 March 1737: Richard Gist conv. 100 a. (*) to Robert Banneky and Benj. Banneky (HWS#M: 58).

STRAWBERRY HILLS (See DIVISION)

2 Nov 1702: Thomas Thurston conv. 200 a. (*) to John Mortimer of AA Co., Gent. (HW#2: 207).

3 March 1730: John Deaver conv. 50 a. pt. Turkey Hills and pt. (*) to Benjamin Jones. JD's w. Hannah cons. (IS#L: 138).

4 Aug 1730: Benjamin Jones conv. 100 a. (*) and Turkey Hills to John Browne (IS#L: 1).

4 Aug 1730: John Browne conv. 81 a. The Division, pt. (*) and Turkey Hills, back to Jones. JB's w. Mary cons. (IS#L: 3).

2 Nov 1731: John Deaver, Sr., carpenter, conv. 200 a. (*) to Thomas Deaver, blacksmith. JD's w. Hannah cons. (IS#L: 156).

27 Nov 1740: Dinah Jones, widow of Benjamin Jones, conv., pt. Turkey Hills and 50 a. Division (pt. (*)) which BJ bought from John Brown(?), to William Bradford; BJ conv. the land to WB and by his LWT directed his w. to make the conveyance (HWS#1-A: 481).

21 Oct 1749: William Bradford of BC conv. to his s. John George Bradford pt. of two tracts: (*) and Turkey Hills, conv. to WB by the execs. of Benjamin Jones (TR#C: 315).

STREETS ADVENTURE

23 June 1707: 100 a. surv. for Francis Street (MHM 16: 121n; pat. 1709; MPL DD#5: 532).

1718: Francis Street conv. (*) to Richard Gist. This is the land on which St. Thomas Church, Garrison Forest stands (MHM 15:213).

18 Aug 1722: Richard Gist of BA Co. and w. Zepporah conv. to Christopher Choate, Choate's Fancy, being pt. of Green Spring Traverse, and pt. of (*) (IS#G: 111).

STREIGHT

25 Aug 1767: John Gosnell and w. Sarah conv. 63 a. (*) to David Bradford (B#Q: 26).

STRIFE

1685: 185 a. surv. for Tobias Sternborow, betw. the branch of Back R. and Gunpowder R., beginning at a bounded white oak by the Herring Run (MHM 9: 74 and 21: 353).

1714: 268 a. resurv. for Thomas and Daniel Starnborough, sons of Tobias (Card Index, MSA).

SUCCESS (Pt. BEST SUCCESS)

Orig. taken up by Thomas Lightfoot (IR#AM: 8).

10 March 1705: Thomas Hammond and w. Rebecca conv. 250 a. to Matthew Hawkins (IR#AM: 8).

SUCCESS
(See MILLER'S PURCHASE and WITH'S ADVENTURE)

2 Sep 1729: Henry Peregoy and w. Amey conv. 50 a., residue of (*), now called Miller's Purchase, to John Miller, planter (IS#K: 174).

SUCCESS

4 July 1706: Surv. (TR#A: 117).

22 Nov 1706: William Norris, carpenter, conv. 114 a. (*) to Robert Thomas of AA Co., Gent. (TR#A: 117).

SUMMERS DEER PARK

13 June 1764: Richard Summer, of Northampton Co., NC, nephew of John Summer (to whom the tract was granted on 10 July 1730), and elder bro. of John Summer of BA Co., dec., conv. (*) to Richard Williams (B#N: 224).

SUMMERS GIFT

22 da., 2 mo., 1642 (probably 1742): John Summers conv. 1 a. (*) to the General Baptist Church (TB#A: 131).

SURE INHERITANCE

26 Feb 1747: Joseph Gostwick, s. and heir of Nicholas Gostwick, dec., conv. 52 a. (*), left him by his father, to Luke Trotten. Abrella Curtis, w. of Benjamin Curtis, and mother of JG, ackn. her right of dower (TB#E: 665).

SURPLUS

28 May 1707: Francis Watkins of BA Co., planter, conv. Hopewell, Bettor Hope, and (*), to James Crooke (RM#HS: 559).

SURVEYOR'S POINT

26 March 1666: 500 a. surv. for George Goldsmith; later held by John Hall for the orphans of the GG (MRR: 6; MHM 53: 246, 247n).

SUSANNAH AND MARY

4 March 1745: Nicholas Haile conv. 100 a., pt. (*), to his dau. Susanna Green (TB#E: 10).

SUTTON UNDERHILL

20 Oct 1662: Capt. Thomas Howell and w. Elizabeth conv. all but 50 a. of (*) to Nathaniel Stiles (RM#HS: 13).

SWALLOW FORK

3 May 1683(?): 100 a. surv. for Hendrick Inloes in Seneca Creek; later poss. by John Inloes, and still

later by John Leakins for Inloes' orphans (MRR: 66).

28 Aug 1682 [sic]: Hendrick Inloes of Middle River for 4000 lbs. of tobacco conv. 100 a. (*) to John Fuller (RM#HS: 19).

19 July 1687: John Fuller of Middle River conv. 100 a. (*) to Hendrick Enloes, Jr. JF's w. Easter cons. (RM#HS: 234).

13 May 1734(?) (1724?): Henry Enlows conv. 100 a. (*) to Bloys Wright. HE's w. Mary cons. The deed states that the cert. of surv. was dated 1673 (IS#G: 315).

20 June 1733: Bloys Wright conv. 150 a. (*) to his eld. s. Thomas (MCW#VII: 232).

1750: Heirs of Thomas Wright owned 100 a. (*) (1750 DB: 16).

SWALLOWS BILL

8 Dec 1688: Michael Hastings was granted a warrant for 400 a. which he assigned to Edward Boothby, who assigned it to Thomas Richardson who in turn assigned it to Daniel Scott (RM#HS: 385).

16 Dec 1688: 216 a. surv. for Daniel Scott (RM#HS: 385).

21 April 1701: John Chadwell made an affidavit that Daniel Scott has put up a locust post in place of a bounded tree of (*) as the tree had fallen down (HW#2: 65).

SWAN HARBOR (1668)

27 Feb 1668: 200 a. surv. for Oliver Spry on the s. side of Bush R. on the s. side of the Northwest Branch; later poss. by Charles Jones, and later poss. by Edward Smith for CJ' orphans (MRR: 38).

2 Oct 1668: Oliver Sprye, Gent., conv. 200 a. (*) to John Towers; tract on s. side of Bush R., adj. Phills Choice (IR#PP: 70).

2 Sep 1671 (A): John Towers conv. 200 a. (*) to Thomas Jones; adj. Fills Choice formerly laid out for John Colier (G#J: 44; TR#RA: 33).

SWAN HARBOR (1672)

19 May 1672: 80 a. surv. for Charles Gorsuch on the w. side of Back R. and later poss. by Charles Merryman for the orphan of John Boring (MRR: 94).

15 April 1678/9: Charles Gorsuch of TA Co. conv. 80 a. (*) to John Boring, ackn. by Miles Gibson (IR#PP: 31).

8 Feb 1678/9: Sarah Gorsuch gave p/a to Miles Gibson. John Boring; ackn. by Miles Gibson. (IR#PP: 31).

18 Feb 1725: John Boring and w. Pretiosa, and James Boring and w. Jane conv. 50 a. Boring's Pasture, 50 a. Boring's Range, and 80 a. (*), and 189 a. pt. Ferry Range to William Buckner (IS#H: 218).

30 Aug 1735: Thomas Buckner of VA conv. 80 a. (*) to John Boring of BA Co. (HWS#M: 294).

13 Jan 1737: John Boring of BA Co. and w. Sarah sold to Alexander Lawson 80 a. (HWS#1-A: 48).

SWAN HARBOR (1675)

5 Aug 1675: 300 a. surv. for Wm. Palmer on e. side of Swan Creek; land is liable to escheat (MRR: 13).

10 Feb 1708: John Palmer of Towcester in Co. North'ton, bro. and heir of William Palmer, late of MD, dec., gave p/a to John Davison of CE Co., surgeon, to recover 600 a. Palmer's Forest, 250 a. The Grove, 500 a. Palmer's Point, 300 a. (*), and 500 a. Towcester or Tolchester in CE Co., from John Hall of James Presbury (TR#A: 126).

1 Sep 1720: William Mathew of Martin, Co. Surrey, through his atty. Richard Bennett and Thomas Bordley, both of AA Co., conv. 500 a. (*), 250 a. The Grove, 600 a. Palmer's Forest, 500 a. Palmer's Point, and 100 a. Tunington to Josias Middlemore of BC, chirurgeon, TR#DS: 216).

SWAN POINT

5 June 1676: John Owen of Gunpowder R., conv. 100 a. (*) on the s. side of the western branch of Gunpowder, to Edward [sic] Phillips (G#J: 304).

SWANS DELIGHT

9 March 1738: Christopher Durbin Shaw conv. $48\frac{1}{2}$ a. (being $\frac{1}{2}$ of (*)) and 50 a. (being $\frac{1}{2}$ of Swans Fancy) to George Harryman. CDS's w. Susannah cons. (HWS#1-A: 206).

SWANS FANCY

9 March 1738: Christopher Durbin Shaw conv. $48\frac{1}{2}$ a. (being $\frac{1}{2}$ of Swans Delight) and 50 a. (being $\frac{1}{2}$ of Swans Fancy) to George Harryman. CDS's w. Susannah cons. (HWS#1-A: 206).

SWANSON

22 July 1672: Edward Swanson conv. 100 a. (*) to Richard Symes (G#J: 41; TR#RA: 321).

12 June 1701: Michael Judd and w. Mary conv. 100 a. (*), formerly laid out for Edward Swanson, to John Taylor, in exch. for 75 a. Samuel's Delight (HW#2: 111).

12 May 1705: John Taylor conv. 100 a. (*) to Gideon Skaats (IR#PP: 149).

2 Dec 1723: Vaughan Davies of NY City and w. Catherine (only dau. and heir of Gideon Skaats, dec.) conv. to John Dorsey 150 a., Sims Choice, 100 a. (*), and 15 a. Addition to Swanson (IS#G: 283).

3 Aug 1726: John Dorsey conv. Dorsey's Plains, cont. 775 a. by patent, 150 a. Sims Choice, and 100 a. (*) (the latter two were conv. by Vaughn Davies and w. Catherine, dau. of Gideon Skates, dec.) to Daniel Dulany (IS#H: 272).

SWANSON, ADDITION TO

12 May 1705: John Taylor conv. (*), located in the Fork of Gunpowder R., respecting the s. side of the Court House, to Gideon Skaats, chirurgeon (IR#PP: 147).

2 Dec 1723: Vaughan Davies of NY City and w. Catherine (only dau. and heir of Gideon Skaats, dec.) conv. to John Dorsey 150 a., Sims Choice, 100 a. Swanson, and 15 a. (*) (IS#G: 283).

SWIFT'S ADDITION

Oct 1697: 22 a. surv. for Mark Swift and later held by James Crook (MRR#II).

TALBOT'S CARE

7 March 1726/7: Edmund Talbot conv. 80 a. Talbot's Care and 100 a. Senegar (Seneca?) Ridge to Nathaniel Shepard. ET's w. Mary cons. (IS#H: 366).

6 Sep 1748: William Shepard of BA Co. conv. to Stephen Onion his right to two tracts of land: a) 100 a. Seneca Ridge (q.v.), and b) (*), surv. for Edmond Talbot, who sold it to Nathaniel Shepard, father of the grantor (TR#C: 65).

TALBOT'S FOREST

1756: 282 a. for Samuel Worthington.

See PW Plat W.

1783: 284 a. in Middle and Back River Upper Hundred held by Benjamin Powell (1783 TL).

TALBOT'S PLAINS

3 Jan 1716: John Talbott of AA Co., merchant, leases 50 a. (*) to John Spicer (TR#A: 483).

2 Jan 1718: John Talbott of AA Co., merchant, conv. 150 a., pt. of (*), to William Parrish of BA Co. (TR#DS: 25).

28 March 1729; Mary Talbott of AA Co., conv. release to William Parrish; mentions (*), surv. by Edward Talbott (IS#K: 6).

1 Jan 1730: William Parrish conv. 100 a. Gill's Fancy, Mary's Plains, and 150 a. pt. (*) (pt. of 628 a. taken up by Edmund Talbot who devised it to his s. John, whose w. Mary had it resurv. as Mary's Plains), to George Walker. WP's w. Susannah cons. (IS#L: 39).

TALBOTT'S RESOLUTION MANOR

28 May 1719: John Talbott of AA Co. conv. 300 a., being ½ of (*) to Nicholas Gassaway; the other ½ is owned by Henry Hale or Hall. JT's w. Sarah cons. (TR#DS: 57).

TALL HILL (See FALL HILL)

TANYARD (THE)

1702: 393 a. surv. for Nath. Stinchcomb.

See Horvath Plat: Elkridge.

4 June 1712: William Baker and w. Ann conv. 50 a. (*) to Maurice Baker, being ½ of the 100 a. conv. to William Baker by Nathaniel and Hannah Stinchcomb on 30 June 1704 (TR#A: 188).

30 Aug 1735: Edmond Howard conv. 40 a., pt. (*), to Emanuel Teal. The deed mentions the plantation of Edward Teal, dec. EH's w. Ruth cons. (HWS#M: 285). (The tract lies near Patapsco Falls and probably adjoins Robin's Camp, Liverpool, and Frederickstadt Enlarged: MHM 15:219n.)

25 April 1743: William Baker, Sr., conv. 50 a. (*) (except for the pt. sold to his bro. Maurice Baker), to Charles Ridgely (TB#C: 326).

TASKER'S CAMP

18 Aug 1733: Eleanor Smith of CV Co., widow, conv. pt. (*) to her dau. Rachel Smith; if Rachel dies without heirs, land to go to dau. Rebecca Smith (HWS#M: 17).

1783: 200 a. held by Aquila Hall in Gunpowder Upper Hundred; "Capt. Ridgely to pay" (1783 TL).

TAYLOR'S CHOICE

28 July 1667: A 300 a. tract surv. for John Taylor on the eastern branch of Gunpowder R.; later poss. by Stephen Johnson; still later 150 a. poss. by Moses Groom, and 150 a. by Col. Maxwell; interlined, and "now poss. Ann Phelks" (MRR: 35).

15 March 1669/70: John Taylor, Gent., and Arthur Taylor, planter, both of Gunpowder R., conv. John Scott, merchant, of Sarum 300 a. (*), reserving the right to remove trees from two specified nurseries thereon (IR#PP: 82).

23 March 1669/70: John Scott, merchant of Sarum, appointed John Waterton his atty. to obtain from John Taylor and s. Arthur 300 a. (*) (IS#IK: 33).

11 Feb 1704: Ann Felkes conv. 100 a. pt. (*) to her kinsman Moses Groom (IR#PP: 171).

9 March 1719: Moses Groom mortgaged 100 a. pt. (*) to James Maxwell; deed stated he was conv. land by Ann Felkes on 11 Feb 1704 (TR#DS: 189).

29 March 1725: James Maxwell, Sr., Gent., conv. 1 a. (*) to the Vestry of St. John's Parish (IS#H: 67).

2 April 1729: Asael Maxwell left (*) and adj. tract to his w. Hannah (MCW#VI: 120).

TAYLOR'S DELIGHT

See MHM 38:345.
4 Dec 1672: Robert Taylor conv. 100 a. (*) on e. side of Gunpowder R. to Joseph Peircey (G#J: 114; TR#RA: 80).
1 Aug 1673: 100 a. laid out for Robert Taylor.
23 July 1746: Francis Taylor conv. 50 a. (*) to John Risteau. FT's w. Elizabeth cons. (TB#E: 131).

TAYLOR'S DISCOVERY

18 Feb 1725: 505 a. surv. for Richard Taylor on the w. side of the main falls of Gunpowder, adj. Taylor's String.
2 March 1744: Thomas Taylor of BA Co. conv. to Nicholas Haile 50 a. Smallwood, and 80 a. (*) (TB#D: 63).
6 April 1745: Nicholas Haile conv. 100 a. Hooker's Farm (pt. of Gerar), 60 a. Addition to Hooker's Farm, 100 a. Hailes' Forest, 100 a. pt. of Haile's Fellowship, 80 a. pt. (*), 50 a. Smallwood, 200 a. Hailes Discovery, 200 a. Shadrack's Lot, and 200 a. Meshack's Garden, to Christopher Grindall of London, mariner (TB#E: 83).
19 July 1745: Thomas Taylor mortgaged 270 a. (*) to Henry Morgan (TB#D: 246).
28 March 1747: Nicholas Haile conv. 100 a. Hooker's Farm (pt. of Gerar), 60 a. Hooker's Addition, 100 a. Hailes' Forest, 200 a. Haile's Long Grove, 80 a. pt. (*), 50 a. Smallwood, to Christopher Grindall of London, mariner (TB#E: 347).
1750: George Atkinson conv. 80 a. (*) to Joshua Hall (TR#D: 67).

TAYLOR'S FARM

1730: 100 a. surv. for Thomas Taylor (MPL PL#8: 46).
1750: 100 a. owned by William Seabrooke (1750 DB).
20 Jan 1761: William Seabrook conv. 100 a. (*), formerly surv. for Thomas Taylor, to Peter Gosnell (B#I: 37).

TAYLOR'S FOREST

1679: 1800 a. for Thomas Taylor; surv. for Col. Thomas.
1752: Pat. by Charles Carroll, et al.
See PW Plat B; Horvath Plat: Elkridge.
1750: Heirs of John Galloway owned 1800 a. (*) (1750 DB).
c1754: Samuel Galloway owned (*) (IBC: 69).
18 Sep 1761: Caleb Dorsey conv. to John Owings 130 a. pt. (*). His w. Priscilla signed (B#I: 301).

TAYLOR'S GOOD HAP

6 March 1704: 400 a. surv. for John Taylor on the s. side of Deer Creek, adj. land of John Mills, and adj. Margaret's Mount and Bachelors Good Luck.
20 Sep 1742: John Hall, s. of Edward Hall who was a s. and heir of John Hall, dec., conv. Hall's Purchase (a resurv. of all of the land bought of the Kimballs), 50 a. Mascall's Humor, 400 a. (*), and 470 a. Timber Neck, to John Hall, one of the sons and devisees of John Hall (TB#C: 13).

TAYLOR'S HALL

21 March 1703: 1022 a. surv. for Joseph Taylor of AA Co. on the w. side of the main falls of Gunpowder R., adj. to Roberts Forest.
10 July 1704: Pat. to Joseph Taylor; on PW Plat H.
26 Sep 1725: Thomas Colmore, late of London, merchant, now of CV Co., conv. 2022 a. (*) to Thomas Cockey. Colmore had a p/a dated 3 April 1725 from Benjamin Taylor of Warwick, Co. Warwick, England, blacksmith, bro. and heir of Joseph Taylor, and another p/a from Joseph's remaining bro. William Taylor of Theobalds, Co. Hertford, England, yeoman (IS#H: 186, 189; IS#L: 141).

TAYLOR'S LOT

10 Sep 1716: 754 a. surv. for Richard Taylor on n. side of Deer Creek.

TAYLOR'S MISTAKE

30 Sep 1730: John Wheeler and w. Margaret conv. 200 a. (*) to Samuel Brice of CE Co. (IS#L: 31).
10 Nov 1732: Samuel Brice of BA Co., planter, mortgaged 200 a. (*) to William Cox of CE Co., Gent. (IS#L: 306).
6 Oct 1741: William Cox of Philadelphia, granted release of mortgage to Samuel Brice (TB#A: 74).

TAYLOR'S MOUNT

28 July 1661: A 200 a. tract surv. for John Taylor on the s. side of the eastern branch of Gunpowder R. 200 a. later held by Thomas Richardson; later 50 a. held by Thomas Marley; still later 250 a. held by William Adams (MRR: 58).
2 Aug 1670: Arthur Taylor conv. 125 a. (*) (bought by John Taylor from Benjamin Reid), and 100 a. Fall Hill (taken up by said AT) to Richard Winley (IR#PP: 83).
2 Aug 1670: Richard Winley and w. Mary conv. to John Owen land at Gunpowder R., pt. of (*), lying opposite to John Taylor's plantation adjoining the land of John Dixon. Witnesses: Robert Gates, Matthias Stevenson, and John Waterton (IR#PP: 83).

17 Nov 1670: Mary Winley, w. of Richard, appointed John Water on her atty. to ackn. her cons. to sale of (*) to Samuel Tracey and Hugh Williams. Witnesses: John Collier and John Taylor.

16 Dec 1670: Richard Winley and w. Mary for 6000 lbs. tobacco conv. to Samuel Tracey and Hugh Williams, tailor, of Peanketank, VA, 250 a. (*) at the head of Gunpowder R. Testators: John Taylor, John Waterton (IR#PP: 98).

17 Dec 1670: Samuel Tracey, Gent., and High Williams, taylor, of Peanketank, Gloucester Co., VA, appointed John Waterton of Gunpowder R. their atty. to take ackn. of sale of land to them by Richard and Mary Winley (IR#PP: 98).

13 Jan 1670/1: John Owen, planter, of Gunpowder R., for 1700 lbs. tobacco, conv. to William Chapman, planter, land on the w. side of and at the head of Gunpowder R., being the eastern pt. of (*), formerly bought of Richard Winley (IR#PP: 99).

20 Sep 1671: William Chapman, planter, of Gunpowder R., for 1900 lbs. tobacco conv. to John Owins the eastern pt. of (*), adjoining the pt. now held by John Marley and to the land sold to Samuel Tracey and Hugh Williams, WC having bought this land from Owens.

25 May 1672: William Chapman appointed John Waterton his atty. to ackn. the sale to John Owins of a pt. of (*), now in possession of Thomas Morley (IR#PP: 120).

5 March 1671/2: John Owen, planter, conv. to Thomas Marley or Morley, joiner, the tract (*), at Island Point in Gunpowder R., adj. the land of John Dixon, dec. (G#J: 60; TR#RA: 44).

1 Aug 1672: Samuel Tracy, Gent., of Gunpowder R., for 1500 lbs. tobacco, conv. to Richard Winley planter of Gunpowder R., 50 a., pt. (*) (G#J: 39; TR#RA: 29).

2 June 1673: Samuel Tracey, Gent., of Gunpowder R., for 6000 lbs. tobacco, conv. to James Wells and Thomas Richardson, 150 a., pt. (*), adj. the lands of Thomas Marley and Richard Winley (G#J: 158; TR#RA: 115).

6 Nov 1688: John Winley of BA Co. conv. 50 a., pt. (*), to Thomas Richardson (RM#HS: 291, 292).

28 May 1701: Thomas Richardson and w. Susanna conv. 250 a. (*) to John Richardson (HW#2: 61).

22 April 1708: John Richardson of BA Co., Gent., conv. 250 a. (*) to William Adams, of BA Co., planter (RM#HS: 657).

7 July 1702: John Richardson conv. pts. of Dixons Chance, Long Point, and (*) to William Adams of CV Co. (HW#2: 144).

16 Sep 1724: William Trew of KE Co. and w. Martha conv. pt. (*) to Thomas Hatchman (IS#G: 383).

26 Oct 1726: John Taylor conv. 250 a. (*) to Edward Day (IS#H: 312).

1 April 1729: Henry Adams of BA Co., carpenter, s. of William Adams of BA Co., dec., conv. 310 a., pts. of (*), Long Point, and Dixons Chance to Thomas Tolley (IS#I: 296).

29 March 1742: Robert Emms, of Great Yarmouth, Co. Norfolk, England, clerk, s. and heir of Thomas Emms of Great Yarmouth, conv. 125 a., $\frac{1}{2}$ of (*) and 300 a. Dixons Chance, to Edward Day, per p/a to John Galloway of AA Co., merchant (TB#C: 9).

30 Nov 1743: Henry Adams conv. quitclaim to 200 a. Dixon's Chance and 250 a. (*) to Edward Day who is already in possession (TB#C: 381).

1750: Patrick Lynch owned 50 a. pt. (*) (1750 DB: 25).

(See also MHM 15:111, and 53:40, 41n, 46n, and 355n.)

TAYLOR'S PALACE

1 April 1712: Thomas Taylor conv. 100 a. (*) to Walter Bosley; tract now called Bozley's Palace (TR#A: 182).

1 April 1712: Thomas Taylor conv. 100 a. (*), now called Welches Hopeful Palace, to William Welch. The tract was surv. in March 1705 (TR#A: 183).

1750: William Welsh owned 100 a. (*) (1750 DB).

15 April 1752: William Welsh of BA Co. conv. to Thomas Findley 100 a. (*) (called Taylor's Pollard), which Thomas Taylor sold to WW in 1712. WW's w. Averilla cons. (TR#D: 357).

TAYLOR'S PURCHASE

6 June 1727: 1600 a. pat. to John Taylor of London, merchant.

8 Oct 1746: Margaret Higginson of London, conv. (*) to Charles Ridgely (TB#E: 471).

TAYLOR'S RANGE

26 May 1714: 860 a. surv. for Richard Taylor, including 464 a. Roberts Choice, (pt. of *) 1150 a. Ill Will; patent called for Herring Run and Western Run.

Aug 1739: Richard Taylor of Goochland Co., VA, dep. that about 5 years earlier Ill Will and Roberts Choice were resurv. into (*) (HWS#1-A: 279).

TAYLOR'S STRING

8 July 1726: 300 a. surv. for Richard Taylor on s. side of the main falls of Gunpowder, on e. side of Western Run.

13 Oct 1741: Thomas Taylor conv. 300 a. (*) to Richard Snowden (HWS#1-A: 570).

12 Aug 1745: Thomas Taylor mortgaged 300 a. (*) to Edward Stevenson (TB#D: 286).

19 May 1747: Thomas Taylor and his s. John Taylor conv. 300 a. (*) to Edward Stevenson (TB#E: 445).
17 Aug 1747: Edward Stevenson conv. pt. (*) to Joshua Hall. ES's w. Susanna cons. (TB#E: 509).

TAYLOR'S STRING, ADDITION TO
13 Sep 1726: 125 a. pat. to Richard Taylor.
6 Feb 1749: Thomas Taylor and his s. John conv. 125 a. (*) to Joshua Hall (TR#C: 374).

TEAGUE'S PARK
29 March 1745/6: James Tracey of Craven Co., NC, gives p/a to John Ensor to sell (*) and James Meadow to John Cole, Jr. (TB#E: 248).

TEAGUE'S PLEASANT RIDGE
7 April 1759: Benjamin Tracey conv. pt. (*) to Alexis Lemmon (B#G: 389).
11 Nov 1760: Benjamin Tracey assigns to Andrew Smith his lease, called (*), from the Lord Proprietary (B#H: 430).
22 Oct 1761: Benjamin Tracey conv. 67 a,. pt. (*), to Abraham Ensor (B#M: 210).
1783: Abm. Ensor owns 67 a.; Jno. Lemmon owned 333½ a., and Andrew Smith owned 100 a. (*), all in Middle and Back River Upper Hundreds (1783 TL).

TEAGUE'S REVENGE
13 Sep 1762: Charles Bond assigned 113 a. (*) to Jos. Sutton (B#K: 464).

TEMPLE'S CLAIM (Pt. WATERFORD)
4 March 1704: John Wattes of Patapsco R. conv. 50 a. (*) to Miles Temple (IR#PP: 131).

TEN POUND PURCHASE
13 June 1734: Granted to Abraham Cord (TB#E: 48).
2 Nov 1743: Abraham Cord leases pt. Cord's Purchase, pt. French Plantation, 19 a. (*), and pt. French Plantation to Abraham Taylor (TB#C: 365).
10 July 1746: Abraham Cord conv. (*) to Thomas White (TR#C: 541).
18 June 1750: Thomas White, late of BA Co., now of Philadelphia, conv. (*) to John Hall (TR#C: 541).

TEVIS' ADVENTURE
25 Sep 1740: Robert Tevis of AA Co., and w. Margaret conv. 100 a. (*) to Nathan Hammond (HWS#1-A: 448).

TEVIS CHANCE
1754: Surv. for Robert Tevis, Sr.
See Horvath Plats: Wards Chapel; Baltimore/ Carroll Co.
22 Oct 1762: Robert Tevis conv. 111 a. pt. (*) to Nathaniel Tevis. RT's w. Margaret cons. (B#K: 387).

THACKER'S CHANCE
10 April 1727: Richard Thacker of BA Co. conv. 100 a. Gardner's Mill, 367 a. Long Discovery, and 320 a. (*) to Thomas Cockey (IS#H: 358).

THOMAS' ADDITION
10 Aug 1684: 18 a. (*) granted to Thomas Durbin (IS#L: 364).
25 April 1708: Christopher Durbin conv. 18 a. (*) to John Brice. CD's w. Mary is mentioned in the deed but did not give her cons. privately (RM#HS: 604).
19 Feb 1732: John Brice of AA Co., Gent., with the cons. of Madame Sarah Brice, conv. 18 a. (*) to Philip Jones, Jr., and other tracts (IS#L: 364).

THOMAS AND JOHN COCKEY'S MEADOWS
1783: 500 a. held by Thomas Cockey Deye in Middle and Back River Upper Hundreds (1783 TL).

THOMAS AND MARY'S REPOSE
7 Nov 1745: Amos Garrett, s. and heir of Bennett Garrett, dec., conv. 268 a. (*) and Roberts Choice, which Bennett Garrett bought from Thomas Burchfield, to William Daugherty (to whom BG had given a bond to) (TB#D: 396).

THOMAS' ADVENTURE
2 Sep 1688: 165 a. surv. for John Thomas; later held by the said Thomas (MRR: 86).
3 Dec 1725: Thomas Matthews and w. Sarah conv. 165 a. (*), pat. 19 July 1688 to Col. John Thomas, and now called Partridge's Chance, to Buckler Partridge of Bristol, merchant (IS#H: 208).
1783: Jno. Partridge owned 83 a. (*) in Patapsco Lower Hundred 1783 TL).

THOMAS' BEGINNING
15 Sep 1741: Benjamin Wheeler conv. 370 a. (*) and 30 a. the Green Spring to his s. Thomas, but Thomas is not to have possession until after the grantor's death. Elizabeth Wheeler signed (HWS#1-A: 546).
14 March 1743: Thomas Shey and w. Ann conv., 50 a. (*) and 65 a. Addition to Thomas' Beginning to John Diggs, Jr., of BA Co. (TB#C: 465).

THOMAS' BEGINNING, ADDITION TO

14 March 1743: Thomas Shey and w. Ann conv. 65 a. Thomas' Beginning and assigned 50 a. (*) to John Diggs, Jr., of BA Co. (TB#C: 465).

THOMAS' CHANCE

1745: 500 a. for John Thomas.

See PW Plat N.

THOMAS' CHOICE (c1739)

1729: Stephen Gill conv. 120 a., pt. (*), to John Price (IS#K: 69).

28 July 1739: Stephen Gill conv. 100 a. (*), land bequeathed to him by his father Stephen Gill, to John Price of Garrison (HWS#1-A: 252).

THOMAS CHOICE (1746)

1746: Laid out for Thomas Levins

See MHM 25:333 for notes on location; on PW Plat W.

THOMAS' DELIGHT

23 Feb 1767: Thomas Vaughan of BA Co. conv. 25 a. (*) to Mordecai Ford (B#P: 550).

THOMAS' FROLICK

1783: 40 a. in Mine Run Hundred owned by William Pearce (1783 TL).

THOMAS' LOT

5 June 1734: John Wheeler of BA Co. conv. 71 a. (*) to Abraham Burkholder of Conestoga, Lancaster Co., PA, JW's w. Margaret cons. (HWS#M: 58).

6 Aug 1746: Thomas Cole of BA Co. conv. to his s. Thomas, pt. of Christopher's Lot and (*) (TB#E: 120).

THOMAS PARK

1732: 200 a. pat. by Thomas Boring (Card Index to Patents).

11 July 1746: Thomas Boring conv. (*) to Charles Ridgely. TB's w. Elizabeth cons. (TB#E: 164).

THOMAS RANGE

5 Sep 1683: 150 a. surv. for John Thomas (MRR: 75).

29 May 1688: John Thomas conv. 100 a. (*) to John Bennett of AA Co. Jane Thomas signed (RM#HS: 254).

13 May 1699: William Herbert and w. conv. (*) and Ball's Addition and Bennett's Range to Nicholas Fitzsimmons (HW#2: 21).

THOMPSON'S CHOICE

12 March 1679: James Thompson had surv. 1000 a. (*), on the ridge of Gunpowder R.; later 800 a. poss. by Geo. Parker, and 200 a. held by Arthur Thompson, bro. of James (MRR: 35).

4 Jan 1693: James Thompson of BA Co., Gent., conv. to Gabriel Parrott of AA Co., Gent., 200 a. pt. (*). JT's w. Anne cons. (RM#HS: 364-365).

On 25 Aug 1702 Arthur Thompson of Clement's Bay, SM Co., sold to Joseph Wilson of CV Co. 1000 a. in BA Co. called (*), formerly the estate and inheritance of James Thompson of CV Co., dec., bro. of Arthur, except 200 a. which James Thompson sold to Gabriel Parrott of AA Co. Ackn. 25 Aug 1702 in PG Co. Court. No w. came. (G: cites PCLR TL#2: 703).

17 Dec 1722: Gabriel Parker [sic] of CV Co. sells to Edward Reynolds 200 a. of (*), pt. of 1000 a. pat. to James Thompson, who sold 200 a. to Gabriel Parrott. GP's w. Anne cons. (IS#G: 181).

16 April 1742: Richard Snowden of AA Co. conv. 600 a., pt. of (*) (orig. granted to James Thompson of SM Co., Gent., to Thomas Gittings of BA Co. (TB#A 137).

11 June 1747: John Baldwin of CE Co., Gent., and w. Mary conv. 200 a. (*) to Stephen Onion (TB#E: 502).

5 Dec 1749: Thomas Reynolds of CV Co. conv. 200 a. of (*) to Thomas Gittings (TR#C: 359).

THOM(P)SON'S FORTUNE

19 Nov 1715: Edward Williams of Paspotank R. in Sawyer's Creek, NC, conv. 100 a. where Matthew Green's widow and Robert Smith, shoemaker, dwell, 200 a. Lodowick's Ridge, 150 a. Matt's Addition, 100 a. (*), 300 a. United Friendship, and 150 a. Williams' Fortune, and all other lands in MD belonging to EW by right of inheritance, to Richard Colegate of BA Co., merchant (TR#A: 373).

July 1731: William Buckner and w. Patience conv. 150 a. Motts Addition, 100 a. (*) and 150 a. William's Fortune to Robert Robertson (IS#L: 149).

29 June 1732: Robert Robertson and w. Sarah conv. 36 a. (*) and 150 a. Williams Fortune, to Jonathan Hughes (IS#L: 311).

THOMPSON'S NEGLECT

2 June 1696: Thomas Preston and w. Mary conv., 100 a. (*) to John Mark (RM#HS: 522).

5 July 1720: Dorothy Groves, w. of William, made her LWT, leaving above tract to her loving uncle John Rollings (TR#DS: 290).

7 July 1720: William Groves and w. Dorothy, conv. their right to (*) to John Rawlings (TR#DS: 245).

19 Dec 1720: John Rawlings, for "love and affection," conv. (*) back to William Groves (TR#DS: 289).

31 Dec 1722: William Groves and w. Sarah conv. 126 a. (*) to Richard Thrift (IS#G: 125).

THOROLD'S NEST

7 March 1733/4: Samuel Chew gives to Richard Jones of BA Co., a receipt for 190 a. Denton, 80 a. Walker's Neck, 100 a. Hooper's Island, 330 a. North Point, 546 a. Old Road, 120 a. Industry, 1000 a. Shawan Hunting Ground, 50 a. (*), 100 a. Luke's Privilege, and 100 a. Bagford (HWS#M: 193).

THREE BROTHERS

2 Aug 1746: Tract was laid out for William and Reuben Boring (grandsons of John Boring) and for John Boring (B#O: 656).

9 Aug 1751: John Keasey, Sr., mortgaged (*) to William Dallam (TR#D: 174).

THREE SISTERS (1680)

1680: 1000 a. for John Welsh; on PW Plat D.

17 March 1708: John Giles and w. Sarah, and Daniel Richardson and w. Elizabeth conv. to James Heath their interest in 1000 a. (*), which had been granted by Lord Baltimore to John Welsh who d. leaving four daus., the afsd. Sarah and Elizabeth (above), and Mary w. of Josias Toogood and Damaris w. of Thomas Stockett (TR#A: 5).

19 Sep 1709: Thomas Stockett of AA Co., and w. Damaris conv. their share of (*) to James Heath (TR#A: 326).

13 Sep 1709: Josias Toogood and w. Mary conv. their share of (*) to James Heath (TR#A: 33).

1754: Greenbury Dorsey, with cons. of w. Sarah conv. Three Sisters to William Oldham. No w. signed (BB#I: 513: Dorsey).

1756: Greenbury Dorsey conv. pt. (*) to John Hammond Dorsey. No w. signed (BB#I: 611: Dorsey).

THREE SISTERS (1717)

3 May 1717: 1000 a. surv. for Benjamin Wheeler (IS#L: betw. 14 and 18); 9 Sep 1718: 1000 a. pat. to Benjamin Wheeler (MPL FF#7: 268 and PL#4: 361).

1 Sep 1730: Benjamin Wheeler mortgaged pt. Pearson's Range and pt. (*), to Josias Middlemore (IS#L: betw. 14 and 18).

15 Sep 1741: Benjamin Wheeler conv. 400 a., residue of (*) to s. Benjamin, 200 a. pt. (*) to dau. Mary Wheeler, and 200 a. pt. (*) to dau. Elizabeth, w. of David Thomas. Elizabeth Wheeler signed (HWS#1-A: 548, 553, 555).

15 Sep 1741: Benjamin Wheeler conv. 200 a. pt. (*) to Jane Butterworth, w. of Isaac. BW's w. Elizabeth cons. (TB#A: 21).

2 Nov 1743: Isaac Butterworth and w. Jane conv. 100 a. pt. (*) to David Thomas (TB#C: 410).

2 Nov 1743: Isaac Butterworth and w. Jane conv. 100 a. (*) to Benjamin Wheeler (TB#C: 412).

2 July 1750: William Few and w. Mary (lately named Mary Wheeler) mortgaged to Thomas White, late of BA Co., but now of Philadelphia, 200 a. (*), the same 200 a. given to Mary by her father Benjamin Wheeler (TR#C: 546).

THURRELL'S NECK

31 July 1661: 100 a. surv. for Richard Thorrell in Back River; later 50 a. held by James Todd and 50 a. were held by Joseph Wells for the orphans of John Wells (MRR).

25 June 1669: Richard Thurrell conv. 50 a. of (*), on the s. side of Back R. to James Todd (IR#PP: 74).

2 August 1698: John Leakins conv. 50 a. of the land (formerly held by Thurrell) to John Wells of BA Co. (TR#RA: 279).

20 Jan 1702: James Todd conv. his 50 a. to John Harryman (HW#2: 265).

24 July 1704: John Oldton conv. an orchard called Leakins, pt. of (*), 1 a., 16 p., to John Harryman. JO's w. Mary cons. (IR#PP: 159).

1730: Robert Burgan and w. conv. 50 a. (*) to Nathaniel Darby (IS#K: 326).

1 June 1732: Robert Burgan and w. Ann conv. 50 a. of the land to Nathaniel Darby (IS#K: 336; IS#K: 326 gives the year as 1730).

20 Sep 1733: Samuel Harryman and w. Comfort conv. 50 a. to Thomas Todd (HWS#M: 3).

TIBBALS

1 March 1669/70: Philip Holege (Holeger) and w. Mary conv. to William Peirce, 200 a. (*) on e. side of Toutson's Creek (IR#PP: 78).

TIBBS UNITED INHERITANCE

1722: William Tibbs pet. to have four tracts: 200 a. Oglesby's Chance (laid out for George Oglesby), 100 a. Emanuel's Hope (in 1684 laid out for Emanuel Celly), 100 a. Emanuel's Rest, and 77 a. Dann, resurv. and any vacant land added. He is now granted one entire tract called (*), beginning on the s. side of a branch of Middle R., cont. 640 a. (MPL CE#I: 430).

25 Sep 1732: William Tibbs, clerk, of BA Co., made a will (proved 13 Oct 1732) leaving his dwell. plant. to his sister Ann (MCW#VI: 233).

29 June 1741: William Jones sells to Thomas Sligh his claim to $\frac{1}{2}$ the estate of Samuel Maccubbin which formerly belonged to his w. Ann Jones (HWS#1-A: 513).

29 June 1741: William Jones and w. Ann conv. 640 a. (*) to William Sligh, s. of Thomas and Sophia,

the conveyance to take effect after the death of Ann Jones; if WS should die before age 21, land was to go to his parents (HWS#1-A: 530).

4 April 1746: William Jones conv. 640 a. (*) to Thomas Sligh (TB#E: 82).

TIMBER CHOICE

1745: 250 a. for James Richards; on PW Plat W.

TIMBER HALL

29 Dec 1720: Surv. for Alexander McComas who conv. it to William Hitchcock (IS#L: 410).

6 March 1727: William Hitchcock, Sr., conv. 50 a., ½ of (*), to his dau. Philizanna and her husband Nehemiah Hicks (IS#I: 57).

8 Aug 1733: William Hitchcock conv. (*) to his dau. Philizanna, w. of Nehemiah Hicks (IS#L: 410).

TIMBER NECK (1665)

21 March 1665: 300 a. surv. for Richard Ball on n. side of Patapsco; later 65 a. held by Davis Elder, and 135 a. by Anthony Demondidier (MRR: 78). The tract is located betw. Dundalk and the mouth of Bear Creek (MHM 15: 113).

29 Dec 1682: Thomas Taylor, Esq., of AA Co., conv. to Anthony Demondidier, Gent., for 95 years the tract (*) at George's Pond on n. side of Patapsco R.; adj. to Lewis Bryen's The Hope. Nathaniel Smith appointed atty. for Thomas Taylor (RM#HS: 24).

26 Oct 1686: Anthony Demondidier conv. 50 a. (*) to Thomas Morris for 89 years as laid out 1 Sep 1686 by Thomas Lightfoot; formerly poss. by Richard Ball, dec., and on 14 June 1678 poss. by Thomas Taylor, Esq. On 15 Feb 1686/7 AD appointed Charles Gorsuch his atty. to ackn. deed of 50 a.

10 Feb 1686/7: Anthony Demondidier gave to Thomas Jones 10 or 15 a. (*) being pt. of 300 a. Martha Demondidier a witness (MR#HS: 220).

18 June 1698: Ann Mountfield of BA Co., spinster, conv. to her husband John Mountfield 50 a. (*) purch. in 1696 (actually 1686) by Thomas Morris, the former husband of Ann Mountfield, from Anthony Demondidier, and given to Ann Mountfield as per record (IS#IK: 251).

8 May 1721: William Everest, eld. s. of Hannah Everest conv. 300 a. (*) to John Gardner. WE's w. Grace cons. (TR#DS: 324).

14 Oct 1743: Luke Trotten and William Hamilton, execs. of John Gardner, conv. 300 a. (*), 60 a. Gardner's Addition, 80 a. Gunworth, and 200 a. pt. Honderton (?) (more likely Kinderton) to Sabritt Sollers (TB#C: 327).

TIMBER NECK (1670)

28 Oct 1670: 200 a. surv. for John Howard; later poss. by his heirs (MRR: 75).

TIMBER NECK (1694)

12 Oct 1694: 146 a. surv. for William Budd at Elk Ridge near the Middle Run, near Patapsco R.; later poss. by William Davis (MRR: 101).

29 Sep 1737: Joshua Earp, s. of John Earp and his w. Mary (dau. and coheir of William Budd), conv. (*) (PCLR PL#8: 558).

TIMBER NECK (1704)

10 Oct 1704: 471 a. pat. by John Hall (MPL WD: 389, DD#5: 141).

20 Sep 1742: John Hall, s. of Edward Hall who was a s. and heir of John Hall, dec., conv. Hall's Purchase (a resurv. of all of the land bought of the Kimballs), 50 a. Mascall's Humor, 400 a. Taylor's Good Hap, and 470 a. (*), to John Hall, one of the sons and devisees of John Hall (TB#C: 13).

TIMBER NECK (1729)

13 March 1729: 100 a. surv. for Charles Wells; 100 a. pat. 29 July 1732 (MPL PL#8: 580; AM#1: 150; WHC: App. 1: 1).

TIMBER NECK

22 Feb 1717: William Bladen conv. 463 a. (*) to Henry Hilliard of AA Co. (TR#RA: 470).

11 Oct 1719: Henry Hilliard of BA Co. conv. 463 a. (*) to Daniel Hilliard. HH's w. Elizabeth cons. (TR#DS: 42).

TIMBER NECK

14 Sep 1726: Orlando Griffith of AA Co. conv. 200 a., being ½ of (*) to Charles Ridgely. OG's w. Katherine cons. (IS#H: 294).

2 May 1752: Orlando Griffith of AA Co. conv. to Charles Ridgely ½ of (*), which was the inheritance of Katherine, w. of OG. OG's w. Katherine cons. (TR#D: 328).

TIMBER PROOF

22 Dec 1672: 200 a. surv. for George Wells in Delph Creek; later held by orphans of Col. Wells, and later by George Wells (MRR: 7).

13 Feb 1726/7: John Smithers of KE Co., Gent., eld. s. of Blanch Smithers, (dau. of Col. George Wells and sister and coheir of George Wells, Jr.) conv. his interest in the following tracts to John Stokes: 800 a. Goldsmith's Hall, 24 a. Matthews Neglect, 400 a. Planter's Delight, 200 a. (*), and 81 a. Watson's Addition (some of which were resurv. into 1150 a. Coheir's Lot) (IS#H: 385).

TIMBER RIDGE

1737: Surv. for Hall and White.

See Horvath Plat: Ruxton and Riderwood.

28 Feb 1746: John Board conv. (*) to William Barney. JB's w. Jemima cons. (TB#E: 305).

27 Aug 1756: Richard Rutter conv. 100 a. (*) to Absolom Barney and Absolom Butler (BB#I: 581).

TIMBER SWAMP (1738)

3 Oct 1738: Pat. to Aquila Paca (MPL EI#2: 763, EI#5: 351).

9 March 1748: John Paca, Jr., conv. 300 a. (*) to Richard Garrison (TR#C: 180).

TIMBER SWAMP (1743)

2 Dec 1743: 31 a. pat. to John Taylor (MPL EI#6: 616, LG#E: 140).

20 June 1752: Charles Taylor conv. to Joshua Hardesty; also 32 a. (*) granted to John Taylor. CT's w. Elizabeth cons. (#D: 366).

TIMBERED LEVEL

1746: Surv. for Samuel Owings.

See MHM 16:209n; Horvath Plat: Owings Mills.

TIPPERARA

1752: 325 a. for Col. William Young; on PW Plat M.

TIPTON'S ADVENTURE

5 Aug 1734: Jonathan Tipton conv. 70 a. (*), adj. Hooker's Ridge, to Richard Hooker (HWS#M: 102).

9 March 1748: Richard Hookers conv. 100 a. Hooker's Ridge and 70 a. (*) to William Wheeler. RH's w. Martha cons. (TR#C: 163).

TIPTON'S LOT

Orig. laid out for Edward Tipton.

3 April 1762: James McCamis of Cumberland Co., PA, conv. pt. (*) to Benjamin Bowen (B#K: 105).

TIPTON'S PUZZLE

5 Aug 1730: Jonathan Tipton conv. 200 a. (*) to William Hunt of London, merchant (IS#L: 10).

5 Aug 1734: Jonathan Tipton conv. 95 a. pt. (*) to Reese Bowen (HWS#M: 118).

30 May 1740: Jonathan Tipton conv. 50 a. pt. (*) and Addition to Tipton's Puzzle to his grandson William Tipton (HWS#1-A: 383).

7 May 1745: Jonathan Tipton conv. 140 a. residue of (*) to Thomas Sheredine (TB#D: 127).

TIPTON'S PUZZLE, ADDITION TO

30 May 1740: Jonathan Tipton conv. 50 a. pt. Tipton's Puzzle and (*) to his grandson William Tipton (HWS#1-A: 383).

TODD'S FOREST

1728: 500 a. for Capt. Lance Todd.

See PW Plat W; Horvath Plat: Reisterstown.

9 April 1745: John Todd of AA Co. conv. 250 a. pt. (*) to John Frasher. JT's w. Ruth cons. (TB#D: 97).

23 July 1748: Lancelot Todd of AA Co. conv. his interest in 250 a. (*) to Thomas Hughes. LT's w. Ruth cons. (TR#C: 20).

1750: Lancelot Todd owned 50 a. of (*) (1750 DB).

7 March 1756: John Frazier made a will mentioning (*) (BAWB 2: 94).

16 Aug 1759: John Murray conv. 250 a. (*) to Joseph Cromwell (B#G: 506).

TODD'S GIFT (Pt. TODD'S RANGE)

6 Aug 1698: James Todd of BA Co., Gent., conv. 27 a. of (*), pt. of a larger tract, to his friend John Wells. No w. signed (TR: 288).

TODD'S PLAINS (Also THE PLAINS)

2 July 1688: 187 a. were surv. for James Todd on the s. side of the main run of Back R., and later poss. by Henry King (MRR: 79).

3 June 1696: James Todd and w. Elizabeth sold 187 a. (*) to Henry King (IS#IK: 8).

18 Jan 1717: Henry King made a will leaving (*) to his s. William (MCW#IV: 161).

Aug 1726: William King conv. 187 a. (*) to Thomas Sheredine (IS#H: 279).

TODD'S RANGE

24 June 1669: Surv. for Thomas Todd on n. side of Patapsco; later held by the orphans of (said) Fowler (MRR#II, MSA: 370).

9 Oct 1695: Thomas Todd of Ware Parish, Gloucester Co., VA, conv. 250 a., pt. of (*), to Stephen Johnson, of AA Co., carpenter (RM#HS: 479).

12 June 1699: James Todd, and w. Penelope, conv. 50 a. of John's Interest (pt. of (*)), to John Harryman (TR: 397).

7 July 1702: John and Eleanor Harryman sold John's Interest, pt. of (*), to Michael Young (HW#2: 155).

4 Aug 1703: James Todd of BA Co. conv. 400 a. (*) to Richard Fowler (HW#2: 280).

3 Aug 1725: Richard and Mary Merchant conv. (*) to Samuel Harryman (MRR#II: 370).

23 July 1746: Samuel Harryman conv. (*) to John Shaw (MRR#II: 370).

28 July 1746: Samuel Harryman conv. 50 a. (*) to John Shaw. SH's w. Comfort cons. (TB#E: 274).
1750: The widow of Luke Darby owned pt. of (*); William Shaw owned 50 a. (*) (1750 DB).

TOM'S CHOICE

27 Nov 1712: Thomas Randall, with cons. of w. Hannah, conv. 221 a. (*) to John Gill, carpenter (TR#A: 275).

TOM'S RESERVE
(Pt. HIS LORDSHIP'S RESERVE)

15 Feb 1744: Benjamin Tasker leased (*) to Thomas Steele (TB#E: 647).
12 Aug 1747: Thomas Steele conv. the residue of his lease of 25 a. (*) to Moses Morgan (TB#E: 647).

TOMBEYE

4 March 1666/7: Abraham Coffin conv 100 a. (*), on e. side of the Bay, to William Toulson (IR#PP: 65).

TOWCESTER

1 Aug 1672: Pat. to William Palmer (G#J: 272).
4 Aug 1674: William Palmer, Gent., conv. 500 a. (*) on e. side of Handly Creek, to John Tarkinton (G#J: 272).

TOWER HILL
(Probably more than one tract)

(date?): 100 a. surv. for Charles Simmons (TB#E: 652).
29 May 1711: Thomas Preston conv. 95 a. (*) to Sarah Skates of BA Co., widow (TR#A: 165).
3 Nov 1714: Daniel McTish (McTavish?) and w. Margaret conv. 100 a. to John Durbin (TR#A: 316).
3 March 1718: Charles Simmons and w. Hannah conv. 200 a. (*) to Thomas Miles (TR#RA: 530).
7 Aug 1723: John Burbin ackn. sale of 100 a. (*) to Thomas Cottrell (IS#G: 224).
8 Aug 1734: Thomas Miles and w. Catherine conv. 100 a. (*), surv. Oct 1718, to William Bond (HWS#M: 136).
6 Nov 1747: Wm. Bond conv. 100 a. (*) and 40 a., Miles Improvement to Thomas Bond, Jr. (TB#E: 652).
1783: Moses Sinclair owned 80 as. (*) in Middle River Lower Hundred (1783 TL).

TOWSONS CHANCE

3 June 1761: William Towson conv. 38 a. (*) to Isaac Risteau. WT's w. Dinah cons. (B#I: 132).

TRACEY'S LEVEL

1670: 200 a. surv. for Samuel Tracey; at the head of Gunpowder R., at the head of one of its branches called Back R., and the head of Lightwood's Creek (MHM 20: 275).
17 Dec 1691: Richard Taylor of AA Co. and w. Ann, conv. 200 a. (*) to Lawrence Richardson, bro.-in-law of Richard Taylor (RM#HS: 349).
3 March 1725/6: John Dorsey, atty. for Hezekiah and Elizabeth Clark of AA Co., conv. Littleworth, 100 a. Love Point, and 200 a. (*), to Thomas Tolley (IS#H: 225).
1732: Thomas Tolley, Gent., left (*) to his s. Walter (MCW#VI: 233).

TRACEY'S PARK

1705: 100 a. pat. by Thady Tracy.
See Horvath Plat: Ruxton and Riderwood.
4 Nov 1724: James Tracey conv. 100 a. (*) to George Hitchcock (IS#G: 397).
12 Feb 1736: George Hitchcock conv. 100 a. (*) (which he had bought from James Tracey on 4 Nov 1724) to dau. Persosha Tye and her husband John Tye, Jr. (IS#IK: 352).
1 Aug 1747: George Hitchcock and John Tye and w. Porsoche [sic] conv. 100 a. (*) to Thomas Foy (TB#E: 506).
19 Nov 1748: Thomas Foy conv. 100 a. (*) to George Haile (TR#C: 166).

TRANSILVANIA

11 Dec 1759: Richard Richards conv. 160 a. pt. (*) to Benjamin Bowen als. Cox (B#H: 58).
19 July 1765: Richard Richards and w. Sarah conv. 16¼ a. (*) to Andrew Stigar, along with 33¾ a. Rattlesnake Ridge (B#O: 338).

TRAPNALL'S INDUSTRY

25 March 1744: 69 a. surv. for William Trapnall (Unpat. cert. #1643).

TREDEVEN POINT

1 July 1671: Granted to Thomas Richardson who on 20 Jan 1673 sold it to James Chilcoat, who sold it to John Turner (HW#2: 16).
28 March 1695: John Turner of AA Co. conv. 150 a. (*) to Joshua Merriken, boatwright. JT's w. Margaret cons. (HW#2: 16).

TRIANGLE (1667)

30 Sep 1667: Pat. to John Hawkins.
30 May 1673: Robert Hawkins, heir and admin. of John Hawkins, dec., conv. to William Dunkerton and Thomas Overton, 150 a. (*) (G#J: 194; TR#RA: 144).

TRIANGLE

Dec 1671: Peter Sterling, chirurgeon, of Gloucester Co., VA, conv. 100 a. (*) and 350 a. Albrough to Luke Raven (G#J: 232).

11 June 1726: Luke Raven conv. 317 a. Luke's Garden, The Outlet and 100 a. (*) to his eld. s. Luke Raven (IS#H: 271).

TRIANGLE NECK

3 May 1673: 100 a. surv. for Hendrick Inloes on the Middle R. (MRR: 67).

1750: Anthony Enloes owned 100 a. (*) (called Triangle) (1750 DB).

1763/4: Anthony Enloes' heirs owned 100 a. (*) (called Triangle) (Aquila Hall's Assessment Ledger: 17).

1775: Abraham Enloes sells 100 a. (*) to Thomas Brown (abst. in TE Gen. Coll.).

1778: Abraham Enloes sells 100 a. (*) to William Godsgrace (abst. in TE Gen. Coll.).

TRIPLE (or TREBLE) UNION (1731)

Oct 1731: (*) granted to Thomas White (HWS#M: 261).

7 June 1732: Thomas White ackn. he has conv. (*) to Samuel Hughes; tract was orig. surv. for White, Hughes, and John Durbin; the last have assigned their rights to Thomas White (IS#L: 243).

7 June 1732: Thomas White assigns 100 a. (*) to John Durbin (IS#L: 245).

9 April 1733: Thomas White conv. 350 a. pt. (*) to William Hughes. TW's w. Sophia cons. (IS#L: 383).

1 June 1733: Samuel Hughes conv. 150 a. pt. (*) bought from Thomas White to Nicholas Banam (Baucom) of BA Co., planter. SH's w. Mary cons. (IS#L: 438).

30 July 1733: Thomas White and w. Sophia conv. 350 a. (*) to William Hughes (IS#IK: 487).

6 Aug 1735: Samuel Hughes makes a deed to correct the earlier deed of 150 a. pt. (*) to Nicholas Bacmob (Bascomb?) (HWS#M: 246).

6 Aug 1735: Nicholas Baucom mortgages 100 a. pt. (*) to Josias Middlemore; includes pt. of where NB now lives, which was granted to Thomas White on 30 Oct 1731, and pt. 150 a. (*) sold to NB by Samuel Hughes. NB's w. Mary cons. (HWS#M: 261).

30 Nov 1739: Nicholas Balkham conv. 150 a. (*) to Jacob Giles (HWS#1-A: 308).

29 Aug 1741: Jacob Giles conv. 100 a., pt. (*), adj. the 150 a. (*), sold by Samuel Hughes to Nicholas Balkham, to Josias Middlemore. JG's w. Johanna cons. (TB#A: 60).

11 June 1745: Jacob Giles of BA Co. conv. 50 a. (*), bought from Nicholas Baucum, to Thomas Copley (TB#D: 273).

31 July 1746: John Durbin of BA Co., s. of John Durbin, dec., mortgages 25 a. (*) to Thomas White. Deed also mentioned 100 a. Betty's Lot, granted 21 Feb 1722 to John Durbin, Sr. (TB#E: 141).

26 Jan 1748: Abigail Copley, widow of Thomas Copley, conv. 50 a. (*) to William Waller. Deed states that the land had been sold by Nicholas Baucom to Jacob Giles, and sold by him to Thomas Copley (TR#C: 212).

7 Aug 1750: John Durbin and w. Mary conv. Betty's Lot and (*) to William Husband of CE Co. (TR#D: 19).

c1754: Daniel Durbin owned pt. of Durbin's Chance and pt. of (*) (IBC: 57).

TRIPLE UNION (1734)

10 June 1734: 325 a. pat. by Richard Gist (MPL EI#3: 325, EI#4: 160.

6 March 1739: Richard Gist conv. to Luke Trotten 137 a. pt. of (*), made up of Resurv. on Martinson, Walton, Addition to Walton's Rest and Arden's Marsh (tracts had belonged to John Arden who sold them to Gist who resurv. them) (HWS#1-A: 355).

6 March 1739: Richard Gist conv. 88 a. pt. (*) to Philip Jones (HWS#1-A: 358).

18 March 1739: Richard Gist conv. 100 a. pt. (*) to Jacob Rowles. No w. cons. (HWS#1-A: 369).

TRIUMPH

Taken up by John Collet, Sr., and George Gouldsmith, dec. (G#J: 34; TR#RA: 26).

8 Nov 1672: John Collett, Gent., conv. 500 a., at Elk R., being ½ of (*), to Robert Hawkins (G#J: 34; TR#RA: 26).

30 May 1673: Robert Hawkins, heir and admin. of John Hawkins, dec., conv. to William Dunkerton and Thomas Overton, 500 a. pt. (*), lately poss. by John Collett, Jr., dec. (G#J: 200; TR#RA: 149).

TRONOLWYN

28 March 1671: Rowland Williams conv. 100 a. (*) to James Ives (Deed an Letter of Atty., IR#PP: 110).

TRUMAN'S ACQUAINTANCE

1729: Thomas F. Greenfield released to Micajah Greenfield 500 a. (*) (IS#K: 100).

TUCKER'S DELIGHT, ADDITION TO

4 Dec 1725: William Tucker conv. 100 a. Tucker's Delight and 150 a. (*) to Thomas Cockey. WT's w. Welthy cons. (IS#H: 216).

TUCKER'S ADDITION

1668: 400 a. surv. for Walter Tucker (MRR: 10).
Later conv. to Peregrine Brown (Archer Notes).

TUCKER'S DELIGHT

4 Dec 1725: William Tucker, with cons. of w. Welthy, conv. 100 a. (*) and 150 a. Addition to Tucker's Delight to Thomas Cockey (IS#H: 216).

TUCKER'S FOUNTAIN

See Horvath Plat: Granite.
18 Feb 1734: George Yeates and w. Mary of AA Co., conv. 50 a. (*) to Thomas Floyd (HWS#M: 131).
18 Oct 1738: Thomas Floyd and w. Zipporah conv. 50 a. (*) and Brother's Expectation and Christian's Lot to William Hamilton (HWS#1-A: 137).

TUNNINGTON

1 Sep 1720: William Mathew of Martin, Co. Surrey, (England?), through his atty. Richard Bennett and Thomas Bordley, both of AA Co., conv. 250 a. The Grove, 600 a. Palmer's Forest, 500 a. Palmer's Point, and 100 a. (*) to Josias Middlemore of BA Co., chirurgeon (TR#DS: 216).

TURKEY COCK ALLEY

8 Nov 1738: Charles Harryman conv. 50 a. (*) to Thomas Wright (HWS#1-A: 130).
22 March 1745: Thomas Wright and w. Mary deed to Thomas Staines, of BA, 50 a. (*) (TB#E: 80).
7 April 1752: Thomas Stains of BA Co. conv. to Thomas Cockey Deye 50 a. pt. of (*). TS's w. Sarah cons. (TR#D: 355).

TURKEY COCK HALL

1708: 200 a. surv. for Richard Gist.
See Horvath Plat: Ruxton and Riderwood.
30 May 1713: Richard Gist conv. 80 a. (*) to Edward Reeston. RG's w. Zipporah cons. (TR#A: 238).
13 Jan 1717: Richard Gist conv. 120 a. Chance, pt. of (*), to Thomas Taylor. RG's w. Zipporah cons. (TR#RA: 444).
14 Jan 1717: Thomas and Elizabeth Taylor conv. 120 a. Chance, pt. (*), to Samuel Merryman (TR#RA: 430).
24 June 1738: Samuel Merryman conv. 120 Chance, pt. of (*) to Edward Riston (HWS#1-A: 91).
1783: Joseph Osborne held 34 a. in Pipe Creek Hundred (1783 TL).

TURKEY FOREST

2 Nov 1739: Charles Carroll of Annapolis conv. 300 a., the eastern half of (*) to Thomas Johnson (HWS#1-A: 296).
2 Nov 1739: Charles Carroll, conv. 300 a., the western half of (*) to William Crabtree (HWS#1-A: 298).
4 Nov 1747: William Crabtree, for love he bears his s. John, conv. him 150 a. pt. (*) (TB#E: 579).

TURKEY HILL (1672)

29 June 1672: 200 a. surv. for John James; located in Bush R. at James Creek; later poss. by Thomas Thurston; still later poss. by John Devor (MRR: 13).
4 Nov 1673: John James conv. to Thomas Thurston 200 a. (*) at the head of Bush R. (G#J: 214).
2 Nov 1702: Thomas Thurston conv. 200 a. (*) to John Mortimer of AA Co., Gent. (HW#2: 209).

TURKEY HILL (1695)

1 Jan 1695: 262 a. surv. for Samuel Sickelmore on e. side of the Little Falls of Gunpowder; later poss. by William Hitchcock (MRR: 69; TR#C: 194).
16 March 1702: Edward Reynolds of CV Co., conv. 262 a. (*) to William Hitchcock, in exch. for 100 a. Hitchcock's Fortune. ER's w. Mary cons. (HW#2: 201).
1 March 1708: William Hitchcock and w. Mary conv. 100 a. (*) to Archibald Rollo.
5 Dec 1744: Asael Hitchcock, Elizabeth w. of Samuel Talbee, and Ann w. of John Burton (Asael, Elizabeth, and Ann were ch. of William Hitchcock) conv. (*) to Stephen Onion (TB#C: 664).
8 March 1748: William Hitchcock conv. (*) and Richardsons Reserve to Stephen Onion (TR#C: 194).

TURKEY HILLS

3 March 1730: John Deaver conv. 50 a. pt. (*) and pt. Strawberry Hills to Benjamin Jones. JD's w. Hannah conv. (IS#L: 138).
4 Aug 1730: Benjamin Jones conv. 100 a. Strawberry Hills and (*) to John Browne (IS#L: 1).
4 Aug 1730: John Browne conv. 81 a. The Division, pt. Strawberry Hills and (*), back to Jones. JB's w. Mary cons. (IS#L: 3).
23 Nov 1731: John Deaver conv. pt. (*) and pt. Deaver's Addition to Richard Ruff, bricklayer. JD's w. Hannah cons. (IS#L: 176).

23 July 1748: Daniel Deaver conv. 1 a. pt. (*) to Thomas White (TR#C: 1).
2 Nov 1748: Dinah Jones, widow of Benjamin Jones, conv., pt. (*) and 50 a. Division (pt. Strawberry Hills) which BJ bought from John Brown(?), to William Bradford; BJ conv. the land to WB and by his LWT directed his w. to make the conveyance (HWS#1-A: 481).
29 June 1745: Richard Deaver and w. Mary conv. 170 a. pt. (*) and pt. Strawberry Hills to their s. Daniel Deaver (TB#D: 370).
3 Aug 1749: Thomas White conv. $\frac{1}{2}$ a. (*) to Richard Ruff (TR#C: 262).
21 Oct 1749: William Bradford of BA Co. conv. to his s. John George Bradford pt. of two tracts: Strawberry Hills and (*), conv. to WB by the execs. of Benjamin Jones (TR#C: 315).

TURKEY NECK

1673: 75 a. surv. for Thomas Long on the s. side of Middle R. (MRR).
17 Nov 1701: John Leakins conv. 75 a. (*) to James Crooke, merchant (HW#2: 115).
7 Aug 1724: James Crooke conv. 74 a. (*) to George Chancey, s. of George (IS#C: 362).

TURKEY RANGE (1707)

10 Nov 1707: 80 a. pat. by Joseph Ellidge of BA Co. (MPL DD#5: 429, PL#2: 261).

TURKEY RANGE

7 Nov 1717: William Noble and w. Elizabeth conv. 92 a. (*) and pt. Noble's Desire to John Walker of BA Co. (TR#A: 61).
2 March 1719/20: Simon Pearson of BA Co., weaver, conv. to Henry Wetherall (for 2200 lbs. tobacco and HW's interest in a conveyance, 5 Nov 1719 from John Walker to HW), for pt. of (*) and Noble's Desire, the tract Pearson's Outlet, 200 a. (RM#HS: 660).
7 April 1720: John Walker and w. Mary conv. 92 a. (*) and Noble's Desire to Simon Pearson of BA Co. (TR#DS: 173).
21 May 1722: Seems to be a repeat of the above deed, but this time Pearson's w. Sarah cons. (RM#HS: 683).
7 Aug 1730: Simon Pearson conv. all of (*), all of Noble's Desire, and all of Pearson's Enlargement, lying near the head of Bynum's Run, to William Buckner (IS#L: 13).
7 Feb 1732: Thomas Buckner of VA conv., back to Simon Pearson the three tracts that Pearson made over to Thomas' bro. William Buckner. George Elliott and w. Patience (widow of William Buckner), relinquish their right of dower (IS#L: 328).
22 Feb 1736: Simon Pearson of BA Co., by virtue of an Act of Assembly, assigned to Edward Hall, late Sheriff of BA Co., three parcels: pt. (*), Noble's Desire, and Pearsons' Privilege (IS#IK: 351).
19 June 1738: Edward Hall, Esq., formerly Sheriff of BA Co. conv. 148 a. pt. of (*), Noble's Desire, and Pearsons' Privilege, to Beviss Spain (HWS#1-A: 86).
17 Aug. 1754: William Noble of Augusta Co., VA, s. and heir of William Noble late of BA Co,. dec., conv. to William Dallam pt. (*) and pt. Noble's Desire (BB#I: 297).

TURLOUGH'S CHANCE

1 Feb 1724/5: Matthew Organ conv. 65 a. pt. (*) to Joshua George of Annapolis; Organ inher. 111 a. of a warrant by the LWT of his son-in-law James Maclone; tract was orig. surv. for Turlough Michaelown (IS#H: 5).

TURNER'S HALL

30 Aug 1740: Joseph and Sarah Thomas conv. (*) to William Mattingly (HWS#1-A: 458).

TUTTLE FIELDS

11 April 1681: 50 a. pat. to Michael Judd (MPL 25:14 and 31:511).
2 Aug 1681: Michael Judd and w. Jane conv. 50 a. of the above 200 a., on n. side of Elk Creek to John Bird (IR#AM: 137).
27 April 1683: John Bird and w. Elizabeth conv. 50 a. on n. side of Elk R., which he had from Michael and Jane Judd, to Benjamin Bennett (RM#HS: 44).
3 Nov 1692: John Bevan and w. Sarah conv. to William Galloway 50 a. which Benjamin Bennett bought from John Bird and w. Elizabeth, and then bequeathed to his w. Sarah, now w. of Bevan.
1 Aug 1693: William Galloway and w. Margaret conv. 50 a. which Galloway had from John and Sarah Bevan, to Thomas Preston (IR#AM: 92).
1 July 1717: Thomas Preston conv. 50 a. on Gunpowder R., where Benj. Bennett lived, to John Bond (TR#A: 425).

TWO NECKS

Taken up by Richard Wright; 21 July 1774: Pat. to Richard and John Collett, and assigned on 10 Jan 1664 by John Collett to John Hawkins (IS#IK: 3; G#J: 204; TR#RA: 154).
30 May 1673: Robert Hawkins, heir and admin. of John Hawkins, dec., conv. 600 a. (*) at Crooked Creek on n. side of Elk R., to William Dunkerton and Thomas Overton (G#J: 204; TR#RA: 154).

TYE'S DELIGHT

1717: 100 a. surv.

See Horvath Plat: Green Spring Valley.

6 Aug 1729: John Tye conv.(*), lying on the back of Garrison Ridge, near the Water Spit Branch, to John Cockey. JT's w. Eleanor cons. (IS#K: 61).

UNCLE'S GOOD WILL

1 Dec 1718: Charles Carroll devised 1000 a. (*) by his will to Margaret McNamara, Elinor Boyd, Joyce Bradford, and Mary McCoy; on 10 June 1730 the tract was divided into four pts. (HWS#M: 365).

10 Feb 1735: Margaret McNamara of Annapolis, widow of Thomas McNamara, conv. 250 a., being $\frac{1}{4}$ of (*) to Thomas Shea (HWS#M: 365).

19 Nov 1737: Thomas Shea and w. Elizabeth conv. 100 a., pt. (*) to Hester Butterworth (HWS#1-A: 37).

2 June 1730: William Maccoy and w. Mary conv. 250 a. (*) to Dr. Charles Carroll (TB#D: 136).

18 Oct 1743: Abraham Boyd and w. Hester conv. 100 a. (*) to Isaac Butterworth (TB#C: 408).

11 May 1748: Charles Carroll of Annapolis conv. the third allotment of (*), 250 a. in all, to Moses Ruth (TR#C: 39).

16 March 1749: Dr. Charles Carroll of Annapolis, chirurgeon, conv. 250 a. (*) to Isaac Butterworth (TB#D: 136).

8 Nov 1749: Moses Ruth of BA Co. conv. to John Hayes the southern half of the third allotment of (*), which Charles Carroll third to said Ruth. MR's w. Esther cons. (TR#C: 331).

9 May 1752: Benjamin Boyd of PG Co., (son of Ellinor Boyd, to whom Charles Carroll devised pt. (*)) conv. 250 a., (*) to Thomas Archer (TR#D: 339).

UNION

4 April 1743: Michael Gilbert of BA Co. conv. to Charles Gilbert (his bro.; both are sons of Garvis Gilbert, dec.) 60 a. pt. (*), which was lately surv. for MG. MG's w. Mary cons. (TB#C: 201-206).

1783: Joseph Peregoy owned 166 a. (*) in Middle River and Back River Upper Hundreds (1783 TL).

UNITED FRIENDSHIP (1671)

30 April 1671: 300 a. surv. for John Grange on the s. side of Patapsco R.; later poss. by the heirs of John Rigby (MRR: 104).

UNITED FRIENDSHIP (1676)

350 a. surv. 12 July 1676 for Edward Reeves and Lodwick Williams on n. side of Gunpowder R.; later Thomas Preston held 175 a. and William Burne held the other 175 a. Burn left the Province and Preston claims the whole (MRR: 61).

20 July 1677: The whole tract was pat. to Reeves and Williams, embracing 175 a. for Reeves under a 471 a. warrant of 26 May 1676 to George Yate, and 175 a. for Williams under a 200 a. warrant of 20 May 1676 (IR#PP: 38).

4 Aug 1679: Edward Reeves conv. 175 a. to William Burne at Middle Creek. ER' w. Anne cons. (IR#PP: 38).

4 March 1690: Richard Askew and w. Mary (widow and extx. of Edward Reeves) conv. $\frac{1}{2}$ of tract, 350 a. in all, to Thomas Preston; the deed states that the tract was taken up by Reeves and Williams, and Reeves was the longest survivor (IR#AM: 68).

12 Nov 1715: Edward Williams of Paspotank R. on Sawyer's Creek in NC, gives p/a to Nicholas Rogers of BA Co., innholder, to sell the land (TR#A: 447).

19 Nov 1715: Edward Williams of Paspotank R. in Sawyer's Creek, NC, conv. 100 a. where Matthew Green's widow and Robert Smith, shoemaker, dwell, 200 a. Lodowick's Ridge, 150 a. Matt's Addition, 100 a. Thomson's Fortune, 300 a. (*), and 150 a. Williams' Fortune, and all other lands in MD belonging to Williams by right of inheritance, to Richard Colegate of BA Co., merchant (TR#A: 373).

5 Dec 1717: Rogers, by virtue of p/a, gives possession of 350 a. to Richard Colegate, from Edward Williams, s. of Lodowick Williams of BA Co. (TR#A: 447).

2 Aug 1751: Edward Norwood mortgaged 350 a. (*) to Isaac Webster and Co. (TR#D: 267).

UNITED FRIENDSHIP (1684)

15 Oct 1684: 700 a. surv. for John Larkins on n. side of Patapsco R.; later held by the heirs of Col. Edward Dorsey and 350 a. by William Chew (RR: 76).

10 June 1728: Charles Dorsey conv. his share of (*) to Francis and Edward Dorsey, in exch. for their shares of Owings' Adventure (IS#I: 149; see also 139).

10 June 1728: Francis and Edward Dorsey conv. 350 a. (*) and 45 a. Addition to United Friendship to Hyde Hoxton. FD's w. Elizabeth cons. (IS#I: 156).

7 Dec 1749: Nathan Richardson, s. of William Richardson of AA Co., dec., conv. 350 a. (*) to Thomas Harrison. (Benjamin Chew of William sold it to Samuel Chew who sold it to William Richardson.) NR's w. Hannah cons. (TR#C: 250).

UNITED FRIENDSHIP (1722)

27 Sep 1722: 180 a. surv. for John Fuller, James Isham, John Elliott and Nehemiah Hicks (HWS#1-A: 543).

4 April 1723: John Fuller, James Isham, John Elliott and Nehemiah Hicks jointly own 180 a. (*); they agree that if any of the four die the share of the deceased will pass to the others, and they will share equally in the expenses of finding minerals (IS#G: 127).

8 Nov 1733: John Elliott conv. his fourth of (*) to James Isham; tract was orig. surv. for Elliott, Isham, John Fuller, and Nehemiah Hicks (HWS#M: 2).

3 May 1741: James Isham, Sr., conv. (his share) of (*) to George Elliott (HWS#1-A: 543).

30 June 1746: George Elliott conv. 180 a. (*) to Henry Morgan (TB#E: 259).

18 June 1752: James Isham conv. to Walter Tolley 180 a. (*) JI's w. Jane cons.(TR#D: 334).

UNITED FRIENDSHIP

6 May 1681: Thomas Lightfoot, carpenter of AA Co. conv. 300 a. (*) to Rowland Vance, planter.

6 Nov 1680: Lightfoot had appointed Miles Gibson his atty. to ackn. sale of tract on s. side of Patapsco R. (IR#AM: 130).

UNITED FRIENDSHIP, ADDITION TO

10 June 1728: Francis and Edward Dorsey conv. 350 a. United Friendship and 45 a. (*) to Hyde Hoxton. FD's w. Elizabeth cons. (IS#I: 156).

UNITED LOT

21 July 1738: George Buchanan and w. Eleanor conv. 50 a. (*) to Roger Matthews (HWS#1-A: 98).

UPPE ELLIES

18 March 1661/2: Oliver Sprye conv. (*) to John Collier (RM#HS: 4).

UPPER ELING

17 Aug 1659: 100 a. surv. for Thomas Sampson; located on e. side of Bush R.; land was escheated and granted by petition to James Phillips (MRR: 13).

UPPER SPRING NECK

4 Aug 1651 (?): 150 a. surv. for Walter Dickinson (See AL#O: 288).

9 Feb 1679/80: Walter Dickenson of TA Co. conv. to Charles Gorsuch: a) his share of 1100 a. laid out for Thomas Thomas and William Batten; b) 150 a. (*); and c) Dickenson. (IR#PP: 48, 58).

1 Aug 1682: Charles Gorsuch and w. Sarah conv. to William Pearle 150 a. (*) (IR#AM: 196).

21 June 1716: Mary Sweeting, widow, conv. land to Philip Washington; in the deed she mentions property due her by inheritance in MD (TR#A: 408).

14 May 1759: Sophia Roberson, of BA Co., lately widow of Thomas Demmitt, William Demmitt, eld. s. of Thomas and Sophia, and Richard Demmitt, bro. of aforesaid Thomas, conv. 150 a. (*) to Robert Wilkinson (B#G: 414).

UPTON COURT

2 Aug 1668: Granted to David Poole; on 10 Nov 1712 David and Josias Poole conv. to John Mackwilliam (TR#DS: 254).

18 June 1720: John Mackwilliam of Philadelphia, conv. 500 a. (*) and 050(?) a. Whetstone Point to John Giles of AA Co. JM's w. Rose cons. (Deed and Letter of Atty. from Mackwilliam to James Stoodard in TR#DS: 254).

1729: John Giles mortgaged (*) to William Buckner, et al. (IS#K: 87).

1729: John Giles mortgaged 50 a. pt. (*) and Whetstone Point to Daniel Dulany and others (IS#K: 200).

15 June 1731: John Giles, innholder, and w. Cassandra, conv. 400 a. pt. (*) to John England and Co., ironmaster; tract is adj. to land John Giles left by LWT to his s. Jacob (IS#L: 99).

1 March 1732: Jacob Giles conv. 200 a. pt. (*) to John Moale. JG's w. Hannah cons. (IS#L: 367).

URINSON

1 Nov 1670: Richard Leeke, tailor, conv. to Thomas Howell, Gent., 150 a. (*) on n. side of Sassafras R., taken up by Neale Urinson and sold by him to Leeke; also 600 a. The World's End, taken up by Francis Child. RL's w. Gwilthin cons. (IR#PP: 85).

10 June 1672: Thomas Howell, Gent., conv. to Nathaniel Garrett 150 a. (*) and 500 a. The World's End. TH's w. Elizabeth cons. (IR#PP: 127).

UTIES ADDITION

19 May 1687: 45 a. surv. for George Utie on the s. side of Rumley Creek; later held by Mark Richardson for the orphans of said Utie, and later held by John Hall (MRR: 4).

31 May 1703: John Hall, trustee of LWT of Mary Utie, has requested Roger Matthews and Thomas Cord of Spesutia Hundred, to view the property including (*), Uties Rumley and Carter's Rest, belonging to Susanna Utie, orphan of George and Mary Utie (HW#2: 235).

28 Feb 1716: Francis Holland and w. Susannah conv. to Anthony Drew 45 a. (*) and 300 a. Uties

Rumley, which had formerly belonged to Susanna's father, George Utie (TR#A: 437).

UTIE'S RUMNEY

15 July 1658: 300 a. surv. for ... Utie; later poss. by Mark Richardson for the orphans of said Utie; later in possession of John Hall (MRR: 4).

31 May 1703: Roger Matthews and Thomas Cord of Spesutia Hundred, at the request of John Hall, trustee of LWT of Mary Utie, have viewed the property belonging to Susanna Utie, orphan of George and Mary Utie; included pts. of (*), Utie's Addition, and Carter's Rest (HW#2: 235).

28 Feb 1716: Francis Holland and w. Susannah conv. to Anthony Drew 45 a. Utie's Addition and 300 a. (*), formerly in possession of Susannah Holland's father George Utie (TR#A: 437).

VALENTIA

1720: 200 a. for Thomas Towson; on PW Plat H.

VALIANT HAZARD

27 Aug 1756: Richard Rutter conv. 100 a. (*) to Absolom Barney and Absolom Butler. (BB#I: 581).

23 Aug 1757: Absolom Butler and Absolom Barney conv. 100 a. (*) to William Barney, Jr. (B#G: 32).

VALLE DUNNAWAY

27 Sep 1728; John Clarke conv. 450 a. (*) betw. Susquehanna R. and Deer Creek to John Bond (IS#I: 214).

VALLEY OF BROAD RUN

8 March 1746: Thomas Farlow assigned the residue of the lease for (*) to William Few (TB#E: 557).

VALLEY OF JEHOSOPHAT (1684)

1684: 2500 a. for Richard Smith; on PW Plat AT.

VALLEY OF JEHOSOPHAT
(See CORBIN'S DELIGHT)

2 Sep 1695: Cert. granted to Capt. Richard Smith; called for Peterson's Branch; includes the southern pt. of Dulaney Valley (MHM 47: 98).

19 Nov 1724: William Dawkins of CV Co., with cons. of w. Ann (dau. and devisee of Richard Smith of CV Co.), and James Dawkins, s. and heir apparent of said William and Ann conv. 1250 a., being $\frac{1}{2}$ of (*) and 500 a. Addition to Daniel Dulany of Annapolis (IS#H: 22).

VALLEY OF JEHOSOPHAT,
ENLARGEMENT OF (1684)

1684: 2000 a. for Richard Smith, Jr.; on PW Plat H.

VALLEY OF OWEN

See Horvath Plat: Elkridge.

7 Sep 1703: 361 a. surv. for Richard Owen (1723 Rent Roll).

27 Oct 1714: Richard Owens, with cons. of w. Rachel, conv. 361 a. (*) to Sarah Brice of AA Co., widow (TR#A: 322).

VARDRE
(Pt. 800 a. BOND'S GIFT)

5 Feb 1735: Edmond Talbot conv. 100 a. (*) to John Higginson. ET's w. Mary cons. (HWS#M: 373).

VARDRE'S ADDITION
(Pt. BOND'S GIFT)

5 Feb 1735: William Talbot conv. 100 a. (*) to John Higginson. WT's w. Mary cons. (HWS#M: 376).

VAUGHN'S DELIGHT

1 April 1760: Christopher Vaughn of MD conv. 50 a. (*) to Richard Richards (B#H: 168).

VERINA

20 July 1669: Thomas Cornwaleys, with cons. of w. Penelope, of Stanhow, Norfolk, England, conv. 1000 a. (*) to George Wilson "of VA in the County of Baltimore" (IR#PP: 78).

1 June 1674: George Willson conv. to William Southbee two adj. parcels on the s. side of Sassafras R.: 125 a. (*), and 50 a. The Slipe (G#J: 270).

VINCENTS CASTLES

13 July 1683: 500 a. surv. for Vincent Lowe; located on the w. side of Susquehanna, adj. Phillips Hope; later poss. by the execs. of said Lowe; still later poss. by the heirs of Col. Burgess (MRR: 15).

VINES CHANCE

Aug 1706: 200 a. surv. for William Vines (MRR).

VINES FANCY

20 March 1697: Pat. by William Vines.

9 Nov 1719; William Vines conv. 60 a. (*) to John Hatherly (TR#DS: 128).

VINEYARD (THE)

2 Sep 1704: 100 a. surv. for Jno. Campbell (1723 Rent Roll).

4 Nov 1707: John Campbell and w. Eleanor conv. 100 a. (*) to Thomas Burton (RM#HS: 563).

30 Aug 1714: Thomas Burton of PG Co. conv. 100 a. (*) to James Potee. On the same day he gave p/a to Daniel Scott, Jr., to ackn. the deed (TR#A: 288).

5 Nov 1734: James Poteet conv. to John Cawdrick 100 a. of S... ...Yard. JP's w. Elizabeth cons., and John Putteet was a witness (HWS#M: 132).
29 Aug 1741: John Cawdrick conv. 100 a. (*) to James Preston, planter. Isabella Cawdrick cons. (TB#A: 5).
1750: James Preston owned 150 a. pt. Dennis Choice, 100 a. Preston's Chance, 100 a. (*), 25 a. pt. Andrew's Addition (1750 DB).
17 Sep 1766: James Preston of BA Co. made a will leaving property to his various sons. His s. Barnard was to have (*) and other tracts (BAWB 3: 48).
1783: Spesutia Upper Hundred: Barnard Preston of James owned 100 a. The Vineyard (1783 TL).

VIOLIN

2 May 1750: John Denton of BA Co., and w. Rachel, in exch. for 100 a. called (*), conv. his moiety of Bachelor's Hope, Bachelor's Meadow, and Salt Peter Neck (TR#C: 510).

WALKER'S NECK

7 March 1733/4: Samuel Chew gives to Richard Jones of BA Co., a receipt for 190 a. Denton, 80 a. (*), 100 a. Hooper's Island, 330 a. North Point, 546 Old Road, 120 a. Industry, 1000 a. Shawan Hunting Ground, 50 a. Thorold's Nest, 100 a. Luke's Privilege, and 100 a. Bagford (HWS#M: 193).

WALKINS' NECK

28 Dec 1669: John Walkin of KE Co. conv. 80 a. (*) to Thomas Todd of BA Co. (IR#PP: 107).

WALLTOWN

4 Aug 1691: Charles Gorsuch, with cons. of w. Ann, conv. 58 a. Sparrow's Nest, 15 a. Hopewell, and 156 a. (*) to Joseph Heathcote of AA Co., planter (IR#AM: 107).

WALNUT HAZARD

2 June 1750: Mary Barney conv. 100 a. (*) to her s. William Barney, Jr. (TR#C: 458).

WALNUT NECK (1663)

18 Aug 1663: 100 a. surv. for Hugh Kinsey; later 45 a. held by Isaac Jackson and 55 a. held by John Wilmot (MRR: 82).
13 May 1701: Thomas Sparrow and w. Sophia conv. 100 a. to Thomas Rider (HW#2: 77).
1 Sep 1702: Thomas Rider sold 100 a. (*) to George Valentine; deed states that Lord Baltimore granted the tract to Hugh Kinsey on 6 Aug 1664, that by right of inheritance it passed to Thomas Sparrow who sold it to Rider (See IR#PP: 139).
25 Sep 1704: George Valentine of AA Co. conv. 100 a. (*) to John Gill (IR#PP: 139).
13 Jan 1725: Stephen Gill, s. and heir of John Gill of BC, dec., conv. 100 a. (*) orig. laid out for Hugh Kinsey to William Punteny of Annapolis, butcher. SG's w. Elizabeth cons. (Prov. Court Deeds PL#6: 129).

WALNUT NECK (?)

1664/5: Richard Gorsuch and w. Elizabeth conv. 300 a. (*) to Thomas Powell (IR#PP: 66).

WALSTON'S ADDITION

12 July 1678: 81 a. surv. for John Walston; later held by orphans Col. Wells, and later by George Wells (MRR: 7).
14 July 1679: 81 a. pat. to John Walston (See RM#HS: 238).
6 Sep 1687: John Walston, Gent., conv. 81 a. (*) to Col. George Wells (RM#HS: 238).

WALTER'S HOPE

3 Nov 1696: Lt. Col. Thomas Richardson and w. Mary conv. 100 a. (*) orig. surv. 29 Oct 1696 and Richardson's Outlet to Walter Morrow (IS#IK: 88).
5 Nov 1716: John Morrow and w. Susannah conv. 100 a. (*) to Thomas Tolley of KE Co. (TR#A: 467).

WALTER TOWN

5 Aug 1723: George Reade, atty. for Thomas Ridge and Thomas Reade of Newport, Isle of Wight, conv. 150 a. James Town, and 50 a. (*), to George Groome (IS#G: 160).

WALTON
(See TRIPLE UNION)

1662: 120 a. surv. for John Walton; located on s. side of Back R. (MHM#21: 341).
10 April 1669: John Walton conv. 120 a. (*) to Thomas Greene and John Arthorne (IR#PP: 80).
10 March 1684/5: William Gaine conv. 156 a. (*) (or Waltum) to Charles Gorsuch (RM#HS: 168).
4 Aug 1691: Charles Gorsuch and w. Ann of Patapsco R. conv. 156 [sic] a. (*) and other lands to Joseph Heathcote (IR#AM: 107).

WALTON'S REST, ADDITION TO
(See TRIPLE UNION)

WANDSWORTH

4 March 1666/7: William Orchard, planter, and w. Susanna conv. 200 a. (*) to Edward Ayres (IR#PP: 58).
15 April 1696: John Deveghe of BC conv. 100 a., pt. (*), to John Hurst (RM#HS: 456).

6 April 1713: Francis Dallahide of BC mortgages 100 a. pt. (*), Daniel's Nest, Hornisham and 200 a. Watertown to William Bladen of Annapolis; mortgage to last until 20 March 1713/4 (TR#A: 227).
23 Dec 1717: Abraham Taylor conv. 100 a. (*) to dau. Lettice and her husband William Doddridge (TR#RA: 435).
6 June 1723: Francis Dallahide, eld. s. and heir of FD, late of BC, dec., conv. 100 a. (*), 50 a. Hornisham and 50 a. Daniel's Neck to James Maxwell, Sr. (IS#G: 160).
6 July 1723: Abraham Taylor conv. 100 a. pt. (*) and other lands to Dr. George Buchanan (IS#G: 184).
5 April 1726: Abraham Taylor and w. Dinah conv. pt. of 200 a. (*) orig. surv. for William Orchard, to James Maxwell (IS#H: 230).

WANN'S CHANCE

3 March 1753: Edward Wann conv. 50 a. (*) to Benjamin Wells. EW's w. Prudence cons. (BB#I: 11).

WARD'S ADVENTURE

31 --- 1721: 50 a. surv. for ? (See HWS#1-A: 82).
15 Nov 1724: Joseph Ward conv. 50 a. (*) to Jacob Roberts or Robinson. JW's w. Bridget cons. (IS#C, 415).
7 March 1728/9: Jacob Robinson of BC, carpenter, and w. Mary conv. 50 a. (*) to John Ward, s. of Joseph and Bridget Ward (IS#I: 271).
9 June 1738: John Ward of BC conv. 50 a. (*) to Stephen Onion. JW's w. Sarah cons. (HWS#1-A: 82).

WARD'S PURCHASE

1 Sep 1742: Benjamin Tasker leased 201 a. (*) to John Ward for 99 years (See TB#E: 414).
17 April 1747: William Dallam, admin. of JW, dec., leased 10 a. pt. (*) to Alexander McComas (TB#E: 414).
17 April 1747: William Dallam, admin. of JW, leased 191 a. (*) to Daniel McComas (TB#E: 417).

WARLERICK

11 Feb 1754: Thomas Stain, with cons. of w. Sarah, conv. 40,a. (*) to John Wilmott (BB#I: 185).

WARRINGTON (1695)

26 April 1695: Surv. (RM#HS: 688).
8 Sep 1695 or 1696: William Hill conv. 50 a. pt. (*) to James Cowdrey (RM#HS: 688).
4 Feb 1726: John Hill, mariner, s. of John Hill, dec., and grandson of John Hill, dec., who orig. purch. the land, conv. 600 a. (*) to Rees Hinton of CE Co. (IS#H: 374).

WARRINGTON (1664)

9 Feb 1664: Surv. for 650 a.
10 Sep 1733: John Baldwin, Sheriff of CE Co. conv. (*) to William Rumsey of CE Co., Gent.; deed mentioned John Smith, formerly Sheriff of CE Co. and w. Jane (IS#L: 434).
25 Sep 1733: William Rumsey of CE Co., Gent., conv. ½ of (*), orig. surv. for 650 a., to John Baldwin of CE Co. (IS#L: 436).
22 Aug 1743: John Baldwin of CE Co., and Sabina Rumsey, widow and extx. of William Rumsey, conv. 1450 a. (*) to William Hill of BA Co. (TB#C: 355).
22 Aug 1743: John Baldwin and Sabina Rumsey conv. 128 a. pt. (*) to Thomas Dawney (TB#C: 322).
15 June 1745: Benjamin Lego, Sr., conv. 150 a. pt. (*) to his s. Benjamin Lego, Jr., but BL, Sr., is to have use of tract for life (TB#D: 237).

WASON'S FARM

4 Sep 1732: Thomas Wason, with cons. of w. Elizabeth, of AA Co. conv. 150 a. (*) to Thomas Cockey of AA Co. (IS#L: 291).

WATER OAK LEVEL

1741: Surv. for James Wells.
See Horvath Plat: Finksburg to Westminster.
27 July 1745: James Wells, Sr., with cons. of w. Anne, conv. 50 a. (*) to Ewen Mackdonald (TB#D: 276).

WATERFORD

May 1679: 200 a. surv. for John Arding (MRR: 89).
3 Nov 1684 [sic]: John Ardin conv. 150 a. (*) on the northwest side of Narrow Creek at Back R., to Mark Child (deed and bond in RM#HS: 158).
4 March 1704: John Wattes of Patapsco R. conv. 50 a. Temple's Claim,. pt. of (*), to Miles Temple (IR#PP: 131).
21 Dec 1709; James Jolly and w. Rachel conv. 50 a. pt. (*) to John Harryman, Sr. (TR#A: 87).

WATERS NECK

14 Oct 1717: Maurice Burchfield, Surveyor General of His Majesty's Customs in the Southern District of America, and Joseph Brown, late of London, merchant, s. and heir of Peregrine Brown, late of London, dec., conv. 100 a. (*) to James Phillips; the deed states that Peregrine Brown made a will naming w. Margaret as extx.; the following tracts in MD were owned by Peregrine Brown at the time of his death: Addition, 400 a.; Bachelor's Addition 50 a.; Bachelor's Hope 400 a.; Chilbury

250 a.; (*) 100 a.; the Maryland Court of Chancery decreed that these tracts should be held to satisfy the debts of Browne (TR#A: 485).

WATERTON (1667)
(Also WATERTOWN, WATERSTOWN)

3 Aug 1667: 200 a. surv. for John Waterton on e. side of Gunpowder R. near the mouth of Holman's Creek; Waterton bequeathed the land to Thomas Read and Thomas Ridge, both of the Isle of Wight, England (MRR: 36).
4 June 1697: Thomas Read of Newport and Thomas Ridge, grocer, both of Southampton conv. 100 a. (*) to Francis Dallahide (RM#HS: 534).
6 April 1713: Francis Dallahide mortgaged Daniel's Nest [sic], Hornesham, 100 a. pt. Wandsworth and 200 a. (*) to William Bladen of Annapolis; mortgage to run until 20 March 1713/4 (TR#A: 227).
24 Nov 1713: Francis Dallahide and w. Sarah conv. (*) to Simon Pearson (TR#A: 253).
24 Sep 1714: Simon Pearson conv. (*) to William Lenox, Jr. (TR#A: 377).

WATERTON (1679)

4 Nov 1679: 50 a. surv. for John Waterton on the w. side of Gunpowder R.; later poss. by Thomas Read and Thomas Ridge; later poss. by Geo. Grover (MRR: 36).

WATERTON'S ANGLE

1 April 1693: John Hall conv. 28 a. Hall's Ridge, pt. of a warrant for 640 a., to his dau.-in-law Isabella Hooper. If she d. without lawfully begotten heirs, land to go to her sister Ann Collier. If Ann dies without legitimate heirs, land will revert to John Hall; if Hall buys 31 a. (*), formerly belonging to John Waterton, (and gives it to Isabella) she is to giver her sister Ann an equal amount of above 218 a. (HW#2: 122).

WATERTON'S NEGLECT

1 March 1692: John Fuller and w. Hester conv. 6½ a. (*) to Thomas Heath (RM#HS: 342).
8 Nov 1695: Thomas Heath and w. Sarah conv. 6½ a. (*) to John Fuller (RM#HS: 493).
20 Oct 1701: John Peters and w. Hester, and John Fuller and his w. Sarah conv. 6¼ a. (*) to William Peckett (HW#2: 146).
2 April 1728: Heathcote Pickett conv. 6¼ a. (*) to his sister Elizabeth who m. Benjamin Jones; Heathcote inher. the land from his father William, who devised the land to his sons William and Heathcote (IS#J: 64).
3 March 1735: Benjamin Jones conv. 6¼ a. (*)and 50 a. Fox Hall to Thomas Franklin (HWS#M: 409).
14 May 1745: Thomas Franklin conv. 46 a. pt. Fox Hall, 32 a. Owners' Landing, and 6¼ a. (*), to John Hammond Dorsey (TB#D: 368).

WATSON'S ADDITION

13 Feb 1726/7: John Smithers of KE Co., Gent., eld. s. of Blanch Smithers, (dau. of Col. George Wells and sister and coheir of George Wells, Jr.) conv. his interest in the following tracts to John Stokes: 800 a. Goldsmith's Hall, 24 a. Matthews Neglect, 400 a. Planter's Delight, 200 a. Timber Proof, and 81 a. (*) (some of which were resurv. into 1150 a. Coheir's Lot) (IS#H: 385).

WATSON'S POINT

2 Aug 1704: Charles Gorsuch deposed concerning George Yate and 50 a. (*) (HW#2: 341).
5 Nov 1753: Thomas Watson, with cons. of w. Mary, conv. 125 a. (*) to Benjamin Wayger of AA Co. (BB#I: 95).
13 Dec 1764: Benjamin Harris, with cons. of w. Hannah, conv. pt. 125 a. (*) to Henry Crooks (B#N: 420).
4 Dec 1766: Henry Crooks, with cons. of w. Margaret, conv. 125 a., pt. (*) to John Baptist Snowden (B#P: 394).

WATSONS TRUST

1751: Surv. for Thomas Watson.
See Horvath Plats: Wards Chapel; Baltimore/ Carroll Co.
13 Dec 1764: Benjamin Harris and w. Elizabeth conv. pt. (*) to Henry Crooks (B#N: 470).

WEATHERALL'S ADDITION

3 March 1735: William Talbot leased pt. (*) and other lands he owned, to Joseph Elledge for 10 years (HWS#M: 391).

WEATHERALL'S LAST ADDITION

7 Sep 1721: Henry Weatherall conv. 400 a., being ½ of Ogg King of Bashan, Pearson's Outlet and (*), to John Roberts of BC (TR#DS: 304).
9 March 1726/7: John Roberts conv. 200 a. (*) pt. Ogg, King of Bashan, Pearson's Outlet, and (*) to Edmund Talbott. JR's w. Mary cons. (IS#H: 313).
2 April 1740: William Talbott and w. Mary conv. 100 a. pt. of Ogg, King of Bashan, Pearson's Outlet, and pt. (*), to John Chocke (HWS#1-A: 376).
4 Aug 1757: James Talbott conv. 50 a. pt. (*) and Pearsons Outlet to Samuel Day (B#G: 45).

3 April 1762: Samuel Day, with cons. of w. Sarah, conv. 50 a. Pearsons Outlet and 50 a. (*) to Robert Patterson (B#K: 49).

WEAVER'S PROVIDENCE

18 Jan 1752: Henry Lewis, eld. s. and heir of Humphrey Lewis, conv. to Daniel Dulany and Co. 40 a. Henry Lewis' w. Caturah cons.(*) (TR#D: 288).

WEBSTERS ENLARGEMENT

30 March 1703: John Webster and w. Hannah conv. 106 a. (*) to John Norrington (IR#AM: 5).

1 Aug 1714: John Norrington and w. Elizabeth conv. 106 a. (*) to Peter Overard (TR#A: 302).

4 June 1718: Peter Overard, saddler, with cons. of w. Mary, conv. 106 a. to Josias Middlemore of London, surgeon (TR#RA: 441).

WEDGE

29 Sep 1674: Pat. (TR#RA: 357).

8 Jan 1673/4: Giles Stevens of Back R., conv. 65 a. (*) on n. side of Back R., to Barnwell Smith (G#J: 236).

20 Feb 1698: Giles Stevens, with cons. of w. Rebecca, conv. 65 a. (*) to George Hopham; land desc. to the grantor as s. and heir of Giles Stevens, dec. (TR#RA: 357).

5 June 1724: William "Hoppin" conv. 65 a. (*) to Thomas Hines and John Harryman (IS#G: 327).

WEE BIT

25 Nov 1726: John Dorsey, Gent., conv. 50 a. (*) and 200 a. Wignall's Rest to James Durham (IS#H: 284).

7 March 1744: Greenbury Dorsey of PG Co. conv. 15 a. pt. (*) to John Hammond Dorsey (TB#D: 45).

1750: 25 a. (*) and 50 a. Isaac Wright's Range owned by the heirs of Isaac Wright (1750 DB: 53).

WEEDINGS CHOICE

1 March 1743: James Weeding, with cons. of w. Elizabeth, conv. 50 a. (*) to Charles Kelly (TB#C: 520).

WEEPIT

April 1704: 15 a. surv. for John Taylor (Rent Roll).

WELCH'S ADVENTURE

1703/04: Surv. for Pierce Welch.

See Horvath Plat: Green Spring Valley.

4 March 1719: James Boring and w. Jane, dau. and coheir of Daniel Welsh, late of BA, conv. 102 a. (*) to Otho Holland (TR#DS: 196).

WELCH'S FANCY

8 April 1731: John Jones grants quitclaim of 100 a. (*) to John Roberts; original deed was dated 13 Dec 1729 (IS#L: 227).

WELCHS FOLLY

1729: John Roberts conv. 100 a. (*) to John Jones (IS#K: 218).

WELCH'S HOPEFUL PALACE

1 April 1712: Thomas Taylor conv. 100 a. (*), now called (*), to William Welch. The tract was surv. in March 1705 (TR#A: 183).

25 April 1752: William Welsh of BC conv. to Thomas Finley 100 a. called (*), being pt. of a larger tract called Taylor's Pollard which Thomas Taylor sold in 1712 to William Welsh, father of afsd. William. WW's w. Avarilla cons. (TR#D: 357).

WELCOME

26 May 1686: Charles Gorsuch conv. 100 a. (*) to David Adams, who had appointed Thomas Scudamore his atty. to take possession in court (RM#HS: 177).

WELLS ANGLES

1698: Laid out for Joseph Wells; cert. calls for Bread and Cheese Branch (MHM 25: 349).

22 April 1702: Joseph Wells, with cons. of w. Katherine, conv. 100 a. pt. (*) to Robert Longland (HW#2: 142).

28 Oct 1703: Joseph Wells conv. 178 a. (*) to Richard Miller (HW#2: 330).

1 Aug 1728: George Insull, with cons. of w. Alice, conv. 100 a. pt. (*) to Joseph Fuller, sawyer (IS#I: 249).

28 July 1746: Thomas Sligh conv. 238 a. (*) to John Sargent except for 20 a. which lies in the tract Welcome and which was sold to Martha and Mary Bowen (TB#E: 113).

WELLS CHANCE

27 April 1739; Charles Wells conv. 50 a. (*) and 24 a. Bonds Increase to Benjamin Tasker, except for a $\frac{1}{2}$ a. reserved for a burying ground; 1/5 of the land for use of Tasker; 1/5 for Daniel Dulany; 1/5 to Charles Carroll of Annapolis; 1/5 for Charles Carroll surgeon; and 1/5 for Charles Carroll of Daniel (HWS#1-A: 244).

WELLS LOT (Pt. GARDESON, q.v.)

13 April 1695: John Thomas conv. 50 a. (*), being pt. of Gardeson, to James Wells, in consideration that Thomas be excused from teaching the said Wells to read and write (RM#HS: 460).

WELLS NECK

1658: Surv. for Richard Wells on Middle R. and Back R., betw. Sue's Creek, Brown's Creek and Booby's Bar; in 1664 it was resurv. as Holly Neck (MHM 25: 236 and 30: 326).

2 June 1726: Edward Evans, with cons. of w. Elizabeth, conv. 50 a. (*) (formerly in possession of John Leakins who sold it to John Wells) to Nathaniel Darby (IS#H: 242).

WELLS' PROSPECT

1750: 100 a. surv. for Alexander Wells.

See PW Plat W; Horvath Plats: Green Spring Valley; Owings Mills.

WELSH'S CRADLE

1740: 2000 a. surv./pat. for William Worthington; on PW Plat W.

WENTWORTH

5 Nov 1703: John Hurst, Gent., and w. Hannah, conv. 100 a., pt. of 200 a. (*), to Francis Dallahide, Gent. (HW#2: 299).

WEST HUMPHRIES
(See EAST HUMPHRIES)

13 Feb 1664/5: Richard Ball agreed to conv. 300 a. (*) on Humphreys Creek at Bear Creek, Patapsco, to Rowland Haddoway. Ball also agreed to furnish warranty from the heirs of Thomas Humphrey, dec. (IS#IK: 22).

14 Aug 1666: Rowland Hathaway conv. 300 a. (*) to Henry Goodericke of AA Co. (IR#PP: 55).

WESTER OGLE

1754: 720 a. surv. for Dr. William Lyon.

See PW Plat WH1; Horvath Plats: Owings Mills; Randallstown; Green Spring Valley.

WESTERN FROLIC

28 Dec 1708; Richard Smithers, with cons. of w. Blanch, conv. 100 a. (*), which was devised to Smithers by the LWT of James Ives, to John Hall (RM#HS: 629).

WESTMINSTER

See MHM 53: 44n-ff.

7 Nov 1705: Christopher and Mary Durbin conv. 38 a. to Samuel Greening; tract was orig. held by Christopher's father Thomas (IR#AM: 12).

5 April 1707: Samuel Greening of BA Co. conv. 38 a. (*) to Henry Dukes (RM#HS: 539).

1 Oct 1719: Abraham and Susannah Shavers conv. 38 a. (*) to Mary Lynch (TR#DS: 171).

3 Aug 1737: James Lenox and w. Mary conv. 38 a. (*) to Philip Jones, Jr. (IS#IK: 513).

4 Nov 1749: John Hall, with cons. of w. Hannah, relict and devisee of Asael Maxwell, dec., conv. 48 square perches (*) to Talbot Risteau (TR#C: 329).

WESTPHALIA

1755: 300 a. surv. for John Ensor, Jr.; pat. to Ruxton Gay; on PW Plat N.

WEST'S ADDITION

8 March 1720: John Hammond conv. 100 a. (*), pt. of Paradise, to Robert West (TR#DS: 297).

18 Feb 1722/3: Robert West, Sr., conv. 100 a. (*) (made up of pt. of Maiden's Mount and Paradise) to dau. Constant Barnes and the heirs of her body (IS#G: 94).

8 Nov 1733: Robert West, Sr., conv. pt. Maiden's Mount and pt. Paradice, now called (*) to his dau. Comfort Barnes; if she d. s.p., then after the dec. of her husband Job Barnes, lands to go to RW, Sr.'s s. Enoch West (HWS#M: 9).

WEST'S BEGINNING

7 Nov 1739: James Lee leased pt. (*) and 45 a. pt. Westwood to Gregory Farmer (HWS#1-A: 295).

6 Aug 1740: Robert West, Jr., with cons. of w. Johannah, conv. 50 a. (*) and 45 a. pt. Westwood to Josias Middlemore (HWS#1-A: 404).

24 May 1741: Joseph Middlemore, merchant, with cons. of w. Frances, conv. 50 a. (*) and 45 a. Westwood to James Lee (HWS#1-A: 504).

25 Sep 1751: James Lee and w. Elizabeth conv. 50 a. (*) to William Cox (TR#D: 308).

WESTS FAVOUR

20 April 1727: 50 a. surv.

28 Aug 1739: Richard Butts, carpenter, with cons. of w. Mary, conv. 50 a. (*) to John Prible (HWS#1-A: 269).

WESTWOOD (1686)
(See NEW WESTWOOD)

11 Nov 1686: 200 a. pat. to Thomas Scudamore (MPL 25: 287 and 30: 329).

25 July 1687: Thomas Scudamore, Gent., of Back R., conv. 200 a. (*) to Joseph Strawbridge. Same date: Scudamore gave bond to Joseph Strawbridge (RM#HS: 236).

20 March 1696/7: Joseph Strawbridge conv. 100 a. Addition to Westwood and 200 a. (*) to Isaac Milner. JS' w. Sarah is mentioned in deed but did not sign (HW#2: 25).

1 Oct 1701: Edward Stevenson, Gent., factor for Peter Pagan of Co., London merchants, conv. 200 a. (*) and 100 a. Addition to Westwood to George Hope (HW#2: 106).

9 Dec 1724: William Houchings and w. Judith, execs., of LWT of George Hope, Sr., conv. 200 a. (*) and 100 a. Addition to Westwood to Samuel Maxwell (IS#H: 89).
5 June 1733: Samuel Maxfield [sic] (Maxwell?) conv. 200 a. (*) and 100 a. Addition to Westwood to Luke Stansbury (IS#L: 374).

WESTWOOD (1710)

1 Nov 1710: 500 a. pat. to Robert West (MPL DD#5: 677, PL#3: 253). (Obviously West was selling the land before he pat. it.)
2 Nov 1708: Robert West conv. 200 a. (*) to John Edwards; this is pt. of a larger tract laid out for RW, whose w. Sarah also signed (RM#HS: 619).
7 March 1709: Robert West conv. 60 a. (*) to Gregory Farmer (TR#A: 48).
3 March 1713/4: Robert West and w. Sarah conv. 100 a. (*) to Mark Whitaker (TR#A: 266).
4 March 1728/9: Robert West, Sr. conv. (*) to s. Robert West, Jr., if s. dies without heirs, land to go to nearest in blood. Priscilla West signed (IS#I: 264).
25 Feb 1739: Thomas Whiteacre of PG Co. conv. 100 a. pt. (*), which was formerly conv. by Robert West to Mark Whitaker, father of the grantor, back to Robert West (HWS#1-A: 382).
7 Nov 1739: James Lee leased pt. Wests Beginning and 45 a. pt. (*) to Gregory Farmer (HWS#1-A: 295).
7 June 1740: Robert West, with cons. of w. Sarah, conv. 385 a. (*) (pat. 18 Dec 1739 to RW as New Westwood) to Josias Middlemore (HWS#1-A: 387).
6 Aug 1740: Robert West, Jr., with cons. of w. Johannah, conv. 50 a. Wests Beginning and 45 a. pt. (*) to Josias Middlemore (HWS#1-A: 404).
24 May 1741: Joseph Middlemore, merchant, with cons. of w. Frances, conv. 50 a. Wests Beginning and 45 a. (*) to James Lee (HWS#1-A: 504).
22 Nov 1750: Josias Middlemore, practitioner in Physick, with cons. of w. Frances, conv., New Westwood and (*) to Ephraim Andrew (TR#D: 239).
25 Sep 1751: James Lee, with cons. of w. Elizabeth, conv. to William Cox 50 a. West's Beginning 45 a., West Wood (TR#D: 309).

WESTWOOD, ADDITION TO

30 Nov 1694: 100 a. surv. for Joseph Strawbridge; later poss. by Edward Stevenson; still later poss. by George Hope (MRR: 107).
20 March 1696/7: Joseph Strawbridge conv. 100 a. Addition to Westwood and 200 a. (*) to Isaac Milner. JS' w. Sarah is mentioned in deed but did not sign (HW#2: 25).
1 Oct 1701: Edward Stevenson, Gent., factor for Peter Pagan and Co., London merchants, conv. 200 a. (*) and 100 a. (*) to George Hope (HW#2: 106).
9 Dec 1724: William Houchings and w. Judith, execs., of LWT of George Hope, Sr., conv. 200 a. (*) and 100 a. (*) to Samuel Maxwell (IS#H: 89).
5 June 1733: Samuel Maxfield [sic] (Maxwell?) conv. 200 a. (*) and 100 a. (*) to Luke Stansbury (IS#L: 374).
1750: Tobias Stansbury owned 100 a. (1750 DB).

WEXFORD

3 Jan 1720: Pat. to William Hunter.
4 March 1724: William Hunter, with cons. of w. Mary, conv. 100 a. (*) to William Bond (IS#H: 62).
3 Nov 1730: William Bond conv. 100 a. (*) to dau. Sarah, w. of Robert Love (IS#L: 58).

WHEELER AND CLARK'S CONTRIVANCE

24 Feb 1714: Surv. for 1000 a.
5 Nov 1716: Benjamin Wheeler of PG Co., with cons. of w. Elizabeth, conv. 615 a. (*) to Robert Clark late of PG Co. but now of BA Co. (TR#A: 443).
15 Sep 1741: Benjamin Wheeler conv. 350 a. pt. Pearson's Range and (*) to s. Ignatius Wheeler. The deed mentioned BW's daus. Eliza, Mary, and Ann. The same day he conv. 315 a. of Pearson's Range to his s. Leonard (HWS#1-A: 549, 551).
4 Nov 1747: Robert Clark, with cons. of w. Eleanor, conv. 615 a. pt. (*) to Ignatius Wheeler (TB#E: 701).

WHEELER'S BEGINNING

19 Aug 1752: John Wheeler and John Cross deed to Abraham Raven 50 a. (*), surv. 7 Oct 1716; also 50 a. Cross' Chance, surv. 6 Feb 1743; Wheeler's w. Elizabeth and Cross' w. Dinah cons. (TR#D: 408).

WHEELER'S POINT

20 Sep 1671: John Wheeler made a will bequeathing 250 a. (*) to his sons Samuel and John (IS#IK: 40).

WHEELER'S UNION

31 July 1746: Thomas Wheeler, with cons. of w. Sarah, exch. Clark's Park with Robert Clark, for 100 a. (*) (TB#E: 106).

WHEELER'S WELL

1724: 100 a. for William Wheeler; on PW Plat H.
March 1728/9: William Wheeler, with cons. of w. Constant, conv. 100 a. (*) to Joseph Headsworth of Annapolis, butcher (IS#I: 276).

28 May 1745: Catherine Headsworth, widow of John [sic], late of Annapolis, butcher, conv. 100 a. (*) to James Moore (TB#D: 116).

WHETSTONE POINT

25 June 1685: Charles Gorsuch, planter, and w. Sarah conv., to Thomas Lightfoot 50 a. (*) and 50 a. Mill Haven. (Could this have been actually 1683 and transcribed inaccurately as 1685?) (RM#HS: 143).

6 Aug 1700: Thomas Hammond conv. 50 a. (*) to Charles Gorsuch (HW#2: 17).

2 March 1708/9: Charles Gorsuch, Sr., conv. (*) to his s. John Gorsuch (RM#HS: 636).

WHETSTONE POINT (1702)

May 1702: Pat. to James Carroll (IS#H: 195).

18 June 1720: John Mackwilliam of Philadelphia, with cons. of w. Rose, conv. 500 a. Upton Court and (50?) a. (*) to John Giles of AA Co. (Deed and Letter of Atty. from Mackwilliam to James Stoddard in TR#DS: 254).

25 Oct 1725: James Carroll of AA Co., Gent., conv. (*) to John Giles (IS#H: 195).

1729: John Giles mortgaged (*) to William Hamilton, Hyde Hoxton, et al. (IS#K: 87).

1729: John Giles conv. 100 a. (*) to John England (IS#K: 130).

1729: John Giles mortgaged 50 a. including (*) and Upton Court to Daniel Dulany (IS#K: 200).

28 Feb 1732: John Giles and w. Cassandra conv. (*) to Jacob Giles (IS#L: 363).

WHIPS PURCHASE

1746: 125 a. for Samuel Whipp; on PW Plat J.

1 Aug 1745: Samuel Whips, with cons. of w. Mary, for brotherly love, conv. 125 a. (*) to his bro. Benjamin Whips (TB#D: 255).

WHITACRE'S (WHITAKER) CHANCE

14 May 1713: John Whiticar and w. Mary conv. 150 a. (*) (adj. to Talbot's Resolution, with only the rights to Phelps Luck excepted) to Charles Hammond of AA Co. (TR#A: 226).

WHITACRE'S ENLARGEMENT

27 Feb 1746: William McComas, s. of John, with cons. of w. Hannah, conv. 32 a. pt. (*) which his father bought from Abraham Whitacre, to Col. John Hall, Jacob Giles, and Isaac Webster, the assignees of Col. Thomas White (TB#E: 310).

WHITACRE'S PURCHASE

25 June 1701: John Whitacre, cooper, with cons. of w. (unnamed), conv. 79 a. to James Barley of AA Co. (HW#2: 63).

WHITACRE'S RIDGE

10 Nov 1696: 150 a. pat. by Robert Love (MPL 38:40).

7 Dec 1697: Robert Love and w. Sarah conv. 150 a. (*) to John Whitaker of BA Co. (IS#IK: 182).

6 June 1702: 250 a. pat. by John Whitaker (MPL DS#F: 421, DD#5: 58).

4 Aug 1715: John Whitaker of BA Co., and w. Ann conv. 125 a. pt. (*) to Samuel Hughes (tract was surv. 11 Aug 1701 for 250 a.) (TR#A: 346).

28 Nov 1716: John Whitaker and w. Ann conv. 100 a., being ⅔ of (*), to Robert Pearson of Murplein Twp., Chester Co., PA; the residue of the tract belonged to Mary Whitaker, relict of John Whitaker, for the rest of her life (TR#A: 535).

3 June 1718: Charles Whitaker conv. 125 a. pt. (*) to Solomon Armstrong; tract was surv. on 11 Aug 1701 for John Whitaker, father of CW; JW bequeathed ½ the tract by will to said CW. CW's w. Mary cons. (TR#RA: 475).

1 June 1719: Samuel Hughes conv. 125 a. pt. (*) to John Gallion. SH's w. Jane cons. Deed stated that tract was granted to John Whitaker for 250 a. on 11 Aug 1701; said John by his LWT left ½ the tract to his s. John, who conv. ½ to said Hughes on 4 Aug 1715 (TR#DS: 28).

20 Aug 1720: Robert Pearson of Chester Co., PA, conv. 150 a. (*) to Aquila Paca (TR#DS: 224).

29 Oct 1725: Solomon Armstrong, with cons. of w. Mary, conv. 125 a., being ½ of (*), to John Powell (IS#H: 196).

2 June 1726: John Powell, tailor, with cons. of w. Phillis, conv. 50 a. pt. (*) now called Whitaker's Venture, to Peter Whitaker (IS#H: 390).

18 March 1727/8: John Powell, staymaker, with cons. of w. Phillis, conv. 75 a. pt. (*) to Charles Whitaker (IS#I: 88).

1730: John Gallion of BA Co. made a will (proved 30 June 1731) leaving pts. of this tract to sons Samuel and Henry (MCW#VI: 200).

13 Dec 1732: John Gallion of BA, planter, eld. s. of JG, dec., conv. to James, Thomas, Solomon, Samuel, Henry, and Joseph Gallion, all devisees of JG, dec., their share of the lands, including (*), devised to them by the said JG (IS#L: 324).

14 May 1734: Israel Whitaker conv. 150 a., being ⅓ of (*) to Aquila and John Paca (HWS#M: 52; cons. of Israel's w. Sarah is on folio 81).

28 June 1740: Peter Whitacre and w. Frances conv. 50 a. pt. (*) to Solomon Gallion (HWS#1-A: 456).

5 June 1746: Samuel Gallion conv. 62½ a. (*), which formerly belonged to Samuel's father Henry Gallion, to William Burton (TB#E: 68).

26 Jan 1748: Solomon Gallion, with cons. of w. Martha, conv. 50 a. (*), now called Whitacre's Venture, to Samuel McCarty (TR#C: 154).

29 Aug 1751: John Whiteacre, with cons. of w. Mary, conv. to Robert Patterson, two tracts of land: Miles' Hill, 100 a., and (*), 75 a. (TR#D: 249).

7 Sep 1751: James Gallion, Jr., s. of John, and James' w. Ruth, conv. pt. of (*) to William Pike (TR#D: 219).

15 Sep 1757: Samuel McCarty conv. 50 a. pt. (*) to James Taylor (B#G: 116).

WHITACRE'S (WHITAKER'S) VENTURE
(Pt. WHITACRE'S RIDGE)

2 June 1726: John Powell, tailor, with cons. of w. Phillis, conv. 50 a. pt. Whitacre's Ridge now called (*) to Peter Whitaker (IS#H: 390).

26 Jan 1748: Solomon Gallion, with cons. of w. Martha, conv. 50 a. Whitacre's Ridge, now called (*) to Samuel McCarty (TR#C: 154).

WHITAKER (See WHITACRE)

WHITE HALL

Jan 1716: 50 a. surv. for Henry Sater (MRR).
See Horvath Plat: Green Spring Valley.

WHITE HALL

14 Oct 1727: Richard King conv. 50 a., pt. of 100 a. (*) to his dau. Ann Marsh (IS#I: 20).

13 June 1728: Richard King, with cons. of w. Mary, conv. 100 a. (*) to Hyde Hoxton and Lloyd Harris (IS#I: 137).

WHITE OAK(S) BOTTOM

1752: 1410 a. for Thomas Matthew; on PW Plat N.

4 Aug 1740: Thomas Matthews, Sr., with cons. of w. Sarah, conv. 150 a. (*) to John Thomas (HWS#1-A: 401).

19 Nov 1742: John and Sarah Thomas conv. 150 a. (*) to Thomas Matthews (TB#C: 70).

20 Oct 1763: Thomas Asken or Askew, with cons. of w. Martha, conv. 132 a. pt. (*) to Nathan Chapman (B#L: 470).

WHITE OAK SPRING

23 Jan 1685: Richard Johns, of CV Co., Gent., with cons. of w. Elizabeth, conv. 150 a. (*) and 300 a. Harboron to Thomas Lightfoot (RM#HS: 172).

WHITE OAK TICKET

1750: Heirs of William Galloway owned 46 a. (*) (1750 DB).

c1754: Moses Galloway owned (*) (IBC: 66).

1763/4: Moses Galloway owned 46 a. (*) (AHAL: 74).

WHITEHEAD'S FOLLY
(Orig. pt. LOW'S RANGE)

5 Aug 1735: James Low and w. Mary conv. 50 a. (*) to Robert Whiteheads (HWS#M: 278).

7 Nov 1735: James Low, with cons. of w. Mary, conv. 50 a. (*) to Robert Whitehead (HWS#1-A: 142).

WIDOW'S CARE

19 Sep 1743: William Hunter and w. Ruth conv. 200 a. pt. of 500 a. (*) to Moses Ruth of CE Co. (TB#C: 328).

WIDOW'S CHOICE

19 Oct 1765: Thomas Stansbury, Jr., conv. $61\frac{1}{2}$ a, Stoney Hill, (q.v.), now called (*), to Reuben Boring (B#O: 608).

WIGNALL'S REST

25 Nov 1726: John Dorsey, Gent., conv. 50 a. Wee Bit and 200 a. (*) to James Durham (IS#H: 284).

7 Dec 1748: John Hammond Dorsey, with cons. of w. Frances, conv. 14 a. pt. (*) to Stephen Onion, James Russell, James Wardrop, James Johnson and Alexander Lawson (TR#C: 127).

WILBURN'S VENTURE

5 April 1680: 100 a. pat. (BB#I: 70).

26 Sep 1753: William Wilburn of FR Co., conv. to Isaac Wood (*) which WW's father, Edward, by his LWT, willed to his s. William and to his dau. Ann, now w. of John Ryan (BB#I: 70).

10 nov 1748: John Ryan and w. Ann conv. 100 a. (*), willed to Ann by LWT of her father Edward Wilburne, to Isaac Wood, carpenter (TR#C: 112).

WILKINSON'S FOLLY

(Later included in Huntington Resurv.: MHM 54:236).

6 June 1705: William Wilkinson, with cons. of w. Tamar, conv. 89 a. (*) to Moses Edwards (TR#A: 284).

31 Oct 1749: John Edwards of BC conv. 899 a. (*) Edwards Lot and Edwards Enlargement (except for that pt. which Moses Edwards, father of John, sold to Thomas Rutter and Jonathan Hanson and 2 a. to St. Paul's Parish, and Huntington, laid out for 135 a.) JE's w. Mary cons. (TR#C: 320).

WILKINSON'S SPRING

27 March 1722: Edward Corbin and w. Jane deed to Tamar Wilkinson, widow, 50 a. (*) and 425 a. Land is All (IS#G: 6).

22 May 1758: Edward Corbin and w. Jane conv. to Robert Wilkinson (*) which they had already conv. to his mother, Tamar Wilkinson (IS#G: 6; B#G: 157).

WILLEN

Laid out for Charles Gorsuch.

28 Oct 1680: Charles Gorsuch conv. 160 a. (*) at the head of Bear Creek on n. side of Patapsco R., to Jonas Boen (Bowen) (Deed and letter of atty. in IR#PP: 53).

27 July 1685: Charles Gorsuch, with cons. of w. Sarah, conv. 100 a. pt. (*), at Chincopinn Neck, to Robert Wilmot (RM#HS: 157).

4 July 1689: Charles Gorsuch and w. Sarah conv. 238 a. comprising (*) and Abington, to Roger Newman of London, merchant (RM#HS: 301).

31 July 1697: Roger Newman conv. 238 a. pt. (*) and pt. Abington to John Francis Holland of AA Co., tailor (IS#IK: 145).

6 Aug 1707: See Eagleston's Addition

6 June 1709: Charles Gorsuch conv. 168 a. pt. (*) to Jonas Bowen (TR#A: 3).

March 1719: John Francis Holland, with cons. of w. Jane, conv. 24 a. pt. Willin, to John Eaglestone, carpenter (IS#G: 97).

24 Dec 1730: Patrick Lynch, who m. Martha, dau. of Jonas Bowen, and Zachariah Gray who m. Rebecca, dau. of Jonas Bowen, submit to arbitration by Thomas Sheredine and John Eaglestone, to divide the lands that Jonas Bowen devised to his daus.: 155 a. Maidens Outlet (orig. laid out for 31 a. and now only 20 a.) and pt. (*) (orig. laid out for 168 a.). Lynch is to have 82 a. (*), and Gray is to have 73 a. (*) and 20 a. Maidens Outlet (HWS#M: 464).

WILLIAM

4 Nov 1701: John Francis Holland and his w. Jane Francis Holland, conv. 240 a. Steir's Progress (formerly taken up by Charles Gorsuch and called Aberle), also pt. (*), to Sarah Steirs, spinster (HW#2: 96).

28 Sep 1732: Surv. again for Sam Hooker.

2 July 1737: Dutton Lane conv. 100 a. (*) to James Boring (IS#IK: 476).

30 Aug 1740: James Boring, with cons. of w. Martha, conv. 100 a. (*) to William Merryman (HWS#1-A: 440).

1 Aug 1741: William Merryman, with cons. of w. Margaret, conv. 100 a. (*) to Samuel Hocker or Hooker (HWS#1-A: 518).

WILLIAM AND MARY

1695: 50 a. surv. for William Horn (Rent Rolls).

WILLIAM AND MARY

Surv. for Gye Mayor.

7 Nov 1747: Gye Mayor conv. (*) and other property to Col. Nathan Rigbie (TB#E: 618).

WILLIAM AND SARA'S INHERITANCE

(Formerly pt. of Robin Hood's Forest granted to Robert Jones and on 22 Oct 1716 conv. by John Hall and w. Martha to Miles Hannis).

26 March 1717: Miles Hannis conv. ⅔ of 150 a. (*) to William Robinson (TR#A: 450).

WILLIAM RESURVEYED

127 July 1762: Samuel Hooker conv. 15 a. pt. (*) to Amon Butler (B#K: 236).

WILLIAM THE CONQUEROR

24 May 1685: 200 a. surv. for William Ramsey on the head of Gunpowder R.; 150 a. later held by Nicholas Day, and 100 a. poss. by William Lenox; still later 150 a. held by Nicholas Day and 50 a. by William Lenox (MRR: 59-60).

12 May 1689: William Ramsey of AA Co. made a will leaving 200 a. Leafe's Choice and 570 a. [sic] (*) to his s. Charles; will was proved 20 June 1689 (MCW#II: 44).

7 Sep 1696: John Ramsey gives p/a to his bro. Charles to ackn. sale of 125 a. pt. Leafe's Chance, now called pt. (*), to William Lennox (IS#IK: 176).

16 Oct 1696: Charles Ramsey and w. Elizabeth conv. 170 a. Leafe's Chance (probably also (*)) to William Lenox (IS#IK: 169).

5 Nov 1696: Thomas Bevan and w. Elizabeth conv. 150 a. pt. Leafe's Chance (in another deed described as pt. of (*)) to Nicholas Day (IS#IK: 120).

16 May 1706: William Lenox and w. Ann conv. 170 a. pt. Leafe's Chance, being pt. (*), to William Robinon (i.e., 120 a. Leafe's Chance and 50 a. pt. (*)) (RM#HS: 606).

1729: William Gosnell conv. 100 a. Leafe's Chance to William Rowles (IS#K: 224).

24 Jan 1730: Charles Baker and w. Providence conv. 1/5 of Leafe's Chance and 1/5 of (*), 125 a. in all, to Josias Hendon (IS#L: 35).

5 March 1745: George Presbury and w. Isabella conv. to Stephen Onion pt. Leafe's Chance & pt. (*), which William & Ann Lenox sold to William Robinson, father of sd. Isabella (TB#E: 34).

3 Dec 1745: Hannah Hendon and Mary Bosworth (daus. and coheirs of William Robinson) and Mary's husband John Bosworth conv. 170 a. being $\frac{1}{2}$ of Leafe's Chance and $\frac{1}{2}$ of (*) to Stephen Onion, ironmaster (TB#D: 428).

21 May 1748: Thomas Day and w. Mary, Laban Day, and Robert Bishop and w. Elizabeth conv. 150 a. (*) to Rev. Hugh Deans. The deed stated that on 5 Nov 1696 Thomas Bevan sold 150 a. (*), called Leafs Chance, to Nicholas Day, grandfather of Thomas, Laban Day and Elizabeth Bishop (TR#C: 10).

7 June 1753: Isham Hendon, s. of Josias, conv. to Stephen Onion his interest in Leafe's Chance and (*). Isham's w. Keziah cons. (BB#I: 8).
20 March 1754: Jacob Rowles conv. two parcels Leafe's Chance, 51½ a., 91½ a., and other lands, to David Rowles (BB#I: 302).

WILLIAM THE CONQUEROR

1752: Surv.; on KN Plat WO.

WILLIAMS ADDITION

Oct 1702: 166 a. surv. for Benj. William (Rent Rolls).

WILLIAMS BEGINNING

9 Dec 1746: Thomas Tipton conv. 50 a. (*) to his s. Thomas and his heirs lawfully begotten (TB#E: 268).

WILLIAMS CHOICE

10 April 1762: Owen Williams, with cons. of w. Elizabeth, conv. 30 a. (*) to Absolom Baker (PCLR DD#2: 32).

WILLIAMS DELIGHT

1742: 25 a. granted to William Ogg.
5 Oct 1767: William Ogg, with cons. of w. Sarah, conv. all of (*) to William Lux, William Lyon, Charles Graham and James Dock (B#Q: 202).

WILLIAMS EXCHANGE

Orig. surv. for George Burgess.
7 Aug 1686: Rebecca Lightfoot, widow of Thomas, conv. 100 a. (*) to John Wilson, Sr. (RM#HS: 282).

WILLIAMS FORTUNE

19 Aug 1670: Surv. for Lodowick Williams; Thompson's Fortune and Williams Fortune were combined by Edward Williams, s. of Lodwick, to Richard Colegate, whose LWT left tracts to his two daus., one of whom was Patience. Patience m. William Buckner who conv. the two tracts to Robert Robertson (IS#L: 311).
19 Nov 1715: Edward Williams of Paspotank R. in Sawyer's Creek, NC, conv. 100 a. where Matthew Green's widow and Robert Smith, shoemaker, dwell, 200 a. Lodowick's Ridge, 150 a. Matt's Addition, 100 a. Thomson's Fortune, 300 a. United Friendship, and 150 a. (*), and all other lands in MD belonging to Williams by right of inheritance, to Richard Colegate of BC, merchant (TR#A: 373).
July 1731: William Buckner and w. Patience conv. 150 a. Motts Addition, 100 a. Thompson's Fortune and 150 a. (*) to Robert Robertson (IS#L: 149).
29 June 1732: Robert Robertson and w. Sarah conv. 36 a. Thompson's Fortune and 150 a. (*), to Jonathan Hughes (IS#L: 311).

WILLIAMS LOT

6 April 1738; William Demoss of Orange Co., VA, conv. (*) to James Billingslea (HWS#1-A: 92).
1753: James Billinglsea conv. 18 a. to William Grafton (BB#I: 199).

WILLIAMS RIDGE

8 April 1676: Lodwick Williams mortgaged 200 a. (*) at the head of Bough Creek on the s. side of Bush R., to Samuel Boston, High Sheriff (IS#IK: 58).
6 March 1682/3: James Mills, merchant, exec. of Capt. Samuel Boston, dec., conv. 200 a. (*) to James Phillips (deed, bond and letter of atty.: RM#HS: 28).

WILLIAMSON'S HOPE

8 July 1743: Thomas Williamson, with cons. of w. Eliz. conv. Hope's Addition and (*), in all 89 a., to Samuel Griffith (TB#C: 272).

WILLIAMSON'S PURCHASE
(See also KNAVERY DISCOVERED)

1 Sep 1709 John Frizzell, now of BA Co., conv. (*), being pt. of Knavery Discovered, to Patrick Duncan (TR#A: 30).
On the same day Patrick Dunkin conv. 50 a. of that tract to Thomas Williamson (TR#A: 38).
27 June 1713: John Frizzell conv. 150 a. pt. of Knavery Detected, to William Pumphrey; w. Elizabeth cons. (TR#DS: 143).
3 Oct 1721: Frizzell and w. Elizabeth sold pt. of the tract to William Forest (RM#HS: 664).

WILLIAMSTON

20 feb 1664/5: Pat. to Nathaniel Stiles.
7 Nov 1671: Nathaniel Stiles, Gent., conv. 500 a. (*), on e. side of Steelpone Bay, to Thomas Howell, Gent. (IR#PP: 122).

WILLS CHANCE

1707: 50 a. for John Wills; on PW Plat B.

WILLS FOREST

24 Aug 1748: William Rogers conv. 100 a. to Peter Medcalfe (TR#C: 74).

WILMOTS CHANCE

22 Oct 1757: Richard Wilmot conv. 50 a. pt. (*) to Peter Gosnell (B#G: 72).

WILMOTS CHOICE

6 March 1709; Elizabeth Roberts, widow, owning Roberts Forest in her own right by the LWT of Capt. Thomas Roberts, conv. 100 a. of Roberts Forest, now called (*) to John Wilmot, Jr. (TR#A: 72).

WILMOTS FOLLY

2 July 1688: 140 a. surv.

11 April 1741: John Wilmot, Sr., with cons. of w. Rachel, conv. 140 a. (*) and 50 a. Wilmots Neglect to William Chetynd and Samuel and Osgood Gee and others of the Principio Co. (HWS#1-A: 486).

WILMOTS NEGLECT

7 Sep 1727: 50 a. surv.

11 April 1741: John Wilmot, Sr., with cons. of w. Racel, conv. 140 a. Wilmots Folly and 50 a. (*) to William Chetynd and Samuel and Osgood Gee and others of the Principio Co. (HWS#1-A: 486).

WILMOTS RANGE

26 da., 6 mo., 1730: John Wilmot, with cons. of w. Rachel, conv. 200 a. (*) to Charles Ridgely (IS#L: 72).

WILSONS CHOICE

22 May 1742: Samuel Wilson, with cons. of w. Rebecca, conv. 52 a. pt. (*) to Jacob Bull (TB#A: 234).

4 June 1742: Samuel Wilson, with cons. of w. Rebecca, conv. 50 a., pt. 100 a. (*), in fork of Winters Run, to Alexander Thompson (TB#A: 238).

WILSONS RANGE

18 Nov 1686: 100 a. surv. for John Wilson; located on n. side of Bush R.; later poss. by Stephen Freeland (MRR: 13, 33).

23 Nov 1693: John Wilson, Sr., Gent., of AA Co., conv. 100 a. (*) to Stephen Freeland (RM#HS: 430).

24 Jan 1744: John Wilson, with cons. of w. Mary, conv. 100 a. (*) to Isaac Webster (TB#D: 8).

WINCHESTER'S LOT

1752: 973 a. for William Winchester; on PW Plat M.

WINDLEYS

16 Jan 1740: William Slade, s. and heir of William Slade, dec., conv. 100 a. (*) to Bezaleel Foster (HWS#1-A: 460).

WINDLEY'S FOREST

1667: Taken up by Richard Windley, bought by Edward Ward who bequeathed it to his w. Ann, now w. of Lemuel Howard, and to his dau. Camilla Ward who d. intestate (TB#C: 668).

1667: Surv. for Richard Windley; cert. calls for Cat Creek; lies in the vicinity of Bradshaw; tract later poss. by John Taylor; in 1746: resurv. into Onion's Inheritance (MRR; MHM 25:364, 53:241).

3 Nov 1668: Richard Windley and w. Mary conv. 100 a. (*) to Oliver Sprye (IR#PP: 71).

1 Nov 1670: Godfrey Harmer and w. Mary conv. 100 a. (*) to Roger Hill (IR#PP: 89).

12 Sep 1685: Thomas Lightfoot conv. 300 a. Fortune and 100 a. (*) to Benjamin Williams (RM#HS: 156).

9 May 1717: Benjamin Williams of AA Co., with cons. of w. Margaret, conv. 295 a. Fortune and 100 a. (*) to Edward Ward of AA Co. (TR#A: 457).

6 March 1717 (1717/8): Edward Ward conv. 50 a., being $\frac{1}{2}$ of (*), to John Bradshaw (TR#A: 520).

10 Dec 1740: John Bradshaw of PG Co., with cons. of his mother, Mary Dallahide, conv. 50 a., $\frac{1}{2}$ of (*), to Stephen Onion (HWS#1-A: 470).

9 Jan 1744: Lemuel Howard and w. Ann conv. 295 a. Fortune and 50 a. pt. (*) to Stephen Onion (TB#C: 668).

WINDLEYS REST

27 Feb 1677; Pat. to Richard Windley who m. the sister of Arthur Taylor (RM#HS: 467).

1686 [sic]: 200 a. surv. for Richard Windley, on the s. side of Back R., on the w. side of Windleys Branch (MHM 20: 274).

5 June 1695: John Taylor (son of Arthur Taylor whose sister Mary m. Richard Winley) conv. 200,a. (*) to John Fuller (RM#HS: 461).

8 Nov 1695: John Fuller, with cons. of w. Hester, conv. 200 a. to Thomas Heath (RM#HS: 467).

7 July 1702: Francis Dallahide, with cons. of w. Sarah, conv. 200 a. (*) to William Slade (HW#2: 174).

WINTERS RUN

5 June 1688: 200 a. surv. for John Lee, and later held by Philip Greenslade (MRR: 51).

2 Aug 1684: Joseph Gallion, and w. Sarah, conv. 200 a. (*) occupied by Gallion, on the s. side and at the head of northwest branch of Bush R., to Philip Greenslade, mariner (deed, bond, and letter of atty. in RM#HS: 96).

25 Aug 1724: Philip Greenslade of Barnstaple, Co. Devon, fuller, s. and heir of Philip Greenslade, dec., and Joan, relict and admx. of said Philip, leased 200 a. (*) to Joseph Farmer of Birmingham, Co. Warwick, England, merchant (IS#G: 266, 268).

WISKE als. DANBY, MANOR OF

1659: Surv. on North West R., now Back R. (MHM 25:326).

8 Sep 1665: Mathias Decosta, and w. Elizabeth, conv. 700 a. (*), on northeast side of the s. branch of Northeast R., to Thomas Ireton (IS#IK: 5).

WITH'S ADVENTURE

1 June 1731: John Miller and w. May conv. Success (orig. held by Henry Peregoy and now called With's Adventure) to George With (IS#L: 125).

WITHERINGTON

1699: Robert Benger left 70 a. (*) to his w. Deborah (MCW#II: 188).

15 Jan 1700: John Shaw of CE Co. conv. to Alexander Graves of BA Co., 100 a. Hopewell, 100 a. being ½ of Salisbury Plains, 70 a. Witherington, 80 a. Shadwell's Range. and 100 a. Smith's Range (HW#2: 53).

WITHERS

7 March 1670/1: Nathaniel Stiles, Gent., conv. 200 a. (*) and 300 a. Bayley to Richard Whitton (IR#PP: 100).

WITTBY (or WITTLY)

15 Dec 1739: Michael Gilbert and w. Mary, dau. of Martin Taylor, Sr., and heir of Martin Taylor, Jr., both dec., conv. ⅓ The Adventure and 60 a. being ⅓ of (*) to Benjamin Bond (HWS#1-A: 324).

4 Nov 1742: Jonathan Hughes, tailor, and w. Jane, dau. of Martin Taylor, conv. ⅓ (*) to Benjamin Bond (HWS#1-A: 164).

WITTEN

25 Aug 1698: Thomas Preston, Gent., and w. Mary conv. 86 a. (*), betw. two branches of Lodowick's Creek to Martin Taylor (TR#RA: 286).

WOLF HARBOR (See WOLF'S HARBOR)

WOLF'S DEN

See Horvath Plats: Owings Mills; Green Spring Valley.

31 Oct 1746: John Clark, cordwiner, and w. Susannah conv. pt. (*), orig. surv. for John Berry, ditcher, to William Gist (TB#E: 232).

19 Dec 1751: John Berry, the Younger, s. of John Berry, the Elder, dec., conv. to William Gist, (*) (TR#D: 263).

WOLF'S GROVE

1 May 1746: Benjamin Tasker, Agent, and Recorder for Lord Baltimore, leased 187 a. (*), being pt. of His Lordship's Reserve, to Peter Wolf, for 99 years (TB#E: 337).

WOLF'S HARBOR

20 June 1689: 318 a. surv. for Samuel Sicklemore on n. side of Gunpowder R., on the w. side of the mouth of Custer's Creek (or Foster's Creek); later described as having been taken away by a surv. of Fosters Neck (MRR: 69).

2 March 1696: Samuel Sickelmore conv. 100 a. pt. (*) to John Anderson; Samuel's w. Sarah cons. (IS#IK: 67).

1 Nov 1698: John Anderson of BA Co., planter, and w. Jane, conv. 100 a. pt. (*) to Samuel Sicklemore, merchant (TR#RA: 372).

27 Oct 1706: Samuel Sicklemore of BA Co., Gent., gives p/a to w. Sarah to collect debts, pay debts, and sell all land except land where she lives called (*) (R#HS: 560).

14 June 1711: Samuel Sickelmore, Sr., conv. (*) to Samuel Sickelmore. Samuel, Sutton, and Hannah Sickelmore are all to live together until they marry and they are to teach Thomas Wriothesly Sickelmore to read and write (TR#A: 244).

10 March 1713: Samuel Sicklemore and w. Ruth conv. pt. (*) to Robert Cutchin (TR#A: 263).

13 April 1714: Samuel Sicklemore and w. Ruth conv. pt. (*) to John Roberts (TR#A: 297).

31 Jan 1732: Robert Cutchin conv. Hollands Adventure and (*) to Brian Taylor (IS#L: 332).

8 March 1743: Winifred Cutcheon, widow of Robert, conv. Hollands Adventure and (*) to Stephen Onion of Gunpowder Iron Works, merchant. Cutcheon had formerly conv. the land to Brian Taylor by Winifred Cutchin had not conv. her doer rights (TB#C: 427).

17 Aug 1743: Everard Taylor of CV Co. conv. pt. Howard's Adventure, and pt. (*) to Stephen Onion (TB#C: 318).

WOLF'S HARBOR NECK

22 Nov 1742: Stephen Roberts, s. and devisee of John Roberts, dec., conv. his interest in pt. (*), and Lots 6 and 7 in Joppa, which were devised to him by his father to John Roberts, another s. and devisee of John Roberts (TB#C: 219).

WOLF'S NECK

10 Oct 1672: Robert Chapman of KE Co. conv. (*) at Swann Creek on the s. side of the western branch of Gunpowder, to Thomas Phillips or Phelps of AA Co. (G#J: 161; TR#RA: 117).

5 March 1684/4: Lancelot Todd of AA Co., and w. Sarah, who is dau. and heir of Thomas Phelps, late of AA Co, dec., conv. 150 a. (*) to Edward Philkes (RM#HS: 116).

31 Jan 1732: Robert Cutchin conv. Holland's Adventure and (*) to Brian Taylor (IS#L: 332).

WOODCOT (Pt. MY LADYS MANOR)

30 March 1739: Thomas Brerewood, formerly of Horton (England?), now of BA Co., conv. 413 a. (*) to William Brerewood of SO Co., MD. William is to pay money to his father Francis Brerewood (HWS#1-A: 231).

WOODENS VENTURE

15 June 1759: 40 a. surv. for John Wooden (WHC: App. 1, p. 2).

WOODLAND NECK

28 Feb 1669/70: Samuel Collet, Gent., conv. 250 a. (*) at the head of Musketo Creek, to John Tarkenton (IR#PP: 80).

3 Aug 1674: John Tarkinton and w. Prudence conv. 250 a. (*) and 250 a. The Grove, to William Palmer, Gent. (G#J: 276).

WOODPECKER HALL
(Pt. ENLARGEMENT)

Enlargement was orig. taken up by George Goldsmith, Sr.

15 May 1718: Mary Wells, widow, conv. 11 a. (*) to John Hall (TR#RA: 439).

WOODS ADDITION

4 Nov 1737; Joshua Wood conv. 50 a. (*) to Charles Anderson, carpenter (HWS#M: 27).

WOODS CHOICE

23 Feb 1748: Joshua Wood conv. to Abraham Taylor several tracts formerly owned by Joshua Wood, father of the grantor: Woods Choice, Hobsons Choice, and 254 a. Benjamin's Choice (TR#C: 157).

WOOD'S CLOSE

7 Sep 1638 [sic]: Thomas Mitchell of BC gives clear title to 100 a. to (*) to Joshua Wood; deed states that tract was surv. 2 Oct 1719, but grant was not issued to (Thomas Mitchell?) until 10 June 1734 (HWS#1-A: 102).

2 Oct 1719: Surv.; 10 June 1734: 200 a. pat. by Thomas Mitchell (HWS#1-A:1-02; MPL EI#2: 74, EI#3: 306).

20 May 1720: Thomas Mitchell and w. Martha conv. 100 a. (*) to Mathew Molton (TR#DS: 175).

15 April 1723: Thomas Mitchell and w. Ann conv. 100 a. being ½ of (*) to Joseph England (IS#G: 216).

13 April 1734: Joseph England and w. Margaret of KE Co., conv. 100 a. being ½ of (*) to William Gallenbe in exch. for tract Denbee in Kent (HES#M: 45).

28 Nov 1735: William Gatenbe of KE Co. conv. 100 a., 12 of (*) lately in poss. of Joseph England, to Joshua Wood of BA Co., carpenter (HWS#M: 336).

7 Sep 1638: Thomas Mitchell of BC gives clear title to 100 a. to (*) to Joshua Wood; deed stated that tract was surv. 2 Oct 1719, but grant was not issued to (Thomas Mitchell?) until 10 June 1734 (HWS#1-A: 102).

WOODS END

23 Sep 1727: Thomas Sheredine, with cons. of w. Tabitha, conv. 250 a. (*) to John Hallaway (IS#I: 13).

WOODS RESQUE

29 April 1725: Joshua Wood and w. Martha conv. pt. (*) to Obadiah Pritchard (IS#H: 117).

25 July 1733: Margaret, Samuel, and Obadiah Prichard conv. pt. (*) to Samuel Howell (IS#L: 403).

WOODS VENTURE

2 June 1725: Joshua and Martha Wood conv. 100 a. (*) to Richard Jenkins (IS#H: 105).

WOOLEY'S RANGE

14 Aug 1736: John and Ann Wooley conv. 100 a. (*) to John Jones (IS#IK: 329).

10 Sep 1737: John Wooley conv. 100 a. (*) to Thomas Logsdon (HWS#M: 15).

WOOLSEY'S RANGE

1754: 100 a. for John Woolsey.

See PW Plat P; Horvath Plat: Pikesville.

WORLD'S END

4 March 1666/7: Francis Child conv. 500 a. on the n. side of Sassafras R., pat. to Child, to Richard Leake, tailor (IR#PP: 67).

1 Nov 1670: Richard Leeke, tailor, with cons. of w. Gwilthin, conv. to Thomas Howell, Gent., 150 a. Urinson on n. side of Sassafras R., taken up by Neale Urinson and sold by him to Leeke; also 600 a. (*), taken up by Francis Child (IR#PP: 85).

10 June 1672: Thomas Howell, Gent., with cons. of w. Elizabeth, conv. to Nathaniel Garrett 150 a. Urinson and 500 a. (*) (IR#PP: 127).

5 Sep 1738; John Holloway, with cons. of w. Elizabeth, conv. 150 a. (*) to Abraham Vaughn (HWS#1-A: 100).

2 March 1742: Abraham Vaughan, with cons. of w. Caty, conv. 150 a. (*) to Skelton Standiford (TB#C: 193).

WRIGHTS FOREST

1 May 1732: Jacob Wright conv. 100 a. (*) to Patrick Lynch (IS#L: 400).
22 Jan 1735: Patrick and Martha Lynch conv. 100 a. (*) to James Lenox (HWS#M: 368).
12 Jan 1737: James Lenox, with cons. of w. Mary, conv. 100 a. (*) to Thomas Dulany (HWS#M: 46).
2 July 1744: William Dulany conv. 100 a. (*) to Thomas Brerewood (TB#C: 524).
14 May 1745: William Dulany, with cons. of w. Mary, conv. 100 a. (*) to Thomas Sligh and Chas. Crook (TB#D: 139).

WYFALL

4 March 1667/8: Michael Bellicon conv. 100 a. (*) at Sassafras R. to the estate of Mr. Richard Bennett (IR#PP: 62).

YAPP

14 Aug 1666: Nathaniel Stiles, Gent., conv. 500 a. (*) at a creek in Sassafras R., to Joseph Gundry, merchant (IR#PP: 56).

YATES ADDITION

29 Nov 1715: John Yates conv. 86 a. (*) and 182 a. Yates Forbearance (out of 770 a.) to John Israel (TR#A: 385).

YATES CONTRIVANCE

4 Dec 1725: Joseph Harp, with cons. of w. Ruth, conv. ⅓ of 400 a. (*) to Thomas Cockey, for the life of Ruth (IS#H: 215).
23 Aug 1726: George Yate of BA Co. conv. 144 a. Forbearance and 400 a. (*) to Col. Thomas Cockey. The land desc. to the grantor by virtue of his being the eld. s. and heir of his father George, per the latter's will, or by the deaths of his younger bros. before they reached the age of 21 (IS#H: 281).
28 Oct 1741: Robert Chapman conv. 100 a. (*) to William Hammond (TB#A: 31).

YATES' FORBEARANCE (1673)

17 July 1673: 140 a. surv. for George Yates near the main falls of Patapsco R. (MRR: 80).

YATES' FORBEARANCE (1683)
(See ADVENTURE)

15 June 1683: 770 a. surv. for George Yates on the n. side of Patapsco R.; in possession of the said Yates; still later held by John Yates and s. (MRR: 80).
See PW Plat B2-6, Horvath Plat: Elkridge.
1 July 1710: John Yates of BA Co., planter, conv. 100 a. Adventure, being pt. of (*) to Joshua Sewell. JY's w. Elizabeth cons. (TR#A: 84).
1 July 1712: George Yates of BA Co., conv. 382 a., being ½ of 770 a. (*), granted to George's father George (i.e., John) Yates; to John Israel (TR#A: 208).
5 March 1715: John Yates and w. Elizabeth of BA Co. conv. 100 a. (*) to Robert Chapman (TR#RA: 473).
29 Nov 1715: John Yates conv. 86 a. Yates Addition and 182 a. (*) (out of 770 a.) to John Israel (TR#A: 385).
12 Nov 1716: Joshua Sewell of AA Co., and w. Mary conv. 100 a. Adventure, being pt. of Yates Forbearance, to Richard Colegate (TR#A: 511).
14 July 1727: Samuel Heighe, with cons. of w. Sarah, relict of John Israel, conv. to Charles Carroll of Annapolis, Sarah's right of dower of ⅓ interest in 182 a. residue of (*), purch. from John Yates, 385 a. purch. from George Yate, 87 a. from John Yate and 100 a. pat. by John Israel (IS#I: 29).
23 Dec 1749: Robert Chapman of BC, wheelwright, s. and heir of Robert Chapman, who d. intestate, conv. to Daniel Dulany 100 a. Yates' Forbearance and 106 a. Smith's Forest. RC's w. Margaret cons. (TR#C: 385).

YATES' INHERITANCE

22 Aug 1668: 170 a. surv. for George Yates on the s. side of Patapsco; later poss. by Anthony Johnson; still later poss. by the heir of John Howard (MRR: 80).
11 March 1683/4: Edward Filkes of AA Co., planter, conv. 140 a. pt. of 170 a. to Thomas Pattison of same co.; tract was pat. 4 Sep 1668 to George Yate, deeded by him on 29 March 1668 to Francis Waters; on 1 Jan 1671/2 Water conv. 140 a. of the tract to John Jacob, who conv. the same on 1 March 1671/2 to Felkes; Edward's w. Ellen cons. (RM#HS: 106).
11 March 1683/4: Felkes gave bond to Thomas Pattison that he would perform the covenants (RM#HS: 106).
8 Aug 1693: Gilbert Pattison and w. Ann conv. 170 a. of tract to William Johnson and John Richardson (IR#AM: 95).
16 Dec 1696: William Johnson and John Richardson, both of AA Co., conv. 170 a. to Anthony Johnson; refers to deed of 8 Aug 1693: Anna w. of John Richardson gave cons. (IS#IK: 134).
9 Oct 1702: Anthony Johnson of BA Co. conv. 170 a. (*) to John Howard; w. Katherine cons. (HW#2: 177).

YORK'S CHANCE

1676: 125 a. surv. for William York (MRR).

18 June 1723: Elizabeth York of CE Co., only dau. of William York, late of BA Co., dec., gave a quitclaim of (*) and Bridewell Dock to her uncle George York. William York of BA Co., by his LWT of 23 Nov 1690, left his lands to his sons: William, Oliver, John, George, and James. William and Oliver disposed of their land, but left George with 250 a.; this deed gave George a clear title (IS#G: 204).
1750: George York owned 125 a. (*) (1750 DB: 7).
20 April 1750: George York conv. 62 a. (*) and 20 a. Bridewell Dock to Edward York (TR#D: 122).
20 April 1750: George York conv. 62 a. (*) and 25 a. Bridewell Dock to John York (TR#D: 124).

YORKS HOPE

16 Nov 1664: 200 a. surv. for William York on the northernmost side of Gunpowder; John Yeo had a mandamus on the land and it was granted to him; Yeo is since dead leaving no heirs; his relations live in the w. of England (MRR: 11, 30).
1664: 200 a. in Spesutia Hundred surv. for William York (MHM 19: 351); 200 a. in Gunpowder Hundred surv. for William York (MHM 10: 23).
31 July 1669: William and Elizabeth York conv. 200 a. (*) on n. side of Gunpowder R., to Walter Mackenall and w. Jane (IR#PP: 73).
4 April 1683: Robert Jones, s. and heir-at-law of Thomas Jones, conv. 200 a. (*) and 73 a. Jones Addition to John Yeo (Deed and letter of atty. RM#HS: 49, 53).

YOUNG MAN'S ADVENTURE

4 Nov 1741: Thomas Coale, with cons. of w. Mary, conv. to William Coale of AA Co. following tracts: Young Man's Adventure (granted to William Coale), Martin's Addition and Martinton (TB#A: 22).

YOUNG'S DELIGHT

9 March 1746: Jacob Young deeded to John Bosley 50 a. (*) and 19 a. The Hopyard (Hector's Hopyard?), JY's w. Eleanor cons. (TB#E: 532).

YOUNGS ESCAPE

12 Nov 1731: Samuel Young, Sr., of AA Co. conv. 1200 a. (*) to his s. Samuel Young of CV Co. (IS#K: 330).

YOUNG'S LOT

1679: 300 a. for Theodore Young; on PW Plat B2-6.

YUPP (See YAPP)

LOTS IN BALTIMORE TOWN (Pre-1729)

For a detailed study of the development of lots in Baltimore Town, see "Parceling Out Land in the Vicinity of Baltimore, 1632-1706," by Garrett Power, "Pt. 1" in MHM (Winter 1992) 87 (4) 453-466, and "Pt. 2" in MHM (Summer (1993), 88 (2) 150-180.

Lot 99

3 Feb 1710: John Gill, carpenter, conv. (*) to Capt. William Fowle, mariner, of London. Gill had taken up the tract and built on it, but the tract had earlier been taken up by Col. Thomas Hammond (TR#A: 121).
5 June 1716: John McWilliams, late of Liverpool, merchant, conv. (*), formerly taken up by John Gill, to Capt. William Fowle (TR#A: 372).

LOTS IN BALTIMORE TOWN (1729)

Unplaced Lots

23 May 1736: John Risteau, merchant, with cons. of w. Catherine, conv. a lot to Rev. Joseph Hooper, minister of the Gospel (IS#IK: 363).

14 March 1743: Christopher Gist mortgaged 100 a. Counterscarpe, 83 a. Milford, Gist's Inspection, 500 a. Joshua's Lot, 50 a. Gist's Meadows, and 2 lots in Baltimore Town (TB#D: 438).

28 March 1746: James Richard, atty. for Stephen Theodore Jannsen, conv. 100 a. Counterscarpe, 83 a. Milford, Gist's Inspection, 500 a. Joshua's Lot, 50 a. Gist's Meadows, and 2 lots in Baltimore Town to William Cromwell and Tobias Stansbury, who have paid the mortgaged (TB#D: 438).

25 Dec 1748: Charles Carroll of Annapolis, Gent., conv. 2 lots to Alexander Lawson (TR#C: 41).

15 Oct 1752: Thomas Harrison conv. 2 a. of land in Baltimore Town to Stephen Onion and William Young (TR#D: 313).

Lot 1

6 Dec 1745: Charles Carroll of Annapolis, Gent., conv. Lot 1 (which Charles Carroll of Annapolis, by his LWT of 1 Dec 1718 bequeathed to his sons Charles and Daniel, and which Daniel, by his LWT of 1 April 1734, authorized Charles to sell all lands under 500 a.) to William Hammond (TB#E: 47; TR#C: 504).
20 Dec 1751: William Hammond mortgaged Lots 1 and 5 to Alexander Lawson (TR#D: 265).

Lot 2

11 Sep 1745: Charles Carroll of Annapolis, Gent., conv. Lots 2, 3, 4 (which Charles Carroll of Annapolis, by his LWT of 1 Dec 1718 bequeathed to his sons Charles and Daniel, and which Daniel, by his LWT of 1 April 1734, authorized Charles to sell all lands), to Robert Hollyday, physician (TB#D: 325).

Lot 3

11 Sep 1745: See Lot 2.

Lot 4

11 Sep 1745: See Lot 2.

Lot 5

6 Dec 1745: Charles Carroll of Annapolis, Gent., conv. Lot 5 (which Charles Carroll of Annapolis, by his LWT of 1 Dec 1718 bequeathed to his sons Charles and Daniel, and which Daniel, by his LWT of 1 April 1734, authorized Charles to sell all lands under 500 a.) to William Hammond (TB#E: 47, TR#C: 504).

20 Dec 1751: William Hammond mortgaged Lots 1 and 5 to Alexander Lawson (TR#D: 265).

Lot 6

20 April 1750: Charles Carroll of Annapolis, conv. Lots 6, 17, and 18 to Dr. William Lyon (TR#C: 430).

Lot 9

6 April 1744: James Walker of AA Co. conv. (*) to Nicholas Rogers (TB#C: 463).

Lot 10

22 Sep 1738: Joshua Hall, with cons. of w. Diana, conv. to William Rogers (HWS#1-A: 115).

Lot 13

12 July 1749: Charles Carroll of Annapolis conv. (*) to Charles Croxall (TR#C: 243).

Lot 17

1748: John Boring, in consideration toward his loving s. John, and my grandsons: William and Reuben Boring sons of his s. Thomas, and John Boring, s. of my s. John, granted to s. John: Lot 18 in Baltimore Town, and to grandsons, lot 17 in Baltimore Town, and to grandson John, 100 a. (*) (TR#C: 371).

31 Oct 1749: John Boreing in consideration toward my s. John Boreing as to my grandson (that is to say) William Boreing and Rueben Boreing, sons of my s. Thomas, and John Boreing, s. of my aforesaid s. John Boreing ... grant to my s. John and my said grandson William, Rubin and John viz ... s. John Lot 18 in Baltimore Town and two negros. Grandsons Wm. and Rubin Lot 17 in BT and two negros. Grandson John, Boreings Meadows, 100 a. and 1 negro (TR#C: 371).

19 Feb 1750: Thomas Boring and his bro. John conv. to Sarah Boring, widow, for love and affection, lots 17 and 18 in Baltimore Town, these being the habitation of John Boring, father of said Thomas and John (TR#C: 368).

20 April 1750: Charles Carroll of Annapolis, conv. Lots 6, 17, and 18 to Dr. William Lyon (TR#C: 430).

17 June 1765: William Boring, with cons. of w. Martha, and Reuben Boring, with cons. of w. Nancy, (William and Reuben are two of the grandsons of John Boring), conv. pt. (*) to Mark Alexander (B#O: 386).

17 June 1765: Same grantors conv. to Gist Baughn pt. of Lot 17 (B#O: 652).

Lot 18

31 Oct 1748: John Boreing for love and affection, conv. s. John lot # 18 in Baltimore Town; grandsons William and Reuben, sons of Thomas, lot 17; grandson John, s. of John, 100 a. Boring's Meadows (TR#C: 371).

19 Feb 1750: Thomas Boring and his bro. John conv. to Sarah Boring, widow, for love and affection, lots 17 and 18 in Baltimore Town, these being the habitation of John Boring, father of said Thomas and John (TR#C: 368).

20 April 1750: Charles Carroll of Annapolis, conv. Lots 6, 17, and 18 to Dr. William Lyon (TR#C: 430).

Lot 28

19 March 1750: Sarah Boring, widow, conv. Lot # 28 in Baltimore Town, to Moses Rutter (TR#D: 151).

Lot 23

9 April 1746: Charles Carroll of Annapolis, Esq., conv. Lots 23, 24, 25, and 57 to James Richard (TB#E: 78).

Lot 24

9 April 1746: See Lot 23.

Lot 25

9 April 1746: See Lot 23.

Lot 26

1754: Sarah Boreing to Wm. Askew. Lots 26, 27 and 28 (BB#I: 344).

Lot 27
26 May 1748: Charles Carroll of Annapolis conv. (*) to Leonard Barneets (TR#C: 3, 5).
1754: Sarah Boreing to Wm. Askew. Lots 26, 27 and 28 (BB#I: 344).

Lot 28
26 May 1748: Charles Carroll of Annapolis, Gent., conv. (*) to Joshua Hall (TB#E: 723).
19 March 1750: Sarah Boring, widow, conv. (*) to Moses Rutter (TR#D: 151).
1754: Sarah Boreing to Wm. Askew. Lots 26, 27 and 28 (BB#I: 344).

Lot 29
19 March 1750: Moses Rutter conv. Lot # 29 to Sarah Boring, widow (TR#D: 152).

Lot 30
26 May 1748: Charles Carroll of Annapolis conv. (*) to Daniel Barnetz (TR#C: 6).

Lot 31
26 May 1748: Charles Carroll of Annapolis conv. (*) to Daniel Barnetz (TR#C: 6).

Lot 32
26 May 1748: Charles Carroll of Annapolis conv. (*) to Fetus Hartway (TR#C: 8).
12 June 1750: Vitus Hartway, sadler, with cons. of w. Elizabeth, conv. (*) Edmund Talbot (TR#C: 496).

Lot 33 (See also lot 1)
6 Dec 1745: Charles Carroll of Annapolis, Gent., conv. Lots 1, 5, 33, 34, and 66 to William Hammond (TR#C: 504).
3 Jan 1749: William Hammond conv. (*) to Edward Talbot. WH's w. Sarah cons. (TR#C: 372).
3 April 1750; William Hammond, with cons. of w. Sarah, conv. to Lloyd (Lyde) Goodwin $\frac{1}{2}$ of Lot 33 (TR#C: 504).
23 Jan 1752: Edmund Talbot conv. (*) Thomas Ward (TR#D: 282).

Lot 34 (See also lot 1)
6 Dec 1745: Charles Carroll of Annapolis, Gent., conv. Lot 34 to William Hammond (TR#C: 504).
3 April 1750; William Hammond, with cons. of w. Sarah, conv. to Lloyd (Lyde) Goodwin $\frac{1}{2}$ of Lot 34 (TR#C: 504).
6 Aug 1750: William Hammond, with cons. of w. Sarah, conv. to John Ridgely pt. of Lot 34 (TR#C:).

Lot 36
24 July 1742: Luke Trotten conv. (*) to William Rogers (TB#A: 213).
8 Dec 1746: William Rogers, with cons. of w. Sarah, conv. (*) to Joseph Mayo, Jr., of AA Co. (TB#E: 269).

Lot 37
24 July 1742: Philip Jones, Jr. conv. (*) to William Rogers (TB#A: 216).
8 Dec 1746: William Rogers, with cons. of w. Sarah, conv. (*) to Joseph Mayo, Jr., of AA Co. (TB#E: 269).

Lot 38
12 Dec 1730: James Jackson conv. (*) to Samuel Peele of AA Co., merchant (IS#L: 41).
1 July 1749: William Hammond, Gent., conv. to Sebastian Sadlemire, baker, $\frac{1}{4}$ pt. of (*). WH's w. Sarah cons. (TR#C: 290).

Lot 39
1 July 1754: John Sheppard, tailor, mortgaged Lots 39, 40 and 41 in Addition to Baltimore Town to William Andrews, Patrick Gray and Thomas Sligh ... (BB#I: 261).

Lot 40
1 July 1754: See lot 39.

Lot 41
1 July 1754: See Lot 39.

Lot 42
24 July 1742: William Hammond conv. (*) to William Rogers (TB#A: 211).
28 July 1746: William Rogers, with cons. of w. Sarah, conv. (*) to George Buchanan (TB#E: 117).

Lot 43
24 Sep 1743: William Rogers, with cons. of w. Sarah, conv. (*) to Darby Lux (TB#C: 369).

Lot 44
24 Sep 1743: William Rogers, with cons. of w. Sarah, conv. (*) to Darby Lux (TB#C: 369).

Lot 45
19 Aug 1730: William Hammond conv. (*) to George Hurt (IS#L: 20).

Lot 47
5 Nov 1731: David Robinson, blacksmith, with cons. of w. Elinor, conv. (*) to Richard Gist (IS#L: 192).

Lot 50
19 Jan 1729: Taken up by Lloyd Harris
4 May 1737: Lloyd Harris mortgaged (*) to Richard Bennet (IS#IK: 449).

Lot 51
19 Jan 1729: Taken up by John Gorsuch.
26 April 1731: John Gorsuch conv. (*) to Lloyd Harris (IS#L: 112).
4 May 1737: Lloyd Harris mortgaged (*) to Richard Bennet (IS#IK: 449).

Lot 54
6 Feb 1729: Taken up by Charles Ridgely
7 Nov 1748: Charles Ridgely, Gent., conv. (*) to Thomas Harrison (TR#C: 110).

Lot 56
30 Aug 1731: Christopher Gist, with cons. of w. Sarah, conv. (*) to John Steward of AA Co., shipwright (IS#L: 159).

Lot 57
9 April 1746: See Lot 23.
1 May 1749: James Richard conv. (*) to John Anter of London, mariner (TR#C: 228).

Lot 59
31 Dec 1736: Richard Gist, Gent., conv. (*) to Elizabeth Stone (IS#IK: 348).
14 July 1744: William Rogers and w. Sarah conv. (*) to Daniel Bowly (TB#C: 675).
20 Aug 1745: Eliza Bowly, widow and extx. of Daniel Bowley conv. (*) to William Hammond (TR#D: 294).

Lot 60
6 Dec 1745: Charles Carroll of Annapolis, Gent., conv. Lot 1 (which Charles Carroll of Annapolis, by his LWT of 1 Dec 1718 bequeathed to his sons Charles and Daniel, and which Daniel, by his LWT of 1 April 1734, authorized Charles to sell all lands under 500 a.) to William Hammond (TB#E: 47).

Lot 61
9 Dec 1751: Thomas Harrison conv. pt. Lot 61 to George Michael Hartman (TR#D: 306).
9 Dec 1751: George Michael Hartman mortgaged Lot 61 to Charles Peirpoint (TR#D: 285).

Lot 66
6 Dec 1745: Charles Carroll of Annapolis, Gent., conv. Lot 66 to William Hammond (TR#C: 504).

Lot 87
9 Dec 1751: Thomas Harrison conv. Lots 87 George Michael Hartman (TR#D: 306).
9 Dec 1751: George Michael Hartman mortgaged pt. of Lot 87 to Charles Peirpoint (TR#D: 285).

LOTS IN ADDITION TO BALTIMORE TOWN

Lot 59
15 April 1751: Christopher Strangeways conv. ½ of (*) to John Ensor, Jr. (TR#D: 337).
Lot 61
29 Oct 1751: Henry Cummings, surgeon, conv. (*) to Oliver Noyce of London, mariner (TR#D: 315).

LOTS IN JONES TOWN

Lot 1
1 Oct 1742: Luke Trotten and William Hamilton, execs. of John Gardner, conv. (*) to Edward Hall (TB#C: 42).

Lot 13
6 Nov 1751: Matthew Coulter conv. (*) to William Rogers (TR#D: 314).

LOTS IN JOPPA TOWN

Lot 1
17 June 1727: James Maxwell conv. (*) to Thomas White (IS#I: 35).
2 April 1728: Thomas White conv. (*) to Rev. William Gawthrop (IS#I: 74).

Lot 2
2 April 1729: Roger Matthews, Gent., conv. (*) to Edmund Jenings of Annapolis and Joshua George of CE Co. (IS#I: 307).

Lot 4
13 Jan 1747: Greenbury Dorsey, with cons. of w. Sarah, conv. (*) to Talbot Risteau (TB#E: 631).

Lots 6 and 7
22 Nov 1742: Stephen Roberts, s. and devisee of John Roberts, dec., conv. his interest in pt. Wolf's Harbor Neck, and Lots 6 and 7 in Joppa (which were devised to him by his father), to John Roberts, another s. and devisee of John Roberts (TB#C: 219).

Lot 7
6 June 1728: Asael Maxwell, Gent., conv. (*) to William Lowe (IS#I: 117).
6 June 1728: William Lowe, with cons. of w. Sarah, conv. (*) to Joseph Calvert (IS#I: 123).
22 Nov 1742: See Lot 6.

Lot 8
6 June 1728: Asael Maxwell conv. (*) to Joseph Calvert (IS#I: 120).

Lot 9
6 June 1728: Asael Maxwell conv. (*) to Joseph Calvert (IS#I: 120).

Lot 16
1 April 1729: William Lowe, with cons. of w. Sarah, conv. (*) to Robert Cutchin (IS#I: 311).
10 Aug 1733: Robert Cutchin, with cons. of w. Winifred, conv. (*) to John Roberts (IS#L: 413).

Lot 18
Orig. taken up by John Hall, Thomas Sheredine, Samuel Ward and Hannah Ward, and then by Asael Maxwell, none of whom lived on it (TR#C: 188).
19 May 1749: John Hall, with cons. of w. Hannah, relict and devisee of Asael Maxwell conv. (*) to Talbot Risteau (TR#C: 188).

Lot 19
8 June 1727: Thomas Sheredine, with cons. of w. Tabitha, conv. (*) to Richard Hewett, innholder (IS#H: 439).
15 Jan 1742: Samuel Tipton and w. Mary conv. (*) to Henry Morgan, mariner (TB#C: 166).
1 Aug 1749: Henry Morgan, merchant, conv. (*) to William Young. HM's w. Sarah cons. (TR#C: 241).

Lot 21
10 March 1748: William Dallam conv. (*), which had been issued to Dallam on 18 March 1746, to Nicholas Ruxton Gay (TR#C: 167).

Lot 22
Orig. taken up by David Hughes who neglected to build on it.
19 July 1727: Taken up by Jonathan Hughes.
8 June 1734: Jonathan Hughes conv. (*) to John Crockett (HWS#M: 79).

Lot 25
Sep 1728; Aquila Paca conv. (*) to Rev. William Cawthron (IS#I: 210).

Lot 29
Taken up by Catherine Hollingsworth.
27 Feb 1731: Catherine Hollingsworth, spinster, conv. (*) to Stephen Hollingsworth (IS#L: 66).
25 Nov 1731: Stephen Hollingsworth conv. (*) to John Hiigginson (IS#L: 179).
15 May 1734: John Higginson (mortgaged?) (*) to Charles Hynson and James Calder (HWS#M: 115).
2 Dec 1735: John Higginson, with cons. of w. Ann, conv. (*) to Stephen Hollingsworth (HWS#M: 350).
18 Oct 1745: James Isham, blacksmith, conv. (*) to Edward Day, innholder (TB#D: 320).

Lot 30
8 Sep 1731: Taken up by John Higginson.
2 Dec 1735: John Higginson, with cons. of w. Ann, conv. (*) to Stephen Hollingsworth (HWS#M: 350).
18 Oct 1745: James Isham, blacksmith, conv. (*) to Edward Day, innholder (TB#D: 320).

Lot 31
3 Dec 1730: Samuel Maccubbin, having neglected to build on it, conv. (*) to Abraham Johns; property became forfeit to the person first interested: Asael Maxwell who by his LWT devised it to his w. Hannah (formerly) Johns. (HWS#M: 110).
9 Aug 1734: Hannah Johns conv. (*) to William Cook (HWS#M: 110).

Lot 34
3 March 1742: James Isham, Sr., and James Isham, Jr., conv. (*) and Lot 35 to William Thompson, tailor (TB#C: 254).
5 June 1746: William Thompson, tailor, conv. (*) and Lot 35 to John Bond (TB#E: 102).

Lot 35
3 March 1742: See Lot 34.
5 June 1746: See lot 34.

Lot 39
18 Aug 1744: James Isham, Jr., blacksmith, conv. (*) to William Dallam and Geo. Presbury (TB#C: 685).

Lot 40
26 Nov 1730: Jeremiah Sutton, with cons. of w. Ann, conv. (*) to Mary Hollinsworth (IS#L: 36).
25 Nov 1751: Mary Jackson, widow, formerly Mary Hollandsworth, conv. to Robert Bishop of Joppa Town, innholder (*) (TR#D: 271).

UNIDENTIFIED TRACTS

These deeds for unidentified tracts do not include any for lands at Sassafras or Bohemia Rivers.

29 Dec 1658: John Baypole, merchant, late of London, conv. all his goods, chattels, debts, etc., to his friend Godfrey Bayley, Gent., late of London (IS#IK: 23).

5 Nov 1660: Matthias Cornelius assigned 50 a. to Peter Mounsen (IS#IK: 20).

10 Nov 1660: Peter Jacobson conv. 75 a. pt. of 200 a., to Marcus Severson (RM#HS: 1).

14 March 1661/2: Richard Gorsuch conv. to Thomas Powell pt. of 300 a. surv. for RG in 1659 by Robert Clarke (RM#HS: 5).

10 Aug 1662: Gerrit Waytes of Gloucester Co., VA, mortgaged land at North Point to Thomas Powell (RM#HS: 9).

9 Oct 1662: John Collett conv. 200 a. on the s. side of Steelpone Bay, e. by Charme Creek, to Edward Carter of Nansemond Co., VA (RM#HS: 14).

3 Nov 1663: Abraham Morgan and w. Ann conv. 300 a. on the s. side of Bohemia R. to Thomas Browning. On 5 May 1665, AM, widow, stated she and her husband had been paid for the land (IR#PP: 59).

9 Nov 1664: John Collett has conv. land to Thomas Skelton (IS#IK: 2). The deed was ackn. at August Court 1665 (RM#HS: 13).

10 Jan 1664/5: Richard Collett, w. cons. of w. Elizabeth, conv. 600 a. at Two Necks in Elk R. to his bro. John Collett (IS#IK: 3).

20 July 1664: Richard Stevenson conv. land to Richard Hensworth (RM#HS: 11).

-- Aug 1665: Daniel Jones conv. land to John Collett (RM#HS: 13).

4 Aug 1665: John Collett conv. land formerly belonging to JC and his bro. Richard, to John Hawkins (RM#HS: 11, 13).

20 Aug 1665: James Souchard conv. 300 a. on the w. side and at the head of Fishing Creek to George Strong (IR#PP: 60).

13 Sep 1665: Matthias de Cost conv. 700 a. to Thomas Ireton (RM#HS: 13).

12 April 1666: George Goldsmith conv. 100 a. to his bro.-in-law John Collett to hold in trust for 21 years, land will then revert to any of GG's ch. (IR#PP: 120).

14 March 1667/8: Mary Goldsmith, widow of George, conv. 400 a. at Morgan's Creek, on the w. side of Bohemia R., to Ann O'Mely, formerly w. of Abraham Morgan, dec. (IR#PP: 70).

4 Aug 1668: John Lee and William Osbourn conv. 240 a., on the e. side of a branch of Rumley Creek, in two tracts to Miles Gibson (IR#PP: 64).

2 Nov 1669: James Phillips conv. 100 a. at Leigh Neck to Christopher Tapley, boatwright, and Francis Elling (IR#PP: 76).

30 Jan 1670/1: Elizabeth Booker, widow, and Richard Booker, Gent., in exch. for 200 a. in New Kent Co., VA, conv. to Rowland Williams 500 a. at St. Thomas Branch, on the n. side of Bohemia Back Creek (IR#PP: 96).

1 Feb 1669/70: Charles Gorsuch conv. land to Thomas Roper (IS#IK: 39).

26 March 1670: Francis Trippas and w. Anne conv. 150 a. on the e. side of Bush R., and covered by two patents, to William York (IR#PP: 81).

16 May 1670: William Clapham, of Lancaster Co., VA, w. cons. of w. Jane, through Thomas Todd, his atty., conv. 500 a., near the mouth of Bear Creek on Patapsco, to Richard Ball. (Scisco: 19).

2 Sep 1671: John Towers conv. 200 a. to Thomas Jones, adj. Fills Choice formerly laid out for John Colier (G#J: 44) or (TR#RA: 33).

5 Sep 1671: John Vanheck, Gent., and w. Sarah conv. to Thomas Hawker 300 a. at Fendall's Creek, which was formerly conv. by JV to him (TR#RA: 79).

30 May 1673: Robert Hawkins, ropemaker, gave bond to William Dunkerton and Thomas Overton on behalf of himself and w. Hannah as warranty to 1,050 a. of land sold to WD and TO (G#J: 210; TR#RA: 159).

3 Sep 1674: John Lee and w. Florence conv. 200 a., at the head of the northeast branch of Bush R., to Joseph Gallion (G#J: 294).

18 Jan 1676/7: Anna Todd conv. all her property to her ch. (IS#IK: 57).

8 Feb 1678/9: Sarah Gorsuch gave p/a to Miles Gibson. John Boring; ackn. by MG (IR#PP: 31).

2 Aug 1683: Michael Judd and w. Jane conv. 200 a. at Bow Creek in Bush R. to John Nicholls (RM#HS: 70).

4 Sep 1683: William Osbourne ackn. he had conv. land for the court house to the County Commissioners (Scisco: 69).

22 Sep 1683: 100 a. surv. for Daniel Lawrence at the head of Bush River. DL d. without heirs, and it is reported that Thomas Lightfoot bought the land (MRR: 18).

10 Oct 1683: George Skipwith and w. Elizabeth conv. to Thomas Thurston the land, plantation and other goods and chattels which TT had conv. to his dau. Elizabeth Skipwith on 27 Oct 1676 (RM#HS: 60).

2 June 1685: Charles and Sarah Gorsuch conv. 120 a. on the e. side of Old Road Creek (part of 1,100 a. formerly laid out for William Batten and Thomas Thomas) to Robert Burman (RM#HS: 134).
25 June 1686: William Osbourne and w. Margaret conv. land adj. to the Court House land to James Phillips (RM#HS: 185).
20 July 1686: Thomas Richardson and w. Rachel conv. 200 a., which was granted to TR in 1685, to Robert Love (RM#HS: 197).
20 Aug 1686: Thomas Lightfoot conv. 400 a. at Born Branch to Amos Nicholls of PA (RM#HS: 208).
30 Aug 1688: Thomas Stockett, s. and heir apparent of TS late of AA Co., dec., conv. 200 a. at Point Comfort to Jacob Loten (RM#HS: 284).
2 July 1689: Charles Gorsuch and w. Sarah conv. 100 a. to Richard Wilmot (RM#HS: 304).
5 July 1689: Robert Wilmot and w. Jane conv. land on Patapsco R. to Charles Gorsuch (RM#HS: 303).
9 Jan 1691/2: Nathaniel Anderson assigned land lately purch. from William Loney and w. Jane (dau. and sole heir of Thomas Overton) to Edward Boothby (RM#HS: 386).
10 March 1692/3: William Hill conv. land formerly owned by father John Hill to Mary Love, if she will live in the dwelling where WH's dec. father JH lived, and to assist in home affairs to what should be needful toward WH's accommodation (RM#HS: 383).
28 May 1694: Capt. Thomas Richardson assigned 200 a. to Nicholas Day; pt. of 400 a. granted to Michael Hastings on 8 Dec 1688, and assigned by MH to Edward Boothby, who assigned it to TR (RM#HS: 486).
6 June 1694: John Love conv. to Francis Robinson 200 a. which Lord Baltimore granted to Thomas Richardson, and which TR conv. to Robert Love, who willed it to JL (RM#HS: 433).
4 Nov 1694: John Love of Gunpowder R. conv. to Francis Robinson 200 a., which Lord Baltimore granted to Thomas Richardson in 1685, and which TR conv. to Robert Love, who willed it to JL (RM#HS: 433).
4 Oct 1695: Robert Blunt, of TA Co., s. and heir of RB of KE Co., dec., conv. 200 a. called ... Times to James Todd (TR#RA: 339).
24 Nov 1697: Michael Yeakley and John Pettett of London, merchants, gave p/a to Richard Colegate, factor in Maryland (TR#RA: 329).
7 March 1699: Edmund Hensley, through his atty. Francis Dallahide, conv. 200 a. at the head of Vinnum's Run to John Anderson and William Wright (TR#RA: 355).
5 May 1700: Elizabeth Green, spinster, conv. to Edward Stevenson 100 a. which she inher. from her father Anthony Demondidier, by his LWT dated 2 Oct 1693 (HW#2: 51).
3 April 1703: James Murray conv. land to Christopher Gardner, to make good the title to land conv. by JM on 29 March 1701 (TR#A: 390).
3 May 1703: Thomas Daniell, of AA Co., w. cons. of w. Elizabeth, conv. 200 a. on Curtis Creek to Stephen Warman of AA Co. (HW#2: 231).
23 Feb 1703/4: Michael Judd conv. 75 a., being $\frac{1}{2}$ of ... Delight, to Samuel Sickelmore and Gideon Skaats (HW#2: 321).
10 July 1704: James Barley and w. Johanna conv. 79 a. ... Purchase to John Dorsey (HW#2: 371).
6 April 1705: John Fuller and w. Sarah conv. 200 a. John Nicholas' land on Bow Creek, land formerly held by William Orchard (IR#AM: 57).
30 Dec 1707: James Isham and w. Julian conv. their dwelling plantation to Charles Baker (TR#A: 44).
3 Nov 1708: John Christian, w. cons. of w. Margaret, conv. 75 a. at head of Jones Falls to William Talbot (RM#HS: 621).
2 Aug 1709: John Christian conv. 100 a. adj. to Expectation to Thomas Randall (TR#A: 7).
30 Dec 1709: James Isham and w. Julian gave bond to conv. certain land to Charles Baker if certain covenants were performed (TR#A: 44).
6 May 1711: John Hillen, cordwainer, w. cons. of w. Mary, conv. 93 a. to Mordecai Price (TR#A: 149).
5 March 1715: Hugh Jones conv. 5 a. to John Wilmot, Sr. (TR#A: 382).
1 Aug 1717: Thomas Preston conv. to Thomas Bond 20 a. pt. of land formerly owned by TP, dec., father of the grantor (TR#A: 441).
20 Nov 1718: Samuel Brown leased 150 a. to David Thomas (TR#RA: 485).
26 Feb 1719: Joseph Connoway, w. cons. of w. Rebecca, conv. 100 a. ... Neck to John Connoway (TR#DS: 123).
2 July 1719: Thomas Worthington conv. land to Caleb Dorsey (TR#DS: 3-5 to 7-8).
2 July 1719: Samuel Dorsey, elder bro. and heir-at-law of Benjamin Dorsey, and w. cons. of w. Jane, conv. 200 a. to Caleb Dorsey (TR#DS: 6).
23 Jan 172-: Herbert Prichard conv. to Richard Gist all the lands that lately belonged to John Order, father of Mary Prichard, or which belonged to any of the sons and daus. of JO and which descended to said MP (IS#G: 81).
3 Nov 1720: Nicholas Gassaway conv. 300 a. to Joshua Merriken (TR#DS: 232).

5 April 1721: Hannah Orrick, widow, conv. 410 a. being ½ of ... to Gideon Howard (TR#DS: 328).

30 June 1721: Thomas Ramsey conv. to Simon Pearson, weaver, all tracts on the w. side of the Chesapeake Bay to which TR held title (IS#G: 1).

20 Nov 1721: Joseph Gallion for love and affection, conv. all his property (after his dec.) to his friend John Taylor (IS#G: 27).

1722: John Miles appointed his w. Mary his extx. for life over his entire estate; she had power to conv. his plantation over Deer Creek to JM's well beloved son; if she did not, land was to go to the s. after the death of said Mary; if s. dies, land was to go to Martha Litton, and if she d., then to the nearest in blood to her (IS#G: 136).

9 Feb 1722: William Lenox, carpenter, left all his estate to his w. Bethia, but if she should have a child, then equally to both (IS#G: 63).

15 Dec 1722: George Ogg, Sr., conv. all his property to George Ogg, Jr., on condition that GO, Jr., would take care of his mother and bro. John, both incapable of caring for themselves, and that he would pay his sister Katherine Risteau £25 when she needed it (IS#G: 56; see similar deed dated 16 Dec 1723 in IS#G: 232).

7 July 1723: Richard Fowle of Stepney Parish, Middlesex, mariner, conv. to Philip Smith of London, merchant, 118 perches of land formerly taken up by John Gill, in consideration of town lands in a town called Whetstone, and formerly bought by Capt. William Fowle (IS#G: 146).

23 Sep 1723: John Gorsuch, w. cons. of w. Elizabeth, conv. 2 a. formerly in possession of Charles Carroll, to Richard Gist (IS#G: 227).

26 Jan 1724/5: John Jones conv. to his bro. William Jones 50 a. of land adj. to Mate's Affinity formerly taken up by Emanuel Ceeley and Edward Dowse (IS#H: 88).

31 March 1725: Robert Love, s. of John Love and grandson of RL, both dec., conv. 200 a. at head of Gunpowder R. to Thomas White of Joppa (IS#H: 137).

4 May 1725: Richard Smithers conv. all his real estate in MD to John Stokes (IS#H: 126).

2 June 1725: Thomas Mitchell, w. cons. of w. Ann, conv. all his real estate in MD to Joshua Wood (IS#H: 109).

6 Nov 1725: David Prece of Chester Co., PA, w. cons. of w. Susanna, conv. 250 a. to James Crouch of AA Co. (IS#H: 205).

15 Nov 1725: Luke Raven, a member of the Church of England, disclaimed all responsibility for his w. Elizabeth, dau. of Thomas and Mary Hughes, who left him from 9 Dec 1724 to 13 March 1724/5, and from 17 June 1725 to the present date (IS#H: 207).

18 July 1727: Cadwallader Jones conv. all his lands, household, stuff, and implements to his friend Jacob Herrington if JH provides CJ w. sufficient meat, drink, washing, and lodging for life, and permits CJ to occupy the premises, and will do the same for Avarilla and Frances Jones, ch. of CJ (IS#I: 1).

9 Feb 1728: John Roberts made a will devising 400 a. in The Forest, where John Sumner lived, to his daus. Ann, Frances, and Lucina (MCW 6: 93).

2 April 1728: Abraham Taylor conv. 100 a. to William Burney (IS#I: 100).

19 July 1728: Moses Groome, one of the heirs of Ann Felks, widow of Edward Felks (late of BA Co., dec., who also had a bro. Charles Felks of England, now also dec.), conv. his right and claim to ⅓ of the land which EF owned at the time of his death, to Thomas White (IS#I: 144).

4 Oct 1728: Frances Grant, widow of Hugh Grant, conv. all her estate, including land on the Susquehanna R., to Miles Foy in anticipation of their marriage; if MF should die, FG will have a right to all the estate for her life (IS#I: 317).

Aug 1729: Thomas Harryman conv. 50 a. to Joseph Broadick (IS#L: 56).

19 Sep 1729: George Goodwin, tailor, and w. Elizabeth, conv. 100 a. C...'s Adventure to Edward Fell (IS#K: 103).

15 Feb 1730: Simon Pearson, weaver, conv. land which SP purch. from Thomas Ramsey to Josias Hendon (IS#L: 95).

3 June 1730: Thomas Franklin, w. cons. of w. Ruth, conv. 100 a. ... Chance, surv. 10 June 1729, to John Sumner (IS#K: 308).

8 March 1732: Alexander McKenley leased 100 a. of his dwelling plantation to Samuel Cooper (IS#L: 335).

9 March 1732: Daniel Dulany, of Annapolis, leased to Thomas Lomax 250 a. which DD was lately conv. by John Dorsey (IS#L: 337).

10 May 1732: Richard Colegate conv. to Robert Robertson all his interest or interest by inheritance to all lands within 2 miles of a certain creek (IS#L: 262).

8 June 1732: Spry Godfrey Gundry, and w. Mary, conv. to his bro. James Maxwell several tracts which desc. to SGG from his ancestors. SGG's w. Mary cons. (IS#l: 255).

4 Sep 1732: Thomas Wickes conv. land to Thomas Harris (IS#L: 282).

9 Nov 1732: Simon Pearson, weaver, conv. to Isaac Webster all lands which SP on 15 June 1731 had any right to from Thomas Thurston, of BA Co., dec. (IS#L: 319).

28 April 1733: Walter Dallas sold 500 a. he bought from John Gorsuch (which had orig. been taken up by Robert Gorsuch, and descended to his s. Robert, Jr., who d. intestate and without heirs), 100 a. each to Benjamin Tasker, Charles Carroll, Daniel Dulany, Charles Carroll of Annapolis, and Daniel Carroll of Prince George's Co. (IS#L: 372).

8 Aug 1734: Thomas Brasher and w. Sarah conv. 10 a. adj. Grafton's Gift to Isaac Webster (HWS#M: 109).

22 Jan 1735: John Norton conv. $57\frac{1}{2}$ a., devised him by his father, JN, dec., to Patrick and William Lynch. JN's w. Margaret cons. (HWS#M: 370).

22 Jan 1735: James Lenox and w. Mary conv. to Patrick and William Lynch, all land devised Mary by her father Robuck Lynch (HWS#M: 371).

5 March 1735: Nehemiah Hicks gave quitclaim for 45 a. (part 180 a. surv. 27 Sep 1722 for John Fuller, James Elliott, John Isham, and Nehemiah Hicks) to John Isham (HWS#M: 390).

2 March 1736: Isaac Groce conv. 100 a. on s. side of Salt Peter Creek, adj. to Shadwell's Range, to John Leage (IS#IK: 354).

29 Oct 1736: Joseph and Woolquist Cromwell divided the land they inher. by the LWT of their father, William Cromwell of AA Co. (IS#IK: 316).

1 Dec 1736: Jacob Giles leased 20 a. in St. George's Parish, which had been granted to JG by the Court of Chancery, to John Higginson (IS#IK: 341).

27 Feb 1737: John Yates conv. 100 a. to William Hamilton (HWS#M: 55).

17 March 1737: Hugh Mackdaniel, of PG Co., and w. Elizabeth, relict of John Yates, conv. to William Yates 33⅓ a. of 100 a. granted to said JY, and which was the dower of aforesaid Elizabeth (HWS#M: betw. 59 and 62).

13 June 1737: Michael Rutledge mortgaged 50 a. of land and other property to Samuel MacCubbin, Jr. (IS#K: 454).

9 Dec 1737: James Phillips leased land to Roger Matthews (HWS#1-A: 51).

30 May 1738: James Isham, innholder, and Mary Warren, widow of Thomas Warren, being about to marry, JI conv. all his land and movables to his s. James Isham of Philadelphia, blacksmith, at the elder JI's decease (HWS#1-A: 74).

27 July 1738: James Phillips leased 100 a., pt. of a larger tract, to James Gallion for 21 years

16 Sep 1738: John Wilmot, of AA Co., w. cons. of w. Hannah, conv. 70 a. and 30 a. to William Houchins (HWS#1-A: 113).

27 Feb 1728/9: Mary Bucknell gave bond to conv. 50 a. of land, cattle, etc., to Charles Bailey if Mary's s. Henry should die within 6 years from date (HWS#1-A: 255).

1 Feb 1739: Richard Gist conv. 1 a. to John Frazer (HWS#1-A: 348).

24 April 1739: William Beasman, s. and heir of Joseph Beasman, conv. 50 a. to Elizabeth Beasman, widow of JB (HWS#1-A: 202).

7 June 1739: Peter Carroll conv. to James Carroll land now in PC's possession; deed to take effect after PC's death (HWS#1-A: 240).

2 Oct 1739: Francis Hynes and w. Frances conv. to William Worthington, 133⅓ a., pt. of 400 a. which John Roberts willed to his daus. Ann, Frances, and Lucina (HWS#1-A: 285).

4 June 1744: John Sumner and w. Isabella conv. 1 a. to Rev. Henry Loveall, Thomas Miles, Sr., William Talbot, William Grafton, and Edmond Hays, Jr., elders of the Church of Jesus Christ called General Baptists or Covenanters (TB#C: 482).

11 Dec 1744: William Pritchard of ... Co., VA, s. and heir-at-law of Herbert Pritchard of BA Co., conv. to Paul Garron, carpenter, 150 a., including 50 a. bought by HP and 100 a. bought by HP from Richard Gist on 23 June 1721. PG was one of the witnesses (TB#D: 118).

4 Aug 1746: William Fell assigned to John Ensor his share of a lease for 20 a. (leased on 14 March 1739 to WF and JE for a mill seat on both sides of the Great Run of Jones' Falls) for the remainder of the term (TB#E: 123).

9 Aug 1748: John Martin of PG Co., s. and heir of JM, late of TA and BA Co,., dec., conv. to William Lynch 100 a. orig. granted to JM of BA Co., grandfather of the present JM (TR#C: 43).

25 Aug 1748: Walter Billingsley conv. to William Wilson 100 a., being pt. of land surv. for Edward Talbot who bequeathed it to his s. John, who sold it to John Parker, who in turn conv. it the grantor (TR#C: 79).

2 Feb 1749: George Buchanan conv. his dwelling plantation to his s. Lloyd Buchanan (TR#C: 369).

14 April 1749: Mary Tiftin of Arlington Street, Picadilly, Middlesex, spinster, residuary legatee and administratrix of William Tiftin, master of the merchant ship Lydia, dec. at BA Co., gave p/a to Henry Harrison of Philadelphia (TR#C: 338).

15 Nov 1749: Henry Harrison of Philadelphia, atty. for Mary Tiftin, gave p/a to Tobias Stansbury (TR#C: 341).

27 June 1759: Dutton Lane conv. land to his dau. Mary Murray (B#G: 484).

INDEX

An asterisk (*) indicates the page number of the primary section in which the history of the tract or lot is described.

-D-

-K-

-S-

Made in United States
Cleveland, OH
27 July 2026

41186397R00168